THE RISE
of
Napoleon
Bonaparte

Robert B. Asprey

BASIC
BOOKS

A Member of the Perseus Books Group

Copyright © 2000 by Robert Asprey

Published by Basic Books,
A Member of the Perseus Books Group

The Rise of Napoleon Bonaparte was
originally published in the United Kingdom by Little, Brown as
The Rise and Fall of Napoleon Bonaparte: Volume One.
The Basic Books edition is published by
arrangement with Little, Brown.

A CIP catalog record for this book is
available from the Library of Congress.
ISBN 0-465-04881-1

01 02 03 / 10 9 8 7 6 5 4 3 2 1

To Tim
with gratitude, respect and love

Contents

CONTENTS   xiii

List of Illustrations

MAPS

PERMISSIONS

Grateful acknowlededgment is made for permission to quote from
the following sources:

Chandler, David G. *The Campaigns of Napoleon*, 1967,
Weidenfeld & Nicolson, 1967.

Bruce, Evangeline. *Napoleon & Josephine – An Improbable
Marriage*, Weindenfeld & Nicolson, 1996.

Thomazi, August Antoine. *Napoléon et ses marins*, Berger-
Levrault, 1950.

Sutherland, Christine. *Marie Walewska Napoleon's Great Love*,
Weindenfeld & Nicolson, 1997.

Bertrand, Henri-Gratien. *Napoleon at St. Helena – the Journals of
General Bertrand*, Doubleday, 1952.

Graig, Gordon. *The Politics of the Prussian Army 1640–1945*,
Oxford University Press, 19955.

Thiry, Jean, *Napoléon en Italie*, Berger-Levrault, 1973.

Thiry, Jean, *Les Années de la Jeunesse de Napoléon Bonaparte*,
Berger-Levrault, 1975.

A NOTE TO THE READER

Ever since his untimely death at the age of 51 on the forlorn island of St. Helena in 1821, Napoleon Bonaparte has too often been the victim of biographical and historical exuberance, of unhealthy literary passions that treat him either as demi-god (mainly French authors) or as devil incarnate (mainly British authors). The interpretive pendulum continues to swing, most recently toward devil incarnate in three lengthy books by American, British and French authors.

I object to either interpretation which, by distorting either his achievements or failures, gives the reader a lopsided view of one of the most fascinating persons of all time who dominated one of the most contradictory periods of the world's history.

Napoleon's relatively short life is a story of massive successes and disastrous failures, intense loves and violent hatreds, genius and stupidity, vision and cupidity, arrogance and ignorance, intrigue and treachery, short-term satisfactions and long-term frustrations – of unfettered power once intended for the public good but in time diluted by overweening ambition and conceit.

Napoleon was not the father of chaos, as his detractors would have us believe. He was heir to chaos both at home and abroad. We tend to forget the appalling conditions of abject human servitude that fomented the French Revolution; the devastating period of terror invoked by Robespierre and his Jacobin followers; the inept and corrupt administration of the Directorate which followed the overthrow of the Jacobins. These miserable and chaotic years shaped the young Bonaparte's thinking to bring forth his active participation in a *coup d'etat* followed by the creation of the Consulate and the Empire – and a reasonably successful attempt by the new ruler to restore order in a torn nation while leading it to what he believed was its rightful role in the consolidation of Europe.

Neither was Napoleon the father of the wars that accompanied the process, as his detractors would also have us believe. Almost constant warfare was a legacy of the revolutionary chaos, a series of wars invoked by European and English rulers determined to topple the dangerous interloper and restore Bourbon feudalistic rule to France.

As European armies suffered repeated defeats owing to Napoleon's military mastery, the desire of their governments for revenge continued to grow. It was fueled on the one hand by Napoleon's determination to build a French empire in an attempt to unify a discordant Europe, on the other hand to force the English government to share its control of the seas: too often overlooked is the singular fact that in the first decade of the nineteenth century Britain controlled five-eighths of the world's surface – its oceans – compared to Napoleon's relatively slight and always tenuous European holdings.

The long Anglo-American alliance has tended to make many Americans forget the humiliations suffered by our colonial forefathers, the painful war that gave birth to our nation, the subsequent maritime insults to our fledgling navy and merchant ships, the war of 1812 and the burning of Washington. In Napoleon's day the Royal Navy indisputably ruled the seas to provide its masters with a virtual monopoly of colonial trade that Napoleon was determined to break.

Since the English government had no intention of relinquishing its rule of the seas the results were inevitable. It was the English crown which dishonored its signing of the Treaty of Amiens to declare war on France in 1803; that bankrolled numerous Bourbon *émigré* attempts on Napoleon's life; that subsequently spent millions of pounds sterling in subsidizing a series of armed coalitions to make war on the French tyrant. And, because of Napoleon's strategic errors, both military and political, it was the English crown that emerged the winner to continue enlarging its vast overseas empire throughout the nineteenth and twentieth centuries.

If Napoleon ultimately failed in his grand design to make the seas neutral and to form Europe into a cohesive union of non-warring states, he nevertheless accomplished a great deal in his short reign. His legal reforms embodied in the famous Code Napoléon were alone sufficient to bring lasting fame. Add to that his insistence on the revolutionary principle of equality, one example being his dictum of promotion on grounds of performance rather than birth; his founding of the Bank of France and a national university, of schools, hospitals, orphanages, workhouses; building of roads, tunnels, canals, ports and extension of the primitive telegraph system; his encouragement of and contribution to the arts and sciences – his alleged geometric theorem remains well known; his sponsorship of smallpox vaccination and other unpopular public health measures; his attempts to introduce a unified coinage in his empire; his repeated experiments and successes in agrarian and animal husbandry; his beautification of Paris and other cities.

Militarily he introduced tactical mobility so necessary to battlefield improvisation of which he was a master. Napoleon used time as a precious clock: "We don't march, we fly," General Berthier wrote early in the first Italian campaign. But rapid movement depended on willing troops, and here was Napoleon's real secret of success. No commander in history has so inspired his troops to march, often without adequate food or wine, on occasion without shoes, frequently with meager clothing in dreadful weather. Time and again, in Italy, Egypt, Austria, Germany, Prussia, Russia, and finally France, he asked his men to do what often appeared to be impossible – and they did it. His tricks were many, their sum spelled unexcelled leadership.

His political contributions were real enough even if some were accidentally inspired. Our United States as we know them would never have emerged but for his providential sale of the immense Louisiana territory – an act calculated to strengthen America against England. His creation of the Cispadane and Cisalpine republics planted the seeds of a future Italian nation. His Egyptian campaign, although a strategic failure, resulted in the discovery of the Rosetta Stone and, ultimately, in the building of the Suez Canal. His admittedly nebulous plans for a cohesive Europe, had they been realized, might possibly have led to two centuries of peace as opposed to body- and soul-destroying wars.

Such however was the scope of his ambition, such his unbridled belief in physical force, such his arrogance derived from ignorance of naval strategy and the potential of guerrilla warfare, such his error in confusing his country's destiny with his own, such the strength and determined resistance of aristocratic and oligarchic rule, that in the end his own ambitious dreams fell victim to the nightmare of defeat followed by abdication, exile and six years of very cruel imprisonment on St. Helena island.

As with all of us, Napoleon was a sum of his parts which is why I have treated him, warts and all, as a human being, as child, student, man, soldier, general, lover, husband, father, ruler, emperor, conqueror and statesman. His story is an intensely dramatic saga, presented in terms not of our day but of his. I hope you enjoy the result.

ACKNOWLEDGMENTS

I am greatly indebted to a number of people and institutions for helping me with this book. I want to thank the staffs of the Bodleian Library, the Codrington Library of All Souls College and the New College Library, all at Oxford; the London Library and the British Museum Library; the Library of Congress; the Army and Navy Club Library in Washington, D.C.; the New York City Library; the Vassar College Library; the Bibliothéque Nationale in Paris; and the Biblioteca Nacional in Madrid.

Among many friends who aided my work in one way or another are Gordon and Sheila Seaver, David and Christine Sutherland and Jacques W. Kleynhans in England; Philippe and Danièle Delamare in France; Edward and Irma Sommer in Spain; Robert Andreen, David Bradford, Elle Gohl; Caroline Gifford; Lila and David De Campo; my literary agent, Matthew Bialer, of the William Morris Agency; the "fathers" of the book, two fine editors, John Hermann and Stephen Fraser; my publishers, Jack McKeown of Basic Books and Alan Samson of Little Brown, London; my American editor, Donald Fehr, and my English editors, Becky Smith and Jean Maund.

My old friend, Graham Rosser, has spent many hours during the last several years in correcting and often improving my translations from a wide variety of French sources, and I am grateful. I am equally indebted to my sister, Winifred Asprey, to whom this book is dedicated, for the many hours devoted to the careful proofing of a long manuscript. The maps are the work of the English cartographer, Samantha A. Kirby, to whose talent, care, patience and good temper I pay deep homage.

Robert Asprey

Clearchos was a true soldier and war was his passion . . .
When he could have kept at peace without shame or
damage, he chose war; when he could have been idle, he
wished for hard work that he might have war; when he
could have kept wealth without danger, he chose to make it
less by making war; there was a man who spent upon war
as if it were a darling lover, or some other pleasure.

Xenophon

Clisson was born for war. While yet a child he knew the
lives of the great captains. He thought out the principles of
the military art at a time when those of his age were at
school and were running after girls. As soon as he was old
enough to carry arms he marked every step by brilliant
actions. He had reached the first rank in the army though
but a youth. Fortune constantly favored his genius. His
victories followed one another and his name was known to
the people as one of their dearest defenders.

The opening lines of Napoleon's novella,
Clisson et Eugénie, written after the breakup
of his romance with Eugénie Désirée Clary.

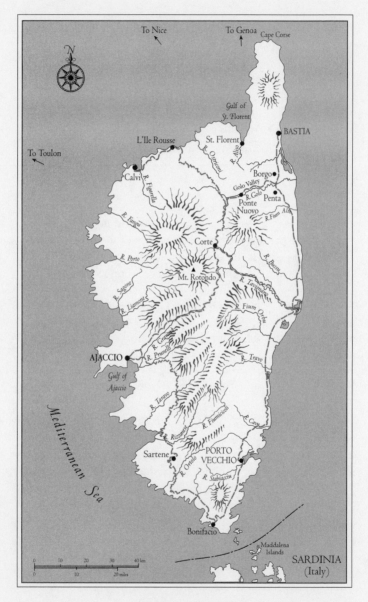

To Nice

To Genoa

Cape Corse

N

Gulf of
St. Florent

To Toulon

L'Ile Rousse

St. Florent

BASTIA

R. Ostriconi

R. Aliso

Calvi

Borgo

R. Figarella

Golo Valley

R. Golo

Penta

Ponte
Nuovo

R. Tartagine

Corte

R. Fium Alto

R. Porto

Mt. Rotondo

R. Bucesi

R. Sagone

R. Tavignano

R. Liamone

R. Fium Orbo

R. Gravone

AJACCIO

R. Prunelli

R. Travo

Gulf of
Ajaccio

R. Taravo

R. Fiumicicoli

R. Cavu

R. Rizzanese

Sartene

PORTO
VECCHIO

R. Ortolo

R. Stabiacciu

Mediterranean Sea

Bonifacio

Maddalena
Islands

SARDINIA
(Italy)

0   10   20   30   40 km

0   10   20 miles

Napoleon's Corsica

IN THE BEGINNING

Corsica, 1769

Cold and hungry, saddened and weary in defeat, their rude clothes in shreds, boots worn through, the small band of rebel fighters continued the slow climb to mountain sanctuary. The beaten ones had been on the move for over a month, losing the French pursuers in dense forests while living on berries and game, occasionally shooting a wild boar while traversing open heathland softly carpeted by the sweet-smelling *maquis* bush, finally to reach the mountains, taking shelter when rains turned narrow trails to treacherous rock-strewn slides, sleeping fitfully in copse or cave, gouging what food they could from the increasingly barren land, drinking from torrential streams before fording the cold and dangerous torrents, slipping and falling, cutting and bruising exhausted bodies on hidden sharp rocks. One of the band was a 19-year-old woman named Letitia Buonaparte who was nearing the end of her strength – not surprising since she was six months heavy with child. In crossing one torrent Letitia slipped and would have been swept away but for a providential hand that pulled her to safety and a brief rest before the climb continued.

*

For almost a year Corsican rebels had been fighting a war without much hope of victory. They were led by Pasquale Paoli, an intelligent and forceful general of 44 years, a big man famous for persuasive oratory and determined actions. Thirteen years earlier he had liberated Corsica in a war that forced the Genoese overlords from the island. Paoli's subsequent rule had resulted in the numerous administrative and economic reforms that so impressed a young Scots traveler, James Boswell, and it had brought about an increasingly proud but all too temporary independence.

Paoli had not reckoned with neighbor France. King Louis XV, having suffered a severe loss of prestige in the Seven Years War (1756–1763), sought redemption in the Mediterranean, specifically its fourth largest island, Corsica, over 100 miles long from north to south and some 50 miles across at its widest point. A vindictive Genoese republic, whose always-avaricious bankers hoped to recoup earlier losses in Corsica, hastened to cooperate. In 1764, by a neat bit of legal trickery Genoa ceded its residual rights to major Corsican ports to France, which subsequently garrisoned the towns with troops. Four years later (in return for a large sum of money) Genoa ceded all claimed rights to the island to France which now strengthened its garrisons to a total six regiments commanded by Lieutenant General Comte Marbeuf.

Such high-handedness was too much for the proud and fiery Paoli whose isolated and independent islanders were among the most warlike peoples of the world. His protestations to European courts went unheeded: "We are treated like a bunch of sheep coming to market," he complained to the Vienna court.[1] He won limited British support for what that government saw as a relatively painless way of "increasing its commercial and political influence in the Mediterranean."[2] But before this ally could act, the French preempted matters in the summer of 1768 by opening a military campaign designed to gain control of the Golo valley, essential to opening cross-island communications between the important ports of Bastia and St. Florent, ten miles apart on the island's northern neck. An incensed Paoli now called his countrymen to arms. The scattered cantons and villages enthusiastically responded by temporarily calling a truce to various vendettas in order to furnish armed bands, altogether some 2,500 proud, strong and determined men very much at home in the inhospitable mountains.

French troops easily attained initial objectives, the mountain ridges that sheltered the target valley, before garrisoning the key towns of Ponte Nuovo and Penta, each protected by a series of outposts. But thinly spread French units operating in strange and difficult terrain became easy targets for the partisans. In mid August one band captured the Penta garrison, other bands put a Corsican royalist regiment of volunteers to flight. An alarmed Versailles court hurriedly sent reinforcements under the less than able Lieutenant General Claude de Chavelin who replaced Comte Marbeuf in overall command.

The shift in command solved nothing. Fighting day and night in tortuous terrain, the rebels repeatedly surprised and decimated isolated French outposts. The important town of Borgo was surrounded and in October, after suffering over 2,000 casualties, the entire garrison surrendered.[3] Talk of retreating to the ports was cut short by the arrival of more French battalions.

By year's end the war was a standoff despite the presence of thousands of French troops and an expenditure of some 30 million livres.[4] Worse, in December Paoli signed a treaty with England that would bring his hard-pressed fighters guns and bullets along with a subsidy of 25,000 francs a week – but, despite the one-man lobbying efforts in London of James Boswell, no troops. Paoli's losses had been heavy, many of the partisans were grumbling about leaving their homes, replacements were few. One band that did form at this time was led by a young patriot, Charles Buonaparte.

Paoli now committed a major error. Hoping to cut enemy communications with supply ports he ordered an all-out attack against a strongly defended French position. This was seized after an 18-hour battle, but French reserves soon arrived to force a partisan retreat, leaving behind some 500 dead and wounded, about a fifth of the entire fighting force.

That winter of 1769 brought still more French battalions to the island, and also Lieutenant General Comte de Vaux, an experienced commander who replaced the inept de Chavelin. De Vaux carried orders to open a massive campaign that the French king hoped would result in a final glorious victory.

Led by de Vaux and Marbeuf the French marched in early May, their objective Paoli's headquarters in Corte. Two extended and very weak partisan lines blocked their way. Seizing village after village, the French systematically isolated the rebel groups which, having lost tactical cohesion, undertook a series of brave but very costly and ineffectual attacks. During one of them a French officer, seeing that the Corsicans had no doctors or field hospitals, asked a prisoner, "What do you do when you are wounded?" The answer was brief: "We die."[5]

And die they did. On 9 May the French attacked Ponte Nuovo, a brief but bloody battle that killed 200 partisans and sent the survivors in flight to the mountains or the coast. Paoli and a few followers finally reached Porto Vecchio to escape on an English ship that sailed in mid June. The French were not sorry to see him go. In General de Vaux's words, his capture "would have been more embarrassing than useful."[6]

The exhausted remnants of Charles Buonaparte's band reached the sanctuary of Mt. Rotondo in late May. Subsequently learning of Paoli's flight and of de Vaux's offer of clemency they decided that their war was over. Charles joined other rebel leaders in surrendering to de Vaux whose terms were generous: the rebels could return to their homes and jobs without punishment.[7]

Charles and his pregnant young wife, Letitia, arrived back in Ajaccio that summer. On a hot August day Letitia was attending Mass when birth pains forced a hurried exit from the church. Reaching her house, she threw herself on a couch and soon gave birth to a male child. He was named Nabolione Buonaparte.

Notes

1   Iung, I, 17. See also Chuquet (*Jeunesse*), 1 ff.
2   Iung, I, 17.
3   Thiry (*Jeunesse*), 12.
4   Iung, I, 21–2. The livre was roughly equivalent to the French gold franc.
5   Nasica, 15. See also Chuquet (*Jeunesse*), 4–5.
6   Iung, I, 27.
7   Nasica, 21–2.

CHAPTER ONE

THE BOY
1769–1778

*Impressions received in childhood cannot be
erased from the soul.*

Frederick the Great, King of Prussia

THE CHILD ARRIVED at an awkward time in the young and almost penniless couple's life. Despite or perhaps because of French clemency to the surrendered rebels Corsica remained dangerously divided, the patriot clans of poor country peasants waiting only for the return of Pasquale Paoli and the day of revenge, the generally moderate and relatively well-off town patricians only too willing to accept the perquisites promised by French rule.

Charles Buonaparte, motivated as much by economic necessity as by political preference, enthusiastically accepted the French overlords and in return was appointed a *juge-assesseur* or court assistant in the Ajaccio jurisdiction at a meager salary of 900 livres a year.[1] He and Letitia sorely needed the small income. The Buonaparte clan, originally from Tuscany, had lived in Ajaccio since the late sixteenth century. The successive families, although enjoying a comfortable existence as benefited an Italian patrician heritage, had not amassed a great or even considerable fortune.[2] Charles' father had died when the boy was 17 years old. What should have been a helpful inheritance had been largely dissipated by the father in an expensive series of unsuccessful legal actions, the *Process Odone*, undertaken to recover

the father-in-law's estate which had fallen into the hands of wily
Jesuit priests. Charles would unwisely continue the legal battle
which he could ill afford and which possibly contributed to his
early death. Meanwhile he had to content himself with a house in
Ajaccio and some small country holdings. His grand-uncle,
Archdeacon Lucien, was quite well off but was extremely careful
with his money, particularly since he frowned on Charles' prodi-
gal ways.[3]

Despite bleak prospects Charles had married when he was 18,
his bride the 14-year-old Letitia Romalino, a strikingly forceful
and attractive girl whose father had left her a small house and
vineyard outside of Ajaccio. Letitia's background differed considerably from that of her husband. Raised in the country with
almost no formal education, she had early matured as an attractive, hard-working, naturally shrewd and intelligent woman with
a deep knowledge of Corsican manners and mores, including the
all-too-frequent *vendetta* or revenge killings practiced through the
centuries by disparate clans.

Their first two children died in infancy. Their third child,
Joseph, was born in 1768. Charles had subsequently moved the
family to join General Paoli in Corte. Working in the local administration, he had been rapidly caught up in Paoli's rebellion and
claimed to have written the stirring proclamation that called the
montagnards to arms before himself taking to the hills with his
young wife.[4]

Charles was now 23 years of age, tall, good-looking, easy-going,
something of a clothes-horse, elegant in appearance and manner
but generally of an empty purse (and too often an empty head
despite a rude education in the law). Forever the opportunist,
Charles wasted no time in exploiting his newly-found allegiance,
petitioning the authorities to grant him the title of nobility formerly held by his father, an achievement finally accomplished
with the support of the French governor of Corsica, General
Comte de Marbeuf.[5] Three years later, supported by the same
protector, he was appointed to the Commission of Twelve, a
group of prominent Ajaccians which was to advise the French

intendant but was rarely called upon. Marbeuf's altruism may
have arisen from a seamy motivation – at least some biographers
believe that he enjoyed Letitia's charms – and there is some evidence that on one occasion Napoleon wondered aloud as to the
identity of his real father.[6]

Charles' prospects suddenly brightened when the Jesuits were
expelled from French lands. Surely, he believed, the property
stolen from his father would revert to make him (by Corsican
standards) a rich man. He was mistaken. The title reverted to the
state, whose guardians had no intention of returning it to Charles.
He could not afford to take the case to court, but he would never
cease trying to win a favorable decision for *Process Odone* by
buttering-up one official after another, both in Corsica and in
Paris, all to no effect.[7]

Failure to recover the property was a great blow to the young
Buonapartes whose family continued to increase. Lucien was born
when Napoleon was six, Marie Anne was soon on the way (and
four more would follow). Charles was far too caught up in various
enterprises to pay much attention to the *ménage* which in any
event was not a Corsican man's role. This was Letitia's job and,
aided by a charwoman, a wet-nurse and an elderly aunt, she performed it well. The problem child was Nabolione who by his own
admission was a self-centered brat whose family nickname was
Rabulioni (the Disturber).[8] "I was a little handful," he recalled
many years later. "Except my mother, nothing and no one could
impose the slightest restraint on me."[9] A small boy, he was skinny,
pale and unkempt, given to fearful temper tantrums, his shrill
voice and flashing eyes dominating his siblings. "I feared no one,"
he went on, "I would thrash one, scratch the other; I made myself
redoubtable to all."[10] To all except his mother who frequently
gave him a good spanking, but who also took quiet pride in the
exceedingly bright and ever curious boy.

The children were not well educated, largely the fault of an
inadequate teaching system. Nabolione learned only a smattering
of church history and the catechism – this from Archdeacon
Lucien – and he was taught a rudimentary knowledge of the

alphabet. He spoke the Corsican dialect of Italian but remained totally ignorant of the French language.

Unlike older brother Joseph he was extremely gregarious, running off to the docks to listen to Corsican sailors relive past battles, and sometimes he was taken out on fishing boats. He also became a great favorite of French garrison soldiers who made him a uniform and cut him a toy sword. He led a street gang which frequently fought other gangs in sometimes bloody combats.[11]

But Nabolione also loved solitude. He enjoyed long horseback rides in a countryside redolent of the natural perfumes of *maquis* and myrtle and a dozen other fragrances awakened by blue sky and bright sun shining on hills of heather and groves of lemons and oranges, olive and chestnut trees. This was Paoli country, a land of bleating sheep and frisky goats, of barking foxes and rooting wild pigs. From the mountainfolk he learned of the rebellion and became a passionate admirer of the exiled general. Not everyone had succumbed to the French whose soldiers continued to hunt down the fugitives – "bandits" as they were called – who defied the French flag and, if caught, paid with their lives.

The total experience should not be understated, not so much because of family quarrels and bellicose brawls as from an unconscious osmosis of peculiarly Corsican traits – an intense family loyalty, an inner toughness that shielded one against adversity, an imagination fired by a thousand myths and beliefs, a temper quick to avenge an insult real or imagined, an inability to forgive a wrong until it was avenged (the Corsican *vendetta*) and, finally, an independent spirit as wild and free as the wind that pounded waves onto 300 miles of coast.

Those who remembered him as a boy recorded his intense curiosity, his never-ending and often mature flow of questions, his impatient movements and his long, brooding silences. From their diverse words emerge the portrait of a tough little boy wise beyond his years.

This was just as well. Nabolione's father can be criticized for many shortcomings, but Charles was determined to place his children favorably. This required a good education, which was impossible in Corsica, and he could not afford to send them to school in Italy or France. But he could and did petition the French king to educate them at the throne's expense, a laborious process that required several years to accomplish mainly because Charles had to obtain legal proof of his four quarters of nobility in order for his sons to be eligible for appointment. Finally all was in order for father and sons to depart for France. Joseph and Nabolione were to enter school at Autun in Bourgogne, their way opened by Comte Marbeuf's brother, the Bishop of Autun. The little party included Letitia's half-brother, 15-year-old Joseph Fesch, who would enter the prestigious seminary of Aix-en-Provence, while hopefully father Charles persuaded the French king to allow his sons to be further educated at the crown's expense, Joseph for the church, Nabolione for the army.

On 15 December 1778, the group sailed from Corsica. The future Napoleon Bonaparte was nine years old.

Notes

1   Marcaggi, 15 ff. See also Browning (*Boyhood*), 26, 34; Chuquet, I, 56–8.
2   Nasica, 28–30. See also Iung (*Bonaparte*), I, 30. I have relied almost entirely on Corsican and French sources for these opening chapters. For a satisfactory if somewhat embellished account in English, see Browning (*Boyhood*).
3   Nasica, 31–6. See also Carrington, 588–607.
4   Thiry (*Jeunesse*), 12. But see Carrington, 590.
5   Nasica, 28–30.
6   Bartel, 42–7. See also Chuquet, I, 58–60; Masson (*Jeunesse*), 21; Thiry (*Jeunesse*), 18. Thiry, loyal to the traditional French school, indignantly rejects the notion. Nonetheless Napoleon later gave Madame Marbeuf a liberal pension and was also extremely generous to their son. Napoleon added credence to his mother's infidelity in a letter written to General Gourgaud on St. Helena: "It was often said that Paoli was my father. It could well have been so, but

it is untrue. He was impotent." See Gourgaud, II, 332; Carrington, 596–602, for an equivocal view. Marbeuf, incidentally, had a daughter by his second wife.

7   Nasica, 31–6. See also Marcaggi, 15 ff.; Iung, (*Bonaparte*), I, 60–1.
8   Chuquet, I, 14.
9   Fortescue, 84.
10 Iung (*Bonaparte*), I, 63. See also Chuquet, 78.
11 Nasica, 55–61.

CHAPTER TWO

AUTUN, BRIENNE AND THE ÉCOLE MILITAIRE
1779–1785

*. . . reserved and studious, he prefers study to any type of
amusement, finding pleasure in the reading of good authors;
very applied [to the study of] abstract sciences, little curious as
to the others, [having] a thorough knowledge of mathematics
and geography; quiet, loving solitude, capricious, arrogant,
extremely inclined to egoism, speaking little, spirited in his
answers, quick and harsh in his replies, having much pride and
boundless ambition, this young man deserves to be encouraged.*

Report of Napoleon's examiner, École Militaire, Paris,
August 1785[1]

THE BUONAPARTE BOYS were soon installed in the secular school at
Autun where Catholic monks taught a curriculum largely devoted
to the humanities. One of Napoleon's teachers, Abbé Chardon,
recalled years later his student's "grave and pensive character,"
describing him as a lonely boy who learned his lessons easily and
quickly.[2] The good father taught him for three months during
which Napoleon learned conversational French (which he spoke
with a strong Corsican-Italian accent that he would never lose).
Joseph was of a different set, as gregarious, soft and timid as his
younger brother was cold, hard and aggressive. As a result
Napoleon soon became a natural target for school bullies with
whom he sometimes came to blows. On one occasion, when someone accused the vanquished Corsicans of having been cowards,
Napoleon, according to Abbé Chardon, calmly and cooly replied

that the French would never have seized Corsica had they been four to one, but that they had been ten to one. When the priest remarked that Paoli was a good general Napoleon responded, "Yes, sir, I would wish to be like him."[3]

Meanwhile father Charles' importunate stay in Paris had paid off, and in March Napoleon entered the royal military college of Brienne.

The school loomed high over the plains of the northern province of Champagne. It was a product of intended military reform, one of ten regional military colleges created only three years earlier to replace the educational decadence and innate snobbishness of the two traditional military academies of Paris and La Flèche. The theory was to democratize (within the day's context) the education of aspirant officers, or at least to moderate the arrogance of these young nobles. This effort had fallen flat, the new colleges quickly reverting to the role of preparatory school full of young aristo-crats, rich and poor, desirous of entering the famed École Militaire in Paris.

Napoleon was one of sixty court-appointed scholars. The crown paid 700 livres a year for the support of each; another sixty boys were private students whose families had to pay a hefty tuition fee. Students wore a blue jacket with red cuffs and collar and blue serge breeches. Teaching was in the hands of the Minimes monks of the Order of St. Benoît. The standard of teaching was poor – Napoleon easily passed his French entrance examination after only three months of tutelage at Autun. The curriculum covered ancient literature, the Latin classics – though it is difficult to believe in the depth claimed by Arthur Chuquet – ancient and modern history, geography, mathematics, voice, danc-ing, playing musical instruments and religious studies – Napoleon received his first communion at Brienne.[4]

His character did not immediately change. He easily accepted the spartan existence, a tiny room, a bed of straps holding a straw mattress and a single blanket even in winter, wholesome but tiresome meals, the usual punishments for infraction of regulations. Lacking Joseph's soft company he became even more isolated, gloomy and resentful. A fellow cadet, Louis Antoine Fauvelet de Bourrienne, later wrote that Napoleon's "ardent wish to acquire knowledge was evident from the commencement of his studies . . . his conversation [with teachers and comrades] almost always bore the appearance of ill-humor, and he was certainly not very amiable. This I attribute to the misfortunes his family had sustained and the impression made on him by the conquest of his country."[5]

Owing to his father's various commercial failures, he remained very poor and resentful. He continued to be bullied, his tiny frame the butt of jokes, his pronunciation and his strange first name – now Napolliene – mimicked, his ancestry insulted. He continued to fight back and more or less held his own, but he would carry the mental scars for life. He may also have carried other scars. The "nymphs" of Brienne were famous in other military schools for homosexual practices. Napoleon might well have been fair game for older and stronger boys; he later said that "brought up among the monks he had experienced the vices and the dissoluteness of the monastries."[6]

In spring of 1781 – he was 12 – he wrote miserably to his father asking to be removed from Brienne if he could not have an allowance. He did not wish to spend the money on weekly treats, but only to show his fellows that he could afford them had he wished. The appeal did not succeed. Poor Charles was in no position to send him even a few livres, nor did he have any intention of withdrawing his son from the school. The archives offer no more such letters, and it seems probable that Napoleon's concentrated studies taken with daydreams of Corsican independence helped him to submit to or even rise above such social and economic vicissitudes; judging from later correspondence he may also have received some financial support from his Uncle Fesch.[7]

His attitude seemed to improve during the next two years, probably because he was maturing and doing well academically.

Bourrienne recalled Napoleon making a snow fort in the great courtyard and leading the attack on the besieged "soldiers." The artillery, snowballs packed around stones, was sufficiently dangerous for the monks to pronounce a permanent ceasefire.

Napoleon was weak in Latin and refused to learn German, but he worked hard on French under the firm but kind tutelage of Abbé Dupuy. He excelled in mathematics, progressing to algebra, geometry and trigonometry. He enjoyed geography but his passion was history, particularly the lives of great men so dramatically presented by Plutarch (in translation). Possibly influenced by his protector, Comte Marbeuf, at some point he opted for a naval career. That he continued his arduous studies is confirmed by a report from an official inspector of schools who examined him in autumn of 1783. Monsieur de Kéralio described him as "slightly above four feet ten inches in height, well built, and in excellent health, obedient, polite and respectful; very correct conduct and has always distinguished himself in mathematics; his knowledge of history and geography is passable; he is rather weak in social conversation and in Latin." The examiner concluded that he "will make an excellent naval officer," should he be accepted in the École Militaire of Paris.[8]

Our next intimate glance of the boy comes from his father who was not only in severe financial straits but who had been suffering from a stomach complaint for some time. His efforts to regain the Odone inheritance were in bureaucratic limbo. One hopeful project, a mulberry nursery, designed for cultivation of silk worms, would not mature for another few years. Meanwhile he had to pay Louis and Lucien's tuitions at Autun while providing for three infants at home. He had managed to get seven-year-old Marie Anne admitted by royal warrant to the exclusive convent of St. Cyr at Versailles, which not only guaranteed her eight years of formal education but also a dowry for what undoubtedly would lead to an advantageous marriage. Countering this gain was Joseph Buonaparte's sudden decision to go into the army rather than the church, thus presenting Charles with another problem. In spring of 1784, having borrowed 500 livres from the governor of Ajaccio, he departed for France to escort Marie Anne to her new school, stopping at Autun to see Joseph and to pick up Lucien who would enter school at Brienne. Once free of these tasks he intended to consult specialists about his own deteriorating health.

Charles had not seen Napoleon for six years. He found a pubescent boy whose skin was tinged yellow, the result he decided "of the irregular functions of his organs and the preoccupations of his impatient mind. The extreme vivacity of his expression and the nervous contraction of his thin lips denoted the rapid flow of ideas which bubbled in this adolescent brain."[9]

The father respected this young brain sufficiently to discuss Joseph's decision to reject the offer from the Bishop of Autun of a profitable church benefice in favor of becoming a soldier. Napoleon agreed that this would be a foolhardy act. As he explained in a long letter to Uncle Fesch, Joseph possessed neither the requisite physical strength and health nor the necessary academic drive to become an army or a naval officer. He would need at least two years of mathematics to train for the navy, four or five years of study for the engineers (and then he would still be only a student) and three years to become an artillery officer (the infantry was too tiresome and unproductive to be considered). Contrarily he could enjoy a brilliant and lucrative career in the Church – as a bishop he could easily support the entire Buonaparte family. He hoped that Uncle Fesch would persuade Joseph to reconsider. If not, Joseph should return to Corsica and become a lawyer.

In this same letter he informed his uncle that the nine-year-old Lucien had been enrolled in the college of Brienne, a tall boy of almost four feet who was studying Latin and other subjects. "He knows French very well and has entirely forgotten Italian." He assured Uncle Fesch that Lucien would write to him more often. No doubt with his older brother standing over him, Lucien added a paragraph in somewhat uneven French, thanking his uncle for all the kindnesses of the past and promising to work harder in the hope they would continue.[10]

Napoleon's own hope for a naval career collapsed following his sponsor Comte Marbeuf's sudden death, after which rival students outmaneuvered him to win the few available places. A distraught Charles Buonaparte now persuaded the war minister to admit Napoleon to the École Militaire in Paris as a "gentleman-cadet" of artillery, subject to his passing an entrance examination. He also persuaded the inspector-general of military schools to admit Joseph to Brienne, courtesy of the king, again subject to his passing an entrance examination. He failed however to obtain a royal warrant for Lucien to study at Brienne – the boy would remain there as a private student. After taking the waters for his failing health the harassed father picked up Joseph at Autun and returned to Ajaccio.

Napoleon passed his official examination in mid September, the examiner noting, "Commanding character, imperious and opinionated." The candidate had no knowledge of literature, having concentrated solely on history, geography and mathematics from whence came "his predominant ideas."[11] In late October 1784 Napoleon and four other Brienne graduates entered the École Militaire in Paris.

Napoleon spent nearly a year at the École Militaire just off the Champ de Mars close to the Hôtel des Invalides, one of some 120 *cadets-gentilhommes* (student noblemen) between 13 and 15 years of age supervised by nearly as many teachers and staff. The cadets who were the guests of the king, the pensioners, paid nothing; private students paid 2,400 livres a year. Assigned to a cell-like room shared by Alexander des Mazis who was a year older, Napoleon was fitted with an elegant winter uniform – blue jacket lined in red and topped with a yellow collar (which in May would be replaced by an equally elegant summer uniform) – and was issued accessories that included a dozen each of shirts, collars, handkerchiefs and stockings. He ate in a main hall, 30 cadets to a table who were served five-course meals that varied from dinner and supper *with* meat to dinner and supper *without* meat. His studies included foreign languages, history, geography, mathematics, drawing, dancing, fencing, horsemanship and only one military course, fortification.[12]

He was not popular. Des Mazis was his only close friend. Fortunately he made notes of their stay, commenting on Napoleon's "fiery temper and rebellious nature." On one occasion he knocked down a bigger boy and was hauled before the captain commandant to defend himself. "I was insulted, I have revenged myself," he said. "That is all."[13]

Despite the improvement in creature comforts the school was not to his liking. He later objected to the striking differences between rich and poor cadets, the former in his opinion contaminating the latter with their constant display of self-conceit and vanity. He also objected to the number of servants and grooms, to the costly and luxurious stables and to five-course meals. Would it not be better, he wrote, for these officer candidates to eat humble regulation bread, brush their own uniforms, clean their own shoes and boots? Forced to live modestly as many of them would have to do in an army career, they would become physically more robust, better able to withstand the vagaries of weather, to hold up to the stress of battle "and to inspire respect and blind devotion from the soldiers serving under their command."[14] Napoleon intended to send his criticism to the war minister, Comte de Ségur, but he wisely consulted his old master at Brienne who, horrified, promptly advised him to forget it – which he did. Ironically, he might have found a friend at court. Ségur had been fighting unsuccessfully against these rich menus, pointing out among other drawbacks that the staff consumed almost half of each day's provisions.[15]

Des Mazis described his room-mate as often walking alone "at a rapid pace . . . his arms crossed, his head lowered as in later portraits," oblivious to other cadets, sometimes smiling or gesturing. His conversation was always serious but interesting. "Corsica most often was the subject of our talks," des Mazis noted. "He hoped that one day it would become a free and independent state."[16] He was a good student but held an "overwhelming distaste" for the study of the German language which he seems to have regarded in Voltaire's words as fit "for soldiers and horses, necessary only for the march."[17] He enjoyed fencing lessons and was very tough and aggressive despite his small size, but he preferred leading the attack or defense of redoubts made from snow.

His stay suddenly darkened in early 1785. His father, facing more obstacles than ever in pursuit of the Odone inheritance, decided that despite ill-health he must escort Joseph to the artillery school at Metz and then further petition Paris officials to respect his claim. Charles collapsed in Marseilles and was taken to a specialist in Montpellier where he died from what was diagnosed as stomach cancer. He was 38 years old. Letitia's half-brother, Joseph Fesch, now an ordained priest, was at his bedside, but Charles angrily rejected his intended ministrations, wanting only "to die quietly."[18]

Despite assertions of later French historians, Napoleon did not seem unduly upset at the news. Aside from a letter to Archdeacon Lucien in Ajaccio, he sent his mother a short and rather stiff letter of commiseration. Des Mazis noted that when a priest wished to take him to the infirmary, as was the custom with a personal tragedy, he refused, remarking that he had no need of consolation.[19] Perhaps he was even relieved that his father's suffering had ended, and that his death would cause Joseph's return to Corsica to look after the indigent Buonaparte family.

Napoleon and his fellows were examined in August 1785. The report of his examiner, perhaps the famous mathematician-astronomer Laplace, is quoted at the beginning of this chapter. Of 58 commissioned aspirants, Napoleon ranked a poor forty-second; his friend des Mazis placed fifty-sixth. Never mind their showing, they had won the right to wear the cherished sword presented only to graduates of the École Militaire.

So equipped they departed for their assigned regiment and new adventures at Valence.

Notes

1 Iung (*Bonaparte*), I, 125.

2 Iung (*Bonaparte*), I, 70.

3 Iung (*Bonaparte*), I, 72–3. See also Chuquet, I, 79–80; Marcaggi, 20 ff.

4 Chuquet, I, 85–8, 102–7, 204. See also Bourrienne, I, 7–8, who commented on the poor quality of teaching; Iung (*Bonaparte*), I, 78–9; Browning (*Boyhood*), 46–8.

5 Bourrienne, I, 6–7. See also Marcaggi, 20 ff.

6 Chuquet, I, 111.

7 Iung (*Bonaparte*), I, 84. See also Chuquet, I, 114–15, who argues not very convincingly that this letter is not authentic; Browning (*Boyhood*), 60–4, for an English translation of Napoleon's letter to Uncle Fesch; Coston, 35–6.

8 Iung (*Bonaparte*), I, 93.

9 Iung (*Bonaparte*), I, 97.

10 Iung (*Bonaparte*), I, 97–9.

11 Iung (*Bonaparte*), I, 110

12 Chuquet, I, 182–211, 232–3.

13 Bartel, 256.

14 Iung (*Bonaparte*), I, 118.

15 Chuquet, I, 208, 210–11.

16 Bartel, 259.

17 Asprey (*Frederick the Great*), 397.

18 Iung (*Bonaparte*), I, 119. See also Thiry (*Jeunesse*), 36–7. Thiry, following many French historians, has Charles returning to the Catholic faith on his deathbed, and he also describes Napoleon as "lively affected." See also Chuquet, I, 212–13.

19 Bartel, 259.

CHAPTER THREE

THE STUDENT:
VALENCE AND AUXONNE
1785–1789

*Tactics, evolutions, the science of the engineer and the
artillerist can be learned from books, almost like geometry, but
the knowledge of the heroic facts of war can only be acquired
by study of the history of wars, the battles of great captains,
and by experience.*

Napoleon on St. Helena[1]

IN TRAVELLING TO their new post, the young lieutenants
Buonaparte and des Mazis spent what little money they had on
books in Lyons and would have had to walk the remaining fifty
miles to the regimental garrison at Valence but for a kindly
artillery officer who paid their fare. Here they were well received
by des Mazis' brother, Gabriel, a captain who soon familiarized
them with their new surroundings.[2]

The change from formal school routine could not have been
more welcome. Napoleon rented a small room in the private home
of Monsieur Bou, capably run by his aging daughter, Marie
Claudine, for which he paid 10 francs a month. Along with other
junior officers he took his meals in an inn, L'Hôtel des Trois
Pigeons, at a monthly cost of 35 francs. Regimental expenses
amounted to a monthly 15 francs, which meant that 720 francs a
year of basic expenses had to be met from the meager annual pay
of 1,120 francs.

As a subaltern in a company of bombardiers Napoleon spent
two months on probation, first as an ordinary gunner, then as a

non-commissioned officer. Only in January 1786 was he accepted as a lieutenant entitled to wear the blue uniform with red facings, gold trimmings, yellow buttons marked with the regimental number and gold-trimmed and embellished epaulettes. Thus attired, he was entrusted with garrison and field duties. Although he relished the new freedom and responsibility of his rank he did not enjoy the off-duty company of most of his fellow officers, having soon realized that the social discrimination current at Autun, Brienne and the École Militaire was also prevalent in regiment La Fère, itself a microcosm of the entire French army.

This army, once the pride of the Sun King (Louis XIV) and the scourge of all Europe, had been in steady decline since the latter half of his long reign (1643–1715). Its massive failure in the Seven Years' War (1756–1763) during Louis XV's reign (1715–1774), when France was allied with Austria and Russia against Prussia and England, had cost France a considerable loss of colonies and an immense loss of prestige.

During the two decades following that disastrous war some able generals – Bourcet, Guibert, St. Germain, Gribeauval and Broglie among them – had attempted to introduce reforms ranging from proper recruitment and training, decent pay and improved food for the troops to officer promotion based as much on seniority and merit as on royal favor.

The reforms were long overdue. Cadet Napoleon Buonaparte's previous criticism of the caste system had been voiced years earlier by a minister of war, General Comte St. Germain, who strongly condemned

the distinction between court and provincial nobility,
between the rich and the poor. The former at once comes
by the senior grades as its right; the latter, by the sole
misfortune of birth and poverty, is condemned to stagnate
in the junior grades. This practice is doubly pernicious: the
first group does not have to work in order to succeed . . .
the second does not work because it would be useless. Thus

all ambition is destroyed, but without ambition man is nothing and can only vegetate.

The French army, the minister thundered, was only a dumping ground for useless nobility, for a dozen types of generals, colonels and lieutenant colonels "not one of whom has real and active functions," who devote themselves exclusively "to their affairs and pleasures . . . who do nothing, who learn nothing, stagnating in idleness, in the most profound ignorance."[3]

Owing to the indolent kings, Louis XV and the present ruler, Louis XVI, each dominated by the powerful feudal nobility who controlled the army, the reforms did not materialize. St. Germain attempted to organize scattered regiments into brigades and divisions to be stationed about the country, both to get rid of command deadwood and to increase the army's efficiency and mobility. Like their Prussian counterparts, these units would train all year round. This reform was scorned by generals who refused to leave Paris even for a mere four months of duty in the provinces, one reason being that they did not know how to give orders, another that they were too decrepit to appear in front of the troops.[4] St. Germain also failed in attempts to reorganize the war ministry and rid it of corrupt and inefficient officers and civilians.

Although such subordinate generals as Jean Baptiste Gribeauval courageously pushed through a few reforms, mainly in cavalry and artillery, the grand edifice remained untouched, the all-powerful court nobility in full command. In 1775 the king named seven new marshals whose qualifications were virtually nil, a fact not lost on a cynical French public which categorized them on the basis of the seven deadly sins: for example the Duc d'Harcourt, the idle one; the Duc de Noailles, the avaricious one; the Duc de Duras, the lustful one; the Comte de Noailles, the arrogant one, and so on. In 1776 the kingdom supported 535 general officers of whom 20 were marshals, 167 lieutenant generals, 364 brigadier generals and no fewer than 1,500 general staff officers. In 1789 the roster would number 966 brigadier generals and

1,918 general staff officers, which worked out at one officer for 75 men and one general officer for 157 men. The highest ranking officers, princes of the blood, received 60,000 livres a year (plus vast perquisites), another 21 generals 30,000 livres, 114 lieutenant generals 10–12,000 livres, and several hundred aides and orderlies very comfortable incomes.[5]

Almost fifteen years after St. Germain announced his first reforms, Marshal Duc de Broglie wrote that

> the principal cause [of the poor showing of French armies] is the total ignorance from the subaltern to lieutenant generals of the duties of their profession and of all the details in which they should enter. Thus the result is that the lieutenant and the captain neither train nor manage nor command their companies, nor do the colonels, brigadiers and lieutenant generals know how to lead their regiments, brigades, to employ them in battle or maneuver them correctly.[6]

Fortunately for Napoleon each artillery regiment was located next to an artillery training school, and not all of Gribeauval's criticism applied to the Valence school, the best in the army. If Napoleon did not take to most of his fellow officers, he did take to both the theoretical and practical teachings that filled his days with courses in advanced mathematics, the workings of cannon, howitzers and mortars, manufacture and storage of powder, the mechanics of forges and foundries, positioning and defense of batteries, diverse cannon ranges, artillery in attack and defense, sieges, the fine points of fortifications, map-making and map-reading – all the intricacies of his profession, three days a week of classes, three days in the field.

Although he studied hard and learned quickly he did not seem too preoccupied with his future career. His off-duty hours were devoted to the ground floor of a building close to his lodgings; the attraction here was a small bookshop run by Monsieur Aurel who had set aside a private reading room for officers, and from whom Napoleon could rent books and even on rare occasions buy one. Here he immersed himself in historical and political studies that often kept him up a good part of the night.

Aside from these studies and professional duties he continued reading James Boswell's history of Corsica which, taken with Jean Jacques Rousseau's explosive libertarian writings, particularly *L'Emile* and *Le Contrat social*, and Abbé de Raynal's equally fiery *L'Histoire philosophique de deux Indes*, excited him tremendously as a portent of Corsican liberation. Letters from his family brought him even closer to the island and in early spring he made his first notes on what would become an unfinished history of Corsica, a written vendetta against French rule that for the next four years would haunt him. It was perhaps this impassioned resentment combined with acute homesickness, improper diet and overwork that brought on an adolescent melancholy manifested by a brief treatise on loneliness and the feasibility of suicide.

"Alone in the midst of mankind," he wrote, "I return to my room to muse and to succumb to all the force of my melancholy. Wither does it turn today? It turns to death . . . Because I have to die anyway, should I not kill myself?"[7] Like Prince Hamlet however he cast off his melancholy to live another day, his spirits raised by meeting some kindly townspeople, courtesy of the Bishop de Marbeuf. One of them, Caroline de Colombier, would take her place in Napoleonic history as his companion on an early morning walk in the hills during which they munched succulent cherries.

Such light moments were rare. After a day of professional studies or drilling, he was soon poring over Parisian newspapers in Aurel's shop or making more notes for his history of Corsica. This routine was suddenly broken when his company was ordered to put down a riot of silkworkers in Lyons. The trouble was over (and three ringleaders hanged) before his unit arrived, but the troops remained for a month. Napoleon thoroughly enjoyed the expedition and would like to have spent the rest of his life in Lyons, as he informed Uncle Fesch, adding somewhat pompously, "but one must follow one's destiny and above all comply to the exigencies of one's profession. A soldier should not attach himself to any thing other than his flag."[8]

From Lyons the detachment rejoined the regiment which had been transferred to Douai. There Napoleon learned that grand-uncle Lucien was very ill, and that the Ajaccio administration had refused to pay further subsidies in support of his mother's young nursery of mulberry trees, which had forced her to cancel her contract. This was adequate excuse for him to claim leave which was granted, commencing the first day of September 1786.

Despite family worries, Napoleon spent a couple of weeks visiting Uncle Fesch, still at Aix, then young Lucien. He finally arrived in Ajaccio in mid September to a riotous welcome by his mother, his brother Joseph and the younger children. Joseph, who had not seen him for several years, found him to be a serious student soon immersed in the books that he had brought with him, a trunk full of the works of Plato, Plutarch, Cicero and Tacitus (in French translation), along with Montaigne, Montesquieu and Raynal.[9]

Napoleon soon discovered a changing political climate. Agents of Pasquale Paoli, supported by English gold and directed from Tuscany by Paoli's brother, Clement, were actively propagandizing in Corsican hinterlands that were off-limits to French officials and soldiers. Napoleon apparently did not directly involve himself in this sedition, yet he did not hesitate to speak of his desire for Corsican independence to his pro-French family. His mother was too preoccupied with domestic problems to pay much attention; neither could she appreciate her officer son's infatuation with the French Enlightenment in the form of Voltaire and Rousseau's writings, nor his fulminations against tyrant France. Grand-uncle Lucien did lend a willing ear but he was old and ailing, intent only on guarding a hoard of gold stashed under his bed, not the most interesting companion for a rebellious 17-year-old. Napoleon as usual preferred his own company. He passed active and happy days in trying to resurrect the wreck of Mellili house – Grand-uncle Lucien refused to lend him the necessary cash – working in the salt marshes and trying to cope with the moribund mulberry nursery.

He often rode alone in the countryside, breathing in the air tinctured with the sweet fragrance of orange blossoms, drinking the crystal-clear water from mountain streams, daydreaming in a favorite grotto high in the hills, and relishing the sight of the sea. Probably as a result of a meeting with Abbé Raynal in Marseilles he resumed work on the history of Corsica, studying Italian (so his brother Joseph tells us) in order to read appropriate histories of this tragic island.

He also began writing an historical novel and a play, besides finishing a short story (which unfortunately for his literary reputation has survived).[10] The winter passed all too quickly. In April 1787 he requested and was granted an extension of leave for another seven months on rather suspect grounds of illness. This saw him through the grape harvest, and in mid September he left for Paris where he hoped to recoup the money he claimed was owing on the subsidy for the mulberry nursery.

Paris was a lonely city for a lonely young man. Living in a cheap hotel, he had few if any friends and little enough money for food, let alone for theater and opera. One night in late November when passing the Palais Royal, he came on a young prostitute huddled in a doorway. Struck by her pale skin, soft voice and timid manner, he listened to her tale of misery, sermonizing her appropriately and then took her off to bed (later regretting it), a somewhat bizarre experience which he recorded in a strange mixture of sadness and distaste.[11]

The effect was temporary. A few days later he was back at work, drawing up an outline of the misfortunes of Corsica which he believed would cause his compatriots "to shed tears" in reading.[12]

His petition to the government for the mulberry subsidy having failed – and being otherwise disillusioned by wealthy Parisians given over to extravagant pleasures at odds with what he deemed to be patriotic duties – he persuaded the war minister, Gribeauval, to intervene on his behalf and was given another six months of leave. This may seem unbelievable to the reader, but frequent long leaves – generally paid and often extended – were quite usual, a practice held over from royalist days.

Napoleon returned once again to Ajaccio to resume his former routine. With the history of Corsica still dominating his thoughts, he spent most of his time interviewing elderly islanders who had fought in the wars of independence. He probably roughed out an introduction and the first two chapters of his work at this time, choosing to tell the story in the form of letters introduced by a fictitious veteran of the wars. If so, it was about his only solid accomplishment before rejoining his regiment in the spring of 1788.[13]

Regiment La Fère had moved to Auxonne, a small town in the Bourgogne about 20 miles southeast of Dijon. Napoleon would spend the next 15 months here, a period that played a major role in his military and general education.

He lived modestly with other junior officers in uncomfortable barracks, his private routine broken only by regimental duties. The small and serious second lieutenant however was soon noticed by the artillery school's commandant, General Baron du Teil, who at 66 was a highly qualified professional artilleryman. Du Teil appointed the young lieutenant to a special commission that was to study certain effects of heavy gun and mortar fire.[14] This complimentary assignment brought him into close touch with the legendary Professor Jean Louis Lombard – a mathematician now in his seventies who had translated a classic work, Benjamin Rolins' *Principles of Artillery*, into French – and also with Captain Gassendi who had taught him at Valence and who would become a friend. Alexander and Gabriel des Mazis were still on hand and he also made friends with an older civilian *commissaire* of war, Jean Marin Naudin, who had served for fifteen years in Corsica.

Social life even with friends was practically non-existent: "I go to bed at ten and get up at four in the morning," he informed his mother, adding that he ate only one meal a day in order to stay in good health.[15] Not surprisingly he came down with anemia and fell victim to a serious fever (probably malarial, induced by unhealthy air from fog-ridden winds, marshes and stagnant over-flows of the Saône river) from which he only slowly recovered while continuing with his unhealthy regimen.

Alexander des Mazis, who loved women and parties, could not understand Napoleon's intellectual isolation. "What is it to me what happened a thousand years ago?" he rhetorically asked his friend. "Of what importance to me are the puerile discussions of mankind? Don't you sense the emptiness of your heart [sitting] in the middle of your room?"[16] Napoleon probably replied that the heart was a matter of knowledge, of books and hard work. His heart was doubtless very full in late summer when he wrote excit-edly to Uncle Fesch that General du Teil had appointed him to command 200 men in construction of a training polygon, "a work that demanded great [mathematical] abilities," but an honor resented by lieutenants and captains who were senior to him.[17] (Apparently something went wrong with the project and he and his sergeant were jailed, the sergeant for eight days, Napoleon for twenty-four hours.)

This was but a brief interruption to his studies. He particularly enjoyed Professor Lombard's lectures as well as his recent treatise on cannon and howitzer fire, and he was soon deep into studies of infantry and artillery tactics recommended by du Teil. Away from the classroom he sighted and fired the big guns, mastering the technical details necessary to a qualified commander. Cooped up in his small rooms he read through such works as *De l'usage de l'artillerie nouvelle* written by du Teil's brother, Jean Chevalier du Teil. He wrote endlessly on tactical matters, lengthy studies on powder, velocity, the advantages of rifled cannon, the speed and rotation of cannon-balls. Internal evidence from his writings, along with common sense, suggests that he was familiar with Guibert's famous *Essai général de tactique*, and he may well have discovered Bourcet's unpublished work, *Principes de la guerre de montagnes*, which would have been of particular interest since

Bourcet had been military adviser to the Comte de Vaux, the general who defeated Paoli and subdued Corsica.[18]

Away from classes, firing ranges and his books and notebooks he had little to do with fellow officers, both because of his extreme poverty and because he regarded the bulk of them as frivolous fools (particularly the aristocrats). In return they looked on him as much too serious and pompous, and on occasion he was the unwilling butt of barracks jokes.[19] In truth he had little time to give anyone. When not reading professional treatises he was taking copious notes from thick volumes of ancient and modern history, geography, political philosophy and biography. Thirty-six notebooks survive of his revelations which he often turned into monographs, including one that questioned royal authority. "There are very few kings," he dangerously concluded in a brief outline of the work, "who do not deserve to be dethroned."[20] He wrote essays on the ancient governments of the Persians, Greeks, Scythians, Egyptians, Carthaginians, Assyrians, Arabs, Turks, French and English, describing and analyzing governments, laws, religions, manners and customs. He read or reread (in translation) philosophers from Plato to Rousseau. Frederick the Great of Prussia fascinated him, particularly his military campaigns, as had earlier those of Alexander, Hannibal, Caesar and others. He studied the history of the East and West Indies; laws and makers of laws through the ages; natural sciences and particularly Buffon.[21] "I have no other resource here than work," he informed Grand-uncle Lucien, ". . . I sleep very little because of my illness . . . I eat only once a day."[22]

Many years later he would recall those days at Auxonne. "When I had saved two écus of six livres I would hurry like a happy child to the bookstore. I went often to look at the books with the sin of envy; I coveted [them] for a long time before my purse allowed me to buy. Such were the joys and seductions of my youth."[23]

In spring of 1789 Napoleon was sent with a small detachment of troops to quell a riot in nearby Seurre. Although it had subsided by the time the soldiers arrived, they remained for three weeks. Napoleon spent the time in an intensive study of revolutions, not so much because of the increasingly unstable political situation in France as because of his desire to foment such in Corsica.

He had reworked the opening chapters of his Corsican opus and he now hit on the idea of enlisting the support of General Pasquale Paoli, the deposed Corsican leader living in London. "I was born when the country [Corsica] was dying," his letter to Paoli began. "Thirty thousand Frenchmen vomited onto our coasts, drowning the throne of Liberty in waves of blood . . . The cries of the dying, the groans of the oppressed, the tears of despair surrounded my cradle of birth."[24] The purple prose continued in strong anti-French rhetoric that would have summarily ended his career, if not his life, had the authorities read it. Fortunately he sent a copy of the introduction to his former teacher at Brienne, Abbé Dupuy, for critical reading. Dupuy replied that he liked the idea but that the choice of words, the arrangement of material and some of the harsh conclusions needed considerable modification. Napoleon did not accept the criticism with much grace, but did send the old gentleman the first two chapters. These drew further critical remarks, including the need for additional research and a more mature presentation, not to mention a veiled warning: "This language is too strong in a monarchy."[25]

Lieutenant Buonaparte was in youthful limbo and it was a particularly difficult time for him. He must have thought that he was wearing his father's shroud of failure while struggling to survive on the meager income from a country and an army for which he felt but slight attachment and, when it came to Corsica, considerable revulsion. Perhaps he did not realize that a salvation of sorts was on its way – marked by the meeting of the French *Estates générales* in June. The bubbling pot of political, social and economic discontent was about to explode into what history knows as the French Revolution.

Notes

1   Wilkinson (*Rise*), 144.

2   Bartel, 260. See also Chuquet, I, 232–3, 423; Browning (*Boyhood*), 89–90.

3   Iung (*Bonaparte*), I, 136–7.

4   Iung (*Bonaparte*), I, 170.

5   Iung (*Bonaparte*), I, 139–42.

6   Iung (*Bonaparte*), I, 135.

7   Iung (*Bonaparte*), I, 168. See also Browning (*Boyhood*), 281–4, for the diary entry and English translation.

8   Iung (*Bonaparte*), I, 166.

9   Thiry (*Jeunesse*), 50–1. See also Browning (*Boyhood*), 100.

10 Iung (*Bonaparte*), I, 175–8.

11 Chuquet, II, 15. See also Masson, *Fonds Libri*, I, 181; Browning (*Boyhood*), 311–14, for the letter and English translation.

12 Chuquet, II, 47.

13 Masson, *Fonds Libri*, I, 200–1. See also Chuquet, II, 52.

14 Chuquet, I, 353–5, 479. See also du Teil, 65–73. General du Teil would be shot for treason in 1794.

15 Iung (*Bonaparte*), I, 203–4.

16 Chuquet, II, 1–2.

17 Iung (*Bonaparte*), I, 187.

18 Chuquet, I, 340. See also du Teil, 71–87; Wilkinson (*Rise*), 8, 18–19; Bartel, 172–3; Colin, 134–7; Epstein (*Modern Warfare*), 10–13.

19 Chuquet, I, 343–5. See also Browning (*Boyhood*), 109–10.

20 Chuquet, II, 25.

21 Masson, *Fonds Libri*, I, lists sixty of Napoleon's writings of which twenty-seven were written at Auxonne. See also Masson and Biaggi, II.

22 Chuquet, I, 309.

23 Thiry (*Jeunesse*), 68–9.

24 Coston, I, 134, II, 87. See also Iung (*Bonaparte*), I, 195.

25 Chuquet, II, 49–51.

CHAPTER FOUR

THE REVOLUTION AND THE REBEL: AUXONNE AND CORSICA 1789–1791

. . . against oppression insurrection is not only a right but the most sacred of duties.

Déclaration des droits . . . Paris, August 1789[1]

EVENTS IN FRANCE moved rapidly that spring and summer of 1789. In early May at the instigation of his finance minister, Jacques Necker, King Louis XVI called a meeting of the *Estates générales*, the first in 175 years. This body consisted of representatives from the First Estate (clergy), the Second Estate (nobility) and the Third Estate (commoners), who met at Versailles, ostensibly to discuss the touchy matter of taxes. As ordained by tradition, each estate debated in a separate chamber. As was also traditional, the protests of the common-folk were stymied by the unyielding rhetoric of the other two estates whose priests and aristocrats were opposed to any variation of a feudal system of government. The impasse ended in mid June when the commoners declared themselves "the sole representatives of the country" and called for a national assembly.[2]

This led a few days later to the famous meeting known as the *Jeu de paume* which brought about the unprecedented presence of the three estates in one hall. Once again the king adjured the delegates to confine debate to tax matters, of course in separate chambers. With that he left, followed *en masse* by clergy and nobility. The commoners, however, defying in Mirabeau's words "the force of bayonets," refused to depart. Their defiance soon paid off when they were joined by eighty penitent priests and half a hundred nobles. A frightened crown ordered in troops who refused to march. Louis caved in and again ordered the estates to meet as a national assembly. He was still not the villain of the piece in the eyes of most of the commoners who, correctly regarding him as the unwilling but weak captive of a powerful and greedy feudal nobility, shared the belief that disobedience and rebellion were necessary weapons to free the king from his keepers.

Had Louis been stronger (and brighter) he could probably have salvaged the situation by agreeing to relatively minor compromises, followed by dissolution of the assembly. But he was not strong, nor did radical members of the assembly want to disband with the country on the verge of a revolution from which they expected to profit. It was radical Jacobin agents who organized the Paris mobs that on 14 July 1789 tore down the tollgates of the capital and stormed the Bastille prison, murdering its governor and the provost of Paris in the process of freeing a few prisoners.

While panic-stricken princes and nobles fled Paris, the king and his finance minister met with rebel leaders in the Hôtel de Ville. There they learned of the illegal election of a liberal mayor and the appointment of General Marquis de Lafayette to command the national guard. Louis' acceptance of these *faits accomplis* was yet another capitulation of his authority – the historian Louis Madelin dates the downfall of the throne from this episode.[3]

An intimidated and confused king next accepted the *cocarde nationale* – the tri-colored rebel badge worn on the hat – and in early August approved assembly decrees that declared equality of taxes, abolition of feudal rights and privileges, and the preparation of a constitution that would strip the throne of power by transferring it to the assembly – roughly the notion of a constitutional monarchy.[4]

Louis' virtual abdication of royal authority at first resulted in nation-wide euphoria, but this was soon dampened by armed bands seizing landowners, burning their estates and committing other crimes against defenseless citizenry. This brutal but understandable manifestation of centuries-old hatred of feudal and ecclesiastical privileges was to find expression in the preface to the new constitution, the famous *Déclaration des droits de l'homme et du citoyen*, source of the fiery quotation at the beginning of this chapter.[5] Here was a license for mob rule, and the radical leaders of the assembly did not hesitate to turn their mobs loose, against not only the king and court but also their more conservative colleagues.

In early October armed bands stormed into Versailles palace, forced their way into the hall of the assembly, roughed up some terrified deputies, pushed into the palace itself, murdered the guards who were covering the flight of Queen Marie Antoinette and finally confronted the king. Accepting General Lafayette's advice, Louis agreed to move the royal residence to the Tuileries in Paris. A frightened assembly followed the court to the capital, henceforth to meet in the large hall of the riding school in the Tuileries.

From there the assembly would pretend to guide the destinies of the new and revolutionary France, oblivious to the fact that it had already succumbed to an evil as great as that of feudal oppression – the rule of the extreme left.

Neither Auxonne nor regiment La Fère escaped the pervasive revolutionary air. A few days after the fall of the Bastille a major riot broke out in the town when a rebel mob knocked down the gates and sacked the tax office. Local civil guards and regimental soldiers quickly broke up the riot but only after one regimental detachment had refused to march against the rebels. In August a group of soldiers mutinied and forced the regimental commander to hand over a slush fund that was designed for their welfare. The soldiers then got very drunk, spilled into the streets and gathered up officers who were forced to drink and dance with them.[6]

This must have been about the last straw for Napoleon, who recently had taken "the new oath 'To the nation, the law and the king' prescribed by the Constituent Assembly."[7] Despite his own transgressions he realized that an army without discipline was nothing but an armed mob, an affront to legal authority and very dangerous to anyone who would dare confront it. A disciplined army offered the young lieutenant little enough of a future; a mutinous army a very uncertain one. Corsica on the other hand needed him, as did his family. Shortly after the riot he wrote to Uncle Fesch that "the sad state of my family distresses me the more because I see no remedy for it."[8]

But perhaps a remedy was at hand? Napoleon had learned that the strong Paoli faction was intent on gaining independence from France. If this were so, the Corsican national guard would perforce play a vital role; who more qualified than he, a professional officer, to lead it? Turning his back on France once again, he applied for six months' leave. This granted, he sent Uncle Fesch preliminary instructions to prepare the ground for his own plan of rebellion in Corsica.[9]

Before sailing from Marseilles he called for a second time on the well-known Abbé Raynal, the septuagenarian outré liberal whom he regarded as a revolutionary hero for wanting to relieve oppressed humanity. Raynal again received him graciously and encouraged him to complete the history of Corsica.[10]

Napoleon arrived in Ajaccio in late September to find his family in worse financial straits than ever. Outwardly the island was almost as he had left it. "Laws, regulations, taxes, administration, all were as if there had been no *Estates générales*," wrote a later historian, "no Constituent Assembly, no 14th of July."[11]

The old masters of Corsica, protected and subsidized by the French, still ran the island – garrison forces still sported the white cockade. But in addition to the royalists, two other political movements existed, one being the Paolists led by Paoli from London, the other the young liberals. Although two royalist deputies had been sent to the *Estates générales* at Versailles – General Comte Matteo Buttafuoco as deputy of the nobility and Abbé Peretti as deputy of the clergy – Corsican voters had elected two patriots, Cristoforo Saliceti and Colonna di Cesari Rocca, as delegates of the commoners. In the subsequent national assembly, Buttafuoco and Peretti sat on the right or conservative side, Saliceti and Colonna on the left or liberal side.

As royalist supporters of the French occupation of Corsica, Buttafuoco and Peretti had become increasingly unpopular at home while Saliceti and Colonna were the hope of young Corsican liberals. Of the two, Saliceti would become the man of the future. A tax assessor trained in the law he was a convinced liberal with a keen and subtle mind.[12] He was also a realist who scorned the notion of an independent Corsica which he believed at best would be a minnow soon swallowed by bigger fish. Saliceti instead favored the close attachment of Corsica to France, an arrangement desired by many young and ambitious Corsicans tired of being confined to a small island where they were held down by a conservative élite. Here he was opposed not only by the island's royalists but also by old guard patriots who demanded complete independence. In London, Pasquale Paoli was pumping for the French assembly to make Corsica a loose French protectorate to which he would return to rule as virtual dictator.

Napoleon, enthusiastically supported by brother Joseph who had recently returned from studying law in Italy, at once threw himself into the Paolist movement in Ajaccio. Headed by Philippe Masseria, whose father and brother had died in liberating the island from the Genoese, its ultimate goal was to seize the French fort in Ajaccio and force the French overlords to depart. First however it was necessary to replace the French puppet Committee of Twelve by a rebel central committee. Napoleon soon enlarged this goal to include the formation of an island-wide armed militia to be paid for by the islanders, thus free of French control. A formal petition calling for these changes was coldly received by Buttafuoco in the French assembly and by the French war minister who would submit it to the crown only if the

Committee of Twelve in Ajaccio approved it – which of course they did not.[13]

The rejection caused a general protest from the rebels whose activities had brought increasing anarchy. Napoleon wished to call the citizenry to arms, seize the citadel and chase the French garrison from the town. This threat was countered by the arrival of French *commissaires* and a Swiss regiment from Corte who dissolved an incipient national guard and closed down the Jacobin club.

Recognizing the futility of armed resistance for the time being, Napoleon wrote a lengthy letter of protest to the national assembly, a document which refuted every objection to an island militia posited by the Committee of Twelve and in so doing hotly attacked its members. Signed by Napoleon and his fellow rebels it was sent to the Corsican deputies, Saliceti and Colonna, in Paris. On Napoleon's part this was a remarkable if not foolhardy act which could have resulted in a court-martial and possibly a death sentence for treasonous behavior as a French officer. Perhaps he reasoned that the major schisms produced by the revolution both in the French government and in the assembly would protect him. Or perhaps he didn't care, for again he courted arrest by going to Bastia where he distributed the revolutionary cockade to local patriots while fomenting a mutiny against the legitimate government.[14]

Despite intense political confusion in France, both its government and assembly had reason for major concern regarding this restless island. Continuing local uprisings, some successful, brought a strong reaction in Paris from former island governors who argued that Corsican "savages and bandits" could never be brought sufficiently to heel to accept complete annexation, and that France should withdraw its forces and save the vast sums spent on the occupation. Such defeatism did not sit well with Corsica's royalist delegate Buttafuoco, whose advice to the French court was brief and brutal: "Bribe some Corsicans, have no pity on the others, just send troops to make them obey you and you will get the better of these shabby people who deceive themselves with grand words and in reality lack the courage to fight for their objectives."[15] This simplistic appreciation was approved by the court. General Comte de Narbonne, a former island governor, was ordered to form an expeditionary force to land in Corsica.

The French assembly in general did not agree with the proposed punitive action, a dissent ably farmed by Saliceti who, by dexterous maneuvering with his fellow delegates, had formed a significant power base in this body. He wanted Corsica to become an "integral part of the French nation," the new *revolutionary* nation which would guarantee young Corsicans the opportunity to build prosperous futures in France and in addition would allow exiled Corsicans to return to their homes.[16]

The contretemps was solved by two powerful assembly leaders, Constantin Volney and Raquetti de Mirabeau, who demanded assembly approval of Corsica's integrated status – only then would the insurrections cease. The legislators agreed and also passed (over royalist opposition) Mirabeau's motion to give amnesty to exiled Corsicans. Although Paoli's own proposal for the island's future had not yet been submitted to the assembly, the old general swallowed his annoyance and wrote a fulsome letter saying that he was overjoyed by Corsica being made a province of France. The French court in turn canceled Narbonne's punitive expedition and also ordered certain restraints on army interference in Corsican affairs.[17]

This twist of events caught Napoleon and his friends by surprise since the assembly decree mentioned neither their desire for a central committee nor for a Corsican national guard. In this interim period Napoleon contented himself by reviving the proscribed national guard unit in Ajaccio, in which he would serve as a mere private while continuing to make fiery speeches at the reopened Jacobin club.

He also returned to the frayed and altered manuscript of his Corsican history. He now reworked the material into two letters that covered the former centuries of Corsica's convoluted history but stopped short of Paoli's war of independence. This effort, entitled *Lettres de Corse*, was sent off to the long-suffering Raynal.[18]

Early in 1790 disturbing rumors swept through Corsica to the effect that the French government, contrary to assembly decrees, intended to abandon the island so that the Genoese could occupy it prior to General Paoli's return. Major outbreaks between locals and French troops followed at Calvi, Bastia and St. Florent, nor was the situation calmed when Paoli arrived in Paris that spring to be given an audience by the king.

It was certainly an exciting time, and in Napoleon's mind a crucial one so potentially important to his future that he audaciously asked for an additional few months of paid leave on medical grounds. His request granted, he revived the original plan of seizing the Ajaccio fortress and, following the Jacobin example in Paris, turning the city into a revolutionary commune.

The good citizens of Ajaccio wanted nothing to do with this hare-brained scheme and now turned on the principal instigator, not least because of his anti-church statements that indicted the Catholic hierarchy as a major instrument of bigotry playing on man's superstition and ignorance to maintain the feudal status quo. Rather than becoming the master of Ajaccio who would strike a deal with Paoli, Napoleon suddenly and understandably found himself almost a pariah. Adding to this humiliation, Paoli enjoyed a hero's return, his official mission being to reorganize what had become a department of France. He capably managed the task within a couple of months during which he formed an elected directorate of which he was president.

What of the pariah? Suspected of further plotting, he could no longer walk city streets without an escort of friends and without hearing screamed threats such as "Death to the Jacobins. Death to the officer."[19] On one occasion he was manhandled by enraged penitents of a religious procession and was rescued only with difficulty. Although he attended the autumn sessions of the Corsican assembly, his meeting with Paoli was a disaster brought on in part by the young officer's candor. Having listened to the old general explaining his military defeat by the French, Napoleon unwisely remarked that Paoli's deployment of his troops had made defeat inevitable.[20] Further disagreements increased the general's *froideur* to the extent that he foisted off the young upstart with a promise of eventual command of a small national guard.

Despite his disappointment and somewhat precarious existence in Ajaccio, Napoleon remained an active member of the Jacobin club which in part caused him not only to overstay his leave but to ignore a ministry of war order for all officers to return to their regiments. He next wrote a long and vilifying letter to Matteo Buttafuoco in Paris, an extremely unwise act that again could have endangered his life. In the event, it drew a rather sad reply from Buttafuoco – who attempted to justify his royalist conduct as that of a man who had acted only with good intentions – and also a reprimand from Paoli to whom he had sent a copy.[21]

The errant lieutenant lingered on for another month until it became clear that the French government would not permit Corsica to form its own national guard. In early February 1791 he left for France, taking his brother 12-year-old Louis with him. He was 22 years old.

Notes

1   Madelin (*Jeunesse*), 84.
2   Madelin (*Jeunesse*), 80–5, for a splendid recital of these events.
3   Madelin (*Jeunesse*), 82 ff.
4   Madelin (*Jeunesse*), 83.
5   Madelin (*Jeunesse*), 84.
6   Chuquet, I, 357–9. See also Iung (*Bonaparte*), I, 203.
7   Wilkinson (*Rise*), 6–7.
8   Iung (*Bonaparte*), I, 189–90.
9   Iung (*Bonaparte*), I, 204–6.
10 Chuquet, II, 53–4.
11 Colin, 160.
12 Iung (*Bonaparte*), I, 213–14.
13 Chuquet, II, 73 ff. See also Iung (*Bonaparte*), I, 218.
14 Colin, 61.
15 Iung (*Bonaparte*), I, 230.
16 Iung (*Bonaparte*), I, 231–3.

17 Iung (*Bonaparte*), I, 237–9.
18 Chuquet, II, 53–4, 111. The letters are in Masson, *Fonds Libri*, I, 127 ff.
19 Iung (*Bonaparte*), I, 272–7.
20 Thiry (*Jeunesse*), 96.
21 Chuquet, II, 138 ff. See also Iung (*Bonaparte*), I 240–53.

CHAPTER FIVE

AUXONNE, VALENCE, CORSICA, PARIS
1791–1792

*I do not see him stopping short of either the
throne or the scaffold.*

· *Commissaire* of War Simon Antoine
Sucy on Napoleon's revolutionary zeal,
Valence, July 1791[1]

NAPOLEON RETURNED TO a France that was slowly tearing itself to
pieces. Power was in the hands of the national assembly, or rather
in the grasp of some powerful leaders intent on creating an autocratic centralized state which they would govern. These deputies,
known as the *légistes* – about 300 of a total 1,500 – were commoners, most of them lawyers from families that for centuries
had served royalty throughout France. As opposed to their
brethren, at this stage they "had one clear idea, one program, one
tradition," and that was to transfer the power of the throne to
themselves.[2]

They were variously opposed by many nobles and religious
members of the assembly as well as by a large number of bourgeois
liberals. The latter wished to reduce the power of a government, or
at least regulate it by checks and balances similar to those written
into the recent constitution of the thirteen American states, notably
a two-chamber system of legislation familiar to England. In subsequent debates on the new constitution the majority, always
disparate in thought and reluctant in action, were soon run over by
the *légistes* flying the doctrinal flag of the omnipotent sovereign
state. By spring of 1790 local parliaments had been banished, the

traditional regions or *pays* of France arbitrarily divided into 83
departments, church properties nationalized and the clergy forced
to accept a restrictive civil constitution (the aetiology of the "constitutional clergy" as opposed to the "refractory clergy," the priests
who refused to sign).

There were problems. It soon became evident that the desire of
numerous deputies for a constitutional monarch was shared by
vast numbers of people in the provinces who had welcomed the
abolition of feudal privileges and other reforms, but who wanted
the monarchy retained despite the obvious failings of the present
king. This desire increased as the revolution ran away with itself
to leave anarchy in its wake. Napoleon hit on this shortly after his
return to France in early 1791 when he found the Dauphiné peasantry "very firm in their stirrups," ready to die for preservation of
the constitution.[3]

Here was an anomalous situation in that the powerful band of
légistes, frightened by the thought of a refurbished monarchy and
attendant reprisals from a counter-revolution, had methodically
eliminated traditional governing bodies and local authorities by
instituting a system of autonomous departmental and municipal
directorates and communes which, each acting independently and
often in opposition with each other, was producing a paralysis of
administration that reached to the assembly itself. To cope with
the resultant anarchy, in 1791 the assembly sent specially empowered representatives (*représentants en mission*) to the departments
to act as minor and often brutal dictators in their own right, an
unwelcome presence that soon would become synonymous with
the ghastly period known as "the Terror."

The *légistes* themselves were split as to the form of a future government. A faction headed by Jean Paul Marat (the Cordeliers)
wanted to transform the monarchy into a republic; another equally
radical faction fiercely opposed the notion – "I would not like
Cromwell any more than Charles I," said Camille Desmoulins.[4]
The debates were still raging in June 1791 when King Louis XVI,
Queen Consort Marie Antoinette and the court departed, secretly
leaving Paris with the intention of crossing the border. Recognized

and arrested at Varennes, they were brought back to Paris where the king though retaining his throne was made a virtual prisoner of the assembly. The question remained: was there to be a monarchy or a republic, and if a monarchy what would be the king's position? The king and a large number of assembly members wanted the crown to retain the power of absolute veto over legislative acts, others argued for a qualified veto, still others for no power of veto. After more acrimonious debate he was granted the power of qualified veto. In September 1791 the king accepted the new constitution despite concern over the means of implementing it and providing for an effective administration, a concern that soon enough would be justified.[5]

The army to which Napoleon returned had not escaped revolutionary tempests. The earlier mutiny which he had experienced at Auxonne in 1789 had triggered a series of uprisings in garrisons throughout France. In Nancy alone three regiments had mutinied, shaky order being restored only with the greatest difficulty and with the commanders giving in to many of the soldiers' demands. An alarmed minister of war, La Tour du Pin, appealed repeatedly to the frightened and confused assembly to guard against "the development of this military democracy, a type of political monster that has always devoured the empires that have created it."[6] Although the assembly "deplored" the situation its only remedy was to transfer responsibility for punishment to an already hobbled king. Army prestige suffered additionally when a strong assembly faction that included Maximilien Robespierre insisted that the French government renounce war as a means of conquest, a brave resolve at a time when France was surrounded by enemies waiting to pounce, but one that was formally incorporated in the new constitution – and was interpreted by bellicose neighboring kingdoms as a sign of internal weakness.

Napoleon found regiment La Fère in Auxonne much as he had left it, although its name had been changed to the more prosaic First Regiment of Artillery and some of its royalist officers had departed to join the growing group of exiles abroad. Brushing off a chilly reception by the regimental commander and most of the officers he easily slipped into his old routine, renting two small rooms for himself and young Louis whom he at once began tutoring in mathematics, history and geography.

His new life was not easy. He could no longer afford *pension* meals, instead eating with Louis in their rooms, often no more than bread and water. Shortly after his return he was impatiently waiting for a few francs owed by his mother. "I have the greatest need for the money," he informed grand-uncle Lucien, hitting him up at the same time for 300 francs so that he could go to Paris to lobby again for money owing on the mulberry plantation.[7]

Encouraged by Abbé Raynal, he had earlier returned to work on the Corsican history and had submitted at least part of the manuscript to Paoli in Corsica along with a request for certain pertinent records and reminiscences. Paoli informed Joseph Buonaparte that he had received the work "which would have made a much greater impression if it had said less and if it had shown less partiality."[8] Paoli wrote Napoleon that he could not find the desired records and "at present had no time to open his files and search for them." He added somewhat harshly that Napoleon was too young to write history.[9]

Napoleon's circumstances improved slightly in June when he was promoted to first lieutenant which increased his pay to 100 livres a month. The promotion also brought an unwanted transfer to the Fourth Regiment of Artillery at Valence. He was already in debt for new uniforms – he would leave Auxonne owing a cloth merchant 100 livres, besides other minor debts – and now he would have to pay for further alterations.[10]

That aside he still had a number of civilian friends at Valence and soon found life much more to his liking. Taking rooms once again in Mademoiselle Bou's comfortable house, he was soon spending hours across the street in Pierre Aurel's bookshop where he closely followed newspaper reports of the king's flight to

Varennes and his humiliating return to Paris. He broke study periods by drinking coffee in a nearby café where he was given generous credit (repaid many years later), eating cheaply with other junior officers in the Hôtel des Trois Pigeons (Louis being fed by Mademoiselle Bou). He also became friends with three other lieutenants – ardent royalists with whom he vigorously argued in favor of revolutionary goals – who often criticized his quick temper and imperious manner of speech. Another friend was the older civilian *commissaire* of war, Simone Antoine Sucy, whose prescient judgment is quoted at the beginning of this chapter.[11]

Although Napoleon had never approved of the humiliations heaped on the king and the royal family, he agreed at this point with those assembly radicals who wanted Louis XVI dethroned and a republic established, hotly criticizing the monarchists who maintained that a republic was impossible solely "because it is impossible."[12] These and other radical views did not sit well with his old bourgeois friends who daily were witnessing the dissolution of the *ancien régime*. But as conservative doors closed to him other doors opened. A large number of officers belonged to a revolutionary club which met in Aurel's bookshop, a group soon joined by Napoleon who propounded many of his ideas in noisy debates with such verve that he was called "the little Jacobin." A convinced republican, in early July he did not hesitate to sign an oath of loyalty to the constitution and to the assembly.[13]

The revolution having removed the supposed thunder from his *Lettres sur la Corse*, he temporarily abandoned the work in favor of a new project: an essay contest held annually by the assembly of Lyons, the winner to receive 1,200 livres put up by the *philosophe* Raynal (who probably suggested that he compete). The subject for 1791 was: "What truths and what sentiments are most important to inculcate in human beings for their happiness?" He had discussed the subject with Joseph in Ajaccio and had made some rough notes on which he based his finished effort.[14]

His long and rambling essay was as intellectually and stylistically deficient as his earlier writings, the bulk of the work being rehashed precepts of Rousseau couched in Roussean style with (now and then) some platitudinous insights into the turbulent and often disordered mind of the contestant: "Men of genius are meteors destined to burn in order to enlighten their world." Again, "Energy is the life of the soul as well as the main impulse of reason . . . The strong man is good; the weak alone is bad . . . The father says to his son: be a man, but be one truly. Aim to master yourself; without fortitude, my son, there is neither virtue nor happiness." These and other offerings did not favorably impress the judges who in August announced that the prize was being withheld in view of the poor quality of all submissions. One judge called Napoleon's essay "a very pronounced dream," another faulted it as "too poorly arranged, too disparate, too incoherent and too badly written to hold one's attention."[15]

Prior to this discouraging result Napoleon had decided to return to Corsica and had applied for leave. Judging from a letter of late July to a friend, he had concluded that although a European war was inevitable it was still some time away.[16] Family concerns were weighing heavily on his mind, among them the need for Joseph to be elected a deputy to the new Paris assembly. Since this could come about only with General Paoli's personal backing Napoleon decided to lobby the general in person, and in so doing win command of the newly authorized volunteer Corsican guards and promotion to lieutenant colonel for himself. After considerable difficulty, resolved only by the intervention of General du Teil, he obtained three months' leave and in September left for home with Louis in tow.[17]

Napoleon's ambitious plan was doomed from the beginning. Pasquale Paoli, president of the department of Corsica and commandant of its national guard, had become a very powerful and popular dictator, particularly with the old clans which saw the French Revolution as a means of gaining Corsican independence. Paoli had chosen the delegates – including Pozzo di Borgo and Marius Peraldi, now bitter rivals of the Buonapartes – to the national assembly *before* the formality of an election which only confirmed his choice. As it turned out Napoleon arrived in Corsica after the election, his only solatium being a crumb thrown to Joseph by Paoli who appointed him to the island directorate in Corte.

His family found him considerably changed, more abrupt and brusque. "A word from Napoleon was an order for the entire family," a friend of the Buonapartes recalled.[18] In this he was supported by his mother and by old Archdeacon Lucien who, on his deathbed some weeks after Napoleon's arrival, turned to him and in coarse Italian dialect said, "As for you, Nabolione, you will be a great man."[19] His subsequent legacy considerably eased the perpetual financial problems of the family.[20]

There remained the matter of Napoleon's hoped-for command of the national guard. When it became evident that Paoli was not going to offer him *any* command, Napoleon and his Jacobin friends arranged his election as deputy lieutenant colonel of the Ajaccian volunteer battalion. Since his superior, Lieutenant Colonel Quenza, had no military experience, Napoleon held virtual command. He seems at this time to have definitely shifted career aspirations to Corsica, perhaps hoping he could force Paoli to give him top command of the guard, perhaps even thinking of leading a coup against Paoli.

Whatever his thoughts, he did not sail for France when his leave expired in December. Instead he immersed himself in family affairs, battalion training and local politics. During a visit to Joseph in Corte he met the famous traveler, Constantin Volney, whose work on Egypt he had studied at Auxonne. Volney had come to Corsica to buy an estate for the cultivation of cotton and citrus fruits. Napoleon ushered him about the island and was probably responsible for his purchase of 600 hectares of land which Volney named *mes petites Indes*.[21]

At some point Napoleon persuaded his pliant commanding officer to request that their battalion should replace the French guard in the Ajaccio fortress. When Paoli furiously rejected the idea, Napoleon talked Quenza into ordering an attack on the citadel which was made in April. After three days of stand-off fighting and a number of deaths, French reinforcements ended the effort, which again returned Napoleon to pariah status.[22]

Worse was to follow. The affair was duly reported to the ministry of war in Paris where Napoleon was already in deep trouble. On the first day of 1792 he had been entered on the regimental roll at Valence as "being in Corsica, leave expired." A few weeks later his name appeared on the muster roll at the ministry of war with the comment, "Has abandoned his posting and has been replaced 6 February 1792."[23]

As Joseph pointed out to his recalcitrant brother, it was obviously the time for damage control, if it were not too late. Napoleon agreed – at the end of May he was living in a cheap hotel in Paris, preparing himself to face the music of his martial masters.

Notes

1   Thiry (*Jeunesse*), 107.
2   Madelin (*Jeunesse*), 88.
3   Nasica, 161–2. See also Madelin (*Revolution*), 15–16.
4   Madelin (*Jeunesse*), 100.
5   Madelin (*Jeunesse*), 104.
6   Madelin (*Jeunesse*), 99. See also Iung (*Bonaparte*), II, 2–56, on the state of the French army at this time.
7   Coston, I, 181–2. See also Iung (*Bonaparte*), II, 69–80.
8   Thiry (*Jeunesse*), 106.
9   Masson, *Fonds Libri*, II, 99–100.
10 Chuquet, II, 156. See also Coston, I, 152.
11 Thiry (*Jeunesse*), 107.
12 Madelin (*Jeunesse*), 121.
13 Chuquet, II, 185–6. See also Thiry (*Jeunesse*), 107–8; Browning (*Boyhood*), 138–9; Iung (*Bonaparte*), II, 84–5.
14 Chuquet, II, 210–12. See also Browning (*Boyhood*), 145.
15 Madelin (*Jeunesse*), 124–6. See also Iung (*Bonaparte*), II, 117, for the criticism of two judges; Browning (*Boyhood*), 145–53, for a more favorable appraisal; Chuquet, II, 217 ff., for a harsh analysis and criticism.

16   Madelin (*Jeunesse*), 128–9. See also Coston, I, 174; Masson, II, 209, for the letter.

17   Browning (*Boyhood*), 156. To plead his case Napoleon traveled to the general's château in Isère where he remained for several days of lengthy discussions on military affairs. After he departed the general remarked to his daughter, "He is a man of great powers and will make a name." See also Chuquet, II, 228–9; du Teil, 108–9.

18   Nasica, 176–7. See also Chuquet, II, 231.

19   Madelin (*Jeunesse*), 164. See also Coston, I, 191; Masson, II, 336.

20   Chuquet, II, 231.

21   Chuquet, II, 238–40. See also Iung (*Bonaparte*), II, 116; Browning (*Boyhood*), 157–8.

22   Chuquet, II, 259–88. See also Madelin (*Jeunesse*), 165.

23   Chuquet, II, 294–5. See also Iung (*Bonaparte*), II, 118–20; Madelin (*Jeunesse*), 116; Colin, 166–7.

CHAPTER SIX

THE PARIS CAULDRON
MAY–OCTOBER 1792

. . . the revolution is the mistress of the hour. One cannot
struggle against it, one must accommodate one's self to it.

Napoleon to Alexander des Mazis, Paris,
August 1792[1]

NAPOLEON ARRIVED IN Paris at a particularly crucial time. Owing to
schisms in the court, the assembly, the government, the army and
the people, the revolution had reached a major crossroads.

The main player was the new assembly, elected the previous
September, a far from homogenous group either in whole or in the
noble, clergy and commoner parts. The preponderant voice was
still that of the *légistes* of the Third Estate, but these newly elected
deputies were mostly younger lawyers who did not have the same
desire as their predecessors to preserve a monarchy subordinated
to the revolutionary state. Since the most eloquent of this group
came from the Gironde, their faction was named the Girondins
(and sometimes the Brissotins), leftist and moderate but mili-
taristic republicans.

The Girondins soon found themselves in ideological contradiction. Recognizing the value of the throne as an antidote to
spreading anarchy, none the less they had become slaves to their
own revolutionary oratory, their target (for want of a better one)
the already debased monarchy. The situation might have remained
stymied in view of the king's extensive if often muted support
both in the assembly and in the country, but now the threat of
invasion by Austria and Prussia (with Russia and England on the

sidelines) radically changed matters. The Austrian emperor and the Prussian king were not at first warm to the notion of invasion but eventually were brought round by royalist pressures and English gold. Their stumbling change in attitude was pre-empted by the Comte d'Artois and vociferous royalist émigrés who in July published the Coblenz manifesto, a formal threat of foreign intervention unless King Louis XVI was restored to his rightful authority.[2]

The manifesto was a red flag to a radical bull. Louis XVI recognized it as such and formally called home the émigrés who refused the royal decree. This reinforced the belief of many assembly deputies in a connivance between the throne and the foreign powers. The assembly now decreed that any émigré who did not return to France by year's end would be suspected of treason, which could result in a death sentence and confiscation of all property. The king's veto of this decree, along with an equally harsh law that any "refractory" priest who refused to take the "constitutional" oath would be imprisoned, merely reinforced the prevalent belief in the assembly and Jacobin clubs that the throne would welcome foreign intervention. This being the case, some deputies argued, would it not be a good idea to fight a preventive war, to attack before being attacked?

By end of 1791 a considerable number of deputies were turning away from the old assembly's pledge against war, pointing to an increasing need, as one deputy put it, "to consolidate the revolution."[3] This notion quickly won favor in Jacobin clubs throughout France and brought thousands of young volunteers to the army. But not all deputies of the Third Estate agreed. Maximilien Robespierre, one of the most vocal of the assembly, argued that a war could cause the revolution to fail if in the royal tradition the king personally led his soldiers to victory, thus reinstating royal absolutism; or it could bring forth a general who if victorious would establish a dictatorship; or it could bring defeat because of the court's treachery.

These arguments washed off the pro-war faction in the assembly which was pushing its case because of increasing resistance to the revolution by monarchists, Catholic bourgeoisie and peasants in the provinces. Its argument for war was strengthened from abroad where the new German emperor, Francis II, and King Frederick II of Prussia were said to be ready to march, their armies augmented by a French *émigré* force, the Condé legion. Violent and dangerous denunciations of the throne both in the assembly and in Jacobin clubs caused terrified ministers to resign, the king himself bowing to the radical threat by replacing them with Jacobin nominees. General Charles François Dumouriez became minister of foreign affairs and Colonel Servan minister of war. In late March Dumouriez sent the Vienna court a blunt ultimatum which was answered in kind. A few weeks later a chastened king agreed to the necessity of fighting a "preventive" war and the assembly almost unanimously approved the decision to make war "on the kings."[4]

This was not only unfortunate, it was stupid. Neither government nor throne was stable. The country was in no condition either financially or militarily to fight a war. The three under-strength armies that guarded the frontier from the English Channel to Switzerland were commanded by General Comte Jean Baptiste Rochambeau, distinguished veteran of the American War of Independence, and by Marquis de Lafayette and General Luckner who were not experienced army commanders. Large numbers of veteran staff and command subordinates had fled abroad, their places taken by young and willing but woefully untrained bourgeois "patriots". The troops no matter how eager were ill-disciplined and ill-trained. The result was inevitable. Ten days after the declaration of war Rochambeau's army was in retreat, pressed hard by Austrian divisions counter-attacking from the Low Countries.

The news threw Paris into panic. Embarrassed radical war-mongers at once blamed the court, accusing the queen of betraying secrets to Vienna. The minister of war recalled the "constitutional" guard of "patriots" from the king's palace, an ominous move when taken in conjunction with his bringing some 20,000 armed Jacobins from the provinces, the *fédérés* who were encamped around the capital. Presumably pressed by his queen, Louis fired two radical ministers, Roland and Servan, accepted Dumouriez's resignation and replaced the three with moderates. Roland and Servan instantly became martyrs of the Jacobin cause, the pretext for a popular demonstration to demand their recall.

Came 20 June, the day of a great celebration on the Terrace of the Monks in the Tuileries to mark the third anniversary of the fateful day of the *Jeu de paume*. At least that is what it said in the big print. In the small print it was rabble day in the form of 8,000 *fédérés* storming into the assembly to intimidate centrists and rightists, then rumbling on to the royal palace to invade court apartments. Confronted by the king the leaders demanded that he approve the controversial decrees concerning *émigrés* and "refractory" priests which he refused to do. Jostled and insulted, he was held for three hours before the demonstrators reluctantly departed.

News of the incident quickly spread to the provinces, to bring written protests from directors of almost all the departments (including Paris), with some volunteering to send their provincial national guard battalions to protect the king. To the further consternation of the left, General Lafayette, once known as "the first republican of France" but long since disillusioned with the Jacobins, left his command at Metz to denounce them before the assembly. Hated by both Jacobins and the court – "Better to perish," the queen said, "than to be saved by Monsieur de Lafayette,"[5] – he was prevented from taking over the national guard because he had failed to bring the necessary instrument: his army. His somewhat peculiar foray stymied, he returned to Metz and a few weeks later went into voluntary exile.

The enemy threat meanwhile seemed to have lessened. Despite the precipitate flight of Rochambeau's corps the Austrians had not invaded nor had the Duke of Brunswick's Prussians moved. Among other considerations Emperor Francis feared that if he marched first Frederick William would slip away to leave Austria at war with France to Prussia's ultimate advantage. It also appeared that internal convulsions in France could bring capitulation without war. Meanwhile the two powers would continue to threaten France with invasion unless its king regained authority.

Internal convulsions there were, and they were leading to one of the most gigantic political convulsions in history. The recent failure of the Jacobin mob to break the king's back had only whetted radical appetites for his dethronement and the establishment of a republic. The assembly remained divided, but the consensus seemed to agree not on dethronement but on a temporary suspension of powers. Maximilien Robespierre also agreed and in late July asked for such, to be followed by a national convention that would write a new constitution to embody the important principles established by the revolution.

This was not good enough for the most radical of the Jacobins, and their fiery leader, Georges Jacques Danton. Realizing that they were still in the minority in their demand for dethronement, they continued to prepare another coup to achieve it. Ironically a strong impetus came from outside France, from the *émigrés* who had persuaded the commander in chief of the Prussian army, the Duke of Brunswick, to issue a new royalist manifesto: if the French king were not restored to full authority, France would be invaded and whoever dared to touch the royal family would be summarily beheaded.

Jacobin reaction to the Brunswick manifesto was swift and deadly. Late on the night of 9 August, Paris church bells summoned Jacobin leaders to Danton's headquarters in the Hôtel de Ville, prelude to an attack on the Tuileries by the *fédérés* the next day. The commander of the national guard had been murdered, only the Swiss Guards protected the king. A ranking official of the department of Paris, Pierre Louis Roederer (of whom we shall hear more), had preceded the mob to the royal apartments where he had persuaded the king that resistance was hopeless – he and his family must take refuge in the assembly. For some time a beaten man Louis obeyed, walking slowly across the Terrace of the Monks. Meanwhile the Swiss Guards had withdrawn into the court and were fighting for their lives. Louis sent them an order to cease fire and come to the assembly, then watched as they were literally torn to pieces in trying to pass through the screaming, bloodthirsty mob.

Danton next informed the terrified assembly that the king would be formally dethroned and a convention convened to write a constitution. Although the assembly voted the throne as "suspended" rather than eliminated, it also voted into power a provisional executive council – all radical Jacobins headed by Danton – to run the country until the convention met in late September. Two days later the suspended king was imprisoned in the Temple. This time the provinces did not intervene; the Brunswick manifesto had persuaded a majority that the crown had sold out to the enemy who was preparing to invade France.

The interim government belonged essentially to Danton, who though titularly minister of justice was temporary dictator. His major concern was to build an effective defense. Lafayette's defection had brought General Dumouriez back to command an army in the Ardennes. Supported by Danton, the old general had melded veteran royalist soldiers and hordes of new and eager if undisciplined volunteers into a reasonable force to shield Paris. General Kellermann had taken over Lafayette's army at Metz and was ready to support Dumouriez if necessary.

These preparations were made just in time. Only nine days after the attack on the Tuileries, the Prussian army with the Condé legion again at its side moved across the undefended border, seized Longwy fortress, accepted the surrender of Verdun fortress and began to cross the Argonne hills which opened onto the Champagne – and the road to Paris.

Once again panic claimed the French capital. Desperately wanting a diversion, Danton found it by filling the prisons with randomly selected "suspects." When news of Verdun's fall reached Paris in early September the Paris commune sent its goons to the prisons to enjoy a three-day orgy of killing.

During the next crucial weeks as elections to the convention took place Danton, known now as "the Titan," continued to reinforce the northern armies. The Austrians meanwhile had crossed the border to besiege Lille and the Prussians had pushed through the Ardennes to gain the roads to Paris, only eight days away.

The new convention, which consisted primarily of radicals headed by Danton and Robespierre, met on 20 September 1792. On that same day, the Prussian army reached the plateau of Valmy to be greeted by a nasty surprise. Good for his word, Kellermann had brought the army of Metz to Dumouriez whose forces were blocking the Paris road at St. Menehould. The Prussians had been told to expect no resistance; now suddenly they were on the receiving end of an artillery barrage from Kellermann's massed guns. Before they could regroup, French infantry sent them running. Hotly pursued they did not stop until they had recrossed the frontier, having abandoned (to French amazement) their recent prizes of Verdun and Longwy fortresses. The Austrians at once raised the siege of Lille and withdrew to the Low Countries. French divisions followed the retreating armies and shortly would invade and conquer Prussian and Austrian lands.

"Paris is in the most serious convulsion," Napoleon wrote to Joseph Buonaparte in late May. "It is flooded with strangers, and the discontented are very numerous . . . The news from the frontiers is always the same; it is probable that our troops will retire in order to carry on a defensive war. Desertion is very frequent among the officers. Our position is critical in every respect."[6]

As he may have judged, his own position vis-à-vis the war ministry was not as precarious as it seemed. To protect his own prestige Pasquale Paoli had treated the attack on the Ajaccio citadel as a silly blunder more than a crime. Although the war minister wanted Quenza and Napoleon courtmartialed, this was a matter for an exasperated and overworked justice minister who threw out the whole case.

As he may also have judged, the exodus of royalist officers had left the army, particularly its cavalry and artillery, dangerously short of qualified leaders – only six of the fifty-six officers of Napoleon's class remained in the army.[7] Shortly after his case had been dropped he was not only restored to duty but was promoted to captain to date from the following August provided he renounce his commission in the Corsican volunteer battalion. Meanwhile he was to remain in Paris.[8]

As an army captain without a job and precious little money, Napoleon once again was facing a rather uncertain future. An old classmate from Brienne, Louis de Bourrienne, returned to Paris at this time. He was also poor, as he later wrote, but not as poor as Napoleon. "Every day we conceive some new project or other . . . for some profitable speculation."[9]

Napoleon now took a good look at the revolution. Although he had admired it from the beginning, he had witnessed only isolated aspects such as the Auxonne riots and regimental mutiny which he disapproved of and helped to suppress. In Paris he saw for the first time something of the machinery of revolution in the form of assembly debates so disorganized and virulent as to at once offend his intelligence in general and logic in particular. "These wretched men," he called the deputies in a letter to Joseph, caring only for their vanities and self-interest made the country's position "very critical."[10]

Two weeks later he informed Joseph that everything "is taking a revolutionary turn." There were three camps, he wrote, one of the "decent people," the monarchists loyal to the constitution, General de Lafayette, most of the officers, the government and the ministers, the Paris *directoire*; one of the majority of the assembly, the Jacobins "who call themselves republicans wanting to eliminate the throne" in favor of a senate, and the rabble; and the third who regard "the constitution as absurd and would like a dictator."[11]

On that fateful day of 20 June he watched with fascinated horror as thousands of screaming *fédérés* spilled into the Tuileries. Turning to Bourrienne he shouted: "Why have they let in all this rabble? They should sweep off four or five hundred with the cannon and the rest would set off fast enough."[12] He regarded the demonstration as unconstitutional and a dangerous example. He was no more sympathetic to Lafayette's unauthorized appearance in Paris and his provocative adjurations to the assembly; it was perhaps necessary, he wrote, "but it was very dangerous for the public liberty."[13] Nevertheless he recognized the winds of change as evidenced in his words quoted at the beginning of this chapter, written in trying to persuade his friend Alexander des Mazis not to emigrate.[14]

Other than these judgments Napoleon remained politically unaligned during the summer, seemingly more involved with the study of astronomy than with the question of the king's dethronement. Disillusioned with the monarchy, disgusted with the pusillanimous bickering assembly, revolted by the actions of the Jacobin-inspired rebels, this child of the revolution was for the moment homeless, looking forward to having his promotion to captain confirmed and rejoining his regiment.[15]

The massive *fédéré* attack in August found him staying in the Tuileries with another friend of Brienne days. As the mob reached the grounds, Napoleon in uniform walked to the Carrousel, ignoring the angry, shouted threats of the invaders. From there he watched the attack on the château followed by the king's retreat to the assembly and the killing of the Swiss Guards, a slaughter that he would recall with horror many years later.[16] However, he held scant sympathy for the king's surrender to the mob. "If he had mounted his horse," Napoleon wrote Joseph that evening, "victory would have remained with him."[17]

Recognizing that victory seemed likely to remain with the revolution he hit upon the cunning notion of transferring to the naval service which at that time employed army artillery officers to command ship batteries. In late August he petitioned the naval minister to respect his rank of lieutenant colonel in the Corsican volunteers (which he had recently renounced) and appoint him lieutenant colonel of artillery in the navy.[18] When this stratagem did not work, he made a sudden decision to return to Corsica.

This was no simple matter. Napoleon did not wish to resign his new rank of captain, but he had to have a valid reason for leaving France at such a critical time. This conveniently arrived with the closure of the royal convent of St. Cyr which forced his sister Marie Anne (named Elisa by her schoolmates) to return home. A certificate from the mayor of St. Cyr stating that the young lady should be accompanied by a family member proved to be a ready passport. On 10 October brother and sister sailed from Marseilles, the trip having been paid for by the local district of Versailles.

Notes

1   Bartel, 210–11.
2   Madelin (*Jeunesse*), 138.
3   Madelin (*Jeunesse*), 139–40.
4   Madelin (*Jeunesse*), 143–6.
5   Madelin (*Jeunesse*), 152.
6   Browning (*Boyhood*), 179–80. See also Masson and Biaggi, I, 387.
7   Chuquet, III, 55.
8   Chuquet, III, 15–18. See also Madelin (*Jeunesse*), 168; Bartel, 210–11.
9   Bourrienne, I, 16.
10 Masson and Biaggi, I, 387.
11 Masson and Biaggi, I, 389–90. See also Chuquet, III, 8; Thiry (*Jeunesse*), 123.
12 Madelin (*Jeunesse*), 170. See also Coston, I, 214.
13 Masson and Biaggi, III, 393. See also Bartel, 210; Iung (*Bonaparte*), II, 189–90.
14 Bartel, 210–11.
15 Masson and Biaggi, II, 403.
16 Lavalette, I, 72–90, whose chasseur company participated in the gory action. See also Thiry (*Jeunesse*), 130.
17 Chuquet, III, 9–10. See also Masson and Biaggi, II, 402.
18 Chuquet, III, 255. See also Iung (*Bonaparte*), II, 201.

CHAPTER SEVEN

END OF A DREAM
CORSICA 1792–1793

Paoli and Pozzo are to be arrested and our fortune is made.

Lucien Buonaparte to Napoleon, Toulon,
c. March 1793[1]

WHY DID NAPOLEON want to return to Corsica at this time? He knew that his family was out of favor with Paoli, and he probably knew that Paoli was suspected by Cristoforo Saliceti and the Jacobins of wanting to establish an independent Corsica (to be swallowed up by England). He also knew that Paoli ruled the island and that Pozzo di Borgo, now a sworn enemy of the Buonapartes, was Paoli's executive agent.

Why then did he return? Perhaps he recognized himself as an ideological orphan who would be necessarily adrift in France during the coming consolidation of the revolution. Perhaps it was the Corsican call of homeland and family mixed with a desire for vengeance on his enemies and the need to further brother Joseph's political fortunes. Perhaps he saw a chance to win more immediate fame by serving as a battalion commander in a Corsican expedition against Sardinia. However, none of these reasons really holds up in the light of his ardent belief in the principles of the French Revolution and his awareness of the dangers that France faced from abroad.

Something must have occurred in Paris to prompt him to this sudden move. We know that Cristoforo Saliceti was a firm believer in Corsican unity with France and that he had become an important voice first in the assembly and now in the convention. Could Saliceti have sent Napoleon back to Corsica to report on Paoli's activities and even to foment a coup against him? Could he have promised Napoleon his favor for the future if he would serve the government as a secret agent?

Once in Corsica, Napoleon *acted* as if he were sponsored by a powerful protector. With the ink scarcely dry on his brevet as captain in the French army, he immediately reinstated himself as deputy commander in the Ajaccio battalion of volunteers in the rank of lieutenant colonel (a commission that he had formally renounced upon accepting reintegration into the army). Lieutenant Colonel Quenza, his untrained superior, was only too pleased to place the battalion in his able deputy's willing hands – to a written complaint by a battalion officer of some unpunished faults, Napoleon replied: "This is the last time that any such thing happens; henceforth I shall be there and everything will proceed as it should."[2]

Saliceti's close relationship with the young captain is confirmed by his long letter to Napoleon in early January 1793 in which he complained of the feeble efforts of the Paoli regime to put Corsica in a proper state of defense at this time of crisis when France found itself "on the eve of a maritime war and on the point of having all the powers of Europe on its hands."[3] That they were as one on Corsica's future cannot be doubted. In a letter to French ambassador Sémonville shortly after the execution of the king and queen in January, Napoleon wrote that "the Convention has without doubt committed a great crime, and I deplore it more than anyone; but, come what may, Corsica should always be united to France. This is the only way Corsica can exist. My friends and I, I assure you, will defend the cause of this union."[4]

It was probably more than coincidence that the war minister instructed Napoleon to report on the most suitable defense of the island (an assignment that was to exercise a remarkable influence on his tactical thinking). Following the precepts of Guibert, Bourcet and the Chevalier Jean du Teil, Napoleon wrote that it would be impossible to defend all of the island's numerous gulfs

and bays as had been the ill-chosen policy of the last twenty years.
It followed that the problem was to identify the most strategically
important gulf, "choose it well and fortify it with all the resources
of art" and defend it to the hilt. His choice was St. Florent because
its harbor could hold a large fleet and because of its proximity to
France, and he submitted a detailed plan of fortifications after
personally taking "the distances and the soundings."[5] He also proposed to defend Ajaccio by flanking artillery batteries of the outer
and inner harbors.[6] A copy of his report was sent to Paoli who
merely remarked that the island's defense was a French concern.[7]

As Napoleon had hoped, the French minister of war ordered
General Paoli to support an expeditionary force 6,000 strong to
seize Sardinia while a land force, having occupied the rich states of
Nice and Savoy, moved into the Piedmont to end King Victor
Amadeus' rule. Paoli's military commander, his nephew Colonel
Colonna Cesari, ordered the Ajaccio battalion to spearhead the
landing by seizing and fortifying a small island of the Maddalena
group north of the target as a base for further movement.

The prospect of battle so delighted Napoleon that he did not
smell a rat in the form of Paoli. This is understandable in that
Paoli not only had been his hero and inspiration for a long time –
in exile he would still speak fondly of the old boy – but also
because Paoli had remained on friendly terms with Letitia
Buonaparte in a vain attempt to regain the family's political support. Nevertheless it was a very serious error. A skin less thick
than Napoleon's might have been penetrated by Paoli's scarcely
disguised hostility of former occasions. The return of this "brat
without experience," as he privately referred to Buonaparte, displeased him to the extent that earlier he had ordered Colonel
Colonna to have nothing to do with "the rogue Napoleon."[8]

Nor did Paoli willingly accept the order to seize Sardinia, "the
natural ally of our island," as he explained to Cesari, adding that
"the King of Piedmont has always been the friend of the
Corsicans and of their cause." Neither did he like the prospect of

Napoleon coming to the fore in a combat capacity. He had tried to humble this upstart earlier by words; now he would do so by action. "Do whatever is necessary," he brutally concluded to Colonna, "to see that this unfortunate expedition goes up in smoke."[9]

The ill-equipped but eager Ajaccio battalion sailed in late February, seized the small target island and set up a battery which opened fire on a neighboring fortified island. But now Colonel Colonna, allegedly faced with a threatened mutiny by sailors of the protective corvette, canceled the operation and ordered the Ajaccians to sail for home. Though Napoleon hotly argued against this, he and Quenza were forced not only to give in but to throw their two cannon into the sea. It was a Pyrrhic victory for Paoli however in that Napoleon now considered him to be not only a traitorous enemy of France but also a personal enemy.[10]

Up to this time Napoleon had sided with the Ajaccian Jacobins, *faute de mieux*. Henceforth he was a proponent of Bartolomeo Arena's vendetta against the general to whom he sent a strongly worded protest concerning the failure of the expedition – copies of which went to the war minister in Paris, to the commanding general of the Army of the Alps and to Saliceti and two other *représentants* at Toulon.[11]

Paoli's reputation in Paris had already taken a severe knock, the result of Bartolomeo Arena's denunciations which Saliceti had submitted along with pertinent official reports to the convention. These had prompted a scathing attack by the famous author and legislator, Constantin Volney, on Paoli's probity and dictatorial administration, harsh words published in the Paris newspaper, the *Moniteur*.[12] Suspicion of treasonous behavior caused the government to summon the general to Paris, and it was strengthened when Paoli refused to make the trip because of his advanced age.[13]

Saliceti and two other *commissaires* were now sent to the island to investigate the allegations against Paoli; they arrived at Bastia, his headquarters, in early April. It was at once an undeclared war. Paoli's police had earlier arrested Bartolomeo Arena; the newly arrived commissioners released him and denounced Paoli's arbitrary acts and squanderous financial ways to their Paris superiors. Aware of the inquisition suggested by Saliceti's arrival, Paoli had moved to Corte, taking the treasury with him and leaving the commissioners to face a very hostile island directorate and population.

Forced to move carefully, Saliceti traveled to Corte to repeat the convention's invitation to come to Paris, and was again refused. Still determined "to put the fish in the net," in Saliceti's words, he returned to Bastia where he again wrote to Paoli.[14] At this crucial point Paoli learned through an intercepted letter that the convention had ordered his and Pozzo di Borgo's arrest.

Enter Lucien Buonaparte, 18 years old. Lucien was a very bright lad, as spirited, ambitious and restless as his older brother. While Napoleon had been preparing for the Sardinian expedition Lucien had befriended a new arrival in Corsica, the Marquis de Sémonville, recently appointed French ambassador to Constantinople, whose ship had stopped at Ajaccio. A devout revolutionist, Sémonville wanted to address the Jacobin club. Not knowing the language he asked Lucien to interpret for him, and was so impressed that he hired him as secretary to his embassy. Unable to reach the Turkish capital because of the British blockade they had returned to France, Lucien remaining in Toulon as a fiery Jacobin and frequent speaker at the local Jacobin club. At some point he had angrily accused Paoli, as he wrote his family, of being a traitor who wanted to deliver Corsica to England, an accusation which caused the convention to order Paoli's arrest. Paoli's police had intercepted Lucien's letter with its unfortunate phrase quoted at the beginning of this chapter.[15]

Napoleon meanwhile had been named inspector of artillery by the commissioners, but he was only too aware of the dangers which an island-wide insurrection posed to family fortunes. Accordingly he wrote soothingly to Paoli, but he was too late. An improvised Paolist assembly condemned the Buonapartes to "perpetual execration and infamy" which in Corsican language spelled a death sentence.[16]

Such was the pro-Paoli sentiment in Ajaccio that a friend

warned Napoleon to leave the town before he was assassinated. He wisely accepted the advice. After several days of harrowing adventures including arrest and escape he joined the hard-pressed commissioners. A hastily organized expedition to seize Ajaccio came to nothing. With the island in full insurrection Letitia Buonaparte barely managed to get her family to the coast, where luckily they were picked up by Napoleon and after more adventures finally boarded a ship to France. A few weeks later the commissioners, threatened with being taken hostage, followed them.

Notes

1   Marcaggi, 59–60.

2   Coston, I, 221–3.

3   Thiry (*Jeunesse*), 135–6.

4   Madelin (*Jeunesse*), 207–8.

5   Wilkinson (*Rise*), 15. See also Colin, 172–3; *Fonds Libri*, Masson et Biaggi, II, 451 ff.

6   Wilkinson (*Rise*), 16, 21. See also Thiry (*Jeunesse*), 136; *Fonds Libri*, Masson et Biaggi, II, 448–50.

7   Thiry (*Jeunesse*), 137.

8   Madelin (*Jeunesse*), 204. See also Chuquet, III, 89; Thiry (*Jeunesse*), 136; Colin, 166–8.

9   Thiry (*Jeunesse*), 138. See also Iung, II, 212–34.

10 Madelin (*Jeunesse*), 210. See also Nasica, 320–9, for a highly exaggerated account of Napoleon's role in the expedition.

11 Thiry (*Jeunesse*), 142; *Fonds Libri*, Masson et Biaggi, II, 439 ff.; Colin, 168.

12 Madelin (*Jeunesse*), 210. See also Chuquet, III, 92.

13 Madelin (*Jeunesse*), 210.

14 Madelin (*Jeunesse*), 211.

15 Marcaggi, 59–60.

16 Madelin (*Jeunesse*), 214. See also Chuquet, III, 135.

CHAPTER EIGHT

NAPOLEON GOES TO WAR
JULY–SEPTEMBER 1793

Fate has sent us a miracle.

Représentants Saliceti and Gasparin
to the Committee of Public Safety,
Beausset, October 1793[1]

THE BEDRAGGLED FAMILY shuffling onto the Toulon docks, meager possessions in hand, was down but not out. Probably through Lucien, whose incriminating letter had led to their final disgrace, the Buonapartes found rude quarters in a Toulon suburb. To solve the immediate problem, lack of money, Joseph left for Paris to lobby the convention for funds to support Corsican refugees and Lucien went to work as a menial guard in a military depot in Var.

Napoleon himself, his precious captain's commission in hand, struck out for the headquarters of the Army of Italy at Nice, the newly-won town on the Riviera. Probably to his surprise, considering his over-leave of nearly two years, the 24-year-old captain was favorably received by Lieutenant Colonel Dujard of his old regiment who now commanded the army's artillery park. Such had been the mass emigration of royalist officers that trained professionals were worth their weight in gold, particularly since the recent *levée-en-masse* had raised 300,000 recruits who had to be quickly trained not only to fight Austria, Sardinia, England, Holland and Spain but also to counter a number of serious domestic insurrections.

Dujard not only cleared Napoleon's reinstatement with the war ministry in Paris, but he also obtained his promotion to *capitaine commandant* or senior captain. General Chevalier du Teil, brother of Napoleon's former mentor and now commander of the artillery of the Army of Italy (which included the coastal batteries of Provence), soon sent him off to organize a much-needed convoy of powder from Avignon magazines.

The French government, indeed all of France, had changed considerably in Napoleon's absence. Almost all members of the new ruling convention were commoners, the bulk of them the *légistes* of the earlier assembly. They initially formed three legislative factions: the Girondins, leftists who had swung to the revolutionary right; the Plain, conservatives of the center; and the Montagnards, ultra-radical Jacobins. Girondins and Montagnards were alike in their loyalty to the principles of the revolution and their belief in the new republic. They differed when it came to governing their creation, the Girondins (far from homogeneous) tending to be more moderate and the Montagnards more violent. At first the Girondins had seemed to control the convention, but they soon clashed with the Montagnards, claiming that the radical leaders Jean Paul Marat, Georges Jacques Danton and Maximilien Robespierre were trying to establish a dictatorship.

This fundamental difference, moderation versus brutality, had asserted itself in late 1792 soon after French troops had successfully gained what were called the "natural frontiers" of France. How were the new acquisitions – Belgium, Holland, the Rhineland, Savoy and the county of Nice – to be administered? The Montagnards wanted the northern states annexed to France but the Girondins, fearing that this would bring on a prolonged European war, argued for their independence under a sort of protective custody by means of which they would serve as buffer states against any future enemy aggression.

This difference of opinion was exacerbated by the debate over King Louis XVI's fate. Most of the Girondins, along with a great many French subjects, wanted the king tried before the convention. The Montagnards led by Robespierre – a proponent of "virtuous terror" – demanded his execution without trial. Had the Girondins maintained a solid front Louis probably would have been spared. They split however and he lost his head, a fate soon to overtake many of the divisive Girondins including those who voted for the king's death.

The effect of the regicide was enormous both within and without France. Royalist dissidents inside France at once gained new recruits for their insurrectionary forces. The Austrian-Prussian-Sardinian coalition revived and was soon joined by England, Spain and the Kingdom of the Two Sicilies. This led to a coastal blockade of France by English warships, an infusion of English gold to support a major uprising in the Vendée and an Austrian counter-offensive in the Low Countries followed by a Prussian counter-offensive on the Rhine.

To cope with this "state of siege" the Montagnards forced through such measures as an all-powerful Committee of Public Safety responsible for the executive policies of the central government, the Committee of General Security to enforce those policies – in other words a police function – and a Revolutionary Court designed to eliminate all enemies of the state. Although the Girondins had played a major role in bringing about this dictatorial stance, it is to their credit that many of their numbers now fought against what shortly was to become a major tragedy. The new fist of power already had struck hard. Members of the convention who were aristocrats or priests were proscribed as being sympathizers of the Vendée uprising. A revolutionary Army of the Interior was formed and revolutionary committees controlled by omnipotent *représentants en mission* were established in the provinces to carry out the often harsh ukases of the Committee of Public Safety and the Committee of General Security.[2]

Events continued to play into Montagnard hands as the uprising in the Vendée "in the name of God and the King" spread rapidly through all of the Anjou, and as the Austrians advanced in Belgium to threaten the French flank. Robespierre ably exploited the crisis by attacking the "soft" Girondins as nothing more than unpatriotic reactionaries.

Enter General Charles François Dumouriez, until now the hero of the day. A monarchist, Dumouriez was already upset both by the proselytizing zeal of Jacobin agents that turned originally cooperative Belgians away from French rule, and by the convention for permitting the execution of the royal family which had brought about a new coalition against France. His written complaints were not well received by the convention, which sent the Jacobin leader Danton to Dumouriez to straighten him out.[3]

Dumouriez meanwhile had learned what any general should know, that a dozen victories can disappear with one defeat – in this case his setback by the Austrians at Neerwinden in March 1793. Despite Danton's persuasive arguments for him to rescind his letter, the proud old general refused. Danton returned to Paris convinced that Dumouriez had to go. His fellow members of the Committee of Public Safety agreed and Dumouriez was ordered to report to Paris.

Dumouriez already had decided on this move. Unlike Lafayette who earlier had unwisely come to the capital without his army, Dumouriez planned to bring his troops to deliver the country from Jacobin oppression. He had gone so far as to conclude a treaty with the Austrian commander who promised not to invade Belgium in his absence. But when Dumouriez learned that his army would not follow him he turned three convention deputies over to the Austrians, followed by his own defection.[4]

Now the cat was really among the pigeons, the latter being the Girondins whom the Jacobins, particularly those of Marat's Paris club, attacked as traitors. Although the "traitors" fought back it was a losing battle that in June 1793 culminated in the Jacobin Army of Paris surrounding the convention to force the proscription of over twenty deputies, among them most of the Girondin leaders. Thirteen were imprisoned in the Tuileries, the others escaped to the provinces.[5]

The result was a series of bourgeois uprisings in many parts of France. The bourgeoisie of Lyons already had put their Jacobin mayor to the guillotine. The citizens of Avignon, Marseilles, Toulon and Bordeaux rose in furious protest which spread through the entire Dauphiné and Franche-Comté. But this resistance was doomed from the beginning. A major ideological conflict developed when leading royalists attempted to take over the burgeoning movements, as at Lyons, or where they already were the leaders, as in the Vendée. Wherever royalists appeared Girondin support faltered to further weaken already slim insurrectionary forces. The external threat from foreign armies, exploited by the Jacobins, also caused large numbers of Frenchmen to back away from what was rapidly becoming a civil war.

During the summer the revolutionary army in collusion with local revolutionary committees cleaned out most of the trouble spots in Normandy and the Midi. A few towns such as Avignon, Lyons, Marseilles and Toulon continued to hold out. As soon as troops entered a town or village, Jacobin *représentants* followed to send royalists, Girondins and anyone else suspected of "treason" to the guillotine.

By the end of October 1793 the Montagnards controlled most of France, their power ruthlessly consolidated by the civil *représentants*. Twenty of the proscribed Girondin leaders had been sent to the guillotine which would claim thousands more in the period known as "the Terror," one of the cruelest purges in modern history.

Republican troops had not yet cleared Avignon of insurgents when Napoleon arrived in the area in late July. The revolutionary cleansing action against minor resistance was commanded by Citizen General Jean François Carteaux, a fine-looking man with a sweeping black cavalry moustache, an ultra-radical, former enlisted dragoon and painter of "battles and portraits" with no command experience. With scornful astonishment Napoleon watched the floundering tactics of ill-trained, poorly led and badly disciplined troops. Nevertheless the town was taken, the *représentants* moved in and a guillotine went to work, a ghastly scene largely avoided by Citizen Captain Buonaparte who was rounding up wagons in surrounding villages for his convoy of gunpowder.[6]

He was still at Avignon when Marseilles fell, its inhabitants suffering the usual bloodbath, in this case by courtesy of the Jacobin *représentants* Louis Fréron and Paul Barras. The murderous experience of the Marseilles population caused royalists in Toulon to chase out the revolutionaries and surrender the port and its French ships – including a squadron of 18 warships and several frigates – to an English squadron whose commander, Admiral Samuel Hood, at once landed troops to defend the port for the arrival of King Louis XVIII.[7]

The Committee of Public Safety responded to this setback by ordering General Carteaux to march his army on Toulon while General Lapoype of the Army of Italy brought in a corps from the east. Thus commenced the siege of Toulon with Carteaux's army of some 8–10,000 troops deployed on the western side, Lapoype's corps of about 5,000 on the eastern side, the two forces separated by enemy-held forts on the rugged slopes of Mt. Faron.

While these events played out, Napoleon was busy loading barrels of gunpowder onto confiscated carts. This was not a happy time for him. Among the persons expelled from Toulon were Letitia Buonaparte and her children who finally reached Marseilles to find a haven of sorts in a refugee hotel. Understandably worried about his family, Napoleon was also upset by his own prospects. He wanted glory more than anything in life. He was no closer to achieving it than ever and he would certainly not find it in his present menial position. He needed a battlefield but the Army of Italy was not ready to go to war. He had no desire to join Carteaux's rag-tag army to fight what in many respects he considered a civil war. But if he deplored the excesses of the rabble let loose by the Montagnards, he equally objected to the dissident Girondins stirring up insurrections in the provinces – "culpable crimes," he later wrote, in view of the foreign menace that could only be thwarted by a unified France.[8]

He displayed his displeasure with the Girondin shunt in a work called *Souper de Beaucaire* (*Supper at Beaucaire*), written when he was at Avignon and published at his own expense. At least one later commentator has called this a brilliant work, but it is difficult to imagine why. It was obviously conceived as much to win favor with Jacobin overlords as to vent his fear of invading continental armies. This brief monograph brought together (at a coincidental supper meeting in a Beaucaire inn) a Jacobin soldier, a citizen from Nîmes, a manufacturer from Montpellier and a citizen from the Marseilles insurrection. The main message came from the Nimian who criticized the Girondin for fomenting dissent when the country was threatened from abroad: "Are you not aware," he asked the others, "that this is a fight to the death between patriots and the despots of Europe?" The message was clear: true patriots had to support Montagnard radicals.[9]

The most interesting aspect of the work stems from the soldier's remarks on artillery. When the man from Marseilles boasted of the heavy guns defending his city the soldier defended the use of lighter guns, and when the former said that the city could withstand a siege the soldier replied that only veterans can resist the uncertainties of siege warfare: it was an elementary truth "that he who remains in his entrenchments is beaten." (The soldier's doctrinal statements were taken from the Chevalier du Teil's treatise on artillery and are found in the notebooks prepared by Napoleon at Auxonne.)[10]

Napoleon tipped his motivating hand by sending a copy to the nearby Jacobin *représentants*, one of whom was his old ally of the Corsican débâcle, Cristoforo Saliceti. He and his colleague Gasparin welcomed the work and had more copies printed and distributed (the task of Napoleon's bookshop friend of Valence days, Marc Aurel, who recently had been appointed "printer to the revolutionary army").[11]

Meanwhile the author had written directly to no less than the war minister, Bouchotte, requesting a promotion to lieutenant colonel and a posting to the Army of the Rhine. Bouchotte had never heard of him but nonetheless ordered the local *représentants* to check on his loyalty and ability and, if these were adequate, to look after him – an interesting commentary on the state of the French army at this time.[12]

Although the frustrated captain didn't know it, he was about to be saved from impoverished oblivion in both mind and pocket by an unusual combination of revolutionary circumstances. The republican siege of Toulon had soon bogged down, not surprising in view of difficult terrain, enemy defenses, the ill-trained revolutionary army and Carteaux's military ineptness. The prospect of a prolonged siege did not appeal to the Committee of Public Safety which now ordered *représentants* Saliceti and Gasparin, in headquarters at Beausset, to supervise Carteaux's operation.

Toulon was a very old port dating perhaps from the fourth century. King Louis XIV (1643–1715) had used the engineering genius of Sébastian Vauban to convert it into a well-protected and secure naval base. The port, which faces the sea to the south, lies at the foot of Mt. Faron whose steep slopes, giving way to a belt of small fortified hills, form a semi-circular amphitheater with the port as the stage. A large outer harbor with a generous entrance gives way to a more restricted inner harbor flanked by jutting promontories made to order for protective artillery batteries.

In September 1793 the inner harbor was home to a host of English, Spanish and surrendered French warships, while the town and surrounding hills were defended by English, French royalists, Piedmontese and Neapolitan troops – estimates range from 14,000 to 18,000 – fighting under the British flag.[13] The British ground commander General O'Hara, and Lieutenant General David Dundas, were so depressed with quarreling troops of poor quality and other problems of defense that their official reports to London seemed to indicate a desire to evacuate the newly-won port.[14]

The republican army commanded by General Carteaux in headquarters at Ollioules village northwest of Toulon had managed to seize two important hills on the western side of the inner harbor, Montauban and Six-Fours, a brisk action in which his artillery commander, Captain Dommartin, had been badly wounded and evacuated. A second and smaller republican force commanded by General Lapoype in headquarters at the village of La Valette was on hand, but was separated from Carteaux by the fortified Mt. Faron foothills.

It was at this point that *représentants* Saliceti and Gasparin, who had already asked Paris to send a replacement for Dommartin, arrived from their Beausset headquarters to oversee the siege.

Napoleon meanwhile had learned that his fellow-Corsican was at Beausset and had interrupted his return journey to Nice to call on him. Saliceti and Gasparin received him warmly. "Fate has sent us a miracle," they informed the Committee in Paris, adding that they had removed Captain Buonaparte from the Army of Italy and had sent him to Ollioules as provisional commander of Carteaux's artillery.[15]

Notes

1   Madelin (*Jeunesse*), 241.

2   Caldwell, 94–106.

3   Madelin (*Jeunesse*), 189–94.

4   Macdonald, 13–32.

5   Madelin (*Jeunesse*), 198–9. See also Caldwell, 94–106.

6   Chuquet, III, 178.

7   Thiry (*Jeunesse*), 162. See also Bellune, 25–9.

8   Madelin (*Jeunesse*), 237.

9   Chuquet, III, 160. See also Iung (*Bonaparte*), II, 354, 372.

10 Wilkinson (*Rise*), 18–19. See also Chuquet, III, 166–7; Colin, 173; Browning (*Boyhood*), 230–8.

11 Madelin (*Jeunesse*), 238. See also Coston, II, 200–9, for the entire manuscript.

12 Madelin (*Jeunesse*), 234. See also Du Teil, 120; Chuquet, III, 153.

13 Madelin (*Jeunesse*), 240. See also Napoleon, *Correspondence*, Volume XXIX, *Siège de Toulon*, 5 [hereafter: Corr., followed by volume number, item number, place and date]; Chuquet, III, 173; Du Teil, 142; Colin, 177–82, who argues that had Carteaux and Lapoype continued their advance in early September they would have met

comparatively slight resistance and could have seized the port. The interested reader, once on the heights of Mt. Faron (via a dangerous, twisting, narrow road), needs only a pair of binoculars and a little imagination to recreate the challenge faced by Napoleon.

14 Browning (*Boyhood*), Appendix IV, 346–53, for the exchange of letters.

15 Aulard, *Actes du Comité*, VII, 79–80.

CHAPTER NINE

THE BATTLE OF TOULON
NOVEMBER–DECEMBER 1793

It is the artillery that takes the forts and the
infantry that only helps.

Napoleon to the Committee of Public
Safety, n.p., 25 October 1793[1]

NAPOLEON WAS NOT well received at Ollioules. Carteaux's plan, as
the old ruffian explained to the young newcomer, was to continue
the siege by methodically attacking the protective forts until the
time came to make an assault on the port. He had no need for a
new artillery commander, he said, since his present batteries on
Montauban Hill were sufficient to support the infantry attacks.
Captain Bonaparte however was welcome to remain at headquarters and share in the glorious victory "without having to exert
himself."[2]

Carteaux probably thought that this ended the matter even
though the artillery commander of a French army, even a *provi-*
sional artillery commander, enjoyed virtually autonomous
authority when it came to the cannon – and this was especially so
if that provisional commander had been appointed by the
représentants of the all-powerful Committee of Public Safety. As
for Napoleon hanging around army headquarters . . . the old general had scarcely ceased his harangue before his subject was in the
field making his own reconnaissance.

Napoleon was horrified by what he discovered. As he later
informed the minister of war the army had no artillery park, only
a few cannon and mortars with meager powder and ball dumps,

The Siege of Toulon
November–December 1793

none of the necessary accessories and no responsible commanders – "from the general to the most junior aide, everyone directs
and changes at his will the deployment of the guns." The
Montauban batteries were hopelessly out of range of the forward
infantry. Surveying enemy positions, spyglass to the eye, he realized the futility of widespread infantry attacks by an army with
limited offensive capability against difficult, well-fortified targets
backed by heavy guns of anchored warships. The key to the capture of Toulon, he saw, was similar to the defense of Ajaccio
harbor in Corsica. In the present case it was either to force the
enemy ships to leave the inner harbor or, if the wind were wrong,
to set them on fire with red-hot cannon-balls. Once the ships were
gone, be it by wind, be it by fire, the French could easily overcome
the weakened garrison.[3]

How was this to be accomplished? First by acquiring heavy
guns and mortars along with ample powder, cannon-balls and
gun carriages from artillery depots along the coast and inland,
and then positioning them to help the infantry seize two forts on
the western promontory, Eguillette and Balaguier, that commanded the narrow entrance of the inner harbor. Enemy ships
bombarded with red-hot cannon-balls would either have to evacuate the harbor or be captured or sunk. This was the plan
Napoleon offered to *représentants* Saliceti and Gasparin who
quickly passed on its substance in a report to the Committee of
Public Safety that they recommended be read to the Convention.[4]

Although Napoleon was reviled by Carteaux and his staff offi-
cers – Carteaux henceforth rudely referred to him as either
"Captain Cannon" or "the Greenhorn" – he shrugged off the
hostility and moved the cannon from Montauban Hill to set up
two forward batteries that soon cleared La Seine of enemy ships.
These were not ordinary batteries. An ordinary officer would
never have questioned the traditional numerical designation.
Napoleon changed numbers to names: "the battery of the
Montagnards," "the battery of Sans Culottes," "the battery of the
Jacobins," "the battery of the Convention," to name a few. An
ordinary officer would not have paid much attention to the

cannoneers who brought the guns to life. To Napoleon the cannoneers were all-important because it was they who made the
batteries either speak victory or remain dumb in defeat. Napoleon
lived with his men, ate and drank with them, trained them, swore
with and at them, praised and chastised them, listened to them
and when the going got tough led them. He treated his crude,
often illiterate troops, often dregs of society, like a patient father,
and they responded in kind as did subordinate officers and non-
commissioned officers. Captain Jean Baptiste de Muiron would
become a loyal follower and dear friend, leaving Napoleon only in
death on the battlefield. Captain Auguste Frédéric Louis
Marmont and Sergeant Andoche Junot would remain with him
almost to the end as would Louis Gabriel Suchet, Louis Charles
Desaix, Gérard Christophe Duroc and the older Claude Victor
Perrin (known to history as Marshal Victor).

Napoleon meanwhile had kept hammering home the necessity
of seizing the western promontory forts. "Take l'Eguillette," he
told Carteaux, "and before eight days you will be in Toulon."[5]
Backed by the *représentants*, Napoleon's persistence finally caused
Carteaux to order the desired attack. The effort was timid in the
extreme, probably on Carteaux's orders, and was easily repulsed.
But it caused the enemy ground commander, General O'Hara, to
reinforce the two fortifications and build a new redoubt, Fort
Mulgrave, on a protective fronting hill called Cairo (a position so
strong that French soldiers soon called it "little Gibraltar").

This was a real blow to Napoleon's plans for a quick tactical
coup. His fury was shared by Saliceti who reported the débâcle in
detail to the Committee of Public Safety, glumly adding: "We
consider our joint plan, then, a failure and the expedition of
Toulon . . . becomes a lengthy affair which will succeed only with
time and [additional] forces."[6]

Napoleon did not agree, and it is greatly to his credit that he
stuck to his guns, scouring artillery parks up and down the coast
for more cannon and mortars, requisitioning wagons, horses and
teamsters, arranging for 100 sacks of earth a day from Marseilles,
building workshops to repair cannon and muskets.

Bonaparte on the Bridge of Arcole,
17ᵗʰ November 1796

By early October according to his later account he had "100 pieces of large caliber, some long-range mortars, some cannon of 24, and some provisions," and had set up two more batteries opposite the strong enemy position on hillock Cairo, the foremost of which he aptly named "the battery of Men without Fear." His impressive accomplishments were rewarded by promotion to *chef de bataillon* (battalion commander), and soon afterwards the temporary rank of *adjutant-général*.[7]

But Carteaux remained as difficult as ever. A slave to siege mentality, he ordered Lapoype's corps to attack the enemy forts that separated the two French forces, an effort that failed with heavy losses. The enemy retaliated by attacking the French batteries and were beaten off only with considerable difficulty and extreme bravery by the defenders, including the army's artillery commander.[8]

Napoleon already had written to *représentant* Gasparin that he could no longer serve under "this old painter, who manifestly does not possess the least notions of the military art."[9] Perhaps as a result of this letter the *représentants*, including Barras, Fréron and Augustin Robespierre – the 29-year-old brother of the Jacobin "dictator" Maximilien Robespierre – decided that Carteaux must go. The Committee of Public Safety, disturbed by the slow progress of the siege, had preempted the decision. Carteaux's replacement, General Doppet, arrived in Ollioules in mid October.

The new army commander was an elderly physician from the Savoy. Napoleon found him as ignorant of military affairs as Carteaux, but more intelligent except when he allowed his ultra-radical Jacobin beliefs to cloud his thoughts. A new commander of artillery arrived shortly after Doppet, General Chevalier Jean du Teil, Napoleon's former commander at Nice, who at once approved "all of Napoleon's moves and plans," a judgment readily accepted by Doppet.[10] Owing to du Teil's physical infirmities – at 55 he could scarcely walk or mount a horse – and to his liking for Napoleon whom he called "his comrade Buonaparte," Napoleon had a freer hand than ever. By his ceaseless energy that brought in new cannon and munitions for more batteries, and by his physical bravery, he soon won Doppet's total blessing. "In all the visits that I have made to our posts," Doppet later wrote, "I have always found Napoleon at his post; if he needed rest he slept on the ground wrapped in his cloak, he never left his batteries."[11]

The pleasant relationship abruptly ended when a forward French infantry unit, goaded by Spanish defenders of the Cairo redoubt, impulsively attacked the fort, a wild effort soon joined by an entire division with Napoleon in the lead. The battle was going favorably for the French when one of Doppet's aides lost his head to a passing cannon-ball, a dreadful sight that caused the old general to call off the action. Napoleon lost his temper, shouting within earshot of Doppet, "The fucker who ordered the retreat causes us to lose Toulon."[12] Napoleon knew perfectly well who the villain was and furiously reported him to the *représentants*.

General du Teil had also let him down in his daily battles with Doppet's staff officers – to the extent that Napoleon wrote in protest directly to the Committee of Public Safety. After briefly reviewing his basic plan and orienting the Committee regarding his battery positions, he pointed to the urgent need for a powerful train of siege artillery: "It is the artillery that takes the forts, and the infantry that only helps." There were plenty of guns and carriages at Marseilles, he went on, but no one there was capable of doing anything. He next complained of his daily struggle "against the ignorance" of his superior officers and "the base passions that engendered them," and asked for a general of artillery strong enough "to impose on a bunch of ignoramuses of the [army's] staff" in order "to destroy their prejudices and implement what theory and experience have demonstrated as axioms to any qualified artillery officer."[13]

A week later he wrote to a ranking official at Valence, begging him to round up 300 horses and oxen and 150 carts to serve his artillery needs. He next appealed to an old friend in Nice, Lieutenant Colonel Gassendi, to send 8,000 or 10,000 spare musket parts which he would find at St. Etienne; he had been sent the wrong caliber bombs for his recently arrived mortars and wanted a large shipment of the correct size; he needed quantities of pioneer tools, particularly hatchets and pickaxes which Gassendi would find in supply depots at Grenoble and Valence; he wanted a small pontoon train in order to cross marshes swollen by rain; his wheelwrights lacked heavy tools which Gassendi would find at Lyons along with signal rockets and incendiary shells which he also needed.[14] Finally he asked Gassendi to visit the chaotic Marseilles arsenal where there was a siege train of heavy cannon and mortars that he had to have, imploring him not to "lose a quarter of an hour."[15]

This all-out effort resulted in the arrival of some heavy guns but insufficient powder and balls. Obviously up against a very inefficient and hostile military bureaucracy and in frustration Napoleon again wrote directly to the war minister, Bouchotte, to hammer home what was necessary to seize Toulon – "the only practicable plan." He followed with another detailed briefing on how this was to be accomplished; what armament he had started with; what he had acquired – an exact count of cannon, mortars and munitions including gun calibers, locations and targets for the eleven batteries he had created; an inventory of all the guns, mortars and munitions that the Army of Italy had sent to Antibes and that he wanted; all the items in the Marseilles arsenal and yards essential for a siege train – information undoubtedly excessive for an over-burdened war minister but certainly welcomed by later historians. Bouchotte sent the lengthy document to the Committee of Public Safety which already had come up with its own plan based almost entirely on Napoleon's original work.[16]

The upshot of this flurry of letters was the replacement of Doppet by a proper army commander, General Jacques Coquille Dugommier. Born in the West Indies, a veteran of 40 years' service, he had made his reputation in the American Revolution and more recently in the Army of Italy. Fifty-five years old, a tall man with white hair and piercing eyes, in Napoleon's later words, "he was an extremely brave man . . . he loved the troops and they loved him." He was good-natured but spirited, very energetic and fair with instant understanding of the tactical situation, composed and resolute in combat.[17] Having been briefed in detail by the *représentants*, Dugommier wisely gave Napoleon *carte blanche* – and never regretted it.

Owing largely to Napoleon's stubborn determination and to pressure from Paris the *représentants* met with the army high command at Ollioules in late November. The army having been significantly reinforced, Dugommier and Napoleon persuaded all functionaries to agree to a major attack on the Cairo redoubt as preliminary to an assault on the key forts, l'Eguillette and Balaguier; the enemy to be diverted by intense fire from the other batteries on various forts and on Toulon itself, by a series of feint attacks on redoubts and forts, and by Lapoype's small corps striking at Mt. Faron defenses.[18]

Alerted by French preparations along the line, General O'Hara attacked first, hitting hard the northernmost battery whose capture would have opened the way to Ollioules. This was the battery of the Convention, several pieces of 24 on a hillock over a mile northwest of Toulon. O'Hara's several thousand troops attacked at 5 a.m. on 30 November, overran the position and spiked the guns. Dugommier and Napoleon arrived with reinforcements to launch a counter-attack during which the general, in Napoleon's later words, fought "with a truly republican courage."[19]

While cannoneers unspiked the guns to turn them on the retreating enemy, Napoleon led a counter-attack on Fort Malbousquet, the last obstacle on the western side of the port, which reached the *chevaux de frise*, a wall of sharp wooden spikes. There the attack ran out of steam, but nevertheless it was noteworthy for the capture of General O'Hara. "The morning has been too beautiful for me not to tell you about it," Napoleon wrote to a friend, going on to describe the seven-hour action that killed some 400 enemy, "mostly British," and captured many more including a Spanish colonel, an English major and 20 junior officers at a cost of 150 French wounded and 50 dead.[20] Napoleon called on General O'Hara that evening to ask what he wanted. "To be left alone and to owe nothing to pity," was the gruff reply.[21]

Promoted to *chef de brigade* (brigadier general) Napoleon continued preparations for his long-dreamed-of assault on the forts.
After a final council of war it opened in mid December with five
days and nights of an artillery barrage that hurled tons of the
deadly balls at the enemy. The morning of the assault was so
heavy with rain that the *représentants* wanted it postponed, but
Napoleon successfully argued that this would waste a costly bombardment and that the rain would impede the defenders as much
as the attackers. As usual he was in the van and had a horse shot
from beneath him. Accompanied by his faithful Captain Muiron,
he fought on foot in the final assault and was bayoneted in the left
calf – but Cairo redoubt now belonged to the French whose cannoneers commanded by Captain Marmont turned the guns
around to fire on the retreating defenders while the French
infantry regrouped to continue the action. The vicious assault
however had caused the defenders of l'Eguillette and Balaguier to
run away, leaving their guns unspiked. A jubilant Napoleon was
setting up reverse batteries in the two positions when he learned
that General Lapoype's attack had captured the Mt. Faron
defenses. "Tomorrow," he told his men, "at the latest the day
after, we shall take supper in Toulon."[22]

He was not far out. The following morning Admiral Hood
ordered his captains to weigh anchor before enemy guns closed the
narrows. His ground troops, seeing preparations to sail, fled from
their positions to fight their way aboard ships. While rearguard
troops set fire to the arsenal, powder magazines and anchored
French ships, small craft jostled with each other in carrying panic-
stricken royalists through burning waters to the departing
vessels.[23]

Once these had cleared the harbor, dodging red-hot cannon-
balls, Napoleon turned his guns on Toulon – already racked by
explosions so severe that they were heard by troops on duty in the
Alps. Three days later French troops entered the smoke-covered
port. Within minutes the royal flag of the *fleurs-de-lys* flying
over the city hall was replaced by the tri-colored flag of the new
republic.

Notes

1   Corr. I. Nr. 1, n.p., 25 October 1793.
2   Coston, I, 266–7.
3   Corr. I. Nr. 4, Ollioules, 14 November 1793. See also du Teil, 150–1; Iung (*Bonaparte*), II, 386; Colin, 186–7; Madelin (*Jeunesse*), 242; Wilkinson (*Rise*), 21.
4   Madelin (*Jeunesse*), 242. See also Colin, 186–7, 208.
5   Chuquet, III, 180. See also du Teil, 150–1.
6   Madelin (*Jeunesse*), 244. See also Chuquet, II, 179–81; du Teil, 152.
7   Corr. XXIX. *Siège de Toulon*, 6. See also Madelin (*Jeunesse*), 246; du Teil, 153.
8   Chuquet, III, 186. See also du Teil, 155; Bellune, 32–8.
9   Madelin (*Jeunesse*), 247. See also Chuquet, III, 191.
10 Madelin (*Jeunesse*), 247. See also du Teil, 162; Doppet, 205–7.
11 Madelin (*Jeunesse*), 247–9. See also Doppet, 205–7; Chuquet, III, 198–200; du Teil, 138, 177, 187–8.
12 Madelin (*Jeunesse*), 248. See also Corr. XXIX. *Siège de Toulon*, 12; Coston, I, 287.
13 Corr. I. Nr. 1, n.p., 25 October 1793. See also Colin, 208–9.
14 Corr. I. Nrs. 2, Ollioules, 3 November 1793; 3, Ollioules, 4 November 1793. See also Corr. XXIX. *Siège de Toulon*, 8; Chuquet, III, 198; Colin, 345; *pièce* 4; Coston, II, 229, *pièce* e.
15 Corr. I. Nr. 3, Ollioules, 4 November 1793.
16 Corr. I. Nr. 4, Ollioules, 14 November 1793. See also Colin, 201.
17 Corr. XXIX. *Siège de Toulon*, 14.
18 Corr. I. Nr. 8, Ollioules, 25 November 1793. See also Chuquet, III, 202–4.
19 Corr. I. Nr. 10, Ollioules, 30 November 1793.
20 Corr. I. Nr. 10, Ollioules, 30 November 1793.
21 Browning (*Boyhood*), 258. See also Chuquet, III, 210.
22 Madelin (*Jeunesse*), 252. See also Corr. XXIX. *Siège de Toulon*, 19; Chuquet, III, 212–6. Years later Napoleon told Las Cases that he knew he was truly angry when "I felt my left calf pulsing" – Las Cases, III, 300; Bellune, 56–71.
23 Madelin (*Jeunesse*), 253, citing Coston, II, 229, *pièces* f and h.

CHAPTER TEN

THE RIVIERA AND DÉSIRÉE CLARY
DECEMBER 1793–JUNE 1794

*Once the changes I have ordered [in coastal defenses] are
made, you may be certain that they will be on a more
respectable footing than ever.*

Napoleon to *représentant* Maignet, Port la Montagne,
25 February 1794[1]

THE MOST CONSEQUENTIAL of the rewards reaped by Napoleon
from the successful denouement of the Toulon drama was the
enthusiastic support of Augustin Robespierre. In command conferences at Beausset and Ollioules, the 29-year-old brother of the
Jacobin "dictator," he had come to admire Napoleon's intelligence,
self-confidence and determination so evident in his forceful pre-
sentations to *représentants* and generals, his blunt, unyielding
letters to the minister of war and the Committee of Public Safety,
and his obvious professional expertise and courageous exploits in
battle. By the time Toulon fell Gasparin was dead and Augustin
had largely replaced Cristoforo Saliceti as principal protector of
the young general.

Représentant Louis Fréron had scarcely begun sending dissident Toulonese to the guillotine – he would soon be cutting off
200 heads a day – when an exhausted and feverish Napoleon
returned to his batteries to consolidate the recent victory. Toulon
was a real treasure, he wrote to a friend. The English had fortified
the port and its surroundings more strongly than ever and almost
all the cannon had been restored to service. They had left behind
an enormous quantity of baggage and tents; they had failed to

burn 15 French ships; powder magazines, lumber yards, most of the arsenal and the rope factory had survived the retreating arsonists. He had placed additional guns in the forts guarding the harbors and was investigating a special type of blast furnace to produce red-hot cannon-balls. To his delight, three unsuspecting Spanish brigs had dropped anchor in the inner harbor only to be captured, and he was eagerly awaiting the arrival of a Spanish warship.

In early February, Augustin Robespierre ordered his protégé, who had been appointed artillery commander of the Army of Italy, to inspect and report on coastal defenses from the Rhone river to Menton. Napoleon welcomed the assignment since it allowed him to move with his small staff – Junot, Muiron and shortly young Louis Buonaparte – to Marseilles where his family was located.

Judging from extant reports filed from Toulon, St. Tropez and Antibes during the next four months he could not have spent much time with the family. The proper defense of Marseilles was crucial to French fortunes but, as he soon reported to the war minister in Paris, one of its most important forts, St. Nicholas, could not "defend itself for a quarter of an hour . . . all the adjacent batteries defending the roadstead are in a ridiculous state. The most absolute ignorance of all the principles has governed their lay-out. They are not in a position to sustain a volley; they would be enfiladed, and the cannoneers of certain guns are completely unprotected [owing to the incorrect placement of breastworks]." He had done what was possible to put things right, he went on, and he had also established necessary forges and made plans for installing blast furnaces.[2]

The state of most other coastal batteries was equally appalling, "badly laid out and badly constructed," the fault of local architects who had not consulted artillery officers. An immense amount of money had been wasted on poor construction, the fault of paymasters who, ignorant of technical requirements, had refused to listen to qualified artillery and engineer officers. The cannoneer companies in Marseilles and other places provoked special scorn:

"They are not drilled and are as ignorant as from the first day . . .
This was largely the result of using sailors in shore batteries – they
should serve on ships and be replaced by members of the national
guard." A serious shortage of powder and proper-sized cannon
existed along the entire coast.[3]

Napoleon's efforts to repair this dismal state of affairs met with
only limited success in that he encountered considerable opposition from various port officials, recalcitrant generals and admirals,
who were over-protective of their turf. He did manage to remove
sailors from shore batteries and replace them with ground troops.
Some neglected batteries were repaired and new ones built, and
some of the forts received welcome shipments of powder and ball.
Further improvements were left to local officials and to artillery
and engineer officers whom he had instructed in detail, as he
informed a local *représentant* in a report quoted in part at the
beginning of this chapter.[4]

A more immediate success came in providing sanctuary harbors and in protecting coastal shipping from hungry predators of
the British blockade. By end of January he had established new
batteries on Hyères island to ensure a safe haven for French
ships in need. To free shipping between St. Tropez and
Cavalaire, the area where most convoys were attacked, he
ordered new batteries mounted on the protective capes. Once
these were functioning, he informed the Committee of Public
Safety, "I expect that [sea] communication from Nice to
Marseilles will be free and will be able to operate even in view of
enemy squadrons."[5]

Napoleon's efforts were interrupted in April when Augustin
Robespierre recalled him to Nice for a more urgent project. The
fall of Toulon had freed forces necessary for the long-desired invasion of Italy. Now the two-fold objective was to seize Turin, the
capital of Piedmont, thus removing Victor Amadeus from his
throne, then to wrest Lombardy from its Austrian overlords.

A major difficulty existed however. The previous two years

had been spent in fighting a series of generally isolated frontier actions, a war of posts that rarely involved more than one or two thousand troops, if that. "None of the generals [of the Army of Italy]," a later historian wrote, "had commanded anything other than an isolated column, and the most able of them, General André Masséna, had never had more than 3,000 men under his orders in the course of operations. Influenced exclusively by the experience of this campaign and without previous military studies, these generals had no concept of a conventional war and a system of combined operations."[6]

Little wonder that the proposed operation already had caused a major rift between *représentants* and generals of the Army of the Alps and those of the Army of Italy, the former wanting to make a major attack by descending from the Alps directly on Turin, the latter by moving down the coast, then swinging inland to march on the capital. Most of the members of the Committee of Public Safety favored the latter strategy, and for good reason. Lord Hood's naval blockade of the French coast, taken with Piedmontese privateers sailing out of Oneglia, had sorely restricted coastal transports from Genoa in supplying the Army of Italy with vital food. The army at this time required 300 tons of provisions a day from Genoa, and more troops would soon arrive to increase the requirement.[7]

In view of the limited qualifications of this army's generals (including commander in chief Dumerbion), it is not surprising that Augustin Robespierre, undoubtedly seconded by Cristoforo Saliceti, called Napoleon – an "officer of transcendent merit" as he described the young general to Robespierre senior – to Nice to write the invasion plan.[8]

Napoleon completed the work in early April. It was based in part on the strategical precepts of Bourcet whose *Treatise on Mountain Warfare* Napoleon is believed to have studied, and on the tactical precepts of Feuquières, Guibert and the younger du Teil. The work was enthusiastically accepted by the *représentants* and General Dumerbion, far less so by the principals of the Army of the Alps.[9]

A preliminary operation involved 20,000 troops commanded by General Masséna. Piedmont was defended by perhaps 45,000 troops commanded by General Colli, but his divisions were spread over a large area. He was not an aggressive commander, nor were his soldiers well trained or spirited. The campaign lasted less than a month and resulted in seizure of Oneglia port, capture of a vital fort, Saorgio, retreat of the Piedmontese from the equally vital mountain pass, the Col de Tienda, and occupation of the heights of Tanaro and Limone – in short, mastery of 70 miles of Alpine and Appenine crests, the springboard for the jump into Piedmont proper.[10] (See map, Chapter 13.)

Controversy still surrounds the extent of Napoleon's personal participation in this victory, but it seems that General Dumerbion, 61 years old and a victim of gout which according to Napoleon kept him almost constantly in bed, relied heavily on his artillery commander-planner to oversee the operation, as did the *représentants*. On one occasion a directive written by Napoleon and signed by the *représentants* criticized Masséna's tactics as deviating from his orders. Napoleon was present at a meeting of the *représentants* with Masséna, and he seems to have continued to direct operations in company with Robespierre.[11]

The fighting was still going on when Napoleon returned to Nice in late April to write the operations order for the second phase of the campaign. His nine-page plan, completed a month later, is extant and also shows the influence of Bourcet's teach-ings.[12] In essence it called for the Army of the Alps, which during April had seized the mountain passes leading from Savoy and the Dauphiné into Piedmont, to make a diversionary attack from the north and to protect the flank of the reinforced Army of Italy as it pushed into Piedmont.[13] Though accepting the plan in general the principals of the Alpine army, already annoyed because of their earlier subordinate role, pushed for a larger share of the tactical action. In an attempt to satisfy the critics, Napoleon rewrote the plan without changing its basic strategy that called for considerable troop reinforcements for the Army of Italy. Published a month later, it was taken to Paris by young Robespierre for presentation to the Committee of Public Safety.[14]

Napoleon meanwhile had returned to normal military duties. Very much the imperious commander he continued to immerse himself in details, for example in ordering the arrest of a corporal in command of a battery "for leaving his post [to] look for wine in Antibes," and in complaining to ranking officials that port admirals and generals were obfuscating his efforts by hoarding cannon that he needed elsewhere.[15]

Fortunately he found time to relax. He had moved his family to a small villa in neighboring Antibes, another step upward for the Buonapartes whose fortunes were slowly reviving. Owing to Saliceti's favor Joseph had become a civilian *commissaire* or supply quartermaster to the army, a traditionally lucrative position which had allowed him to court and finally marry Julie Clary whose natural beauty was enhanced by being the daughter of a rich Marseilles businessman. Napoleon in turn became enamored with Julie's sister, the 14-year-old Désirée, equally beautiful and also fiery, whom he actively courted (and soon seduced) when not figuring out where such and such a division should be deployed in the forthcoming campaign, or where a new battery should be erected on the French coast.

In the process of courting Désirée, Napoleon quarreled with Cristoforo Saliceti. Some historians have claimed that the breach originated from jealousy, the one of the other concerning Désirée. More likely it was the inevitable result of Napoleon's friendship with Augustin Robespierre and Ricord. Relations between Saliceti and his fellow *représentants* had steadily deteriorated as Maximilien Robespierre tightened his dictatorial control over the Committee of Public Safety, that is to say of France itself. Saliceti had disagreed with the decision to subordinate the Army of the Alps to the Army of Italy and this had won him the enmity of his colleagues, to the extent that he filed an official protest at being eliminated from command councils.[16] Despite Corsican ties and

Saliceti's previous favors to the Buonapartes and himself, Napoleon sided with Robespierre and Ricord, not unnaturally since they were backing his strategy. Whatever the reason, discord grew to the extent that Saliceti charged his former protégé with haughty "grandeur." The upshot was Saliceti's transfer to the Army of the Alps which, as we shall see, would result in a dramatic blow to Napoleon's fortunes.

Compounding what fate already had in mind for the young general was a mission to Genoa ordered by Ricord in mid July. In theory Napoleon was to persuade the ruling *doge* to remain neutral in case of a French invasion of Piedmont. In fact he was to size up the republic's military strength in case the *doge*, prompted by English gold, proved awkward.[17]

The mission has too often been overlooked by Napoleonic chroniclers. It graphically demonstrated the extent of Napoleon's growth in a very short time. Despite the differences in age and position he treated the *doge* more as an equal than a ruler. He quickly read the shallow depth of the man and his ultra-conservative advisers, accurately measured the republic's military strength and, going and coming, gained an immensely valuable knowledge of the varied mountainous and coastal terrain, all so important to a future campaign.

He returned to Nice in late July a wiser man by far, certainly a more confident officer, increasingly certain of his future including his love for Désirée Clary.

Notes

1   Corr. I. Nr. 20, Port la Montagne, 25 February 1794.

2   Corr. I. Nr. 13, Marseilles, 4 January 1794. See also Corr. I. Nrs. 12, Ollioules, 24 December 1793; 14, Marseilles, 20–25 January 1794; Colin, 217–18.

3   Corr. I. Nrs. 14, Marseilles, 20–25 January 1794; 16, Marseilles, 12 February 1794; 17, Marseilles, 12 February 1794; 19, Port la Montagne, 23 February 1794.

4 Corr. I. Nr. 20, Port la Montagne, 25 February 1794.
5 Corr. I. Nr. 21, St. Tropez, 28 February 1794.
6 Colin, 225.
7 Colin, 237. See also Wilkinson (*Rise*), 45.
8 Colin, 228.
9 Colin, 232–3. See also Wilkinson (*Rise*), 48–50; Madelin (*Jeunesse*), 259–60; Iung (*Bonaparte*), II, 430–60, for details of Napoleon's several plans written at this time.
10 Corr. I. Nr. 27, Colmars, 21 May 1794. See also Colin, 241–51, for a good account of this campaign.
11 Colin, 248–52, 256.
12 Corr. I. Nr. 27, Colmars, 21 May 1794. See also Wilkinson (*Rise*), 53–5, with plates that compare Bourcet's 1744 plan to Napoleon's effort; Iung (*Bonaparte*), II, 430–60.
13 Corr. I. Nr. 27, Colmars, 21 May 1794.
14 Corr. I. Nr. 30, Nice, 20 June 1794, for the entire plan.
15 Corr. I. Nrs. 29, Nice, 16 June 1794; 31, Antibes, 25 June 1794.
16 Madelin (*Jeunesse*), 266.
17 Coston, II, 278–9.

CHAPTER ELEVEN

FALL AND REDEMPTION
JUNE 1794–MAY 1795

*My conscience is the tribunal which judges my conduct. This
conscience is calm when I question it.*

Napoleon writing from his jail cell to Andoche Junot,
Fort Carré, Antibes, August 1794[1]

FATE IS A conveniently accepted phenomenon whose validity often
dissipates when cogent events are more closely examined. While
Napoleon was fighting the battle for Toulon and planning to push
the Austrians out of Italy, the French Revolution continued to run
its erratic often inane course. A prolonged, vicious and bloody
power struggle among revolutionary leaders and factions had
resulted in rule by the Committee of Public Safety led by
Maximilien Robespierre.

The insane period known as "the Terror" (September
1793–August 1794) had begun under his aegis as ancillary forces,
particularly the Committee of General Security and the
Revolutionary Tribunal, attempted to purge France of counter-
revolutionary elements – we have seen facets of this civil war at
Lyons, Marseilles and Toulon. The extended purge did eliminate
several thousand opponents of whom commoners far outnumbered royalists, and it also stilled dissident pro-royal rightist and
centrist voices to make the legislative assembly little more than a
rubber stamp to the committee's desires. The purge also devoured
a good many pro-revolutionary elements, in particular the leaders
of the once-powerful Girondins. As merciless accusations and
killings continued, as charge and counter-charge reverberated

through revolutionary ranks, severe resentments developed, not only at provisional levels, for example the quarrel between the *représentants* of the Army of the Alps and the Army of Italy, but also within the top committee itself.

The Montagnards were scarcely an homogeneous body devoted to a single leader pursuing a common policy. Robespierre, a *petit bourgeois* who preached a convoluted policy of "revolutionary virtue", had never fully controlled the committee, particularly its veteran member Lazare Carnot who was responsible for having revived the moribund revolutionary army, still less some of the members of the militant ancillary offshoots. We have met a few of the committee's provincial agents, the *représentants* or political *commissaires* who controlled the revolutionary armies as the Terror continued to take its dreadful toll. But as the fathers of the revolution continued to be devoured by Robespierre's dictatorial rule, opposition increased within both the committee and the assembly, the latter finally beginning to awaken from its cowed somnolence. In the early months of 1794 dissident voices began to challenge the arbitrary and despotic methods of Robespierre and his trusted lieutenants.

A major point of discordance arose in June with the arrival of Napoleon's plan for the second phase of the invasion of Italy. Robespierre at once favored it as part of a series of French offensives on all fronts. Lazare Carnot volubly disagreed, wanting the French armies to remain on the defensive in order to avoid the danger of a European coalition forming against France. Somewhat grudgingly a compromise was reached and Carnot agreed to a limited operation to seize one or two Piedmont forts.[2]

Augustin Robespierre arrived in Paris in early July along with another trusted *représentant* from the Army of the Rhine, Louis de St. Just. According to the French historian, Louis Madelin (among others), this was because Robespierre had recognized the growing challenge to his leadership and needed the help of trusted subordinates to eliminate it. Subsequent events would seem to confirm this, but the younger Robespierre also used the occasion to plead for reinforcements for the Army of Italy and for a much more extensive offensive than that approved by Carnot. In support of his cause Augustin presented two documents prepared by Napoleon. One was a somewhat modified plan for the invasion of Italy, the other a brilliant study of grand strategy entitled "A Note on the Political and Military Position of our Armies of Piedmont and of Spain . . ."[3]

Napoleon did not agree with either Robespierre or Carnot's strategy. He rejected a defensive strategy out of hand unless momentarily necessary. But he equally rejected a simultaneous attack on Austria and Spain because it would disperse rather than concentrate military strength on a single target, namely Italy, which for strategic, tactical and political reasons he favored attacking.

The new studies undoubtedly would have reopened the debate on offensive versus defensive strategy had not an unforeseen change in government occurred. Supported by Augustin and St. Just, Maximilien began arranging for the murder of three committee members (Carnot among them), a number of *représentants* (including Paul Barras, Jean Lambert Tallien and Joseph Fouché) and a score or more of recalcitrant deputies in the assembly.[4] Fouché was denounced as an "atheistic criminal" by Robespierre and went into hiding from where he formed a new opposition group. In late July 1794, Robespierre denounced this group to the assembly and called for further "purification" of both the assembly and the Committee of Public Safety. As Madelin later wrote, Robespierre "blundered in naming no one, thus everyone believed himself the target . . . [his opponents] had only one thought: to kill the dictator before he killed them."[5]

The denouement of this savage drama occurred on 27 July 1794, the famous day of 9 Thermidor, when St. Just mounted the assembly platform to denounce "the traitors." Before he could speak he was chased from the podium by a furious Tallien. In the ensuing uproar the Robespierre faction steadily lost ground, Maximilien's own frantic words being drowned out by the continual pealing of the speaker's bell. Downtrodden liberal deputies, at last awake and passively supported by conservative members, decreed the arrest and banishment from the assembly of the Robespierre brothers, St. Just and other important lieutenants. Arrested by police of the Paris commune, the miscreants were later released and took refuge in the old Jacobin headquarters, the Hôtel de Ville, where fiery assistants urged Robespierre to call for a general insurrection. He wasn't up to it. Worn down by the sudden overturn of fortune, fearful of moving outside his rigid concept of the law, the prematurely old and tired man was not to be hurried. As he was about to sign the insurrectionary proclamation a group of soldiers led by Paul Barras burst into the room to gun down him and some of his supporters. In case anyone missed the point, the perforated bodies were sent to the guillotine the next day.[6]

Robespierre was not the first dictator to be toppled, nor was the resultant confusion new to history. In a nutshell, the demise of tyranny returned the country to anarchy. The Montagnards basically responsible for the overthrow were motivated mainly by a desire to save their own skins, not to do away with the reigning Terror. They were soon surprised, however, to learn that their rebellion had introduced a strong counter-revolutionary movement. This was marked in Paris by a significant strengthening of the center and right in the assembly, and by the appearance on Paris streets of groups of armed young men intent on rooting out and destroying remnant Jacobin "terrorists." The ardent and often bloody activities of these vigilantes, derisively termed *muscadins* (social fops) by the Jacobins, soon won an immensely popular following of ordinary citizens revolted by Jacobin excesses, a movement that quickly spread to the provinces.

The problem for the revolutionaries was now to keep the revolution alive. Robespierre's control organization composed of ultra-Jacobins – the Committee of Public Safety and its enforcement bodies – fell with the master. An assembly reshaped by the recall of almost a hundred banished deputies and not least by radical Montagnards who joined the popular tide, attempted to replace the centralized authority of the committee by no fewer than thirteen quasi-executive committees, a power dilution that eventually filtered down to the provinces with concomitant weakening of central authority – a development not without effect on the career of the 25-year-old Brigadier General Napoleon Buonaparte.

Napoleon had never attempted to hide his preference for Jacobin rule insofar as it promised an end to tyranny and the establishment of an egalitarian republic. Nevertheless he did not like certain aspects of the formative period: he loathed the mob attacks on the Tuileries, and he approved neither of the execution of King Louis XVI nor of the hideous excesses of the Terror. Yet what were the alternatives? Certainly not a monarchy and rule by a host of feudal lords. Certainly not rule by assembly, a mumbo-jumbo of screeching lawyers who could scarcely agree on the time of day, a disastrous regime that threatened to plunge the country into anarchy and open its borders to foreign invasion. No one could deny that Robespierre's quasi-dictatorship, despite or perhaps because of its excesses, had brought a semblance of order to a torn country.

That was one consideration.

The other consideration was personal: Napoleon's star. The Corsican dream finally shattered, his future as an impoverished captain had appeared bleak. But within only a few months this dreary picture had brightened. Had it not been for his pro-Jacobin sentiments, for a series of admiring and helpful *représentants*, he would probably still have been escorting powder convoys along the French coast. Many persons go to the grave with unrecognized abilities, having failed either to find opportunity or to recognize it when it came. In July 1795 Napoleon did not so err. And as he revealed his exceptional talents so his star still appeared to be rising and his future seemed bright.

Having made a full report to *représentant* Ricord upon his return from Genoa, Napoleon resumed his duties with accustomed zeal in late July – before the provinces had learned of

Robespierre's fall. The fateful news arrived on 5 August when the principals at Nice learned not only of Robespierre's death but also that the *représentants* of the Army of the Alps would henceforth control the destiny of the Army of Italy. Ricord left at once for Paris to join Augustin Robespierre in what turned out to be a futile attempt to save both their lives.[7]

This left Napoleon in a very uncomfortable position. He knew that he was disliked by *représentants* Albitte and Laporte of the Army of the Alps who so vigorously had disputed his plan for the conquest of Italy. He knew also that he had angered his old protector, Cristoforo Saliceti. Enemies now became inquisitors determined to bring about the downfall of young Robespierre, Ricord and Napoleon by charges of peculations and treasonous behavior. These accusations provided more nails for the coffins of Augustin and Ricord who signed their own death warrants by refusing to recant. As for Napoleon, General Dumerbion was ordered to arrest and incarcerate him on grounds of possible embezzlement and traitorous behavior stemming from his recent mission to Genoa, and to seal his papers for shipment to Paris.[8]

So we find our suddenly toppled general incarcerated in a small cell at Fort Carré, Antibes, where he awaited his fate with admirable sang-froid. "I have been somewhat affected by the catastrophe of Robespierre, whom I loved and whom I believed pure," he wrote to a friend, "but were he my father I personally would have stabbed him to death had he aspired to tyranny."[9] A few days after he had been interrogated in detail he wrote heatedly to his persecutors, complaining of being disgraced without having been heard, and pointing to his services to the republic. "Destroy the oppression that surrounds me," he thundered, "and restore me to the esteem of patriots."[10] His aide-de-camp, Andoche Junot (now a lieutenant), feared the worst and offered to help him escape. Napoleon replied: "People are being unjust toward me, my dear Junot, but it is sufficient to be innocent; my conscience is the tribunal which judges my conduct. This conscience is calm when I question it, therefore do nothing that would compromise me."[11]

Napoleon's belief in himself was soon justified. Four days after he had written to Junot the *représentants* Albitte and Saliceti began eating crow to finally inform the Committee of Public Safety, headed now by Lazare Carnot, "that from the examination of [Napoleon's] papers and all other available information," there was nothing positive to warrant his further detention.[12] General Dumerbion hurried to extol his superior military talents so necessary to the Army of Italy. Napoleon was not completely cleared however. He was given "provisional liberty" but instead of being restored to his old command he was assigned to Dumerbion's staff (at half-pay).[13]

Dumerbion certainly needed his help. Carnot had summarily canceled plans for the second phase of the Italian invasion and had ordered the troops withdrawn from forward positions.[14] This move had brought an enemy advance and occupation of the evacuated areas. No soldier likes to yield hard-won positions. Nothing threatens more to destroy morale which in this case was already low due to a sick-list of 15,000 caused in part by living on meager rations in inhospitable mountains. Napoleon, breathing the fresh air of freedom (if somewhat tenuously), at once recognized the depth of the new threat and graphically presented his estimate of the situation to his commanding general. "Give me your plan," was the reply, "and I will do my best to execute it."[15] (See map, Chapter 13.)

Napoleon's plan was already made and now quickly handed over. According to a latter-day scholar, it was based on his study of Maillebois' 1745 campaign and it was simple enough: a three-pronged attack by Masséna, Laharpe and Cervoni to push in the Austrian advance posts at Montenotte and, with one force shielding the port of Vado, move on to strike the juncture of the Austrian and Piedmontese armies at Ceva. This plan had partially succeeded when the *représentants*, who had approved it without gaining permission from Paris, began to fear an Austro-Sardinian counter-attack and forced Dumerbion to withdraw.[16]

At the instigation of the *représentants* Napoleon submitted still another plan for the invasion of Piedmont, but this was disapproved by the committee which instead decided on an expedition to recover

Corsica. Thanks to an effective British naval blockade of Toulon this effort failed before it got started. Napoleon had volubly disapproved of the attempt and he next disapproved of a plan proposed by the committee to occupy Rome in order to avenge frequent papal insults to France. He sensibly argued that not only was the Army of Italy too weak to undertake such an expedition but that, as in the case of the Corsican effort, it would result in a disaster unless France first won control of the Mediterranean from the British – indeed, a trial sortie from Toulon led to a sharp naval battle with losses on both sides and with the French fleet holed up in the waters of Hyères (protected by batteries that Napoleon had placed there).[17]

As had happened prior to the siege of Toulon, Napoleon was not pleased with his situation in an army for which he saw no future, and he now requested assignment to one of the northern armies. While waiting for a reply he resumed his romance with Désirée Clary, which had now lasted off and on for well over a year. One story has it that he asked her father for her hand but was dismissed with, "One Buonaparte in the family is enough." Father however had died in early 1794 and their romance had continued despite Napoleon's travels and various dalliances: one with a general's wife, one with his landlord's daughter. It now picked up steam to the extent that they became formally engaged.

In early May 1795 he received orders to report to the Army of the West which meant that he would be fighting a counter-insurgency war against the rebel Vendéeans. This not being to his taste – he would forever scorn this type of warfare possibly because he never did understand how to fight it – he set about lobbying in his usual manner to have the orders changed. He had to move carefully. The assignment was a clear indication that certain officials in the war ministry still regarded him as Robespierre's untrustworthy protégé. Seventy-four Jacobin generals had already lost their jobs, some their lives, and only recently Napoleon had had reason to fear for his life. On the credit side he could count on the support of remaining Jacobin sympathizers as well as on his combat record. But nothing could be done until he reached Paris.

Leaving behind a tearful Désirée he departed from Nice with his small staff – Junot, Marmont and brother Louis.

Notes

1   Corr. I. Nr. 35, Antibes, 16 August 1794.

2   Colin, 287–90.

3   Colin, 443–7, for this study in full.

4   Madelin (*Jeunesse*), 266. See also Carnot, 63–8.

5   Madelin (*Jeunesse*), 267–8. See also Mathiez ("Robespierre"), 5–31, for a spirited defense of the man whom George Sand called "the greatest man of the Revolution and one of the greatest in history."

6   Madelin (*Jeunesse*), 269. See also Fouché, 43–9.

7   Madelin (*Jeunesse*), 304–5.

8   Madelin (*Jeunesse*), 304–6. See also Coston, II, 205.

9   Madelin (*Jeunesse*), 307. See also Coston, II, 286–8.

10   Madelin (*Jeunesse*), 307. See also Coston, II, 289–91.

11   Corr. I. Nr. 35, Antibes, 16 August 1794.

12   Madelin (*Jeunesse*), 307. See also Aulard (*Actes*), XVI, 321.

13   Madelin (*Jeunesse*), 308. See also Coston, II, 292, 307; Corr. XXIX. *Précis des opérations de l'armée d'Italie*, 42.

14   Madelin (*Jeunesse*), 308. See also Colin, 289.

15   Madelin (*Jeunesse*), 309. See also Colin, 316; Corr. I. Nrs. 36, Loano, 15 September 1794; 37, Cairo, 23 September 1794.

16   Wilkinson (*Rise*), 58–61, for details of this action. See also Thiry (*Jeunesse*), 229–30.

17   Madelin (*Jeunesse*), 309–10. See also Colin 289; Coston, II, 340–8, 363, for a large number of letters and orders from September 1794 to January 1795 signed by Napoleon as "*commandant d'artillerie.*" One wonders if a missing decree perhaps issued at the time of his joining Dumerbion's staff did not fully reinstate him; Corr. XXIX, *Précis*, 42. Napoleon does not mention any interruption in his command role.

CHAPTER TWELVE

JOSÉPHINE BEAUHARNAIS
MAY 1795–MARCH 1796

I awake full of you, your face, our intoxicating evening, have
excited all my senses . . . I take from your lips, from your heart
a scalding flame . . . Mio dolce amore, a million kisses, but
give none to me for they set my blood on fire.

Napoleon to Joséphine, Paris, c. December 1795[1]

NAPOLEON SPENT NEARLY two weeks visiting old friends in Avignon, Valence and Lyons, which suggests that he was more than confident of arranging a change of orders upon reaching Paris. If so he was to be sadly disappointed. By late May another shift in revolutionary affairs had consigned most of his Jacobin supporters to the political dustbin, leaving his immediate fate to a new member of the Committee of Public Safety. This was an old Girondin, Monsieur Aubry, who hated Jacobinism and who was in charge of military assignments. In his eyes Napoleon was "the friend of Robespierre," therefore evil. To worsen matters Aubry had been an artillery captain for 45 years, with no battle experience. Resentful of Napoleon's meteoric rise, he greeted him coldly and informed him that he was going to the Army of the West as an infantry brigade commander.[2]

Napoleon would have none of this nonsense. Hoping that time might alter matters – a less than forlorn hope in view of the turbulent political situation – he obtained a brief leave on grounds of poor health, but as a sign of ultimate compliance he did send his horses to Nantes. Unfortunately they were captured by rebel Chouans, to make the situation even more awkward. Meanwhile he sat out the time in a cheap hotel (three francs a week) in the Latin Quarter, a penurious existence shared by Junot and Marmont who later wrote feelingly of their poverty.[3] The trio continued to suffer from rampant inflation of already exorbitant prices. Louis Antoine Bourrienne, Napoleon's school-mate at Brienne now living in Paris, tells us that Napoleon sold his now horseless carriage for 3,000 francs in *assignats* – heavily discounted paper money which did not go very far.[4] "Soon one will no longer be able to live," Napoleon wrote his brother Joseph in Genoa, "the harvest is impatiently awaited."[5]

Bourrienne recalled that Napoleon had become "pensive, melancholy and anxious," which is scarcely surprising. Marmont had soon departed for duty on the Rhine (escorting young Louis to school at Châlons-sur-Marne), and Junot was caught up in family affairs. Although he saw Saliceti frequently the former *représentant* was now a fugitive, hiding out with his mistress, and would soon slip away to sanctuary in Venice. That their relationship was still strained is evident from Napoleon's letter to his old mentor saying that, despite Saliceti's recent treatment of him, he had no intention of turning him over to the police.

But Napoleon was young and the delights of Paris soon outshone the nasty twists of fortune. Junot later recalled their many strolls on the boulevards crowded with expensive carriages and overdressed fops riding fine horses. If he were upset by not hearing from Désirée Clary whom he still hoped to marry, if on occasion he felt sufficiently sorry for himself to contemplate suicide, he was still entranced by this great metropolis rapidly recovering from the ghastly days of the Terror.

Paris was again a city of luxury, of wondrous arts, elegantly dressed ladies handed down from magnificent carriages by richly uniformed coachmen, of libraries, exhibitions, free lectures on the arts and sciences, lovely parks and gardens, fêtes and fairs of every variety. Nor did he and Junot neglect such Parisian fleshpots as the Palais Royal. In July he wrote to Joseph: "It is here in Paris that the honest and prudent man, who involves himself only in his own affairs, has the freedom to live as he wishes."[6]

As perhaps Napoleon had surmised, his professional status was improving as a result of military setbacks suffered by the Army of Italy now under General Kellermann's command. An Austro-Sardinian attack had recently forced Kellermann's right wing to retreat from its forward positions, thereby opening the port of Vado to the enemy. Once again English warships and Sardinian corsairs had cut the vital coastal shipping from Genoa to Marseilles. A disturbed government now consulted Napoleon, its acknowledged expert on Italy, despite his semi-disgraced position. He responded by writing a series of lengthy memoranda that stressed the necessity of a counter-offensive, not only to recapture the port and restore vital sea communication with Genoa, but also to invade the Piedmont.[7]

His rehabilitation might have ended there, but in August his nemesis, Aubry, was replaced by a more sympathetic man with the melodious name of Doulcet Pontécoulant. The transfer happened in the nick of time since the war ministry had summoned its errant general to a physical examination which probably would have signaled his departure for the Army of the West. Instead, thanks to Pontécoulant he was assigned to the ministry's bureau of topography which was responsible for the planning and operations of all the armies. In this capacity he pushed his plans for the invasion of Piedmont with the hope that he would be assigned to carry them out. But in another twist of the political rope Pontécoulant was dismissed, to leave his protégé's future in the hands of hostile bureaucrats in the war ministry.

Up again, down again, up again. Owing to the threat of Russian and British expansionism in the Middle East relations between France and the Ottoman empire had warmed to the extent that the Turkish sultan asked the French government to send a military team to Constantinople to reshape his artillery and engineer corps. The request at once awakened the imagined magic of the East in Napoleon's mind and he hastened to apply as commander of the mission – "a wonderful opportunity for glory," as he informed Désirée.[8] Although Pentécoulant had favorably endorsed his application, some members of the Committee of Public Safety objected to sending abroad "such a distinguished officer" at so critical a time.[9] The compliment pleased Napoleon. "The Committee has thought it impossible that I leave France so long as the war continues," he wrote Joseph. "I am going to be restored to the artillery, and probably I will remain on the Committee."[10]

These were restless, difficult weeks. Among other problems was young Lucien Buonaparte, who had made a poor marriage and then got himself arrested for subversive activities. Napoleon finally got him released and brought to Paris where he was trying to find him a job. Désirée was another concern. In early September, when his professional position seemed assured, he wrote Joseph that if he remained in Paris he was thinking of marriage. He was looking for a house and would be grateful if Joseph would press the matter with Désirée – "it is necessary that the affair is concluded or broken off. I await your response with impatience."[11] But only a week or so later he was suddenly notified that he had been struck from the list of active-duty generals "for having refused to report to the post to which he had been assigned." Yet on the same day this same Committee of Public Safety confirmed his appointment to command the military mission to Turkey.[12]

Napoleon was now a general with one foot employed and one foot on a banana skin, an ambiguous situation about to be resolved by yet another political event. We have noted that a strong royalist revival was taking place in Paris at this time. Although Napoleon subsequently scorned the weak assembly, he remained faithful to the republic of "the patriots" which was being increasingly challenged by royalist sympathizers in that summer of 1795. In letters to Joseph he condemned the royalist insurgents of the south, writing in late July of his hope "that soon a firm and better organized government will put a stop to all that." He cheered when an English attempt to land a large expeditionary force at Quiberon in Brittany was soundly defeated. Nevertheless he remained concerned with royalist and radical agitation, complaining to Joseph of the weak government and the political anarchy responsible "for the tragic state in which the country finds itself." In late August he wrote ominously of "the storms that are perhaps forming." A month later he wrote that "the time appeared critical."[13]

The time was not only critical, it was explosive. The new constitution of September 1795 replaced the Committee of Public Safety with an Executive Directory of five persons. The 750 deputies of the national convention were formed into a Council of Five Hundred, the remaining 250 into a Council of Ancients, each with specific legislative powers to complement the executive function. To prevent losing control of government to royalists and radicals in a general election, the convention also decreed that its present members remain, with only one-third having to seek re-election each year.

The storm broke on 3 October when over 25,000 national guardsmen and volunteers under command of General Danican took to arms in an attempt to topple the government. It caught Napoleon in the open; not until evening did he find shelter in the Tuileries where Paul Barras, appointed president of the Directory by panic-stricken legislators, was calling for loyal republican officers to take arms. Probably to Napoleon's horror he was joined by (among others) his nemesis of Toulon days, General Carteaux. No matter. This was no time for personal rancor; the situation was all-too critical. Only about 5,000 troops were on hand and in a chaotic state. The rebel General Danican was an experienced if not particularly competent commander who was positioning two large armed columns for an assault on the Tuileries the next day.

Napoleon appeared in Barras' headquarters literally as a savior, though an impoverished one. Paul Thiébault, a cavalry officer serving under General Menou's less than inspired command, had never heard of him – "his puny figure and statuesque face, his untidy dress, his long lank hair and his worn-out clothes still betrayed his straits . . . but from the first his activity was astonishing."[14] He instantly saw that the defenders would be overwhelmed since they were disorganized, outnumbered and, worst of all, had no cannon. The nearest guns, he knew, were in the Sablons artillery park near Neuilly, and rumor had it that Danican had already sent a force to seize them. As luck would have it Major Joachim Murat, a diehard Jacobin and a hard-charging cavalry officer, had also reported for duty. Napoleon sent him and his troopers flying, and only just in time. Having cut his way through an enemy force Murat returned with the guns that same evening and Napoleon at once deployed them.

The next day – the famous 13 Vendémiaire in French history – Danican's columns moved to attack. Another stroke of luck for the defenders: heavy rain dampened aggressive spirits, the advance faltered, then stopped. Danican had not realized that some troops have to be led more than others, that the insurgents were untrained, more a mob than an army. Instead of placing himself at their head he remained in headquarters, dispatching a host of aides who failed to move the units from wet and chilly inertia. Not until mid afternoon did the attack resume, this time the troops gaining entrance to a key street, the rue Honoré. The word quickly spread inside the Tuileries to plunge assembly members into the worst of depressions, that caused by fear.

Cannon fire suddenly shook assembly halls. The parliamentarians did not at first realize that these were republican guns firing on a horde of insurgents who had reached a church on the rue Honoré. Napoleon had anticipated the advance, had positioned his guns here, had watched the disorganized advance, had finally flung down a blue-coated arm, had watched murderous grapeshot tear enormous holes in humanity, had seen the survivors stupefied, then had relaxed as Murat's cavalry tore into the fleeing mob to cleanse the key streets for occupation by the infantry.

The battle was over by noon the next day. Government troops held the city's key points, the insurgents had taken refuge in the suburbs and countryside. Barras was the hero and played the role to the hilt, appearing in the cheering assembly with his officers though naming none of them. But Louis Fréron, the Jacobin *représentant* of Marseilles and Toulon days, had fallen in love with the voluptuous Pauline Buonaparte. Wanting to marry her he needed Napoleon's favor, so now he stood in the assembly to single out in praise *"le général Buona-parte"* who was responsible for the victory. The accolade caused a mild sensation that resulted in Napoleon's promotion to full general and appointment as second in command of the Army of the Interior.

Parisian society reacted predictably: who was this savior, "where did he come from, what had he done, what extraordinary services has he performed to merit our attention?"[15] In no time the talk of elegant salons centered on Napoleon's feats at the siege of Toulon, his important role in the Army of Italy, his arrest, his unjust assignment to the Army of the West which, had he not refused it, might have cost the republic its existence. Napoleon was soon a hero – before the month ran out he had replaced Barras in command of the Army of the Interior.

This was a great turnabout. Bourrienne and his wife, upon leaving for the country some weeks earlier, had said goodbye to an impoverished young brigadier general. Upon their return they found Napoleon a highly-paid army commander living in a splendid house tended to by numerous lackeys, driven about in a superb carriage, entertaining old friends at grand luncheon parties – but caring little for them and no longer addressing them "in the style of familiar equality."[16] His small figure and youthful face were now seen in the most exclusive salons, at the most coveted fêtes, balls and garden parties. All eyes were on him – including those of the very sensuous and highly covetous mistress of Paul Barras, Joséphine de Beauharnais.

The probably apocryphal but pleasant enough story (later related by Napoleon on St. Helena) has him in his new and exotic office when a handsome lad of some 14 years was announced. One of the general's early tasks had been to disarm all Paris civilians and the boy had come to request the return of his dead father's sword.

Empress Joséphine dancing naked before Barras in the winter of 1797

The Empress Joséphine

The request granted, the youth's mother called in person to thank the benefactor – from which beginning a lively romance developed. The boy was Eugène de Beauharnais, the woman was Joséphine de Beauharnais, born Tascher de la Pagerie. The initial meeting probably occurred at her instigation in Paul Barras' magnificent mansion but no matter, the explosive result was the same.[17]

Joséphine was a gracious and elegant creole of French parents from Martinique in the French West Indies. She had been married at 16 to 19-year-old Alexandre Vicomte de Beauharnais who brought her to Paris in 1779 and later deserted her and their two children, Eugène and Hortense. After several years of very loose, often scandalous living she had become reconciled with the viscount, who meanwhile had enjoyed a noteworthy career as president of the Constituent Assembly and commander in chief of the Army of the Rhine. Their new life was savagely ended during the Terror. They were imprisoned; he was guillotined only a short time before the overthrow of Robespierre, a fate narrowly missed by Joséphine before her release from jail.

At the time of her meeting with Napoleon she was 32, a scarcely desirable age in the Paris of that day. She had been mistress to a number of well-placed lovers, General Louis Lazare Hoche (with whom she had cohabited while in prison) among others. She had hardly any money other than what came from male friends, chief of whom was Napoleon's benefactor, Paul Barras, who claimed her as mistress. Together with her two children she lived in a scantily furnished small house in the rue Chantereine, an altogether unsatisfactory and highly precarious existence that she longed to improve.

Joséphine was more handsome than beautiful, gracious in or out of distress, a fine face albeit marred by blackened teeth which she tried not to show when smiling, long chestnut hair, beautifully alive eyes, a small slightly turned-up nose, a lovely voice sounding more of West Indian somnolence than of Parisian clatter. Coquettish, flattering, sympathetic and giving, she had a supple figure with invitingly long arms and legs. "It was said of her," wrote a principal biographer, Frédéric Masson, "that she even went to bed gracefully."[18]

Napoleon had surely never met the like in the course of his several provincial love affairs. In a word he was smitten. Gone was the vision of Désirée Clary as if she had never existed. Despite the heavy demands of his new position – Napoleon was revising his plans for the invasion of Italy, reorganizing the national guard and the police and making careful deployments of regular army units to ensure the peace in Paris – he became almost a daily visitor to the little house in the rue Chantereine. Here in her salon, no matter its modest proportions, he met and was readily accepted by such personages as Comte Ségur (the elder), the senior General Caulaincourt and many others – some distinguished, some not, some aristocrats, others commoners, many of them were or had been Joséphine's lovers. Napoleon soon became an ardent lover, a love that was heartily if perhaps insincerely returned as he showered her with passionate notes.

Despite the passion there were some bad moments in the ensuing courtship. Joséphine's children, Eugène and Hortense, feared a marriage and were upset at the thought of losing their mother. Everyone in Napoleon's family was inalterably opposed to a marriage that would remove or at least temporize Napoleon's financial support. Signs of future incompatibility also appeared. In a letter written over a year later to Joséphine, Napoleon referred "to the memory of your mistakes and of the distressing scene fifteen days before our marriage."[19] Had this involved another man for Joséphine or, less likely, another woman for Napoleon? Whatever the scene, it had obviously blown over, at least for a time.

Sentimental writers and readers for nearly two centuries have wept over Joséphine's subsequent experiences and premature death without taking into account that she married Napoleon under false colors, a deceit that regrettably carried on into the marriage with disastrous results. She represented herself as four years younger than she was, and as a woman of comfortable means which she wasn't. She desperately wanted and needed a permanent sinecure. Barras wanted rid of her, at least as a full-time mistress. A deal was struck: she would marry Buonaparte if Barras appointed him commander in chief of the Army of Italy.[20]

Barras was delighted. He was tired of her expensive tastes, he was also annoyed with the flaccid attitude of General Schérer who had replaced Kellermann in command of the Army of Italy, and who refused to move against the enemy. Without question he was upset and probably a little afraid of Napoleon's newly found popularity both with political figures and the ordinary people of Paris.

Napoleon missed all this by a mile. A great deal of future misery on both sides might have been avoided had mother Letitia been on hand. It would have taken the shrewd Corsican about five minutes to see through the false pretensions, the gestures, the powder and rouge, the seductive smile (that hid her teeth), to come up with the facts. Joséphine would have become a quick discard.

They were married in a Paris registry office in March 1796. Napoleon arrived late to the annoyance of Joséphine and the principal witness, Paul Barras, but he obligingly upped his age to 28, while Joséphine reduced hers to 29. A slight problem arose on the wedding night when Joséphine's dog, a pug named Fortune, refused to vacate her (and its) bed. Asserting conjugal rights Napoleon attempted to remove the snarling wretch only to be bitten in the leg.

The groom left Paris two days later to take command of the Army of Italy. Joséphine promised to join him as soon as possible.

Notes

1   Napoleon *Lettres* (Tulard), 46, Paris, n.d. 7 a.m.
2   Corr. I. Nrs. 41, Paris, 22 June 1795; 55, Paris, 17 August 1795. See also Madelin (*Jeunesse*), 311–12.
3   Marmont, I, 34–63.
4   Bourrienne, I, 28.
5   Thiry (*Jeunesse*), 237.

6 Corr. I. Nr. 45, Paris, 18 July 1795. See also Corr. I, Napoleon's letters to Joseph of June–July–August which describe Paris in the summer of 1795.

7 Corr. I. Nrs. 49–53, Paris, July 1795; 57, Paris, 23 August 1795; 60, Paris, 30 August 1795; 75, Paris, 12 October 1795. See also Colin, 330–4; Wilkinson (*Rise*), 66–8.

8 Madelin (*Jeunesse*), 313.

9 Madelin (*Jeunesse*), 313. See also Corr. I. Nrs. 61, Paris, 30 August 1795; 64, Paris, 5 September 1795; Thiry (*Jeunesse*), 246.

10 Corr. I. Nr. 64, Paris, 5 September 1795.

11 Corr. I. Nrs. 64, Paris, 5 September 1795; 65, Paris, 6 September 1795.

12 Madelin (*Jeunesse*), 314.

13 Madelin (*Jeunesse*), 315. See also Corr. I. Nr. 56, Paris, 20 August 1795.

14 Thiébault, I, 260. See also Lavalette, I, 154–72.

15 Madelin (*Jeunesse*), 319.

16 Bourrienne, I, 32–3.

17 Thiry (*Jeunesse*), 268. See also Coston, I, 425.

18 Masson (*Napoleon and the Fair Sex*), 56.

19 Napoleon *Lettres* (Tulard), 77, Milan, 8 June 1796.

20 Fortescue, 59.

CHAPTER THIRTEEN

THE ARMY MARCHES – I:
THE INVASION OF PIEDMONT
MARCH–APRIL 1796

Hannibal forced the Alps, we shall outflank them.

Napoleon to his generals on the heights
overlooking the Piedmont plain,
17 April 1796[1]

DURING THE JOURNEY to Nice Napoleon divided his time between writing passionate love letters to Joséphine – one mailed at each post stop where horses were changed – and reading from a great pile of carefully selected books. He arrived in Nice, general headquarters of the Army of Italy, in late March 1796 and almost immediately was in conference with his skeleton staff.

This staff was an interesting collection. General Berthier, its chief, was 42 years old. The son of an ennobled engineering officer at Versailles, he was educated as a topographical engineer before gaining an army commission. During the American revolutionary war he served with distinction on Rochambeau and Lafayette's staffs, then held a series of senior staff posts and in 1792 rejoined Rochambeau and was promoted to brigadier general. Put on ice by suspicious Jacobin rulers, he thawed out after their fall to serve in the Vendée where he was wounded. In 1795 he became chief of staff to General Kellermann, who commanded the Army of the Alps, and was promoted to major general. A year later he volunteered to join Napoleon and was appointed chief of staff of the Army of Italy. He was a small man with an unusually large head, a nervous type who stuttered and

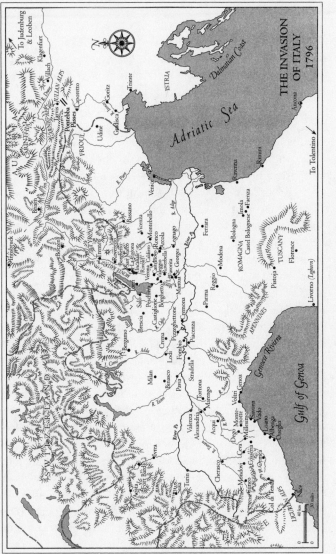

The Invasion of, Italy, March 1796–April 1797

bit his fingernails, something of a clothes-horse, a pedantic man but an extremely able and conscientious administrator who worked twenty hours on end if necessary to get Napoleon's orders written and dispatched to the right person.[2]

Joachim Murat was two years older than Napoleon. An innkeeper's son, he received a good seminary education which he cut short in 1792 by enlisting in the cavalry as a private. He was promoted to major the following year. His brilliant performance in rescuing the cannons during the Paris uprising to give Napoleon his famous "whiff of grapeshot" brought him an appointment as aide. Tall and broad-shouldered, he too was a clothes-horse but, unlike Berthier, greatly admired by the ladies. He was also a spirited and very brave man, though without much between the ears.

Auguste Marmont came from the Burgundian aristocracy and was formally educated in royal military schools. An artilleryman, he was 22 years old. Having made his mark with Napoleon during the Toulon, Army of Italy and Paris days, Napoleon recalled him from the Rhine to appoint him aide with the rank of major.

Andoche Junot, the son of a wealthy Burgundian farmer, had joined a group of local volunteers in 1792 and had fought so furiously that his fellows called him "the Tempest." Napoleon had taken him on as secretary during the siege of Toulon as much for his sense of humor as for his legible handwriting. He subsequently made him an aide, promoting him first to captain, then to major.

Napoleon appointed his aides but he inherited his commanders, each as different from the other as "the night the day." André Masséna was the senior of three divisional group commanders. Born to an impoverished family in Nice (then part of the Sardinian kingdom), he ran away to sea as a boy. Eventually joining the army, he was promoted to sergeant-major but then left the ranks in favor of a three-year stint of cross-border smuggling. In 1792 he joined the revolutionary army, to end as a general in the Army of Italy where he and Napoleon had met. He was a small man, 38 years old, self-taught, extremely brave and a fine tactician with a keen eye for women and money, possibly in reverse order.

In stark contrast stood Jean Sérurier, 53 years old, with more than thirty years' service in the royal army. A tall and generally mournful man, he was a strict but fair disciplinarian though too stolid and unimaginative to be anything more than a mediocre general.

Finally we have Charles Pierre Augereau, 38 years old, son of a poor stonemason, product of the Paris gutters. He joined the royal cavalry in his late teens, became one of the best fencers in the army, fought numerous duels (he was said to have killed a young officer who struck him), fled to Switzerland, fought with the Russians against the Turks, served in Frederick the Great's army, hoboed around Greece and Portugal, and taught fencing and dancing for a living. Augereau joined the revolutionary army in 1792 and a year later was a general of division. In the next few years he fought the royalists in the Vendée and the Spanish in the Pyrenees. A tall, well-built man, he spoke gutter French, swore at everyone, constantly bragged about his exploits and stole whatever he could get his hands on. He was also an extremely brave and good commander – and the troops loved him.

Napoleon's initial reception by these generals was not warm. "More Jacobins and more revolutionaries than republicans, impatient of all restraint, of all authority," they did not at once take to their young and authoritative new commander.[3] They were older than he, they had fought more battles and they resented what they regarded as a political appointment. About the only quality that they had in common other than wounds was that none had commanded an army. Napoleon's initial position brings to mind Frederick the Great's general, Friedrich Wilhelm von Seydlitz, whose appointment to command the cavalry at the battle of Rossbach displeased generals senior to him. He settled matters at once with a simple statement: "Gentlemen, I obey the king and you obey me."[4] Replace the authority of King Frederick by King Directory and the point is made, but now add to it Napoleon's tersely confident and expert explanation of what he and they were going to do with the Army of Italy, and the conversion was complete. Having established command authority, Bonaparte, as he now spelled his name, never relinquished it.

Napoleon had already made his plan for the invasion of Italy. The army would march down the coast, wheel inland near Savona, break through the Austro-Piedmontese (Sardinian) guardians of the mountain passes and force the main Austrian army to retreat to the northeast. He would then defeat General Baron de Colli's Piedmontese army to remove the Sardinian king, Victor Amadeus III, from the war. Next he would push the Austrian General Baron de Beaulieu from the rich Austrian provinces of Lombardy and the Milanese. Depending on circumstances he would then either seize the base fortress at Mantua to effectively end Austrian rule in Italy or, screening Mantua, would push north to the Tyrol to join Moreau and Jourdan's armies coming up from the Rhine, defeat the Austrians and end the war.[5]

The initial phase did not appear easy. About 40,000 of the Sardinian king's 60,000 troops were strung out along the Alps in well-provisioned and well-defended fortresses. Colli's field army of some 20,000 men was composed largely of Piedmontese veterans who were presumably capable of stiff resistance despite long years of inactivity. Beaulieu commanded about 32,000 Austrian troops, including 3,000 highly rated cavalry (of little value in Piedmontese mountains). A British naval squadron controlled coastal waters from where the ships could interdict French army supply lines and also troops if they were forced back to the coast. Even if initial attacks succeeded there was no reason to expect light resistance.

But comfort could be gleaned from enemy problems. Difficult, compartmented terrain with few roads limited communication between widely dispersed Austrian and Piedmontese forces, the Piedmontese in mountain fortresses and entrenched camps, the Austrians only beginning to emerge from winter quarters on either side of the Po river in Lombardy. Piedmontese generals were at odds with the Sardinian king's anti-French stand. The Vienna court however distrusted this king's loyalty which prevented a

unified Austrian-Piedmontese command. Morale was low owing
to severe supply difficulties that in part accounted for nearly one-
third of the Austrian troops being on the sick-list. Traditional
Austrian command shortcomings and jealousies had only been
exacerbated by Beaulieu's arrival: a 72-year-old officer, a Belgian,
of little distinction (and dismal future). Nor was his principal
general, Argenteau, highly rated, at least by the British agent in
Genoa who wrote: "The miserable Argenteau is only fit to make
war in the boudoirs of women."[6]

Tradition ruled the army which consisted mainly of 40-year-
old veterans, most of them unfit for vigorous campaigning. The
infantryman carried a long muzzle-loading flint musket with
about the same range as the French *fusil* but much heavier.
Strategic and tactical thinking had not changed for a century.
Austrian generals preferred position warfare, their corps never far
from supply depots, with as little fighting as possible. When they
moved it was a matter of creeping, ponderous columns with little
if any tactical flexibility. If they did attack it was by compact,
slow-moving lines particularly vulnerable to sharpshooting skir-
mishers, the French *voltigeurs* and *tirailleurs*. Tactical initiative on
the part of younger officers was almost unheard of. "Austrian
generals were disciplined by rule," wrote a later historian, "and
accustomed to execute the letter of an order. In proportion as
rank descended, conduct became more mechanical, until the
private soldier was a mere automaton."[7]

The French also had problems. Small units held the mountainous area from the Col di Tenda to the coast between Loano and
Savona. The army's condition, never prosperous, had worsened
considerably in Napoleon's absence. In theory some 42,000 effectives, in fact it numbered about 30,000 hungry, unpaid, poorly
equipped and extremely dispirited officers and men. These unfor-
tunates, when not slogging through snow-jammed mountain
passes in pursuit of ill-chosen objectives or fighting off rapacious
and bloodthirsty brigands called the Barbets – rebellious peasants, criminals and deserters from the Piedmontese army[8] – had
been idling on mountain crags for two years, suffering Alpine

snows and blizzards in tattered uniforms and worn or often no
shoes, their feet covered only by 'woolen coverings stolen from the
peasants. Some of the officers were dressed in goatskins.'[9]

The army's artillery consisted of 24 light mountain guns, 200
transport mules and fewer than 3,000 underfed horses. Neither
generals nor senior officers were mounted, and they were usually
as hungry as their men. Divisions lacked qualified artillery and
engineer officers, pontoon trains, money to pay the troops and
buy provisions, and seemingly had little hope of getting any. The
few hospitals were overflowing and were no more than centers of
pestilence for pathetically undernourished victims. In January
1796 one brigade had reported 600 deaths in 20 days, caused by an
epidemic in a Savona hospital. Little wonder that the army's
former commander, General Schérer, when pressed by the
Directory to activate Napoleon's plan of invasion, replied "that the
man who had drafted the plan ought to carry it out."[10]

In addition to this sorry picture a battalion mutiny greeted
Napoleon's arrival. He put it down swiftly and forcefully, court-
martialing the negligent commanding officer and ringleaders and
disbanding the unit while carrying on in his own very distinct
style to turn a moribund mob into a fighting army. His confidence was never to fade. Only a day or two after his arrival, when
he faced the military equivalent of cleansing the Augean stables,
he privately reported to Lazare Carnot of the Directory, "There
are great obstacles, but the greatest have been surmounted." And
to the Directory: "The administrative situation is dreadful, but
not hopeless."[11]

Napoleon's energy and activity were incredible. When not dictating his ukases to a secretary to be passed on to Berthier, who
would then turn them into official orders, he was with the troops.
His remarkable oratory spread over them like sunshine, his fecund
mind dealing with the scores of problems that confronted him. He
issued over a hundred orders in the first three weeks of his command. Incompetent officers were relieved, injustices and unfair
treatment investigated but in part remedied; he tore into corrupt
civilian supply *commissaires*, and he praised and cajoled others

and soon his troops were eating good bread and meat. He forced local banks to grant loans so that he could pay the soldiers – they would have to deal with the Directory for repayment.[12]

But Napoleon needed more than money and rations to make a fighting army. He needed hope, and to gain hope he impetuously offered his men a blank check on the bank of conquest. "Soldiers, you are ill-clothed, poorly fed; the government owes you much, it has given you nothing . . . I will lead you to the richest plains in the world. Rich provinces and great cities will be in your power; you will find there honor, glory and riches."[13] Thus the pronouncement of a major Napoleonic (and Lazare Carnot) tenet, that of his armies living off the land. It was scarcely original. Years earlier Guibert had written "that the war should feed the war."[14] Napoleon had read Guibert – and agreed.

Furious activity in the Army of Italy continued as Napoleon moved headquarters to Albenga near the coast in the first week of April. Reinforcements from coastal divisions and the Army of the Pyrenees had to be sorted out and distributed, generals assigned to organize the infantry into regular and light demi-brigades, the former about 3,000 strong, the latter 1,000–1,500, four demi-brigades to a division. Horses and mules were rounded up to transport heavy cannon; old muskets were replaced; uniforms and shoes procured; existing supply channels were corrected and new ones opened. Spies were sent into Piedmont, villages were fined for not meeting supply requisitions. Marching orders were written and distributed and provisions collected – for the troops, one day of fresh meat, one day of vegetables, one day of salted meat; for the horses, 10 lbs of hay and half a bushel of oats a day. Letters had to be written to the Directory complaining of insufficient funds; more letters to the Genoese government, threatening retaliation if French patriots continued to be molested and comfort given to "the émigrés and enemies of the [French] Republic."[15]

In a remarkably short time the army was as ready as possible, which was not saying much. The infantryman at least was supplied with essentials. He carried a flint muzzle-loading musket, the model 1777 *fusil* with bayonet and long smooth-bore barrel which weighed about 11 lbs and fired a 10½-ounce lead ball. Maximum range was about 330 yards, but at 200 paces half of the shots would be wasted. The other half could be effective enough: a ball penetrated nearly two inches of oak, over four inches of pine. A veteran could charge the piece in 10 or 12 seconds and fire five rounds a minute without aiming.[16] A soldier carried 80 cartridges, 40 in his pack and 40 in the cartridge pouch.

Napoleon had hoped that mountain snows would shield the movements of the advance guard, Laharpe and Menier's divisions, a total 17,000 troops under General Masséna's command marching down the coast to Voltri, about nine miles short of Genoa. Beaulieu learned of the march however. Thinking that Napoleon intended to cut his communications with Genoa, he led a strong force to counter the threat. General Argenteau took command of the weakened center outside the village of Montenotte to protect communications north to Alessandria and Milan. While General Cervoni's outgunned French brigade at Voltri was making a night withdrawal on Savona, Napoleon marched the main force inland only to be attacked by Argenteau's mixed Austrian-Piedmontese corps.

Breaking through one French position after another, Argenteau's drive was halted only by a final defensive post whose commander, the brave Colonel Rampon, refused to surrender though vastly outnumbered and short of ammunition. His courageous stand allowed General Laharpe to close the field and on the following morning to defend against a renewed attack, Argenteau having been hastily joined by Beaulieu's corps.

For some hours the battle seesawed, but then a fresh brigade brought up by General Masséna arrived, in Napoleon's words, to "sow death and destruction on the enemy's flank and rear." The survivors escaping only with difficulty to Millesimo.[17] According to Napoleon the battle cost Beaulieu 1,500 casualties and 2,500 men taken prisoner. He probably did not exaggerate. Argenteau, seriously wounded, informed Beaulieu: "Yesterday I beat the enemy, and today I have been almost destroyed. My loss is very great."[18] Napoleon reported some 400 French causalities.

The French now smelled Piedmontese blood. General Augereau's elated brigades quickly pressed on to attack General Provera whose small corps was holed up in the formidable castle of Cosseria. An assault failed at a cost of 900 French casualties but the next day Provera, lacking food, water and ammunition, surrendered. Sérurier's corps in reserve at Ormea meanwhile had been ordered to march on Ceva, while Masséna advanced on Dego where he would be joined by Napoleon and Laharpe's division. Napoleon's subsequent attack on Dego was a brilliant display of generalship – we shall see it repeated time and again: simultaneous assaults on flanks, center and rear, an action so swift that the overwhelmed enemy succumbed to "death, fright and flight." Among several thousand prisoners were one lieutenant general, "twenty or thirty colonels or lieutenant colonels," the better part of several regiments and all of the artillery. Argenteau's battalions, though badly hit, managed to escape.[19]

Napoleon and Laharpe now marched in the hope of joining Augereau and Sérurier's corps for an attack on Ceva, Masséna being left to guard Dego. But the victors grew careless. "Overcome by privation and hunger," General Roguet later wrote, "the soldiers impatiently scattered themselves in the environs of Dego seeking food and shelter." No outposts, no patrols. Early the next morning a strong Austrian force appeared from mist and rain to send the surprised and disorganized French in retreat. Napoleon perforce had to send Laharpe back to Dego where Masséna had managed to scramble together some demi-brigades. A day-long counter-attack regained the town, but at a cost of nearly 1,000 casualties, the Austrians losing an estimated 1,700 men.[20]

Although Napoleon did not yet realize it, he had separated the Austrians from the Piedmontese in accordance with his original strategy. "The [Austrian] army is in a very bad situation," Beaulieu informed the Vienna court on 16 April. ". . . I am endeavoring to collect the relics of the troops at Acqui . . . [after which] I shall take a position which will be the most advantageous for the security of what is left of my army and the defense of Lombardy. I beg your Majesty to consider what can be hoped from an army which hardly amounts to 16,000 men."[21]

Augereau's corps of 6,500 determined soldiers was meanwhile either bridging or fording fast-flowing mountain streams in moving to join Sérurier's corps and strike the entrenched camp of Ceva defended by General Colli's 6–7,000 Piedmontese. Although the camp held after a day's hard fighting, Colli, fearing that he would be outflanked, withdrew during the night to a strong position on the Tanaro river. Napoleon now aware that Beaulieu was in full retreat ordered an all-out attack on Colli's force, an effort weakened by one column failing to cross the rain-swollen Tanaro and by another giving itself over to food and wine. Once again however Colli retreated, first to Mondovi and then north toward Turin, his losses amounting to nearly 10,000 men, 11 colors, 8 cannon and a great deal of supply and equipment left in Ceva and Mondovi.[22]

Pushing hard, Napoleon's divisions reached Cherasco which Colli had hastily evacuated, leaving behind 28 cannon and valuable magazines. All was now ready for the final march on the Piedmont capital, Turin, some 20 miles to the north, when Colli, following his king's orders, requested an armistice to be followed by peace negotiations in Paris.

The request placed Napoleon in an awkward situation. As he explained to Colli, he was not empowered to negotiate with the enemy. However he knew that the Directory wanted peace in order to remove the Sardinian king from alliance with Austria. He was also aware that his supply lines from the coast had broken down as a result of commissariat inefficiency, British naval bombardment, lack of wagons and horses and, not least, difficult terrain. His fast-moving divisions were tired and hungry. Too many soldiers had abandoned their units to plunder the countryside – a number of regiments stood at little more than company strength. Despite Beaulieu's reverses the Austrians were still superior in men and guns, their excellent cavalry had not come into play, and he would soon be reinforced from the Tyrol. The French divisions suffered serious shortages. Food was still scarce, uniforms and shoes shredded; the demi-brigades lacked cannon; there was no siege artillery. Notwithstanding repeated promises from Paris, Napoleon still lacked qualified artillery and engineer officers, not to mention pontoon bridge equipment. He himself was approaching exhaustion, as were his staff officers, commanders and troops.

With these factors in mind, he agreed to an armistice provided the Sardinian king would turn over some major fortresses complete with defenses, munitions and provisions (which he would purchase). In addition he would retain the lands he had conquered along the Stura river and would have the right to cross the Po river at Valenza and march across the king's lands in Lombardy in order to attack the Austrian army.

In informing the Directory of his decision Napoleon painted a bleak picture of his command, pointing to broken promises of reinforcements; but he also stated the advantages of an armistice that would allow him to retain control of what he had won, not to mention his gaining time to "seize all of Austrian Lombardy as far as [fortress] Mantua and chase Beaulieu from Italy." His somewhat repetitive and ambiguous dispatches were entrusted to his brother, Joseph, accompanied by Junot, the latter carrying 21 Austrian and Piedmontese battle colors to present to the Directory along with assurance of the army's "devotion to the constitution."[23]

Napoleon remained only a few days at Cherasco, "the most beautiful land in the world," as he informed the Directory. His advance had opened communications with Nice via the Col di Tenda which would allow him troop reinforcements along with food and wine to (hopefully) reduce troop pillaging. More to the point was the appearance of the Piedmontese peace envoys, one of whom later recalled the general's "grave and frigid courtesy" and his "hard and biting sarcasm" as he delivered an ultimatum: either accept his conditions immediately or he would resume his offensive.

His conditions accepted, his lines of communication seemingly secure, he jubilantly informed the Directory that he would march the next day, force Beaulieu to retreat behind the Po river, seize all of Lombardy and in less than a month would hope to be in the Tyrol to join the French armies coming from the Rhine and carry the war into Bavaria. He wanted 15,000 men from the Army of the Alps to give him a total 45,000 effectives: "If you continue to give me your confidence and approve these projects, I am certain of success: Italy is yours."[24]

With that the Army of Italy marched to the banks of the Bormida river where it wheeled to the northeast in pursuit of the Austrians.

Notes

1 Corr. XXIX, 89.
2 Macdonell, 9. See also Thiébault, I, 269; Scott, 62–73.
3 Bouvier, 44. See also Marmont, II, 146–54.
4 Asprey (*Frederick the Great*), 471.
5 Colin, 338–52.
6 Burton, 11.
7 Burton, 8–12.
8 Bouvier, 15. See also Marmont, II, 144–6.
9 Burton, 19. See also Jackson, 39–43.
10 Thiry (*Jeunesse*), 282, citing Marmont, I, 93. See also Rose (*Life*), I, 75; Bouvier, 1–22.
11 Corr. I. Nrs. 94, 95, Nice, 28 March 1796.
12 Rose (*Life*), I, 79.
13 Corr. I. Nr. 91, 27 March 1796.
14 Colin, 349.
15 Corr. I. Nrs. 120, Albenga, 5–7 April 1796; 129, Savona, 10 April 1796.
16 Bouvier, 20–1.
17 Corr. I. Nrs. 143, 148, Carcare, 14 April 1796. See also Marmont, II, 156–65, for his eyewitness account of this string of battles.
18 Wilkinson (*Rise*), 103.

19 Corr. I. Nr. 165, Carcare, 15 April 1796.

20 Wilkinson (*Rise*), 115–17. See also Marmont, II, 158–61.

21 Wilkinson (*Rise*), 118. See also Thiry (*Italy*), 52. We feel sorry for Argenteau, but more so for the system that brought him to command. Blamed by Beaulieu for the Austrian defeat, and unable to state the location of his corps when asked, he was arrested and courtmartialed, but was allowed to retire to his estates (and boudoirs) owing to the influence of friends at court.

22 Corr. I. Nrs. 203, 213, Lesagno, 22 April 1796; 251, Cherasco, 27 April 1796.

23 Corr. I. Nrs. 220, 222, 223, Carrù, 24 April 1796; 256, Cherasco, 28 April 1796.

24 Corr. I. Nr. 257, Cherasco, 28 April 1796.

CHAPTER FOURTEEN

THE GENERAL
APRIL 1796

I am very content with General Bonaparte. He is talented.

General Berthier to General Clarke of the ministry of
war in Paris[1]

It is impossible to make a more brilliant campaign . . .
General Bonaparte is successful and he deserves to be; his
reputation consolidates itself daily, and his most recent
moves are not less brilliant.

Auguste Marmont to his father,
Cherasco 26 April 1796[2]

FOR A MAN who had never commanded a division let alone an
army Napoleon performed remarkably well in the opening phase
of this Italian campaign, demonstrating a revolutionary tactical
agility based on a remarkable respect for and use of time and
space. Guibert and Bourcet may have provided the inspiration
but it was Napoleon who accomplished a tactical tempo unheard
of by his contemporaries, a speed that allowed him to disperse his
divisions as necessary yet repeatedly to concentrate them at the
crucial moment: "We do not march, we fly," in Berthier's words.[3]
Time and again his columns surprised inferior numbers of the
enemy, either to fight them under favorable circumstances or to
send them running.

This was by careful calculation more than by chance, the result
of superb leadership that transformed a disparate bunch of
demoralized officers and men into a hard-charging army. Once the

fighting started he was rarely out of touch with even his most advanced units, a tremendous accomplishment in mountainous terrain and one explained by his own fervid activity and by the intrepidity and ingenuity of his aides who sometimes carried orders to the most far-flung units. Although his generals on occasion questioned and even scorned his orders, they soon enough realized that these orders were producing victories one after another.

Nor did it take them and their troops long to realize that the new commander in chief was on their ideological side, that he not only shared but constantly exhibited the revolutionary *esprit de corps* so dear to their hearts. This was an army on the move, he told officers and men alike, an army fighting to preserve revolutionary ideals that promised mankind a kinder life. "Everything tells us that today and tomorrow will make their mark in history," he wrote in an order to Masséna early in the campaign.[4]

But if one eye strayed to posterity, the other remained fixed on the instant. He was everywhere, ordering, praising, encouraging, scolding, dictating new orders, munching a piece of bread and cheese bummed from a private, snatching an hour or two of sleep by a campfire. He was never far from battle, never far from officers and men whose victories he shared, whose losses he suffered. His touch was human whether questioning a tired soldier about his home village, or trying to console a dying youth, or joking with a general or an aide – often tweaking the man's ear-lobe, which soon became the hallmark of his approval and good humor. Generous with praises and promotions, he frequently called the Directory's attention to meritorious and courageous performances; words printed in the *Moniteur* soon to reach all the provinces to be read by parents, siblings and sweethearts of the fighting men as they moved from one great victory to another, words published in Lazare Carnot's *Journal des Defenseurs de la Patrie* to be read army-wide.[5]

Napoleon allowed his generals far more command independence than is generally supposed, on occasion requesting a plan of attack, in one instance calling a council of war to decide if an attack were feasible. Although he did not easily suffer tactical incompetence he respected the fortunes of war, favorable or adverse. He learned "with sadness" that a detachment of Cervoni's division had been taken by surprise in a village. Rather than complaining he issued orders for a new attack: "There is no need to be shaken, my dear General, by the small setback that you have received; it will be only the prelude to your victory."[6]

Even with a string of victories it was not easy to keep this army together. The mountainous country showed no signs of the happy land earlier promised by Napoleon. Rations were in short supply and booty was scarce. Not being able to feed bodies, Napoleon turned to minds. His various proclamations, orders of the day and bulletins (published in the *Moniteur*), were clever concoctions of praise and challenge, of appeals "to vanity and the love of glory," in designating the common soldier to be the guardian of the new republic which he must at all costs defend from countless enemies. One such issued in late April read:

Soldiers! In fifteen days you have won six victories, taken twenty-one standards, fifty-five cannon, several fortresses, you have conquered the richest part of the Piedmont; you have taken fifteen thousand prisoners, killed or wounded more than ten thousand men . . . deprived of everything, you have made up for everything. You have won battles without cannon, crossed rivers without bridges, made forced marches without shoes, bivouacked without brandy and without bread . . . The greatest obstacles are without doubt surmounted; but you still have battles ahead, cities to take, rivers to cross. Is the courage of any of you weakening? Would any of you prefer to return to the mountains and suffer the abuses of military slavery? No – not for the conquerors of Montenotte, Millesimo, Dego and Mondovi. Every single one of you wants to extend the glory of the French race; to humiliate those arrogant kings who dare think of putting us in irons; to dictate a glorious

peace which will indemnify the country for its immense
sacrifices; everybody wants, upon returning to their
villages, to be able to say with pride: "I served with the
army that conquered Italy."[7]

Napoleon had much to admire in his army, but also much to
regret. Almost from the beginning of the campaign his troops
(including officers) went on a rampage of pillaging and plundering, excesses including rape and murder that, as he informed the
Directory, "make one ashamed of being a man."[8]

This was partly his own fault for having employed command
flatulence in his initial proclamation to the army. In pointing to
the riches of Piedmont and Lombardy he probably meant that his
quartermasters would be able to keep magazines filled with vegetables, fruit and meat while his paymasters found cash to make
up back pay. He was presumably counting on the Directory to furnish him additional funds and other assistance. When that august
body failed him, his lack of horses, mules and carts taken with
inefficient and corrupt *commissaires* in the supply depots soon
resulted in shortages of bread, wine and brandy which not unnaturally caused widespread plundering.

The brigandage took several forms, the most common being
small groups of soldiers sneaking away from their units to scour
farms and villages for women, wine and food (probably in that
order). Both officers and men were guilty of unyoking enemy
horses and mules from captured artillery pieces, either for unauthorized personal use or to sell, this at a time when quartermasters
desperately needed road transport for munitions and rations. As
Napoleon made clear to the Directory, he understood all too well
the reasons for this breakdown in discipline; as he made clear to
his officers and men, he would not tolerate it. But despite his
harsh decrees the pillage increased to an alarming degree. "In all
the villages, in all the farmhouses, in all the hamlets, everything is
pillaged and devastated," complained one officer. ". . . One steals
from the unfortunate inhabitant of a cottage his bedsheets, his

shirts, his clothes, his shoes, in short, everything . . . if he does not give money he is killed."[9]

Napoleon now ordered his generals to arrest any culpable officer and send him to prison in Antibes. Any officer or man inciting others to pillage would be shot instantly. Anyone absent from his unit in combat would be subject to punishment ranging from being stigmatized by his fellows to busted in rank and, if either a grenadier or a carabinier, formally degraded at the head of his battalion and sent to hard labor.[10] On 26 April he laconically reported to the Directory that "the pillage is much less . . . I have shot three men and sent six to hard labor beyond the Var." Several privates and a corporal who had stolen some vases from a church were to be shot on the morrow: "In three days discipline will be strongly established, and an astonished Italy will admire the good behavior of our army as much as it admires our courage."[11]

Napoleon somewhat lessened the severity of these measures by a careful distinction between pillage and the "spoils of war." Any soldier turning in a captured work-horse would be paid one *louis* (a gold coin worth 20 francs); captured cavalry horses were regarded as legitimate prizes and could be sold to army officers or civilian transport agents; detached units that captured horses or mules would be paid upon delivering them to the artillery park.[12]

The spoils of war also included arbitrary "contributions levied on any person, village or town" unfortunate enough to get in the way of war. Owing to an extreme shortage of cash – the Directory had promised him over a million livres but paid him only 300,000 – Napoleon seized some statuary on the approach march and put it to auction, "which should give us thirty to forty thousand livres."[13]

Early in the campaign he ordered General Sérurier "to employ all possible means, be it by agreement, be it by force, to make the Genoese furnish us with mules." At one point General Joubert was ordered "to rest your troops and take everything that you find in the neighboring villages."[14] Similar orders authorized commanders to exact contributions of bread, meat, wine and anything else necessary for troop welfare. Following the battle of Mondovi he ordered the inhabitants to supply at once nearly 40,000 rations of biscuit, 8,000 rations of meat and 4,000 bottles of wine; on the following day they were to deliver 8,000 rations of meat and another 4,000 bottles of wine.[15] They were to turn over all properties, arms and ammunitions that belonged to the king of Sardinia or that they had purchased, and if they failed to do so they would be brought before a military tribunal.[16]

This was only a beginning. As Napoleon informed the Directory: "the province of Mondovi alone will give us a million [francs] in contributions," and he intended to exact millions more from the Duke of Parma in order to pay for his next campaign.[17]

Napoleon's correspondence with the Directory offers numerous and sometimes telling insights into his character. He almost always exaggerated the facts in his favor when reporting on a battle, minimizing his own forces and losses, inflating enemy strengths and casualties, but this is a hallmark of most commanding generals, and it was also intended to throw off the enemy in case the courier was intercepted. His frequent reports offered generally lively battle scenarios along with trenchant complaints, particularly in his private correspondence with the minister of war, Carnot. Early in the campaign he informed the minister that, owing to the machinations of a rear-echelon general, "I can not hide from you that I am aided neither by the engineers nor the artillery; I do not have, despite the order that you have given, one officer that I have requested . . . I do not have one engineer capable of reconnoitering Ceva . . . not one who has made a siege or who has done duty in a fortress." The company of light artillery which Carnot had ordered had not arrived, the inevitable result "when bureaucrats wish to command."[18] Lack of light artillery was not only annoying but also dangerous in view of the enemy's superior strength in cavalry which would show as the campaign reached more open terrain.

Later in the month he returned to the charge, writing to Carnot: "I cannot conceal from you how much that counter-order that you have authorized to the company of light artillery . . . hurts my operations." Nothing that the Bureau of Engineers and Artillery should have sent him had arrived, "not one officer . . . not one artisan, not one company of horse artillery . . . I can suggest only the ill-will of the Bureau of Artillery. If I had had light artillery, I would not have lost the brave General Stengel [killed during a cavalry charge], and I would not have found myself stopped on a plain by a cavalry more numerous and better mounted than mine."[19] He was less severe when it came to diplomatic affairs, indeed in reporting negotiations with the Turin court to the Directory he was even servile but this was little more than Socratic humility.

The sum of his lengthy dispatches amounted to a *fait accompli* – he would march into Lombardy knowing full well that the Directory would not recall him so long as it received money and treasures. At the end of April the army marched east in pursuit of more honor, more glory – and more plunder.

Notes

1   Thiry (*Italy*), 95.
2   Marmont, I, 318.
3   Thiry (*Italy*), 94–5.
4   Corr. I. Nr. 138, Carcare, 12 April 1796.
5   Marten, 406–7, 413 ff.
6   Corr. I. Nr. 194, Lesegno, 26 April 1796.
7   Corr. I. Nr. 234, Cherasco, 26 April 1796. See also Burton, 5.
8   Corr. I. Nr. 220, Carrù, 24 April 1796.
9   Reinhard (*Italy*), 27.
10   Corr. I. Nr. 214, Lesegno, 22 April 1796.
11   Corr. I. Nr. 233, Cherasco, 26 April 1796.
12   Corr. I. Nrs. 166, Carcare, 15 April 1796; 221, Carrù, 24 April 1796.
13   Corr. I. Nr. 121, Albenga, 6 April 1796.
14   Corr. I. Nr. 154, Carcare, 14 April 1796.
15   Corr. I. Nr. 202, Mondovi, 21 April 1796.

16 Corr. I. Nr. 214, Lesegno, 22 April 1796.
17 Corr. I. Nrs. 233, Cherasco, 26 April 1796; 266, Cherasco, 29 April 1796.
18 Corr. I. Nr. 175, Carcare, 16 April 1796.
19 Corr. I. Nr. 224, Carrù, 24 April 1796.

CHAPTER FIFTEEN

THE ARMY MARCHES – II:
THE INVASION OF LOMBARDY
MAY–JUNE 1796

We no longer understand anything; we are dealing with a
young general who is sometimes in front of us, sometimes in our
rear, sometimes on our flanks; one never knows how he is going
to deploy himself. This kind of warfare is unbearable and
violates all customary procedures.

An Hungarian officer captured at the battle of Lodi to
Napoleon, whom he had not recognized[1]

ANXIOUS TO PROTECT the citadel and supply magazines of Milan, a
tired and discouraged General Beaulieu retreated first behind the
Po and then the Tecino rivers to defend Pavia which he believed
would be on Napoleon's line of march. Having been considerably
reinforced, his main army numbered 20–25,000 troops. Another
5,000 under General Liptoy were to cover his left flank, the
Piacenza area on the Po river southeast of Pavia, while additional
detachments screened the riverline north and west of that city.[2]

Aware of Beaulieu's general dispositions, Napoleon marched on
Tortona, "a very beautiful fortress that cost the king of Sardinia fifteen million livres to build and which held one hundred bronze
cannon and had room for three thousand troops." From here some
detachments under General Sérurier marched north of the Po, their
subsequent feints and ostentatious preparations for a river crossing
confirming Beaulieu's belief that his enemy intended to cross at
Valenza. Napoleon meanwhile positioned his divisions for a march
south of the Po on Piacenza, where he would cross the fast-moving

river some 5–600 yards wide. If Beaulieu should guess his plan and move the bulk of his force to guard the crossing at Piacenza, Napoleon would double back rapidly to cross at Valenza.[3]

The march on Piacenza was led by General Dallemagne whose 5,000 infantry were commanded by Lanusse, Lannes and Augereau while Laharpe commanded 1,500 horse. Led by Colonel Lannes the vanguard swept through a few Austrian cavalry patrols to enter the town, seize the ferry and all available boats and rafts, cross the river and hold a precarious bridgehead against other enemy cavalry. A boat bridge was soon constructed, the rest of the corps crossing at night, their way lighted by carefully prepared straw torches. This rapid movement, accurately described by Napoleon as "the most audacious of the campaign,"[4] allowed the army to push northward and defeat Liptoy's corps at Fombio which cut his communications with Beaulieu at Pavia. The brisk fight in which Dallemagne, Lanusse and Lannes distinguished themselves, and in which the brave General Laharpe was accidentally shot and killed by some panic-stricken French soldiers, yielded quantities of wheat and flour and enough medical supplies to equip hospitals for 15,000 men.

Beaulieu now marched on the new threat, clashed indecisively with the French and withdrew to Lodi on the western bank of the Adda river. Leaving nearly 10,000 troops here, he continued his retreat to join Liptoy's shattered corps at Pizzeghettone from where he would soon depart with the bulk of his army to Cremona and on eastward to the fortress-base of Mantua, thus exposing Milan and yielding the rich province of Lombardy to the victorious (and very rapacious) French.[5]

"One more victory and we are masters of Italy," an elated Napoleon informed Carnot.[6] He now sent Dallemagne's advance guard supported by Masséna and Augereau to seize Lodi. Marmont's hussars and Sugny's light artillery, the guns "pulled by the carriage horses of the Piacenza nobility,"[7] pushed back the pickets to open the way for Lannes' grenadiers. The swift French advance had caught the enemy by surprise, leaving no time to close the gates of the old walled town. A dispirited rearguard soon retreated over a narrow wooden bridge about 200 yards long to join the bulk of the defenders on the eastern side of the river. Perched on a church steeple Napoleon positioned his few guns whose accurate fire prevented the Austrians from destroying the bridge. While Sugny deployed newly arrived cannon on either side of the bridge, Napoleon ordered an assault spearheaded by carabiniers and grenadiers and supported by sharpshooters wading out to small islands to pick off the defenders.[8]

Taking a long, narrow bridge defended by musket fire and cannon firing grapeshot is never an easy task, but neither is its defense when one's army is in disordered retreat, enemy cannon are belching forth murderous balls and *mitraille*, sharpshooters are firing from island flanks, enemy infantry fire never ceases – and when angry men charge with leveled bayonets.

The attack opened at six in the evening by drums beating the *pas de charge*. It succeeded owing to Lannes, Masséna, Berthier, Cervoni and Dallemagne leading repeated charges of very brave French grenadiers. The defenders fought stubbornly, but after suffering perhaps 2,000 casualties they gave up in favor of retreat to the east. Napoleon's active role in the fighting won the acclaim of his soldiers who that night extolled him as *le petit caporal*, "the little corporal" who wins battles, a nickname that would stick to him.

Napoleon himself was euphoric, claiming only 150 French casualties, a slight loss owing to "the promptitude of execution and the sudden effect that the mass and the formidable fire of the intrepid columns have produced on the enemy army." His detailed account of the battle sent to the Directory praised numerous generals and other officers.[9] Chief of staff Berthier was directed to obtain the names of the men of the assault sections so that these could be sent to the respective *départements* in France for publication in local newspapers.

*

Napoleon's original intention had been to follow Beaulieu to Mantua, besiege and capture the fortress to force the Austrians from Italy, then march north to join the Army of the Rhine and carry the war into Bavaria.

He was still at Lodi when he learned that the armistice in Germany remained in force and that the Army of the Rhine was in camp, not in the field as he supposed. Beaulieu was about to gain 10–15,000 reinforcements. Napoleon's own reinforcements had not yet arrived, his divisions were tired, uniforms were in tatters, the often hungry men too thin, the emaciated horses exhausted. Serious pillaging in some areas was bringing on local insurrections. Even more upsetting was a new instruction from the Directory which negated his notion of marching into the Tyrol. Instead he should divide the army, sending its weaker portion into the Milanese under General Kellermann's command while he marched with the remainder to Leghorn to seize all enemy ships and merchandise there, and threaten Rome and the papacy along with Naples (the kingdom of the Two Sicilies).[10]

Napoleon had no intention of being replaced center-stage even by the hero of Valmy or by confining his victorious campaign to a plundering expedition when on the verge of forcing the Austrians from Italy. Believing that he could rely on his steadily rising popularity in France and also on the increasing cupidity of the directors, he replied at length, invoking his demonstrated patriotism and devotion to the republic, his accomplishments and, not least, plain military common sense. "I believe it very unwise," he wrote, "to divide the Army of Italy in two; it is equally contrary to the interests of the Republic to give its command to two different generals." The proposed expedition would be a trifling affair, he went on, providing it was carried out by one general. Unity of command was essential to all future military operations, as was complete confidence in the commander. After reminding the directors of his victories to date he concluded, "Each man has his way of making war. General Kellermann has more experience and makes it better than I; but the two of us together will make it very badly."[11] In a somewhat self-pitying letter to Lazare

Carnot asking for his support, Napoleon insisted that a joint command would be a total disaster: "I am not able to serve voluntarily with a man who believes himself the first general of Europe; moreover I believe that one poor general would be preferable to two good ones. War like government is an intuitive affair."[12]

This awkward issue was still unresolved when in mid May the army marched on Pavia and Milan. In the capital of Lombardy the French were received as liberators by all classes who were soon sporting the tri-color cockade on their hats while generously entertaining the new arrivals. The soldiers of Augereau's division on the first night washed down quantities of fresh bread and meat with 6,000 bottles of wine.[13] Masséna was presented with the keys of Milan, his troops meanwhile investing the fortress held by some 2,000 soldiers. Napoleon's arrival occasioned another celebration as the exuberant Milanese greeted him as a liberating hero. Enthusiastically responding from headquarters in the palace, he hosted balls and receptions, holding court to writers, scholars, artists and politicians from all over Lombardy who flocked to petition for the long-awaited independence from nearly a century of Austrian rule. The general-turned-viceroy seemed to favor the notion, authorizing newspapers and political clubs to print and say what they liked, establishing provisional municipal councils composed of patriots, ordering a national guard to be formed, and asking the Directory in Paris if it intended to turn his conquest into a republic under French hegemony.[14]

The enthusiastic reception by the Milanese may well have turned Napoleon to liberating-hero thoughts which were quite in keeping with his egotism, latent Jacobin instincts, mercurial imagination and Italian-Corsican blood. One thing was certain however: the directors intended no such political innovation, regarding the Italian campaign as ancillary to the German theater of war. Napoleon moreover had already excited the greed of the financially strapped Directory with his confident notion of not only waging war on the cheap but also of sending millions of francs in cash and treasures to Paris. The Directory's message was now clear: rape the land and get out.[15]

Some historians have blamed the Directory for Napoleon's locust-like policies (a fiction later perpetrated by the general himself), in one instance citing an order dated 7 May 1796 which would not have reached him for another eight to ten days. The directors were assuredly culpable but it was Napoleon who had in large part inspired the culpability. From the beginning he had pointed to the potential riches and without notifying the Directory had scouted out golden geese. "Send me a geographical, historical, political and topographical report on the imperial fiefs around Genoa," he instructed Faypoult, the French minister in Genoa, on the first day of May, "so that I can make all possible profit from them. Send me a report on the dukes of Parma, Piacenza and Modena; their armed forces, the location of their fortresses, and what constitutes the riches of their lands; above all, send me a report of the paintings and statues . . . that are to be found at Milan, Parma, Piacenza, Modena and Bologne."[16] On 4 May he ordered General Pelletier to collect from the imperial fiefs in his command area (within 48 hours) 250,000 francs in cash, 200,000 horned cattle and 200 pack mules. Pelletier in addition was to raise 50,000 livres from the *seigneur* of Arquata, "a raging oligarch, enemy of France and of the army"; if he failed to comply his chateau was to be destroyed and his lands laid waste.[17] Two days later he informed the Directory that he was sending a force to take 6 million francs from the Duke of Modena and intimidate both Rome and the Grand Duke of Tuscany. In the same dispatch he asked for three or four artists to select what was suitable "to send to Paris."[18]

On 9 May in reporting his successful crossing of the Po river, he notified the Directory that in return for neutrality the Duke of Parma would pay 2 million French livres in cash and would furnish 1,200 harnessed draft horses, 400 harnessed cavalry horses and 100 saddle horses; 20 paintings to be chosen by Napoleon and within 15 days 1,100 tons of wheat, 550 tons of oats and 1,200 cattle. Should he default on the time schedule, a French corps would occupy his lands.

A week later he reported that in return for an armistice the Duke of Modena had agreed to pay 7.5 million livres of which 3 million would at once be paid to the army, the rest to be paid to a Genoese banker within a month. In addition the duke would provide 2.5 million livres' worth of provisions, gunpowder and other munitions, and 20 paintings to be chosen from his gallery or from his states.

This largesse was largely the responsibility of the Directory's *représentants*, Saliceti and Garrau, but meanwhile the Directory had formed a Commission of Science and Arts in Italy of which the leading lights were the mathematician Gaspard Monge and the chemist, Claude-Louis Berthollet, supported by an artist, sculptor and naturalist, who were to arrive in Milan in early June.[19]

Money and treasures continued to roll in. Six to eight million livres in gold and silver were already at the Directory's disposition in Genoa. If wished, Napoleon would send a million livres to the Army of the Rhine. Already he had sent General Kellermann, commanding the Army of the Alps, 10,000 livres in silver, and would soon send him 200,000 more.[20]

His own division commanders were to requisition everything needed to keep their units combat-ready. Officers and men suddenly received many months of back pay and would continue to receive half of their pay in cash as opposed to paper *assignats* so discredited that it was difficult to cash them even at a considerable discount on their paper value.[21] Napoleon's decree – unique in the French army – suddenly changed hardship to comparative luxury. Officers and men now became smartly dressed and addicted (as Stendhal later noted) to the pursuit of the good life, of beautiful women and other pleasures.[22]

On the basis of this development a later historian concluded that the Army of Italy now became "an army of mercenaries devoted to Bonaparte."[23] This is unfair. The Army of Italy was already devoted to Bonaparte and would remain so. It would also remain a republican army inspired by a mission to free a downtrodden people from feudal and religious slavery. To pay them in cash was to show the commander's extreme gratitude – one more facet of already inspired leadership that helps to explain the soldier's demonstrated willingness to endure extremes of hunger, exhaustion and cold, the pain of wounds and the supreme sacrifice of life to accomplish his mission.

While French locusts continued to scavenge, Napoleon tried to justify the plague to the Lombardians, arguing in one proclamation that 20 million livres extracted in contributions was little enough payment for liberation from the Austrian yoke, indeed that it was "a feeble retribution" for such a rich country.[24] In an attempt to appease the educated classes, he offered profitable havens in France for artists and scientists and broadcast plans to reopen the University of Pavia.[25]

This was more than altruism. Napoleon was getting ready to continue his campaign against the Austrians in the Venetian provinces and he wanted to leave a peaceful, well-organized and supportive Lombardy behind him. He had been receiving intelligence on enemy positions all along from Lallement, the French agent in Venice, and in mid May sent him a further 6,000 livres: "Send spies to Trente, Mantua and the road to the Tyrol, and let me know when the boats of Trieste have departed for Mantua. Spare neither money nor efforts . . . Send me an accurate map of the Venetian states."[26] Two days later his generals received marching orders. On 20 May his soldiers were read a long proclamation that praised past exploits and called for future sacrifices – always the prelude to further action.

As had happened before and would happen again, Napoleon now fell victim to chimerical thinking. Shortly after arriving in Milan he had informed the Directory that the city "is very inclined to liberty,"[27] a sentiment to which he clung. The French notion of liberty however was distinctly at odds with the Milanese concept, as became obvious in a very short time.

Nobles, priests and landowners, already furious at having to pay a cash contribution of some two million francs, soon abhorred Napoleon's encouragement of local Jacobins who wished "to abolish religions, confiscate private fortunes and set fire to the mansions of merchants, bankers and landowners."[28] Neither educated Italians nor the lower classes would applaud French rule when the centuries-old art treasures of Italy were being shipped to Paris almost daily. Nor could property holders and peasants rejoice when their already stripped lands and warehouses had to supply tons more of grain, thousands of cattle and horses and other provisions to the French, and when properties were daily ravaged by individual soldiers despite Napoleon's asseveration to the Directory that "the pillaging is checked [owing to the abundance of supply] and the discipline reborn in this glorious army."[29]

The army's requirements were enormous. One directive ordered procurement of 2,000 draft horses, enough cloth for 15,000 coats, 50,000 jackets, 100,000 shirts and 20,000 hats. These were to be provided from various provinces within eight days and paid for by enforced contributions.[30] In addition to authorized contributions, generals such as Masséna stole almost at will from hospitals, charitable and religious foundations. Such were the violations that Cristoforo Saliceti (himself amassing a large fortune) complained to the Directory that, if they continued, Napoleon's mission "would certainly become difficult."[31] As Stendhal would later sardonically write of the Milanese, "The good people did not know that the presence of an army, however liberating, is always a calamity."[32]

Either Napoleon's intelligence agents missed various signs of discontent or he ignored their reports. Ignorant and arrogant he had left Milan to join the main army at Lodi, pleased with a large cheering crowd that saw him off. The blow fell at Lodi where he learned that the good people of Pavia, supported by 5–6,000 peasants, had captured the 300-man garrison and were trampling the French tri-color underfoot while waiting for peasant reinforcements. Horrified by the work of "the nobility, the priests and the Austrian agents," as he put it,[33] he immediately sent Lannes with a small task force which arrested hostages, killed about a hundred rebels defending the village of Binasco and burned it. Back in

Milan where an uprising had also occurred along with several in the countryside, Napoleon issued a proclamation offering amnesty if the rebels put down their arms within twenty-four hours and swore a new vow of obedience to the French republic; failing this they would be treated as rebels and their villages burned *à la* the recent "terrible example" of Binasco. General Despinoy, commanding the Milan garrison, was ordered to root out the insurgents in and around Milan, showing no pity to the concerned villages, and to establish a military court that would sentence to death anyone convicted of having taken part "directly or indirectly" in the Milan insurrection.[34]

Returning to Pavia, Napoleon ordered an all-out assault which stormed the town gates to send the rebels to roof-tops (from where they showered soldiers with tiles) and to basements to be ferreted out, a good many being sabered or shot. Also he ordered members of the town council to be executed, 200 priests and nobles sent as hostages to France and the town turned over to pillagers. He furiously reprimanded the garrison for dereliction of duty – its captain was tried by a military court and shot. He reported these sordid events to the Directory, adding optimistically that "all is completely quiet today, and I don't doubt that this lesson will serve as an example to the Italian people."[35]

Victory at Lodi meanwhile had deferred the Directory's notion of a divided command. The Army of Italy was to continue military operations as planned. Thus blessed, Napoleon returned to his war against the Austrians.

Notes

1   Corr. XXIX, 122.
2   As previously state these strengths vary depending on the source. Thiry (*Italy*), 109, for example, allows Liptoy a corps of 6,000 infantry and 2,000 horse. Wilkinson (*Rise*), 135, credits Beaulieu with a total 21,400 troops. Rose (*Despatches*), 113, credits Liptoy with 10,000 men at Lodi.

3 Wilkinson (*Rise*), 138. See also Corr. I. Nr. 337, Tortona, 6 May 1796.

4 Corr. I. Nr. 382, Lodi, 11 May 1796.

5 Wartenburg, I, 45–9.

6 Corr. I. Nr. 366, Piacenza, 9 May 1796.

7 Corr. I. Nr. 382, Lodi, 11 May 1796.

8 Numerous commentators have criticized Napoleon for failing to have his cavalry ford the river to envelop the defenders. Napoleon was far too skillful to have neglected this possibility. In a report to the Directory shortly after the battle, he wrote that the cavalry had to ford the river on foot which prevented their timely arrival. Whether they did or did not ford the river is beside the point because Napoleon would have kept up the impetus of the infantry attack, realizing that the retreating Austrians lacked time to establish a defense in depth.

9 Corr. I. Nr. 382, Lodi, 11 May 1796. See also Marmont, I, 167–75. Marmont commanded a regiment of hussars in this action, which later earned him the award of a saber of honor.

10 Thiry (*Italy*), 113. See also Miot de Melito, I, 50–3.

11 Corr. I. Nr. 420, Lodi, 14 May 1796.

12 Corr. I. Nr. 421, Lodi, 14 May 1796.

13 Thiry (*Italy*), 136.

14 Rose (*Life*), I, 96–7. See also Corr. I. Nrs. 437, Milan, 17 May 1796; 454, Milan, 19 May 1796; 455, Milan, 19 May 1796.

15 Rose (*Life*), I, 97. See also Corr. I. Nr. 437, Milan, 17 May 1796; Thiry (*Italy*), 143.

16 Corr. I. Nr. 280, Acqui, 1 May 1796.

17 Corr. I. Nr. 324, Tortona, 4 May 1796.

18 Corr. I. Nr. 337, Tortona, 6 May 1796.

19 Aubry, 170–1.

20 Corr. I. Nr. 478, Milan, 22 May 1796.

21 Corr. I. Nrs. 422, Milan, 17 May 1796; 478, Milan, 22 May 1796.

22 Reinhard (*Italy*), 25–6. See also Stendhal (*Life*), 236.

23 Reinhard (*Italy*), 26.

24 Corr. I. Nr. 453, Milan, 19 May 1796.

25 Corr. I. Nrs. 491, 492, Milan, 24 May 1796.

26 Corr. I. Nr. 441, Milan, 17 May 1796.

27 Corr. I. Nr. 427, Milan, 17 May 1796.

28 Thiry (*Italy*), 159.
29 Corr. I. Nr. 478, Milan, 22 May 1796.
30 Corr. I. Nr. 471, Milan, 21 May 1796.
31 Thiry (*Italy*), 159.
32 Thiry (*Italy*), 158.
33 Corr. I. Nr. 493, Milan, 25 May 1796. See also Marmont, I, 179, who claimed that 30–40,000 peasants had rebelled.
34 Corr. I. Nrs. 493, Milan, 25 May 1796; 536, Peschiera, 1 June 1796; 494, Milan, 25 May 1796; 504, Brescia, 28 May 1796.
35 Corr. I. Nr. 536, Peschiera, 1 June 1796.

CHAPTER SIXTEEN

THE ARMY MARCHES – III
CONSOLIDATION
JUNE–JULY 1796

*[My grenadiers and carabiniers] are playing and laughing
with death . . . nothing exceeds their boldness unless it is the
cheerfulness with which they make the most forced marches;
they sing in turn of country and love.*

Napoleon to the Executive Directory, Peschiera,
1 June 1796[1]

HAVING RETREATED ACROSS the Mincio river, the Austrian General
Beaulieu established a defensive line along its banks, his right on
Lake Garda, his left some 20 miles south on the forbidding but
somewhat weakened fortress of Mantua which he soon strengthened with reinforcements from the Tyrol (violating Venetian
neutrality in the process). Although Beaulieu was a broken reed –
the British observer in Austrian headquarters, Colonel Thomas
Graham, remarked on his "downright dotage" – his beaten army
had somewhat revived and now numbered nearly 40,000 of whom
about 13,000 formed the Mantua garrison.

By late May the French army stood west of the Mincio, ready
to pounce. From headquarters at Brescia, a town of 50,000 inhabitants, Napoleon informed Venetian overlords that he had come to
deliver "the most beautiful country of Europe from the iron yoke
of the arrogant house of Austria." Pointing to the traditional
French-Venetian friendship, he explained that the army would
observe the strictest discipline, that religion, government, tradi-
tions and private property would all be respected, and that any

subsistence furnished to the [French] army "would be fully paid for in cash" (a promise soon to be broken).[2]

Napoleon scarcely exaggerated the beauty of the country, as any visitor to the Lake Garda region will attest. The traditional gateway to the heart of Italy, its cold, swift-running mountain rivers, narrow valleys and crisp air had been enjoyed by Attila the Hun nearly fourteen centuries earlier when Pope Leo arrived in his camp on the Mincio to buy protection of the papal lands.[3]

The French commanding general seemed every bit as confident as Attila according to a young French diplomat who was minister to the Grand Duke of Tuscany at Florence. Miot de Melito, who came to army headquarters to discuss Neapolitan affairs, later described Napoleon's moderate height, his thinness, powdered hair cut squarely across his forehead above the ears then falling to his shoulders, his uniform tunic buttoned to the top, decorated only with a narrow gold-embroidered strip, hat sprouting tri-colored plumes, in short not much to regard at first sight except for the lively inquisitive eyes, the abrupt but animated gestures, the high, creased forehead, the curt speech and very incorrect grammar. The military task, Napoleon explained, was to seize Mantua fortress and advance into central Italy. He favored a nego-tiated armistice with Naples. Shuffling papers while they talked, he suddenly broke off to give orders to waiting generals "who maintained toward him an attitude of respect, I may even say of admiration. I saw none of those marks of familiarity . . . conso-nant with republican equality. He had already assumed his own place, and set others at a distance."[4]

Napoleon's tactical challenge was to cross the Mincio, cut through Beaulieu's defensive line, set up a protective flank to the north and turn south to invest Mantua. Knowing that Beaulieu had to protect major supply lines, the roads (scarcely more than tracks) east of Lake Garda climbing sharply northward on either side of the Adige river, Napoleon sent Kilmaine's cavalry and Augereau's infantry up the west side of the enormous lake to make Beaulieu fear an end run around its northern tip.

Beaulieu was suitably fooled. Occupying the small Venetian fort of Peschiera on the southern end of the lake (another violation of Venetian neutrality), he extended his right as far north as Roveredo, consequently weakening his defense of Mincio. Murat's cavalry now cleared western approaches to the river of enemy men and horses, their first important action in the campaign but one that yielded nine Austrian cannon, two standards and 2,000 prisoners. The main force followed to cross the Mincio and seize Borghetto and Valeggio.

Napoleon established forward headquarters in Valeggio while waiting for Masséna's division to come up from the Mincio. But Masséna's troops preferred eating to marching. Napoleon was ill and was soaking his feet in hot water when a detachment of Austrian hussars charged into the town. He escaped only by jumping barefooted onto his horse, an unpleasant incident which caused him subsequently to form an elite corps of bodyguards, the famous *Guides* of which we shall hear more.[5]

Hoping to cut Beaulieu's retreat northward, Napoleon next sent Augereau to block Peschiera and the roads eastward but he was too late: the defenders had evacuated the fort to join their retreating brethren. The French pursued as far as Rivoli, where they learned that Beaulieu had crossed the Adige and destroyed the bridges.

Napoleon and his soldiers could still feel pleased. In less than two days of fighting, Beaulieu had been driven north with a loss of 1,500 men (including prisoners), 500 horses, five cannon and a number of caissons loaded with ammunition. As he informed the Directory he could not sufficiently praise his grenadiers and *carabiniers*, his words quoted at the beginning of this chapter. To make the directors as cheerful as his troops, he was sending them 2 million livres in cash with another 4 or 5 million to come; he was also sending a hundred of "the most beautiful horses that are to be found in Lombardy" to replace their own indifferent carriage nags.[6]

The first task completed, Napoleon ordered Masséna to Verona east of the Mincio and Augereau to Castiglione west of the

Mincio, their patrols to keep an eye on the Austrians to the north. Napoleon himself was in almost constant movement, inspecting divisions and detachments; setting up artillery parks; rebuilding the defenses of Peschiera; dispatching generals to force local officials and priests to swear allegiance to the French republic, to disarm all civilians and seize whatever cash was in local safes; arranging for armed boats to patrol Lake Garda; ordering bridges built over the Po and boats collected on its banks; and a variety of other tasks undoubtedly unwelcomed but soon carried out by already tired generals.

Fearful of the approaching *canicule* or "dog-days" of early July to mid-August, which were particularly dangerous in swampy areas around Mantua, he ordered hospitals built at Verona, Peschiera, Brescia and Crema with arrangements to evacuate more seriously ill patients to Tortona, Alessandria, Milan and Pavia. At Verona, a town of 60,000 population, he informed the city fathers of his displeasure at their acceptance of the future French king, Louis XVIII, who only recently had fled to Germany with 1,500 émigré followers. Verona was a beautiful city, he reported to the Directory, particularly its old Roman amphitheater which, seating 100,000 spectators each of whom could easily hear and understand an orator, made the Champ de Mars in Paris look shabby.[7]

He was distinctly unimpressed with two envoys sent by the Venetian senate to determine his future intentions. Instead of encouragement they received a Napoleonic scolding for the reception accorded to the pretender's brother, Comte d'Artois, and for having allowed the Austrians to seize the Venetian fortress of Peschiera. He had reported these transgressions to Paris, he told them, but had not yet received a reply. He believed it possible for the Venetian senate to repair the damage to republican *amour-propre* by furnishing everything necessary to his army (as opposed to his earlier pledge to pay for all provisions). Harsh, yes, but clever and cunning. A few days later he notified the Directory that he had arranged this quarrel in case it wished to milk Venice for 5 or 6 million livres. If the Directory held more radical intentions, he should be notified and would strike at the right moment.[8]

The way now stood open for an investment of Mantua (colo-
nized by the Romans in 220 BC). The fortress built by the
Austrians nearly a century earlier stood on the west bank of the
Mincio in the middle of three lakes connected to land by five
dikes, some defended, that extended in spoke-like formation from
the mother hub.

General Sérurier commanding the siege troops soon seized
these to push the defenders into the fortress proper so that Colonel
Chasseloup of the engineers could begin preparing siege lines.
Protected on north and south by water and marsh, the Austrians
could only be attacked from or could only attack besiegers on the
east and west. In view of the fortress' natural strength and recent
reinforcement an assault would not be easy.[9] If Napoleon's total
force now numbered some 60,000, he could still spare only 10,000
combat troops to blockade the target until siege artillery and more
troops were available.

Meanwhile the Directory was pressing him to march southward on Leghorn, Naples and Rome. With this and other
considerations in mind he returned to Milan in early June.

Napoleon was not eager to march south at this time. Following
Miot de Melito's visit he had received diplomats from the courts of
Naples and Rome and had signed an armistice with Naples which
was sent to the Directory as a virtual *fait accompli*. Under its terms
the Naples court would recall its four cavalry squadrons from
Beaulieu's army, some 2,400 horse which had impeded the French
advance through Lombardy and more recently from the Mincio; it
would also recall its warships and frigates from the English
squadron based on Naples. Pope Pius VI also seemed more than
eager to sign an agreement which Napoleon estimated would be
worth many millions in cash, *objets d'art* and provisions.[10]

As Napoleon pointed out, it thus seemed fruitless to march, at
least before the surrender of Mantua fortress. Not only was he
strapped for men, but Vienna was sending General Würmser with
30,000 troops from the Rhine to Italy. He had only 6,000 men

available for an expedition, but "should we have twenty thousand
it would not suit us to make a twenty-five-day march in July and
August in order to look for sickness and death."[11] A march on
Rome would be particularly difficult, he privately informed Lazare
Carnot, in view of the vast spaces and supply problems not to
mention the resistance foreseen from the fanaticism of the peoples.
He ended this letter on a pleasant enough note however: he was
sending a million livres in cash to Basle for the Army of the Rhine,
and another 8 million at Genoa were at the Directory's disposal. In
a letter to the minister of finance on the same day he wrote that in
a short time another 10 million livres would be at his disposition.[12]

Napoleon for some time had been begging Joséphine to join
him and she finally had agreed to do so. He had expected her
arrival in early June, the major incentive for his move to Milan.
But there he found neither Joséphine nor letters – indeed he
learned that she was still in Paris. His disappointment was obvious
to all as he drowned it in hard work. Joséphine aside, he had good
reason to be pleased. "Lombardy is completely quiet," he reported
to the Directory. "Everyone is singing political songs and accus-
toming himself to liberty." Crowds of youngsters wanted to join
the French army, he continued, but since that was legally ques-
tionable he was thinking of organizing a native battalion with
French officers.[13]

The arrival of Monge and Berthollet also helped for now the
evenings were filled with mathematical and scientific discussions.
They and their fellow commissioners could scarcely believe what
they found waiting to be packed and sent off to France. An inventory of treasures taken from the Bibliothèque Ambroisienne in
Milan and from various academies, museums and churches in
Parma and Piacenza listed 34 items, among them a 1,100-year-old
manuscript written on Egyptian papyrus, one of Virgil's manuscripts annotated by Petrarch, de Vinci's *Head of a Woman* and
paintings by Raphael, Luini, Rubens, de Leyde, Calabrese,
Ferrari, Salvator Rosa, Corregio, Van Eyck and others.[14]

This was only a beginning. Still pressed by the Directory,
Napoleon now agreed to lead a limited expedition southward

before the Austrian General Würmser could arrive with reinforcements. Its first objective was to reestablish French authority
in troubled areas, its second to collect needed weapons, its third to
turn loose Monge and his fellows in scouring operations.

After alerting General Augereau to march a small task force on
Bologna, Napoleon, closely followed by Monge and Berthollet,
hurried to Pavia and ordered its castle completely renovated, the
moats cleared and filled, the interior furnished to hold 2,000
troops. A day later he was in Tortona to deal with a new series of
uprisings in the imperial fiefs. Rebels in one village had assassinated 150 French soldiers. Napoleon replied in kind. Lannes with
1,200 infantry, cavalry and artillery "burned the houses of the
rebels," Napoleon reported to the Directory; 15 ringleaders
"judged guilty by a military court" were shot.[15] He accused the
Genoese government in large part for fomenting the rebellion and
demanded the prosecution of certain responsible persons by
name. If Genoese territory was not purged of these assassins,
Napoleon warned the senate, "I shall burn the towns and villages
where a single Frenchman is assassinated . . . [and] I will burn the
houses which gave refuge to the assassins."[16]

Napoleon now marched on Bologna, his columns stopping at
Modena to accept the surrender of its fort which yielded 5,000
fusils of an excellent make, 50 well fitted-out cannon and quantities of food and wine.[17] Splendidly received in Bologna, many of
whose approximately 50,000 citizens deeply resented papal rule,
he found his military and civil *commissaires* busy stripping the
area of anything worthwhile. Among the plunder were another
114 cannon which with the other captured pieces would form the
siege artillery at Mantua.

From headquarters at Bologna he sent the Directory a series of
detailed reports on the military and political situation. He was
plainly worried by hearing that Beaulieu was actively recruiting
and would soon be joined by Würmser's new corps some 30,000
strong. He already had sent a column of troops to reconnoiter the
area around Lake Como and distribute an edict similar to that
issued to the Venetians: we are your friends so long as you do not

betray us, but if you betray us you will suffer "the fire of heaven," your homes will be burned, your lands devastated.[18]

Considering the tasks on hand, Napoleon was not as strong militarily as he should have been. Not counting troops tied up in rear-area duties, the field army numbered over 40,000. Masséna was defending the Adige with only about 15,000 men, Sauret the area between Lake Garda and Lake Iseo with 4,500 and Despinoy in Milan with 5,200. Entrenchments necessary for the siege of the Milan citadel were now completed. Its surrender would ease the manpower shortage but it was apparent that the Austrian garrison would continue to defend it.

Another problem, in addition to Joséphine's absence, excessive heat and his usual impatience, concerned the civilian role in army administration in which he found "no order, no effort, no spirit." Army requisitions to civilian *commissaires* were not being properly filled. Contributions from towns and individuals were at a standstill owing to constant changes in collection policy. There was no standard operating procedure; the numerous civilian supply *commissaires* were working in opposite directions from his own headquarters and were disagreeing among themselves, the result of conflicting orders from the Directory. To end this disruptive conflict it was vital for the Directory "to regulate the functions of your various *commissaires* and agents . . . and particularly that you settle my relations with them and the amount of authority delegated to me in diplomatic and financial operations."[19]

On the bright side was the political atmosphere of his latest conquest. Several centuries of oppressive papal domination had created an intense hatred of Rome from where a succession of popes had progressively subverted the traditional privileges of this rich country. One of his first acts after imprisoning the cardinals of Bologna and Ferrara was to authorize the Bolognese senate "to declare null and void all the decrees of Rome prejudicial to its liberty."[20] The *grands seigneurs* at the head of government were moderate and wise men, Napoleon reported to Paris, who wanted freedom from Rome and a return to their ancient constitution, matters that they were sending a delegation to Paris to discuss. He believed that Bologna, Ferrara and the Romagna could easily form an aristocratic-democratic government which, considering its two ports on the Adriatic, could rival Venice, annul the papal power and in time draw Rome and Tuscany into the folds of liberty.

Meanwhile the Bolognese were being more than cooperative in the matter of contributions. We can almost hear Napoleon's abrupt voice pick up speed and enthusiasm while dictating to a secretary the predatory results of his campaign. Paintings taken from Parma were on their way to Paris. They included Corregio's *Saint Jerome* which the country unsuccessfully offered to buy back for a million livres. Paintings taken from Modena were also on their way. Commissioner Barthélemy was choosing 50 works, including Raphael's *Sainte Cécile*, from the Bologna treasures. French agents in Pavia were culling plants and various biological exhibits to enrich Parisian gardens and museums.[21] The country already had enriched French coffers by almost 10 million livres in cash from imposed contributions, local treasuries and the sequestered contents of official pawnbrokers' safes. Nearly 5 million more livres were paid in kind, a lengthy list that included 1,000 cattle, 1,500 horses, 20,000 uniforms, 6,000 pairs of shoes, hundreds of yards of cloth and numerous wagon-loads of silk and hemp. The army had also gained thousands of muskets, nearly 200 cannon and quantities of munitions.[22]

Napoleon's armistice with the pope called for the release of all political prisoners and the restitution of their properties, the closing of all ports under papal jurisdiction to all powers at war with France, French occupation of the important Adriatic port of Ancona, acquisition of 100 paintings, busts, sculptures or vases and 500 ancient manuscripts. The pope would pay 15.5 million livres in French money and 5.5 million in goods, manufactures and provisions.[23] Although Napoleon was pleased that the booty would exceed that called for by the Directory, he was annoyed with the principal *commissaires* – Saliceti included. He would have been able to have 30 million in cash and 10 million in provisions had the supply *commissaires* not informed the papal representative that the French were unable to march on Rome at this time.

More loot poured in when General Vaubois' division, joined by
Napoleon and a small staff, seized the port of Leghorn, the last
Austrian refuge in the Mediterranean. The Leghornese had
severely disrupted French commerce and were now terrified of
French vengeance. "The shops were closed," an aide noted, "the
streets empty, people had hidden themselves and sent all their
daughters to the countryside."[24] These words came from Captain
Joseph Sulkowski, a young Polish prince and rabid revolutionary
who had taken French citizenship to fight for the cause of liberty.
Brilliantly educated, fluent in half a dozen languages, he had been
appointed an aide thanks to the influence of one of Joséphine's
aunts. Although the French arrived too late to prevent either two
French ships from being captured by an English frigate or 40
richly loaded English merchant vessels from sailing, Napoleon
estimated that the English warehouses would yield 7–8 million
livres' worth of goods.[25]

Leaving a garrison at Leghorn, Napoleon stopped briefly at
Florence, conferred with Miot de Melito, dined with the Grand
Duke and departed the next day for Bologna. The Bolognese,
Sulkowski observed, were all wearing the French revolutionary
cocarde, not from attachment to the French cause but rather "from
a tacit order of the pope . . . and I presume . . . that the Holy
Father would hasten to attach one to his tiara at our mere
approach."[26] Sulkowski was struck by Napoleon's "astonishing
activity" and by the rapidity of their march: "As we traveled neither to see the country's curiosities nor to reflect on the antiquities,
but rather to assert . . . the power of the Republic of Italy, our stay
everywhere was only momentary."[27]

Back in Bologna, Napoleon received the welcome news that the
other French armies at last had crossed the Rhine to begin a new
campaign in Germany, and that his own siege of the Milan citadel
had abruptly ended with Austrian surrender. His mission in central Italy now accomplished, it was time to return to the war.
Moving army headquarters to Roverbella from where he would
supervise the siege of Mantua, he ordered the bulk of the army to
recross the Po river.

Notes

1   Corr. I. Nr. 537, Peschiera, 1 June 1796.
2   Corr. I. Nr. 514, Brescia, 29 May 1796.
3   Rose (*Life*), I, 101.
4   Miot de Melito (1873 ed.), I, 83–7.
5   Thiry (*Italy*), 171–2. See also Marmont, I, 182–4.
6   Corr. I. Nr. 537, Peschiera, 1 June 1796.
7   Corr. I. Nrs. 559, Verona, 3 June 1796; 570, Brescia, 5 June 1796; 581, Roverbella, 5 June 1796.
8   Corr. I. Nr. 582, Milan, 7 June 1796.
9   Corr. XXIX, 117–18, for a detailed description of the terrain.
10   Corr. I. Nrs. 570, Brescia, 5 June 1796; 583, Milan, 7 June 1796.
11   Corr. I. Nr. 583, Milan, 7 June 1796.
12   Corr. I. Nrs. 589, 591, Milan, 8 June 1796. See also Thiry (*Italy*), 186.
13   Corr. I. Nr. 610, Milan, 11 June 1796.
14   Corr. I. Nr. 444, Milan, *c*. May 1796. See also Aubry, 172–3.
15   Corr. I. Nrs. 631, 633, 634, Tortona, 14 June 1796; 639, Tortona, 15 January 1796. See also Thiry (*Italy*), 201.
16   Corr. I. Nr. 640, Tortona, 15 June 1796.
17   Corr. I. Nr. 663, Tortona, 21 June 1796.
18   Corr. I. Nr. 629, Tortona, 14 June 1796.
19   Corr. I. Nr. 664, Bologna, 21 June 1796.
20   Corr. I. Nr. 665, Bologna, 21 June 1796.
21   Aubry, 173–5.
22   Corr. I. Nrs. 709, Bologna, 2 July 1796; 663, Bologna, 21 June 1796; 694, Pistoja, 26 June 1796.
23   Corr. I. Nrs. 710, Bologna, 2 July 1796; 685, Pistoja, 26 June 1796. See also Aubry, 176–7.
24   Reinhard (*Italy*), 94. See also Miot de Melito (1873 ed.), I, 96–101.
25   Corr. I. Nr. 707, Bologna, 2 July 1796.
26   Reinhard (*Italy*), 95.
27   Reinhard (*Italy*), 96–7.

CHAPTER SEVENTEEN

THE GENERAL AND HIS LADY
MAY–JULY 1796

*I am in despair. My wife is not coming [to Milan]. She has
some lover who is keeping her in Paris.*

Napoleon to Lazare Carnot, Milan, June 1796[1]

TO READ OF Napoleon's myriad activities during this month of
June – his defeat of Beaulieu, his other military and political
accomplishments, his subjugation of central Italy and the pope,
his outpourings of directives, decrees, analyses, all this after an
extremely rigorous campaign in the Piedmont and Lombardy – it
is sad to learn that the heart within his meager body was in the
way of being broken.

Joséphine wielded the hammer. She had promised to join her
husband who had been living on her words. Despite the demands of
his new command he had frequently written to her, pouring out his
heart in the fashion of an immature lovesick swain. He repeatedly
had begged her to join him and had scolded her for not doing so.

Joséphine saw no reason to yield the delights of Paris life in a
dreary provincial capital, particularly since she was spending her
nights and probably days in the arms of lovers including those of
a dashing young hussar lieutenant, Hippolyte Charles. She greeted
her husband's missives with either a cruel silence or with equally
cruel short and cold replies that touched on patently false reasons
for procrastination.

Driven to desperation Napoleon had informed her in late April
that he was sending an aide, Joachim Murat, to Paris on official

business, and that she was to return with him. Murat subsequently reported that Joséphine was pregnant and in his opinion
could not stand the trip. Joséphine was not pregnant – she never
again would be so – but the false news drew long letters of sympathy, hope, reiterated love and his sadness because she could not
come to him. "I impatiently await Murat so as to learn in the
greatest detail everything you do, everything you say, the people
you see, the clothes that you wear."[2]

Ah, irony!

To his immense delight Joséphine suddenly agreed to come to
Milan with her two youngsters. The full correspondence is not
extant but it appears that Napoleon expected her arrival in early
June; thus his hurried return to Milan only to learn that she was
still in Paris.

Devastated, Napoleon immediately wrote at length and pathetically: "My heart was open to joy: it is full of sadness . . . Your
love for me has been just a passing fancy . . . it appears to me that
you have made your choice and that you know whom to turn to to
replace me. I wish you happiness . . . if fickleness, I do not say
perfidy, is able to obtain it . . . You have never loved me." After
reviewing his immense love for her in maudlin detail, he continued, "Your portrait was always over my heart; never a thought,
never an hour without looking at it and covering it with kisses." It
was cruel of her, he went on, to have made him hope for a love
which she did not feel. "But the reproach is not worthy of me . . .
I have never believed in happiness. Every day death hovers about
me . . . *Adieu*, Joséphine; stay in Paris, do not write me, and at least
respect my asylum. A thousand daggers pierce my heart; do not
push them in further. *Adieu*, my happiness, my life, everything
that existed for me on earth."[3]

The busy days in Milan passed rapidly but still no letter arrived
from Joséphine. On 11 June he wrote to her again:

> Joséphine, where shall one send this letter? If it is to Paris,
> my misery is then certain, you no longer love me! I have
> only to die . . . my tears flow . . . no peace of mind or

hope . . . your conduct . . . but ought I to accuse you? No. Your conduct is that of your destiny. So lovely, so beautiful, so gentle, should you be the instrument of my despair? . . . *Adieu*, my Joséphine . . . embrace your lovely children: they write me charming letters . . . I shall love you all my life.[4]

His state of mind at this time is emphasized by his lament to Lazare Carnot as quoted at the beginning of this chapter.[5]

But there was no goodbye to the sensuous Joséphine. She owned a secret compartment in his mind which he could not close. While quelling the rebellion in the imperial fiefs he had waited daily on the dusty road outside Tortona for the arrival of her carriage. One day in taking her portrait from his pocket he dropped it and the glass broke. He turned pale, Marmont later wrote, "and said to me, 'My wife is either sick or unfaithful.'"[6]

His overwhelming love for her had soon caused him to regret the harsh words written from Milan. Grasping at a new straw, he now wrote that "drowned in grief" he perhaps had written "too strongly" to her. When word had come that she was dangerously ill, attended by three physicians, the thought of her dying had filled his soul with serpents of desolation. "I do not believe in immortality of the soul. If you die, I shall at once die, but from despair or prostration." Would she forgive his earlier letters that stemmed from the depth of his love? Although Murat assured him that her illness was not serious, he would not rest easy until she informed him of its exact nature. If it continued he would be with her in five days. A hundred times he had wished to leave for Paris, but his sense of honor and duty had prevailed over his heart. He wanted her to write twice a day "to remove the pain that consumes me. Come, come quickly, but take care of your health."[7]

A day later he wrote: "My life is a perpetual nightmare . . . I have lost more than life, more than happiness, more than repose; I am almost without hope. I am sending you a courier. He will remain only four hours in Paris and then will bring me your reply." After expressing further contrition for his wrongs he begged her to tell him the nature of her illness. "If it is danger-ous . . . I shall leave immediately for Paris." He was totally beside himself, his mind conjuring up fantasies: she was already at Lyons on the way to him; or she was ill in bed, "suffering, more beauti-ful, more attractive, more adorable; you are pale and your eyes are languishing." She must know that he thinks incessantly of her, "that never has an hour passed without thinking of you; that never has the thought of another woman come to me." The letter ends on a strange note: "Do you remember that dream where I removed your shoes, your clothes and made you come entirely into my heart? Why has nature not arranged things in this way?"[8]

Napoleon's next extant letter was written eleven days later from Tuscany. He had received only two notes of three lines each from her, he complained, and was again in a state of despair: she was enjoying Paris too much to come to him, she loved everyone more than she loved him. Despite his hurt he still loved her, still expected her to await him at Milan where as soon as possible he would be "in her arms, at her feet and on her breast."[9]

Napoleon did not know that two days earlier his beloved had left Paris for Milan. The traditional explanation is that the Directory had pressed her to go for fear that her distraught hus-band would abandon the army and come to Paris. She may also have been warned by Joseph Bonaparte, Junot and possibly Murat that he was approaching the breaking point. Joséphine must also have realized that her husband was becoming a hero not only in Paris but throughout France, which made a future with him look much brighter. Whatever the reason she departed in the com-pany of Joseph, Junot, her little dog Fortune, Lieutenant Hippolyte Charles and other protégés.[10]

Napoleon learned of Joséphine's arrival a few days after he had returned from Bologna to Roverbella. At once he departed for Milan and the arms of his beloved. Such were official pressures that the reunion lasted only 48 hours, and it does not seem to have been as idyllic as he had anticipated.

A letter written after his return to headquarters spoke of his joy in having been with her, of his delight in passing the night in her arms. But he also asked her never again to be jealous, never to cry: "Your tears deprive me of reason, they burn my blood." Was there a quarrel? Was she jealous of an imagined or reputed lover? Of the army? Or had she staged a scene in order to hide her own infidelities? We don't know. Apparently she complained of an illness because he begged her to get well and join him as soon as possible.[11]

He wrote again the next day to repeat his attestations of love which were somewhat watered by a brief and unromantic recital of his attack on Mantua fortress. He wished to know what she was doing and if she were amusing herself. He enclosed a letter to him from her son, Eugène, and asked her to send some gifts to him and Hortense. He had spent the previous night on the shores of a lake looking at a silvery moon and thinking of her: "I saw you asleep, one of your hands was around my neck, the other on your breast. I pressed you against my heart and felt the throbbing of yours." The letter ended strangely: "A thousand kisses as passionate as you are cold, unending and always faithful love. Before Joseph [Bonaparte] leaves [Milan], I wish to speak to him."[12]

He wrote again the following day to complain that he had not heard from her for two days. A courier had brought two letters for her, one from Paul Barras and one from Madame Tallien. He had taken the liberty of reading them and, although she had given him permission to do so, he feared that she would be annoyed: "I would like you to give me complete permission to read your letters. With that there would no longer be remorse or fear."[13]

Another curious letter followed. He was sending her some taffeta from Florence that would make a beautiful skirt: "You see that I am generous, this cost me more than thirty livres." He would send her a lovely robe from Bologna if she would give him her preference in color and quality. He would also in time find suitable places for her *protégés*, by whom he presumably meant Hippolyte Charles and a merchant named Hamelin.[14] Although he was leaving on a tour of inspection, he hoped that she would soon join him at his headquarters "in order never again to leave me." Came then an abrupt change of mood: perhaps she had found the lover in Milan whom she came to find? "The thought remains with me . . . I am assured, by the way, that you have known for a long time and *intimately* this gentleman whom you recommend to me for a [business] undertaking. If this is true you would be a monster." The thought vanished as he completed the letter. "What are you doing right now? You are sleeping, no? And I am not there to inhale your breath, to behold your charms, and overwhelm you with my caresses . . . *Adieu*, beautiful and good, beyond compare, all divine; a thousand amorous kisses everywhere, everywhere."[15]

He finally heard from her and responded at once with two long letters. He could not come to Milan owing to the serious military situation. Instead she should come to Brescia. He was upset by her jealousy of the ladies of Brescia for whom he cared very little. He was sorry to have opened her letters and would not do so again, but he was plainly annoyed by her continuing relationship with Paul Barras: "I believe however that in a country where everyone is watching you, you should shelter yourself from the shade of suspicion and boastings of the most superficial and inconsequential man of the eighty-seven deputies of France." All arrangements had been made for her journey, but the letter ended on a negative note: "My heart is crushed by sadness, I don't know why. Would it be possible that one day you will no longer be able to love me??? A thousand tender kisses, you hold my heart in yours."[16] Another letter sent that evening was extremely disjointed, at one moment complaining of her cold letters and again suggesting that she had a lover, at another moment proclaiming his immense love: "But what I know for sure is that without you there is no longer either happiness or life . . ."[17]

Joséphine finally arrived in late July – two days later Napoleon was fighting for his life.

Notes

1   Coston, I, 466.
2   Napoleon *Lettres* (Tulard), 71, Lodi, 13 May 1796.
3   Napoleon *Lettres* (Tulard), 76–8, Milan, 8 June 1796. See also
    Marmont, I, 187–8.
4   Napoleon *Lettres* (Tulard), 78–80, Milan, 11 June 1796.
5   Coston, I, 466.
6   Thiry (*Italy*), 202.
7   Napoleon *Lettres* (Tulard), 80–4, Tortona, 14 June 1796.
8   Napoleon *Lettres* (Tulard), 84–9, Tortona, 15 June 1796.
9   Napoleon *Lettres* (Tulard), 90–2, Pistoja, 26 June 1796.
10 Thiry (*Italy*), 204.
11 Napoleon *Lettres* (Tulard), 93–5, Marmirolo, 17 July 1796.
12 Napoleon *Lettres* (Tulard), 95–7, Marmirolo, 18 July 1796.
13 Napoleon *Lettres* (Tulard), 98–101, 19 July 1796.
14 Napoleon *Lettres* (Tulard), 101–3, Marmirolo, 21 July 1796.
15 Napoleon *Lettres* (Tulard), 101–3, Marmirolo, 21 July 1796.
16 Napoleon *Lettres* (Tulard), 104–6, Castiglione, 22 July 1796.
17 Napoleon *Lettres* (Tulard), 106–9, Castiglione, 22 July 1796.

CHAPTER EIGHTEEN

THE AUSTRIANS ATTACK:
THE BATTLE OF RIVOLI
JULY–SEPTEMBER 1796

*The fortunes of war are changeable, my dear general; we shall
retrieve tomorrow or the day after what you have lost
today . . . Nothing is lost as long as courage remains.*

Napoleon to General Masséna, Montechiaro,
29 July 1796[1]

GENERAL BEAULIEU'S HUMILIATING exodus from Italy did not sit
well with either Emperor Francis or members of the Aulic
Council in Vienna. To revive Austrian fortunes Beaulieu was
replaced by General Würmser who, heavily reinforced, was to
cut through what were believed to be relatively weak French
defenses, relieve the besieged fortress of Mantua and drive the
insolent enemy from Lombardy.[2]

The choice of Würmser to accomplish what patently was a
major task merely affirmed the Austrian army's command
poverty. Seventy-two years old, the Alsation-born general had
made a sort of reputation in the Rhine campaign but was scarcely
up to the challenges of the Italian theater. "The zeal of this good
old man is not enough," Colonel Graham reported to London,
"and there is nothing else." Stricken with the same "downright
dotage" displayed by Beaulieu, he first erred in accepting a far too
complicated operations plan, probably drawn up by a chief of
staff who failed to respect either terrain difficulties, the army's low
morale or the strength of the French in both spirit and tactical
excellence.[3]

In late July Würmser marched to signal a three-pronged attack by an army that numbered around 47,000 men.[4] Commanding the center corps about 24,000 strong, he moved down the narrow rocky valley of the Adige, his troops probably not appreciating the overwhelming natural beauty of the area. On his right a force of some 17,500 commanded by General Quasdanovich moved down the western side of Lake Garda, its mission to seize Brescia and cut French communications with Milan, then wheel left to join Würmser's two columns on the southern end of the lake for the final march on Mantua fortress. On Würmser's left a small force commanded by General Davidovich marched on Vicenza and Legnago, the latter only 25 miles east of Mantua, its mission to screen Würmser's flank and if necessary join in the battle for the fortress.

Upon his return from Bologna, Napoleon meanwhile had reorganized his divisions so that "at the first movement of the enemy," as he informed the Directory in mid July, "the army will pass rapidly from the defensive to the offensive."[5] His mission as he now saw it was to protect the siege of Mantua. When this bastion fell, hopefully within six weeks, he would march northward, force the enemy from the upper Adige, push into the Tyrol and in conjunction with General Moreau's Army of the Rhine carry the war into Bavaria and if necessary march on Vienna.

To screen the all-important siege, Masséna's corps of about 15,000 men was holding a line that ran east from Torri on Lake Garda to the Adige before bending down the river to a few miles below Verona, a line extended to Ronco by General Despinoy's much smaller corps. On his left, Augereau's corps about 8,000 strong carried the line southwest to where locks could be opened to flood the low country if necessary. West of Lake Garda, Sauret with about 3,000 men defended a line from Salo on the lake westward to Lake Iseo. Cavalry and artillery units covered other particularly vulnerable points. Discounting General Sérurier's force of 10,000 besieging Mantua and a sick-list that would soon number 5,000 men, Napoleon was holding a line nearly 60 miles long with about 30,000 effectives.[6]

In general he was pleased with the military situation, though he urgently pestered the Directory to send more troops. Masséna's people had more than distinguished themselves in a series of skirmishes and attacks on Austrian outposts. Sérurier's *braves* were also functioning well, having smashed two strong sorties from the fortress while engineers worked around the clock to open siege trenches in mid July. Inevitably major problems arose, mainly the sick-list increasing at about 50 bodies a day owing to hot and pestilential air and insufficient vinegar, wine and brandy rations (soon to be remedied). Long-overdue reinforcements had arrived from France but numbered only 4,000 men. His generals were not moving fast enough in organizing static defenses, and it may have been impossible for them to have done so.

The political situation was also favorable. Napoleon's recent foray into central Italy had paid off handsomely. Subsequently there had been some trouble in Leghorn owing to royalist agitators from Genoa who turned formerly cooperative merchants against the French administration, but he was sending more troops to handle that problem. Good relations were particularly important at this time, as he explained to the Directory, because a large contingent of Corsican refugees would soon arrive in Leghorn. Here they would form an expeditionary force under General Gentili to land in Corsica and force the detested English from the island, and they would have to be furnished with food, arms and boats. Deputations from Bologna and Ferrara were on their way to Paris to plead for independence under French protection. The sneaky Genoese and Venetians were misbehaving, but for the time being he would leave them alone – until Mantua fell.

As/the weeks of July and August passed, as a lovesick and lonely Napoleon continued to condemn and forgive and beg Joséphine to come to him, the old fortress of Mantua refused to fall despite the most appalling conditions within. This was what Würmser had counted on and what he now used to his advantage.

At 3 a.m. on 29 July, Napoleon learned that a surprise attack had driven back Masséna's forward positions at La Corona north of Rivoli, and that Würmser's columns were advancing on Verona. A second surprise attack by Quasdanovich had pushed Sauret from Salo on the western shore of Lake Garda, and the Austrian vanguard was moving on the all-important but lightly defended supply depot of Brescia.

Napoleon reacted instantly and well. Upon learning that Brescia had fallen, he ordered Masséna and Augereau to abandon the line of the Adige and fall back on the Mincio. Historians who later portrayed him as a nervous wreck at this point cannot have read his orders to his generals, for example one written to Masséna on that fateful day:

> The fortunes of war are changeable, my dear general; we
> shall retrieve tomorrow or the day after what you have lost
> today . . . burn your bridge; reorganize your force; fall back
> a little tonight from the enemy, do what you can to obstruct
> his passage [of the river]. Fall back on the Mincio [river]
> but cover Castelnovo . . . where I shall be shortly after
> midnight. Nothing is lost as long as courage remains.[7]

Napoleon next ordered Sérurier to abandon the siege of Mantua – leave the siege guns in the trenches, burn the gun carriages, evacuate what he could of the remaining guns, throw what could not be saved into the lakes, and send all available troops north to the main army. Sérurier could carry out only part of the order and Würmser joyfully notified his emperor that he had captured 179 cannon and had entered Mantua fortress.[8] The Austrian commander failed to realize that Napoleon was concentrating his forces to prevent Quasdanovich from joining him, that he intended to attack the one or the other depending on circumstances (as he had done in the initial invasion of the Piedmont).

Suchet, Louis Gabriel 1770–1826

Victor Perrin 1766–1841

The seven-day battle was a disjointed affair – Holland Rose accurately defined it as a "series of maneuvers rather than of prolonged conflicts."[9] Chances at first seemed bleak for the French. Controversy still surrounds Napoleon's behavior, which has been criticized and even condemned as halting and indecisive, mainly on the prejudiced evidence presented years later in the memoirs of a very disgruntled turncoat, Marshal Pierre Augereau. If however Napoleon showed signs of indecision there was good reason. He was tired, having been on the move for weeks. His fecund mind was juggling a host of military and political problems, and he was emotionally entangled with Joséphine's nearness. Although he did not say so he was probably upset by the failure of his advance posts to anticipate the Austrian march.

His critics have pointed to Augereau as the savior of the day, a suggestion warmly endorsed by Augereau's own subsequent account of the action. It is true that he was the single general who in the darkest hours refused any notion of a retreat recommended by other members of a war council, and it is also true that his troops continued to fight like lions in repairing the situation and recapturing Castiglione. This latter feat of arms, carried out against numerically superior forces, saved the day as Napoleon always freely admitted. By blocking Würmser's planned attack at a critical moment, it allowed Napoleon to defeat Quasdanovich before turning on Würmser's strong columns to force them into disordered retreat to end the campaign.

But no objective observer can deny that Napoleon's early orders set the stage for his eventual victory; that almost all officers and men fought like lions, Junot for example, who personally killed six enemy while leading an attack, a compliment returned by his receiving six saber slashes before falling in a ditch and being left for dead; Major Suchet, who won promotion for his courageous leadership, as did Captain Thiébault and countless others who fought long and hard. Nor should it be overlooked that on 30 July when the French world was falling in, Napoleon ordered as many as possible of the sick and wounded evacuated to Milan; nor that in the heat of battle he ordered the governor of Brescia to prepare bread rations for 5,800 prisoners of war; nor that, although summoning a council of war (which he rarely did), he dismissed the generals without having divulged his own plans; nor that his subsequent and very forceful orders resulted in victory.[10]

The result of these seven confused days of fighting once again emphasized the quality of French arms even against a poorly commanded if numerically superior army. Napoleon reported that in five days the Austrians suffered 6,000 casualties, the loss of 12–15,000 prisoners, 70 cannon and all infantry supply wagons before retiring north of Roveredo and Trente, figures considerably elevated in Colonel Graham's report from Würmser's headquarters which also contained a blistering critique on Austrian commanders.[11] Napoleon reported French losses of 2,000 casualties and 1,300 prisoners (they were probably two or three times that), with guns lost at Mantua and elsewhere. He was immensely satisfied with the performance of infantry, cavalry and artillery, reporting to the Directory many brave deeds by many brave men (not neglecting his own contribution).

But he could not ignore the fact that this was something of a Pyrrhic victory. Würmser may have been beaten, but he had reinforced Mantua with men and provisions to upset Napoleon's timetable. Nor was there any hope of a new siege so long as the French lacked men and guns and the pestilential season continued. Napoleon now counted 15,000 sick and wounded, and the worst month was to come. For the nonce, all he could do was to throw a blockade around the fortress (whose defenders were also suffering from the pestilence) while he worked to put his own army back in shape.

Napoleon Bonaparte was probably the most resilient commander in history. Heaps of moldering humans and horses had not yet been tossed into mass graves – a task for local peasants – thousands of French and Austrian sick and wounded not yet attended to; exhausted soldiers not yet rested, divisions not yet reassembled; supply lines not yet reopened; promised reinforcements not yet arrived . . . when he decided to turn his back on Mantua and open an offensive in the north if the French armies in Germany could close on Innsbruck. Once he had "swept away" the fugitive Austrians, he planned either to join the other French armies or to seize Trieste and march from there on Vienna. In late August he informed the Directory: "Everything here is satisfactory. We are waiting for the first news [of General Moreau's advance on Innsbruck] before we advance into the Tyrol; however if this is delayed a few days we shall make a provisional advance on Trente."[12]

Meanwhile the political situation had become uncomfortably complicated. On the credit side was the obvious desire of the peoples of Bologna, Ferrara and above all Milan to seek freedom from Austrian and papal bondage. This was complemented by the British evacuation of Corsica which now returned to French control.

The other side of the political ledger was not so good. The King of Sardinia, having disbanded his provincial regiments, had brought renewed attacks by the dreaded *Barbets* falling on convoys and even killing a French general. Napoleon replied by dispatching a small force whose commander earlier had reported the annihilation of the bands.[13] A more serious problem arose when the King of Naples led an army of 24,000 men into papal territory, threatening to march on Rome and from there to join Würmser or move on Leghorn to join with the English in driving out the French. Napoleon reacted by noisily assuring the pope of his protection while threatening the "perfidious and stupid" court of Naples with severe countermeasures.[14]

Napoleon was again upset with civilian supply *commissaires*, a large number of whom had fled the field during the recent crisis. He was fed to the teeth with their scandalous exactions in the field and depots, and he now recommended to the Directory that only veterans of the line who had served in several campaigns and had proved their courage should be appointed to these lucrative posts: "Any man who esteems life more than the national glory and the esteem of his comrades should not be part of the French army."[15]

His criticism was not confined to *commissaires*. He deeply resented a series of vicious personal attacks by Parisian journalists, accusing them of being royalist agents. This was undoubtedly true in part, but the barbs were also in keeping with the deterioration of life in the capital. Referring to the Bolognese offer of a million livres to keep Correggio's *Saint Jerome* in Bologna, Madame Monge wrote bitterly to her husband who was collecting the paintings: "It seems to me that I would give all the saints of Paradise for much less at a time when we are worshipping an *écu* of five francs. *Objets d'art* certainly hold less attraction when one is dying of famine . . . Not a day passes without a suicide, women as well as men."[16] Napoleon nevertheless was growing increasingly sensitive to the charges against his generalship and would have welcomed three or four months of leave during which they would be dissipated, a suggestion at once voided by the Directory who placated him with suitably strong praise.[17]

While the army commander was wrestling with these peripheral concerns, he was also concentrating on preparations for his new campaign. Supply requirements were enormous. His *commissaires* had to stock Peschiera fortress with 120,000 rations of biscuit, 240,000 rations of brandy, oats for 2,000 horses for ten days, 3,000 pairs of shoes, flour to bake 120,000 more rations. Boats on the Adige river would transport 60,000 rations of biscuit, 120,000 rations of brandy, 60,000 rations of flour, and oats for 4,000 horses for ten days.[18]

The news he had been wanting arrived in late August: General Moreau's Army of the Rhine was moving through Bavaria toward Innsbruck. In early September, Masséna crossed the Adige to push back Austrian outposts and move north. Simultaneously Augereau's corps marched on the heights to Masséna's right while Vaubois moved up a corps west of Lake Garda. A series of sharp actions culminated in the capture of Roveredo, the enemy retiring on Trente. After a vicious fight in extremely difficult mountainous terrain, Masséna's people won the city to cause Würmser's retreat to Bassano with Vaubois hot on his heels.

Writing from Trente on 6 September, Napoleon informed the Directory that "the only thing to do now is to march on Trieste. . . The plan which was adopted and which was good for the month of June counts for nothing at the end of September." Cold filled the air and soon snow would fall. He was marching on Bassano and wanted instructions once he had seized the place. He personally favored the capture of Trieste from where he could carry the war into "the heart of Italy" if that was desired.[19]

As Napoleon knew only too well it was the enemy, not the Directory, who would decide his subsequent moves. After fighting through the gorges of the Brenta, Masséna and Augereau blasted their way into Bassano, the fiery Jean Lannes once again distinguishing himself, to take 5,000 prisoners, 35 cannon and carriages, 200 baggage wagons and five standards while nearly capturing Würmser and his staff. He now learned that Würmser, believing the French would march straight on Innsbruck, had set off with 8,000 men for Verona to cut French communications. This forlorn effort terminated with Würmser and the remnants of his army, about 5,000 foot and 1,500 horse, taking refuge in Mantua fortress to join a desperately sick and hungry garrison. They were fortunate. Had a confused French battalion commander not abandoned a vital bridge, the Austrians would have been captured.

Nevertheless it was a most rewarding ten days. "The enemy has lost, my sweetheart," Napoleon informed Joséphine, "eighteen thousand men taken prisoner, the rest are dead or wounded . . . Never have we had such an uninterrupted and great success . . . A thousand passionate kisses."[20]

In reporting the conclusion of the second phase of the battle for north Italy, Napoleon again praised numerous officers and men for outstanding bravery and tremendous accomplishments. In the final days of this two-week campaign, no fewer than eight of his generals had been wounded. The troops constantly performed tactical miracles. In two days of moving on Trente and the Brenta gorges Masséna and Augereau's men marched 50 miles in some of the most difficult terrain in the world to fall like wildcats on a surprised enemy. His artillery, cavalry and engineers all performed brilliantly.

But not all generals drew accolades. As he reported to the Directory, Sauret was a good soldier but not intelligent enough to be a general. Garnier, Meunier and Casabianca were not suitable for even battalion commands in a war as active and serious as this one. Macquart was a brave man devoid of talent. Gaultier was good for a desk job but not war. Despinoy was indolent and lacked boldness. He had performed very well in rear-area duty at Milan and "very badly at the head of his division." It was he who decided Napoleon henceforth to judge men only by their actions.[21]

As for Napoleon now at Ronco: "I have been here, my dear Joséphine, for two days sleeping in an uncomfortable bed, eating poor food and very provoked to be far from you. Würmser is surrounded . . . The moment that this affair is ended I shall be in your arms to cover you with the most tender kisses. I kiss you a million times."[22]

Notes

1   Corr. I. Nr. 797, Montechiaro, 29 July 1796.
2   Rose (Life), I, 105.
3   Rose (Despatches), 118, 121.
4   Rose (Life), I, 105. Rose based the figures on official Austrian records. See also Corr. I. Nr. 725, Roverbella, 6 July 1796, where Napoleon reported to the Directory an enemy strength of 67,000 including 8,000 at Mantua. This would appear to be a highly exaggerated figure (for reasons previously discussed), but it has been accepted by a host of French historians including Thiers and, more recently, Thiry.
5   Corr. I. Nr. 755, Verona, 12 July 1796.
6   Corr. I. Nrs. 725, Roverbella, 6 July 1796; 755, Verona, 12 July 1796.
7   Corr. I. Nr. 797, Montechiaro, 29 July 1796.
8   Rose (Life), I, 110.

9   Rose (*Life*), I, 115.
10 Corr. I. Nrs. 804, Montechiaro, 29 July 1796; 808, Desenzano, 30 July 1796.
11 Rose (*Despatches*), 122–3. Colonel Graham reported on 15 August 1796 from Austrian headquarters at Trente that the total "loss of the [Austrian army] (exceeding 15,000 men in killed, wounded, prisoners and missing and 60 pieces of cannon) has so completely destroyed the spirit and confidence of all ranks that I cannot flatter myself with the hopes of being able to send your Lordship any favorable intelligence." Two days later he reported the Austrian loss "as infinitely greater than he had imagined." He followed this report with a blistering critique of Austrian commanders. See also Corr. I. Nr. 842, Castiglione, 6 August 1796.
12 Corr. I. Nrs. 889, Brescia, 14 August 1796; 925, Milan, 26 August 1796.
13 Corr. I. Nrs. 852, Verona, 8 August 1796; 907, Brescia, 18 August 1796; 925, Milan, 26 August 1796. See also Wilkinson (*Rise*), 37–8.
14 Corr. I. Nrs. 907, Brescia, 18 August 1796; 927, Milan, 26 August 1796.
15 Corr. I. Nrs. 925, Milan, 26 August 1796; 937, Brescia, 30 August 1796. See also Corr. I. Nr. 881, Brescia, 12 August 1796.
16 Thiry (*Italy*), 213.
17 Corr. I. Nr. 858, Verona, 9 August 1796.
18 Corr. I. Nr. 940, Brescia, 30 August 1796.
19 Corr. I. Nr. 968, Trente, 6 September 1796.
20 Napoleon *Lettres* (Tulard), 114–15, Montebello, 10 September 1796.
21 Corr. I. Nr. 890, Brescia, 14 August 1796.
22 Napoleon *Lettres* (Tulard), 116, Ronco, 12 September 1796.

CHAPTER NINETEEN

THE BATTLE OF ARCOLA
NOVEMBER 1796

Never has a field of battle been as disputed as that of Arcola.

Napoleon to Lazare Carnot, Verona,
19 November 1796[1]

NAPOLEON WAS STILL not well when he returned to Milan and Joséphine's arms. If ever a commander deserved a carefree rest it was this small, thin and very tired man, but neither illness, fatigue nor Joséphine could claim him for long, and orders, reports and letters were soon flowing from his headquarters.

His military situation, as he informed the Directory, was "uncertain." Splendid as it was, the recent victory over Würmser spelled only brief respite. French army defeats in Germany and Moreau's retreat to the left bank of the Rhine had allowed the frustrated Emperor Francis to shunt thousands of reinforcements to his troops in the Tyrol and the Frioul, there to build a new army under command of General Baron Joseph Alvintzy in yet another effort to relieve the Mantua garrison. Frequent reports from spies led Napoleon to believe that Alvintzy would eventually command 50,000 troops and would probably strike in late October.[2]

Napoleon's paper command just about equaled Alvintzy's planned strength, but his effectives fell far short. About 19,000 of his nearly 50,000 troops were deployed in the north guarding invasion passes, while 9,000 resumed the blockade of Mantua. Another 4,000 were tied up in line-of-communication fortresses.

However, 14,000 were in hospital and another 4,000 were recovering from wounds.[3]

In view of the Austrian buildup he desperately needed 23,000 replacements, not only grenadiers but also seasoned cavalry, gunners, teamsters, engineers and artillery officers. He also needed 25,000 *fusils* (his troops did not like captured Austrian muskets because of their excessive weight) and more cannon.[4] His campaign already had produced 20 million livres for the Republic, not counting the pay and maintenance of his army. He would double this sum in the forthcoming campaign – *if* the Directory sent him 30,000 troops.[5]

There was no possibility of renewing the siege of Mantua until early in the new year owing to heavy rains and continuing sickness. Instead he had "hermetically sealed" the fortress by General Kilmaine's force of two divisions (Sérurier being *hors de combat* from illness and replaced by General Sahuguet). Mobile columns were prowling through surrounding areas to disarm civilians, arrest dissidents (and buy back horses which French troops had illegally sold to civilians).[6]

Elsewhere in the battle zone units were kept on high alert, strengthening defenses and polishing tactics. "The enemy is still far from your walls," Napoleon warned the commandant of Legnago, "but such are the ways of war that you could be besieged from one moment to the other."[7] He paid particular attention to his line of communications, ordering special inspections of rear-area forts. In mid October he reported to Paris that the rapacious *Barbet* bands had been virtually destroyed by General Garnier's force.[8]

These developments were to the good, but a large sick-list and overall troop weakness continued to plague him. He was desperately short of funds which was telling on the morale and physical state of the army.[9] Rear-area generals, some of them royalist sympathizers, were holding up troops consigned to Italy. One General Willot was a rabid royalist who should be relieved of command: not only was his repressive policy fomenting civil war in the Alpes Maritimes but he was deliberately sabotaging the replacement process.

The second problem was an old one, the extensive corruption and rapacious acts of supply *commissaires* and army agents who were failing in almost every respect to meet army needs. Their peculatory antics knew no bounds. We can envision him pacing the parquet floor of his Serbollini palace while dictating to a scribbling secretary: "I am here surrounded by thieves." These scavengers, often working in collusion with officers and enlisted men, were making life a hell for the Milanese and Mantuan citizenry by illicit and often brutal private requisitions of money and property. Napoleon was doing his best to lessen "the weight of the army" on the civil population, but the situation in Mantua was out of hand. With only a few exceptions the *commissaires* everywhere were making illegal fortunes at the time when the army was "without a *sou*." He had declared personal war on these *fripons*, many of whom he named along with a recital of their embezzlements of millions of livres by illegal sale of military property: "They steal in such a ridiculous and brazen way that, if I had a month of time, there would not be one who would not face a firing squad." Although he repeatedly had them arrested and tried, they easily bought their freedom. Everyone was corrupting everyone else; it was a fair, "everything was for sale." The only solution, even if partial, was to replace corrupt and inefficient civilians with experienced and honest men.[10]

If Napoleon's military position was uncertain, his political situation was "very bad." Rome was in an uproar. Monge and his colleagues had been forced to leave, abandoning (at least for a time) the spoils of statuary, paintings and books along with two million francs in ingots. As Napoleon bluntly informed the Directory it had made a terrible mistake in breaking the armistice with Rome. The papacy had subsequently armed its peoples and stirred up nascent hatred of the French infidels to become the nucleus of a powerful coalition that included Venice and Naples. To counter this new threat France had to make friends, not enemies, in Italy.

The Directory should at once make peace with Naples, Venice and Parma; it should form an alliance with Genoa and if possible with the court of Turin; it should further place Lombardy, Modena, Reggio, Bologna and Ferrara under formal protection. If the Directory insisted on making war on Rome and Naples, Napoleon would need 25,000 additional reinforcements. He was extremely upset that he had not been consulted concerning negotiations with these states which in view of the "incalculable influence of Rome" he would have prolonged: "Whenever your general in Italy will not be in the center of things, you will run great risks."[11]

Having suitably admonished the Directory for past errors and advised it as to a future course of action, he returned to his own plan which would soon result in an extremely controversial *fait accompli*: the establishment of the Cispadane Republic, the forerunner of the Cisalpine Republic that in one way or another would influence French and Italian fortunes for years to come. Gaspard Monge had come up with this title for the union of Modena, Reggio, Bologna and Ferrara which caught on marvelously well with the Italians, as he wrote his wife: "You see that I am godfather of a beautiful baby."[12] The creation was inspired in part by Napoleon's still fervent belief in the ideals of the French Revolution, in part by impulses from Charlemagne's lobes that were neighbors to those of Alexander the Great in his ever-active brain.

We need to remember that Napoleon carried the torch of liberty upon entering Italy. If it flickered weakly in the languid air of Piedmontese peasantry, it revived in Lombardy and, after a brief crisis, in the Milanese. It positively flared in central Italy where officials in Bologna, Ferrara, Reggio and Modena seemed to welcome the French presence in preference to the papal yoke despite the very heavy contributions levied on respective treasuries and estates. Napoleon had encouraged these formerly Austrian and papal states to send delegates to Paris to seek French protection at the same time as he encouraged local patriots to form protective militias. At his instigation the Milanese were arming a legion of

3,500 soldiers commanded by French and Italian officers and armed with captured Austrian *fusils* – all at the expense of Milan which would have to raise the funds by requisitioning silver from the churches. He was already using Milanese troops to escort prisoners since his own escorts were so understrength that 4,000 out of 5,000 prisoners escaped *en route* to prison camps. These troops were working out well, as were Venetian troops incorporated into French patrols in an effort to prevent troop pillaging in north Italy. He wanted an alliance with the Duke of Parma who in return for the province of Mantua come the peace would now furnish him with a regiment of foot troops and a battalion of pioneers, the latter necessary to repair fortifications at Peschiera and elsewhere. His star performer had been Reggio's small militia which recently had intercepted and captured 150 Austrian soldiers cut off from Mantua fortress while foraging.[13]

In defiance of Directory orders to leave politics to Paris, and in connivance with the political *commissaire* at Bologna, Napoleon surreptitiously organized a congress of one hundred delegates from the former papal states. Meeting in mid October, the delegation included nobles, priests, cardinals, merchants and "generally esteemed and patriotic gentlemen" who authorized an armed Italian legion of 2,800 men and voted to send representatives to Paris to ask for "liberty and independence." The congress of Modena, Napoleon informed the Directory, was a tremendous success, a rousing display of enthusiastic patriotism: "I shall not be astonished if these states and Lombardy with a population of two to three million don't produce a great shock in all Italy." Perhaps as important, he envisioned the new legions as vital protection to his flanks and rear for the imminent battle with Austria.[14] Adding to this success was the English evacuation not only of Corsica but of the Mediterranean which now allowed French ships to proceed unharmed to the Adriatic.

As opposed to these gains, Napoleon's tentatives to Würmser in Mantua to surrender and to the Vienna court to make peace had been met only with silence. The courts of Rome and Naples and the senate of Venice had continued to arm. Genoa, Turin and

Pavia remained unknown quantities, home to active and disruptive royalist elements. Massive Austrian reinforcements were strengthening Alvintzy's army, in sad contrast to the limited number of replacements received by Napoleon.

The French commander was still wrestling with this mercurial political picture and was still waiting for promised troops when in late October he learned that the Austrian vanguard had reached the Piave river to open a new offensive.

The Austrians had still not learned how to wage war in northern Italy, the inevitable result of a stubborn emperor misadvised by an Aulic Council; of old and useless generals forever dreaming of decisive actions by military maneuvers as complex as they were obsolete; of subordinate commanders who owed their rank to court favoritism as opposed to education and ability; and of a plodding peasant army of old and tired veterans motivated by little more than hope of a daily bread ration.

General Baron Alvintzy was typical: yet another septuagenarian, veteran of the Turkish and Netherlands wars, a brave man but scarcely an able general qualified to detect weaknesses in staff-prepared plans. On paper the new plan as drawn up by chief of staff Weyrother – whom we shall meet again at Ulm and Austerlitz – was relatively simple: the main army about 75,000 strong to march southwest in three columns from province Frioul, destination Vicenza-Verona; simultaneously General Davidovitch with a corps variously estimated as between 18–25,000 bodies to move down the Adige valley, scatter French defenses and join Alvintzy in Verona for a final effort to rescue the defenders of Mantua fortress – all this to take place in extremely difficult, well defended terrain that would require a great deal of exquisite timing and sustained good fortune.

As with past Austrian offensives this one started well by Davidovitch pushing in Vaubois' defenses at Corona while Alvintzy's main army caused Masséna to yield Bassano and begin a tactical retreat over the Brenta river toward Vicenza. Here he was met by Napoleon who had come up with Augereau's division and the army's reserve cavalry. For several days the outnumbered French fell back in good order, often clashing sharply with the Austrians usually to the latter's cost.

Early on 6 November the French marched to attack Alvintzy's corps. Fighting continued all along the line the next day. But that night two of Vaubois' regiments panicked to bring on a general retreat that ended only on the Rivoli plateau at a heavy cost of 3,000 casualties (including those taken prisoner) and six guns.[15]

The threatened collapse of Napoleon's inadequately defended northern shield brought immediate crisis which he resolved by rushing from Verona to the windswept plateau to tongue-lash the errant troops back into action. They had shown "neither discipline, constancy, nor bravery," he told them, having fled panic-stricken from a position "where a handful of soldiers should have stopped an army." They were no longer French soldiers, they no longer belonged to the Army of Italy – a harsh sentence to be inscribed on their standards. The effect was immediate: tearful promises to redeem themselves if given another chance. Napoleon gave them the chance; he also subordinated Vaubois by placing Masséna in overall command of the threatened sector.[16]

Having reestablished the threatened position he hurried back to Verona to confront Alvintzy. Advancing from Montebello, the Austrian commander had reached the protective hills of Caldiero from where his lines ran south, his left resting on the Arcola marshes. Upon learning that additional Austrian columns were closing on Caldiero, Napoleon attacked at once even though outnumbered two to one. Masséna had almost won Caldiero and Augereau its southern heights when enemy resistance increased and a fierce rain suddenly turned to blinding sleet which halted the action. After a sleepless night the French withdrew to Verona with a stated loss of 800 casualties and 150 men taken prisoner.[17]

If initial reverses left Napoleon chastened, they also brought forth an accusatory fury expressed in a lengthy dispatch to the Directory. Such were the army's inferior numbers and overall exhaustion that "perhaps we are on the eve of losing Italy." He

The Marshal Berthier 1753–1815

Murat, Joachim 1767–1815 Marshal of France

Junot, Andoche 1771–1813 French General

Masséna, Andre 1758–1817 Marshal of France

had received a mere handful of reinforcements; his divisions had been fighting hard for two weeks; both he and the enemy had suffered heavy casualties but Alvintzy could more easily sustain them because of numerical superiority:

> The [French] wounded are the elite of the army; all of our field grade commanders, all of our best generals are *hors de combat* . . . the army . . . is exhausted. The heroes of Lodi, Millesimo, Castiglione, Bassano have died for their country or are in hospital . . . We are abandoned in a remote part of Italy . . . What remains of the army sees death as certain . . . Perhaps the death knell is ready to sound for the brave Augereau, the intrepid Masséna, Berthier, myself . . . Within a few days we shall make another effort. If fortune smiles on us, Mantua will be taken and with that, Italy.[18]

Sensing almost certain disaster if he remained in Verona, Napoleon somehow rallied the discouraged troops to a final and extremely daring attempt to outflank Alvintzy. After feigning a retreat northward the army turned to make a 25-mile night march to Ronco where it crossed the Adige. Masséna's columns then moved along a narrow dike on the left of a canal while Augereau simultaneously advanced on the right of the canal intending to cross the Alpone river at Arcola to strike the enemy's rear while Masséna hit his flank. A third trail ran down the Adige where a brigade was to cross and come up in support of the attack.[19]

This was a typically brilliant Napoleonic stroke that might soon have broken the Austrian back but for an unforeseen development probably due to over-haste at a crucial time. Unknown to the French, Alvintzy (in anticipation of a march on Mantua) had placed a strong body of Croat and Hungarian infantry with two cannon at Arcola to guard his left flank. The unpleasant surprise revealed itself when Augereau's advance guard commanded by General Verdier, one of the heroes of Castiglione, overran some outposts on the causeway to approach the bridge – and was shot to ribbons by an enemy firing from loopholed cottages behind and on its flanks. As Augereau brought up the rest of his division, the enemy received reinforcements. To gain the bridge the French had to cross over 200 yards of narrow, flat, open ground which was soon named *la terrible chausée* (the terrible causeway).[20] After watching several futile and costly assaults in which no fewer than five generals including Bon, Lannes and Verdier were seriously wounded, Napoleon jumped from his horse, pulled together some troops by appealing to "the conquerors of Lodi bridge," wrapped a flag around his sword and started toward the bridge, shielded by a few men including a favorite aide, Major Muiron. Enemy fire again shattered the effort, Muiron falling dead at Napoleon's feet.[21]

The grenadiers had had enough. With this last failure, attack turned to retreat, to frightened, screaming men crowding the dike, their only desire to escape certain death. Napoleon nearly found death himself when in the press of the mob he slipped from the causeway into a swamp where probably he would have drowned but for the quick work of his brother, Louis, and Marmont assisted by two soldiers.

After a tense night of stand-off, heavy fighting continued without the French breaking the defense. Masséna's effort to the west had fared much better, his march culminating in the defeat and withdrawal of an enemy corps which lost 400 dead, 1,500 taken prisoner, two standards and seven cannon.[22] Augereau's people however were hit hard but, personally rallied by Berthier, managed to hold.[23]

Vaubois meanwhile had been forced to retreat from Rivoli. If his new line caved in, then Davidovitch would fall on Napoleon's flank while Alvintzy struck his center, a potential disaster that probably would have been exploited by Würmser leading a force from Mantua to strike the French rear. Fortunately for the French a third day of fighting that included a brilliant ambush, a feigned cavalry charge, reinforcement by troops from the south and Augereau's final and successful attack at Arcola caused Alvintzy to break off the action and withdraw to the northeast.

After making two more unsuccessful attacks, Alvintzy was hit in turn, severely beaten and forced to retreat on Verona. While cavalry pursued him, Napoleon sent Masséna to reinforce Vaubois at Castelnovo as Augereau marched to cut Davidovitch's retreat. But Davidovitch, learning of Alvintzy's departure, swiftly about-faced to the north, although not in time to prevent some 1,200 of his rearguard from being captured before he reached his old position at Trente. As a final irony, at this inopportune moment Würmser led a force from Mantua that was quickly forced back inside its walls.[24]

There was no denying a major victory and Napoleon hastened to report it to the Directory. The enemy had lost at least 4,000 dead and as many wounded, 4–5,000 men taken prisoner, four standards and 18 cannon. The French put their losses at 200 dead and 900 wounded, but these are all highly dubious figures.[25]

As usual Napoleon poured praise on officers and men, asking Directory approval for numerous promotions. His star performer (aside from the brave Muiron) was General Lannes who, still recovering from an earlier serious wound, received two more wounds at Arcola bridge and was evacuated. Subsequently learning of Napoleon's own unsuccessful attempt to storm the bridge the fiery Gascon left his bed, forced himself to mount and galloped to the action. Unable to dismount because of his wounds, he was hit a third time (but somehow survived). Staff generals and officers "displayed an activity and bravery without example: twelve or fifteen had been killed . . . not one whose uniform was not riddled with balls."[26] The artillery had "covered itself with glory," and he asked that the faithful Andréossy be promoted to *chef de brigade*.

Only one general had disappointed him. This was Vaubois, who lacked the necessary temperament and knack for division command.[27] Napoleon also found the infantry not up to that of former battles: "fatigue and the absence of veterans have deprived them of that impetuosity" necessary for the capture of the whole Austrian army – a disturbing observation that will be heard again.[28] Napoleon failed to mention his own tactical error, later remarked on by Marmont and others, which was his initial failure to order up troops from Legnago to outflank Arcola and attack it from the rear; but very few generals in history have admitted to their own mistakes.

Notes

1   Corr. II. Nr. 1197, Verona, 19 November 1796.
2   Corr. II. Nrs. 1086, Milan, 11 October 1796; 1094, Modena, 17 October 1796; 1182, Verona, 13 November 1796.
3   Corr. II. Nr. 1055, Milan, 1 October 1796.
4   Corr. II. Nr. 1055, Milan, 1 October 1796.
5   Corr. II. Nr. 1094, Modena, 17 October 1796.
6   Corr. II. Nr. 1086, Milan, 11 October 1796.
7   Corr. II. Nr. 1038, Milan, 27 September 1796.
8   Corr. II. Nr. 1094, 17 October 1796. He did not report that he was ill again as he informed Joséphine – see Napoleon *Lettres* (Tulard), 118, Modena, 17 October 1796.
9   Corr. II. Nrs. 1147, 1148, Verona, 3 November 1796.
10 Corr. II. Nrs. 1055, Milan, 1 October 1796; 1059, Milan, 2 October 1796; 1078, Milan, 8 October 1796; 1082, Milan, 9 October 1796; 1086, Milan, 11 October 1796; 1088, Milan, 12 October 1796. See also Aubry, 183–4.
11 Corr. II. Nr. 1078, Milan, 8 October 1796. See also Corr. II. Nrs. 1059, 1060, Milan, 2 October 1796.
12 Aubry, 182.
13 Corr. II. Nrs. 1059, Milan, 2 October 1796; 1063, Milan, 3 October 1796; 1076, Milan, 8 October 1796; 1085, Milan, 11 October 1796.
14 Corr. II. Nrs. 1082, Milan, 9 October 1796; 1095, Modena, 17 October 1796; 1106, Verona, 24 October 1796.
15 Corr. II. Nr. 1182, Verona, 13 November 1796.
16 Corr. II. Nr. 1171, Verona, 8 November 1796. See also Rose (*Life*), I, 122. Napoleon's technique was not original – see Asprey (*Frederick the Great*), 532, 538.
17 Corr. II. Nr. 1182, Verona, 13 November 1796. See also Rose (*Life*), I, 113, who along with other historians puts French losses much higher: 2,000 casualties and 750 taken prisoner; Burton, 75, accepts Rose's figures.
18 Corr. II. Nr. 1182, Verona, 13 November 1796.
19 Thiry (*Italy*), 357. See also Reinhard (*Italy*), 176, Marmont, I, 251–6.
20 Reinhard (*Italy*), 185.
21 Corr. II. Nrs. 1199, Verona, 19 November 1796; 1324, Milan, 28 December 1796. Napoleon felt the loss of Muiron very deeply, as

he informed the widow who subsequently received many marks of his favor including the naming of a frigate in his honor. See also Reinhard (*Italy*), 176–9, and Marmont, II, 256–9, for graphic accounts of the battle.

22 Reinhard (*Italy*), 180.

23 Reinhard (*Italy*), 180.

24 Corr. II. Nr. 1216, Verona, 23 November 1796. See also Reinhard (*Italy*), 182.

25 Corr. II. Nr. 1196, Verona, 19 November 1796. As usual, later authorities cite contradictory figures. See also Reinhard (*Italy*), 182: Captain Sulkowski, who was on the scene, reported 3,000 Austrian casualties and 5,000 taken prisoner. He also cited 14 French generals either killed or wounded.

26 Corr. II. Nr. 1196, Verona, 19 November 1796.

27 Corr. II. Nrs. 1196, Verona, 19 November 1796; 1217, Verona, 24 November 1796. Napoleon however respected Vaubois' bravery and sent him to command Leghorn prior to assuming command in Corsica.

28 Reinhard (*Italy*), 179, 186. Captain Sulkowski attributed the decline to over-excessive desire for pillage; others to the good life brought on by the troops having been paid in cash; still others to attrition from previous campaigns of the best commanders and elite troops, what Reinhard called *l'élimination à rebours*.

CHAPTER TWENTY

THE SECOND BATTLE OF RIVOLI
JANUARY 1797

It is said that the Roman legions marched twenty-four miles a
day; our brigades have marched thirty while also fighting.

Napoleon to the Directory, 18 January 1797[1]

NAPOLEON LATER WROTE that the battle of Arcola was a milestone in
his life (an emotion previously experienced after the battle of Lodi),
the dawn of his fortune. It certainly sealed his fame within the
army. News of his impulsive and very brave act at the bridge spread
like wildfire through the ranks. Perhaps he now realized that he
could accomplish miracles with this army that was devoted at least
in part to spreading the revolutionary flame of liberty – if to Italy,
why not to all of Europe? Perhaps he believed that this victory
would allow him to further twist the Directory to his own desires?

But now it was time for a private reward. "At last my adored
Joséphine, I live again," he wrote two days after the battle. "Death
is no longer before my eyes, and glory and honor are still in my
heart. The enemy is beaten at Arcola . . . Mantua will be ours in
eight days, and I will soon be in your arms to give you a thousand
proofs of my love . . . I am a little tired . . . A thousand and a thousand tender and amorous kisses."[2]

There would be no amorous kisses. Napoleon remained in
Verona for another eight days writing frequently to Joséphine to
express his concern at her silence: "Don't you know that without
you there is neither happiness nor life for your husband?" He also
wrote of his anticipation of seeing her at her toilette:

[her] small shoulder, a small white breast soft but firm;
above that a small head bound with a kerchief *à la Créole*,
good enough to eat. You know well that I do not forget the
small visits; you know well, the little black forest. I give
you a thousand kisses and impatiently await the moment
to be there . . . To live inside a Joséphine is to live in
paradise. To kiss the mouth, eyes, shoulder, breast,
everywhere, everywhere.[3]

Two days later he wrote:

What are you doing all day, then Madame? [using the
formal *vous*] What is so important as to take you away from
writing to your good lover? . . . Be on your guard, Joséphine,
one beautiful night, the doors broken open and here I am in
your bed. You know! The little sword of Othello![4]

And the following day [back to the informal *tu*]:

I hope soon, my sweet friend, to be in your arms. I
passionately love you.[5]

Came now the horrible moment of truth. The little black forest like
Birnam Wood had moved (not to Dunsinane but to Genoa, with
Hippolyte Charles as chief woodsman): "I arrive in Milan. I hurry to
your apartment. I have abandoned everything to see you, to crush
you in my arms . . . You were not there . . . You cannot believe my
unhappiness."[6] It is not surprising that this terrible and very cruel
blow to an exhausted man brought a physical relapse so severe that
he was scarcely able to mount his horse, along with stomach spasms
of such intensity that he believed himself poisoned.[7]

As if this were not sufficient he received another surprise, a
professional one in the form of an emissary sent by the Directory.
This was a 23-year-old general, Henri Clarke of the bureau of
topography, whose mission was to negotiate an armistice with the
Austrians. Such was the dangerous state of affairs within France, was

the Directory's reasoning – the people's almost unanimous desire for peace, an empty treasury, threatening anarchy – that peace had to be made with Austria or the revolution stood in danger of foundering.

Napoleon could not believe this stupidity. Bridling his temper, he informed the directors that an armistice would only allow Alvintzy to reinforce Mantua which was on the verge of surrender, its garrison mostly sick while trying to survive on half-rations of bread, *polenta* (Italian gruel) and horsemeat. There were no medicines, no wine. In his opinion the fortress would fall within a month – he was shortly intending to fire-bomb it. Once it fell not only Austria but also Rome would make peace with France, bringing new territories to the republic and massive funds to fill empty army and republic coffers. An armistice would not only void these gains but would hasten the recovery of Alvintzy's army in the Tyrol where it was already receiving reinforcements.

Meanwhile he had to deal with young Clarke whom he correctly considered a "political general" foreign to the battlefield and "a spy" of the Directory, "a man of no talent, only conceited."[8] Instead of confrontation, however, Napoleon turned on his famous charm, soon convincing Clarke of the fatuity of his mission and in the process making the man a fervent admirer who informed the Directory in early December:

> There is no one here who does not regard [Napoleon] as a
> man of genius. He commands a great ascendancy over the
> individuals of the republican army . . . His tactical
> perception is sure. He carries out his resolutions with
> energy and strength. His coolness in the most lively actions
> is as remarkable as his extreme readiness to change his
> plans when unforeseen circumstances demand it.[9]

Failure of either the Vienna court or of Alvintzy to respond favorably to Clarke's overtures soon ended his mission, at least for the present.[10] Napoleon shunted him off to Turin where he received orders from the Directory to subordinate himself to the army commander's wishes, a change of mind resulting from the French victory at Arcola followed by Napoleon's persuasive analysis of the situation.[11]

Napoleon meanwhile was dealing with the usual myriad civil and military affairs from his Milan headquarters. His diverse concerns ran the gamut of army administration: special cash allowances to generals for their tables and extraordinary expenses (including spies); orders for horses to be rough-shod for winter; bonus payments to Major Bessières' guides who had fought valiantly at Arcola; funds for division bands; payments to officers returned from enemy captivity; a depot-school to train supernumerary company officers; fines for soldiers who had lost their bayonets; long lists of deserved promotions and numerous other decrees and directives.[12]

Internal security was a major concern in both the battle and the rear areas. In the former it was largely a matter of careful infantry and artillery deployments, combat readiness (instilled by Napoleon's frequent personal inspections), constant vigilance reinforced by reports from patrols and spies and by certain controls over civilian workers such as special uniforms and identification cards.[13] A new system of relay signals by cannon fire was introduced. The guardians north of Rivoli were to fire so many cannon rounds to signal an attack, so many if a vital position were forced, so many if the attack were defeated, signals repeated by neighboring units leading all the way to headquarters. Napoleon also established a series of interim posts from which mounted orderlies could bring important dispatches to him more quickly.[14]

Security presented a different problem in rear areas where "rabid priests" and royalist agents continued to inflame local populations. Napoleon's reply to insurrectionary outbreaks in Modena and elsewhere was standard: a mobile column to seize and shoot the ringleaders, burn the houses of recalcitrant offenders, take hostages if necessary, and compel villagers to swear oaths of allegiance to local officials and to the French republic.[15]

Royalist agents and Austrian spies were everywhere. One suspicious character arrested near Mantua in late December turned out to be a young Austrian officer who admitted to carrying a letter from

Emperor Francis intended for the beleaguered General Würmser. The document however was not *on* him but *in* him, in a small phial which was eventually retrieved. This was a common technique of the Austrians, Napoleon explained to the Directory, probably unknown to other French commanders who should be warned. The phial was coated with Spanish beeswax and was often held in the stomach for several days. If an upset caused the spy to disgorge it, he merely dipped it in elixir and reswallowed it.[16] The message in this case was of particular value: once a fresh Austrian offensive raised the French blockade, Würmser would march 5,000 troops to Rome where he would take command of the pope's new army.[17]

Alvintzy had partially rebuilt his shattered army with the help of reinforcements from the Rhine and spirited volunteers from Vienna (including some nobility) and had joined Davidovitch at Roveredo, a total of somewhere between 30,000 and 45,000 troops for yet another drive on Mantua. A slave to converging tactics, the old general ordered no fewer than six columns to attack Joubert's 10,000 light infantry posted north of Rivoli.[18]

The Austrian plan was curiously inept. One column was to advance *east* of the Adige river with the most uncertain mission of providing artillery support to its brethren. A second and main column of 8,000 troops commanded by Alvintzy was to march on the village of Incanale, then struggle up a steep, winding trail about three-fourths of a mile to the plateau above the town. Three columns were to attack from the Mt. Baldo area, and a final column was to snake around the French left to strike from the rear. A separate corps of 9,000 men under General Provera, another Piedmont veteran, would march on Masséna's division guarding Verona, a move to be supported by another force marching on Augereau's position east of Legnago. If necessary Alvintzy and Provera were to make independent attacks to raise the blockade of Mantua (commanded once again by Sérurier) and allow·Würmser to escape to Rome.

The action began on 7 January with an attack east of Legnago that pushed Augereau's outposts back on the town. Napoleon was in Bologna with a strong detachment hoping to force Rome into submission when he learned that Alvintzy was on the move. The news brought him and his troops hastening back to Verona where early on 12 January Provera unsuccessfully attacked Masséna's forward posts. Having in theory concentrated French attention on the south, Alvintzy moved against Joubert's outposts on the Corona and early the following day forced him to withdraw to the plateau above Rivoli and shortly to order a general retreat.[19]

Napoleon at Verona was at first in doubt as to the enemy's main effort, but from what he later termed *différents indices* – various signs of which one may have come from a turncoat Austrian officer[20] – he had reasoned that by mid afternoon the real threat was at Rivoli which he reached shortly after midnight.[21] After surveying enemy campfires and rallying the disorganized regiments in his inimitable fashion, he ordered a pre-dawn attack that pushed through to the far end of the plateau. A few hours later Masséna and Berthier's vanguards arrived, but during the day the French were slowly pushed back, at one point nearly being outflanked by a column on Masséna's left where two demi-brigades gave way without a fight, a crisis overcome by Leclerc and Sulkowski intercepting the retreating troops to restore the situation.[22]

While fighting continued on the plateau, Alvintzy's main column began the difficult climb up the ravine from Incanale. Napoleon recognized the new threat and managed to clear a vital ridge in order to take the enemy under flanking fire while Joubert's infantry and Leclerc's cavalry tore into the exhausted vanguard as it reached the plateau. This master-stroke sent the entire column into confused retreat compounded by the massive explosion of an ammunition wagon. Joubert's troops now fell on the three remaining columns to send them running. When informed that the sixth Austrian column had gained the French rear, Napoleon, aware that fresh troops from Verona were closing on the field, quietly said, "We have them now."[23] With that he rode off to meet a new crisis posed by Provera closing on Mantua. Joubert subsequently sealed victory by a brilliantly executed night attack followed by a vigorous pursuit which recovered all the lost ground and more.[24]

Meanwhile Napoleon had hurried south where Provera's corps, encumbered by a large convoy of provisions and cattle, had diverted Augereau's attention sufficiently to make a night crossing of the Adige to close on Mantua, but had failed to break through the fortified suburb of St. Georges. At this critical point, the night of 15 January, Napoleon arrived followed by Masséna's exhausted but still spirited division. Provera next tried a pre-dawn attack on La Favorita while a force under Würmser sortied from the fortress only to be driven back by Victor's demi-brigade. Fighting furiously, Victor's soldiers cut Provera from St. Georges which (as Napoleon reported to the Directory) threw the Austrians into complete confusion, "cavalry, infantry, artillery all pell-mell."[25] With Masséna and Sérurier's divisions closing in for the kill, Provera wisely surrendered.

Napoleon reported that in all Alvintzy had lost 6,000 dead or wounded and 25,000 taken prisoner, 60 cannon and 24 standards.[26] French losses, he claimed, amounted to 700 dead and 1,200 wounded.[27] Alvintzy was very nearly captured but escaped to join the remnants of his army beyond the Piave river. French troops would soon occupy all positions earlier held and once again would be masters of the Tyrol.

The immense victory, Napoleon stated, was entirely due to the fantastic leadership of his generals and the bravery of his troops: "It is said that the Roman legions marched twenty-four miles a day; our brigades have marched thirty while also fighting."[28]

Napoleon himself did not escape unscathed. "I have beaten the enemy," he wrote Joséphine the day after Provera's surrender. "I am exhausted. I beg you to leave immediately for Verona. I need you because I believe that I'm going to be very sick. I give you a thousand kisses. I am in bed."[29]

Notes

1   Corr. II. Nr. 1399, Verona, 18 January 1797.
2   Napoleon *Lettres* (Tulard), 121–2, Verona, 19 November 1796.

3   Napoleon *Lettres* (Tulard), 123–4, Verona, 21 November 1796.
4   Napoleon *Lettres* (Tulard), 124–5, Verona, 23 November 1796. We wonder whether the "little sword of Othello" was a threat or a sexual implication.
5   Napoleon *Lettres* (Tulard), 126, Verona, 24 November 1796.
6   Napoleon *Lettres* (Tulard), 127–8, Milan, 27 November 1796.
7   Thiry (*Italie*), 370.
8   Rose (*Life*), I, 130–1, See also Miot de Melito, I, 150–1.
9   Thiry (*Italie*), 386.
10 For details of Clarke's mission: Corr. XXIX, 205–6.
11 Thiry (*Italie*), 323.
12 Corr. II. Nrs. 1294, Verona, 19 December 1796; 1295, Verona, 20 December 1796; 1311, Verona, 21 December 1796; 1339, Milan, 31 December 1796.
13 See, for example, Corr. II. Nr. 1287, Milan, 15 December 1796.
14 Corr. II. Nrs. 1301, Verona, 21 December 1796; 1367, presumed Milan, presumed 7 January 1797.
15 Corr. II. Nrs. 1246, Milan, 8 December 1796; 1256, Milan, 10 December 1796; 1261, 1264, Milan, 11 December 1796; 1365, Milan, 7 January 1797.
16 Corr. II. Nr. 1319, Milan, 28 December 1796. See also Thiébault, I, 283–4, for General Dumas' unique interrogation and treatment of the prisoner.
17 Corr. XXIX, 212–13.
18 Wartenburg, I, 94, and Chandler (*Napoleon*), 113, offer figures apparently taken from official French bulletins. But see Rose (*Life*), I, 134, who puts Alvintzy's strength at less than 30,000.
19 Corr. II. Nr. 1399, Verona, 18 January 1797. See also Reinhard (*Italie*), 199–210.
20 Rose (*Life*), I, 133–4.
21 Corr. II. Nr. 1378, Verona, 13 January 1797.
22 Reinhard (*Italie*), 203.
23 Rose (*Life*), I, 136.
24 Reinhard (*Italie*), 205, for Joseph Sulkowski's moving account of this action.
25 Corr. II. Nr. 1399, Verona, 18 January 1797.
26 A somewhat exaggerated claim, but see Corr. II. Nr. 1408, Verona, 21 January 1797, in which Napoleon informs the minister of war in

Paris that 20,000 prisoners captured in the recent battle were being sent under guard to Grenoble.

27   Corr. II. Nr. 1399, Verona, 18 January 1797. Other sources state that the French losses were considerably higher.

28   Corr. II. Nr. 1399, Verona, 18 January 1797.

29   Napoleon *Lettres* (Tulard), 132–3, Roverbella, 17 January 1797.

CHAPTER TWENTY-ONE

VICTORY
JANUARY–APRIL 1797

Up to now, Prince Charles has maneuvered worse than Beaulieu and Würmser. He has made extremely clumsy mistakes at every step.

Napoleon to the Directory, Goritz,
25 March 1797[1]

THE ITALIAN CAMPAIGN entered a new phase in January of 1797. Jourdan and Moreau's abysmal defeats in Germany and retreat across the Rhine, combined with the dismal failure of General Hoche's expedition to topple British rule in Ireland, had caused a reluctant Directory to regard Napoleon Bonaparte as the republic's savior, a well-earned accolade that he was already enjoying in most of France.

Italy was no longer a secondary theater of war. Napoleon could now expect a reinforcement of 30,000 troops which he deemed necessary to carry the war across the Tagliamento river and through the Frioul into Austria proper. Savoring his new importance he at once asked the Directory for 1,000 cavalrymen: "It is said that heavy cavalry is not used in other armies, but I value it and use it very much." He also wanted trained artillerymen and combat-experienced engineer and artillery officers. He needed some generals and adjutants-general, but "I beg you not to send those who have served in the Vendée because they understand nothing of war." He wanted only distinguished commanders "because our way of making war is so different." He would like to have some young soldiers who would be taught "to make the war of movements and maneuvers . . . [responsible for] our great successes."[2]

Meanwhile there was much to be done: Joubert suitably reinforced to work his way up the Adige (constructing a series of defensive positions in case of retreat) to culminate in the occupation of Trente; Masséna and Augereau to march on Joubert's right to clear and hold the gorges of the Brenta and to support Joubert when necessary.[3] These missions were accomplished by early February and were complemented by General Würmser at last surrendering Mantua fortress with its 16,000 sick and starving men. Napoleon allowed them the honors of war with the right to return to Austria after pledging not to fight the French for a year – Würmser later wrote to thank him and warn of a plot to poison him.[4]

In the interim Napoleon had moved south to deal with the recalcitrant Pope Pius VI. Ever since the armistice with Rome had broken down, the papal court had been insulting the French flag. More recently the pope had formed a new army whose regiments totaled perhaps 15,000 men commanded by a former antagonist in the Piedmont, General Colli. This corps had joined an Austrian force working up the coast from Ancona to threaten Bologna (where Gaspard Monge and his fellows were collecting precious books and manuscripts for shipment to France). Corpses were still being buried at Mantua when Napoleon sent Victor (recently promoted to division general) with 5,000 troops to Bologna.

Victor was joined by Napoleon on the first day of February 1797. The general in chief at once issued a proclamation to the effect that France was justified in entering papal lands whose peoples were assured of peace, protection and security (so long as they behaved themselves) – a document widely distributed both locally and to numerous European courts. Several thousand French émigré priests were also assured that they would not be harmed and that bishoprics and convents would come under French protection.[5] General Lannes (still recovering from wounds) who commanded Victor's advance guard had just won a brisk action at Imola, killing several hundred defenders and capturing another 1,000 men along with 14 cannon and eight standards.[6] The French immediately marched on Faenza but were stopped by a papal force at Castel Bolognese, a nasty and bloody battle in which the Romans fought "better than expected." The papists retired to defend Faenza, a brave but futile effort that allegedly caused them to be put to the sword and the town pillaged – despite Napoleon's contrary claim to the Directory.[7]

This ended further resistance. Napoleon had earlier informed Cardinal Mattei, the pope's nephew, that his target was neither the pope nor the peaceful Roman citizenry but rather the perfidious courtier fanatics in the pay of foreign powers who were sabotaging papal relations with France. Mattei, he suggested, should urge the pope to make peace and save the blood of his subjects.

As Victor's troops continued triumphantly down the Adriatic coast, finally seizing Ancona (Colli having hastily evacuated his army by sea), Napoleon followed, glumly complaining of a bad cold and sullen peasants to Joséphine but gleefully reporting his gains in money and land to the Directory. "Ancona is a very good port," he wrote in mid month. "One goes from there in twenty-four hours to Macedonia, and in ten days to Constantinople . . . We must retain Ancona at the general peace, and we must always keep it; this will give us a great influence over the Ottoman Porte [Turkey], and will make us masters of the Adriatic sea." As for loot, the magnificent convent of "[Notre Dame de] Lorette held a treasury of approximately three million livres . . . The province of Macerata . . . is one of the most beautiful and without contradiction the richest of the Papal States."[8]

A few days later he was at Tolentino from where he wrote to Joséphine of the good news but scolded her for her silence and complained again of his cold. A papal delegation led by Cardinal Mattei now arrived to make a peace that would bring France undreamed-of riches. In informing the Directory of this unauthorized negotiation, Napoleon was neither humble nor contrite:

it had been necessary to act swiftly to prevent the King of Naples from entering the negotiations; it would bring an additional 30 million livres to the French treasury, which was ten times more than the value of Rome itself; the treaty would help lead to a general peace; and the critical situation in the north was such that he soon had to return to his army.[9]

The Directory could scarcely fault the terms of the Treaty of Tolentino. The pope agreed to sever all relations with the allied powers, to disband his new regiments, to close his ports to all but French and neutral shipping, to cede the province of Avignon to France along with the legations of Bologna, Ferrara and the Romagna, to pay France 15 million livres in cash or diamonds in addition to the 15 million still owing from the former armistice, and to turn over more manuscripts and works of art. Marmont left for Rome at once to pay Napoleon's respects to the pope and to arrange for the takeover of the treasures. He was well received not only by the pope but by the accommodating ladies of Rome – "a husband spoke of the love affairs of his wife without embarrassment or annoyance," he wrote. Monge and his fellow commissioners, reinforced by another two artists and the famous violinist, Kreutzer, arrived soon after to begin a task that would keep them busy until July.[10]

Napoleon's principal reason for accepting the peace with Rome (soon ratified by the papacy and a few months later by the Directory) stemmed from reports of Austrian reinforcements pouring in from the Rhine to rebuild Alvintzy's army. This force was now to be commanded by Archduke Charles, the emperor's 25-year-old brother, reputedly the best of the Austrian generals. Spies reported that his troops were on the move and presumably would soon strike.

During February the Army of Italy received 20,000 reinforcements including the veteran general (and husband of Napoleon's old love, Désirée Clary), Jean Baptiste Bernadotte, a hot-headed Jacobin egoist who almost at once challenged chief of staff

Berthier to a duel (quashed by Napoleon). Looking at a total of about 50,000 effectives, roughly Charles' estimated strength, Napoleon decided to attack. His plan was all the more daring in that he violated his usual tactics by geographically isolating one corps: Joubert with three divisions and a cavalry brigade to move north through the Tyrol from Trente to Brixen, then wheel east to cross the Carnic Alps and rendezvous with the main army; that army of four divisions commanded respectively by Masséna, Guieu (who had replaced Augereau), Bernadotte and Sérurier (with Napoleon never far in the rear) to cross the Tagliamento river and march northeast on Udine, then advance on a broad front, Masséna on the left and the other divisions echeloned to his right; Masséna to cross the Pontebba passes of the Julian Alps and close on Tarvis to be followed by the other three divisions; the four divisions to cross into Austrian territory to be joined by Joubert in the valley of the Drava.[11]

The offensive began auspiciously by pushing Archduke Charles behind the Tagliamento. "The enemy appears very uneasy," Napoleon wrote Masséna on 13 March, "and once more finds himself caught with his pants down after executing his adopted plan. Everything presages our great success."[12] Two days later he qualified this ebullience in a long operations order to Joubert which warned that under certain circumstances he might find himself beaten and "even obliged to take refuge in Mantua." Should this happen he was to play for as much time as possible to allow the main army to extricate itself.[13] Napoleon's major worry at this point centered on the Austrian right flank and was considerably eased when he learned that Masséna had sent that column flying with a haul of 800 prisoners including its commander, the disreputable General Lusignon.[14]

He was further encouraged when the first few days of driving rain suddenly changed to beautiful weather that eased the rigors of marching and fighting in difficult mountainous terrain – he now expected to reach the Austrian border within two weeks. But the further he advanced into Germany, he warned the Directory, the more enemy forces he would find:

Order, I beg you, the crossing of the Rhine [by General
Moreau] for it is impossible that with fifty thousand men I
can face all circumstances. If the armies of the Rhine cross
promptly and come into action, the [Austrian] emperor is
lost . . . But if I am allowed to be overpowered, I shall have
no other resource than to retire into Italy, and all will be
lost.[15]

His fears were groundless; the Austrians continued to be driven
back at all points. Joubert won several battles to gain Botzen,
taking a few thousand prisoners, before seizing Brixen where he
turned eastward. Masséna pushed through the tight Pontebba
passes to attack the strongly defended border town of Tarvis, a
stubborn battle fought in three feet of snow that cost him nearly
1,000 casualties but put the Austrians in flight across the border to
Villach with a loss of several thousand men. The remaining three
divisions crossed the Isonzo river to push the enemy from the
Venetian towns of Gradisca and Goritz, taking large numbers of
prisoners and quantities of much needed provisions and weapons.

Napoleon now sent Guieu north to join Masséna at Tarvis, a
pinching maneuver that resulted in still another victory (including
the capture of three Austrian generals). Guieu pushed his enemy
to an important border fort whose 500 grenadiers surrendered
after a brisk fight. "By the laws of war," Napoleon reported to the
Directory in words that were to be sharply reversed a couple of
years later, "the five hundred soldiers should have been put to the
sword, but this barbarous law has always been ignored and never
practiced by the French army."[16] Meanwhile Bernadotte and
Sérurier advanced on Guieu's right, the entire force debouching
into Austrian territory, first to Villach in the rich valley of the
Drava, then pushing on to Klagenfurt, capital of Carinthia, fighting here, fighting there, altogether a brilliantly coordinated
offensive soon capped by Joubert's victorious corps rejoining the
main army.[17]

None of this had been easy. Had it not been for the *élan* of
French officers and men and the poor leadership and general

demoralization of the Austrian army, it could not have happened so quickly if at all, as is emphasized by Napoleon's remarks quoted at the beginning of this chapter.[18]

That did not mean the enemy could not recover, particularly if Moreau failed to cross the Rhine. Napoleon's ignorance on this point would continue to keep him on tactical tenterhooks as he pushed deeper into Austria, and as he received reports of General Laudon's corps marching down the Adige and of a peasant rebellion against French rule in several cities which forced him to release a division in support of his weak garrisons there.

This explained his agonized appeals to the Directory for Moreau to move. "If I had twenty thousand men more," he wrote Carnot, "I believe that I would be at Vienna in two weeks."[19] Lacking such, lacking siege artillery, worried about his line of communications, his own limited food and ammunition, the potential Austrian threat from the Tyrol on the left and Istria on the right, aware that Charles would be reinforced as he continued to retreat, his belief that the capture of Vienna (even if possible) probably would not end the war, he correctly feared for the future of his command which was his primary reason for sending a peace tentative to Prince Charles at the end of March.[20]

His tactical worries soon vanished. In early April the defenses of Judenburg north of Klagenfurt melted away to leave the road open to Leoben, indeed to Vienna. At this point Charles gave in to the omnipotent and omnipresent French steamroller. On 7 April his plenipotentiaries, the generals Bellegarde and Merveldt, arrived in Judenburg to sign an armistice soon to be followed by the preliminaries of the peace of Leoben.

Why did Napoleon make this peace when he had the Austrians on the run? We have already noted some of the military reasons that prompted the armistice, which can scarcely be faulted. But there were also personal and political factors at work. Louis Bourrienne, Napoleon's schoolmate at Brienne, arrived in army headquarters at this time, having been summoned months before to serve as the army commander's private secretary. Bourrienne later recalled that Napoleon was not "very well satisfied" with the peace preliminaries but had gone ahead because the Director had notified him that "he must not reckon on a diversion in Germany."[21]

Bourrienne found a new Napoleon, a popular and powerful army commander only too well aware of his ability to work magic on the battlefield: "I saw him suddenly great, powerful, and surrounded with homage and glory."[22] The Italian campaign which was widely publicized in France had made him a national hero. He was disgusted with the Directory's failure to send the armies of the Rhine into Germany, and he was also aware of his nation's increasing desire for peace.

Napoleon already had informed the Directory of his intention to make the peace providing that Prince Charles and the Vienna court agreed to an armistice. "You will certainly realize," he added, "that the conditions . . . would be much more advantageous, in the current circumstances, than the instructions that you have given to General Clarke."[23]

These conditions would influence the future of Europe and would also reflect on the political acumen of their author and of the Directory. Clarke not yet having arrived from Turin, Napoleon negotiated the treaty with the emperor's plenipotentiaries. Three options were sent to the Vienna court and to the Directory, but where the Vienna court replied within three days the Directory's reply could not reach Napoleon before he signed the final preliminaries. There was nothing submissive in his interim report to Paris dated 16 April. "If one of these three options is accepted by Vienna," he wrote, "the preliminaries of peace will be signed on April 20th."[24]

Once the Vienna court had accepted an option, Napoleon signed – having informed the Directory that "although our military position is brilliant, we have not dictated the conditions [of the peace]; the court has evacuated Vienna; Prince Charles and his army have fallen back to the Rhine; the people of Hungary and all parts of the hereditary states have risen in mass and at this moment their advance guard is on our flanks; the Rhine has not been crossed [by Moreau and Hoche]; the Emperor was just this moment to leave Vienna and put himself at the head of his army."[25]

Napoleon sent two documents to the Directory for ratification. The first contained the preliminary articles of peace and was fairly routine. Within three months France and Austria were to conclude a definitive peace based on the integrity of the German empire. Emperor Francis renounced all rights to the Belgian provinces known as the Austrian *Pays Bas* or Low Countries, and he recognized the borders of France as decreed by the laws of the French republic in return for suitable territorial compensation to injured parties. Once the Vienna court ratified the peace, France would evacuate all the presently occupied Austrian provinces.[26]

The second document, the preliminary secret articles of peace, was much more complex. Its first article contradicted the public treaty in that the Austrian emperor renounced all of his Italian states except a portion of the Venetian mainland. France in turn agreed to turn over the Legation states – Bologna, Ferrara and the Romagna – to Venice in return for the rest of the Venetian mainland not tendered to Austria. The Italian lands acquired by France would form an independent republic.[27]

In submitting these documents to Paris, Napoleon pointed out that "the Lombard Republic finds itself not only confirmed but increased . . . We shall have in the heart of Italy a republic with which we communicate by the states of Genoa and by the sea, which gives us, in all future wars in Italy, an assured connection."[28] In Napoleon's mind the treaty would tie Austria more closely to France and place France between Austria and Prussia, and by lessening the influence of Prussia "will enable us to hold the balance [of power] in Europe."[29]

Shortly after beginning the return march to Italy, Napoleon learned that the northern French armies were on the point of crossing the Rhine. Bourrienne later recalled that so "great was [Napoleon's] agitation of mind" that he wished to return to Leoben to invent some pretext in order to break the recently signed preliminaries, but was talked out of it by Berthier and others. Three days later when he was in the Venetian states he learned that the armies had crossed the Rhine and had won considerable victories against the Austrians. Since this would have entirely altered his position at Leoben, it is difficult not to conclude as Bourrienne (and probably Napoleon) did that the Directory had been intentionally deceitful.[30]

There was not much that could be done about that, at least for the moment, but at least he could make the Venetian rebels pay for their recent crimes against the French flag.

Notes

1   Corr. II. Nr. 1632, Goritz, 25 March 1797.
2   Corr. II. Nr. 1402, Verona, 20 January 1797.
3   Corr. II. Nrs. 1412, 1413, Verona, 23 January 1797; 1428, Verona, 28 January 1797; 1429, 1430, 1431, Verona, 29 January 1797.
4   Thiry (Italie), 453. See also Burton, 90; Marmont, I, 257–8.
5   Corr. II. Nrs. 1434 (footnote), Bologna, 1 February 1797; 1498, Macerata, 15 February 1797. See also Thiry (Italie), 459 ff.
6   Corr. II. Nr. 1448, Faenza, 3 February 1797.
7   Reinhard (Italie), 228.
8   Corr. II. Nr. 1497, Macerata, 15 February 1797. See also Aubry, 188–90: Monge wrote that the papal army had evacuated a large part of the treasury, a statement confirmed by Marmont, I, 261, who was sent to take over the loot and found only "large pieces of silver plate, worth about one million francs"; Reinhard (Italie), 222–5.
9   Corr. II. Nr. 1510, Tolentino, 19 February 1797.
10 Corr. II. Nr. 1511, Tolentino, 19 February 1797; Aubry, 190–202; Marmont, I, 265.
11 Corr. II. Nrs. 1582, 1583, 1584, Sacile, 15 March 1797. See also Reinhard (Italie), 289–90, for Sulkowski's tactical insights.
12 Corr. II. Nr. 1573, Conegliano, 13 March 1797.
13 Corr. II. Nr. 1582, Sacile, 15 March 1797.
14 Corr. II. Nrs. 1583, Sacile, 15 March 1797; 1587, Sacile, 16 March 1797.
15 Corr. II. Nr. 1590, Valvasone, 17 March 1797.

16 Corr. II. Nr. 1632, Goritz, 25 March 1797.

17 Reinhard (*Italie*), 288–94, for Captain Sulkowski's tactical account of the advance. See also Thiébault, I, 307–20, for highlights of Masséna's advance of 200 miles in 25 days while fighting 18 battles.

18 Corr. II. Nr. 1632, Goritz, 25 March 1797.

19 Corr. II. Nr. 1637, Goritz, 25 March 1797.

20 Reinhard (*Italie*), 301. See also Corr. II. Nr. 1677, Klagenfurt, 31 March 1797.

21 Bourrienne, I, 56.

22 Bourrienne, I, 55.

23 Corr. II. Nr. 1666, Klagenfurt, 1 April 1797.

24 Corr. II. Nr. 1735, Leoben, 16 April 1797.

25 Corr. II. Nr. 1745, Leoben, 19 April 1797.

26 Corr. II. Nr. 1743, Château d'Eggen-wald, 18 April 1797.

27 Corr. II. Nr. 1744, Château d'Eggen-wald, 18 April 1797.

28 Corr. II. Nr. 1745, Leoben, 19 April 1797.

29 Corr. III. Nr. 1756, Trieste, 30 April 1797. See also Rose (*Life*), I, 141.

30 Bourrienne, I, 56–8.

CHAPTER TWENTY-TWO

MONTEBELLO – THE KING WITHOUT A CROWN APRIL–JULY 1797

Everyone had bowed before the brilliance of his victories and the haughtiness of his manners. This was no longer the general of a triumphant republic, this was a conqueror in his own right, imposing his laws on the vanquished.

Miot de Melito on Napoleon at Montebello,
c. May 1797[1]

NAPOLEON HAD DECIDED to destroy "the atrocious and bloodthirsty government" of Venice once he had brought the Austrians to heel, and he was in no mood to wait for formal approval from Paris. He had considerable justification. The recent uprising against French rule had been organized by the Venetian *doge* and carried out over Easter by mainland peasants who massacred several hundred French soldiers, some in hospitals in Verona and elsewhere. This uprising, what Napoleon acidly termed the Sicilian Vespers,* was followed by a seizure of a small French ship that had taken refuge in the harbor of Venice and the coldblooded slaughter of its captain and crew.

News of the latter action reached Napoleon in Trieste. He at once ordered the seizure of all Venetian merchant ships in Trieste and Ancona, a rich haul of some 50 vessels, many loaded with valuable cargoes.[2] Back in Milan in early May he turned General

---

*A major rebellion against French rule in Sicily in 1282 signaled by the ringing of vesper bells on an Easter Monday.

Augereau loose to disarm mainland peasants, send all officials to the city of Venice, arrest anyone responsible for the uprising and murders and levy enormous fines and requisitions on the citizenry.[3] Threats to attack the city of Venice caused its terrified senate to accept a treaty which transferred government by hereditary aristocracy to government by the people. It also brought France 3 million livres in cash, naval provisions worth another 3 million, three warships, three frigates, 20 paintings and 500 manuscripts of choice.[4]

Having subjugated and virtually eliminated a 600-year-old republic, Napoleon turned to the overthrow of the conservative government of Genoa whose anti-French behavior had long been a sore subject. French minister Faypoult and *commissaire* Saliceti had been intriguing in the capital for months in favor of liberal politicians. An armed dispute between liberals and conservative peasants in which several Frenchmen were killed provided the pretext for Napoleon to threaten military intervention. The upshot brought Genoese envoys running to Napoleon's elegant country retreat, the castle of Montebello near Milan, in late May to negotiate a secret convention in favor of France.

There remained the earlier established Cispadane and Cisalpine republics, the former consisting of the papal legations of Bologna, Ferrara and the Romagna south of the Po river along with the duchy of Modena; the latter the Lombardian territories and the former Venetian lands north of the river. Napoleon's revolutionary enthusiasm concerning the Italian lands had undergone a marked change owing to his disillusionment with the Piedmontese, later with the Lombardians and the Cispadanes whose liberals during his absence had succumbed to clerical anti-French pressures. Nevertheless he regarded the alliance of these lands as vital to the security of army communications in case peace negotiations with Austria broke down and war was resumed, or in case the ailing Pope Pius VI died and the King of Naples marched on Rome.[5]

Mainly for these reasons he continued to receive Italian notables while working out a suitable constitution (modeled on that of France) for the new republic. To ensure that matters went his

way, the new leaders – presidents, directors, ministers and legislators – were by his appointment rather than being elected. And it
was also by his permission that the former Venetian districts along
with the tiny Cispadane states would eventually be allowed to
join this republic.

Shortly before the end of the recent campaign a tired and dejected
Napoleon informed the Directory that he wanted only to turn
over his command and retire in France. That is the last we shall
hear of this sentiment for some time. Part of the reason for his
volte-face was Joséphine, but a larger part was his new regal role
which he played to the hilt in the pseudo-monarchical trappings of
Montebello.

He had chosen a superb setting. Visitors could not fail to be
impressed by the appearance of the elegant old château looming
high on a hill to overlook the rich and fertile Lombard plains. It
was approached by a long, bowered road lined with a guard of
richly uniformed Polish soldiers. In luxuriously furnished drawing
rooms distinguished guests mingled with Napoleon and
Joséphine, generals and aides, civilian *commissaires*, diplomats
from a dozen states, the cream of Milanese and Italian society – all
reveling in the new-found luxury provided by rich tables served
by a large Italian staff and by the excitement of couriers arriving
day and night with the latest news from Paris and other continental capitals. Several senior officers had been joined by their wives;
others such as Berthier, Murat, Leclerc and Marmont enjoyed
Italian beauty – in Berthier's case the arms of his mistress, the
beautiful Madame Visconti.

Joséphine's 17-year-old son, Eugène Beauharnais, was on hand.
Napoleon, who was very fond of both Eugène and Hortense,
appointed him a lieutenant and personal aide-de-camp, the beginning of a distinguished military career. Mother Letitia turned up
with daughter Marie Anne (henceforth called Elisa) to explain
away the girl's marriage to a dull Corsican, Felix Bacciochi, and to
sweet-talk Napoleon out of a commission in the French army for

Felix and a dowry of 30,000 francs for Elisa. Napoleon was probably glad to see his sister settled since she shared Lucien's
anti-Napoleon views and in general was a nuisance. In June came
the marriage of another sister, the beautiful and over-sexed 16-
year-old Pauline – "the prettiest creature ever seen and the wildest
ever imagined," to quote one of his favorite generals – with
Charles Leclerc (along with a dowry of 40,000 francs).[6]

Napoleon could afford to be generous. The recent campaign
had brought in 7 million francs with more to come, and the pope
had already turned over 8 million francs' worth of diamonds as a
first installment of the agreed payments. In addition to the hefty
take from Venice, Napoleon was anticipating a contribution of
2.4 million francs from the city fathers of Trieste in return for the
departure of French troops. Another 5 million was to come from
the Duke of Modena, along with 13 or 14 million in provisions
and supplies owed by various states.[7]

Despite the regal trappings life at Montebello was more exciting for some than for others. To the young Colonel Marmont
(who had turned down Napoleon's offer of Pauline's hand), it was
"movement, grandeur, expectation and gaiety. At this time our
ambition was entirely secondary, our duties and our pleasures
alone occupied us."[8]

Joséphine might not have shared this sentiment. Napoleon's
mother and sisters spared no opportunity to make life difficult for
her. Napoleon was often tied up with official matters, which left her
to deal with a tiresome succession of receptions and balls attended
by people with whom she had little in common. Smaller gatherings
were equally dull, a far cry from the exciting social intrigues and
gossip familiar to Parisian *soirées*, not to mention frequent and
expensive shopping expeditions in exclusive Paris boutiques.
Napoleon often deserted her to play a silly card game (in which he
invariably cheated but usually refunded his winnings), leaving
Joséphine to small talk or a game of backgammon. On occasion
however he would take over the company to tell wild stories, as
Bourrienne reported, often in darkness with dagger props, bizarre
stuff that frequently drew screams of fear from the ladies.[9]

Perhaps the most pleasant times, at least for Napoleon, were more intimate outings such as an excursion to nearby Lake Maggiore where on a spring night he and Joséphine sat hand in hand listening to the gorgeous voice of the La Scala operatic diva, Madame Grassini, turning the beautiful countryside into paradise. Napoleon was still deeply in love with Joséphine despite her capricious and often cruel behavior, and on such occasions he relished her nearness. "In the carriage," so an adjutant related, "he would take marital liberties which were apt to be embarrassing to [General] Berthier and me. But it was all so simple and natural that there was no ground for offense."[10]

These intimate occasions were all too few. Day after day supplicants of a dozen varieties filled a large tent erected in front of the château. Day after day Napoleon met with scores of persons most of whom wanted *something* from "the conqueror in his own right," as the diplomat, Miot de Melito, put it.[11] Among the latter were the terrified Genoese who soon signed a secret convention that ended rule by oligarchy in favor of rule by the ordinary citizens, prelude to what would become the new Ligurian Republic.[12]

The Austrian peace negotiator, Monsieur Gallo, arrived as did his French opposite, General Clarke. In late May the Vienna court ratified the peace preliminaries. The principals conferred throughout June, a seemingly endless process owing to the Vienna court invoking every conceivable pretext to delay matters in the hope that a revolution in France would break out to restore Bourbon rule. In late June the plenipotentiaries were still haggling when negotiations were moved to Udine.[13]

Napoleon remained in Italy for another seven months, an important period that tells us a great deal about this man. We do not find extraordinary changes in his military role, with the exception of his building a new fleet based on warships acquired from Venice. He remained the consummate general who demanded well-disciplined, well-trained and highly-motivated troops. He wanted his divisions combat-ready (for reasons soon to become clear) and he wished to be kept informed of enemy strengths and movements. He also wanted his soldiers properly armed, clothed, equipped, trained, fed and otherwise looked after. Newspapers with articles that might lower morale or adversely influence republican beliefs were prohibited, but the troops were kept informed of local and homeland news by newspapers produced at headquarters such as the *Courrier de l'armée d'Italie* and the *Journal de Milan*.

He had earlier scolded a general for allowing his men to be caned, a practice "entirely contrary to our principles and manner of discipline laid down in the Army of Italy." A few days later he relieved another general of his command for failing to drill his brigade properly. More than once he pounced on his generals for allowing officers and men unauthorized leave which led to unhealthy debauchery in the cities. A report that some of his precious guides were insulting ladies and behaving badly "in public places where despite orders they ramble about at night" brought a sharp reprimand to the unit commander and a threat to dissolve the company unless it cleaned up its act.[14]

He also did his best to look after troop welfare. He tried to prevent unfair distributions of either solid or liquid rations. Displeased with the poor quality of cloth for uniforms, he ordered a special investigation that resulted in the punishment of corrupt merchants. "The low quality and high prices" of shoes and boots caused him to order new models with strict supervision of manufacture. Learning that some bakers were using a dangerously inferior flour mixture for army bread so as to bake white bread for private sale, he ordered an investigation that resulted in the court-martial of a depot quartermaster in Milan. Another order named special area investigators to visit all hospitals to confirm the number of claimed patients, to check on employee honesty and to hear complaints from patients. Inept civilian administration of the hospitals, he complained to minister of war Schérer, would cost 1,500 deaths unless remedied.[15]

Napoleon could not however be everywhere in his widespread command. Numerous abuses continued owing to a lack of qualified army inspectors, command ineptness, and to circumstances outside his control such as civilian responsibility for army supply, administration of hospitals and other matters. No one familiar with his official correspondence and the attestations of numerous officers can suggest that he did not *try* to remedy such evils, and he undoubtedly succeeded in part which is greatly to his credit.

Equally creditable was his constant effort to improve troop morale. He realized that an army has to have a *raison d'être* which soldiers can readily grasp if they are going to successfully surmount the thousand and one privations that are suffered in combat and often in garrison. The *raison d'être* of the Army of Italy was the propagation of the French Revolution and defense of its established principles against enemies abroad and, increasingly, at home. Napoleon never let his officers and men forget their patriotic responsibility, and as a result he commanded the best and most powerful army in Europe.

Ceremonial parades and reviews played a dual military and political role. Who else would dictate that the stirring hymn of the revolution, the *Marseillaise*, would be played only at general reviews or when attacking the enemy, never at ordinary drills? General reviews usually celebrated some revolutionary event such as Bastille Day (14 July) which in 1797 called for division reviews throughout the army's area. Beginning in June, Napoleon personally drew up the most elaborate plans which with modifications filled several pages. Not only was the birth of liberty to be celebrated but each demi-brigade was to receive a new battle standard carrying a special accolade: "Brave Eighteenth. I know you; the enemy will fall back before you"; "The Twenty-Fifth has covered itself with glory," and many more such. Centerpoint of each celebration was a large pyramid whose sides were inscribed with the names of all soldiers killed in the Italian campaign. As troops stood at attention a cannon fired six rounds for each of the three generals who had been killed, five rounds for each general of brigade and three rounds for each adjutant-general. It was a day the soldiers would not forget, perhaps not so much for its impassioned proclamation and fiery speeches as for their receiving double rations of meat and wine.[16]

His methods were not always this grand but they were still effective. Consider two young soldiers who had helped to pull the army commander from a muddy swamp at Arcola, an act seemingly overlooked until some months later they were summoned by their commanding officer and presented with 25 livres each as a personal gift from Napoleon. Learning of a brave retired soldier with virtually no resources, he asked the Directory to arrange a pension. An army laundress who had plunged into the Po river to save a soldier's life was presented with a laurel crown for bravery. One hundred expensively wrought and engraved sabers were presented to soldiers who had displayed extraordinary bravery in combat, and these characteristically were awarded with a great deal of pomp at a general review.[17]

Deserving officers and civilian *commissaires* were not neglected. A particular mark of Napoleon's favor was to send a general to deliver captured standards to the Directory with a note of praise for the bearer, be it Berthier, Sérurier, Bernadotte, Augereau or other chosen ones. On Bernadotte: "This excellent general . . . is today one of the officers the most essential to the glory of the Army of Italy." His reports to the Directory often praised generals for their performances, character and unquestionable loyalty to the republic. On occasion this praise was qualified, as in the case of General Clarke whom he did not personally like but who "in conducting the [peace] negotiations has been good and loyal; he has not displayed great talent but he has ample good will and zeal." Such was the effort of Admiral Brueys in building the new Adriatic fleet that Napoleon presented him with an expensive telescope on behalf of the Directory. Upon receiving a special flag from the legislative corps in honor of the battle of Arcola, Napoleon sent it on to General Lannes, noting that in view of Lannes' incredibly courageous and loyal performance at the battle it was only fitting that he should have the flag.[18]

Napoleon had good reason to keep his army strong and alert and this reason intensified as the political situation in France worsened.

A large part of the Directory's failure to live up to past promises of reinforcements and supplies to the Army of Italy stemmed from deep and intense political divisions in Paris and the countryside.

Although the Jacobins held the majority of seats in the Directory, they were greatly at odds with the legislative councils and increasingly with the people. The average citizen had had quite enough of the French Revolution with all of its horrors, including what began to look like endless war beyond its borders. Many bourgeoisie and peasants, having purchased confiscated lands, had become satisfied with the status quo and had shifted political loyalties to center and right, a development that greatly benefited the steadily reviving royalist movement.

Recent elections of members of the Council of Five Hundred and the Council of Ancients had resulted in positive gains for this movement that was led by the one-time hero of the revolution, General Jean Charles Pichegru, and was based at the Paris suburb of Clichy. The stated aim of the Clichy Club was to restore the Bourbon monarchy. Such was increasing royalist preponderance in the councils that a conservative rightist had been elected to the Directory to sit with its four Jacobin members – one of whom, Lazare Carnot, was moving ever closer to the political right. Paul Barras and two others continued to hold the fort in defense of revolutionary principles and laws, but owing to numerous plots and intrigues it was a fort with a lot of holes in its defense. The result was an uncomfortable stand-off since under the constitution the Directory could neither dissolve the councils nor veto their decrees, but neither could the councils override the Directory.[19]

Napoleon at Montebello was privy to a good part of this dangerous situation which continued to ferment as spring turned to summer. He was convinced that the royalists intended to restore Bourbon rule. His police had recently arrested the Comte d'Entraigues in Venice and had seized incriminating documents to that effect. Napoleon himself was an early target of the royalists in the assembly who distributed a paper in the Army of Italy accusing him of being a war criminal for his armed descent on Venice – a paper deeply resented by the soldiers whose comrades had been assassinated by Venetian insurgents. Napoleon replied with a furious note to the Directory in which he asked to resign his command and which he followed with a lengthy justification of his military intervention there and a warning "to the cowardly advocates and gossips of Clichy" that the time had passed when they could have French generals guillotined; indeed that he commanded 80,000 soldiers who could easily appear at the gates of Clichy suburb.[20]

Although Napoleon vigorously proclaimed his loyalty to the republic on every conceivable occasion, there is considerable doubt as to his loyalty to the Directory. He had become increasingly disenchanted with this body during the Italian campaign and was still smarting from its ambiguous if not deceitful behavior of holding up and then releasing the armies of the Rhine when it was too late to accomplish the total military defeat of Austria. During the few months of precarious peace he had become more and more upset with the growing royalist movement at home. Propaganda broadcast by a host of royalist newspapers was filtering through to his army (despite rigid military censorship) to cause increasing dissatisfaction with the government.

He was uncertain just how to act. He knew that his army was loyal to himself and the republic. He seems to have hit upon a strategy of careful intimidation. In early July he informed the Directory that he could only attribute the delaying tactics of the Vienna court in the peace negotiations "to the interior situation of France," a not-so-veiled threat for that body to take remedial action against the royalist threat.[21] He next sent an aide, Lavalette, to Paris, ostensibly to brief the Directory on the political situation in Italy but in reality to discover the situation in the capital. Lavalette, described by Bourrienne as "a man of good sense and education, pleasing manners, pliant temper, and moderate opinion",[22] duly reported (in secret cipher) that the standing of the three Jacobin members of the Directory was so precarious that Napoleon should back off from any overt support until matters became more settled.[23] We can assume that further reports concerning the spineless Directory and the growth of the royalist insurgency confirmed Napoleon's belief that this was the explanation for the Vienna court's current haughtiness and the renewed buildup of its army. He made his position clear in a harangue to the troops on Bastille Day: "Soldiers . . . we swear on our new battle flags: Implacable war to the enemies of the Republic and to the Constitution of the Year III [1794]."[24]

Napoleon sent this rhetoric to the Directory along with a very angry letter. Newspaper reports of royalist machinations, he wrote, "have raised army indignation to the full," the soldier asking if his reward for fighting a six-year war was to be threatened with assassination upon his returning home. "Circumstances become more aggravating every day, and I believe, Citizen Directors, that this is the moment when you should make a decision."

What should that be? "With one blow alone you can save the Republic . . .: Arrest the émigrés; nullify the influence of the foreigners. If you need force call in the armies. Destroy the newspaper presses in the pay of England, more sanguinary than Marat ever was."[25]

It was almost as if he had declared war on the Directory. No longer did he merely suggest, he stated: Without any question Vienna along with the rest of Europe was waiting to see what happened in France. If the Directory smashed the royalist presses and closed down the Clichy Club it would not only show the foreigners that there would be no counter-revolution, but it would also remove the uneasiness that excited all the soldiers "and which will end by some explosions the consequences of which one cannot foresee." What use are our military victories, he concluded, when the intrigues in the interior annul everything?[26]

He next sent the Directory a petition signed by 12,000 soldiers in support of the republic and constitution. Again he warned of the "extreme discontent" of his troops with the "sinister direction" that things were apparently taking in France. Should the present government fall, "the Army of Italy will be almost exclusively impelled by the desire to march to the aid of liberty and the

Constitution."[27] Bourrienne later recalled that the army commander's intention of marching on Paris in case the Clichy Club gained
ascendancy was well known to the Army of Italy.[28]

While trying to move the Directory to action, Napoleon began
to think that the only solution to the stalled peace process was to
reopen the war against Austria. Still hoping however to eliminate
the interior threat to the republic, he sent General Pierre
Augereau, perhaps the most ardent revolutionist of all his generals (certainly one of the most corrupt), to Paris, ostensibly because
of the general's personal affairs but in reality to cooperate with the
three Jacobin members of the Directory in smashing the royalist
menace.[29] He next sent General Bernadotte to back up Augereau,
his flimsy pretext being to present some recently discovered standards to the Directory. Simultaneously a stream of preparatory
orders for a new offensive flowed from the Milan headquarters to
his dispersed generals.

Notes

1   Miot de Melito (1873 ed.), I, 150.
2   Corr. III. Nrs. 1758, 1759, Trieste, 30 April 1797.
3   Corr. III. Nr. 1767, Milan, 5 May 1797.
4   Corr. III. Nrs. 1795, Milan, 14 May 1797; 1803, Milan, 16 May
    1797.
5   Corr. III. Nr. 1811, Milan, 19 May 1797.
6   Rose (Life), I, 153; Levy, 6, 17; Thiébault, I, 340; Miot de Melito,
    I, 91–5.
7   Corr. III. Nrs. 1799, Milan, 14 May 1797; 1806, Milan, 18 May
    1797; 1870, Montebello, 6 June 1797; 1875, Montebello, 6 June .
    1797; 1903, 1907, Montebello, 12 June 1797; 1917, Montebello, 13
    June 1797.
8   Thiry (Italie), 569–70. See also Marmont, I, 286–7.
9   Rose (Life), I, 157.
10 Ludwig, 100.
11 Thiry (Italie), 571. See also Miot de Melito (1873 ed.), I, 150.
12 Corr. III. Nr. 1869, Montebello, 6 June 1797.

13 Corr. III. Nr. 1969, Montebello, 30 June 1797.

14 Corr. III. Nrs. 1747, Leoben, 20 April 1797; 1751, Palma, 24 April 1797; 1961, Milan, 25 June 1797; 2094, Milan, 11 August 1979; 2130, Passariano, 28 August 1797.

15 Corr. III. Nrs. 1960, Milan, 24 June 1797; 1961, Milan, 25 June 1797; 2084, 2085, Milan, 9 August 1797; 2087, Milan, 9 August 1797; 2128, Passariano, 28 August 1797; 2123, Milan, 22 August 1797; 2128, Passariano, 28 August 1797.

16 Corr. III. Nrs. 1879, Montebello, 7 June 1797; 2009, Milan, 13 July 1797.

17 Corr. III. Nr. 2127, Passariano, 28 August 1797.

18 Corr. III. Nrs. 2083, Milan, 9 August 1797; 2192, Passariano, 13 September 1797; 2260, Passariano, 26 September 1797; 2339, Milan, 10 November 1797; 2413, Paris, 6 February 1798.

19 Rose (*Life*), I, 159.

20 Corr. III. Nr. 1971, presumed Montebello, 30 June 1797.

21 Corr. III. Nr. 1978, Montebello, 2 July 1797.

22 Bourrienne, I, 82. See also Lavalette, I, 218–40.

23 Rose (*Life*), I, 161.

24 Corr. III. Nr. 2010, Milan, 14 July 1797. See also Iung (*Bonaparte*), III, 182–5.

25 Corr. III. Nr. 2014, Milan, 15 July 1797.

26 Corr. III. Nr. 2018, Milan, 17 July 1797.

27 Corr. III. Nr. 2023, Milan, 18 July 1797.

28 Bourrienne, I, 81.

29 Corr. III. Nr. 2043, Milan, 27 July 1797. See also Bourrienne, I. 82.

CHAPTER TWENTY-THREE

THE TREATY OF CAMPO FORMIO
AUGUST–NOVEMBER 1797

[Napoleon's] praises are sung by everybody. People
were embracing each other in the street in pronouncing his
name. Workers drank to his health . . . Theaters played
appropriate works in his honor. To win applause actors had
only to mention his name.

Paris police report, 28 October 1797[1]

OTHER THAN THE army and Joséphine the one bright spot in Napoleon's existence during spring and summer of 1797 was a new star in the East, this in the form of the Ionian islands, one of the prizes from the rape of Venice. In late May possibly to their astonishment the directors in Paris had learned of their general's decision to employ his new navy in sending a task force of about 2,000 troops to seize the islands of Corfu, Zante and Céphalonie along with all the Venetian holdings in the Levant. The commander of the expedition, General Gentili, was to act only as an auxiliary of the new republic of Venice. If however the "people of Corfu are inclined to independence he is to encourage their desire."[2]

The people of Corfu, Napoleon reported in late July, were very much inclined to independence. Gentili's proclamations, which invoke the memory of classical Greece, Athens and Sparta, had inspired an historical reawakening. French troops had landed to the cheers of islanders gathered on the beaches. The *papa* or chief of religion greeted the general with a humble speech that bemoaned the people's ignorance of arts and sciences owing to the oppressive Venetian government. It had not always been like this, he explained, proudly handling Gentili a precious copy of Homer's *Odyssey*. Neighboring islands showed the same desire to enjoy liberty, to educate their peoples and to profit from commerce by escaping from "the tyranny of oligarchs" with the help of French protection.[3]

Gentili's subsequent reports raised Napoleon's enthusiasm to fever pitch. Whereas the Italian states were exhausted by the French presence of two years, the Ionian islands possessed great riches waiting to be exploited. This was but a prelude to what he had in mind. He already had informed the Directory that the island of Malta was of "major interest" to France, and suggested that Spain, France's ally, should seize it before the King of Naples claimed it.[4] Moreover:

> the Turkish empire is crumbling every day; the possession
> of these [Ionian] isles will enable us to prop it up for as
> long as this will be possible, or to seize it, or to take our
> share of it. The time is not far away when we will perceive
> that, in order to truly ruin England, it will be necessary for
> us to seize Egypt.[5]

To the new French minister of foreign affairs, Charles Maurice Talleyrand-Périgord, who had written him a very flattering letter, he replied in kind while emphasizing the importance of holding the islands and also reported the enthusiasm of the neighboring Albanian *paschas* for friendship with France. "Corfu and Zante," he concluded, "make us the masters of the Adriatic and the Levant."[6]

Napoleon's letter to Talleyrand marked the beginning of a long, at times productive, at times tortuous, relationship made the more exciting by its inherent intellectual, moral and political acrobatics that often rose to Olympian heights only to plunge to Satanic depths.

Talleyrand was fifteen years older than Napoleon, scion of an ancient, aristocratic family. Crippled by a childhood accident, he

Talleyrand, Périgord, Charles Maurice de 1754–1836
Grand Chamberlain

had been schooled from a young age in theology but at age 21 was expelled from his seminary for keeping a mistress. Undaunted, he continued his studies and was ordained a few years later.

An active career in church politics eventually gained him a bishopric and an influential voice at the meeting of the States General in 1789. Contrary to his earlier conservative beliefs he here made his mark as one of the more radical revolutionary bishops. Excommunicated by the pope for advocacy of numerous clerical reforms, he resigned from the church to take up a diplomatic career.

In 1792 he was sent to London to try to dissuade William Pitt's government from joining Austria in a coalition against France. The failure of this effort combined with revolutionary turbulence in France caused him to spend two years in the United States where he made a great deal of money from financial investments. In 1796 he returned to a more sympathetic political climate and in the following year was appointed minister of foreign affairs, his sponsor being Madame de Staël – daughter of the deposed and scorned finance minister, Jacques Necker.

Although each knew of the other's reputation they had never met, but their early correspondence makes clear that each increasingly respected the other's intelligence, political and military acumen and drive, and they undoubtedly sensed the possibility of a profitable future alliance. The pith of this correspondence ostensibly concerned current peace negotiations with the Austrians as well as Italy's political situation; indeed it covered both subjects *ad nauseam*.

But as Napoleon's plans for the Italian lands waned so his enthusiasm for the east waxed. Seeing that the Directory lacked enthusiasm for his new venture, or that it was too hard-pressed politically to show much interest, Napoleon continued his hot-sell to Talleyrand, perhaps unknowingly foreshadowing the future.

In September he informed the lame aristocrat that the Naples court had its eye on the Ionian group. "I think that henceforth the main maxim of the [French] Republic should be never to abandon Corfu, Zante, etc. We should, to the contrary, solidly establish ourselves there; we will find there immense commercial resources, and [the islands] will be of great importance for us in the future of European developments." So far as that went, he added, it would be a good idea to take the lightly-defended island of Malta whose inhabitants, suffering from widespread hunger, were disgusted with the rule of the oligarchic knights and were very pro-French.

Napoleon then turned to the distant future. "If peace with England would oblige us to cede the Cape of Good Hope, it would be necessary for us to seize Egypt . . . one would be able to sail from here with 25,000 men, escorted by eight or ten ships of the line or Venetian frigates, and take it." Egypt had never belonged to a European nation, he pointed out, nor did it belong to the (Ottoman Porte's) Grand Seigneur. "What would be the Porte's reaction to a French expedition to Egypt?"[7]

Talleyrand liked the idea but the Directory at first rejected an attack on Malta because of its neutrality. However, as the directors learned of Russia and Austria's intentions to seize the island they changed course. In late October, Napoleon received authority to prepare an expedition under Admiral Brueys' command. He now sent an agent, one Poussielgue, ostensibly to inspect the ports of the Levant but in reality to set up local support in Malta for a French landing.[8]

As for Talleyrand's optimism concerning the future of the Italian states, Napoleon unsympathetically replied: "You know only a little of the people here . . . you imagine that liberty does great things to a lazy, superstitious and base people . . . This is a nation very enervated and very mean-spirited . . . one of [the King of Sardinia's] battalions and one of his cavalry squadrons is stronger than all the Cisalpine united."[9]

Despite his personal feelings Napoleon was in no position to write off the Italian adventure, at least until a satisfactory peace was achieved with Austria. In an effort to speed up negotiations at Udine, in late August he transferred army headquarters to Passariano, a beautiful château about ten miles distant from Udine.

Here he would shortly learn that General Augereau had unleashed his troops in a successful coup against ultraconservative deputies in the assembly, along with a host of royalist officials, judges, recently returned émigrés, priests and journalists who were either summarily deported to French Guiana or otherwise forced to leave the country.

The Clichy Club was closed, its printing presses subsidized by English gold were smashed. Among the victims was Lazare Carnot who escaped to Genoa; another member of the Directory, Barthélemy, was deported as was Jean Charles Pichegru, the motivating force of the Clichy Club, a revolutionary turned general who two years earlier had become a national hero for having seized the Austrian Netherlands.

After detailing events of the coup to Napoleon, Augereau concluded: "Paris is tranquil, and everyone is astounded at an event which promised to be awful, but which passed over like a *fête* . . . It now remains for the wise energy of the Directory and the patriots of the two councils to do the rest."[10] A week later he sent an aide to Napoleon with

> some dispatches from the Directory, where much uneasiness is felt at not hearing from you. No less uneasiness is experienced on seeing in Paris one of your *aides-de-camp* [Lavalette], whose conduct excites the dissatisfaction and distrust of the patriots, toward whom he has behaved very ill . . . Fresh troops having been summoned to Paris, and my presence at their head being considered indispensable by the Government, I shall not have the satisfaction of seeing you as soon as I hoped. This has determined me to send for my horses and carriages, which I left at Milan.[11]

General Bernadotte, who had remained discreetly in the background during the coup, informed Napoleon that

> Paris is quiet. The people at first heard of the arrest of the deputies with indifference. A feeling of curiosity soon drew

them into the streets; enthusiasm followed, and cries of
Vive la République, which had not been heard for a long
time, now resounded in every street . . . The Government
is presently powerful enough to elevate public spirit; but
everybody feels that it is necessary the Directory should be
surrounded by tried and energetic Republicans.
Unfortunately a host of men, without talent and resources,
already suppose that what has taken place has been done
only in order to advance their interests.[12]

What was Napoleon to make out of all this? The coup had seemingly removed the royalist threat to the Paris government, at least
temporarily, but it had brought some disturbing side effects. One
was increased resistance in the already agitated countryside.
Napoleon informed the Directory a week after the coup that he
had sent troops to keep the peace in Lyons and Marseilles, and if
the situation subsequently demanded it he would "march there
with the utmost rapidity."[13]

More disturbing was Augereau's elevation from a subordinate
to an independent and almost equal position to Napoleon in the
military hierarchy. Neither was Napoleon pleased with the
harsher aspects of the coup, particularly the summary treatment
of the legislators and other victims. Nor would he have failed to
note Bernadotte's remark that "unfortunately a host of men without talent and resources already suppose that what has taken
place has been done only in order to advance their interests."[14]
Radical extremism had earlier challenged revolutionary principles. Was it now to challenge the laws of the republic? Napoleon
did not immediately acknowledge Augereau's reports, and when
he did it was in subdued tones: "The entire army [of Italy] has
applauded the sagacity and energy that you have shown on this
vital occasion . . . It is only with sagacity and a moderate mind
that the welfare of the country can be established in a stable
manner."[15]

*

The *coup d'état* did not immediately lend impetus to the peace negotiations. The villain remained the Austrian minister of foreign affairs, Baron Thugut, who according to the Viennese envoys had sold himself to England and was holding out for a war that neither the Vienna court nor the people wanted. The envoys did not dare to challenge Thugut's instructions: "They speak very little," Napoleon informed Talleyrand, ". . . privately, each looks right and left and in a low voice tells [me] that Thugut is a rogue who should be hanged but that he is the true sovereign of Vienna."[16]

As the impasse continued and the Austrians increased military preparations, in early September Napoleon issued preliminary marching orders to his divisions. Austria was ready for war, he warned the Directory, with 100,000 troops on the Austro-Italian border. Owing to the demands of rear-area garrisons he had only 50,000 effectives. But what worried him most was the internal condition of France. "Can one reestablish [internal] tranquility without the army?" he asked Talleyrand. "Can one do without the greatest part of the troops that are [in France] right now?" If so, he continued, it would probably be advantageous for him to beat the gun and open a new campaign against Austria.[17]

These overtures were not well received in Paris where rumors of his ambiguous attitude toward the coup were circulating. Even before the coup, members of the Directory and certain important officials had resented his long periods of silence broken by explosive reports couched in intemperate language.

The situation came to a boil in late September with the appearance in Milan of an officer from Paris who, under the war minister's auspices, spread word to the soldiers of the Directory's discontent with Napoleon's ambiguous post-coup attitude and who, more ominously, carried a letter, defamatory from Napoleon's standpoint, from Augereau to the army's division commanders.

The army commander at once complained to the Directory that "it is obvious that the government is acting toward me approximately as [it did] toward Pichegru after *Vendémiaire*." He again asked to be relieved of his command – the second time in less than three months – both because of this undeserved and "horrible mark of the ingratitude of the government," and because his deteriorating health strongly demanded "repose and tranquillity." He followed this with a similar request a few days later: "I am unable to mount a horse. I need two years of rest."[18]

His anger further increased when the new president of the Directory, Paul Barras, sent his secretary, one Bottot, to Passariano. Napoleon judged him to be nothing more than a spy and treated him accordingly. According to Bourrienne, Napoleon "accused the government, at table, in Bottot's presence, of horrible ingratitude. He recounted all his subjects of complaint, in loud and impassioned language, without any restraint, and before twenty or thirty persons."[19]

How much of this anger was genuine and how much was playacting is anyone's guess. As perhaps he had anticipated, his sharp letters to the Directory drew an almost craven reply from its president, insisting that he remain at his post.[20] This was no great sacrifice. Gaspard Monge described life at Passariano as pleasant in the extreme, the evenings often devoted to long scientific discussions. Joséphine arrived in mid September, the erudite poet Arnault was on hand, as was General Louis Desaix.

A year younger than Bonaparte, Desaix was a small, ugly man with a saber scar across his face, a brilliant military reputation gained on the Rhine, and a keen and active mind. Though from an aristocratic family, he was a simple, humble man, devoted to women – and to his soldiers of whom he had a fount of stories such as the private who had drunk too much wine and was stumbling along repeating between hiccups, "Red and white, red and white, if you can't agree with each other, out you both go." He responded eagerly to Napoleon's soaring imagination, particularly his suggested designs on Egypt. Before departing he gained Napoleon's promise to take him along on the next campaign.[21]

The already tense diplomatic situation was exacerbated by the arrival of a senior Austrian diplomat, 44-year-old Count Louis de

Desaix de Veygoux, Louis Charles Antoine 1768–1800

Cobenzl, who was to revive the dormant negotiations. At first it seemed that his presence impaired more than improved matters. Marmont described him as "extremely ugly and grotesquely fat . . . very opinionated, a social butterfly, light and superficial," in unpleasant contrast to the conciliatory Gallo and the gentlemanly General Mersefeld.[22] Napoleon instantly disliked him – "he is not always ready to discuss things but is certainly used to having his own way," he informed Talleyrand; he was a wind-bag who kept repeating ridiculous demands, although hinting that the emperor would like to make common political cause with France in order to oppose the ambitious plans of Prussia.[23]

Napoleon held good reason to continue the talks. The season was now too advanced for a new campaign and in any case he was leery of having to count on General Augereau who had been appointed commander of the 120,000-strong Army of the Rhine: "You know him, and you know the measure of his talents and likewise of his courage," Napoleon told Marmont. "[The directors] have taken his idle chatter for genius and his bragging for heroism."[24] Napoleon also needed a free hand in case the ailing pope died and the Naples court decided to march an army on Rome.

As negotiations continued a see-saw course, the Vienna court began to realize that its hopes of a royalist coup in France had been dashed and with that became more amenable to a peace despite some stormy sessions. Contrary to the Directory's instructions, Napoleon agreed that in return for French possession of certain areas including the left bank of the Rhine, the Austrian *Pays-Bas* or Low Countries (Belgium), the Savoy, the county of Nice and the Ionian islands, Austria would gain Istria on the Dalmatian coast in the Balkans, the city of Venice and the Venetian mainland up to the Adige and Po rivers. Austria would further recognize the new Cisalpine Republic, which included its ancient holdings in Italy, as an independent state. The treaty also called for a subsequent congress at Rastadt to settle the peace of the German empire.[25]

Napoleon signed the Treaty of Campo Formio (a village between Passariano and Udine) in mid October and, as a sign of gratitude, entrusted it to Berthier and Monge for delivery to the Directory. He expected heavy criticism from the directors, he informed Talleyrand, but he insisted that France could not gain a more favorable treaty without resuming the war and conquering two or three Austrian provinces. "Was this possible? Yes. Probable? No." The bulk of French army strength was deployed on the Rhine and was not combat-ready. The bulk of Austrian strength, now estimated at 150,000 troops plus reserves, was on the Italian border, ready to strike Napoleon's numerically weaker army. Snow already covered the mountains whose passes would soon be closed, thus preventing a French advance. Finally and not least, peace with Austria would demolish the enemy coalition to end a land war which had steadily grown more unpopular in France.[26]

The Directory did not readily accept the peace terms and probably would not have ratified the treaty except for Napoleon's intense popularity with the people. News of the peace had raised him to demi-god status. Aware of the public mood the directors had little choice. Not only did they ratify the treaty but they nominated its creator to represent France at the coming congress of Rastadt.

Napoleon regarded the treaty as a stepping stone to new heights. "The league of European oligarchies being now broken up," he wrote Talleyrand, "France should profit by the opportunity to seize England bodily – in Ireland, Canada, India."[27] The real villain of the peace was England. The English monarchy, he insisted, had to be eliminated before its corrupt intrigues destroyed France. "This done, Europe is at our feet."[28]

Back in Milan however his strategic thinking underwent a major change. He now wanted a direct invasion of England which would require adequate naval strength, 36,000 well-commanded troops and 30 million livres in cash. Despite his own precarious health he suggested, somewhat obliquely, that he would be available as overall commander.

Talleyrand liked the idea and it was probably his influence that persuaded the Directory to accept it. Napoleon immediately plunged into action without waiting for authority. He alerted a number of his generals to prepare for a march back to France where their troops would join a new Army of England. His artillery commander was to form a train of cannon of the same caliber as those of the English (presumably to utilize captured English munitions), and the present cumbersome ammunition caissons were to be replaced by light, collapsible, two-wheeled wagons of Napoleon's design for landing on English beaches.

After making a final tour of his Italian states – "every place through which he passed, the greatest honors were paid him," Bourrienne reported[29] – the conqueror left the country in mid November. At Rastadt he exchanged ratifications of the new treaty with the Austrian envoys, Metternich and Cobenzl, presented them with elegant gifts, graciously accepted Emperor Francis' gift of six priceless Lippizaner horses, looked briefly into the negotiations and, in accordance with new orders from the Directory, swept grandly off to Paris.

Notes

1 Thiry (*Italie*), 689–90.

2 Corr. III. Nrs. 1828, 1829, 1830, Montebello, 26 May 1797.

3 Corr. III. Nr. 2061, Milan, 1 August 1797. See also Coston, I, 474–5.

4 Corr. III. Nr. 1828, Montebello, 26 May 1797.

5 Corr. III. Nr. 2103, Milan, 16 August 1797.

6 Corr. III. Nr. 2106, Milan, 16 August 1797. See also Talleyrand, I, 256, 259; Talleyrand (O . . . du C . . .), 231–2; Bertrand (Pierre), 4–5; Boulay, 275.

7 Corr. III. Nr. 2195, Passariano, 13 September 1797. See also Coston, I, 478; Boulay, 275 ff.

8 Coston, I, 481–2, 485, 494–5.

9 Corr. III. Nr. 2292, Passariano, 7 October 1797.

10 Bourrienne, I, 83.

11 Bourrienne, I, 83–4.

12 Bourrienne, I, 84.

13   Bourrienne, I, 84–5.

14   Bourrienne, I, 84–5.

15   Corr. III. Nr. 2254, Passariano, 23 September 1797. See also Iung (*Bonaparte*), III, 204–9.

16   Corr. III. Nr. 2153, Passariano, 6 September 1797.

17   Corr. III. Nrs. 2154, Passariano, 7 September 1797; 2220, 2221, Passariano, 19 September 1797.

18   Corr. III. Nr. 2255, Passariano, 25 September 1797; Coston, I, 488–9.

19   Bourrienne, I, 94.

20   Coston, I, 489–91.

21   Thiébault, I, 365; Marmont, I, 295. See also Aubry, 204–5

22   Marmont, I, 288.

23   Corr. III. Nr. 2263, Passariano, 28 September 1797.

24   Thiry (*Italie*), 677–8; Marmont, I, 300–1. See also Macdonald, 52, who witnessed Augereau's review of the Army of Germany shortly after his appointment as commander: "His dress was startling; he was covered with gold embroidery even down to his short boots, thus contrasting strongly with our simple uniforms . . . [addressing the soldiers before the review he] spoke of the bravery of his troops, but without even mentioning the leader of the Army [of Italy, Napoleon]. He said that the soldiers were very well treated there, and that there was not a man among them, bad character as he might be, who had not ten gold pieces in his pocket and a gold watch. This was a hint to our fellows."

25   Corr. III. Nrs. 2296, Passariano, 10 October 1797; 2304, 2305, Campo Formio, 17 October 1797. The text of the treaty and its secret clauses are included. See also Aubry, 204.

26   Corr. III. Nr. 2307, Passariano, 18 October 1797.

27   Fortescue (*Heritage*), 141.

28   Corr. III. Nr. 2307, Passariano, 18 October 1797.

29   Bourrienne, I, 105.

CHAPTER TWENTY-FOUR

PARIS INTERLUDE
DECEMBER 1797–MAY 1798

*True conquests, the only ones which leave no regret, are those
made over ignorance. The most honorable and useful
occupation for nations is to contribute to the extension of
human knowledge. The true power of the French Republic
should consist henceforth in allowing no single new idea
to escape its embrace.*

Napoleon in accepting membership in the National
Institute of Sciences and Arts, Paris,
26 December 1797[1]

THE TIRED GENERAL reached Paris in early December, an intentionally quiet arrival followed by a secluded week in the small house on
the *rue Chantereine* (Joséphine was still in Milan). Other than a
lengthy meeting with Talleyrand, some generals, a few diplomats
and politicians, Gaspard Monge and other scientists, long sessions
with brothers Joseph and Lucien who briefed him on the latest
political developments, he kept a low profile to the disappointment
of thousands of Parisians anxious to give him a hero's welcome.

A week later he broke isolation to appear in a simple field uniform as guest of honor at a magnificent ceremony in the
Luxembourg palace where he presented the ratified Treaty of
Campo Formio to the directors. Introduced by Talleyrand's flattering speech, Napoleon replied briefly but in fervidly patriotic
terms, congratulating the overlords for having introduced representative government to replace twenty centuries of rule by
religion, feudality and royalty, but nonetheless reminding his

audience that the future welfare of the French people would depend on the best possible laws.[2]

The speech was greeted by tremendous applause from several hundred distinguished guests. The president of the Directory, Paul Barras, replied at far too great length, then threw his pudgy arms around Napoleon as did the other directors in turn, much to the general's discomfiture. All told it was a night of supreme hypocrisy since Napoleon held the directors in contempt and they held him in jealous fear. They could not have been very happy when their guest was cheered by thousands of waiting citizens upon leaving the palace.

Homage continued in the following weeks as he was honored by a hymn set to music, an opera and assorted eulogistic poems as enthusiastic crowds acclaimed him the savior of France. The directors hosted another lavish banquet in the gallery of the Louvre to honor his acquisition of artistic masterpieces from Italy. Theater managers vied in providing special performances and boxes for him and his friends. His little street was renamed the *rue de la Victoire*, and crowds daily gathered outside the house (which Napoleon was soon to buy as a gift to Joséphine) hoping to catch a glimpse of the famous man.[3]

Napoleon treated newly-acquired fame with great care and considerable cynicism. It would not last, he assured Bourrienne. "The people of Paris do not remember anything. Were I to remain here long, doing nothing, I should be lost. In this great Babylon one reputation displaces another. Let me be seen but three times at the theater and I shall no longer excite attention; so I shall go there but seldom." Henceforth he preferred a box shaded by curtains, and more than once refused to show himself to the audience. Was this to indicate a romantic modesty or to safeguard his person? He knew only too well that the supposed adulation was spiced with evil, that there were people who would have welcomed his demise, including a few ambitious generals such as Augereau. Bourrienne tells us that he received a note from a woman warning that he was to be poisoned – police tracked her down only to find her throat slit and body mangled. Aware that the public interest was fickle, he remarked to Bourrienne that "the people would crowd as fast to see me if I were going to the scaffold."[4]

He did treasure one honor – his fully deserved election to the prestigious National Institute of Sciences and Arts. Not only was he a keen student of each, he was also an ardent patron as confirmed by his recent Italian campaign. In Milan he had spent long hours in discussions with artists and scientists. Upon learning that the famous sculptor, Antonio Canova, had lost his Venetian pension by moving to Rome, he at once offered him the protection of the army and payment of the pension. More than anyone else he was responsible for the wholesale theft (acquisition if you will) of many of Italy's priceless treasures. He worked the members of the Committee of Sciences and Arts hard but he treated them well and backed them to the hilt. In closing down the mission he officially praised its members who returned to France singing his praises. He subsequently appeared at meetings of the Institute and on occasion read a paper to the critical savants. After Joséphine's return to Paris their small house was frequented by men of letters, one of the most notable being the famous mathematician-astronomer, Pierre Laplace, to whom Napoleon had brought some new Italian calculations of the orbits.

He did not warm to constant invitations from fashionable French hostesses however. The celebrated Madame de Staël did everything possible to attach him to her *salon*, without success. He was civil enough to her at their infrequent meetings but most of her aggressive letters went unanswered and she never penetrated his exterior coldness. A woman used to getting her way, her frustration increased with each failure, as indicated in a lengthy and hostile *mémoire* which concluded: "I have never been able to breathe freely in his presence."[5] At one of Talleyrand's receptions she sought Napoleon out to ask loudly what type of woman he most admired. "The one who produces the most children," he replied, turning his back on her.[6]

Napoleon was soon deeply involved in planning for the invasion of England. Bourrienne later suggested that he never really intended to cross the Channel, a dangerous statement because nobody – not even a private secretary – really knew what Napoleon intended, and because it stands considerably at odds with the written record.

In mid December the general wrote a lengthy operational study of the project which he expanded during the next two months, adding the most precise orders for assembling battle fleets, collecting landing craft, building artillery parks, forming divisions and brigades, naming specific units and commanders, organizing ammunition and supply magazines, and countless other details.[7] Some of these tasks were never carried out, some only partially, but in aggregate they suggest that if Napoleon was a genius on land he was not as clever on water.

This was not altogether his fault. He had been trying for two years to resurrect a defunct navy, sending the maritime authorities at Toulon several million francs for this purpose while simultaneously attempting to build a powerful squadron around the nucleus of warships seized from Venice. Sabotaged by poorly educated naval officers and engineers (the best had fled the country) and by corrupt and inefficient civilian administrators, his effort failed. As confusion mounted and time ran out he slowly lost confidence in what was from the beginning an over-ambitious project.

Napoleon faced the ugly truth in February when, accompanied by Lannes, Sulkowski and Bourrienne, he spent two weeks inspecting assembly ports, interrogating naval officers, engineers, quartermasters, sailors, fishermen, smugglers – anyone who could provide him with pertinent information on force readiness and the problem of a Channel crossing. Almost everything he learned was negative. The necessary warships to protect troop convoys were virtually non-existent, the result of bureaucratic confusion and human idleness. Without battle fleets to counter English predators the operation could not succeed – and that was that.[8]

He returned unexpectedly to Paris to write his report (nearly catching out Joséphine who had revived overly cordial relations with Paul Barras). It began: "Whatever our efforts we will not acquire mastery of the seas for several years. To effect a landing in

England without such mastery is the most difficult and hazardous operation ever attempted."[9] Although willing to continue the present naval building program, he believed it best to postpone the invasion for another year, but he also wanted to keep the threat visibly alive to the enemy. In the interim he suggested a campaign to seize Hanover and Hamburg from the British, or alternatively an expedition in the Levant to threaten British commerce with India and the East Indies. If neither were feasible then the Directory should make peace with England (which would give French diplomats added clout at the Rastadt negotiations).[10]

Talleyrand meanwhile had been trying to interest the Directory in an expedition to Egypt earlier contemplated by Napoleon. About the time that the general left Paris to inspect the Channel ports, the foreign minister delivered a lengthy *mémoire* extolling this project which originally had been proposed by Gottfried Wilhelm Leibnitz to King Louis XIV in 1672,[11] and revived by the Duke of Choiseul in 1769 as a suitable replacement for the loss of New World colonies. A few years later Baron de Tott's favorable report on the country caused a number of influential French writers including Constantin Volney to favor an expedition. "Never has a project more extensive or more important in its results yet more simple in its means of execution been presented to the Executive Directory," Talleyrand wrote in his usual persuasive style. In addition to the obvious trade advantages awaiting this extension of French suzerainty, there was a major strategic consideration: the conquest of Egypt would be a most effective blow to English commerce without the risk of a dubious cross-Channel landing.[12]

The proposed strike eastward held considerable appeal for all concerned parties as Talleyrand undoubtedly had foreseen. The Directory regarded it as a much more certain and safe way to replenish an empty treasury while threatening British control of India, all under the guise of spreading the revolution to the oppressed Egyptian *fellahin* or peasantry. Perhaps as important it also offered a convenient means to send the immensely popular and thus dangerous young general a long way from Paris. For

Napoleon it was an opportunity to conquer exciting new worlds while the inept and corrupt directors continued to dig their own graves. It offered Talleyrand a clear field in which to exercise his own talents in establishing a position so secure as to survive whatever political vicissitudes lay ahead (or so he supposed), a motive cleverly obscured by his apparent willingness to serve as French ambassador in Constantinople.

Once the directors asked Napoleon to estimate the requirements in men, munitions and money, events moved rapidly. Napoleon replied in early March, in effect stating his own terms. He called for an expeditionary force of nearly 25,000 infantry, 3,000 horses and 1,500 artillerymen. Although the cavalry and most artillery units would leave their horses behind – he reckoned that thousands of Arabian mounts could be easily acquired in Egypt – they would carry saddles. Officers would take horses, three for each general of division, two for each lesser rank. The force would include engineer and labor companies and a bridge train.

The expedition would sail from six ports commencing in late April, each ship carrying water for one month, provisions for two months, their destination known only to a few. The convoys were to be protected by a host of warships, frigates, corvettes and smaller armed vessels. Cost was estimated at 8–9 million francs. Napoleon's report included details as to which units and what guns would be loaded on what ships at which ports. This and a host of following orders offer a valuable lesson in what 150 years later would be known as combat loading – and this must be attributed to the military genius of its author.[13]

The Directory accepted these requirements and in mid March put Napoleon in titular command of the expedition. It was an enormous challenge. The first problem was money – the treasury was *in extremis*. This was solved by turning General Brune loose in occupied Switzerland from where he would shortly empty Berne coffers of a good many million francs. Simultaneously General Joubert was unleashed to raise what he could in Holland, as was General Masséna in Rome. The combined plundering effort yielded enough money for immediate needs but there was nothing left over to repair more than the most serious naval deficiencies, even had time permitted.

Next came the matter of organization. Napoleon recalled General Berthier from Rome (his command taken over by Masséna) and appointed him chief of staff to what was still called, for deceptive purposes, the Army of England. He had already begun the herculean task of fitting out the expedition, and in the weeks ahead his orders covered almost every conceivable detail. "I never saw Napoleon so active," Bourrienne noted. ". . . Orders and instructions succeeded each other with extraordinary rapidity. If he wanted an order . . . he ran to the Luxembourg [palace] to get it signed by the directors . . . [his] orders flew like lightning from Toulon to Civita Vecchia (where General Desaix was organizing his contingent)."[14]

Despite a workload impossible for an average person to comprehend, much less sustain, Napoleon did not appear to be overly concerned with military aspects. He did not seem to fear the presence of a reported British fleet in the Mediterranean and he apparently believed that the Egyptian host would receive him as a liberator, that the people would rise in armed rebellion against the dreaded Mamelukes. Conquest of course was necessary, first the capture of the island of Malta which would serve as an interim base, then the subjugation of all Egypt.

Once these preliminaries were out of the way the real task would be that of colonizing, of civilizing this vast country according to French lights, of restoring it to its former grandeur but this time with the French flag flying overhead (in company with that of the Turkish sultan). Napoleon's earlier studies had assured him that Egypt held untold treasures. To ferret them out would be the task of Gaspard Monge and Claude Berthollet who were to recruit teams of scholars, mathematicians, engineers, physicists, chemists, geologists, archeologists, geographers, astronomers, linguists, botanists, draughtsmen, physicians and surgeons – altogether 167 top-rank civilians including some of the biggest names in French arts and sciences, the mathematician-physicist

Fourier, the balloonist Condé, the engraver Denon, these and other professionals each with young acolytes to do the necessary foot- and fieldwork, a total force of about 500 civilian savants. In addition to quantities of scientific equipment ranging from butterfly nets to microscopes to excavating tools to hot-air balloons to printing presses (acquired by Monge from the Vatican along with French, Italian and Arabic fonts), the scientists carried large private libraries – Napoleon's library alone consisted of over 300 volumes divided into sciences and arts, geography and voyages, history, poetry, novels and political and moral philosophy. The latter category included the old and new Christian testaments, the Koran, the Hindu *Vedas* and Montesquieu's *Esprit des Lois*.[15]

No part of this gigantic effort, military or civil, was easy and it is to the credit of Napoleon and his underlings that progress was so rapid. In mid April a secret decree named him general in chief of the Army of the Orient. This document, which he had written, was followed with two more that authorized him to seize the island of Malta and the country of Egypt and justified the deeds. Malta's ruler, the Grand Master of the Order of Knights of St. John of Jerusalem, had openly declared war against the French Revolution, provided sanctuary for French royalists and sought protection from one or more enemies of France with the intention of paralyzing French trade in the Mediterranean. The landing in Egypt was justified on two counts. The ruling Mameluke beys, bought by English gold, were daily perpetrating horrific cruelties on French merchants in Egypt; French ships needed a new route to the East Indies, the former one having been blocked by English seizure of the Cape of Good Hope. His mission therefore was to hoist the French flag over Malta and Egypt, march through the isthmus of Suez, take control of the Red Sea and chase out English merchants, protect the indigenous peoples of Egypt and maintain good relations with the Turkish sultan's lieutenant, the Grand Seigneur, Pasha Abu Bakr, in Cairo.[16]

It would seem then that Napoleon had abandoned the quasi-role of either Caesar or Charlemagne for that of Alexander the Great, that henceforth he would devote his immense talents and energy to winning control of Egypt as prelude to planting the French flag in India and other lands – to England's commercial ruin.

Napoleon's capricious mind however always contained options. A good many historians later agreed with Bourrienne in claiming that Napoleon held no notion of invading England, either in 1798 or later. How then to explain another *mémoire* to the Directory written at this time, a document which strongly suggests that he may have regarded the Egyptian expedition as a play within a play, that his grand design may still have been the invasion of England. "In our position," he wrote, "we have to make constant war on England, and we can make it. Whether we are at peace or war, we need to spend forty or fifty millions to reorganize our navy." Napoleon wanted no fewer than 35 ships of the line to be built at Brest, ready to sail in September only five months away, and he also wanted 400 gunboats and 400 fishing boats in Boulogne harbor in the same month. With the English fleet parceled out in America, the West Indies and the Mediterranean, 40,000 French troops could cross the Channel from late October to late December (thus in darkness) and almost certainly succeed in landing on English beaches against virtually no resistance.[17]

This is a curious document but its content should not be rejected out of hand. Was it momentary fantasy or strategic insight? We believe it to be the latter and that it explains Napoleon's ambiguous answer when asked by Bourrienne how long they would be gone. "A few months," he replied, "or six years; it all depends on events."[18]

Whatever other thoughts were flowing in this turbulent mind, they did not hinder the work of the moment. As April drew to a close the immense armada consisting of six different convoys each with naval shepherds was ready to sail from as many ports to a destination still unknown but to a few.

Napoleon was on the point of leaving Paris for Toulon – he had written the naval commander, Vice Admiral Paul Brueys, to prepare "a good bed for a man who will be seasick for the entire journey" – but a last-minute diplomatic wrangle that threatened a new war with Austria kept him in Paris until early May when the crisis passed.[19]

Traveling incognito with Joséphine he reached Toulon to be recognized almost at once by soldiers whom in an impromptu harangue he compared to those of the Roman legions and who cheered his proclaimed promise of "great destinies to fulfill, battles to fight, dangers, fatigues to overcome."[20] A week of final feverish orders followed before he kissed Joséphine good-bye and boarded the flagship L'Orient. Early on 19 May 1798, the escorts weighed anchor followed by the main convoy of some 200 sails.

Notes

1   Corr. III. Nr. 2392, Paris, 26 December 1797.
2   Corr. III. Nr. 2385, Paris, 10 December 1797. See also Talleyrand, I, 259–60.
3   Bourrienne, I, 109–13; Iung (Bonaparte), III, 241.
4   Bourrienne, I, 112.
5   Ludwig, 110–11.
6   Thiry (Egypt), 21.
7   Corr. III. Nrs. 2386–2419, Paris, 12 December 1797–23 February 1798.
8   Napoleon later claimed that he had already written off the English landing and that his trip to the coast was camouflage to cover preparations for the Egyptian expedition. See Corr. XXIX. "Campagne d'Egypte et De Syrie," 362–3. This was dictated almost twenty years after the event and does not jibe with his writings of 1798 nor with contemporary statements of concerned persons. See also Marmont, I, 347–8; Boulay, 708.
9   Corr. III. Nr. 2419, Paris, 23 February 1798.
10 Corr. III. Nr. 2419, Paris, 23 February 1798.
11 Corr. VIII. Nr. 6976, Namur, 4 August 1803. One of his generals sent Napoleon Leibnitz's manuscript proposing this expedition. "This work is very curious," Napoleon replied.

12　Benoit, 16, 20. See also Talleyrand, I, 262–3.
13　Corr. IV. Nr. 2426, Paris, 5 March 1798. See also Corr. IV. Nrs. 2427–2540, Paris, 5 March–22 April 1798, which cover most logistical and operational aspects.
14　Bourrienne, I, 117–18.
15　Corr. IV. Nr. 2458, Paris, 28 March 1798.
16　Corr. IV. Nrs. 2491, 2496, Paris, 12 April 1798.
17　Corr. IV. Nr. 2502, Paris, 13 April 1798.
18　Bourrienne, I, 120.
19　General Bernadotte had been sent as ambassador to Vienna, an unfortunate choice in view of his revolutionary fanaticism and known arrogance. Worsening relations reached crisis proportions when, in protest against a Viennese celebration in honor of soldiers who had fought in Italy, he hoisted an enormous tri-color flag marked *"Liberté, Egalité, Fraternité,"* over his embassy and hosted a dinner to honor French victories in Italy. A furious crowd pushed into the embassy, broke windows and managed to tear down and burn the French flag. Bernadotte was ingloriously hustled out of the capital under military guard. Paris hotly protested, but after mutual saber-clanking the affair was finally settled by Talleyrand and Thugut.
20　Corr. IV. Nr. 2570, Toulon, 10 May 1798.

CHAPTER TWENTY-FIVE

THE CONQUEST OF EGYPT – I:
THE BATTLE OF THE PYRAMIDS
APRIL–JULY 1798

Soldiers! Forty centuries are looking down on you.

Napoleon to his troops prior to the battle of
the Pyramids, 21 July 1798

THE NAVAL OPERATION went well, the ships sailing close to the beautiful Italian coast, a precaution against the reported presence of Admiral Horatio Nelson's feared squadron. The weather held fair, the winds favorable with an occasional calm as smaller craft joined the convoy, now an armada of some 400 vessels sailing slowly but smoothly past the coasts of Sardinia, Sicily and Pantelleria – still no sign of enemy warships.

Despite fears of *mal-de-mer* Napoleon soon left his "good bed" (and extremely comfortable quarters) to instruct inexperienced sailors in cannon drill (the ship carried 120 guns) or to promenade while a band played lively military airs. He spent evenings in long conversations with civilian savants on a wide variety of subjects – science, philosophy, history, religion – his opinions dominating the proceedings. Even before sailing he had dictated the organization of the covering battle squadrons to Admiral Brueys to whom he also gave his views on naval battle tactics: "What I say is perhaps contrary to standard procedures in some circumstances" but he nevertheless went on to defend his words. At times he seemed pensive, walking the quarter-deck, contemplating sea and sky; at times he took to bed and had an aide read to him; on occasion he prowled the ship, talking to soldiers and sailors, questioning petty

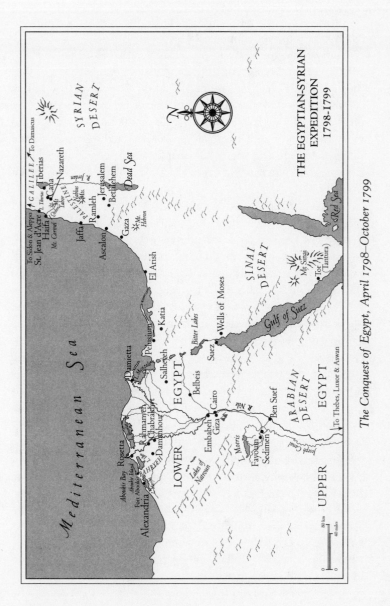

The Conquest of Egypt, April 1798–October 1799

officers and officers, often displaying an impressive knowledge of technical details and shipboard lore.[2]

The voyage to Malta lasted just over three uneventful and tedious weeks. Napoleon had a good idea of what he would find there, his interest in the island having begun during the Italian campaign. French spies in one form or another had been reporting on the dictatorial but now shaky rule of the old chevaliers who were out of favor with a population that had paid too much tribute for too long. He also knew that, thanks to his agent Poussielgue's work, some French members of the Order of St. John favored a French takeover.

He was taking no chances however. No sooner was the island fortress in sight on 9 June than he ordered Admiral Brueys to deploy his ships around perimeter forts, a move followed by troops landing and quickly seizing the dilapidated structures, an easy task since their dispirited defenders fled panic-stricken into the town. Initial germs of fear quickly produced an epidemic of surrender. Several centuries of rule disappeared overnight. As reward the Grand Master and his cooperative chevaliers received European sanctuary, generous pensions and indemnities for property losses. Napoleon in turn gained a necessary advance base whose armories held 1,200 cannon, 30,000 muskets, 7,000 barrels of powder, a splendid harbor, two warships and four galleys holding 700 chained Turkish slaves, a capital protected by granite walls so thick that Napoleon was horrified by the thought of assaulting them, a remark answered by his senior engineer, the one-legged General Louis Maximilien Caffarelli, "Yes, General, we are fortunate that there is someone within to open the gates for us."[3]

After garrisoning the island with 4,000 French troops commanded by General Vaubois, Napoleon reorganized its government, created municipal committees and local courts, abolishing feudal laws, proclaiming citizen equality and other such measures – all at the expense of the Knights whose treasury and private funds amounted to around 5 million francs. Most of the loot went to Paris, some to local administrations, but Napoleon added 700,000 francs to his war chest, much of it in gold and silver ingots from melted-down religious relics. He also took a corps of about 2,000 Maltese troops aboard ship along with the liberated Turkish slaves and some younger knights.

Nine days after its arrival the armada, decks loaded with juicy Maltese oranges, weighed anchor: destination Alexandria, Egypt.

The voyage to Alexandria lasted thirteen days. The weather remained fair, winds favorable. Napoleon used his time in drawing up a series of complicated landing orders that demonstrated an intimate knowledge not only of units and commanders but also of the target area. The latter could only have come from intelligence reports, probably from the French consul at Alexandria and from merchant ship captains and commercial travelers. He also dictated a stack of contingency orders that covered the establishment of hospitals and lazarets, police units and disciplinary arrangements, and pay and quartermaster procedures.

Shortly before arrival the soldiers learned that they were going to deliver the peoples of Egypt from the tyrannical rule of the Mameluke beys, the first step in setting the stage for England's final demise. "You are going to undertake a conquest of which the effects on world civilization and commerce will be incalculable. You will give England the most positive and painful blow before delivering the death blow."[4] Long marches and battles were to come, but the troops were to remember that this was a colonizing expedition, its mission to win over the "common people" while turning the country into a prosperous French colony. The common people were Mohammedans who believed that "there is no other God than God, and Mahomet is his prophet."[5] French soldiers were at all times to respect religious beliefs and practices, they were to leave the women alone, they were not to pillage nor extort money nor ever to gather in front of or enter a mosque. Those found guilty of rape or pillage would be shot. The crime of a man would be the crime of his unit which would be held responsible for identifying him. If the guilty one was not discovered, financial restitution would be taken from the company pay-chest.

Two other proclamations were distributed, each translated into Arabic. The first was directed to the ordinary people and was similar to those earlier distributed to the Lombardians and the Venetians, the gist being that the French had come to liberate and protect, not to oppress, to build, not to destroy. The Mameluke tyrants must be driven from the land which would be returned to its former prosperity and beauty. Accordingly the people should receive the soldiers as friends. Villagers must turn in their arms, swear obedience to the new rulers and fly the French tri-color next to the Turkish flag. Any village resisting French rule would be burned. The people were to continue normal religious practices led by sheiks, magistrates and priests: "Each person will thank God for the destruction of the Mamelukes and will cry: Glory to the Sultan! Glory to the French army, his friend! a curse on the Mamelukes and happiness to the peoples of Egypt!"[6] These words were to be carried into the country by the Turkish galley slaves freed in Malta. At the same time, a Turkish officer would secretly carry a personal letter to the pasha in Cairo who would learn that Napoleon promised to oust the Mamelukes and return the country to the Turkish sultan's authority.[7]

As with most amphibious landings, ancient or modern, the invaders received a host of surprises on the first day of July 1798. One was the discovery of hidden reefs along the western coast that prohibited dispersed landings, the second a sudden upsurge of wind that kicked up a cruel sea dangerously crowded with ships. Under normal circumstances the landing should either have been delayed or, perhaps better, transferred to Aboukir Bay east of the target area. But that morning Napoleon had learned from the French consul that three days earlier Horatio Nelson had turned up with a powerful squadron to seek provisions, water and information concerning the French fleet. Refused on all counts – the Mameluke commandant thought that his ships might have been carrying Turkish troops to seize the port – Nelson had scuttled off to the northeast. But who knew when one of his ships or even the entire squadron would return?

Napoleon's priority now was to get his troops and guns ashore as rapidly as possible. The third surprise was the amount of time that task required. The *chaloupes* or small landing craft were launched only in late afternoon, an awkward business which claimed a score of lives from drowning. The first troops landed late that evening, mostly seasick men clutching heavy muskets and weighed down with 60 cartridges, a canteen of water, clothes and rations for four days. Only token forces of the three spearhead divisions reached shore by dark, Menou and Kléber each with 1,000 men and Bon with 1,500. Napoleon landed about 3 a.m., reviewed the troops under a bright moon, then ordered a march on Alexandria some four miles away, leaving Desaix with a small force to hold the beachhead.

The fourth surprise consisted of hostile Arabs who dogged the columns throughout the night, firing on flanks and rear and beheading any soldier unfortunate enough to have fallen out of ranks. (Soldiers taken prisoner and returned a few days later reported "grotesque and horrible" details of the sexual customs of these men of the desert.)[8] The small force reached Alexandria's walls by dawn soon to be hit with the fifth surprise, one of the hottest suns in the world that caused men to empty canteens that could not be refilled. Standing on the pedestal of Pompey's Pillar, the 88-foot-high red marble column, Napoleon noted "the jagged wall of the Arab fort . . . the minarets of the city, the masts of a Turkish caravelle moored in the port." Then the attack kicked off, Kléber's grenadiers on the left storming neglected but stubbornly defended walls, Bon's people battering in Rosetta gate, Menou's men thrusting into the fortress complex, difficult and often bloody tasks watched by Napoleon from the pillar where he and sweat-soaked aides, having run out of water, assuaged thirst with carefully horded Maltese oranges before following the troops into the village.

House-to-house fighting continued into the afternoon with

"each house a citadel" in Napoleon's words, but now the commandant, Mohammed el-Koraïm, with a small force, was pushed into the lighthouse fortress – once Alexander the Great's *pharos*, one of the Seven Wonders of the World – from where he wisely capitulated. The battle cost the French perhaps 40 dead and 100 wounded. Menou had been shot or struck by rocks no fewer than seven times and Kléber had received a head wound.[9]

Napoleon opened his new headquarters in the village on the following day. Kléber was appointed military commander who, once recovered, would rule through a governor, the former commandant el-Koraïm, and a divan or small committee of prominent locals. Napoleon carefully spelled out his ruling policy to Kléber: "It is necessary to accustom these people little by little to our views and opinions, meanwhile allowing them great latitude in their interior affairs, above all not to interfere with their system of justice which, being entirely founded on the divine laws, follows the precepts of the Koran."[10] Kléber's priority projects were to establish two hospitals for the troops, one for the sick, the other for the wounded, and to set up printing presses to turn out 4,000 copies of Napoleon's proclamation in Arabic.

Napoleon meanwhile was coping with further surprises. Admiral Brueys had failed to block the "new" port with the result that hordes of local boats, the *djermes*, loaded with produce, had fled along with four large merchantmen, thus earning the admiral a reprimand. Napoleon was still very much concerned with Nelson's whereabouts. "It is indispensable," he informed Brueys, "to moor the ships so as to be able to maneuver in accordance with any future events, and to protect against the superior forces that the English could have in these waters." Brueys was to sound the "old" port and if the depth were satisfactory to anchor his fleet there. If not he was to unload all troops, artillery and supplies as rapidly as possible and then drop anchor in Aboukir Bay, providing he could defend himself there. Otherwise he was to take the bulk of his warships to Corfu.[11] In the event, the entrance to the old harbor was judged to be too shallow for the warships which Brueys then anchored in the bay.

In the interim Napoleon had made precarious peace with local Arab chieftains whose men earlier had harassed the French columns. In return for their cooperation he promised, once master of Egypt, to restore their former lands, a gesture that resulted in his purchase of 300 horses, 500 camels, rental of another 1,000 camels with drivers and the release of twelve French prisoners. Having fashioned a rudimentary administration in Alexandria he turned to the march on Cairo.

Desaix's division with Reynier's in support already had been sent south to Damanhour about 35 miles inland. Menou was now assigned to command Rosetta province from where Dugua's division, aided by naval Captain Perrée and General Andréossy's river flotilla of armed *chebecs* – small three-masted ships with overhanging bow and stern – would parallel the main army's march to Cairo.

Napoleon was correctly anticipating a major battle with the Mameluke hordes. On 3 July when he was still fretting because neither his few cavalry mounts nor the rest of his cannon had been unloaded he advised Desaix in the unlikely event of an enemy attack "to screen your cavalry, show the enemy only your infantry platoons . . . do not use your light artillery. It is necessary to save it for the great day when we shall have to fight four or five thousand enemy horse."[12]

The message reached Desaix as his troops were plodding on over land which was hard and parched owing to the Nile's stubborn refusal to flood, the allure of Damanhour, described as grander than anything Italy offered, before their eyes. What a frustrating business it was. They kept seeing lakes and villages in the distance only to disappear as they approached. (The phenomenon of the mirage was not yet known to the western world.) But finally there was Damanhour in flesh and blood. Damanhour! A filthy little stinking village but at least it furnished water and shade, a grove of date palms, fresh vegetables and meat to fill empty stomachs before the trudge to the next village of El Rahmanyeh.

Despite delays and frustrations Napoleon marched with the bulk of the army on 6 July. The march was another horror of thirst, hunger and infuriating mirages. His new friends, the Arab chiefs, meanwhile had received a *fetfa* or decree from the *ulémas* or clerical magistrates in Cairo who ordered them to take up arms against the infidels. Overnight the promised horses and camels vanished to be replaced by 1,800 bloodthirsty enemy. Riding swift, agile horses, hiding in the least wrinkle of land, they struck like lightning from flank and rear to mutilate and kill luckless laggards, to keep exhausted columns on weary alert as they stumbled on under burning sun with neither water nor wine to assuage soul-consuming thirst. "We were crushed by thirst and exhaustion," François Bernoyer reported to his beloved in France. "My throat was parched, my breath a burning vapor."[13] As Napoleon would later write, "Everything to the soldier was new, and everything was unpleasant."[14]

Owing to the heat and lack of water – Desaix's advance columns had emptied some wells, marauding Bedouins had filled others with rocks and sand – the troops suffered terribly, some dying from dehydration, some committing suicide. Somehow the rest held out for another few days to join Desaix's force at El Rahmanyeh on the Nile, officers and men racing the last few hundred yards while peeling off sweat-encrusted uniforms to plunge into the cooling water.

Their joy was brief. Napoleon had learned from spies that the principal Mameluke commander, Mourad-Bey, had reached the village of Chabrakhyt on the Nile with 3,000 Mameluke horse and 2,000 Janissaries or foot soldiers supported by two artillery batteries and a fleet of 60 boats of which 25 were armed; he was followed by Ibrahim-Bey commanding another smaller Mameluke force.

Though woefully short of cavalry – only 200 lame mounts – on the night of 12 July the French marched to meet the enemy while Perrée and Andréossy were ordered to attack the enemy flotilla with their small fleet.

Mourad-Bey's right, consisting of mounted Mamelukes, rested on the village, a line extended into the desert by about 2,000

Arabs, a total 15–18,000 warriors including swarms of Bedouins who buzzed around French flanks and rear. Napoleon deployed his army in a line a little over two miles long; his left on a village close to the Nile, his right on a village near to the desert. Desaix who held the right formed his division into battalion squares about 300 yards across the front and 50 yards on the sides. Vial (commanding in place of the wounded Menou) similarly deployed on the left as did the three other divisions across the line at 6–700-yard intervals, with the reserve some 2,000 yards to the rear holding defended villages. Of 36 cannon in line, 18 could fire on the same point.

The field remained quiet for several hours. There was no sign of Perrée's fleet, the fault of an adverse wind. From time to time isolated combats took place, a Mameluke or two attacking an advanced post of *tirailleurs*: "The Mameluke displayed all his skill and courage," Napoleon later wrote. ". . . He was one with his horse which appeared to share all his wishes; the saber hanging from the wrist, he held his carbine, his blunderbuss, his four pistols, and, having fired six weapons he outflanked the platoon of sharpshooters and passed between them and the line with wonderful dexterity."[15] These preliminaries over, the French watched seven richly clad chiefs confer on a small hillock.

The magnificently dressed warriors riding "perhaps the best horses on the continent" immediately attacked, repeatedly striking front, flank and rear of battalion squares without penetrating the hedgehog formations of bristling bayonets supported by devastating musket and artillery fire. After suffering an estimated 300 casualties the Mamelukes broke off the fight, disappearing as suddenly as they had appeared.

Perrée's ships meanwhile arrived to begin a fierce battle as his small fleet closed on enemy boats only to be outgunned. Seeing the problem, Napoleon moved the army forward, the Mamelukes looking on from a distance, the Arabs fleeing after some resistance. Musket and cannon fire soon rescued the beleaguered fleet, the enemy boats either sailing off or being sunk or captured. It was a narrow escape. Perrée was wounded. Berthollet and Monge, the leaders of the civilian contingent who were on a chebec which was sunk, were saved only with difficulty. Of a total 3–400 French casualties three-quarters were sailors.

This brief action was only a prelude to the big battle so heartily desired by Napoleon who at once continued the march on Cairo, another eight days of burning heat, limited water and biscuit rations, no wine, an occasional grove of date palms, the troops mainly surviving on a fruit new to them, the *pastéque* or water-melon which grew profusely but caused severe diarrhea unless the flesh was boiled. Napoleon later wrote feelingly about this march constantly harassed by Arabs, the troops hating everything about Egypt, the stupid peasants, the plains without shade, the wretched Nile of dirty, muddy water, the ugly and ferocious Bedouins, their women dirtier still. The soldiers grew increas-ingly melancholy and some drowned themselves in the Nile.

On 20 July when 15 miles south of Cairo, Napoleon learned that the combined forces of 23 Mameluke beys with 60 cannon were entrenched near the village of Embabeh not far from the famous Pyramids of antiquity.

At dawn the following day the French advance guard ran into enemy posts and pushed on to the main position. The rest of the army closed the field about 9 a.m. The French soldiers were look-ing at some 6,000 of Mourad-Bey's Mamelukes, each attended by three or four foot servants, drawn up on the western or left bank of the Nile, their left on the village of Giza, their right of about 20,000 foot troops resting on Embabeh, a rudely entrenched line seven or eight miles long. They looked on at least 40 cannon, and some of them saw beyond Giza in the direction of the Pyramids thousands of rudely armed Janissaries, Arabs, Coptics, Abyssinians and peasant *fellahin* – those whom the French had come to liberate – who stretched the line another few miles. Behind that unpleasant-looking host a large fleet of Arab gunboats guarded the river, and across the river were another 1,000 or so mounted Mamelukes commanded by Ibrahim-Bey, not to mention thousands of civilians, men, women and children, who had come from Cairo to watch the slaughter of the infidels.

As the soldiers stared perhaps they discerned Mourad's richly decorated tent, perhaps they watched him riding the line, greeting each bey, telling the warriors that this was a battle for Egypt's (and their) survival, that Allah had sent this miserable dust-covered, tired and hungry rabble as meat for flashing scimitars – all glory to Allah.

And as the Mamelukes stared at their enemy perhaps they saw Napoleon followed by his staff officers and aides riding the line, greeting each general, repeatedly invoking the troops to do their duty for army and France, a dramatic performance climaxed by his pointing to the Pyramids and declaring: "Soldiers! Forty centuries are looking down on you."[16]

Napoleon chose to fight the big battle with tactics similar to those employed at Chabrakhyt (which must have seemed an eternity ago to his exhausted troops). This time there would be no fleet action owing to an adverse wind. Divisions deployed in echelons of mutually protective battalion squares, the artillery filling the intervals, the *tirailleurs* carefully placed. Moving up toward Embabeh, moving toward Mourad's horsemen, he deployed Bon on the left, Vial on the right and Dugua in reserve on Vial's flank (where Napoleon stationed himself). Reynier and Desaix's divisions deployed ahead and to the right of the assault divisions to block what Napoleon believed was Mourad's natural line of retreat. This move caused the Mameluke commander to open the action by sending a corps to attack Reynier and Desaix.

Although surprised, the brigades quickly deployed in battalion squares, the troops holding steady, showing great courage as enemy hooves thundered through packed sand up to fifty yards from their ranks. Grenadiers and gunners stood ready, a few fell, the rest waited patiently for the command to open fire. The command was given, slaughter ensued. The survivors fell back, regrouped, brave men who tried again, this time aiming for intervals between squares. But now flanking fire barked a loud farewell to drive what was left of them from the field.

Bataille des Pyramides

Napoleon next moved Bon on the Embabeh defenses with Vial coming up to cover him. Bon's columns commanded by Rampon were assaulting enemy defenses when Mourad-Bey sent in a fresh corps which attacked at full gallop, riders screaming, scimitars gleaming. The French columns halted and faced to the front, bayonets at the level, while supporting squares fired muskets and cannon to create more carnage and send the Mamelukes into frenzied retreat up river toward Giza. But Vial had blocked their route with a battalion of sharp-shooting *carabiniers* who either killed the victims or forced them to jump into the Nile where they drowned.

Thus the battle of the Pyramids, which lasted only a few hours and was a clear victory for the French. Mourad and remnant followers escaped southward into Upper Egypt. Ibrahim-Bey, whose horsemen had not joined the fighting, fled eastward with his small corps, taking the Turkish pasha with him. At Mourad-Bey's orders the fleet was set on fire which devoured quantities of weapons and provisions not to mention a vast fortune of gold lost for ever on the river bottom.

Napoleon's subsequent report to the Directory claimed the lives of 2,000 Mamelukes and countless *fellahin* and Janissaries at a cost of some 30 French soldiers killed and 120 wounded. The French captured 50 cannon and 400 camels laden with rich personal baggage. The victors were amazed at the richness of the clothing worn by the fallen – elaborate silks thickly embroidered with gold and silver, the pockets holding at least 300 and sometimes 500 gold louis of immense value. Soldiers who had seized an Arabian horse were paid five louis for each mount, the beasts going to the still almost immobile cavalry.

The general in chief was particularly pleased with the tactical transition of the brigades in this "entirely new type of war" which demanded great coolness and patience foreign to the impetuous character of the French soldiers. As he had supposed, artillery played a vital role in the victory – its chief, Dommartin of Toulon days, was promoted to general of division. In the following weeks scores of officers and men would receive well-earned promotions and other rewards for heroic deeds. Unfortunately for the soldiers, this was a mere sample of what would soon follow.

Notes

1   Corr. IV. Nr. 2816, 21 July 1798.
2   Corr. IV. Nr. 2540, Paris, 22 April 1798. See also Bernoyer, 17–21.
3   Benoit, 59. See also Marmont, I, 358–61.
4   Corr. IV. Nr. 2710, *L'Orient*, 22 June 1798.
5   Corr. IV. Nr. 2710, *L'Orient*, 22 June 1798. See also Bernoyer, 44.
6   Corr. IV. Nrs. 2712, *L'Orient*, 24 June 1798; 2723, Alexandria, 2 July 1798.
7   Corr. IV. Nrs. 2719, *L'Orient*, 30 June 1798; 2734, Alexandria, 3 July 1798.
8   Corr. XXIX, 433; Marmont, I, 374.
9   Corr. IV. Nr. 2765, Alexandria, 6 July 1798. See also Bernoyer, 46.
10   Corr. IV. Nr. 2778, Alexandria, 7 July 1798.
11   Corr. IV. Nr. 2728, Alexandria, 3 July 1798.
12   Corr. IV. Nr. 2724, Alexandria, 3 July 1798.
13   Bernoyer, 50.
14   Corr. XXIX, 439.
15   Corr. XXIX, 442–3. See also Miot (Jacques), 63–4, whose detailed description of the Mameluke bridle suggests use of a choke-bit.
16   Corr. IV. Nr. 2816, 21 July 1798. Napoleon's words have frequently been challenged, but are confirmed in a letter home written by Bernoyer on 22 July 1798 – see Bernoyer, 59.

CHAPTER TWENTY-SIX

THE CONQUEST OF EGYPT – II:
THE GREAT SULTAN
JULY–AUGUST 1798

*Only those who saw him in the vigor of his youth can form an
idea of his extraordinary intelligence and activity. Nothing
escaped his observation . . . in a few weeks he was as well
acquainted with the country [Egypt] as if he had lived in
it for ten years.*

Louis Antoine Bourrienne, Napoleon's secretary[1]

NAPOLEON SPENT THREE days in Giza from where he published
another proclamation that promised to protect the people against
the villainous Mamelukes while fully respecting their liberty and
religion. He received here a steady flow of notables from Cairo
who were assured of his peaceful intentions to build a new and
prosperous Egypt.

Having won the battle of the Pyramids, Napoleon turned to the
defense of his conquests against Mameluke remnants and sympathizers, Arab brigands, Bedouin marauders, Turkish rebels, the
British navy and in due course the Turkish empire. He at once
sent General Desaix five miles south to build a fortress complex
guarding the Nile. Giza was turned into an armed camp and Cairo
defended by forces based in the citadel commanded by General
Dupuy. Captain Perrée's boats prowled the Nile to safeguard communications with the sea whose ports, Alexandria, Damietta and
Rosetta were garrisoned accordingly, along with major towns in
the neighboring provinces.

Once removed to elegant headquarters in Cairo, a bey's mansion off the great square of Ezbekyeh, he turned to administration. Known now to the Egyptians as the Sultan El Kaber (the Great Sultan) he appointed a divan of nine sheiks to govern Cairo, to build hospitals, police markets and slaughterhouses, purify the stinking air by burying the dead who were often left rotting in the streets, and cleaning up the most filthy areas.

Each occupied province was headed by a French general called a governor-commandant who ruled through a divan of seven notables. As had been the case under Mameluke rule the collection of taxes was entrusted to an intendant, usually a literate Coptic who was also to teach his French counterpart "the customs and language of the country."[2] The new governors were to see that villagers swore obedience to the new masters and that the French tri-color flew overhead. They were also to disarm the villagers to prevent local wars, build hospitals and roads, map the countryside and chart the Nile, reorganize civil and criminal courts in favor of justice and perform countless other tasks for the people's good.

All this would not be easy. Expecting to find treasuries like those he had plundered in Italy, Napoleon instead found very little cash. Expecting to buy thousands of horses to mount his cavalry and pull his guns, he found very few. Expecting to build limbers for cannon and palisade defenses for forts and outposts, he found almost no wood.

Shortage of cash was a major factor in his ultimate undoing. Napoleon and the Directory had expected the occupation to pay for itself and more. He had landed with somewhere between 1 and 4 million francs in cash, yet he was looking at an army-civil payroll of about a million francs a month not to mention enormous expenditures for provisions, uniforms, weapons and transport. Although he had gained a plethora of grains, rice, vegetables and sheep, he could not pay the troops in produce. In desperation he ordered Kléber in return for produce to redeem the silver and gold ingots that had been taken from Malta and sold to Alexandrian merchants; the Cairo mint would turn them into coins. Meanwhile his governors were to scour their provinces and

seize Mameluke houses, warehouses, goods and cash. He allowed
Mameluke wives to return to their mansions in Cairo but in turn
they must pay contributions, in the case of Mourad's wife 600,000
francs, lacking which she would be reduced to living in an apartment tended by only six slaves.[3] In short order governors were
levying hefty contributions on rich merchants: those of Damas to
pay 100,000 talari (about 500,000 francs), those of Damietta
150,000 francs, those of Rosetta 100,000. French commandants
were also to requisition horses to mount the cavalry, camels to
carry ammunition and rations on patrols, and boats to ship produce from Cairo to the Mediterranean ports.

These severe measures which stood at odds with all the splendid words of various proclamations were not well received. Tax
collections lagged in all provinces. Cash contributions were either
non-existent or slow in delivery. Horses, camels and boats of all
kinds mysteriously disappeared in hidden reaches, as did entire
herds of cattle and sheep.

For a brief time Napoleon rolled with events. If cash was short
then provisions would have to suffice. In early August, ironically
as we shall see, he ordered Admiral Brueys to send ships loaded
with produce to Malta to bring back 220,000 lbs of biscuit,
100,000 pints of wine, 30,000 pints of vinegar, 30,000 pints of
brandy and 65,000 lbs of lard. His governor at Malta, General
Vaubois, was to establish a bartering service with local merchants
for future supply of "the largest possible quantity of wine, brandy,
dry raisins and wood" – objects entirely lacking in Egypt – in
return for "coffee, sugar, indigo, grains and all types of merchandise of the Indies." It was only a matter of time, he believed, until
the Directory would send him money and soldiers along with
a troop of actors, ballerinas, 100 French women, wives of his
soldiers, 20 surgeons, 30 pharmacists, 10 physicians, some blacksmiths, distillers, 100 gardeners with families and all types of
seed. Each convoy from France would carry 200,000 pints of
brandy, 1 million pints of wine, thousands of yards of cloth, and
soap and cooking oil.[4]

This was in the future of course. But Napoleon had to live in the present and as local opposition mounted and problems rolled back on him like the boulder on Sisyphus his temper grew short. As had happened in Italy his somewhat naïve optimism regarding liberated natives soon collided with ugly reality. Before leaving Alexandria he had informed the Directory in Paris that "this nation is nothing less than that portrayed by travelers and writers: it is quiet, proud and brave." This happy appraisal scarcely jibed with Arabs beheading laggard troops or kidnapping civilian scientists who once ransomed (if lucky) reported gross sexual violations on their bodies by Arab males.

Napoleon presumably regarded such events as acceptable blips in the colonizing process, for on 10 July he wrote General Dugua that "the country is superb. All goes well for us here." He was not quite so upbeat after the battle of the Pyramids when from his new headquarters in Cairo he informed the Directory:

> It is difficult to see a country more fertile and a people
> more miserable, more ignorant and more stupid. They
> prefer to have a soldier's button to an *ecu* worth six francs.
> The villagers have no knowledge of scissors. Their houses
> are a bit of mud furnished only with a straw mat and three
> or four earthen pots. They eat and in general consume very
> little of anything. They don't know how to use grinding
> mills so that we have constantly bivouacked on immense
> piles of grain without being able to have flour. We eat only
> vegetables and meat. The little flour they have is made by
> stones or in some larger villages by mills turned by cattle.

Moreover, he went on, "we have been constantly harassed by groups of Arabs who are the biggest thieves and scoundrels in the world, assassinating any Turks or French who fall in their hands. General of Brigade Mireur and several aides and general staff officers have been murdered by these wretches. Hidden behind dikes and in ditches on their excellent small horses – woe to any [French] who are further than a hundred yards from the columns."[5]

As Napoleon soon discovered, the Turks were proving as hostile as Arabs and Mamelukes. He responded as he had done in Italy, first with repeated threats and then with brute force. "It is necessary that you treat the Turks with the greatest severity," he informed one governor. "Every day here I have three heads cut off and displayed in Cairo: this is the only way to subdue these people." (A few days later he congratulated the governor for having five rebels shot.)[6]

Upon leaving France, Napoleon supposed that his conquest would be welcomed or at least condoned by both the sultan in Constantinople and his deputy, the impotent Turkish pasha in Cairo. Whatever doubts the sultan held, Napoleon reasoned, would be assuaged by the persuasive presence in Constantinople of the new French ambassador, Monsieur Talleyrand.

Nelson's cruisers having effectively severed communications between France and Egypt, Napoleon had no way of knowing that Talleyrand was still in Paris, never having intended to leave the center of power for a distant capital. Nor could he know that English, Austrian and Russian envoys had persuaded the Turkish sultan to abandon his traditional alliance and declare war on France, which he would do in August.

The net result was that the favorable *firmans* or decrees anticipated and desperately needed by Napoleon were never written: instead, sheiks and peasants were ordered to fight the infidels. In early August, Napoleon learned that a number of sheiks had joined their forces to the Mameluke nuclei who were becoming increasingly active in their respective areas. Hoping to neutralize the Mameluke leaders Napoleon sent the Austrian consul in Rosetta on a secret mission to Mourad in Upper Egypt to inform him that it was in Napoleon's interest "for Mourad-Bey to serve as my right arm." If Mourad stopped attacking French forces Napoleon would appoint him governor of a province over which he would exercise complete autonomy and in time would offer him "great advantages."[7] Mourad eventually spurned the peace tentative and, as we shall see, General Desaix spent the better part of a year trying to run him to ground – without success.

(J. Christopher Herold tells the exciting story well in his book, *Bonaparte in Egypt*.)

Napoleon fared no better in rooting out Ibrahim-Bey, whose Mamelukes had also been joined by peasant forces of several Arab sheiks. When this corps attacked General Leclerc's cavalry division Napoleon responded by leading a punitive expedition composed of Lannes and Dugua's divisions some 75 miles eastward to Ibrahim's headquarters in the village of Salheyeh on the edge of the Syrian desert. The expedition almost captured the Mameluke leader who after a brisk battle (in which he was wounded) fled into the desert with his followers and his immense treasury. Napoleon next sent him a peace offer similar to that received by Mourad-Bey, with an equally negative result. Meanwhile Napoleon began converting Salheyeh into a major fort garrisoned by Reynier's division which was to open road communications with Damietta and send numerous spies into Syria.

Having received no reply from Ibrahim, Napoleon started back to Cairo. He had not proceeded very far when a courier brought news that his entire fleet of warships had been destroyed in Aboukir Bay by Horatio Nelson's fleet.

Nelson, Rear Admiral Sir Horatio – one of eleven children of a Norfolkshire parson; now 40 years old; went to sea as a boy, commissioned a lieutenant at 19, promoted to captain at 20, duty in the West Indies, the Arctic, the Indian Ocean and the Mediterranean; lost an eye at Corsica, an arm at Tenerife, won fame at the battle of Copenhagen, rewarded with a knighthood after the battle of Cape St. Vincent, and was promoted to rear admiral in 1797.

In May 1798 Admiral Lord Jervis, whose fleet was blockading Spanish warships in Cádiz, sent Nelson with three cruisers, two frigates and a sloop to see what the French were up to at Toulon. The ships were blown hither and yon by a north-westerly gale (whose aftermath ironically propelled Napoleon's convoys down the Italian coast). After recovering his warships (but not all of his frigates) and receiving additional vessels Nelson set out in pursuit, a cat-and-mouse effort frustrating in the extreme. He correctly believed that his quarry was heading for Egypt as the first step in a grand design of joining up with Tippo Sahib, the Sultan of Mysore, to push the British out of India. "Be they bound for the Antipodes," he assured the First Lord of the Admiralty, "Your Lordship may rely that I will not lose a moment in bringing them to action."[8]

All well and good, but first he had to find them. But where? Upon learning that Nelson was after him, Napoleon diverted the convoy toward Crete. Nelson passed his enemy only a few hours distant – at night. As the chase continued he grew frantic. He found nothing at Alexandria. Were the French even in the Mediterranean, he wondered? Perhaps Napoleon had slipped past Gibraltar to join the French fleet at Brest to carry out a threatened landing in England? Nelson sailed on to Sicily, learned nothing there, took on food and water and sailed for Greece. But now he learned that the French battle fleet was anchored in Aboukir Bay.

The information was correct. Some three weeks earlier Admiral Brueys had anchored his warships and frigates in this bay about fifteen miles east of Alexandria. This was in keeping with Napoleon's order of 3 July, the operative clause reading that, if it were not feasible to anchor the warships in the old port, Brueys should anchor in Aboukir Bay *providing* that he deemed it suitable for defense against a British attack. If not he should depart for Corfu.[9]

Vice Admiral François Paul Brueys d'Aigailliers, 45 years old, an aristocrat, officer of the old royal navy, served with distinction in the American revolutionary war, was promoted to captain in 1792, imprisoned by the Jacobins, eventually released but returned to active duty only in 1796. Landing at Venice the next year in command of a small squadron of Venetian ships seized at Corfu, he at once fell victim to Napoleon's charm and soon embraced his Alexandrian dream of conquering the East, at the same time fully subordinating himself to this general sixteen years his junior.

Brueys' decision to keep his warships anchored in Aboukir Bay seemed rather unwise in view of a detailed report on soundings of the old harbor made by a subordinate, Captain Barré, who concluded that the ships could pass the harbor entrance safely providing that the usual precautions were taken.[10] Brueys was not the most adventurous admiral in the world and Barré's report was somewhat equivocal. Brueys was within his rights to choose to remain in the bay, but in so doing he tacitly assumed responsibility for the safety of his ships, whether static at anchor or active at sea. He chose to remain static, at least for a time, against a possible enemy attack. This was sound enough considering the poor condition of three of his ships, his somewhat understaffed and inexperienced crews, his lack of trained cannoneers and his shortage of food and water, complaints that he had showered on Bourrienne among others.

It is one thing to make a sound decision, another to carry it out correctly. Brueys' first error was to anchor his ships at 50-yard intervals connected by cables in a line about a mile long and a mile and a half from shore. He believed that the enemy would not risk running aground on a protective sandbank by sailing shoreward on the port or left side of his lead ship, a passage further defended by guns on tiny Aboukir island and by a frigate and gunboats. In his mind this left the enemy no alternative other than to strike the right or starboard side of the line defended by some 500 cannon firing from static positions, with frigates and gunboats protecting the tail ships. Perhaps he chose this deployment in the belief that he could still go to sea if circumstances warranted, or if Napoleon suffered a severe land defeat and the army had to be evacuated.

That is not the point however. The point is that he deemed his deployment to constitute an adequate defense against an enemy attack. But working against this assumption was the long distance for small boats to carry shore parties sent to fetch water and food, the lack of food in the immediate beach area and the danger from marauding Arabs – by mid July several sailors had been killed in skirmishes. These and other minus factors should probably have persuaded him to seek safe sanctuary even at risk of running a ship aground. There is some evidence that he had decided on this course, having learned of Napoleon's victory at the battle of the Pyramids.[11]

Brueys was wrong and subsequent attempts to vindicate him and shift the blame on Napoleon are not very persuasive.[12] Either unknowingly or unprofessionally he had left a passage on the port side of his lead ship sufficient for an enemy warship to transit – there is no record that soundings were taken. The cannon placed on Aboukir island were of insufficient range for their mission – there is no record of test firing. By anchoring so far off shore he made provisioning all the more difficult. Finally, had he anchored in a tighter line closer to the shore he could have used at least two of his frigates as distant sentries to prevent a surprise attack.

In view of these shortcomings Napoleon is probably justified in a remark made many years later: "This would not have happened if I had been there."[13]

Nelson's prolonged and agonized search ended in early afternoon on 1 August when Captain Hood signaled that he had sighted the French squadron in Aboukir Bay. Nelson instantly ordered his captains to attack, telling them that "on the morrow . . . he would be either in the House of Lords [ennobled] or in Westminster Abbey]buried]." As his ships closed on the bay he signaled to strike the enemy's starboard fore and center and with that retired to his cabin "with a raging toothache."[14]

Lookouts perched high on the masts of French ships first saw enemy masts at about 2 p.m. Cannon were fired to recall working parties from the beach, an estimated 25–30 per cent of Brueys' 8,000 sailors, only a few of whom returned to their ships. Brueys aboard L'Orient had been ill with colic and dysentery for two weeks which could only have compounded his numerous problems and doubts. He had received no further orders from Napoleon, communications having been cut by hostile Arabs. He could not make up his mind whether to stay and if necessary to fight or to put out to sea. Prompted by his chief of staff, Admiral Ganteaume, and by two rear admirals, du Chuyla and Villeneuve, he chose to remain.

We can only sketch the battle – it has been told in lucid and horrifying detail by a host of able writers including Oliver Warner, J. Christopher Herold, A. Thomazi and Jacques Benoist-Méchin.[15] The opening and ultimately decisive blow was struck by Captain Foley of the *Goliath* who led the attack and who, seeing an anchor buoy between the lead French ship, *La Guerrier*, and the shore, cut sharply to starboard, shot through the narrow channel between the *Guerrier* and the shore, dropped anchor opposite the second French ship and opened a murderous fire, an incredibly daring feat followed immediately by Hood's *Zealous* and three more vessels while the remaining ships bored in on the seaward flank to anchor opposite forward and center enemy vessels. In but a short time enemy was facing enemy, each cannonading the other at minimal and brutal ranges, but the French getting it from both sides, a ghastly massacre witnessed by French sailors of the five rear ships under command of Rear Admiral Villeneuve who, having received no orders from Brueys, almost unbelievably took no part in the action.

The horrendous battle continued through the night, a give-and-take affair of dismasted and sunken ships, of disembodied and drowning men. Brueys was killed soon after the fighting started. Captain Casabianca of *L'Orient* was wounded but remained on the bridge with his nine-year-old midshipman son. Within two hours the 400-man crew of *Le Conquérant*, the second ship of the French line, had suffered 130 dead and nearly a hundred wounded. Nelson on the *Vanguard* received a scalp wound that bled so profusely he thought he was going to die. Pounded by British fire from port and starboard *L'Orient* soon caught fire and an hour or two later blew up, a tremendous explosion that rattled buildings in Alexandria and beyond – Casabianca and his son were blown to bits. At dawn on 2 August the French fleet was reduced to Villeneuve's flagship, *Guillaume Tell*, another warship

and two frigates, a pathetic remnant which escaped that afternoon.

French losses amounted to some 1,700 killed including one
admiral and three captains, 1,500 wounded including one admiral
and six captains and over 3,000 sailors taken prisoner (and later
released on parole). The British lost over 200 killed and nearly 700
wounded. Nine British ships were either totally or partially dismasted and three others were put out of action.[16]

Once Nelson's dead were buried and his ships patched up he
left three warships and three frigates to blockade Rosetta and
Alexandria, the others sailing to Gibraltar for major repairs.
Nelson himself was ordered to Naples where as Lord Nelson he
would soon commence a love affair with Lady Hamilton so passionate as to scorch itself on the pages of history for ever after.

Notes

1   Bourrienne, I, 143.
2   Corr. IV. Nrs. 2858, Cairo, 27 July 1798; 2868, 2870, Cairo, 28 July
    1798.
3   Corr. XXIX, 453. Eugène Beauharnais was sent to inform Madame
    Mourad of the levied contribution. Well received, he was given a
    tour of her splendid palace, shown its *serail* or harem of fifty
    women "of all countries and all colors," plus a splendid meal and a
    valuable ring.
4   Corr. IV. Nrs. 2874, Cairo, 28 July 1798; 2961, 2962, Cairo, 3
    August 1798.
5   Corr. IV. Nrs. 2765, Alexandria, 6 July 1798, 2793, El Rahmânyeh,
    10 July 1798; 2834, Cairo, 24 July 1798. See also Bernoyer, 57–8;
    Boulay, 283–92: the Directory did not receive this and subsequent
    dispatches. According to a letter from the Directory dated 4
    November 1798 (never received by Napoleon), it had received only
    one dispatch dated 19 August 1798 which arrived 14 October 1798.
6   Corr. IV. Nr. 2901, Cairo, 30 July 1798.
7   Corr. IV. Nr. 2920, Cairo, 1 August 1798.
8   Herold, 58.

9   Corr. IV. Nr. 2728, Alexandria, 3 July 1798. My italics.

10   Corr. XXIX, 462–3, for Barré's letter to Napoleon of 19 July 1798,
     which enclosed a copy of Barré's report to Brueys of 13 July 1798,
     and Brueys' reply to Barré of 21 July 1798. See also Boulay, 70–1;
     Corr. IV. Nr. 3259, Cairo, 8 September 1798; Corr. V. Nr. 3439,
     Cairo, 7 October 1798.

11   Corr. XXIX, 466–7. Napoleon at St. Helena claimed that he had
     received a letter dated 30 July 1798, from Brueys: Brueys had
     learned of the French victory at the Pyramids, he had found a pas-
     sage into the old port, buoys were laid and in a few days all would
     be secure.

12   See, for example, Herold, 106–7, who argues that Brueys could not
     have sailed for Corfu because his ships lacked food and water. How
     then did Villeneuve successfully do so immediately after the battle?

13   Thomazi, 51.

14   Herold, 111.

15   Herold, 111–22; Thomazi, 47–56; Benoist-Méchin, 119–148.

16   Herold, 118–22.

CHAPTER TWENTY-SEVEN

THE CONQUEST OF EGYPT – III:
COLONIZATION AND CONFLICT
AUGUST 1798–FEBRUARY 1799

Tell the commander in chief [Napoleon] to assemble all his
troops and go back to Alexandria. I shall pay him 10,000 gold
purses to cover his army's expenses. In doing so, he will spare
his soldiers' lives and save me the trouble of fighting him.

Mameluke leader Mourad-Bey's response to Napoleon's
peace offer, August 1798[1]

NAPOLEON LEARNED OF the naval tragedy during his return from
Salheyeh. Marmont was present and tells us that he received the
news calmly – a disaster, yes, he told his officers, but also a challenge to be met by developing local resources to make Egypt a
self-sufficient base until reinforcements arrived from France. Back
in Cairo he issued a series of damage-control measures: Admiral
Ganteaume to command what was left of the French fleet; General
Kléber to rush the arming of smaller craft in Alexandria harbor;
alert warnings to be sent to the Malta and Corfu garrisons;
Marmont's brigade to occupy Rosetta and prevent enemy landings.

If Napoleon were upset he hid it well in these and a flurry of
further communications. Although he must have realized that the
defeat would resound throughout Europe and the East, his diplomatic tentatives rang with his own invincibility. Under the
impression that Talleyrand was in Constantinople, Napoleon
wrote courteously but firmly to the sultan to extol the advantages
of continuing his traditional alliance with France by a suitable
treaty between the two countries. He sent an emissary with a sim-

ilar message to the governor of St. Jean d'Acre, Ahmed-Pasha Djezzar, and he informed the *sherif* of Mecca that all pilgrim caravans would be protected by French troops while in Egypt.[2]

As reports of the naval disaster filtered in he concluded that Brueys was the villain of the piece. Although he lightly scolded Villeneuve – "If one were to reproach you it would be for not having sailed immediately after the *Orient* blew up" – he also encouraged him to rebuild a battle fleet at Malta. He concluded however that "the generals [admirals] had been beaten rather than the squadron" and he insisted on the battle supremacy of the French fleet in normal circumstances.[3]

To Kléber in Alexandria he was almost cheerful in reporting that his recent foray had captured some of Ibrahim-Bey's cannon and had pushed the Mameluke leader back into Syria. General Desaix with a corps of about 3,000 strong would now go after Mourad-Bey in Upper Egypt while other divisions neutralized rebellious pro-Mameluke groups in the Delta interior. Less than six weeks after losing his fleet Napoleon informed the Directory in Paris that "all goes perfectly here. The country is obedient and is beginning to get used to us . . . I will not be able to be back in Paris in October as I have promised you; but this will only be delayed a few months."[4]

Napoleon's major concern remained that of security against British-Turkish landings, raids by desert Arabs, sneak attacks by villagers against couriers, isolated soldiers and land and river convoys. Coastal forts were daily reinforced and improved. Eighty cannon would soon guard land approaches and 70 more the sea approaches to Alexandria. The port was to stock provisions and munitions for a year. Similar plans were made to defend Rosetta and Damietta. Five hundred troops at the new fort of Salheyeh, Napoleon boasted, could hold "against all the forces of the Turks." In early November he pushed a force to the old desert fort of Katia about 30 miles east of Lake Manzala with orders to turn it into a strongly defended bastion.

Ten years earlier Lieutenant Bonaparte had studied Constantin Volney's *Voyage en Syrie et en Egypte* ("the sole work," Berthier later wrote, "that never led us astray."). Here he learned of Ptolemy's attempt to construct a canal from Suez to the Nile river. In November 1798 General Bonaparte sent General Bon with 1,200 infantry and 200 cavalry across the desert to Suez, a convoy of 1,000 camels carrying rations, water and firewood along with sections of four gunboats to be reassembled on arrival there. Napoleon followed with a team of scientists to explore the eastern shore of the Red Sea (intrigued by the Wells of Moses among other archeological treasures), then a successful search for Ptolemy's canal track.[5] We can only speculate as to the outcome of this exploration had the general not fallen victim to time and fate.

By early September the French flag was flying from the highest point in Cairo and from the tallest minarets in other cities and towns. Boats sailing the Nile flew the blue-white-red flag, and inhabitants wishing to gain favor wore the French *cocarde*. Chambers of commerce were opening in principal cities, provisional registry officers were beginning to record land transactions and issue birth certificates. Businesses, shops and restaurants were being licensed in towns and cities, native police departments established, roads built, canals dredged, windmills introduced, even a limited postal service in the northern provinces.

A major *fête* marked the important opening of the refurbished canal from Alexandria to the Nile and an elaborate countrywide extravaganza honored the birth of the Prophet. City officials were ordered to establish tended garbage and sewage dumps. Cairo was to have street lighting and a hospital for poor Arabs. Armed patrols roamed the provinces not only to discourage or punish local uprisings but, aided by civilian scientists and artists, to investigate scientific phenomena and record major terrain features, village populations, distances between towns, canal depths and roads, data necessary for the drawing of accurate maps.

Napoleon's pet project, the Institute of Egypt for Arts and Sciences, was launched in Cairo with great fanfare. Gaspard Monge was president, Napoleon vice president. Each of its four sections – mathematics, physics, political economy, and literature and arts – was composed of twelve members appointed by Napoleon. Senior members were paid 4–500 livres a month, the most junior members 50 livres. Elegantly housed on Ezbekyeh Square it eventually contained the precious printing presses, chemistry and physics laboratories, workshops and an extensive library.

At the first meeting Napoleon presented six topics for subsequent committee study. These ranged from finding a substitute for hops (essential in brewing beer and nonexistent in Egypt) to purifying water from the Nile, to a study of Egyptian civil and criminal law and education. A few weeks later appropriate committee members were asked to investigate vineyard cultivation; the most suitable place to establish an observatory; the origin and history of the *nilomètre* (the ancient monument that measured the depths of the Nile especially at flooding); the temperature and moisture of the atmosphere and oscillations of the compass; and the quantity and quality of water in various desert areas.

A modern scientific historian tells us that one of the first papers read, an explanation by Gaspard Monge of the heretofore unknown mirage, is the most famous of many contributions, but Berthollet also made important discoveries in physical chemistry as did Desgenettes and Larrey in medicine (the latter employing the word *virus* in his studies), and as others would do in the future.[6]

Napoleon perforce concerned himself almost constantly with the more immediate aspects of colonization. Army morale was shaken initially by agonizing marches, then by loss of the battle fleet and finally by duty in generally uncomfortable places in a land with almost no wine or beer, virtually no bread, and few attractive women. There were no letters from home and long periods of idleness or of standing guard with danger never far away. To bolster flagging spirits he frequently decorated, promoted and otherwise rewarded officers and men for outstanding duty, a fortunate few receiving chased silver muskets, beautifully engraved swords or miniature silver grenades. A soldier who saved General Caffarelli's life during the Red Sea expedition was promoted to corporal and received a saber inscribed on one side: "General Bonaparte to the mounted guide, Louis," on the other, "Crossing of the Red Sea",[7] a typical gesture that in part explained his continued popularity in the ranks.

His generals were given mansions formerly owned by Mameluke chiefs, officers and men were allowed to keep booty taken in battle so long as they sold captured horses and camels to the army. He ordered troop hospitals built in all major garrisons, along with lazarets for quarantined patients and even a convalescent hospital in Cairo. Whenever possible patients were entertained by cheerful music from military bands. (The less fortunate were buried in special military cemeteries.) The excellent work of his chief medical officers, Desgenettes and Larrey, was rewarded by substantial cash gifts to their families.

He constantly tried to improve the quality of rations, particularly the mainstay of the army diet – bread – and set fair prices for all produce and meat. He encouraged various specialty shops to open in Cairo and he sponsored a comfortably fitted-out club for soldiers, Le Tivoli, that included dances with local women. One newspaper, La Décade, carried the latest scientific, artistic, social and archeological activities to outlying garrisons every ten days; a second paper, the Courrier d'Egypte, published what there was of lighter news. As the troops also began to discover, some oriental customs were pleasant. One commissaire later wrote:

> We went to bathe and found endless pleasure in this new way of purifying ourselves . . . We took to the pipe (chebouk) . . . often we smoked eagle-wood with our tobacco, and the perfume mingled very pleasantly with the smoke . . . We had coffee at every meal. We had almost forgotten the use of chairs, and lived stretched out on divans . . . We exchanged our narrow breeches for wider trousers.[8]

Napoleon's own morale was another concern. Sometime in December, according to Bourrienne, he had a number of Asiatic women brought to the mansion for inspection but soon rejected them as being fat and unpleasing. He now took a fancy to a young French woman, Pauline Fourés, an infantry lieutenant's wife who, disguised as a hussar, had accompanied her husband. One thing led to another and Pauline was suddenly living in a house next to Napoleon's mansion, daily promenading in his carriage often accompanied by one or two aides including Eugène Beauharnais. So smitten was the general with her charms that he now dispatched Lieutenant Fourés to Paris on some trifling mission.[9]

Unfortunately for the lovers the cuckold's ship was captured by the English who, learning the situation, cheekily returned him to Egypt. After some embarrassing scenes Pauline divorced him and became Napoleon's official mistress, proudly wearing a miniature of her lover around her neck. Dressed as a general and wearing a tricorn hat she became a familiar sight on her Arab horse, a great favorite of the troops who called her either "Cleopatra" or "our other general." According to Bourrienne, Napoleon was upset by her failure to become pregnant. When an aide discreetly mentioned this she replied: "Upon my word, this is not my fault."[10]

Napoleon Bonaparte was one of those rare individuals who preferred duty to dalliance. His major concern remained the army and its transition to a new kind of warfare, armed occupation of a too often hostile country.

His supreme watchword was tactical cohesion. Insofar as possible, detachments were not to occupy villages so as to become targets for lurking Arabs – one such detachment was completely wiped out. He ordered General Desaix not to divide his forces in trying to envelop Mourad-Bey's Mamelukes, "these maneuvers being too uncertain in the broken landscape of Upper Egypt."[11]

To increase firepower he ordered non-commissioned officers to carry muskets. Cavalry non-commissioned officers and mounted guides were to carry carbines and pistols – "a short saber is of no value against a peasant's pike"[12] – and the guides were taught to fire them at full gallop. He increased mobility by utilizing the amazing strength and staying power of the camel which soon replaced wagon transport. Special harnesses or pillions were fashioned to carry both cargoes and wounded soldiers. A portable bridge for crossing canals was to be developed – it would be 30 feet long, its sections carried by two camels. Early in 1799 he created an elite dromedary regiment, eight companies each of 50 camels, to be ridden by soldiers under 24 years of age, at least 5' 4" tall and with a record of bravery. Wearing gray uniforms with turbans and cloaks, they carried fusils, bayonets and long lances.

Earlier tactics were not fundamentally altered. Generals continued to deploy brigades into battalion squares laced with artillery, tactics successful in a score or more of set-piece fights such as General Vial's victory over several thousand Arabs in September, followed by Desaix's against Mourad-Bey in October at Sedimen which cost Mourad 400 dead and most of his baggage.

Against less discernible and more subversive targets such as spies, rebellious villagers and brigand tribesmen, Napoleon continued to use brute force tactics. In the countryside these were practiced by punitive expeditions ranging from 50–500 troops with a few horse and one or two cannon. A village deemed guilty of harboring assassins was burned, some villagers executed, hostages taken, horses, camels, cows and sheep seized. In time this self-defeating tactic was altered to spare the houses in favor of arresting and executing the chiefs.

In towns the chosen punishment was beheading with the heads then placed on poles and paraded through the streets, a placard announcing the crime. These terrible punishments increased in ferocity as the political situation darkened, as no convoys arrived from France, as tax collectors grew ever more ruthless in collecting the *myry*, as Djezzar (promoted to general in chief of all Syria by the Turkish sultan) mobilized a powerful army, and as agents of

a reviving Ibrahim-Bey infiltrated Egyptian provinces with incendiary appeals for resistance.

A great deal of Napoleon's paper activity could not stand the
litmus test of reality. Perhaps to his credit he would not admit, at
least outwardly, that he was trapped in a hostile country. His continuing orders to form battle fleets in Alexandria, Corfu and
Malta were the stuff of dreams. The large convoys carrying men,
munitions, money and other essentials existed only in his imagination – in six months only one such reached Malta. He had
almost no communication with Corfu, Malta, Italy, Toulon or
Paris. Copies of dispatches sent by five different routes were
almost always intercepted, and the few that got through to Paris
brought little response. By September only one courier from Paris
managed to reach Egypt but in fleeing from murderous Bedouins
lost all but a couple of meaningless fragments of a dispatch from
the Directory dated 6 July 1798.[13] Communications would further
deteriorate, although the Directory would receive more news from
Egypt by one source or another than Napoleon would receive
from it.

His constant efforts to bolster morale and maintain discipline
only partially succeeded. Despite severe punishments, disgruntled soldiers and civilians alike continued to steal rations and
other supplies including most of the wine that had been brought
from France. General Desaix reported from Upper Egypt that
one convoy supposedly carrying 60,000 biscuits delivered only
20,000. Some generals were accused of levying unauthorized cash
contributions from sheiks and peasants, some of converting
material contributions into cash, others of confiscating supply
boats on the Nile. A nasty quarrel developed when Napoleon,
learning that General Kléber had appropriated 100,000 francs
for army purposes that were intended for Admiral Ganteaume,
forced him to return the money while suggesting peculation on
Kléber's part. Although Napoleon in time would apologize, the
damage was done – henceforth Kléber was an enemy. Soldiers in

all units continued to pillage, to invade private houses and to rape and sometimes murder women – two such were publicly executed by a firing squad – and desertions also increased.[14]

So did sickness despite Napoleon's claims of a salubrious climate. In late November he informed the Directory that "we have some eye sickness, a few fevers but no other illness." This was only partially true. The troops had begun suffering from the dreaded eye disease called trachoma soon after their arrival. Treatment was rudimentary, consisting of various drops including copper sulphate which was in short supply, but chief surgeon Larrey insisted that it could be cured by proper continuing treatment which many of the victims failed to maintain. The disease was believed to be caused by wet night air, severe heat, powerful sun rays and dusty air and aggravated by liquor and venereal disease (in reality it is caused by "a nonfilterable virus" and has remained endemic to Egypt). Napoleon advised his stepson, Eugène Beauharnais, to sleep in tents when in the field and keep his eyes covered. If Beauharnais escaped blindness others did not. Two hundred victims shortly would be sent to Alexandria for evacuation to France. Napoleon also failed to mention frequent cases of dysentery along with serious fevers, nor did he report a high incidence of syphilis and gonorrhea. One authority states that 15 per cent of the army was sick by late October, not an unreasonable figure since Desaix's corps of 3,000 was believed to have had 8–900 men on the sick-list.[15]

Proper hospital treatment was often vitiated by inefficient and corrupt officials as well as by lack of adequate equipment and medicines and in some instances uncaring and frightened doctors. Napoleon discovered patients sleeping on the ground in one hospital as late as the end of October, and he never ceased to appoint various commissions to oversee hospital administration. An outbreak of the plague in Alexandria at the turn of the year caused Marmont, then governor, to institute severe control measures. Insofar as possible plague victims were isolated in special hospitals and troop units were moved to open-air bivouacs in the countryside. Any doctor refusing to treat a plague victim was courtmartialed. One guilty surgeon was sentenced to be dressed as a woman and hauled through the streets on a donkey, a placard on his back proclaiming: "Unworthy to be a French citizen, he is afraid to die." He was then imprisoned, to be returned to France on the first boat. As the plague epidemic worsened, Napoleon ordered senior officers to visit hospitals every five days and shoot on the spot any attendants who refused to nurse the sick.[16]

Provincial administration left much to be desired. Napoleon was soon complaining of inefficient and corrupt Coptic tax collectors and of overdue cash contributions that had been levied on merchants and villages. Repeated requisitions for animals brought scant results. A demand to one general to collect 3,000 horses resulted in only a few hundred, another for 50 mules produced 22 animals. Camels continued to be in short supply despite the most strenuous procurement methods. Corruption remained endemic. In late September 500 laborers were being paid to work on Cairo fortifications while only 250 (including women and children) were actually employed – and that is just one instance of many.[17]

The internal security that Napoleon so desired was often ephemeral. Hostile Arabs and Turks lurked everywhere. Such was the fatality rate of couriers that commanders were instructed to use Arab messengers, who often proved untrustworthy. The normal time for a letter to reach Cairo from Alexandria (135 miles away) was five days. Coach service was so threatened that Napoleon formed three companies of Greek soldiers solely for escort duty. On several occasions isolated army detachments were surprised and eliminated by Arab attacks. One *djerme* was attacked on the Nile and its soldier passengers all killed. The northern provinces were hotbeds of insurrection. Spies roamed through the countryside and towns to report the location and strengths of French forces and patrols to lurking enemies.

The French struck back – hard. Miscreants were summarily executed, others taken hostage; severe fines were levied, animals and crops seized. To avenge the murder of one of Napoleon's aides, General Lannes with 500 troops attacked the guilty village, seized its chiefs, turned the village over to troop pillage and left no house standing. A later punishment for errant villages called for all children aged from 12 to 16 to be taken away and held in special camps.[18]

Napoleon's orders during and after the Cairo mutiny in late October were draconian, particularly when he learned of the deaths of General Dupuy and the immensely talented Joseph Sulkowski (who was recovering from earlier wounds).[19] During the fighting the heretofore protector of mosques ordered the bombardment and assault of the great mosque of El Azhar and the execution of rebels who had taken refuge there. Captured rebels were either thrown into dungeons or, if armed, were summarily beheaded. The rebel loss was put at between 2,000 and 2,500, French troop losses at 16 dead plus the killing of 21 wounded and 20 isolated soldiers and civilians. Eleven rebel sheiks were executed and their properties seized while scores of peasants had their heads cut off.[20]

Napoleon's policy generally brought peace but always uneasy and temporary. Troops occupied cities and towns, punitive patrols circulated through the provinces, border forts were secured, roads cleared at least for a while, and the Nile made safe – until the next time a raiding party struck. The truth was that as the old year ran out, Napoleon's position was becoming increasingly perilous. The truth was that the French controlled only the ground of their garrisons and forts and the ground walked on by punitive expeditions – that was the limit of their security, and for good reason.

Napoleon had badly misjudged the Egyptian and Turkish psyche fashioned by centuries-long force of Islamic belief and tradition. He had thought to win over the *fellahin* by a promise of liberty with the material benefits offered by European civilization, but liberty was a concept too remote for the peasant to understand. As one historian put it, "the immense majority of the Egyptians took no heed of this civilization, because they did not yet feel the needs which it satisfied."[21]

The Turkish sultan had certainly suffered a loss of authority

and income from Mameluke rule as had the Egyptian peoples, but
that did not mean that the one or the other preferred foreign rule –
oppressive foreign rule by an infidel Christian general. Napoleon
could pay lip service to the Islamic faith as fulsomely and garru-
ously as he wished, but his words and acts made not the slightest
difference to the majority of the Islamic faithful. The syllogism
was simple and dangerous: the French intruders are Christian,
Christians are our born enemies, therefore the French are our
enemies.

This was more obvious to some than to others. The sultan in
Constantinople understood it well. He may not have liked the
Egyptian rulers, the Mamelukes, but they were better than the
greedy French (with whom he was now at war). His lieutenant, the
general in chief of Persia, Djezzar, understood it well. The first
envoy bearing a placatory letter from Napoleon barely escaped
with his life; he returned to Cairo to report Djezzar's fury as well
as the hatred of the French in Jaffa and Acre. A later courier was
executed.[22]

The *sherif* of Mecca and the fugitive Ahmed-Pasha of Cairo
also understood it well. They did not reply to Napoleon's missives.
Ibrahim-Bey completely ignored a peace offer. Mourad-Bey's
reply is quoted at the beginning of this chapter. Although General
Desaix caught up with Mourad-Bey, beat him in battle and sent
him on the run, he did not bring him to the peace table.
Napoleon's victory over Ibrahim-Bey was only a temporary setback. From their desert and border sanctuaries these leaders sent
streams of fiery messages to interior Egypt. The message was
clear: armed rebellion.

This did not particularly worry Napoleon. Local uprisings
including the Cairo mutiny were relatively easy to suppress with
only minimal French casualties. He believed that harsh measures
such as burning villages and beheading alleged spies and traitors
would prevent future uprisings, but this was a false reading. The
French were up against a religious-inspired stoicism difficult for
the westerner to comprehend – as witness Mohammed el-Koraïm,
the French-appointed governor of Alexandria, who chose to have

his head chopped off rather than pay a relatively modest fine for treachery.[23] If such severe punishments deterred large numbers of Arabs from taking arms, they undoubtedly increased clandestine support of the actual militants.

Napoleon was far more concerned with the threat from external forces. He estimated desert Arabs to number 15,000 horse and 50,000 infantry, but such were their primitive tactics and tribal dissensions that he tended to discount the threat. He was also rather patronizing when it came to the English enemy, regarding the naval blockade as a temporary nuisance. (At the same time, he never ceased to long for news from Europe.) He did not fear a troop landing in the near future – the northern ports were well defended and the storm season was approaching – and he did not seem unduly upset upon learning of the English blockade of Malta.

His major concern stemmed from reports that Djezzar was forming an invasion army 50,000 strong. A newly appointed pasha of Egypt, Abd-Allah, was reportedly at Gaza, a coastal town close to the Egyptian-Syrian border, along with other Egyptian sheiks and their forces as well as Ibrahim-Bey's Mamelukes who had been joined by 2–3,000 Egyptian Arabs.

Here was a challenge, Napoleon believed, that had to be met by French arms – by nothing less than a military expedition across the desert. Its *raison d'être*, as he informed General Desaix, was to complete the conquest of Egypt by pushing Ibrahim-Bey from the country and breaking up enemy contingents in Gaza. Whether this alone prompted his move is a moot question for he simultaneously advised the Directory that after defeating Ibrahim-Bey he planned to eliminate Syrian logistic support of the English fleet (by eliminating Djezzar's army). Some evidence also suggests that eventually he hoped to arm the Christians, Druses and Maronites, seize the *pashaliks* of Damascus and Aleppo to bring a peace with Turkey, then with Turkish support invade India and with the help of Tippoo Sahib, the Tiger of Mysore, push out the English to make France the undisputed master of the East. (Although he did not know it, in early November the Directory had written him to undertake this ambitious effort if he deemed it wise.[24] Neither did he know that despite considerable efforts the Directory was about to abandon the attempt to reinforce his expedition, a decision soon to be confirmed when war with Austria broke out.)

Whatever the real motive(s), when Napoleon learned that a corps of Mamelukes and Djezzar's troops had fortified the village of El Arish, 25 miles inside Egypt, he ordered General Reynier to complete the fortifications of Katia village about 25 miles southeast of Pelusium.

This was completed by mid January 1799. Reynier and Lagrange next marched on El Arish, only 40 miles from Ibrahim's stronghold at Gaza. General Kléber, again commanding his old division, followed Reynier as did Bon and Lannes' divisions. On 10 February 1799, Napoleon turned the Cairo command over to General Dugua and left for the desert to take command of the expedition.

Notes

1   Herold, 146.
2   Corr. IV. Nrs. 3076, Cairo, 22 August 1798; 3110, Cairo, 25 August 1798.
3   Corr. IV. Nrs. 3064, Cairo, 21 August 1798; 3079, Cairo, 22 August 1798; 3228, Cairo, 4 September 1798; 3263, Cairo, 10 September 1798. Gaspard Monge agreed with Napoleon's assessment, albeit with some reservations – see Aubry, 24–9.
4   Corr. IV. Nr. 3259, Cairo, 8 September 1798.
5   Corr. V. Nr. 3808, Cairo, 2 January 1799. See also Corr. XXIX, 507; Aubry, 260–3; Berthier, 5.
6   Corr. IV. Nrs. 2938, Cairo, 2 August 1798; 3083, 3084, Cairo, 22 August 1798; Corr. V. Nr. 3459, Cairo, 12 October 1798. See also Bourrienne, I, 158–9; Herold, 152, 167–73; Aubry, 251–3; Gillespie, 85.
7   Corr. V. Nr. 3819, Cairo, 9 January 1799.
8   Charles-Roux, 248–9. See also Corr. V. Nr. 3389, Cairo, 20

September 1798, for a detailed breakdown of quality, content and prices of rations.

9   Corr. V. Nr. 3774, Cairo, 17 December 1798.

10 Bourrienne, I, 157.

11 Corr. IV. Nrs. 3230, Cairo, 3 September 1798; 3233, 3234, Cairo, 4 September 1798; Corr. V. Nr. 3424, Cairo, 5 October 1798.

12 Corr. V. Nr. 3388, Cairo, 26 September 1798.

13 Corr. IV. Nr. 3259, Cairo, 8 September 1798.

14 Corr. IV. Nrs. 3080, Cairo, 22 August 1798; 3210, Cairo, 1 September 1798; 3236, Cairo, 4 September 1798; 3264, Cairo, 10 September 1798; 3271, Cairo, 12 September 1798; 3338, Cairo, 17 September 1798; Corr. V. Nr. 3398, Cairo, 28 September 1798; 3457, Cairo, 12 October 1798; 3844, Cairo, 12 January 1799. See also Bernoyer, 132–3.

15 Corr. V. Nrs. 3649, Cairo, 21 November 1798; 3761, Cairo, 16 December 1798. See also Herold, 161; Desgenettes (*Histoire*), 13, 16,–18; Larrey (Dominique), 208 ff.

16 Corr. V. Nrs. 3818, Cairo, 8 January 1799; 3861, Cairo, 16 January 1799. See also Desgenettes (*Histoire*), 24.

17 Corr. IV. Nrs. 3090, Cairo, 23 August 1798; 3361, Cairo, 21 September 1798; Corr. V. Nrs. 3394, Cairo, 28 September 1798; 3461, Cairo, 13 October 1798.

18 Corr. V. Nr. 3728, Cairo, 8 December 1798. See also Charles-Roux, 259–61.

19 Napoleon named forts in Egypt after Dupuy and Sulkowski and otherwise honored their memory. Later, as First Consul he ordered a granite column raised in Dupuy's birthplace of Toulouse and inscribed: "To Dupuy and the courageous soldiers of the 32nd demi-brigade, killed on the field of honor." See Corr. VI. Nr. 4492, Paris, 4 January 1800.

20 Corr. V. Nrs. 3322–3324, Cairo, 22 October 1798; 3526, 3527, Cairo, 23 October 1798; 3538, Cairo, 27 October 1798; 3571, Cairo, 3 November 1798. See also Corr. V. Nr. 3785, Cairo, 21 December 1798. Napoleon disbanded the Cairo divan immediately after the mutiny but in late December restored it because of the people's good behavior.

21 Charles-Roux, 248–9.

22 Herold, 147.

‎

23   Corr. IV. Nr. 3248, Cairo, 5 September 1798.

24   Corr. V. Nrs. 3592, Cairo, 10 February 1799; Boulay, 283–92, quoting President Treilhard's letter of 4 November 1798, which Napoleon did not receive. See also Corr. XXX, 14; Aubry, 264–5.

CHAPTER TWENTY-EIGHT

THE CONQUEST OF EGYPT – IV:
THE SIEGE OF ST. JEAN D'ACRE
FEBRUARY–MAY 1799

I saw officers, with their limbs amputated, thrown off the stretchers . . . [having] given money to recompense the bearers. I saw the amputated, the wounded, the infected . . . deserted and left to themselves.

Louis Bourrienne on the French retreat from Syria,
May–June 1799[1]

IT WAS A strange expedition. In addition to some 13,000 troops – four infantry divisions supported by cavalry, artillery, engineers, pioneers, medical detachments and camel transport companies – it included Napoleon and his staff, his special foot and horse guides, a few sheiks and *ulémas*, a number of French savants (among them Monge and Berthollet), wives of a few officers and assorted female camp followers. Three thousand camels and 3,000 mules carried food and water, not only for the humans but for 3,000 cavalry horses as well.

Although Napoleon paid lip-service to supply requirements – "We shall have to spend nine days in the desert without water or forage," he informed the Directory[2] – his preparations seem to have been hasty and incomplete, particularly when it came to adequate provisions and proper clothing for the wet and cold coastal country. He surprisingly underestimated the difficulty of pulling cannon over shifting desert sands, a contretemps that caused him to send heavy siege artillery by boat from Damietta to Haifa.

Worse yet he lacked good intelligence despite countless spies sent out by his generals.

It may be that he anticipated a swift campaign, counting on rich booty including food and forage. He had ample reason to scorn Arab and Turkish battle tactics. Despite contrary evidence he insisted that Turkey was at peace with France and that perhaps Djezzar would not continue to support Ibrahim-Bey.

Part of the trouble lay with chief of staff Berthier who was so enamored of his absent mistress, Madame Visconti, that he had become an increasing problem though not without a lighter side. In an earlier outing to the Pyramids, Berthier had set up two tents, one for himself and one for an altar holding the portrait of his loved one. Napoleon at once organized a contest to see who would be the first to reach the top of the Great Pyramid (easily won by 53-year-old Gaspard Monge). Berthier, taken by the heat, had stopped halfway up and started to descend when Napoleon wickedly called, "You're descending already? *She* is not at the summit, my poor Berthier, but neither is *she* below."[3] (Napoleon later recalled Berthier's shrine, noting that it was often violated by other women.) Finally yielding to Berthier's pleas, he gave him permission to return to Europe. Although the chief of staff's conscience caught up with him and he rejoined the expedition at the last moment, his absence during critical planning undoubtedly told on adequate preparations.

The neglect proved costly. The advance guard, General Reynier's division, left Katia on 6 February with the mission of seizing fort El Arish. This coastal village was supposed to be held by some 1,800 Mamelukes and Turks. To his surprise Reynier found this force backed by a strongly built fort with a garrison of some 1,500 Albanians and Moroccans. Although the French seized the village and invested the fort a week passed with rations daily growing slimmer. The crisis was resolved by a night attack on the Arab-Turkish camp, left unguarded because of the celebration of Ramadan, which killed 400 and captured 900 sleeping soldiers and put the rest to flight. However this achieved very little because the fort continued to hold out. Food was now so scarce that according to a civilian in Kléber's division, which meanwhile had arrived, the troops "were eating camels, horses and donkeys."[4]

This disappointing scene greeted Napoleon on 17 February. He had also received a severe emotional blow during the march from his aide, Andoche Junot, who for some unknown reason bluntly informed him of details of Joséphine's many love affairs and perhaps of her financial peculations from army contracts arranged with the connivance of Hippolyte Charles. "I never saw him exhibit such an air of dissatisfaction," noted Bourrienne, "or appear so much under the influence of some prepossession." After upbraiding Bourrienne for not having confided in him earlier, he angrily swore to divorce her, "a public and open divorce." Although Bourrienne insisted on the falseness of the details Napoleon continued in his fury until it was absorbed by the challenge of El Arish.[5]

A parley between Napoleon and the fort's commandant having led to nothing, field guns opened fire on the thick stone walls, a day's cannonade that finally produced a small breach. This was important because under existing rules of war (anyway in the West) the garrison now had either to capitulate or face execution if captured. The commandant wisely chose to surrender. Napoleon disarmed the Mamelukes and sent them to Cairo, and a number of captives volunteered to serve in the French army. The remainder, in return for swearing not to serve Djezzar for at least a year, retained their arms and marched off in the desert. Welcome booty included 300 horses, 90 camels and large amounts of food for man and beast. Unfortunately the fort also contained "an entire room filled with dying victims of the plague."[6]

The subsequent march to Gaza at once floundered when Kléber's division, now the advance guard, got lost in the desert, an ordeal that produced a minor mutiny quickly settled by Napoleon.[7] Desert hardships were soon ameliorated by the peaceful seizure of Gaza and booty that included French-caliber cannon, quantities of gunpowder, biscuits, barley, pomegranates, dates, fruits and tents as well as welcome relief from desert heat. "We are here in mud and water up to our knees," Napoleon informed General Dugua. "You are indeed fortunate to have the beautiful Cairo sun."[8] To General Marmont in Alexandria, "for three days the sea is as high as the mountains," a welcome change that voided any threat from prowling English cruisers.[9] The surrounding country, "the citrus trees, the olive groves and the irregular terrain resemble almost perfectly that of Languedoc," he wrote Desaix.[10]

Pleasure soon subsided. Scores of camels perished from humidity and muddy ground. Improperly clothed soldiers were hit next by the chilly weather – 700 were soon on the sick-list. Leaving a small garrison at Gaza, Napoleon continued the march to Ascalon where he relived the famous battle of the Crusades which won Jerusalem to the Christians for a hundred years. The march continued to Ramleh and a warm welcome by local Christians. Ten miles further on the army pitched tents outside the fortified town of Jaffa (today's Tel Aviv) perched on a hill overlooking the sea. Having positioned his artillery outside the gates Napoleon sent the commandant, Abdallah-Aga, an ultimatum: either surrender in return for safe conduct of troops and protection of the city or fight and be destroyed.

The commandant unwisely beheaded Napoleon's emissary and chose to fight. French guns opened fire, the wall was breached, angry grenadiers stormed into the town shooting and bayoneting an estimated 2,000 Turkish soldiers and numerous civilians before indulging in an all-night orgy of pillage and rape. "The soldiers' fury was at its height," Napoleon wrote many years later, "everybody was put to the sword."[11]

Worse was to come when 2,500 Turkish soldiers inside the fortress surrendered to two of Napoleon's aides, one of whom was Eugène Beauharnais, in return for a promise that their lives would be saved. According to secretary Bourrienne, Napoleon was furious when the prisoners were marched out: "What do they want me to do with them?" he muttered.[12]

It was a difficult question that might have been answered with another: Why was Napoleon unprepared to cope with a large number of prisoners and what would he have done had the entire garrison initially surrendered? That aside, he held several options as answer to his question. He could return them to the filthy, disease-ridden fortress where they would have to be fed, guarded and eventually buried. He could execute those among them who had violated the oath taken at El Arish by joining the Jaffa garrison and either turn the others loose, which would allow them to reinforce Djezzar, or send them back to Egypt under a guard that he could ill afford to spare. Or he could execute the lot in compliance with the (Western) rules of war, the commandant having chosen to fight after the wall was breached.

Napoleon chose the last measure (which in the Italian campaign he had scorned). Most of the prisoners were taken to a secluded beach and were either shot or bayoneted to death, a hideous act that has been either defended or condemned for the wrong reasons by two centuries of historians. According to Bourrienne, who claimed to be an eyewitness, Napoleon agonized over his decision for two days during which he called two councils of generals who favored execution.[13] The record does not show this. His senior general, Kléber, was already on the march north when he received Napoleon's laconic message dated 9 March: "The garrison of Jaffa numbered about 4,000 men; 2,000 have been killed in the city and 2,000 have been shot between yesterday and today." Similar messages appeared in an order of the day and in a letter to General Dugua in Cairo.[14]

Napoleon did not need a council of war to make his grisly decision any more than he needed one before ordering scores of Egyptian villages burned, or thousands of recalcitrant natives shot or beheaded, or hundreds of children taken from their parents. He was a man of mission and anybody or anything that got in his way was fair game for whatever force he mustered. He had no intention of calling off his campaign because some wretched prisoners had suddenly got in the way.[15] A student of Attila the Hun and Genghis Khan, Napoleon had used terror tactics when necessary ever since landing in Egypt – he had used them in Italy as well. In his mind terror was a weapon. Even while the slaughter was going on he was writing proclamations to Syrian potentates in the provinces of Gaza, Ramleh and Jaffa warning them to ally with the French:

> It is advisable for you to know that all human efforts are useless against me because everything I undertake has to succeed . . . The example offered by Jaffa and Gaza should make you understand that, if I am terrible to my enemies I am good to my friends, and above all mild and merciful with the poor people.[16]

Similar sentiments were carried to the sheiks, *ulémas* and the commandant of Jerusalem. A special message was sent to Djezzar-Pasha:

> The provinces of Gaza, Ramleh and Jaffa are in my power. I have generously treated those of your troops who have submitted to my will. I have been very severe toward those who have violated the rules of war. I shall march within a few days on St. Jean d'Acre . . . become my friend, be the enemy of the Mamelukes and the English . . . Send me your reply by a man who knows your intentions and is furnished with your full powers.[17]

Prior to Napoleon's writing the above words the dreaded bubonic plague had struck French ranks. Scores of enemy soldiers had already died from it – chief physician Desgenettes later wrote of Turkish orderlies throwing bodies in the sea at night. By 9 March 31 French who had developed the telltale pus-filled buboes, prelude to terrible suffering, had died in a rude hospital hastily established in a Greek Orthodox monastery. Desgenettes and Larrey denied that these were plague victims but nonetheless the rumor spread. Desgenettes later described Napoleon's supreme effort to prevent panic:

On March 11th, 1799, General Bonaparte, followed by his general staff, felt it incumbent upon himself to visit the hospital . . . The General walked through the hospital and its annex, spoke to almost all the soldiers who were conscious enough to hear him . . . While in a very small and crowded ward, he helped to lift, or rather to carry, the hideous corpse of a soldier whose torn uniform was soiled by the spontaneous bursting of an enormous abscessed bubo.[18]

A foolhardy act, perhaps, but also a very brave one which one officer noted in his diary "has produced an excellent effect. Already there is less fear."[19]

The coastal town of Akko was born eighteen centuries before the birth of Christ. A choice port because of its natural bay it had subsequently suffered a wide variety of invaders including Alexander the Great, Ptolemy II of Egypt and diverse Romans, Persians and Arabs. In the early twelfth century the crusading Knights of St. John (the Hospitallers) made it their fortified capital, St. Jean d'Acre, which turned out to be their last refuge before flight to Malta in the late thirteenth century. Thenceforth it was largely owned by Ottoman Turks.

The most recent governor was Ahmad Pasha al-Jazzār who took command of the *pashalik* or province in 1775. Al-Jazzār (or Djezzar), which translates to "the butcher," was aptly named since he had devoted large parts of his turbulent career to removing noses, ears, eyes, hands, feet and finally heads from any unfortunate Christian or other enemy who came along.

Despite his ferocious disposition and intense hatred of the French invader, the 71-year-old governor's military position was not especially strong at the time Napoleon marched, a fact that may well have been reported by spies. But now a 35-year-old English soldier of fortune named Sir Sydney Smith entered the picture. Smith had variously commanded a privateer and served in the English and Swedish navies. His path had briefly crossed Napoleon's at Toulon where he commanded a squadron of fire boats. Two years later he was captured off the French coast, accused of piracy and imprisoned in the Temple. Here he was rescued by one Picard de Phélippeaux (shortly before Napoleon sailed for Egypt), who had been Napoleon's classmate and bitter rival at the École Militaire.

A royalist émigré who had returned clandestinely to France to work up resistance to the republicans, Phélippeaux, by a ruse as brave as it was brilliant, had taken Smith back to England, an act that won him a colonel's commission in the English army. Smith in turn was given command of a warship and took Phélippeaux with him to the Mediterranean where he was charged with the blockade of Alexandria. Upon learning that Napoleon had reached Jaffa, Smith and Phélippeaux hurried to St. Jean d'Acre where with Djezzar's blessing they reorganized and strengthened the fortress town's defenses, posting guns and trained cannoneers (taken from the ships) on the walls and in the flanking towers behind a wide and deep ditch.[20]

Napoleon might still have seized the place had his heavy siege guns arrived on schedule, but this was not to be. The ships carrying them reached Haifa waters on 18 March, the day after the French had seized the port. For some reason they delayed entering the port, a fatal error for now Smith's small fleet surprised them to seize six transports and send the others flying, a tragedy witnessed by Napoleon from Mt. Carmel overlooking the bay.[21]

As with the disaster of Aboukir Bay, if Napoleon were unduly upset he hid it well, at once ordering the army to encamp outside Djezzar's walls and commence siege operations. Perhaps he believed that the lost cannon could be replaced in time – he at once sent word to Alexandria to ship new ones – or perhaps he believed they would not be necessary. His camp was easily defensible, the area rich in pasturage, orchards and wheatfields. It offered ample wood and water and mills to grind the grain. Friendly Druse villagers soon began supplying food. He had what he believed to be easy communications with the supply ports of Haifa and Jaffa, his security being increased by posting four mobile corps along the Jordanian border. He also hoped to win support of local sheiks and holy men to whom he had appealed for help, and a number of them who had been cheated out of their lands by Djezzar did join him, some offering troops, others food.[22]

What he failed to realize was the intensity of Djezzar's hatred and the immense boost to Turkish morale caused by Phélippeaux's artillery expertise and by the importance of Smith's ships which could replace powder, ball and rations as needed. Contrarily Napoleon had but limited amounts of munitions which could only be replaced from Haifa and Jaffa, a supply line that soon became less satisfactory owing to a shortage of carts and animals and attacks from marauding natives.

But that was in the future. The first task now was to dig zig-zag trenches leading to the protective ditch or *fosse* fronting city walls, then a communications trench parallel to the towers and walls, a task that required a week of hard work with unwelcome casualties from enemy gunfire. The result was meager: "The trenches do not come up to my knees," General Kléber complained to Bourrienne.[23]

The assault opened on 28 March with a heavy cannonade answered in kind from the walls and from anchored ships. Within two hours 40 French gunners were killed, a large number wounded and all but three cannon knocked out. Light French guns had opened a breach in the wall but at too great a height for soldiers to reach it with scaling ladders. Although the defenders had momentarily panicked, Djezzar revived them sufficiently to send off the French, a discouraging setback noted by one officer in his diary: "Many of us were of the opinion from that moment on that we could never take the place." The attack nevertheless infuriated Djezzar who retaliated by murdering several hundred Christians in the town, a hideous act that Napoleon believed was sanctioned by Sydney Smith, henceforth his blood enemy.[24] A second assault four days later failed, again with heavy French casualties. Napoleon now backed off to wait for replacement siege cannon, an interim period during which Djezzar was substantially reinforced with Turkish troops arriving by sea.

Meanwhile surgeon Larrey had been trying to cope with a growing sick-list of men suffering from violent colics and diarrhea. No hospital yet existed, there was very little wine, vinegar or medicines. Some of the sick would have died but for food provided by local natives. Then had come the first casualties who had to lie on rush beds in the open with no blankets, tormented by a scourge of blue flies so intense that wounds had to be dressed three or four times a day. Fortunately Larrey managed to have three rude hospitals built and forward aid stations established but medicines remained in short supply.[25]

As if all this were not enough Napoleon now received a letter from the Directory dated 3 March 1799, the first since the meaningless fragments that had reached him the previous September. He had learned of European developments up to 1 November from some transient traders who left him a pile of Italian newspapers: General Humbert's disastrous attempt to land an expeditionary force in Ireland; the English blockade of Malta and Corfu; the inactive French and Spanish navies; and various unsettling rumors of warlike movements. Now he learned of the Directory's failure to send convoys to Corfu, Malta and Egypt. The letter was accompanied by "several boxes of newspapers" that brought matters up to mid February and seemed to presage the outbreak of war. At least one historian marks this as the moment when Napoleon decided to return to France just as soon as circumstances permitted.[26]

Circumstances were not cooperative however. Djezzar's appeals to the neighboring governors of Aleppo and Damascus and to the Nablus mountain tribes were soon answered by large armies marching to strike the French flank. Having been informed of the threat by friendly Christians, Napoleon sent General Junot to investigate.

In early April Junot defeated a large cavalry force near Nazareth. General Kléber, with 1,500 infantry sent to reinforce Junot, beat off another group nearly 5,000 strong. In mid April General Murat with only two battalions dusted off still another large army on the Jordan river north of Lake Tiberias, a victory made the sweeter by rich booty.

Kléber meanwhile had moved to attack the Damascun army, a force of some 25,000 horse and 10,000 infantry encamped on a plain below Mt. Tabor. In short order the attacker became the defender. The day-long battle was on the point of being lost by the French when Napoleon arrived with General Bon's division to completely rout the Turks, many of whom were either drowned or killed in trying to escape across a nearby lake. Napoleon celebrated the victory with a *Te Deum* sung in the old church of Nazareth, and by issuing still another bulletin praising the heroic deeds of his troops.[27]

While these violent battles were being fought the siege of Acre continued. Frequent artillery exchanges took an increasing toll of French soldiers including the death of the immensely popular General Caffarelli, but the enemy also suffered heavy losses through making unnecessary sorties, 12 in all, that were decimated by musket and cannon fire. Although Rear Admiral Perrée's three frigates finally landed six siege cannon and numerous provisions and munitions at Tantura (today's Tor) not far from Haifa, Napoleon ordered still another assault before the guns arrived in the belief that a mine exploded under the main tower would end resistance. This effort failed as did subsequent costly attempts.

With all siege guns finally in place Napoleon attacked again, his troops this time seizing the cursed tower and even penetrating into Djezzar's gardens before running out of steam. A final effort made over rotting bodies of Turks and French alike was beaten off, General Bon dying in the attempt.

Napoleon had had enough. Although he would cite a variety of reasons for his subsequent retreat, his hope of seizing Acre had failed beyond redemption. He had inflicted a great many casualties on the enemy however and surely can be excused for believing that he had destroyed, at least for a time, the Turkish-Arab ground threat to Egypt.

The truth was that he could not have carried on much longer. Morale had been savaged by casualties and disease. One French historian recorded a minimum 1,200 combat deaths, 1,000 deaths from disease and 2,300 seriously ill or wounded – over a third of an original 13,000 men.[28] Provisions were becoming increasingly scarce owing in large part to corrupt civilian *commissaires* in Jaffa and Gaza,[29] and munitions were in such short supply that for some weeks cannoneers had been paid to retrieve enemy cannon-balls to fire back. Horses and camels were at a premium. Although the army had gained one redoubt it now faced another just as heavily defended. Ranks thinned, morale low, sickness including the dreaded plague prevalent, the army's time had run out. To top matters Napoleon received another dispatch from the Directory: a second coalition had formed against the republic, a new war had begun and a French army had invaded Naples. "The general in chief henceforth could think only of a way to return to France," Napoleon wrote years later. "Syria, Galilee, Palestine were no longer of any importance."[30]

As countless commanders have discovered, a retreat can be a very costly affair in both spirit and substance. Napoleon attempted to disguise his intentions by four days of bombardment from every functioning cannon, an effort that must have sorely told on the enemy. On 17 May he published a proclamation to the army which as Bourrienne sourly noted "from one end to the other offends against truth."[31]

To their surprise the troops learned that their mission had been accomplished, that

the [enemy] army which was marching to invade Egypt is destroyed . . . the thirty ships that you saw arrive at Acre twelve days ago carried the army that was to besiege Alexandria; but, obliged to hurry to Acre, it there finished its destiny; some of its flags will grace your entry into Egypt . . . [where we are going] because the season of [enemy] landings calls me there . . . [thus] the capture of the castle of Acre is not worth the loss of any more time. [And more ominously], Soldiers, there are more hardships and dangers ahead.[32]

A few days before the troops moved out the more seriously wounded and sick were sent to Tantura. Here Perrée was to load them aboard ships, but unfortunately his frigates (which had been cruising between there and the island of Rhodes and had taken several enemy prizes) were no match for Smith's warships and he had sailed before the tragic victims reached the small port. A few lucky ones were loaded on small boats and arrived safely in Damietta. The remaining sick and wounded followed, some walking, some riding, some carried on stretchers, some supported by one or two soldiers. Thirst, heat, fatigue, depression and fear of the plague soon changed men into primordial beasts as described by Bourrienne at the beginning of this chapter.[33]

The main army marched on the night of 20 May, covered by General Reynier's division which had spent the day fighting off a strong Turkish sortie. It was probably the sight of discarded bodies along the way, taken with the human flotsam found in Jaffa, that brought about a nasty clash between Doctor Desgenettes and Napoleon, the latter wanting the worst plague cases – men who could not survive a day's march – killed by an overdose of opium but the former refusing to consider it, a contretemps apparently solved by placing the opium within reach of the victim to swallow when left on his own. At Jaffa, Napoleon and Larrey managed to load 1,200 of the most seriously wounded and sick on boats for Damietta, leaving 800 to go by land. "It is to General Bonaparte," Larrey later wrote, "that these honorable victims mainly owe their lives."[34]

The subsequent retreat brought many more horrors caused in part by a scorched-earth policy of torching anything – villages, hamlets, crops – that would burn so as to hinder enemy pursuit and any future invasion, in part by leaving some sick and wounded either to die or be killed by marauding peasants. Ten days out Napoleon ordered all horses (including his own) and camels turned over to carry the worst casualties, apparently a temporary dictate in his case since three days later he was again on horseback; nor did Monge (who was recovering from a serious illness) and Berthollet have to abandon their carriage (shared by two pestiferous soldiers).[35]

Pursued by Turks and joined by camp followers and Christians fleeing from Djezzar's wrath, the pathetic columns stumbled back from Jaffa to Gaza, taking hostages from each town, blowing up all fortifications, then crossing the burning Sinai desert to El Arish, finally reaching Katia in early June. Here sick and wounded soldiers were sorted out and sent to various hospitals, the Christian refugees going to Damietta where they would be given parcels of land. To their great relief the soldiers were rested and provided with new uniforms. Napoleon already had sent a contingent to Cairo along with orders to General Dugua to prepare the city for the army's triumphal entry.[36]

On the great day Napoleon was met outside the city by Cairo sheiks and other notables who presented him with heaps of immensely valuable gifts including richly caparisoned camels and horses along with male and female black slaves. General Dugua pulled out all stops. The still tired divisions were greeted by bands playing, flags flying and the homage of the city fathers before being turned loose to enjoy a three-day bacchanalia never to be forgotten by the survivors of the unfortunate expedition.

Notes

1   Bourrienne, I, 192.
2   Corr. V. Nr. 3952, Cairo, 10 February 1799.
3   Aubry, 254–5; Desgenettes (Souvenirs), 14.
4   Herold, 270.
5   Bourrienne, I, 170, 172–3.
6   Corr. V. Nrs. 3969, El-Arish, 17 February 1799; 3984, El-Arish, 21 February 1799; Herold, 272.
7   Corr. V. Nr. 3990, Près de puits de Záouy, 24 February 1799. See also Bernoyer, 140–1.
8   Corr. V. Nr. 3993, Gaza, 26 February 1799. See also Miot (Jacques), 126.
9   Corr. V. Nr. 3994, Gaza, 26 February 1799.

10   Corr. V. Nr. 4000, Gaza, 27 February 1799.
11   Herold, 274.
12   Bourrienne, I, 176. See also Bernoyer, 145–7.
13   Bourrienne, I, 178–9.
14   Corr. V. Nrs. 4012, 4019, 4021, Jaffa, 9 March 1799. See also Corr. XXX.
15   Colin, 376.
16   Corr. V. Nrs. 4022, 4023, Jaffa, 9 March 1799.
17   Corr. V. Nrs. 4025, 4026, Jaffa, 9 March 1799.
18   Herold, 279. See also Desgenettes (*Histoire*), 48–9; Larrey (Dominique), 289 ff.
19   Herold, 279.
20   Herold, 280–3. See also Bourrienne, I, 182–4.
21   Herold, 284.
22   Corr. V. Nrs. 4041, Mount Carmel, 18 March 1799; 4044, Acre, 19 March 1799; 4047, Acre, 20 March 1799.
23   Bourrienne, I, 184.
24   Herold, 291. See also Bourrienne, I, 183–4.
25   Larrey (Dominique), 293–4.
26   Boulay, 83–91.
27   Bourrienne, I, 188. "Bonaparte attached the greatest importance to those [bulletins], personally drawing them up himself . . . It must be confessed that at that time nothing so much flattered self-love as being mentioned in a bulletin . . . he knew that to insert a name . . . was a great honor, and that its exclusion was a severe disappointment."
28   Herold, 299. See also Napoleon, Corr. XXX, 58–9, where he cites 500 dead and 2,500 wounded of whom 1,700 were evacuated to Syria; Berthier, 118.
29   Corr. V. Nr. 4176, Cairo, 14 June 1799. Some of the guilty ones were subsequently arrested and tried.
30   Corr. XXX, 40, 57.
31   Bourrienne, I, 191.
32   Corr. V. Nr. 4138, Acre, 17 May 1799.
33   Bourrienne, I, 192. See also Moit (Jacques), 215–16.
34   Larrey (Dominique), 311.
35   Aubry, 269.
36   Charles-Roux, 267–97.

CHAPTER TWENTY-NINE

THE CONQUEST OF EGYPT – V: HAIL AND FAREWELL JUNE–OCTOBER 1799

The serious and almost alarming turn that the war has taken calls for the Republic to concentrate its forces. The Directory in consequence has ordered Admiral Bruix to employ all the means that are in his power to make himself master of the Mediterranean and to sail to Egypt and bring home the army that you command. He is charged to work with you as to embarkation and transport. You will judge, Citizen General, if you are able to safely leave a part of your forces in Egypt, and the Directory authorizes you, in this case, to give the command to whom you judge the most suitable. The Directory would see you with pleasure at the head of the republican armies that you have so gloriously commanded up to now.

Signed by the three directors, Paris, 28 May 1799 (and never received by Napoleon)[1]

IT WAS ALMOST as if Napoleon had never been absent. After a brief rest in his spacious mansion, no doubt in the arms of Madame Fourés, he again closeted himself for lengthy sessions with his staff in facing old and familiar problems.

Security was still the paramount concern. Provincial commanders in Upper and Lower Egypt were to strengthen present forts and build new ones to further protect Nile shipping and vulnerable borders. In late June he informed General Desaix that he was spending 2–300,000 francs a month on various defensive works.

It is difficult to square this with his frequent assertions that the threat from Syria had been wiped out at Acre; that, as he informed the Directory in Paris, "the entry into Egypt from the side of the Red Sea and Syria" is absolutely closed to an enemy by the forts of Suez and El Arish: "The fortifications of Damietta, Rosetta and Alexandria render an attack by sea impracticable, and assure the Republic forever of the possession of this beautiful part of the world."[2]

Napoleon was talking in two time frames, present and future. Although later detractors have insisted that the Syrian expedition was a costly failure they have failed to take into consideration that at least for a time it did eliminate the threat of an overland Mameluke-Arab-Turkish invasion of the eastern border. This we should remember was one of his stated goals, perhaps the main one.

In late June he informed the Directory that "we are masters of the entire desert, and we have upset *for this year* the plans of our enemies."[3] Napoleon was far too intelligent not to suppose that the Ottoman Porte working with the English navy could hurl vast armies against him if it truly wished. But he did not believe this would happen in the immediate future. He correctly believed he had neutralized the threat from Ibrahim-Bey and Djezzar. He incorrectly believed he had all but eliminated the threat of a major English-Turkish landing on the northern beaches. He assured General Marmont that Commodore Smith, that "young fool," that "captain of fireboats," that "madman," could at most raise a landing force of 2,000 Turks which was not a worry.[4]

This did not mean that he wrote off the threat. In mid June he informed General Desaix that the present season was compatible to enemy landings, but that in all probability there would not be a landing.[5] He was wrong, as we shall shortly see.

Internal security was a different matter. Cairo was relatively quiet, the result both of numerous proclamations of victories in Syria (spiced with captured enemy standards) and of General Dugua's sensible relations with Arab chiefs during Napoleon's absence. Desaix had performed well in Upper Egypt but Mourad-Bey was still on the loose, albeit with a very small force. Lower Egypt was still plagued by local rebellions – no less than five had been quashed during his absence.[6] New orders called for the execution of anyone captured carrying arms. So severe was the bloodbath of prisoners in Cairo that General Dugua suggested replacing the firing squad by a guillotine which "will save us ammunition and make less noise."[7]

A large part of the unrest was caused by Napoleon's need for money. He constantly urged his generals to make their divisions self-supporting by levying frequent contributions, impositions, requisitions of Mameluke properties and enforced tax collections. "You are very rich [from your collections]," he wrote Desaix. "Be generous enough to send us 150,000 francs."[8] General Fougier was suddenly notified to come up with 100,000 francs and 40 good horses.

This need for funds sharply conflicted with the need to win over the people. Ibrahim-Bey, Mourad-Bey and lesser fry would continue to find fertile ground for rebellion, couriers would continue to have throats slit, villages to rebel, soldiers to punish the errants – and so it would go.

The problem was complicated by attrition. The Syrian expedition had cost heavily in men and equipment. In late June Napoleon informed the Directory that since landing in Egypt the army had lost 5,344 men. He needed 5,000 infantry, 500 cavalry and 500 artillery replacements. He also needed thousands of muskets, bayonets, sabers, pistols and pioneer tools. Enigmatic as always, he added, "If in addition you supply us with [another] 15,000 troops we will be able to go anywhere including Constantinople."[9] Meanwhile he attempted to repair his ranks by purchasing 4,000 negro slaves, an effort that apparently failed. He also asked the commandant of Reunion island to send him 3,000 muskets, 1,500 pairs of pistols and 1,000 sabers since so many English ships in the Red Sea and the Mediterranean made it difficult for French vessels to arrive from Toulon.

Not the least of his problems was that of raising army morale, sharply lowered by the recent campaign. Troop commanders were to weed out and punish agitators and increase discipline, but also were to recommend the brave and worthy for promotions, nearly always granted. Generals were variously rewarded. Kléber was given the Mameluke palace that he occupied; Desaix received a fulsomely engraved sword; Belliard and Friant earned swords with diamond-encrusted hilts and gracious letters of gratitude. Typical was the award of a pair of pistols to replace those lost by a cavalry commander in combat: "I can give them to no one who could make better usage of them. Bonaparte."[10] Forts were named for dead generals and other heroes such as Joseph Sulkowski. Numerous officers were promoted and some non-commissioned officers were commissioned. Seriously wounded officers and soldiers were transferred to administrative duties. Egyptian sun and reasonably ample provisions taken with drill and frequent punitive expeditions (which often provided booty) slowly revived tired and dispirited units which was just as well in view of the forthcoming storm.

Nor did Napoleon neglect the more fruitful aspects of colonization. Numerous scientists, engineers, architects, naturalists and artists accompanied various expeditions, observing, measuring, digging, charting, dissecting, drawing, theorizing, discovering; their reports when read and their drawings when viewed today, their meticulous reconstruction of temples and tombs induce a breathless wonder at the vast scope of their activities.

General Desaix's expedition in Upper Egypt was one of the most interesting and productive efforts which unfortunately we can only touch on. Desaix (accompanied by several mistresses) overcame endemic danger, hardships and serious illnesses in never allowing Mourad-Bey much breathing room after initially hammering his force. In contrast to Napoleon however he attempted to win over the *fellahin* population and in so doing accomplished several major goals: he kept Mourad-Bey on the run; he amassed considerable cash from local sheiks; and, his corps becoming increasingly self-sufficient, he penetrated the Nile valley up to the cataracts and Aswan, its archaeological, mineralogical and natural science secrets revealing themselves to such naturalists as

Étienne Saint-Hilaire and Jules César Lelorgne de Savigny and to botanists, engineers, architects and artists, among the latter Vivant Denon, to whom we are grateful for magnificent artistic reconstructions of temples and tombs. Berthier among many others later told the story of the expedition and its dauntless leader, Desaix, deservedly eulogized by Desgenettes: "He left the most honorable memories in Upper Egypt. The people named him Desaix the Fair."[11]

Splendid as were the results of the southern expedition, they were only a portion of the total gigantic effort. Napoleon's demands were almost insatiable. He wanted more studies of the Nile waters. He established a topographical bureau to prepare a general map of Egypt (later printed in Paris and kept a state secret), and he constantly ordered officers and civilians to report in detail on their field trips. Their activity eventually led to discovery of the Rosetta Stone (and years later the reading of heretofore indecipherable Egyptian hieroglyphics). The results of the expedition complete with magnificent illustrations would be published in a massive twenty-four volumes entitled *La Description de l'Egypte*, the first appearing in 1809 and the last several years after Napoleon's death.

Some projects were more immediate than others. In reconvening the Institute he ordered a study made of the bubonic plague. Doctor Desgenettes regarded this as an insult to his professional competence and refused to participate, nor was he pleased when Napoleon asked the Directory to send 18–20 physicians and 60–80 surgeons for further study of the country's innumerable diseases. He continued to build hospitals and lazarets for his sick and wounded, and he became very angry when inspecting a troop hospital in Cairo to discover a lack of such essential medicines as *la pierre infernale* (silver nitrate) used for cauterizing venereal patients; pharmacists not at their posts; patients' complaints about surgeons; lack of sheets, and nightshirts "dirtier than those in the field hospital before Acre."[12]

*

Napoleon's hatred of the English, particularly devil incarnate Commodore Sydney Smith, was matched by his loathing of the elusive Mourad-Bey who seemed to have more lives than a bevy of cats. Having written him off a score of times, Napoleon now suspected that he had been joined in the Bahryeh by some Arabs and Moroccans and was in touch with Smith to plan future evils.

So began a new campaign against the Mameluke leader. "I wish you would add to the services that you have never ceased to give us," Napoleon wrote General Friant in early July, "that very important one of either killing Mourad-Bey or causing him to die from fatigue."[13] A week later Mourad was reported heading for the Natroum lakes northwest of Cairo where Murat was ordered to pounce on him. "The general who will have the good fortune of killing Mourad-Bey will have sealed the conquest of Egypt: I very much hope that fate has reserved this fame for you."[14]

Upon learning that the wily fighter suspected an ambush and had doubled back 15 miles south of Cairo, Napoleon decided to deliver the death blow personally. "I have spent the day racing through the deserts beyond the Pyramids chasing Mourad-Bey," he informed General Kléber.[15] His chase abruptly ended when a courier brought news that a Turkish-English fleet of five warships, three frigates and 50–60 troop transports had dropped anchor at Aboukir Bay and had landed at least 10,000 troops on the beaches.

The frustrated general chasing Mourad in the desert swiftly changed into the superb army commander faced with a major invasion. In the next six days Napoleon covered over a hundred miles to reach the fort of El Rahmanyeh from where aides rushed to deliver deployment orders to Menou, Kléber, Murat and Desaix, the latter to return at once to Cairo.

As it happened there was no need for hurry. Some 8,000 or 9,000 Turkish soldiers had seized small Fort Aboukir at the tip of the peninsula to position themselves in three lines that stretched about half a mile across the flat terrain, their right on the sea, their left on a lake, an apparently strong position fronted

by redoubts and retrenchments laced with cannon and supported by cruising gunboats. This was a substantial enough
beachhead, but a beachhead is only valuable if it supports a
subsequent movement inland. For reasons best known to the
venerable Turkish commander, Hussein Seid Mustafa-Pasha,
his troops remained stationary despite a serious shortage of
water and food.

Hussein's inactivity was fatal because if a beachhead is attacked
and things go wrong for the defenders they have no place to hide.
This is what happened on 25 July when Murat's cavalry and
General Destaing's infantry and artillery tore through the defenses
on the Turkish right while Lannes' infantry simultaneously
pushed through the first line of defense on the left, killing or capturing all who failed to escape. With that the entire defense
collapsed, about 4,000 soldiers throwing themselves into the sea to
drown or be shot. Another 2,000 men fled to the small fort which
was immediately placed under siege. The turkey shoot was over in
only a few hours.

What Napoleon later described as "a large number of [enemy]
wounded and an infinite number of corpses" covered the field. A
few days later 2,500 fugitives in the fort, having been pounded day
and night by mortar and artillery shells, threw down their arms
and rushed forth to embrace French knees and beg for mercy.
They had no food, they had been drinking sea water for days – in
the first twenty-four hours of surrender 400 died from overeating
and overdrinking. The fort contained another 300 wounded and
1,800 dead. "One of the most beautiful battles that I have seen,"
in Napoleon's words, cost the French 100 dead and 400 wounded
including Murat, the hero of the day who was promoted to general of the division. It is only fair to add that Napoleon also
described the drowning enemy as "the most horrible sight that I
have seen," one he would never forget.[16]

Although he exaggerated enemy strength his claim that not
one man escaped was probably correct. While prisoners buried
their dead, the pasha and his son along with 200 officers were
sent to Cairo under guard to be held in the citadel; two prominent

Egyptian officials who had collaborated with the English were publicly beheaded.[17] The seriously wounded enemy were sent back to their ships, an altruistic act that brought unexpected results when the French emissary returned with a gratuitous stack of newspapers, courtesy of Commodore Smith.

Napoleon now learned of European events up to 10 June. The Second Coalition (principal members: England, Russia and Austria) had shattered French armies in Germany, Switzerland and Italy. France had declared war on Austria in mid March (as he had supposed would happen). General Jourdan's French army had moved on the Austrians in southern Germany only to be beaten by Prince Charles at Feldkirch and forced to recross the Rhine. Jourdan's retreat caused Masséna's army in Switzerland to withdraw to the Geneva area and take up defensive positions against the Austrians. General Schérer's army in Italy had been defeated by Kray's Austrians at Rivoli and had recrossed the Adige river, leaving Mantua under blockade. Suvarov's Russian corps now arrived in Italy, the allied command being turned over to the 55-year-old marshal who loved vodka almost as much as war. In late April, Suvarov pushed into Lombardy, seized Milan and marched into the Piedmont to occupy Turin, pushing the French force (commanded now by Moreau) to the Genoa area. The French squadron from Brest, 22 warships and 18 frigates, had reached Toulon harbor only to be blockaded by English cruisers as was a large Spanish squadron at Cartagena. A famine on Corfu had caused the French garrison there to be evacuated to France. Malta was blockaded by an English squadron but had provisions sufficient for two years.[18]

In Napoleon's mind these events were more than setbacks. They were nothing less than calamitous defeats that threatened the life of the republic. How could Jourdan let himself be beaten by Charles? How could Schérer lose what Napoleon's Army of Italy had won at such cost in lives and self-sacrifice? Undoubtedly the fault lay with a pusillanimous, corrupt and divided Directory trying to rule by committee when the nation needed a leader if it were to survive the royalist threat. In his mind there was no doubting the identity of that leader. It was time to return to France.

Napoleon's decision to leave Egypt has been a matter of controversy for nearly two centuries. He has frequently been accused not only of deserting his army but also of deceiving his generals by a hurried and secret departure, his sole purpose having been to return to France to seize power.

In righteous fury his detractors have overlooked several important points. Napoleon from the beginning regarded his mission as open-ended. Although he had promised the Directory to return to France in October 1798, that promise was contingent both on his expedition receiving subsequent reinforcements and on Talleyrand establishing favorable diplomatic relations by serving as ambassador to the Ottoman Porte at Constantinople. Napoleon realized that the situation might become more complex (thus his previously quoted reply when Bourrienne in Paris asked how long they would be gone: "A few months or six years; everything depends on events.").[19]

Once the Directory proved unable to support the expedition Napoleon became sole arbiter of these events. Left in the lurch by Paris he became his own government. A lesser man might have succumbed. Although he reported regularly, at length (and sometimes over-optimistically) to Paris, his dispatches on occasion suggest that the tail was wagging the dog. In reporting the insolence of a Portuguese fleet in appearing off Alexandria in conjunction with English ships, he informed the directors that France should send an army through Spain to seize Lisbon which would complicate English communications and provide much needed material for rebuilding the French navy.

A month later in repeating his needs we read the following: "You will not abandon your army in Egypt; you will send reinforcements, news, and will do everything that I requested in order to put a large squadron in these waters. You will send via Vienna an ambassador to Constantinople."[20]

In early February 1799 he again asked to hear from the Directory so that "I can at any rate learn what is happening in Europe in order to guide myself accordingly."[21] A few days later he informed the directors that if they went to war "against the kings I shall return to France."[22]

In Syria he had suspected that war would soon break out. Upon his return to Egypt he had ordered Admiral Ganteaume as a contingency measure to secretly keep two frigates ready to sail to France.[23] Now that war was confirmed there was no further hope of receiving reinforcements which he must have to march on Constantinople or India. Neither could he remain in Egypt and deprive the government of his military talents, nor his own career of what he believed to be its just due.

This was not a one-sided decision. Napoleon's letter of 10 February reached Paris on 13 April shortly after Jourdan's defeats in Germany and Schérer's in Italy. The looming prospect of invasion prompted Paul Barras to suggest the recall of Napoleon in order to give him the Italian command. Although the directors did not accept the notion, less than two weeks later they reversed course to send him the orders quoted at the beginning of this chapter.[24]

Napoleon's critics have also objected to the manner in which he left Egypt by turning command over to General Kléber and departing before they had personally conferred. Napoleon claimed that he had summoned Kléber to a secret rendezvous and there is evidence to suggest that he did so.[25] He later claimed that his failure to meet Kléber as scheduled was caused by his precipitate departure due to Ganteaume's fear that English warships would return at any moment, and this too may be accurate. The enduring criticism also overlooks Napoleon's extreme need for secrecy. He was undertaking a very dangerous voyage that could well have led to capture or death. Whether he wanted a face-to-face with the truculent Kléber remains a moot question, but had he informed either Kléber or other generals of his plans the word soon would have passed to the army and to enemy ears.

As for his deserting the army, he reasoned that he was trying to save an army that had been deserted by the government. The letter that he left in General Menou's hands for Kléber contained various warnings and cogent instructions along with a personal commitment to send reinforcements of men, arms and munitions just as soon as possible, a commitment he was making not only as a member of the government but as a private citizen. (This was not idle chatter, as will be seen.) If the shipments were not made, if Kléber received no news from France and if the plague continued, then he was empowered to make peace with Turkey in return for the safe evacuation of the army from Egypt. He was sure however that Kléber would appreciate the importance of Egypt to France and would realize that evacuation "would be a misfortune made the greater should we see this beautiful province in other European hands."[26]

Having sorted out the detritus of recent battle Napoleon returned to Cairo on 11 August. Other than Admiral Ganteaume and a few senior staff officers no one had reason to expect his imminent departure as he resumed normal activities in the capital. After ticking off General Desaix for not having come to Cairo for the landing crisis as ordered, he sent him a saber of "very beautiful workmanship" engraved with the words "Conquest of Upper Egypt". He also authorized him to make peace with Mourad-Bey and give him back his country estates if he promised never to keep more than ten men under arms. "However," Napoleon added, "it would be much better if you got rid of him."[27]

He sent tentatives to the Sultan of Morocco and the Bey of Tripoli asking for trade and friendship. He named 25 members of the Institute to sail for Upper Egypt in order to visit all monuments of antiquity and make new descriptions of them. He ordered 3,000 livres paid to surgeons of the recent battle and concerned himself with myriad other details. But he also alerted Bourrienne, Berthier, Lannes, Murat, Andréossy, Marmont, Monge, Berthollet and others (including a Georgian-Mameluke slave, Roustam Raza, given to him as a body servant) to be ready to accompany him on a special mission at very short notice.

Admiral Ganteaume informed him that on 17 August the English-Turkish squadron had sailed and that the road was open for departure. The party left at midnight ostensibly to make a tour of Lower Egypt. Prior to departure he met with Madame Fourés, dressed as a hussar, on whom it was said he bestowed some playful words.

In Alexandria he wrote the above cited letter to General Kléber along with farewell letters to Dugua, Junot, Desaix, members of the Cairo divan and the army. On the night of 22 August the party was hustled into small boats and carried to the waiting frigates, the *Muiron* and the *Carrère*, which hoisted sail at midnight.

The frigates hugged the African coast to avoid enemy cruisers. Progress was slow, the days dragged, innumerable card games palled. Contrary winds held them to about 250 miles in twenty days. But then they struck the equinox and at end of September the *maquis*-tinctured wind announced their approach to Corsica. Anchored in Ajaccio Bay, the small ships were immediately surrounded by excited Corsicans whose officials exempted the newcomers from the normal quarantine period against the plague.

After a six-day delay owing to unfavorable winds, a nostalgic period for Napoleon who met old friends and visited childhood haunts, the ships set out on the short voyage to France, during which they narrowly missed capture by a squadron of English warships. On 9 October 1799, they dropped anchor in the small harbor of Fréjus whose officials also exempted them from quarantine, the general feeling in the town being that "we prefer the plague to the Austrians."[28]

The following day Napoleon departed for Aix-en-Provence from where he informed the Directory that he would soon be in Paris.[29]

Notes

1   Boulay, 125–6.
2   Corr. V. Nr. 4205, Cairo, 23 June 1799.
3   Corr. V. Nr. 4225, Cairo, 28 June 1799. My italics.
4   Corr. V. Nr. 4168, Sâlhey, 9 June 1799.
5   Corr. V. Nr. 4179, Cairo, 14 June 1799.
6   Corr. V. Nr. 4188, Cairo, 19 June 1799.
7   Herold, 316.
8   Corr. V. Nr. 4190, Cairo, 19 June 1799.
9   Corr. V. Nr. 4225, Cairo, 28 June 1799.
10   Corr. V. Nr. 4273, Cairo, 12 July 1799.
11   Desgenettes (*Souvenirs*), 44; Berthier, 121–69; Gillespie, 79–85.
12   Corr. V. Nrs. 4213, Cairo, 25 June 1799; 4225, Cairo, 28 June 1799.
13   Corr. V. Nr. 4253, Cairo, 5 July 1799.
14   Corr. V. Nr. 4271, Cairo, 12 July 1799.
15   Corr. V. Nr. 4285, Gyzeh, 15 July 1799.
16   Corr. V. Nrs. 4314, 26 July 1799; 4323, Cairo, 28 July 1799; 4334, Alexandria, 4 August 1799.
17   Thiry (*Egypt*), 425.
18   Corr. V. Nr. 4341, Cairo, 11 August 1799.
19   Bourrienne, I, 120.
20   Corr. V. Nr. 3439, Cairo, 7 October 1798.
21   Corr. V. Nr. 3936, Cairo, 5 February 1799.
22   Corr. V. Nr. 3952, Cairo, 10 February 1799.
23   Herold, 312.
24   Boulay, 101–2, 125–7.
25   Corr. V. Nr. 4369, Menouf, 19 August 1799.
26   Corr. V. Nr. 4374, Alexandria, 22 August 1799.
27   Corr. V. Nrs. 4337, 4341, Cairo, 11 August 1799; 4357, Cairo, 15 August 1799.
28   Rose (*Life*), I, 215. See also Ludwig, 140; Bourrienne, I, 219; Roustam, 73–80.
29   Corr. V. Nr. 4382, Aix, 10 October 1799.

CHAPTER THIRTY

The *Coup d'État* of 18–19 Brumaire 9–10 November 1799

You have hoped that my return would put an end to so many
evils; you have celebrated it with an alliance that imposes on
me some obligations which I am fulfilling; you will fulfill
yours, and you will support your general with the energy,
firmness and confidence that I have always seen in you.
Liberty, victory and peace will restore the French republic to
the rank that it occupied in Europe, and that it has lost owing
to ineptness or treason.

Napoleon's proclamation to the army, Paris,
9 November 1799[1]

THE FRANCE THAT Napoleon returned to in October 1799 was not
a happy country. Its very existence was being challenged by a
second enemy coalition composed of England, Russia, Austria,
Naples, Portugal and Turkey. The major threat came from
Austrian and Russian armies subsidized by English gold, and
from the English navy which blockaded French ports to reduce
profitable trade to a trickle.

As we have seen, conscript French armies often indifferently
commanded had initially proved no match either for Prince Charles'
Austrians in Germany and Switzerland or for General Kray's
Austrians and Marshal Alexander Suvorov's Russians in north Italy.
This was the series of French defeats recorded in the Directory's
letter of early May that had so upset Napoleon in Egypt.

The picture had continued to darken. An ill-conceived counter-
attack against Suvorov by Moreau's army and a strong corps
under Macdonald marching up from Naples ended in disaster in

mid June when Moreau delayed his advance. Instead of attacking, Macdonald was attacked and decimated at Novi where General Joubert was killed. The defeat left the one-time French masters of Italy holding a weak line that curved from Mt. Cenis southeast to Genoa. Generals Brune in Holland and Masséna in Switzerland maintained only precarious defensive positions. By end of August the coalition armies were forming to invade France.[2]

France was also writhing internally. Despotism ruled the land. Owing to Jacobin resurgence and a host of unjust laws – such as that of enforced loans that put citizens on the brink of if not in bankruptcy, or the taking of hostages from villages suspected of disloyalty – some 45 departments were in the throes of anarchy and civil war. Brittany and lower Normandy were seriously threatened by Chouan and other rebels supported by numerous recalcitrant priests and supplied by English ships. The treasury was almost empty. Understaffed local administrations were struggling to survive. Roads, bridges and canals were in an appalling state, hospitals lacked doctors, staff and medicines, schools remained closed. Armed bands of vagrants, some as large as 800, roamed the provinces, pillaging, burning, raping. The army and police lacked men, money and means. Is it any wonder that Napoleon plaintively asked: "What have you done with the country that I left so powerful?"[3]

The machine that was supposed to remedy these and other evils, the national government, stood close to collapse. Quarrels between royalists, Jacobins, constitutionalists and moderates had reached the point of absurdity within both the Directory and the legislative chambers. Members of the Council of Ancients and the Council of Five Hundred had grown increasingly frustrated by obstructionism of royalists and radicals, and by the Directory's authoritative, often contradictory and almost always ineffectual *ukases*, not to mention its murderous interference in military affairs.

The ministries were also in disarray. Foreign affairs minister Talleyrand had been caught with his hand in the cookie jar – some months earlier he had sought a $250,000 bribe from American peace commissioners who had indignantly and loudly refused to

Macdonald, Jacques Etienne Joseph Alexandre 1765–1840
Marshal of France

pay it – a scandal that forced his resignation at a very crucial time.[4] Minister of war Bernadotte, Napoleon's rival and a fervent Jacobin, was secretly plotting to overthrow the government in favor of restoring leftist rule. Army generals and admirals were fed up with flabby government and would have welcomed any improvement (that did not interfere with their own peculations). Army finances were in a mess: the troops had not been paid for months, corruption was rife at all levels. Political anarchy had produced national lethargy. It was scarcely surprising that the average citizen and soldier had lost faith in government.

Some modern scholars, blithely overriding substantial evidence from earlier sources such as the work of Madelin, Vandal, Gaxotte and Mathiez, have attempted to defend the Directory.[5] It is true that despite eternal and widespread grumbling it was functioning with what Holland Rose termed "spasmodic energy." Bernadotte by a superhuman effort had raised a new army of 100,000 conscripts. General Masséna had driven the Russians from Switzerland, owing in part to his own tactical ability not fully recognized by the Directory, in part to the main Austrian army shifting to southern Germany for political reasons. This left Korsakov's Russian corps and a small Austrian force holding Zurich. Masséna was reinforced and attacked Korsakov in late September before Suvorov's army arrived from Italy, all but obliterating it. Suvorov was now forced into a hurried retreat from Switzerland into Germany. Czar Paul meanwhile was quarreling with England and Austria over the spoils of war and now called Suvorov home. Within France a new system of taxation was being introduced along with stronger counter-insurgency measures against the rebel Chouans.[6]

These various developments were healthy enough but they could not eradicate the continuing squabbling, lassitude, corruption and inefficiency of the Directory. So long as France was poorly governed from the top, it would be treading water before drowning under the weight of threats at home and abroad.

*

Napoleon did not at once plumb the depth of the national malaise. Having arrived in France shortly after the news of his victory over the Turks at Aboukir Bay appeared in the *Moniteur* and other papers, he was received as a conquering hero by hordes of cheering citizens as his carriage passed through festively decorated and illuminated streets in the towns and cities visited on his six-day triumphal journey to the capital. Arriving early on 16 October, he went directly to his house on the *rue de la Victoire*, his buoyant mood no doubt dampened by the prospect of a confrontation with Joséphine.

He need not have worried.

Three days earlier, when Paris had learned that Napoleon was on his way, Joséphine was dining with the new president of the Directory, Louis Gohier, who had taken a fancy to her. It was the worst possible news for Madame Bonaparte. Her various assignations were the talk of Paris salons – she had been living openly with among others Hippolyte Charles, now a wealthy if corrupt businessman – and in addition she was heavily in debt with only Napoleon to turn to. Gohier later described her rapid exit in order to intercept her husband before his brothers could report the details of her infidelities. This frantic strategy failed when her coachman chose the wrong road which caused her to spend two days searching for a man who wasn't there.

Upon returning to her small house she feared the worst and she was right: Napoleon was locked in their bedroom and refused to see her. He called through the door that he was divorcing her and that her trunks were packed for her departure. Wildly distraught, she spent the rest of the day – some accounts say two or three days – prostrate before his door, tearfully pleading her love and promising eternal devotion if only he would relent. All was in vain. It was as if she no longer existed. At wit's end she called in her children, Eugène and Hortense, to plead her case. Napoleon loved Eugène who was his aide and Hortense who was still gentle and sweet. After a long silence the door slowly opened. The next morning brother Lucien dropped by, so the story goes, expecting to find his sister-in-law gone. Instead he found the loving couple in bed.[7] To Napoleon's credit, once he had taken Joséphine back he again became the affectionate and often doting husband – at least for a time.

Young Lucien Bonaparte had developed into an exceedingly able if overly ambitious politician. A deputy in the Council of Five Hundred, he had become so popular that he had recently been elected its president (though at 24 he was six years younger than the prescribed age). A few months earlier Lucien had been instrumental in arranging the appointments of Emmanuel Sieyès and Roger Ducos to the Directory.

This Directory had veered sharply in its responsibility to carry out the terms of the 1795 constitution. Former president Paul Barras, when not seducing ladies and young men, was secretly plotting to overthrow the government in an attempt to bring King Louis XVIII to power – a service for which he allegedly was to be paid 12 million francs.[8] Sieyès and Ducos, supported by Lucien, wanted to overthrow the present government. Two other new members, Gohier and General Moulin, were in the center probably without yet realizing the perfidious nature of their fellows.

We briefly met the former priest, Sieyès, as an important political theorist and one of the more effective radicals in the early days of the revolution. The 51-year-old director had been educated in ecclesiastical studies at the Sorbonne and had risen in church hierarchy to become chancellor of the diocese of Chartres before turning to the role of revolutionary activist. Although a regicide he backed away from the excesses of the Terror – when later asked what he had done during those dangerous years he laconically replied, "I survived."

After briefly serving on the Committee of Public Safety in 1795 he was elected to the Council of Five Hundred and in spring 1799 was appointed to the Directory. Aware of the strong royalist sentiment in both legislature and country and of Barras' plot to return the monarchy, he had decided that only a dictatorship could save the republic.

Toward this end he, Ducos and Lucien Bonaparte enlisted the active support of the temporarily unemployed Talleyrand, Admiral Bruix, minister of police Joseph Fouché, a former civil servant and journalist Pierre Louis Roederer, Pierre François Réal and Jean-Jacques Régis de Cambacérès, a powerful group passively supported by numerous legislators and ranking army and navy officers. All agreed that a *coup d'état* was necessary to replace the Directory with a consulate of three members who would oversee what they euphemistically termed necessary constitutional reforms – translation: dictatorship.

To accomplish this the plotters needed what Sieyès termed "a sword," a military figurehead who after invoking the support of the army to accomplish the task would quietly disappear. Young General Joubert had been the original choice but he was killed at the battle of Novi in Italy. General Bernadotte would have been an alternative, but he was plotting his own Jacobin coup and was not interested. Nor was another Jacobin, General Jourdan, neither were Generals Moreau nor Macdonald.

At this indecisive point Napoleon arrived in a Paris illuminated in his honor to receive a standing ovation in the Council of Ancients and the shouted cheers of thousands of Parisians. Now that the military crisis had subsided he was not well received by the directors. In Sieyès mind he was scarcely the most desirable "sword" in view of his sharp temperament, obvious ability and scarcely concealed ambition. But time was running out. Either Barras or Bernadotte could soon strike. Napoleon was undeniably able and was immensely popular both in the country and in the army. It was a matter, in essence, of *faute de mieux*.

Lucien made him the offer: his support in return for becoming one of three governing consuls. Napoleon did not immediately accept. He was tired and he needed rest and relaxation, particularly in Joséphine's arms. He was entertaining friends such as Pierre Simon Laplace, the brilliant mathematician-astronomer who had recently published *La Mécanique Céleste*, and he reveled in other intellectual companionship. He probably doubted that the coup would succeed – one wonders what would have been his

Lucien Bonaparte, Prince of Canino

decision had the Directory ordered him to rebuild the broken Army of Italy.

But Napoleon also weighed other factors. Although he had been given a hero's welcome by the populace he knew that this type of fame was fleeting, and he also recognized that recent French military victories in Holland and Switzerland – the latter gained by a potential rival, General Masséna – had somewhat tarnished his own unfinished effort in Egypt. Nor had he taken long to discern the national mood, civil and military, in particular the almost universal unpopularity of the Directory. Napoleon had excellent ears: Lucien and Joseph, General Berthier, General Marmont and other officers, aides and civilians who had returned with him. As he wrote Marmont, "When the house is crumbling, is it time to busy oneself with the garden?"[9] Further and very important, he realized that Sieyès (who was anything but a leader) could easily be won over when the time came, and there is also a suggestion that he had the secret support of a large part of the army.[10]

What else could he look forward to? He had no military command. He was facing a hostile Directory which had received him almost insultingly. He had received no tentatives from the Barras and Bernadotte camps, but he loathed both royalists and Jacobinists. In short he was in professional limbo. *Faute de mieux* he accepted the offer.

After extensive if hurried covert planning (joined by Moreau and Macdonald) the action opened early on 9 November in the Tuileries where the august senators of the Council of Ancients had been hastily summoned by Sieyès and Ducos acting without authority of their fellow directors. There the senators were persuaded to approve two decrees. The first called for immediate transfer of both legislative houses to the outlying St. Cloud for reasons of security. The second decree named General Napoleon Bonaparte commander in chief of the troops in and around Paris who were to protect the legislators.

Duly sworn in, Napoleon underlined the emergency created by those legislators "who wished to make trouble and discord" for "a republic founded on true liberty."[11] He then transported his spirited oratory to the beautiful gardens and the waiting troops with whose aid the republic would be established "on the bases of civil liberty [and] internal happiness."[12] He followed this with a proclamation to the rest of the troops concerning these "constitutional acts." The republic, he explained, "has been badly governed for two years," and he continued as quoted at the beginning of this chapter.[13]

Talleyrand and Admiral Bruix meanwhile had called on Paul Barras and coerced him into resigning from the Directory, an unexpected demotion assuaged in part by a bribe of 2 million francs. The two other directors, Gohier and Moulin, repaired to the Tuileries where Napoleon bluntly informed them that the Directory had been dissolved. In fury they returned to Luxembourg palace only to be put under military guard.

The overthrow of government continued on 10 November in the old château of St. Cloud. Bewildered senators gathered in the great hall had finally realized that something was amiss and after affirming allegiance to the constitution they passed a resolution calling for the election of a new Directory. This information brought Napoleon storming into the hall with some grenadiers, a scene that has been described variously both by onlookers and subsequently by often biased historians. The official version of Napoleon's address was published at the time in the *Journal militaire* and some decades later in the official *Correspondance*, an impassioned and lengthy effort several times interrupted by one or more venerable and angry senators. The unofficial but more likely version described a speech delivered in tantrum-like incoherency. Bourrienne for one was appalled – "General, you no longer know what you are saying" – and only with difficulty persuaded him to leave the hall.[14]

An already shaken Napoleon next invaded the Council of Five Hundred which was meeting in the *orangerie* with Lucien in the chair. Seeing the accompanying grenadiers the younger members

Le dix-huit Brumaire 9 Novembre 1799

went wild, screaming "down with the tyrant." A scuffle ensued and there is some evidence that daggers and even firearms appeared as Napoleon was physically assaulted and was extricated only by General Lefebvre and the soldiers, a graceless exit accompanied by shouts of the damning curse of Corsican days, *hors la loi* – outside the law. When Lucien refused to accept a motion declaring his brother an outlaw, he was turned on and was rescued only by more soldiers.

The Bonaparte brothers, Sieyès and the coterie of generals were severely upset, and with good reason. The coup stood at a crossroad. It was one thing to disband the generally scorned Directory, but it was a far more serious matter to challenge the freedom of the elected legislature. But if that body were not quickly brought to heel the conspirators would undoubtedly end on the guillotine. No one realized this more than Sieyès who had a carriage and six horses standing by for a quick escape. Ironically it was he who at this critical moment kept his cool and advised Napoleon to send in the grenadiers.[15]

The next question concerned the loyalty of those grenadiers – was it to their commander or to their legislature? Lucien recovered to mount his horse and address the nervous, somewhat confused soldiers, explaining that a group of armed royalist deputies in English pay were threatening the lives of their fellows. It was up to the soldiers to save the day. Dramatically unsheathing his sword and pointing it at his brother, he swore to run him through if he ever threatened the precious liberty gained by the revolution, words loudly applauded by the waiting generals. Napoleon followed this harangue with an appeal to avenge his insult: "I wanted to speak to the deputies and they answered me with daggers."[16] The soldiers were won over. "*Vive la république!*" was repeatedly shouted from the ranks. "To arms!" Napoleon ordered. The ominous roll of drums filled the air as grenadiers with bayonets at the ready pushed into the *orangerie*, the terrified deputies jumping through windows and crowding through doors.

A few hours later a chastened Council of Ancients and the remnants of the Council of Five Hundred accepted Napoleon,

Sieyès and Ducos as the nation's consuls authorized to direct a provisional government.[17]

Notes

1   Corr. VI. Nr. 4387, Paris, 9 November 1799.
2   Thiébault, II, 16–17.
3   Adye, 21–2. See also Madelin (*Consulate*), I, 34–46.
4   Adams, I, 238–43.
5   Steven T. Ross, "The Military Strategy of the Directory: The Campaign of 1799," *French Historical Studies*, Vol. 5, Nr. 1, 1967.
6   Rose (*Life*), I, 217, 220.
7   Herold, 334–5. See also Bourrienne, I, 224–6; Bruce, 271–4.
8   Herold, 329.
9   Rose (*Life*), I, 218. See also Fouché, 76–81.
10 Corr. VI. Nr. 4387, Paris, 9 November 1799.
11 Corr. VI. Nr. 4385, Paris, 9 November 1799.
12 Corr. VI. Nr. 4386, Paris, 9 November 1799.
13 Corr. VI. Nr. 4387, Paris, 9 November 1799.
14 Herold, 339.
15 Rose (*Life*), I, 224–6. See also Roustam, 91–2.
16 Herold, 340. See also Corr. VI. Nr. 4389, Paris, 10 November 1799.
17 Madelin (*Consulate*), I, 1–23.

CHAPTER THIRTY-ONE

THE CONSULATE RULES
NOVEMBER 1799–FEBRUARY 1800

*We have a ruler who knows how to do everything, who is able
to do everything, and who wants to do everything.*

Emmanuelle Sieyès on First Consul Bonaparte[1]

THE NEW CONSULS were soon at home in the Directory's old and
luxurious offices in the imposing Luxembourg palace from which
they commenced to consolidate their victory. On the basis of
widespread military popularity and known administrative and
military talents, Napoleon easily assumed the overlordship. So
long as he was running the government the army would support
it.

The coup had caught opposition Jacobin and Royalist parties
by surprise. By the time they began to recover, the consuls had
filled ministerial offices with their supporters: Berthier, minister of
war (soon replaced by Lazare Carnot); Talleyrand, minister of
foreign affairs, Lucien Bonaparte, minister of interior; Forfait,
minister of the navy; Gaudin, minister of finance; and Fouché,
minister of police.

Napoleon's popularity was not confined to the armed forces.
The average Frenchman was neither an extreme rightist nor a
radical leftist. He was a person trying to support a usually numerous family, and he had become thoroughly disgusted by a paralytic
government forever quarreling with a politically divisive legislature while the country was falling apart. If he could not expect
Napoleon to solve overnight the weighty problems that confronted

the nation, at least he knew that action would be taken toward solving them.

He was right.

Napoleon always saw affairs in military terms. The successful coup no matter how dicey was in his mind a victorious battle. Any good general knew that a victorious battle should be swiftly exploited if possible, in this case by assuring the nation that better times were ahead.

The deposed legislators had not stopped panic-stricken flight when Napoleon published a proclamation in the *Moniteur* that in fanciful terms informed the good citizens of France of his risk of life and limb by answering the appeal of the Council of Ancients to eliminate the enemies of legitimate government.[2] He followed this by thanking the army and the national guard for saving his life during the coup – certain soldiers and officers would in time receive generous rewards.[3] Two days after the coup the nation was asked to pledge its loyalty "to the Republic one and indivisible, founded on equality, liberty and the representative system." Napoleon personally dictated this decree but generously allowed Ducos and Sieyès to add their signatures.[4]

Almost at once he ordered the writing of a new constitution. The task was given to Sieyès and Boulay de la Meurthe who were to work with a special commission of fifty members, half chosen from the Council of Ancients and half from the Council of Five Hundred. This effort would shortly result in a complex and impressive corpus designed to end internal strife while in theory guaranteeing individual liberties under representative government.[5]

With these formalities out of the way Napoleon turned to the enormous tasks of administration which would fill his days and nights for months ahead. They ranged from borrowing large sums of money from bankers in Paris, Amsterdam and Lisbon, to implementing the metric system of measurement, to annulling harsh treatment of French émigrés who had been shipwrecked and detained, to declaring the *Moniteur* the official newspaper of France, to guaranteeing the freedom of religion and repeal of "unjust laws" – and, most important, to reorganizing and strengthening the army.[6]

To his credit he soon attempted to keep his promise to General Kléber in Egypt by ordering some ships, providing they could evade the English blockade, to carry news of the coup to Alexandria along with cavalry replacements, thousands of muskets, sabers and pistols, thousands of cannon-balls, and even a troupe of actors, comedians and dancers. In early December he published a special proclamation to the Army of the Orient which assured the soldiers that they were not forgotten by their country. Other decrees called for payment of a third of the soldiers' pay to wives who had remained in France, as well as pensions to officers' widows.[7]

Internal security was his most important concern in these formative months. A serious uprising of the Chouans in the Vendée, Brittany and lower Normandy was being fought by the army and there were other uprisings in the Midi or south. The Chouans formed the major threat since they were strongly supported by the English who were stripping the provinces of wheat and who were rumored to be planning a large-scale troop landing at Brest. The victorious coup had somewhat dampened rebel spirits, a development exploited by the new government which eliminated certain harsh counter-insurgency measures such as taking hostages from villages suspected of royalist sympathies and forcing citizens to make loans and contributions to the government, and by propitious treatment of rebellious priests and various partisan chiefs. In late November a number of the latter agreed to an armistice that would lead to a peace (however fragile). Those who refused to see reason – "the brigands, the émigrés, the mercenaries hired by England" – were to be eliminated by military means.[8]

The Consulate also decreed that a deputy representative would be assigned to each *arrondissement* with the task of explaining to the people the reason for the coup and the goals of the new government. These thinly disguised *représentants en mission* (the dreaded Jacobin overseers) were to work with army commanders and trusted republican officials in gauging "the principles and morality of public functionaries" whom they were empowered to suspend or replace for adverse political behavior.[9] Army commanders were to explain to the people that the revolution was ended, that peace and tranquillity would reign, and they were to take military action against those factions which thought otherwise.[10]

External security was also a priority consideration. Although Napoleon was burning with desire to personally drive the Austrians from Italy, he had to move slowly. In early December he ordered Berthier to meet with generals Moreau and Clarke "to work out an operations plan for the new Army of the Rhine" which hopefully would be ready to move into Bavaria by month's end. Meanwhile General Masséna was to command the Army of Italy and was given "extraordinary powers" to revitalize the discouraged units.[11] To support the intended campaign Napoleon was undertaking what almost amounted to a reorganization and certainly a revitalization of the entire army. This effort was well underway by mid December when the new constitution was ready for promulgation.

The document prepared by Sieyès and reshaped to Napoleon's liking was offered to the nation with considerable fanfare that belied its true nature. Rather than a guarantee of democratic government it was basically designed to control if not eliminate the disruptive influences of royalist and Jacobin radicals in order to allow the executive – the new Consulate – to get on with the awesome task of repairing the country's ills. It was more significant for what it guaranteed – a change from anarchy to order – than for what it represented. "Citizens," Napoleon told the nation, "the revolution remains faithful to the principles which gave birth to it. It is finished."[12]

The new constitution was basically a manipulative front for a dictatorship that was to endure for the next fifteen years. It did pay lip service to democratic procedures in that candidates for the new legislature were to be chosen by an extremely complex

electoral process that began with local communities and pro-
gressed through district, department and finally national levels.
However this convoluted process merely furnished a pool of
politicians from which the actual members of the legislature
would be chosen arbitrarily by the Consulate – in essence by First
Consul Napoleon.

The executive branch held most of the real powers. In theory it
ruled through a council of state as conduit to the various ministries; in fact Napoleon frequently dealt directly with his
ministers. He was authorized to appoint all members of the three
legislative bodies, the senate, the assembly and the tribunate; all
members of governmental administration at all levels, national,
departmental, district and municipal; all government ministers; all
ambassadors; all military and naval officers. The three consuls
were to serve for ten years at annual salaries of 150,000 francs.
They would reside in regal splendor in Luxembourg palace, they
would be waited on hand and foot, and would be guarded by a
consulate corps of 2,100 veteran soldiers commanded by General
Murat.[13]

A truncated legislature voted the constitution into law in late
December. In early January 1800 some 3 million voters approved
it with 1,500 voting against it. This was more a vote for Napoleon
than for representative government – indeed the elections of legislative candidates were postponed for a year. Prior to the national
vote Sieyès and Ducos resigned. Sieyès was appointed president of
the new senate and was given a valuable estate (to which he retired
and which soon became a core of opposition to the Consulate).

Sieyès and Ducos were replaced by Jean Jacques Cambacérès
and Charles François Lebrun. The choice reflected Napoleon's initial policy of conciliatory and moderate government. Cambacérès
was 46 years old, a regicide which made him particularly attractive
to the Jacobin element, but he was also a learned jurist, recently the
minister of justice and more recently an active supporter of the
coup, but a man more interested in legal reform than in politics.
Lebrun was 60 years old, a skillful lawyer and politician known as
a moderate liberal who, favoring a constitutional monarchy,

appealed to conservatives needed to support Napoleon's wide-ranging plans.

The First Consul was now free to go to war. Although he wooed Czar Paul I of Russia and celebrated Christmas by writing flattering peace tentatives to King George III of England and to Emperor Francis II of Germany (Austria), he also issued a stirring proclamation to the army: "Soldiers! It is no longer a matter of defending your frontiers but of invading enemy countries . . . When the time comes I shall be with you." He also made a special appeal to the soldiers in Italy to help General Masséna repair the disciplinary lapses of the past. (As always came the carrot with the stick, in this case rewards to officers and men ranging from silver-chased muskets and engraved sabers to double pay for outstanding performance.)[14]

He already had ordered his naval minister to prepare expeditions to the West Indies, the Red Sea, India and China, their mission being to disrupt British trade. Cristoforo Saliceti was to recruit six battalions of Corsicans to seize Sardinia and depose its king. General Moreau, commanding the Army of the Rhine, was to prepare for combat: "The aim of the Republic in making war is to bring peace . . . [if] the court of Vienna's intentions conform to ours then the first wish will be fulfilled . . . if it hesitates, a brilliant victory and the invasion of Bavaria will correct its ideas and carry our arms to the borders of the Hereditary States [of Austria]." As part of this strategy Moreau was authorized to conclude a three-month armistice with the Austrians providing it included the forces of Italy.[15] While Napoleon was careful to compliment Moreau's zeal and military talents he nevertheless sent a special agent to report on the exact strengths of his divisions, their locations and state of readiness.[16]

In early January, Napoleon ordered Admiral Bruix to sail for Egypt with a formidable fleet to carry reinforcements and supplies to General Kléber and to attack any English ships he found there. Simultaneously Admiral Lacrosse was to sail for Madeira to seize whatever English vessels he discovered before sailing on to San Domingo, Jamaica and Cuba. Proceeding to Barbados and the

Bahamas, he was to sweep up the American coast, sinking all English ships encountered, and finally to destroy the Newfoundland fisheries before returning home by the Azores.[17]

These grandiose plans were only in the making when rebellion flared once more in the Vendée, Brittany and lower Normandy. Napoleon's policy of moderation having failed, he turned with a vengeance to armed force. General Hédouville who commanded the Army of the West some 17,000 strong was ordered to break up and disarm the rebel bands: "act as freely as if you were in the middle of Germany." He was to turn over town and city defenses to local national guards and move his troops into the countryside where they belonged. Priority targets were the bands of two principal leaders, Comte Louis de Frotté in Normandy and Georges Cadoudal in Brittany. If Hédouville employed "rigorous and energetic measures" he would have no trouble eliminating them and lesser bands – the problem did not compare with insurgencies in Egypt since the French rebels had neither the gift of terrain appreciation nor the mobility of the Arabs. In Napoleon's mind the success of a counter-insurgency operation depended only on brute power speedily applied with maximum terror: shoot anyone caught with a firearm, burn villages which sheltered or supported rebels, act fast and hard: "Feebleness alone is inhumane." Although Napoleon was willing to negotiate a peace with submissive chiefs and priests, Hédouville was not to forget "that this civil war will be terminated only when the insurgents no longer have arms, and they will be inspired by great fear to a way of life conforming to moderation, good order and justice."[18]

A special proclamation informed the inhabitants of the target areas that moderation had given way to the sword: henceforth no contact under any pretext with rebels; towns with populations of over 5,000 people to furnish mobile columns which would protect smaller towns from rebel raids; any person caught either carrying arms or preaching rebellion to be shot on the spot.[19] Certain rebellious districts no longer enjoyed constitutional protection – the army could go where it wished and act without restraint to accomplish its mission.

Napoleon believed that these various measures would quickly end the uprising. When they failed to do so he did not question the efficacy of his own strategy and tactics which were as full of holes as a Swiss cheese. Instead he relieved Hédouville who "had neither enough energy nor enough adaptability" in favor of General Brune and raised army strength to 60,000. Brune was to force lazy generals who remained inactive in towns into the countryside to lead unceasing punitive drives: "The post of honor is the bivouac and the barns."[20]

At first Brune seemed the right man for the job. In early February an exalted Napoleon informed General Masséna in Italy that "the Vendée is three-quarters pacified; Brune has defeated Georges [Cadoudal] and his band of the Morbihan [a *département* in Brittany]. Everything makes me hope that the war will be over in fifteen days."[21]

Fifteen days passed and the war continued. "Do you wish then," Napoleon asked General D'Arnaud, "to be the only [commander] who will fail to acquire glory . . . or do you believe that you will win glory in keeping your headquarters in a city? Move [so] that your first courier notifies me that you have dispersed, disarmed and destroyed the brigands of the Sarthe, and that day and night you are in pursuit of their dispersed bands." General Gardanne who was fighting around Calvados and the Manche in Normandy was to promise his soldiers 1,000 louis for Frotté's head and 100 louis for the head of each lieutenant. Other commanders were to demand submission and if that failed they were to make all-out attacks leading to Napoleon's beloved "decisive battle." He repeatedly stressed the need to end the insurgency by late February. He was doing his bit on the Paris front: "Every day five or six Chouans here are executed by firing squad. A great number of arrests have been made."[22]

Ironically his goal was achieved at least in part by a conciliatory political-diplomatic approach. Through the mediation of a Vendéean priest, Abbé Bernier, he won over a number of priests and with them the submissions of several lesser but still important rebel chieftains. Cadoudal however refused generous terms in what must have been a nervous meeting of the two in Paris since according to Cadoudal's friend, Hyde de Neuville, Cadoudal wanted only to strangle Napoleon with his bare hands.[23] Napoleon's reaction was not so strenuous: "He seemed to me to be a coarse Breton who perhaps will work for the best interests of the country," he informed General Brune.[24] Although Cadoudal continued to fight, his time was short and he soon escaped to England.[25] Frotté continued to hold out until he was captured, courtmartialed and shot.[26] Although a few bands remained active (and would cause a great deal of future trouble) the target areas were more or less pacified by late February.

The insurgency had brought both gains and losses to the nation. Émigrés were now allowed to return home along with other political exiles, but they were not to regain their properties that had been seized and often sold to private citizens or designated as national lands. Orthodox priests who had refused obeisance to the 1795 constitution were allowed to return to their parishes so long as they promised allegiance to the new constitution.[27]

But these gains palled beside the losses. The only debative body of the legislature, the tribunate, was forced to limit time for debates, virtually a gag order that drew heavy criticism from the liberal thinker, Benjamin Constant, among others. Napoleon had grown increasingly annoyed with the liberal opposition stemming from Madame de Staël's salon and she was relegated to live in the country. In mid February the press learned that it could not print any information "relative to movements of the armies on land and sea," the first step in what soon became harsh censorship and suppression of hostile newspapers and journals.[28]

These military movements were becoming considerable. While Brune's army was fighting the Vendéean rebels Napoleon was planning not only invasions of Sardinia, San Domingo and Minorca, but also a major offensive designed to remove the Austrians from Germany and Italy.

Notes

1   Adye, 17.
2   Corr. VI. Nr. 4389, Paris, 10 November 1799.
3   Corr. VI. Nr. 4443, Paris, 24 December 1799.
4   Corr. VI. Nr. 4391, Paris, 12 November 1799.
5   Rose (*Life*), I, 229–34. See also Miot de Melito, I, 154–8; Madelin (*Consulate*), I, 24–33.
6   Corr. VI. Nrs. 4430, Paris, 19 December 1799; 4439, Paris, 23 December 1799; 4457, Paris, 26 December 1799; 4473, 28 December 1799; 4477, Paris, 29 December 1799. See also Madelin (*Consulate*), I, 11–17.
7   Corr. VI. Nrs. 4393, Paris, 15 November 1799; 4411, Paris, 2 December 1799; 4428, Paris, 18 December 1799; 4438, Paris, 22 December 1799; 4494, Paris, 4 January 1800; 4606, Paris, 15 February 1800; 4612, Paris, 26 February 1800.
8   Corr. VI. Nrs. 4477, 4478, Paris, 29 December 1799; 4488, Paris, 30 December 1799; 4498, Paris, 5 January 1800. See also Rose (*Life*), I, 229; Madelin (*Consulate*), I, 16–18.
9   Corr. VI. Nr. 4395, Paris, 20 November 1799.
10 Corr. VI. Nr. 4493, Paris, 4 January 1800.
11 Corr. VI. Nr. 4437, Paris, 22 December 1799.
12 Corr. VI. Nr. 4422, Paris, 21 December 1799. See also Madelin (*Consulate*), I, 32–3.
13 Rose (*Life*), I, 232–3. See also Corr. VI. Nr. 4459, Paris, 26 December 1799.
14 Corr. VI. Nrs. 4449, 4450, 4451, Paris, 25 December 1799. See also Madelin (*Fouché*), 136.
15 Corr. VI. Nr. 4432, Paris, 21 December 1799.
16 Corr. VI. Nr. 4433, Paris, 22 December 1799.
17 Corr. VI. Nrs. 4494, 4495, Paris, 4 January 1800.
18 Corr. VI. Nr. 4499, Paris, 5 January 1800. See also Madelin (*Fouché*), 136 ff.
19 Corr. VI. Nr. 4506, Paris, 11 January 1800.
20 Corr. VI. Nr. 4523, Paris, 14 January 1800.
21 Corr. VI. Nr. 4565, Paris, 5 February 1800.
22 Corr. VI. Nrs. 4580, 4581, Paris, 11 February 1800; 4589, Paris, 13 February 1800.

23   Rose (*Life*), I, 237–8.
24   Corr. VI. Nr. 4639, Paris, 5 March 1800.
25   Corr. VI. Nr. 4744, Paris, 1 May 1800.
26   Corr. VI. Nr. 4603, Paris, 18 February 1800.
27   Rose (*Life*), I, 235.
28   Rose (*Life*), I, 239.

CHAPTER THIRTY-TWO

PRELUDE TO MARENGO
DECEMBER 1799–MAY 1800

*The goal of the Republic in making the war is to
bring about the peace.*

Napoleon to General Moreau, Paris,
21 December 1799[1]

UPON MOVING FROM Luxembourg palace to the Tuileries in late
February 1800, Napoleon remarked to secretary Bourrienne,
"Well now, here we are in the Tuileries and here we must
remain."[2] By this he meant that he must checkmate all attempts of
either royalists or Jacobins to unseat him and at the same time persuade the French citizenry that the peace so ardently desired could
only result by defeating the armies of the Second Coalition.

The task required enormous dexterity but it was somewhat
eased by his opponents. As we have noted, early in the Consulate
he proclaimed himself peacemaker by sending tentatives to King
George III of England and to Emperor Francis II of Germany
(Austria). As perhaps he had anticipated, his letter to the English
king caused an immediate parliamentary outcry against France.
Lord Grenville in full moral majesty proclaimed that "peace was
impossible with a nation whose war was against all order, religion
and morality."[3] William Pitt in righteous indignation declared
"that the French Revolution was the severest trial which
Providence had ever yet inflicted on the nations of the earth."[4]
After levying similar accusations against the barbaric behavior of
France, King George in his reply called for "the restitution of
that line of princes which for so many centuries maintained the

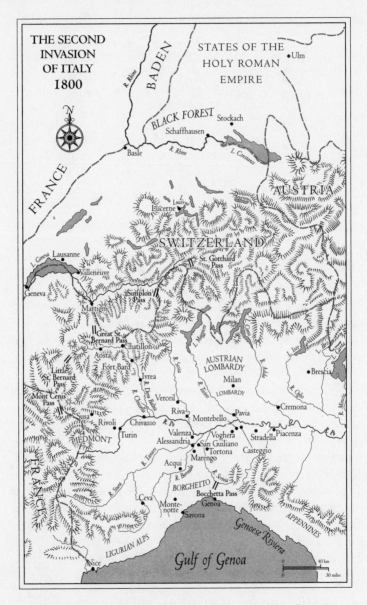

The Second Invasion of Italy (battle of Marengo) May–June 1800

French nation in prosperity at home and in consideration and respect abroad."

Although this demand to reinstate the Bourbon monarchy in France appealed to nervous European rulers, it did not mend the torn fabric of the Second Coalition as the English king had hoped. Suvorov's Russian army was continuing its march northward away from war, and Czar Paul was about to order home another 25,000 Russian soldiers who had been sent to the Channel Island of Jersey to assist a British landing in France. Prussia showed no sigh of abandoning its neutrality, and France was about to end its brief war with the United States – peace preliminaries would be signed at Mortefontaine in February. What the note did produce was a fervid outbreak of patriotic sentiment in France ably exploited by Napoleon in rousing the nation to furnish him "the money, weapons and men" necessary to support a new campaign.[5]

Napoleon's tentative to the Austrian court was not so much harshly treated as it was evaded in an acknowledgment that left matters as they were. He replied that a new peace should be negotiated on the scuttled Treaty of Campo Formio with certain modifications, and he proposed an armistice while this was worked out. Not unnaturally the Aulic Council in Vienna was unwilling to yield the results of recently gained victories in the Rhineland and Italy since it seemed that the French were on the verge of being pushed out of Italy. The surrender of General Masséna's besieged Army of Italy in Genoa would expose General Suchet's small force on the Var to attack, opening the way for an invasion of Nice, Provence and the Savoy.[6]

Thus the court paid only lip service to Napoleon's proposal by agreeing to what became prolonged and meaningless diplomatic exchanges while the war continued. But the net result also benefited him, not only because he was trying to make peace (or so it seemed to the French public) but also because the Austrians, believing that his initial peace-feeler demonstrated weakness, did not pay requisite attention to French preparations for a new campaign.[7]

Napoleon's intentions in Italy were only part of his strategy. While diplomats bustled about exchanging long-winded notes during these winter and spring months of the year 1800, the ever slow-moving French navy was assembling a powerful French-Spanish battle fleet at Brest designed to succor General Vaubois at Malta and General Kléber in Egypt. This accomplished, it would sail to the Balearic islands to seize the Minorcan port of Mahon as a major step toward gaining control of the Mediterranean. Simultaneously Cristoforo Saliceti was preparing an expedition to sail from Corsica to seize Sardinia.

A still larger fleet was to land 6,400 troops in San Domingo to settle a civil war and install General Pierre Dominique Toussaint L'Ouverture as dictator. Toussaint, a negro, was to guarantee the freedom and equality of the blacks in carrying out a policy of conciliation similar to what Napoleon was pursuing in the Vendée, Brittany and Normandy. The battle fleet was then to proceed up the American coast in pursuit of English shipping. Another four frigates were to sail to northern waters between Iceland and Greenland to disperse or capture English whaling ships, and possibly to continue on to Hudson Bay to raid and destroy the principal fur-trading ports. Finally, Talleyrand was to suggest to the Spanish court that since Portugal refused to make peace it might be a good idea to seize a few of its provinces – Napoleon would gladly lend a division of troops if necessary.[8]

Standing above these expensive and extensive ancillary operations was the need to eliminate the immediate enemy threat in Italy. General Mélas could not be allowed to gain a foothold in France which would only bring on a severe political crisis.

Austria's field forces consisted of two armies. One about 100,000 strong was commanded by General Kray in southwestern Germany. The other of lesser strength was commanded by General Mélas in Italy. The overall Austrian position, though still strong, had been weakened by the Russian Suvorov's defeat in and withdrawal from Switzerland the previous autumn. Where once relatively easy communication had existed between Kray and Mélas, this was now reduced to tortuous routes through eastern Switzerland and the Tyrol – in short, they were all but separated at a crucial time in the Italian offensive.

Opposing these armies were General Moreau's Army of the Rhine which would soon number about 120,000 men, and General Masséna's Army of Italy now about a tattered 40,000. Kray's divisions across the Rhine in and around the Black Forest were relatively quiescent despite some sharp skirmishes.

It was a different story in Italy. The Austrian offensive which had recovered most of the lands won by Napoleon had pushed the French army into the port of Genoa from where a ragged line of defense ran northwest to Mt. Cenis. Such had been the earlier deplorable state of this now fragmented army that Napoleon had turned it over to one of his best generals: André Masséna, who had chased Suvorov's Russians out of Switzerland. As Masséna soon reported, the Army of Italy was sick and starving, its soldiers dressed in rags had not been paid for over six months. Ammunition was in dangerously short supply. There were few horses, hardly any carts, no food, no forage – Masséna was putting all soldiers including himself on half-rations. He could scarcely have been overjoyed, then, when in late January he received a lengthy and convoluted order from Paris to attack enemy positions along the Levantine Riviera east of Genoa and execute certain maneuvers that a force in top condition would have found difficult.[9]

Something of his plight rubbed off on the First Consul who in early February sent him 1.5 million francs, a hefty sum followed by further large payments. He also congratulated Masséna on "the firmness that you have employed in reestablishing discipline in your army," but he still wanted a major attack on the enemy, and he would continue to press for offensive actions throughout March and even into April when Masséna's army was starving to death behind Genoa's walls.[10]

Napoleon's unrealistic reaction to Masséna's gloomy reports is curious unless we take into consideration first, the problems

caused by extended and difficult communications, second a pronounced trait in Napoleon's character that we have come across
earlier, a refusal to accept any obstacle to his own wishes.

In communicating with the northern armies the Tuileries could
to a certain extent rely on a primitive semaphore system to expe-
dite important messages. Called the telegraph, this had been
invented a few years earlier by Claude Chappe. It consisted of
towers 6–10 miles apart each with an optical device to flash semaphore signals to the next tower. Each station was manned by two
men, one with a telescope receiving and recording the message,
one working the device to pass it on. Entirely dependent on fair
weather, the system could move a message up to 200 miles a day.[11]

Even with such a system, which was lacking in the south, it is
doubtful that Masséna could have shocked Napoleon into the
remedial action called for in dispatches that required forever and a
day to reach Paris. Napoleon could not have furnished substantial
material aid without endangering his own strategy to reconquer
Italy. Moreover he held the Austrian army in general contempt –
Mélas "is not a very able general," he informed Masséna, "having
neither your military talents nor your energy." Contrary to
Masséna's repeated protestations Napoleon continued to regard, or
at least pretend to regard the Army of Italy as a viable force. In
early March he informed the general that he was forming an Army
of Reserve under General Berthier's command (the First Consul
was prohibited by the constitution from commanding an army)
and was sending an aide with plans for the coming campaign
"where you will see that your role will be most important and will
not exceed the means at your disposal." In mid March he ordered
Masséna to pull in his forces from the northwest in order to
strengthen his defenses around Genoa: "Here are the true military
principles, in acting thusly you will defeat 50,000 men with 30,000
and will cover yourself with immortal glory."[12]

Napoleon's apparent misreading of Masséna's strength strongly
influenced his initial plan for the new campaign. In late December

he had informed General Moreau that if the Austrians did not come to the peace table, "a brilliant victory and the invasion of Bavaria may change its mind and bring our armies to the borders of the Hereditary States [of Austria]." His plate being filled with domestic problems including the Vendéean insurgency, nothing more was heard on the subject for several weeks, but he also sent Moreau over 6 million francs, ordered him to make extensive reconnaissances of the Alpine crossings into Italy and in late January asked for his ideas "concerning the military operations of the forthcoming campaign."[13]

Unlike most of his brethren, French or Austrian, Napoleon was not thinking in terms of a two-theater war. He envisaged a single line of operations running initially from the right or northern bank of the Rhine, ultimately from the Danube, across Switzerland and over the Alps to Genoa.

Moreau's four corps would concentrate between Basle and Lake Constance. Three of these corps would open the campaign by crossing the Rhine between Schaffhausen and Lake Constance to strike Kray's flank and force him to retreat northeast beyond Ulm all the way to the Bavarian border. Moreau would then cut Kray's direct communication with Milan by Lake Constance and eastern Switzerland. Moreau's fourth corps, some 25,000 troops commanded by General Lacourbe, would deploy in Switzerland to protect Moreau's right flank and prevent the enemy from occupying the Alpine passes, the St. Gotthard and the Simplon.

Once Moreau's force crossed the Rhine the newly formed Army of Reserve would close on Geneva. If Moreau ran into trouble Berthier would move to his support. If Moreau's operations proceeded smoothly Berthier would leave a small covering force in Switzerland and, joined by Lacourbe's corps, cross the Alps to fall on Mélas' main force wherever it might be.[14]

This was a brilliant concept of pivotal strategy but it did contain two weaknesses. One was the assumption that the plodding and unimaginative Moreau would advance with requisite speed to protect Berthier's flank, the other that Masséna could hold out in the Genoa area.

Napoleon informed Moreau in late March that the campaign would open a month later. Much of the onus lay on General Berthier and his chief of staff, General Dupont, who were at Dijon trying to form a large army by snagging remnants here, remnants there, willing young volunteers, unwilling young conscripts, demi-brigades from the Army of the West, cavalry squadrons from a dozen scattered posts, artillery from a score of depots. The recruits lacked uniforms, arms and equipment; training was at best rudimentary, if even that.

The logistical task was enormous. In addition to Moreau's immediate needs he was to build a depot at Lucerne containing 100,000 bushels of barley, 500,000 rations of biscuit and a million musket cartridges. Two hundred thousand pounds of lead were sent to General Marmont's artillery depot at Auxonne and other arsenals to be molded into musket and cannon-balls. Blacksmiths and other specialists were to open workshops in Geneva to make horseshoes, rim wagon wheels, manufacture munitions, harnesses, artillery carriages and other vital accoutrements. Money flowed like water: millions of francs to Masséna, to Nice, Dijon, Auxonne, to Moreau's headquarters, to Geneva. But money could not buy time. "No cartridges, no lead," Berthier complained. "The artillery coming from the [Army of the] West is without horses. There is not a single means of transport." Marmont was desperately short of artillery and skilled gunners. By late April many of the workshops had not yet opened in Geneva. Five million cartridges were still in Paris and there was a serious shortage of powder, horses, wagons, gun carriages and provisions.[15] It was a race against time which more than one ranking general and official doubted could be won.

Napoleon's other major problem during these hectic weeks was to raise civilian morale as one way of combating divisive royalist and Jacobin plots. His first step was to adopt an appealing profile of leadership. As opposed to the social excesses and scandalous behavior of previous directors, he and Joséphine, although living regally in the Tuileries, received only the most respectable guests and in general led a restrained social life.

To win national support for his forthcoming campaign he struck in several directions. Young Lucien Bonaparte, now minister of interior, was to have a patriotic song written whose words would fit a familiar tune such as the *Marseillaise*. Lucien was also to supervise construction of granite columns to the memory of soldiers who died "in defense of country and liberty." A column inscribed with the names of the dead would occupy the main square of each departmental capital and the Place de la Concorde in Paris. To win recruits he appealed to the youth to enlist in "an army destined to end the war of the revolution by assuring the independence, liberty and glory of this great nation: to arms! to arms!" Although these stirring words produced thousands of willing volunteers, the opposite side of the coin emerged from Napoleon's later disgruntled remark to one of his generals that "most of the conscripts supplied to the 30th demi-brigade deserted with weapons and luggage before reaching Dijon."[16]

This patriotic hoop-la scarcely appealed to everybody. As criticism mounted so censorship increased. In early April theater owners in Paris and the provinces learned that no dramatic work could be staged without the express permission of the minister of the interior. In Paris the number of theaters was to be reduced. (In the same order, Napoleon desired Lucien to suppress some pejorative lines in a popular song.) Police minister Fouché was to rigorously censor journals and newspapers (and to inform one "Monsieur Payne" that he was behaving badly and if he did not shape up he would be sent back to America).[17]

Meanwhile the forthcoming campaign was heating up. On 9 April Napoleon instructed Berthier to visit Moreau's headquarters and work out an operations plan to fulfill three goals: Moreau's march into Swabia with Berthier's army in support, if necessary; Berthier and one of Moreau's corps to cross into Italy; to leave enough troops in Switzerland to prevent an Austrian attack from the east. Napoleon outlined the plan to General Masséna on the same day. Once Berthier's army crossed into Italy, Masséna should coordinate his movements accordingly so as to attract the attention of the enemy and oblige him to divide his forces, and then join Berthier's army.[18] (At this point Masséna was *in extremis* behind Genoa walls.)

During the next two weeks Napoleon received driblets of information to the effect that the enemy had seized Montenotte and Savona, but that Masséna had beaten off a major attack and had taken 2,000 prisoners. General Suchet's two divisions had fought a separate action and were forced to retire to the line of the Borghetto river, but they also garnered 1,200 prisoners. As Napoleon explained to Berthier, he hoped that Masséna would subsequently have recaptured Savona or at the very least was holding against the Austrian onslaught. Although Napoleon was sending a division of troops as well as munitions and food to Masséna, it was vital for Berthier to come into the action "independently of the Army of the Rhine."[19]

Suddenly the operative word was speed. Berthier was to let Moreau's army take care of itself and, as opposed to the earlier plan, cross the Alps by the western Great St. Bernard Pass, thus shifting his line of communications westward. The road from Aosta to the Po river, he was warned, might prove difficult: "Your greatest effort in all this will be to assure your supplies."[20]

On 26 April Napoleon, learning by the telegraph that Moreau had opened his campaign, prepared to join Berthier. He was still undecided as to tactical goals. "It is possible that it is no longer necessary to go to Milan," he wrote to Berthier, "but that we may be obliged to march with the greatest speed on Tortona in order to extricate Masséna who, if he has been beaten, will be locked in Genoa where he has food for thirty days."[21]

By the time Napoleon arrived in Geneva in early May this new scenario had almost jelled, even though he still refused to accept Masséna's increasingly desperate situation. Masséna and Suchet were to be informed by special courier that the Army of Reserve would be in Piedmont by 10 May and that they should act according to circumstances: once the enemy was weakened by having to meet the Army of Reserve, "they should try to regain

the lost territory." Napoleon's new estimate of the situation credited General Mélas with a maximum 40,000 troops including
cavalry posted in the plains. Neither the Aulic Council in Vienna
nor Mélas in Italy had the slightest notion of the forthcoming
French movement: "I have very certain information that the
Army of Reserve is mocked at in Vienna and in Italy; they do not
believe that it will be ready before August . . . that it is a collection
of conscripts to complement the Army of the Rhine."[22]

Napoleon was about to correct enemy ignorance. Berthier was
to have a million rations of biscuit at Villeneuve within a few
days, enough for the troops to receive a four-day supply.
Additional biscuit would be on hand at Martigny and the village
of St. Pierre. The monks of St. Bernard at the top of the pass
would provide the troops with a ration of wine and cheese, and
barley and oats for the horses. "You see that I concern myself a
great deal with your affairs," Napoleon informed Berthier, "but
this is because in truth the success of the campaign depends on
your operations, and I have no doubt that you will have the glory
of reconquering this beautiful country." Berthier should have no
qualms concerning the operation because his right flank would be
guarded by some 5,000 troops under General Chabran crossing
the Little St. Bernard Pass, his left by General Lecourbe's corps
guarding the St. Gotthard and Simplon passes.[23]

Napoleon next learned that Masséna was blocked in Genoa
where he either would remain or surrender – he had enough food
to hold out until late May. Napoleon ordered him to hold out
until 30 May but in a letter to Suchet changed this to 4 June on the
assumption that the Army of Reserve would be in the Piedmont
by 14 May. Since Mélas would need only eight days to march the
bulk of his army to Aosta, it was imperative for Berthier to get
some troops there first. Berthier accordingly was to start the
march over the Alps as soon as possible. Napoleon would join him
in four days.[24]

Prior to leaving Paris, Napoleon learned by the telegraph that
Moreau had won an important battle at Stockach where he captured 7,000 Austrians, nine cannon and considerable supplies.

His congratulatory message ended: "glory and three times more glory."[25]

Notes

1   Corr. VI. Nr. 4432, Paris, 21 December 1799.
2   Adye, 25.
3   Rose (*Life*), I, 242.
4   Rose (*Life*), I, 243.
5   Madelin (*Fouché*), 136.
6   Rose (*Life*), I, 244.
7   Rose (*Life*), I, 243–4. See also Corr. VI. Nr. 4623, Paris, 27 February 1800; Adye, 59, 61.
8   Corr. VI. Nrs. 4670, Paris, 24 March 1800; 4726, Paris, 22 April 1800; 4727, Paris, 23 April 1800; 4749, Paris, 2 May 1800; 4750, Paris, 3 May 1800.
9   Corr. VI. Nrs. 4458, Paris, 26 December 1799; 4543, Paris, 21 January 1800; 4642, Paris, 5 March 1800. See also Adye, 27–8, 34–5.
10 Corr. VI. Nrs. 4543, Paris, 21 January 1800; 4565, Paris, 5 February 1800; 4642, Paris, 12 March 1800.
11 Crefeld (*Command*), 62.
12 Corr. VI. Nrs. 4642, Paris, 5 March 1800; 4662, Paris, 12 March 1800.
13 Corr. VI. Nr. 4557, Paris, 31 January 1800.
14 Corr. VI. Nrs. 4695, Paris, 22 March 1800; 4710, Paris, 9 April 1800.
15 Corr. VI. Nrs. 4695, Paris, 22 March 1800; 4738, Paris, 27 April 1800.
16 Corr. VI. Nrs. 4683, Paris, 20 March 1800; 4722, Paris, 21 April 1800; 4790, Lausanne, 14 May 1800.
17 Corr. VI. Nr. 4707, Paris, 5 April 1800.
18 Corr. VI. Nrs. 4710, Paris, 9 April 1800; 4712, Paris, 11 April 1800.
19 Corr. VI. Nrs. 4728, 4729, Paris, 24 April 1800.
20 Corr. VI. Nrs. 4729, Paris, 24 April 1800; 4738, Paris, 27 April 1800.

21 Corr. VI. Nr. 4738, Paris, 27 April 1800.
22 Corr. VI. Nrs. 4742, Paris, 28 April 1800; 4747, Paris, 2 May 1800.
23 Corr. VI. Nr. 4747, Paris, 2 May 1800.
24 Corr. VI. Nrs. 4751, Paris, 4 May 1800; 4755, Paris, 5 May 1800.
25 Corr. VI. Nrs. 4758, 4759, Paris, 5 May 1800.

CHAPTER THIRTY-THREE

THE CROSSING OF THE ALPS
MAY–JUNE 1800

I offered peace to the Emperor [Francis II], he has not wished
it. Nothing remains for us but to go after him.

Napoleon to his soldiers, Vevey, Switzerland,
15 May 1800[1]

NAPOLEON ARRIVED IN Geneva on 9 May to assume unofficial command of the Army of Reserve. This force of some 40,000 men shaped up well on paper. An advance guard of two infantry divisions (Watrin and Mainoni), Rivaud's cavalry brigade and an artillery train was commanded by the able and aggressive general, Jean Lannes. The main army consisted of four divisions, two (Loison and Boudet) commanded by General Duhesme, two (Chabran and Chambarlhac) by General Victor. Murat commanded the cavalry, Marmont the artillery and Marescot the engineers. Chabran's small corps formed the right flank. Moreau had grudgingly agreed to provide Lecourbe's strong corps to shield Berthier's left flank but, caught up in operations in Germany, now reneged, substituting General Moncey's far inferior corps to deploy south of Lausanne. An additional corps 4–5,000 strong commanded by General Turreau would move into Italy from the western mountains, push through any enemy and eventually join up with the Army of Reserve.

The first problem was to get that army across the Alps by way of the Great St. Bernard Pass while Chabran crossed by the Little St. Bernard Pass (which subsequently would serve as a second supply conduit).

As Charlemagne had learned many centuries earlier, this route posed an enormous challenge. Once across the snow-covered pass the troops would march down a barren valley to the old Roman town of Aosta to be joined by Chabran's corps. The army would then march on Fort Bard which, defended by Austrian troops, blocked its entry into the rich Piedmont plains. This fort once seized, the march would continue to Ivrea, also defended, in theory arriving there on 19 or 20 May. Moncey's corps in the St. Gotthard area south of Lucerne meanwhile was to carry out false maneuvers and demonstrations to hold Austrian forces there while Turreau's corps marched in from the west to seize the town of Susa and catch up the main army.[2]

Once the army gained Ivrea, Napoleon would choose between two courses of action, depending on what news he received from General Masséna at Genoa. If Masséna continued to fend off the Austrians the Army of Reserve would march eastward, cross the Tecino river and seize Milan to cut Austrian lines of communication. If Masséna were in deep trouble then the army would march directly on Genoa to attack Mélas' besieging corps.[3]

The paper force to accomplish this scenario was considerably reduced in flesh. As Napoleon determined in several days of whirlwind inspections, uncomfortably large numbers of untrained conscripts and volunteers lacked proper uniforms, arms and in some cases even shoes; a large number still had to be taught how to load, aim and fire their muskets. Murat's cavalry was also below par. "A good many squadrons will be going over the pass," Napoleon informed Berthier, "and if . . . [the horses] are not better fed than at present they will arrive in Italy dead." Murat was to reorganize his brigades: "There are neither transport officers nor quartermasters, and the result is that nobody knows where to get supplies."

The problem was not so much a lack of clothing, shoes, provisions, arms and munitions as the means to move them. A serious shortage of wagons, carts, horses and mules would continue to plague future operations – rarely if ever would legs play such a vital role. The artillery lacked trained gunners, cannon, carriages and munition caissons which had not yet arrived from Auxonne.

Although General Moreau had won three battles and was advancing on Ulm, he again reneged on his promise of Moncey's diversionary corps of 20,000 men, earmarking only isolated and far-distant detachments of inferior troops. Napoleon wrote to him to the effect that if he failed to supply Moncey *with the corps ordered by the government* he would be responsible for the failure of the campaign. General Turreau's corps was also an unknown quantity and would remain so for some weeks.[4]

Napoleon reported none of these problems to the consuls in Paris whom he informed on his arrival in Geneva: "The entire army is on the move and in the best possible order . . . All goes very well." This startling optimism so at odds with the actual situation would become a hallmark of the campaign – for good reason. The Consulate's power position was still somewhat fragile owing to the determination of both royalists and Jacobins to topple the new government: "strike vigorously the first to step out of line," Napoleon ordered Fouché in Paris. "This is the wish of the entire nation."[5]

This concern for the preservation of the Consulate (and probably the lives of the consuls) would become a recurring theme in future dispatches and (though often overlooked) would play a major role in the conduct of the campaign.[6] The French people must under no circumstances learn of the teething problems of the Army of Reserve. "For the welfare of France, [military] reverses are essential," Madame Germaine de Staël had said, and there were all too many disgruntled royalists who agreed with her.[7] The French nation must learn of one thing only and that was victory – defeat would probably finish off the Consulate and the republic.

However the military picture was not altogether bleak. Though scarcely a ball of fire, Berthier continued to untangle awkward operational and supply knots. Most of his generals were first-rate, a formidable command group that in a few weeks would be joined by one of the very best, Loius Desaix, who had just returned from Egypt.

Napoleon's arrival also worked wonders. The confused and lackadaisical air that had pervaded the new army soon vanished. As in past campaigns, he seemed to be everywhere at once, an omniscient force, scolding and correcting here, cajoling and praising there, bracing officers to do the impossible, exciting troops by fiery speeches and limitless energy. What seemed to have been a pointless series of exhausting marches suddenly turned into an important mission of saving the peace by winning the war. "I offered peace to the Emperor [Francis II]," he told the troops, "he has not wished it. Nothing remains for us but to go after him."[8] He spent only two days in Geneva where a letter from Joséphine awaited him. "I love you very much," he responded, "write me often and believe that my Joséphine is very dear to me."[9]

The snow-covered Great St. Bernard Pass towers 8,100 feet above the waters of the world. The march began at Villeneuve where the troops received four days of biscuit to get them to Martigny. There they received biscuit for another three days as they trudged up the steep, twisting road, a grueling march of nearly 20 miles to the tiny village of St. Pierre. Here the road gave way to a steep rutted track that led some seven miles to the pass marked by the hospice of the monks of St. Bernard. Once through the narrow pass – the track itself was only eighteen inches wide, hemmed in by enormous crags dangerously pregnant with snow – the troops faced a steep and dangerous descent to Aosta.[10]

Lannes' advance guard marched on 15 May, his mission to cross the forbidding pass, descend to Aosta and move on to seize the vital fortress of Bard. Considering the fragile transport arrangements the march went reasonably well. The troops received advance rations as Napoleon had arranged. As also arranged, the monks of St. Bernard laid out tables in front of the hospice and as each tired and cold soldier filed by he was given two glasses of wine and a small ration of rye bread and cheese – an effort that in one day consumed 1,300 bottles of wine and 83 lbs of cheese.[11]

The true test came in getting the heavy cannon up to and across the pass. Neither gun carriages nor ammunition caissons could carry loads further than St. Pierre. Foreseeing the problem Marmont and Gassendi had special sledges built at Auxonne to carry the ammunition chests, the dismantled carriages and empty caissons. But what of the guns? A cannon of eight with carriage weighed nearly 4 tons, a piece of four with carriage nearly 3 tons, a mortar with carriage 3.5 tons.[12]

Marmont's solution was to remove the cannon from its carriage and place it in a hollowed-out pine tree fitted with a rope harness. A team of soldiers or peasants 100 strong then dragged each gun up the steep narrow track over frozen, snow-covered ground, a feat that required two days per gun. Pulling the sledges proved even more difficult than hauling up the cannon. Since mules were in short supply, many having died from lack of forage, soldiers and peasants had to bear the brunt of this gigantic effort that took seemingly forever to complete. The troops performed magnificently. Despite the danger of provoking sudden avalanches, bands blared martial music along the way while at the most difficult parts of the track drummers beat the charge. One team preferred to bivouac in the snow rather than leave its cannon – once over the pass, its soldiers refused a bonus of 2,400 francs saying that they preferred to exact the sum from the Austrians. Within three days, Napoleon reported to the consuls, despite "ice, snow, storms and avalanches" the entire army and a third of the artillery were in Italy.[13]

Napoleon sent off this report from Martigny where he spent three days in a Bernardine convent in the middle of the Valais and the Alps never seeing daylight, as he informed Joséphine, owing to the workload. Joséphine wished he would write to her daughter Hortense: "I shall write her when she is a great lady: she is still too young; one does not write to children." News of Christine Bonaparte's death was upsetting, and her husband, Lucien, must be very sad: "To lose your wife is to lose, if not glory, at least happiness."[14]

His somewhat nebulous plans had begun to harden. He had recently received a message from General Masséna in Genoa written in late April – a plea to come immediately to lift the siege. Next came a letter dated 11 May from General Suchet in Nice – the Austrians had forced the important pass into France, the Col de Tienda, and the defensive line of the Borghetto which caused Suchet to evacuate Nice and take refuge in the citadel and nearby forts. This was the worst possible news. Napoleon was still very much in the dark as to Mélas' strength and dispositions which he could not determine until he reached Ivrea, if even then, but it was now apparent that his enemy was much stronger than he had supposed. Having ordered Lannes to push on to Ivrea, he reassured Suchet that the enemy would not cross the Var, adding: "I shall be at the foot of the St. Bernard Pass tonight: I shall march on Ivrea from where I shall determine the enemy's latest movements and maneuver accordingly."[15]

At this point Lannes had yet to reach Aosta, and between Aosta and Ivrea was Fort Bard. Bard was a well-known strategical and tactical choke point. Napoleon and at least some of his generals were all too aware of its potential danger, as pointed out by a study of the Franco-Italian-Swiss frontier that he had ordered the previous January. Only a week earlier General Dupont, Berthier's chief of staff, had written that the army would be at Ivrea on 18 May "if the fort of Bard does not delay us."[16] Napoleon's apparent assumption that it would not delay the army is as curious as his earlier remark to Berthier that it was necessary to determine the condition of the roads beyond Aosta. Why hadn't the January report covered this important requirement? Perhaps Napoleon assumed that Berthier had sent forth the necessary spies and that the fort was lightly defended. Or perhaps he didn't give a damn as to its strength – it was in his way, it had to be taken so it *would* be taken – and that was that.

In creeping down the valley of the Aosta millions of years ago an enormous glacier had been split by the jointure of two mountains. Nature had left an opening at their bases however, a narrow gorge about 50 yards wide flanked by the Dora Baltea river. This natural obstacle which guarded Piedmont from the north had eventually been exploited by its defenders building an upper and lower fort that towered over the tiny village. Through the centuries the fort had changed hands several times. In spring of 1800 it was held by 400 Austrian soldiers whose 18 cannon commanded the narrow road below.*

Napoleon informed Berthier on 18 May that he was holding the cavalry at Martigny until he learned of the capture of this "wretched fort of Bard." Lannes was to occupy the heights above the fort as prelude to assault, and was to be informed that "the fate of Italy and perhaps the [French] Republic hangs on [its] capture."[17]

Lannes scouted the heights above Bard the next day to discover a rough track barely adequate for a foot soldier, thus needing considerable widening to accommodate guns and wagons. Berthier meanwhile arrived on the scene and was horrified at the strength of this "very real obstacle" which, as he informed Napoleon, was far more than "we had expected." Plainly discouraged he added that if he could not capture it within three days he would be "in a very awkward position, as he only had provisions enough to last up to the 24th [of May]."[18]

The report did not seem to unduly upset Napoleon, who left Martigny with secretary Bourrienne and aide Duroc in tow on 20 May. At the village of St. Pierre he mounted a mule (which for posterity's sake would be replaced by a magnificent stallion, courtesy of artist David's canvas) for the journey to the pass. Perhaps influenced by the good monks' wine during a brief stop at the hospice, the group reverted to childhood and had a merry old time sliding down a reverse slope.[19]

Once settled in the seminary at Aosta, Napoleon ordered local authorities to round up all available rice, grain and salt to supplement provisions slowly coming in over the Little St. Bernard Pass.

---

*The fort is extant and the drive up to it and back very exciting, an effort well worthwhile not only because it demonstrates the challenge to the French but also because it offers the most wonderful views of this beautiful country.

Berthier's engineers were to recruit a task force of peasants to widen the rude track above Bard "which would have to be very bad to be worse than that of the St.Bernard."[20]

Lannes already had bypassed Bard with Watrin's grenadiers and had defeated a waiting Austrian force. Several miles short of Ivrea he cheered Napoleon with a brief message: "We shall have a fine time. From the reports I have had from people in this district, it looks as if the enemy does not know which way to turn . . . We are in a splendid position here."[21]

It seemed as if nothing could check the irrepressible Lannes. With a comparative handful of infantry, no artillery and no cavalry he went on to attack Ivrea that was defended by a fort and a garrison of 6,000 Austrians with 14 cannon. His totally unexpected appearance threw the enemy into such confusion that in a few hours of fighting Watrin's division seized the town, the fort, all of the cannon and killed, wounded or captured 600–1,000 Austrians at a cost of twenty French casualties.[22]

On the other hand, an attempt to sneak through Bard village at night was foiled by soldiers in the fort illuminating the road with flares followed by cannon fire. General Moncey reported from Lucerne that he had received only 11,000 infantry and cavalry from Moreau instead of the promised force of some 20,000 men. Berthier reported rumors of a large Austrian force approaching Ivrea from the south. Prisoners captured at Ivrea stated that General Mélas was still at Genoa whose garrison was expected to fall in a few days. Chief engineer Marescot quashed Napoleon's plan to seize Bard by bombardment followed by scaling the walls – such an attack required cannon which the army didn't have (shades of St. Jean d'Acre). A blockade would eventually bring surrender, Marescot believed.[23]

The situation then was scarcely encouraging. By Napoleon's own count his fragmented army, a large part of which was still stuck at Bard with the bulk of its meager artillery, was about to come to grips with a newly estimated 66,000 Austrian troops (a figure far short of the mark owing to Mélas having been reinforced). Admittedly these were dispersed from Milan to Nice, but if Masséna caved in at Genoa a large number would quickly move on the French.

One of Napoleon's strengths lay in his respect for the positive. Lannes and Watrin were fighting superbly. Their victory at Ivrea only strengthened his conviction that the Austrians still had not divined either his strategy or his strength. Chabran's vanguard was about to arrive at Aosta with eight cannon, the rest of the division to follow. Moncey's report was a disappointment – it was that damn Moreau who was sabotaging Napoleon's campaign – but at least Moncey now had over 11,000 troops and was preparing to cross the St. Gotthard Pass. The Bard impasse was equally disappointing but the infantry, cavalry and all but the heavier guns were slowly bypassing the place by the improved track. Food shortages were serious – weeks earlier he had warned Berthier that supply would be his chief problem – but that would improve as supply lines developed and as the army reached rich Italian plains. He had received no word from General Turreau, but contact should result once Lannes fought his way into Chivasso.[24]

In Napoleon's mind, therefore, the good outweighed the bad. "The enemy appears to be surprised by our movement," he informed General Brune at Dijon on 24 May, "he does not know what to make of it; he still seems scarcely to believe it." And to Joseph Bonaparte the same day: "Please give 30,000 francs to my wife. The biggest obstacles are surmounted; we are masters of Ivrea . . . We have struck here like a thunderbolt, the enemy in no way expected it and can scarcely believe it." Berthier and his force obviously needed a shot in the arm provided by Napoleon moving his headquarters to a village near Fort Bard. According to a young lieutenant his sudden appearance "electrifies the souls, fortifies the hopes, increases the desires and brings to all hearts the noble ambition to triumph under his eyes." Thus inspired, Loison's division made a night attack on the fort, a costly failure despite Napoleon's claims to the contrary. The bulk of the army now having bypassed the fort – a few cannon, the carriage wheels covered with rags to deaden the noise, even slipped through the town at night – Napoleon and Berthier turned over the effort to General

Chabran and departed for Ivrea. A few days later the Austrian garrison surrendered.[25]

Napoleon faced an anxious moment of truth in the new head-quarters at Ivrea. What now? He had recently learned from Suchet that about 15,000 enemy were in Nice and that Mélas was in Ventimillo. In response to a report that a strong French corps had arrived in Geneva, Mélas had moved General Bellegarde with 5,000 men into the Piedmont. Later reports credited 20,000 Austrian infantry besieging Genoa with another 10,000 standing by in Lombardy; Austrian cavalry regiments were reportedly at Turin and west of Alessandria.

The French counted between 30,000 and 40,000 troops but only a few small cannon. Supply lines were still primitive. But Lannes had fought his way well south of Ivrea and General Turreau's corps was supposed to be on the march from the west to join the main army. General Mélas reportedly had returned to his Turin headquarters but apparently had not recognized the extent of the French incursion and was still concentrating on the siege of Genoa.

According to memoirs dictated nearly twenty years later on St. Helena, Napoleon at Ivrea considered three courses of action: a march on Turin to fight Mélas there; a direct march to relieve Masséna at Genoa; a march on Milan to cut Mélas' lines of communication so as to leave his army either to wither on the vine or to give battle under conditions presumably favorable to the French.[26]

In view of Masséna's predicament Napoleon probably should have marched directly to the relief of Genoa. His orders to move on Milan instead have been harshly judged by later critics. The condemnation is perhaps unfair. Napoleon defended his decision by pointing to a new and more realistic notion of Austrian strength obtained from officers captured at Ivrea. He now reckoned that Mélas, dispersed troops or not, was three or four times stronger than he was. This was certainly a major factor in his thinking – he had always paid the closest attention to relative strengths – if only because he could not afford to be defeated by plunging into a tactical unknown. Earlier he had shown prudence by shifting the crossing of the Alps from the more exposed easterly passes to the safer St. Bernard Passes. His orders often stressed the importance of guarding a secure line of retreat. By marching on Milan not only would he gain the support of General Moncey's 11,000 troops along with vast amounts of food, forage, munitions and hospitals, but also (and not least) two new lines of retreat via the Simplon and St. Gotthard Passes.

Another factor often overlooked by critics was Napoleon's conviction that Masséna could hold out if only because "one besieged soldier is worth twenty besiegers."[27] Add to this the general's own reports of successful forays against the enemy – if Masséna could so fight he could presumably carry on despite his serious situation, or so Napoleon reasoned. Even ignoring this misplaced optimism it is difficult to fault his strategy in refusing to risk a largely unproved army to save a corps when it appeared that a far safer course of maneuver could result in an even more decisive victory.

It was time to act. Lannes was to seize Chivasso on the Po river not far from Turin, which would cause Mélas to believe that he intended to join Turreau between Rivoli and Susa. Meanwhile the main army spearheaded by General Murat's cavalry would march east on Verceil, preceded by General Lechi's Cisalpine Legion of 2,000 Italian volunteers on its left. Lechi was to cross the Sesia river at Riva and push through enemy detachments to open the Sesia valley to supply wagons.

The plan worked beautifully. Lannes won a splendid victory at the Chiusella river and entered Chivasso, the enemy garrison retreating into Turin. This action brought Napoleon to review the victorious troops which he praised to the skies. Here he learned that Turreau's corps had won a major battle a few days earlier at Susa where he captured 1,500 enemy and large quantities of arms, food and munitions. He also learned that Mélas was definitely at Turin and was calling in all available corps.

"All goes for the best here," he jubilantly informed the consuls. "I shall be in Paris before June 19th."[28] And to Joséphine:

> I depart in an hour for Verceil . . . The enemy is very baffled; he still does not understand [what we are doing]. I hope within ten days to be in the arms of my Joséphine who is always charming when she is not crying or playing the role of coquette. Your son [Eugène Beauharnais] arrived this evening . . . he is fine . . . I received the letter from Hortense. I will send her a pound of very good cherries by the next courier. We are [weatherwise] here a month ahead of Paris. I am all yours.[29]

Marching all out, in some cases stopping only to eat, Murat and Duhesme's corps fought a series of skirmishes, crossed the Tecino river under fire and continued to march on Milan. In early June, Napoleon and Berthier followed Murat's advance guard into the capital of Lombardy whose Austrian defenders fled, leaving only a small force blockaded in the old citadel and 1,800 sick and wounded in the hospitals. The new occupants, delighted to find large quantities of food, powder, ammunition and cannon, were in general well received. Napoleon soon informed the consuls in Paris that the rapacious Austrians had taken away everything but the trees of Lombardy. They also had stripped bare the Piedmont and had left the King of Sardinia in Florence with only a cheap carriage, four servants and barely enough money to live on.[30]

General Lannes meanwhile had come up from the Po on the army's right, crossed the Tecino and occupied the important town of Pavia to find large stores of food, 10,000 new muskets, 200,000 lbs of gunpowder, cannon and cannon-balls and, as an unexpected bonus, a number of secret letters from General Mélas to the Aulic Council in Vienna.[31]

Napoleon next pushed Duhesme with two divisions northeast toward Brescia and east toward Cremona, while Murat marched south to cross the Po and seize Piacenza. General Moncey's advance guard had crossed the St. Gotthard Pass and would be followed by the rest of his force.

These movements having been carried out, often against considerable but generally dispirited opposition, Berthier moved army headquarters to Pavia to better direct the major task of crossing the Po in strength – the final move before battle.

Notes

1   Adye, 40.
2   Corr. VI. Nrs. 4792, 4793, Lausanne, 14 May 1800.
3   Corr. VI. Nrs. 4792, Lausanne, 14 May 1800; 4825, Martigny, 19 May 1800.
4   Adye, 87–9, 107. See also Corr. VI. Nrs. 4797, Lausanne, 14 May 1800 – my italics; 4802, Lausanne, 15 May 1800; 4804, Lausanne, 15 May 1800; 4826, Martigny, 19 May 1800.
5   Corr. VI. Nr. 4764, Geneva, 9 May 1800; Fouché, 138–41.
6   See, for example, Corr. VI. Nrs. 4834, Aosta, 24 May 1800; 4849, Ivrea, 27 May 1800; 4867, Milan, 4 June 1800.
7   Madelin (Consulate), 72.
8   Adye, 40.
9   Napoleon Lettres (Tulard), 147, Geneva, 11 May 1800.
10 Corr. VI. Nrs. 4785, Vevey, 13 May 1800; 4852, Chivasso, 28 May 1800. See also Bellune, 110–20; Madelin (Consulate), 237–47. The author recently traced the army's route. As was the case in the earlier march of the Army of Italy up the eastern side of Lake Garda, one can only marvel at the achievement in marching man, beast and cannon up, through and down the pass.
11 Adye, 103.
12 Adye, 105. See also Rothenburg (Warfare), 76–9.
13 Corr. VI. Nrs. 4811, Martigny, 18 May 1800; 4814, 4815, Martigny, 18 May 1800; 4830, Aosta, 22 May 1800; 4846, Aosta, 24 May 1800; 4848, Aosta, 26 May 1800. See also Larchey, 83–7.
14 Napoleon Lettres (Tulard), 150–1, Martigny, 18 May 1800.
15 Corr. VI. Nrs. 4807, 4808, Lausanne, 16 May 1800. See also Adye, 113.
16 Adye, 84.

17 Corr. VI. Nrs. 4812, 4816, Martigny and Aosta, 18 May 1800.

18 Adye, 126.

19 Corr. VI. Nr. 4846, Aosta, 24 May 1800. See also Adye, 128–9; Constant, 5.

20 Corr. VI. Nr. 4828, Étroubles, 20 May 1800.

21 Adye, 135.

22 Corr. VI. Nrs. 4824, Aosta, 21 May 1800; 4852, Chivasso, 28 May 1800. See also Bellune, 124–8.

23 Adye, 124, 133, 144–5.

24 Corr. IV. Nr. 4828, Étroubles, 20 May 1800.

25 Adye, 147, 149. See also Corr. VI. Nrs. 4836, Aosta, 24 May 1800; 4865, Milan, 3 June 1800.

26 Adye, 154–7. See also Corr. XXIX, XXX.

27 Corr. VI. Nr. 4795, Lausanne, 14 May 1800.

28 Corr. VI. Nr. 4849, Ivrea, 27 May 1800.

29 Napoleon Lettres (Tulard), 151–2, 29 May 1800.

30 Corr. VI. Nrs. 4864, Milan, 3 June 1800; 4882, Milan, 4 June 1800. See also Adye, 166.

31 Corr. VI. Nr. 4865, Milan, 3 June 1800.

CHAPTER THIRTY-FOUR

THE BATTLE OF MARENGO
14 JUNE 1800

*I shall soon be in Paris. I cannot tell you more; I am in
the most profound sadness at the death of the man I loved
and admired the most.*

Napoleon to consuls Cambacérès and Lebrun, Italy,
15 June 1800[1]

WHILE HIS GENERALS were setting the scene for a final act Napoleon
remained in Milan with his aides, his 18-year-old body servant
Roustam and his new valet inherited from Joséphine, 21-year-old
Constant Wairy. He savored his popular reception as liberator of
Lombardy. "The First Consul was obliged to show himself frequently to the public," one bulletin announced, because the
enemy "is claiming that this is not he but one of his brothers."[2]
Recognition turned to general adulation which he increased by
playing on people's hatred of Austria's allies, the Croats and the
English. "The *Te Deum* has been sung at the capital of Milan," an
early bulletin read, "for the successful deliverance of Italy from
the heretics and the infidels."[3]

Religion was henceforth to be a major weapon in the winning of
Italy, as a convocation of local priests soon learned:

Persuaded that [the Catholic religion] is the single [one]
able to provide a true happiness to a well ordered society
and to strengthen the bases of a good government
[Napoleon told them] I assure you that I shall endeavor to
protect it and defend it at all times and by all means . . . I

declare to you that I shall consider anyone who makes the least insult to our common religion or . . . [to] your sacred persons as a threat to public peace and enemy of the common good, and will punish as such in the most rigorous and striking [way], if necessary by death.

More was to come as prelude to a future *rapprochement* with Rome that would briefly sparkle before collapsing under the weight of its hypocrisy:

The modern *philosophes* [Napoleon continued] endeavored to persuade France that the Catholic religion was the implacable enemy of the entire democratic system and republican government, and from that resulted the cruel persecution that the Republic exercised against the religion and its ministers . . . [but] I too am a philosopher and I know that, in whatever the society that exists, no man can become virtuous and just if he does not know from where he came and where he goes.

Possibly with the Venerable Bede's parable of the Sparrow and the Mead Hall in mind, he went on:

. . . without religion one walks constantly in darkness . . . and the Catholic religion is the only one that gives to a person certain and infallible enlightenment as to his origin and his final end . . . A society without religion is like a ship without a compass . . . A society without religion, always disquieted, perpetually unsettled by the conflict of the most violent passions, experiences in itself all the furies of civil war which plunges it into a bottomless pit of evil and which sooner or later infallibly brings about its ruin. France, taught by its misfortunes, has finally opened its eyes; it has recognized that the Catholic religion was like an anchor that alone could fix it in its turmoils and save it from the stresses of the storm . . . I assure you that

the churches are reopened in France, that the Catholic
religion regains its former renown, and that the people
view with respect these sacred holy shepherds who have
returned, full of zeal, to the midst of their abandoned
flocks.[4]

Napoleon followed this outburst with an emotional appeal to the
Cisalpine peoples for renewed unity. Simultaneously almost daily
he dictated the all-important bulletins – victory bulletins from
first to last, large portions of which appeared in the *Moniteur* to be
eagerly devoured by the good citizens of Paris – while coping
with new crises that arrived with each courier from the capital.

Some were easier to handle than others. Learning that the
Vendéean rebel, Georges Cadoudal, had returned from England to
Brittany, Napoleon ordered General Bernadotte, commanding the
Army of the West: "If you capture the wretch shoot him within
twenty-four hours."[5]

With future peace negotiations in mind Napoleon asked
Talleyrand to have an anti-Austrian pamphlet written in German
and distributed throughout the Germanic states. The Batavian
(Dutch) government was to be sharply reminded that in accordance with the Treaty of the Hague it was to supply a corps of
7,000 Dutch soldiers very quickly in order not to compromise the
present campaign. Talleyrand was also to send an emissary to St.
Petersburg to pave the way for negotiations with Czar Paul concerning common interests in the event of a breakup of the
Ottoman empire.[6]

Closer to home war minister Carnot was to build a second
Army of Reserve, remount and resupply the cavalry and fill
French arsenals with weapons: "I will not regard the Republic as
consolidated so long as there are not three million muskets in its
arsenals."[7]

So the days passed, words flowing from the First Consul's
mouth one minute and from the general's mouth the next, to keep
secretaries dipping quill pens into an ocean of ink while a regiment of couriers carried inspirational orders of the day to the

troops, operational orders to Berthier and his generals, victory bulletins to Paris.

Probably Napoleon should have been paying more attention to military issues and especially to the enemy during his eight-day stay in Milan. While he was immersed in a variety of matters broken by an occasional relaxing concert and a torrid love affair with the famous diva, Madame Grassini, General Mélas was slowly putting together an army much stronger than Napoleon supposed.

The Austrian general in chief had been so intent on seizing the glittering prize of Genoa from Masséna that he failed to understand what Napoleon was up to. His secret reports to the Aulic Council in Vienna captured by Lannes showed that as of 25 May – ten days after French troops had entered Aosta – he was still ignorant of their movements.[8] But as reports confirmed the strong French march eastward he suddenly realized the danger to his communications. He now raised the siege of Genoa, called in his corps from the Italian-French border and concentrated the army at Alessandria.

Ironically just as General Masséna (who had been wounded and whose hair had turned white during the siege) was about to be saved, extreme circumstances dictated otherwise. Hunger approaching starvation of both soldiers and townspeople – for weeks the troops had been existing on a daily ¼ lb of ersatz bread and ¼ lb of horsemeat, a ration no longer available – caused him to surrender in return for safe conduct of his troops north to the border (where they would soon join Suchet's two divisions). Mélas must have known of Masséna's plight but so powerful was the appeal of a victory without battle that he accepted the terms.[9] Again ironically the subsequent formalities of surrender consumed several days which considerably slowed his troop build-up in Alessandria. The delay gave Berthier time to reinforce Murat sufficiently to defeat a serious attack on his corps at Piacenza. Mélas' communications were now cut, as a captured courier carrying more secret reports to Vienna could attest.

Lannes, Jean 1769–1809 Marshal of France

The confused action was approaching climax. Early on 8 June a courier, 17-year-old Bon de Marbot, arrived with news that Masséna had surrendered and that his army would be allowed to join General Suchet. "I am putting myself in pursuit of the enemy who intends to concentrate at Alessandria," Napoleon informed Suchet. "It is possible that by the time I arrive he will not be ready to fight and . . . [will] retreat, be it toward Turin, be it toward the Genoese Riviera." Suchet was to hold in check as many enemy as possible while moving on Ceva.[10]

Napoleon next had to determine if Mélas intended to fight if attacked, and if so on which side of the Po river and in what strength. He calculated that Mélas could not have all his forces at Alessandria until 11 June, and even then that they would consist of only three divisions – those of generals Elsnitz, Ott and Hadik – or a maximum 22,000 troops. On 9 June Berthier received the following orders: General Lannes who was fighting west of Stradella was to march on Voghera the following day with about 8,000 troops; he would be followed by three divisions to give a total strength of about 23,000 men; Murat's cavalry and Duhesme's divisions were to follow this force and a final division was to march up the north bank of the Po to parallel the main advance.

So far, so good, but now Napoleon wrote: "If the crossing of the Po had delayed you so that you were not ready for these maneuvers, settle for the advance guard taking up a position at Casteggio [just short of Montebello and Voghera]." If, however, he added, any enemy appeared between Stradella and Voghera they were to be attacked "without hesitation" since they would have to be less than 10,000 strong[11] – a serious miscalculation.

An increasingly nervous Berthier read this order while standing on the north bank of the rain-swollen Po which was threatening to wipe out his boat bridges. He at once informed Napoleon that insufficient troops to support the desired attack had crossed the river, and that he was ordering Lannes to march on Casteggio in line with Napoleon's alternate orders.

Napoleon suffered another disappointment with the arrival of

General Moncey's corps which, as he furiously informed war minister Carnot, amounted to less than one-third of its supposed
strength, "and half of that is composed of units which one could
scarcely count on." More favorable was news that Suchet had
fallen on two of Mélas' divisions retiring from Nice, taking 1,500
prisoners from one and all the artillery from another. Hopefully, as
the First Consul wrote Carnot, once reinforced by Masséna's
troops Suchet would march into the Piedmont to force Mélas to
leave some troops in Genoa.[12]

Lannes marched early on 9 June with Watrin's division in the
lead. Around noon, about halfway to Casteggio, Watrin's advance
guard ran into General Ott's reinforced corps some 20,000 strong.
Watrin immediately attacked to open an extremely stubborn
battle fought on open level ground between Casteggio and
Montebello.

For many of the French troops it was their first battle. "I made
the sign of the cross . . . and it brought me good luck," Captain
Coignet (then a conscript private) remembered. Charging into a
hail of grapeshot, "I lowered my head . . . but my sergeant-major
struck my pack with the flat of his saber. 'We do not lower the
head,' he said. 'No,' I replied . . . This was a carnage . . . The men
of our demi-brigade had become lions." Head raised, the 24-year-
old conscript became one of the fiercest lions, to the extent that
after the battle Berthier presented him to Napoleon who tugged
the hero's earlobe in approval, promised him a chased *fusil d'hon-
neur* and a place in the Consular Guard after he had fought in four
campaigns.[13] Victory cost the French a reported 600 dead and
wounded against 3,000 enemy casualties, the Austrians also losing
6,000 prisoners and five cannon.[14]

Napoleon arrived at Stradella the same day, suffering from a
bad cold – "I cannot stand the rain," he complained to Joséphine,
"and I was exposed to it for several hours." Lannes' victory cheered
him however, as did Watrin's miracle in holding his ground with
only one field gun and one mortar until reinforcements arrived. He

now believed that Mélas had concentrated his army at Alessandria. With battle in the air his spirits were high and they rose further with the arrival of his close friend and perhaps the finest of all his generals, Louis Desaix.

To fight what he believed to be a do-or-die "decisive battle", Napoleon (still acting through Berthier) divided the army into four corps headed respectively by Lannes, Desaix, Victor and Duhesme. Each corps contained two divisions, cavalry and artillery, and ranged in strength from over 9,000 to around 6,000. A separate division under General Chabran was posted on the north bank of the Po opposite Valenza to dispute an enemy crossing there. In addition were a strong cavalry corps and an infantry reserve of about 5,000 men.[15]

The French army was strong in numbers but otherwise weak. More cannon and munitions were urgently needed. On 10 June Napoleon ordered Marmont at Pavia to bring up 18 cannon, several thousand cannon-balls and half a million musket cartridges by the next day. Rations were in very short supply, some line units were going hungry, some lacked aid stations, a good many soldiers were barefoot.[16] All of this and more was quite normal however and Napoleon did not hesitate to order the army to march on the enemy.

On 12 June the army advanced to the east bank of the Scrivia river – Lannes on the right, Desaix and Murat in the center and Victor on the left not far from Tortona. What enemy there was had fallen back toward the village of Marengo southeast of Alessandria. The only other sign of the Austrians was some cavalry which made Napoleon fear that, contrary to his most recent assumption, Mélas was running away.

This fear increased when his corps crossed the Scrivia the following day and marched across the wide plain dotted with small farms and vineyards to San Guiliano about three miles from the village of Marengo. Reconnaissance cavalry reported no sign of Austrian troops. If Mélas were going to fight, Napoleon concluded, he surely would have chosen the Marengo plain which greatly favored his superiority in cavalry and artillery. Ergo, he must be running either northward to cross the Po and march on Napoleon's communications or southward to take refuge in Genoa where, supported by the English navy, he could stay for donkey's years. Seeing the battle that he had counted on suddenly evaporating, he made a fateful decision to send Lapoype's division north to join Chabran's blocking division on the Po while Desaix with Boudet's division moved south to block an escape toward Genoa, thus contradicting his cardinal tactical rule of never dividing one's forces at so great a distance in a battle environment.

His reasoning seemed to be confirmed that evening when Gardanne and Victor's scouts reported that the Austrians had destroyed the bridge over the Bormida river that led to Alessandria, itself only lightly held. Still another report arrived from Desaix that Mélas had sent troops southwest to Acqui.

Napoleon's logic had been perverted by an intelligence failure of major proportions, by his contempt for the enemy and by his fear that his highly vaunted Italian campaign would end in a draw or, worse, in defeat.

He was soon to learn that General Mélas had not run anywhere: that the Austrian army, much stronger than he had calculated, was at Alessandria preparing not so much for a major battle as for breaking through the French army and marching east to relieve the threatened forts, particularly Mantua. Mélas had sent no troops to Acqui, the bridge over the Bormida (along with two other bridges) had not been destroyed.

On the morning of 14 June about 30,000 Austrians supported by cavalry and at least a hundred cannon crossed these bridges to move on Marengo, defended by Victor's two divisions supported by Watrin's division and the Consular Guard on the right, in all some 22,000 troops.

The surprise attack was well carried out. By mid morning when General Victor's corps (Gardanne and Chambarlhac's divisions) was getting the worst of it, Napoleon recognized his blunder and sent aides galloping to fetch Lapoype from the north and Desaix from the south. Vicious fighting continued in the afternoon, the cannoneers and sharpshooters of the Guard firing at only 20 paces from their enemy. It was a matter of attack and counter-attack, of cannon captured and recaptured, of uncommon valor repeated a thousand times. The French were outnumbered and outgunned, their ranks repeatedly torn by deadly grapeshot from a hundred cannon.

Toward mid afternoon an enemy cavalry charge smashed into the French left to send it in retreat. And now the French lines, short of men and ammunition, began to fall back on San Guiliano with the enemy pressing ever forward.

Just when the battle seemed lost General Desaix galloped up with Boudet's division on his heels. Joining Napoleon and his generals, each mounted, he was given the picture by the general in chief and asked for an opinion. "The battle is certainly lost," Desaix is said to have replied, "but there is still time to win another" – so long, he added, as a massive artillery barrage preceded the counter-attack.

Napoleon agreed. Marmont massed his remaining guns whose unexpected fire of grapeshot surprised, then halted the triumphant enemy. A battle line was quickly formed with Boudet's division in the center, Desaix leading one brigade, Boudet the other. The sight revived faint hearts to bring tired bodies back to the field. Napoleon rode the ranks – "My children, remember that I am accustomed to sleep on the field of battle."[17] With flags flying and drums beating, the troops charged the center of a surprised and now exhausted enemy while Kellermann's cavalry division attacked from the right. Even the splendid Austrian cavalry could not break the advance but itself was broken by Kellermann's charge and Bessière's reinforced brigade to send it from the field.

Defeat suddenly turned to victory but at a terrible price. Some 6,000 Austrians were either killed or wounded, another 6,000 or more had been taken prisoner along with 40 cannon and 15 battle flags. The French admitted to 600 killed, 1,500 wounded and 900 taken prisoner but their losses were undoubtedly much higher – only 14 of Private Coignet's company of 174 men escaped wounds or death.[18] Among the fallen was General Desaix who, dying, told Boudet to keep it secret so as not to discourage the troops. Upon learning of his death Napoleon was overwhelmed, muttering to an aide, "Why am I not permitted to weep?"[19]

The sudden reversal was too much for the Austrian commanders. Mélas had had two horses shot from under him, he had hurt his arm in a fall, he was old and tired, and it is said that, confident of victory, he had left the field before the Austrian defeat. That night a council of war of weary and dispirited Austrian generals decided to negotiate a surrender in return for free passage of the troops (with arms) to the hereditary territories east of the Mincio river.

On the following day Napoleon informed the consuls of his victory and his losses. "I will soon be in Paris. I cannot tell you more; I am in the most profound sadness at the death of the man whom I loved and admired the most."[20]

Sweating peasants were still tossing the bodies of humans and horses into mass graves when the opposing generals Berthier and Mélas signed an agreement which would send the Austrian army from Lombardy but would allow it to retain the fortresses east of the Mincio. In return Vienna would accept the French as the new rulers of Lombardy and Ancona.[21]

While this document was being prepared for submission to Vienna, Napoleon was dictating a lengthy and emotional letter to Emperor Francis II. Influenced by interrogations of Austrian officers who bitterly criticized the emperor and his foreign minister, Baron Thugut, for having disgraced Archduke Charles and for continuing the war in return for English gold, Napoleon thought to avoid Hannibal's error after his famous victory at Cannae centuries earlier: "You know how to gain a victory, Hannibal," said General Maharbal, "you know not how to use one."[22]

By Napoleon's own admission his letter was written in a radical departure from normal style, indeed in places he sounded more like a modern foreign correspondent than a head of state. His peace tentative of the previous December having failed its

purpose, now from the blood-soaked battlefield of Marengo, surrounded by the wounded and by 15,000 dead bodies [sic], he
wished to appeal again for peace. Why, he asked Francis, considering Austrian control over so many states, did his cabinet (read
Baron Thugut) wish to continue the war? He followed this with
a series of blunt questions and answers of which we can offer
only a few examples.

Is it because of religion and the church? If so, then why isn't
your Majesty advised to make war on the English, Russians and
Prussians of a different faith? Is it because of the French elective
form of government? If so, then why is the Emperor not advised
to demand the suppression of the English parliament or the
destruction of the American congress? The sum purpose of these
and other provocative questions (and answers) was to prove that
"the sole instigator of the present war" was England, that the
danger to the equilibrium and future welfare of the European
nations came not from France but rather from England's mastery
of the seas and of world commerce. Napoleon could have taken
Mélas' entire army prisoner, he wrote, but instead he allowed its
return beyond the Mincio, hoping that Francis would now
embrace the Treaty of Campo Formio which would be supplemented to the satisfaction of both powers. "If your Majesty were
to refuse these proposals, hostilities would recommence; and, if I
may speak frankly, he will in the eyes of the world be solely
responsible for the war."[23]

While Berthier remained at Marengo to oversee the carefully
calibrated departure of the beaten Austrians and to fashion battlefield detritus into a new army, Napoleon returned to Milan to
try to meld political debris left by the Austrian departure into a
new and viable government, a process that called for levying new
taxes and imposing a constitution on the Cisalpine peoples (who
would at once pay 2 million francs toward support of the French
army).

Meanwhile the newly won territories had to be occupied and
administered which meant wholesale shifting of units and commanders. General Masséna arrived and was confirmed in command

of the Army of Italy which would soon absorb the Army of Reserve. General Suchet oversaw the evacuation of Genoa by the Austrian garrison whose commander, the Prince of Hohenzollern, conducted himself "with dignity, openness and honesty." The booty all told was immense, amounting to over 2,000 cannon and supplies of all sorts.[24]

Napoleon returned to Milan "a little tired" and annoyed by heavy rains, but undoubtedly pleased to be with the beautiful Madame Grassini once again. He was still greatly upset over Desaix's death, however, and he would soon learn that by a curious twist of fate General Kléber in Egypt had been assassinated on the same day Desaix died (leaving the inept General Menou in command of the Army of the Orient). A special bulletin announced that Desaix's embalmed body was to be buried under a monument raised on the Great St. Bernard Pass. Designations of demi-brigades, cavalry and artillery regiments and the names of their commanders were to be engraved on a marble slab next to the monument. Napoleon's eulogy included a furious diatribe against the English admiral, Lord Keith, who had intercepted Desaix on his return journey from Egypt and treated him as a virtual prisoner of war. This was the same admiral who was now proving obstructive at Genoa but who to Napoleon's obvious pleasure had been forced by Suchet to sail without the booty he had intended to take with him.[25]

In the midst of this whirlwind activity Napoleon paid the greatest attention to a prospectus sent by his minister of interior, Lucien Bonaparte, for the celebration of 14 July – Bastille Day. The battle standards taken at Marengo were being dispatched to the consuls in Paris. The escort would travel a convoluted route calculated to produce maximum provincial interest in the forthcoming celebrations. Fireworks would prove popular, he agreed, but not the proposed chariot races which appealed only to the ancient Greeks. Lucien was to see that Desaix would be honored by a special oration. The two most famous Italian divas, Billington and Grassini, would be brought to Paris to sing with choir backing "an Italian piece that you will have had composed over the deliverance of the Cisalpine and the Liguria, and the glory of our arms."[26]

Notes

1   Corr. VI. Nr. 4908, Torre dei Garoffali, 15 June 1800.
2   Corr. VI. Nr. 4865, Milan, 3 June 1800.
3   Corr. VI. Nr. 4882, Milan, 4 June 1800.
4   Corr. VI. Nr. 4884, Milan, 5 June 1800.
5   Corr. VI. Nr. 4877, Milan, 4 June 1800.
6   Corr. VI. Nrs. 4860, Navare, 1 June 1800; 4870, 4873, Milan, 4 June 1800.
7   Corr. VI. Nr. 4875, Milan, 4 June 1800.
8   Corr. VI. Nrs. 4865, Milan, 3 June 1800; 4894, Milan, 8 June 1800.
9   Thiébault, II, 35; Marbot, I, 107–19. Both officers were with Masséna in Genoa.
10   Corr. VI. Nr. 4899, Milan, 8 June 1800.
11   Corr. VI. Nr. 4898, Milan, 8 June 1800.
12   Corr. VI. Nrs. 4901, 4903, Milan, 9 June 1800. See also Adye, 196–7.
13   Larchey, 192–9.
14   Corr. VI. Nr. 4905, Stradella, 10 June 1800.
15   Figures vary as usual. See Wartenburg, I, 189, who cites 34,000 French on the spot with another 23,000 too distant to give battle; Chandler (*Napoleon*), 688, gives a field strength of 58,000 with "some 30,000 forming the field force."
16   Corr. VI. Nr. 4904, Stradella, 10 June 1800. See also Larchey, 101–2.
17   Corr. VI. Nr. 4910, Torre dei Garoffali, 15 June 1800.
18   Larchey, 103. See also Rovigo, 270–80.
19   Corr. VI. Nr. 4910, Torre dei Garoffali, 15 June 1800. For detailed accounts of the battle, see Bellune, 160–89; Rose (*Life*), I, 255–9; Wartenburg, I, 164–97; Adye, 223 ff.; Chandler (*Napoleon*), 190–6.
20   Corr. VI. Nr. 4908, Torre dei Garoffali, 15 June 1800.
21   Corr. VI. Nrs. 4911, Torre dei Garoffali, 15 June 1800; 4912, Torre dei Garoffali, 15 June 1800.
22   Asprey (*War in the Shadows*), 45.

23 Corr. VI. Nrs. 4914, Marengo, 16 June 1800; 4941, Milan, 22 June 1800.
24 Corr. VI. Nrs. 4944, 4945, Milan, 23 June 1800; 4952, Turin, 26 June 1800; 4915, Milan, 17 June 1800.
25 Corr. VI. Nr. 4952, Turin, 26 June 1800.
26 Corr. VI. Nr. 4938, Milan, 21 June 1800.

CHAPTER THIRTY-FIVE

THE FIRST CONSUL RULES
JULY–OCTOBER 1800

*You ought not wish to return to France – you would have to
trample across a hundred thousand bodies. Sacrifice your own
interests for the peace and happiness of France – history will
credit you for having done so.*

First Consul Napoleon Bonaparte to the future King
Louis XVIII of France, September 1800[1]

A TIRED MAN found no time for rest. If victory at Marengo vindi-
cated Napoleon's military strategy (but scarcely his tactics), it still
left him with a good many unsolved problems at home. If it
attracted thousands of cheering citizens at each stop of the returning hero, it did not mend serious rifts in the military, the tribunate,
the senate, the assembly and the Institute. If it struck both unwilling admiration and unbridled fear from European rulers, if it
further isolated England and Austria from Russia and Prussia, it
did not bring the favorable peace that Napoleon needed to prevent
England from forming a new coalition against him.

He was trapped in a vicious circle. To gain this peace he must
continue the war. To continue the war it was necessary to retain
support of the French people. But to retain this support it was
vital to implement domestic reforms (many of them controversial)
that had been interrupted by the Italian campaign.

After a night or two in Joséphine's arms Napoleon moved in a
dozen directions (including taking on a new mistress, the myste-
rious Madame D., valet Constant tells us, discreetly housed in an
apartment in Malmaison and in a small house in Paris).[2] Long

days closeted with ministers, generals and secretaries – he some-times dictated to four secretaries at a sitting – were followed by 15-minute dinners. "If you want to dine well," he advised General Thiébault, "dine with Cambacérès; if you want to dine badly, dine with Lebrun; if you want to dine quickly, dine with me."[3] Lengthy night sessions followed with fellow consuls, state coun-cillors, civil and military experts, politicians, diplomats and members of the Institute. If someone dozed he was sharply awak-ened: "Do let's keep alert," Napoleon scolded. "It's only two o'clock. We must earn our salaries."[4]

He certainly earned his. Within days of his return he initiated a tax reform program that in time would replenish an almost empty treasury by reestablishing national credit and financial con-fidence. Almost at once he convened a committee headed by the leading jurist of France, the venerable Tronchet, to write a new legal code intended to turn a jungle of archaic Roman and feudal laws as well as thousands of more recent conflicting and heavy-handed revolutionary edicts into a pleasing pasture of fairness open to the average citizen. Completed in four months, the draft required more than a hundred sessions of editing by the council of state, often eight or nine hours of complex and acrimonious dis-cussion. Napoleon personally chaired over half of these mostly late-night meetings and early revealed an extensive knowledge of the law that surprised and frequently impressed professional members. One such, the historian Thibaudeau, later wrote of his methodical and logical mind "at work on the cumbrous legal phraseology, hammering it out into clear, ductile French."[5] The final draft counted over 2,000 articles that governed most aspects of daily existence.*

While Napoleon was urging his jurists to complete the civil

---

*The civil code became law in 1804. It would be supplemented in a few years by various related codes and in 1807 would be named the Code Napoléon – soon adopted by (or imposed on) in whole or part Holland, Germany, Prussia, Switzerland, Spain and several countries in Central and South America where it rules today.

code, he began negotiating a religious reform designed to stem
religious anarchy that the revolution had brought both at home
and abroad. In line with his flattering speech to the Milanese
priests and his letter to Pope Pius VII a few weeks earlier, he now
persuaded the pope to send an emissary to Paris to work out a
formal *rapprochement* between the church and France. He closeted
this man, Monseigneur Spina, with Joseph Bonaparte and Abbé
Bernier, the latter his ally in the pacification of the Vendée,
"exhorting them . . . to secure the religious peace with the utmost
possible speed."[6]

The negotiations which led to the famous (and controversial)
Concordat between France and Rome were involved, prolonged
and often stormy. It was evident from the beginning that
Napoleon considered himself the master, that the Catholic church
in France would subordinate itself to the state. The Vatican
wanted French priests to once more have the right to collect
tithes – ten per cent of a peasant's income – which was one of the
privileges most hated by peasants in the *ancien régime*. Napoleon
would not hear of it, nor would he even discuss restoring church
lands which had been sequestered during the revolution and subsequently sold to peasants and small landholders. The Vatican
also demanded its traditional right to appoint bishops, but
Napoleon reserved this right for himself though agreeing to papal
canonization for his choices. The Vatican wanted to proscribe *constitutional* priests – the clergy who had supported the revolution as
opposed to orthodox priests who either had fled to the mountains
and forests at home or to impoverished exile abroad. Napoleon
replied that this was a healing reform, that priests were priests no
matter a constitutional or orthodox past.

The First Consul was keenly aware of the various pitfalls ahead
but in his mind the result would justify the effort. The Concordat,
as he preached to his councillors, was the first and major step in a
national reconciliation designed to bring about an armistice, if
not peace, between the 15 million orthodox Catholics and the 17
million non-orthodox or constitutional Catholics of France. In
his mind this step was vital if he were to win continued support

for his policies. This same thinking explained his first moves toward allowing the return to France of some 100,000 French *émigrés* who were judged politically harmless – a momentous and very controversial event that would take place within three months.

Bearing in mind always the dangerous opposition from leftist and rightist politicians and generals, Napoleon also took the greatest care to maintain his popularity within the army. The heroes of Marengo were heaped with honors. Each general who had been wounded received a commendation written "on parchment in the form of a commission with the seal of the Republic." A host of generals received engraved sabers. Some officers and men were awarded inscribed silver muskets and carbines, others miniature silver grenades, ramrods and trumpets. Names and birthplaces were to be carved on a special marble table in the Temple of Mars. A special medal was struck to honor "the entry of [Moreau's] army in Munich and the conquest of all of Bavaria by the Army of the Rhine." Three new branches of the Paris Invalides were to be opened in various cities to care for a total 10,000 wounded veterans. Fifty boys whose fathers had been killed in battle were to be taken into the Paris Invalides as guides for blinded veterans.[7]

The civilian population was scarcely neglected. In addition to major reforms in finance, taxation, law and religion Napoleon embarked on a score of ancillary projects designed to improve the standard of living of the average French citizen. During these summer and autumn months scores of engineers and surveyors crowded around work tables in the Tuileries, drawing up plans to improve old roads and build new ones for both commercial and military purposes. New canals were to be dug, ports deepened and widened, Paris provided with clean drinking water. Provincial museums were to receive paintings, plans were drawn to enlarge the Louvre. Theaters, operas and the arts were granted subsidies – the Comédie Française alone received an annual 100,000 francs – and various educational reforms were studied.

Napoleon had reason to be in a hurry. The military situation was still critical and would remain so. As scores of daily orders attest, his generals more than ever were to keep their units alert and in top condition. There would be no dereliction of duty without punishment. General Brune received orders to replace General Masséna in command of the Army of Italy. That army was in pretty good shape, Napoleon informed Brune, but peculation, seemingly with Masséna's cooperation, was at an all-time high. Brune was to institute widespread reforms. Of even greater concern was the navy which had fallen into dangerous disrepair and was in need of drastic overhauling – a problem never to be satisfactorily solved.[8]

Internal security formed another pressing problem. The elusive Georges Cadoudal who had set the Vendée on fire had returned to France and was again organizing royalist opposition in the Morbihan. Order after order went to General Bernadotte and police minister Fouché to capture and shoot him and his accomplices. Fouché was also to keep a sharp eye on returning *émigrés* and his spies were to investigate reports of new Chouan plots to overthrow the government.[9]

Napoleon's concern was not misplaced. Royalist plots abounded. The previous February, the future Louis XVIII had written directly to Napoleon, proposing that he should return to claim the throne and promising a suitable reward for "the general." His letter having been ignored he wrote once more after Marengo, and again was ignored. Meanwhile agents of the Comte d'Artois, both French and English, were hatching numerous schemes to do away with the First Consul, going so far as to approach such important royalist sympathizers as consul Lebrun, foreign affairs minister Talleyrand, even Joséphine.[10] Another threat came from old republicans in the senate, assembly, tribunate and the military.

The force of this opposition was increased in part by minister of the interior Lucien Bonaparte's turn to the political right, his ultimate desire being to make Napoleon a dictator (to be succeeded by himself). This group included Barras, Merlin de

Thionville and Sieyès along with a coterie of republican generals. Diverse opposition groups in the assembly also wanted a change in government and were approaching various potential candidates including La Fayette, Carnot, Fouché, Talleyrand and the two Bonapartes, Lucien and Joseph. Hatred reigned in the ministries. Fouché and Talleyrand loathed Lucien, Carnot despised Talleyrand and Fouché; Lucien scorned everyone. Each was intent only on furthering his own interests. Dangerous intrigue ruled the councils; the price of dubious loyalty was gold.[11]

Napoleon remained well aware of this diverse opposition which on occasion he adroitly turned to his own advantage, playing off one dissident against another to achieve his own ends. But he also knew that he was idolized by the average citizen and by the bulk of the army including most of the officer corps.

His general policy of conciliation was also proving popular – after all he had appointed Lebrun, whose pro-royalist sympathies were well known, to the Consulate, and had subsequently appointed numerous other potential opponents on the grounds that the one best suited for the post should have the job. His careful handling of influential members of the tribunate and legislative assembly won him considerable support as did his decision to allow the return of *émigrés* (some of whom even came over to his camp). As each week passed he felt himself more secure, to the extent that in early September he privately replied to the pretender Louis XVIII as quoted at the beginning of this chapter.[12]

Remaining remarkably calm, remarkably sure of himself in the midst of turmoil, he shrugged off the discovery of an assassination plot in mid October in which Masséna and Bernadotte were allegedly implicated.[13] When brother Lucien pushed the case for a dictatorship too strongly by distributing an incendiary pamphlet, *Parallèle entre César, Cromwell, Monk et Bonaparte*, Napoleon responded to the outcry by relieving him of his ministerial post and packing him off to Spain as ambassador.[14]

Part of Napoleon's domestic policy was dictated by sheer prudence. Although his position as First Consul was no longer in open jeopardy, it was by no means secure. He still had numerous, important and vociferous enemies. But as the year 1800 moved to an end these voices were going to be largely stilled as one result of his very successful foreign policy.

Notes

1   Madelin (*Consulate*), 94.

2   Constant, 19–20.

3   Thiébault, II, 17.

4   Ludwig, 170. See also Chaptal, 225–6.

5   Rose (*Life*), I, 290. See also Markham, 95–8.

6   Madelin (*Consulate*), 90.

7   Corr. VI. Nrs. 4969, Paris, 5 July 1800; 4988, Paris, 18 July 1800; 5004, Paris, 20 July 1800; 5053, Paris, 7 August 1800; 5064, 5065, Paris, 15 August 1800.

8   Corr. VI. Nrs. 5020, 5021, Paris, 24 July 1800; 5062, Paris, 13 August 1800. See also Rovigo, 295–8.

9   Corr. VI. Nrs. 4960, Paris, 3 July 1800; 4968, Paris, 4 July 1800; 4974, Paris, 10 July 1800; 5001, Paris, 18 July 1800; 5031, Paris, 24 July 1800; 5037, Paris, 28 July 1800.

10 Madelin (*Consulate*), 92–3.

11 Madelin (*Consulate*), 83–4, 94–6. See also Fouché, 146–53.

12 Madelin (*Consulate*), 94.

13 Madelin (*Consulate*), 99.

14 Roederer (*Journal*), 33–40, 50–4; Fouché, 150–3.

CHAPTER THIRTY-SIX

THE TREATY OF LUNÉVILLE
JULY 1800–FEBRUARY 1801

The nation is happy with the treaty, and I am
particularly satisfied with it.

Napoleon to Joseph Bonaparte, Paris,
13 February 1801[1]

UPON HIS RETURN to the French capital Napoleon resumed an intricate, exceedingly clever and ultimately very successful series of diplomatic and military maneuvers which had been interrupted by the crisis of battle. His political goal was to isolate Austria and England from the other European powers, notably Russia, Prussia and Spain, so as to prevent a new military coalition against France.

Anticipating a general armistice that would be followed by peace negotiations with Vienna he moved to put himself in the strongest possible military position in Germany and Italy. He formed a new Army of Batavia (Holland) 20,000 strong (including 7,000 Dutch soldiers), commanded by General Augereau and deployed in the center of Germany. Augereau's mission was to threaten Bohemia in order to cause Vienna to reinforce its fortresses there (thus weakening its other armies); to protect the left flank of Moreau's Army of the Rhine; and to pressure each of the minor German princes into signing a separate peace with France (while paying hefty contributions to support Augereau's presence).[2] Moreau's army which had recently seized Munich was to remain on the Danube and in Bavaria, its right flank guarded by a new Army of the Reserve which would deploy in Switzerland and the Grisons to open communications with the Army of Italy.[3]

These deployments were being carried out when General Moreau, hard on the heels of his beaten and dispirited enemy, accepted an armistice with General Kray to end the fighting. Emperor Francis' envoy, Comte de St. Julien, arrived in Paris and in late July he and Talleyrand signed the preliminaries of peace which were at once ratified by the Consulate.[4]

Not so by the Vienna court (which imprisoned St. Julien for exceeding his powers). Influenced by English gold – the usual figure quoted is something over 2 million pounds sterling – and by the hope that Bonaparte would soon be overthrown, the court refused to ratify the preliminaries, agreeing only to open peace negotiations at Lunéville some 20 miles southeast of Nancy in Lorraine, the first step in a stonewalling campaign that would continue for the next six months.

Perhaps it did not occur to either the Vienna or London courts that Napoleon was not one to sit idly by. Even before the signing of the preliminaries he had opened a diplomatic initiative in Spain, one result of his having concluded preparatory peace discussions with the United States the previous March. In late July, Berthier undertook a secret mission to Madrid, the opening move in a complicated negotiation with the Spanish court.

The Spanish king, Charles IV, and his prime minister (and Queen Marie Louisa's lover) Manuel Godoy (known as the "Prince of Peace" for having worked out an earlier treaty with France), were both impressed and frightened by Napoleon's victory at Marengo. Napoleon wanted Charles to cede his North American territory of Louisiana to France in return for a cash payment and cession of Tuscany in Italy to the Duke of Parma. Berthier was also to persuade the Madrid court to declare war on Portugal, England's ally, in order to seize several Portuguese provinces for trading purposes when it came to peace talks. Finally Berthier was to visit principal naval ports to determine what help Spain could offer France in the maritime war against England.[5]

Napoleon meanwhile had received an offer from the young Prussian king, Frederick William III, who had been on the throne for only three years and who was also suitably impressed by the French victory at Marengo, to serve as intermediary between France and Austria. Napoleon welcomed the gesture with falsely honeyed words, but believed it would be more suitable if Frederick William intervened on behalf of France to bring peace with Russia and with the minor German princes (not forgetting to remind the latter of the Treaty of Basle which ceded the left bank of the Rhine to France).[6]

No less impressed with the victory at Marengo was Czar Paul of Russia whose hatred of England was increasing at the same pace as his admiration for Napoleon. Quick to take advantage of this diplomatic windfall, Napoleon informed the czar that he was outfitting 6,000 Russian prisoners of war (captured in 1799) with new uniforms before sending them home with their weapons.[7]

This clever act began a genuine *rapprochement* between the two rulers. Not only did the czar now urge Prussia to join Russia and France in a triple alliance against England and Austria, but he also sent a special envoy to Paris to negotiate a treaty of alliance (even though the two nations were still at war). As eventually worked out, the czar offered to recognize the "natural frontiers" claimed by France – the left bank of the Rhine, the Maritime Alps and the Pyrenees – and disputed by the German emperor, the English king and the lesser German princes. Napoleon in turn agreed to a number of concessions, but the chief plum was his offer to Paul of the island of Malta if France were forced to evacuate its garrison which had been under siege at Valetta for nearly two years. Few offers could have appealed more to the czar. Along with other rulers he was greedily anticipating the breakup of the Ottoman empire, and now he would gain a powerful base from which to menace further the Turkish sultan.[8] A final word of advice from the czar may have been the seed of later heavy fruit: Napoleon should found a dynasty "and thereby put an end to the revolutionary principles which had armed Europe against France."[9]

*

The desired alliance with Russia soon gained momentum. England's mastery of the seas, a feat of overwhelming national pride that in large part explained its comfortable existence along with its diplomatic truculence, was in some ways becoming an embarrassment. The surrender of the French garrison on Malta to a small Anglo-Maltese force infuriated Czar Paul who, deprived of the prospect of this new base, promptly embargoed all British ships in Russian ports.

Also in September, American envoys met with French opposites at Mortefontaine, Joseph Bonaparte's luxurious château, for formal signature of the peace treaty worked out the previous March. The major clause called for mutual defense against England's claimed "right of search" of any vessel on the high seas.[10] A few days later Napoleon challenged England's presence in the Americas when Spain formally ceded Louisiana and the Spanish portion of San Domingo to France. He followed this coup by making peace with Algeria and Tunisia and by opening peace talks with the Bey of Tripoli.[11]

Meanwhile Czar Paul's special envoy, Sprengporten, had arrived in Paris to discuss a peace and the proposed alliance. Such was the czar's fury over England's seizure of Malta that he even proposed going to war against England (still his ally). As an interim measure he signed treaties with Denmark, Sweden and Prussia – the revival of the defunct Armed Neutrality League of 1780 – an event that caused Napoleon to tell Sprengporten: "Your sovereign and I have been called upon to change the face of the world."[12]

Propitious as were these various developments, the fall of Malta had caused Napoleon to worry more than ever over the fate of his army in Egypt. Once again Admiral Ganteaume was ordered to assemble as rapidly as possible a strong battle fleet to escort the long-delayed convoy of troop reinforcements, munitions and provisions, not to mention a large collection of newspapers and journals and even a theatrical troupe, to General Menou. Talleyrand was to arrange a shipment by private merchants of 2 million bottles of wine, brandy and liqueurs, cloth, medicines and oil in return for rice, coffee, indigo and sugar taken on in Alexandria.

Ganteaume was to take with him as a lowly naval apprentice young Jérôme Bonaparte who, as Napoleon informed the admiral, needed strict discipline to make up for lost time: "Insist that he fulfill with exactitude all the functions of his appointment." Talleyrand and Lucien Bonaparte were to maintain pressure on the Spanish king to strike a blow against English commerce by seizing Portugal and closing its ports to English ships. They were also to persuade the king to send large shipments of provisions and munitions to Egypt. Napoleon simultaneously continued to stroke the *landgraves* – the minor German princes – as his relations with Czar Paul grew ever warmer owing to their mutual resentment of England's naval arrogance.[13]

All this and more had been accomplished while peace negotiations with Vienna were stalled. The special envoys, Joseph Bonaparte and Count Cobenzl, did not even arrive in Lunéville until late October. Although Joseph performed well professionally vis-à-vis the more experienced Austrian, virtually no progress resulted. By late November, Bonaparte realized that the Vienna court intended to prolong talks throughout the winter while repairing its military losses and working with English diplomats in an attempt to plaster together the desired coalition against France.

His repeated adjurations and threats having accomplished nothing, in early December Napoleon ordered his generals to war: Moreau's Army of the Rhine fell on General Kray's force at Hohenlinden, a few miles east of Munich, to win a tremendous victory, the Austrians suffering 6,000 or 7,000 dead and wounded and 12,000 taken prisoner along with 87 cannon.

Moreau followed this crushing victory by crossing the Inn river into Upper Austria. General Macdonald's army meanwhile crossed the Splügen Pass into Italy – an amazing feat in the middle of winter – to press south and close the trap set by General Brune's Army of Italy which moved across the Adige river east into

Venetia. Simultaneously generals Miollis and Murat marched into Tuscany to occupy the important port of Ancona and threaten the King of Naples.[14] On Christmas Day General Moreau signed an armistice with the beaten Kray to end the fighting.

It was a great victory but Napoleon almost did not live to savor it. Shortly before his arrival at the Opéra on Christmas Eve to hear Haydn's *The Creation*, an enormous bomb (known to history as the Infernal Machine) exploded just behind his carriage, blowing other carriages into oblivion and killing and wounding a score or more of his entourage and passers-by, while damaging nearby buildings to the extent that many would have to be demolished.[15] Napoleon escaped physical injury, made a brief appearance before a wildly applauding crowd in the opera house, then returned thoroughly shaken to the Tuileries for a series of emergency conferences.

Owing to rightist influence in the assembly and the tribunate, first blame fell on the leftists, the *anarchistes*, with whom police minister Fouché was accused of being implicated – Roederer among others tells the complicated story in several lengthy chapters of his memoirs.[16] Hysterical reactions continued to abound, with everyone demanding the arrest of the guilty ones. Despite knowing that the *anarchistes* were innocent, to save his own skin Fouché quickly rounded up over a hundred alleged "terrorists" and shipped them off to permanent exile in the Seychelle islands.[17] A few weeks later his police rounded up the true culprits, two renegade agents of Georges Cadoudal who had acted on their own but undoubtedly with Royalist-English-Austrian blessing. Although the villains were executed, the unfortunate innocents remained in exile.[18]

If Napoleon was severely shaken – and who wouldn't have been? – he did not allow his feelings to change the swift course of his diplomatic offensives. From Czar Paul's standpoint he had struck the right note with the American representatives in condemning the English control of the seas. He had not yet learned of Moreau's victory at Hohenlinden when in early December he sent a sharp note to all friendly and neutral states informing them that France would not negotiate a peace with England until that nation recognized "that the sea belonged to all nations."

To his delight the czar responded by declaring war on England and also set about expanding the armed neutrality league into a Baltic League – Russia, Denmark, Sweden and Prussia – designed to cleanse that sea of English ships. Nothing could have pleased Bonaparte more since it complemented his own grand strategy and when the czar proposed a Franco-Russian invasion of India he quickly agreed, albeit with some reservations.[19]

Austria however was not quite supine. Cobenzl continued stonewalling the Lunéville negotiations during January despite Napoleon's threats of renewed fighting. Nor was England sleeping. Reports had reached Paris that Admiral Lord Keith was assembling a fleet to land a British force in Egypt. Admiral Ganteaume's fleet, considerably weaker than that originally ordered by Napoleon, had finally sailed in late January, but could not reach Alexandria for several weeks even if it evaded or sank hovering English warships. As it turned out, Ganteaume soon felt himself forced to return to Toulon where the fleet remained.

Although Napoleon had assured the Spanish court of England's weakness in the Mediterranean, the Spanish showed few signs of furnishing the requested ships and provisions to aid General Menou in Egypt. In early February, Napoleon sent General Gouvion St. Cyr to Madrid to work with ambassador Lucien Bonaparte in overcoming Spanish inertia. "Taking care not to offend Castilian pride," the two were to persuade the court to release their warships and also to march an army into Portugal.[20]

Cobenzl however had more reasons to worry than Napoleon. In early February the fortress of Mantua fell to French besiegers to eliminate the final obstacle to a French offensive in Venetia. Just as important, Czar Paul's increasing bellicosity caused Cobenzl to fear that Prussia might join Russia and France. Hoping to neutralize any such development Cobenzl signed the Treaty of Lunéville in early February 1801.

The treaty's main provisions were those of the earlier Treaty of Campo Formio. Austria accepted French hegemony in almost all of Italy and in the Dutch and Swiss republics. The entire left

La Machine Infernale, 1803

bank of the Rhine from Basle downwards was ceded to France, as was the authority to intervene in the formerly sacrosanct politics of the Germanic states.

Napoleon was quick to compliment Joseph: the treaty "has fulfilled perfectly the government's hope," he wrote. ". . . The nation is happy with the treaty, and I am particularly satisfied with it."[21]

Peace with Naples and a favorable treaty with Tuscany followed in less than a month. King Ferdinand closed Neapolitan ports to English and Turkish ships, and a French corps 10,000 strong under General Soult occupied the three major ports in the heel of Italy (at Neapolitan expense).[22] Ferdinand also withdrew his troops from Rome and the papal territories so as to allow Pope Pius VII's return under French protection. By early 1801 Napoleon was left with only one major enemy – England.

Notes

1   Corr. VII. Nr. 5367, Paris, 13 February 1801.

2   Corr. VI. Nrs. 4961, 4962, Paris, 3 July 1800.

3   Corr. VI. Nr. 4959, Paris, 3 July 1800.

4   Corr. VI. Nr. 5103, Paris, 23 September 1800.

5   Corr. VI. Nrs. 5010, Paris, 22 July 1800; 5034, Paris, 28 July 1800; 5070, Paris, presumed 20 August 1800.

6   Corr. VI. Nr. 5029, Paris, 25 July 1800.

7   Corr. VI. Nr. 5047, Paris, 4 August 1800. See also Madelin (*Consulate*), 88; Rose (*Life*), I, 260–1.

8   Rose (*Life*), I, 260–1. See also Seton-Watson, 61–3.

9   Rose (*Life*), I, 261.

10 Madelin (*Consulate*), 102.

11 Corr. VI. Nr. 5153, 28 October 1800.

12 Madelin (*Consulate*), 102. See also Ragsdale, 274–84.

13 Corr. VI. Nrs. 5193, Paris, 22 November 1800; 5219, Paris, 14 December 1800; 5220, 5221, Paris, 15 December 1800; 5225, 5226, Paris, 16 December 1800; 5232, Paris, 21 December 1800; 5234, 5235, 5236, 5237, Paris, 22 December 1800; 5258, Paris, 7 January 1801; 5275, 5276, Paris, 10 January 1801; 5299, Paris, 15 January

1801; 5304, Paris, 17 January 1801; 5319, 5320, Paris, 23 January 1801.

14 Madelin (*Consulate*), 101; Corr. VI. Nrs. 5229, Paris, 20 December 1800; 5250, Paris, 2 January 1801; 5302, Paris, 17 January 1801; 5309, Paris, 19 January 1801. See also Ségur, II, 113–24; Macdonald, 21–2.

15 Corr. VI. Nrs. 5246, Paris, 28 December 1800; 5323, Paris, 24 January 1800.

16 Roederer (*Journal*), 54–90. See also Fouché, 154–64.

17 Madelin (*Consulate*), 106.

18 Corr. VII. Nr. 6209, Paris, 25 July 1801. See also Roederer (*Journal*), 54–90; Fouché, 154–64.

19 Corr. VI. Nr. 5208, Paris, 7 December 1800; Fortescue, 169; Rose (*Life*), I, 262–3; Corr. VI. Nrs. 5310, 5312, Paris, 20 January 1801.

20 Corr. VI. Nrs. 5270, 5301, Paris, 17 January 1801; 5315, Paris, 21 January 1801; Corr. VII. Nr. 5336, Paris, 4 February 1801. Ganteaume's fleet consisted of seven warships and two frigates which carried 4,000 troops, provisions and munitions for General Menou's hardpressed army; 5339, Paris, 4 February 1801.

21 Corr. VII. Nr. 5367, Paris, 13 February 1801.

22 Corr. VII. Nr. 5333, Paris, 2 February 1801; Rose (*Life*), I, 263–4.

CHAPTER THIRTY-SEVEN

THE PEACE OF AMIENS
FEBRUARY–JUNE 1801

I intend to make Paris the most beautiful capital in the world.

Napoleon to minister of interior Chaptal, Paris,
February 1801[1]

THE TREATY OF Lunéville resulted in rapid acceleration of an already supercharged government. Ministers and councillors of state concerned with internal affairs were flooded with a deluge of *ukases* so various that we can only hit on a few to suggest the scope of Bonaparte's far-reaching interests.

. Minister of interior Jean Antoine Chaptal learned that according to Bonaparte too many departments were claiming support for orphans who in reality had parents – henceforth the state would support a maximum of 30,000 foundlings a year. Chaptal was also ordered to crack down on departmental prefects suspected of interpreting government decrees to their own desires (and occasional personal profit); to determine why the blades of French swords were inferior to those of Sweden; to report why a certain department was lax in combating armed brigands.[2]

Minister of finance Martin Gaudin was to investigate suspected tax frauds, answer numerous questions relating to his report of the previous year's finances and investigate discrepancies in various reports from state councillors.[3]

Minister of war Berthier was to explain why various expeditionary forces that were being fitted out had received only a quarter of the required muskets; why military hospitals were not being improved as decreed; why some French generals in Genoa were raking in "exorbitant sums for secret expenses", and why there were "omissions and confusions" in reports on military strengths and payrolls.[4]

Minister of the navy and colonies Forfait was blanketed with orders ranging from the preparations of squadrons for numerous expeditions to the building of new ships, to pushing admirals Ganteaume and Bruix to sail on assigned missions, to determining how long it would take to assemble 100 gunboats at Boulogne (how many men would each boat hold? how many boats could sail per tide?), to answering complicated questions concerning his financial reports, to raising officers and crews for three warships recently acquired from Spain. In addition he was authorized to grant one Robert Fulton, a visionary American inventor, 10,000 francs to finance trials at Brest of an underwater craft called the *Nautilus*.[5]

The minister of justice was to name a special commission to make a final examination of each of the more than 2,000 articles of draft the civil code (already being examined by 29 separate departmental courts of appeal). Such was the healthy progress of this immensely complicated work that Bonaparte appointed a new commission to write complementary criminal and commerce codes.[6]

Seemingly nothing escaped the sometimes discerning, sometimes heavy but always active hand of the First Consul. In the months ahead corrupt judges would be investigated (and prosecuted if warranted); national forests surveyed and protected; uniforms and codes of discipline and studies provided for cadets at the new military school, the *prytanée* of St. Cyr; military hospitals improved and new ones opened; plans drawn to reorganize the artillery and combine the schools of artillery and engineers.[7]

Of more interest to the average French citizen was a far-reaching and very costly construction program. Even before the treaty was signed, Bonaparte had ordered engineers to work out plans for a canal to connect the Aisne and Somme rivers to the Escaut (Scheldt) in order to facilitate trade with Belgium.[8] In addition to public works earlier touched on, depressed industries such as the textile mills of Lyons were to be revived. Armed brigandage in the provinces was to be stamped out by recruiting additional gendarmes and sending special tribunals with extraordinary powers to 32 departments.

"I intend to make Paris the most beautiful capital in the world," Bonaparte told Chaptal, and he was as good as his word. Architects moved ahead on plans to enlarge the Louvre (so as to display art treasures removed from Italy) and to connect it to the Tuileries. Plans were presented to extend quays on the left bank of the Seine, new bridges to span the river, the Jardin des Plantes to be restored.

Millions would soon be spent in an unsuccessful attempt to bring clean drinking water from the Ourcy river to Paris by canal. Silos would be constructed to store wheat which in case of a poor harvest would be sold to the people at low prices. New streets and elegant boulevards were to be laid down, each named for a military victory in Italy, Egypt and Germany – we cross them today. Public buildings were to be restored, parks created, monuments erected to the brave and dead – we enjoy them today. Arrangements were made to host an autumn industrial and arts exhibition in Paris.[9]

Critics through the ages have complained that many of these projects were never completed, but that is beside the point. A large number were finished and the government's intention to accomplish the rest was obvious. In summer of 1801 the citizens of France were beginning to enjoy the first fruits of victory and peace – the result of Napoleon Bonaparte's all-embracing rule.

In addition to administrative and internal improvements, Napoleon perforce had to concentrate on external affairs at a critical and confusing period in European history. Again we can only mention a few of the political problems to illustrate the workings of his mind.

Not least of his actions in early 1801 was prompted by an

armistice with the kingdom of Naples which allowed him to send General Soult with some 12,000 troops to occupy the ports of the gulf of Taranto and the lower Adriatic sea "until the maritime peace with England" was achieved. Although his stated purpose was to ease communications with Egypt, a subsequent order for a detailed report on all harbors from Ancona to Brindisi suggested deeper motives for the move, as did his instructions to occupy Elba island and to have "very good maps . . . [made] of all the country between the Adige, the Po and the Adda rivers . . . which will probably be the theater of new wars."

Whatever his motive, the loser was Naples which would either pay 500,000 francs a month plus grain to support Soult's force or be invaded. Meanwhile French warships and frigates were ordered (once again) to carry news of the treaty to General Menou in Egypt along with the latest newspapers, munitions, muskets and quinine, not to mention a stirring proclamation from the First Consul congratulating the Army of the Orient on defeating a British attempt to land troops.[10]

In accordance with the Treaty of Lunéville, French army engineers began demolishing forts in Venetia, the Tyrol and Germany while army commanders in these occupied areas prepared to evacuate French troops. Simultaneously negotiations were opened with Switzerland to obtain territory in the Valais, the large southern canton, sufficient to guarantee road communication through the Simplon Pass from Lombardy and further west from Piedmont with France.[11] This territory once gained, a flurry of road and bridge building would last for several years.

As for the New World, General Collet was to sail to Louisiana as captain-general to build a French colony. Another expedition was to carry troops to the French half of San Domingo along with the brevet of captain-general for the negro leader, Toussaint L'Ouverture. Governor Toussaint was to "maintain the peace and encourage agriculture" while making the island a jewel in the French colonial crown. The white colonial prefect received orders to treat Toussaint with kid gloves: "Rally all the inhabitants of the island around him. Tell the [black] people in all possible ways of the glory of the [French] Republic . . . let them know that the time is not far distant where the black legions will appear with glory."[12]

Czar Paul of Russia received special attention. Napoleon wrote to him at length in late February once again complaining of "the arrogance and insolence of the English which have no parallel." He then proposed the basis for what in a few years would become the Continental System: "if the Russians were to block English commerce with the northern powers, if a Russian corps presently in Prussia occupied Hanover to close the Elbe and Weser rivers to British ships, and if Portugal, Naples and Sicily were to close their ports, then the English would have no communication with Europe." Meanwhile it was in the best interest of all Mediterranean and Black Sea powers for the French to remain in Egypt.

> The Suez Canal, which would join the Indian Ocean to the Mediterranean, is already marked out; this is an easy work of short duration which can produce incalculable advantages to Russian commerce. If your Majesty is still of the opinion, as he so often has said, of sharing his commerce of the north with the south, he can join this great undertaking, which would greatly influence the future situation of the [European] continent.[13]

This aggressive, wide-reaching diplomacy inevitably met some snags. Despite minimum English naval strength in the Mediterranean the French admirals would not shake off ingrained indolence and sail for Egypt. Yet it was vital to get help to General Menou, if only a single frigate loaded with muskets and munitions. After receiving innumerable urgent orders to sail, Admiral Ganteaume finally weighed anchor in late February. Probably to his surprise he encountered no enemy warships in departing from Toulon – his squadron even captured a valuable English prize. But in venturing too close to Port Mahon in the Balearic islands he put Admiral Warren on guard which forced him (so he believed) to hustle back to Toulon.

The game now recommenced. Although Napoleon congratulated him on capturing a prize he also pointed out that Admiral Keith had arrived in Rhodes with six warships and 50 troop transports en route to Egypt – Ganteaume must sail as soon as possible. A few days later the admiral was ready with a considerably reduced squadron to carry 4,900 troops commanded by General Sahuguet, along with supplies and munitions. "The maritime peace [with England]," Bonaparte informed Sahuguet in early March, "will be decided by the success of your expedition." Ganteaume received two letters from Napoleon the same day, one an encouraging pep-talk, the other rather more terse: "Go!" Ganteaume went, but not for another two weeks and not very far. When two of his ships collided in a storm, instead of carrying on without them he returned to Toulon for repairs, a timid decision for which he was justly censured.[14]

Napoleon had no better luck with Admiral Bruix who was to sail from Lorient, Rochefort and Brest. Such was the lethargy of preparations that a favorite aide, General Savary, was sent to Lorient to remain there until the ships had departed for Rochefort. Savary later summed up the situation: "All France was on the move except the navy, mired in bureaucratic molasses and general ineptitude that no amount of threats was going to dissolve."[15]

Related to the naval problem was indolent ally Spain. In its recent treaty with France the Spanish court committed itself not only to maintain a sizeable squadron of its own warships in the Mediterranean, but also to turn over others to French control. The main obstacle here, one that Napoleon could not immediately overcome, was the failure of Manuel Godoy, the Prince of Peace, to honor the naval commitment. The First Consul loathed the man whom he believed to be in English pay, but Godoy was the favorite, sexually and politically, of the Spanish queen and as prime minister was titular ruler of the country. The French ambassador to Spain, Lucien Bonaparte, was no help since he was under Godoy and the court's thumb, having been made a very rich young man by generous gifts of diamonds and paintings.[16]

These serious vexations would continue to increase. Nevertheless by mid April the First Consul held a relatively strong position vis-à-vis England and had good reason to be confident of achieving the "maritime peace" so volubly desired. But now two events occurring within a few days of each other radically changed the European situation – to his cost.

A French peace with England should have been a relatively simple matter to negotiate, if only because each power desperately needed to end a costly and in early 1801 virtually stalemated war. At Bonaparte's instigation quiet talks had started in autumn of 1800 when a minor French envoy, one Monsieur Ott, arrived in London ostensibly to arrange a prisoner of war exchange but in reality to discuss the possibility of peace.

Ott's overtures were not well received by William Pitt (the Younger), the 41-year-old prime minister whose morbid, brooding brilliance, fed in part by an unbending hatred of French republicanism and more lately of Napoleon, had guided British fortunes for nearly a decade. Toppled by his support for Catholic emancipation in Ireland which was anathematic to King George III, he was replaced by a man of his own choice, Henry Addington, veteran Speaker of the English parliament.

Addington at age 44, a commoner among the ruling nobility, was certainly not the man to face ongoing crises at home and abroad with, in Holland Rose's words, "the complaisance born of bland obtuseness."[17] England now stood alone against that upstart Bonaparte who had dared to successfully defend the egalitarian principles of the French Revolution, and to incite the European continent and the North American states to incipient rebellion against England's self-claimed and arrogant control of the seas, not to mention supporting (albeit unsuccessfully) a serious uprising in Ireland.

England was also facing a difficult transition as the industrial revolution intensified. Agricultural workers migrating to towns and factories often found either no job or jobs demanding long,

long hours at pittance pay. A series of poor harvests had brought bread shortages and the prices of basic staples were rising dangerously. Although the treasury was far from empty, it had been seriously depleted by nine years of war which had uncomfortably increased the national debt, in part by maintaining an imposing fleet of warships that controlled the waters of the world.[18]

The Second Coalition against France having disappeared into the dustbin of history, Addington's first need was to make peace with the real troublemaker, Napoleon Bonaparte. The trick was to pacify an extremely heavy-handed parliamentary opposition to this move while simultaneously maneuvering for a favorable negotiating position similar to that recently obtained by the French in the war against Austria. The English government had done its best to prolong peace talks at Lunéville in the hope that internal revolution would topple Bonaparte while Austria was rebuilding its army. The British navy had done its part by landing a ground force that seized Malta as prelude to landing an army in Egypt.

However the peace of Lunéville upset English plans. Without Austrian participation there was no longer a nucleus for a new armed coalition against the enemy. England, divided politically, Tories against Whigs, each party looking at an increasingly restive population, needed peace as much as if not more than France. This explained a tentative sent to Paris by Addington's foreign minister, Lord Hawkesbury. Where Pitt had scorned Bonaparte's attempt at talks a few months earlier, so now did Bonaparte reject this effort – until two unexpected events changed matters.

The first was the assassination of Bonaparte's new ally, 57-year-old Czar Paul I of Russia. In his brief reign the impetuous and imperious (some said mad) Paul had alienated the nobility, the army and the bureaucracy, numerous members of each being in English pay. His overly ambitious plan to invade India – he had recently started troops on the march – was the last straw in what appeared to his enemies to be an increasingly dangerous and inconsistent rule. This ended abruptly on a night in late March when an assassin gained his bedroom to plunge a dagger into the imperial heart.

The second event followed a few days later, partly the result of Bonaparte's misinterpretation of Hawkesbury's move to open negotiations. Hawkesbury was not begging. The Franco-Russian threat to British sea power was potentially serious, but it was still only a threat. British naval power was a fact, and so was Admiral Lord Nelson.

Horatio Nelson recently had been recalled to London to answer for his prolonged and flamboyant affair in Naples with Lady Hamilton, as well as for flagrant disobedience of Admiralty orders. The Admiralty cloud under which he arrived however was more than countered by the sunshine of his popular welcome as a national hero. Thus stymied, the Admiralty chiefs reluctantly appointed him second in command to Admiral Sir Hyde Parker's Baltic fleet, which was preparing to destroy a building Danish fleet, mainstay of Czar Paul's newly proclaimed Baltic League, in Copenhagen harbor.

Leaving behind him a pregnant and tearful Emma, Nelson duly reported for duty. Parker received him coldly but did agree that he could lead the attack into Copenhagen harbor which was well defended by shore batteries. By daring choice of a dangerously narrow channel Nelson evaded shore fire to fall on a greatly superior if surprised fleet. Horrified by the ensuing carnage seen through his spyglass, Parker signaled Nelson to disengage. Nelson raised his glass to his blind eye: "I don't see the signal," he muttered – and the battle continued. An hour later he had virtually eliminated the enemy fleet (and the Baltic League).[19]

Napoleon learned of Czar Paul's death in mid April. Taken with the subsequent demise of the Danish fleet it spelled an end to his exaggerated dreams of bringing England to heel either on the high seas or elsewhere – at least for the present.

Paul's successor was his son, the 24-year-old Alexander I, who almost at once repaired relations with England while demanding that France back off from the recently signed Treaty of Lunéville in so far as it granted French hegemony in Italy. Bonaparte curtly responded by sending General Jourdan with a corps of troops to occupy Piedmont (the first step in its annexation), and by leaking reports of his intention to invade England.

But he also sent a letter of condolence to the new czar which included a subtle reference to his father's desire to achieve "neutrality of the seas," as well as his own wish to be at peace with Russia. Recognizing that the political shoe had suddenly shifted to another's foot, Bonaparte also ordered envoy Ott in London to eat crow in reopening peace negotiations, but not before delivering a sharp protest to the English court for its part in sponsoring the December attempt on the First Consul's life.[20]

Lord Hawkesbury was not at first receptive to Ott's overture but as French preparations for an invasion of England continued at Boulogne, as the new Russian czar seemed inclined toward peace with France, as Napoleon consolidated his position in Italy, his troops occupying a new kingdom of Tuscany and elsewhere building roads and forts, and as a Spanish-French army invaded Portugal, he began talks with the French envoy. In late May, Ott informed Hawkesbury that as much as France wished peace it must be "an honorable peace . . . founded on the neutrality of the seas."[21]

Negotiations lasted throughout the summer as Hawkesbury dragged his feet, demanding first one territorial concession, then another, as couriers wore out a fleet of horses and themselves in traveling between Paris and London. As summer drew to a close Napoleon became increasingly nervous. Vocal opposition to his religious and legal reforms was growing. San Domingo was on fire, a general armed mêlée between mulattoes and blacks brought on by a confrontation between Toussaint and an important tribal leader. A French regiment had mutinied in Turin; the Spanish court still had not turned over Louisiana to France; time was running out for a new military campaign on the continent if England remained obdurate; the situation in Egypt was growing bleaker by the month.

In mid September, Ott was ordered to deliver what amounted to an ultimatum. Having ceded Trinidad (which belonged to

Spain) and Ceylon (which belonged to Holland) to England,
Napoleon would cede nothing more, "not a single rock . . . if it
only had a village of a hundred inhabitants." If preliminaries were
not signed by early October he would break off negotiations.[22]

Hawkesbury gave way and the preliminaries were signed – only
a few days before General Menou in Egypt, ignorant of diplomatic developments, surrendered the Army of the Orient to the
English, but under honorable terms that included the evacuation
of troops with arms and artillery to France.[23]

The next act was played at the Congress of Amiens, where
France was represented by Joseph Bonaparte and England by the
venerable Lord Cornwallis. Diplomatic haggling would continue
for nearly another six months, but at least ships could once again
peacefully sail the seas.

As finally worked out, the principal clauses of the treaty called
for England to return the colonies seized from France, Spain and
Holland since the beginning of the war, leaving England only
Trinidad, Ceylon and its holdings in India; England to turn over
Malta to the Knights of St. John within three months to be put
"under the protection of one of the great powers of Europe";
France to evacuate its troops within the same period of time from
Neapolitan and papal lands; Egypt to be returned to Turkey;
Portugal to regain its independence.

The treaty was signed in late March 1802. Although it brought
about a general peace for the first time in nine years many heads
on both sides of the English Channel regarded it more as an
armistice than as an end to the war – unfortunately a correct
appraisal.

Notes

1   Chaptal, 355.
2   Corr. VII. Nrs. 5350, Paris, 6 February 1801; 5354, Paris, 7
    February 1801; 5379, 5380, Paris, 15 February 1801; 5383, Paris,
    17 February 1801; 5391, Paris, 18 February 1801.

3   Corr. VII. Nrs. 5379, 5380, Paris, 15 February 1801; 5407, Paris, 22
    February 1801; 5497, 5498, Paris, 2 April 1801.

4   Corr. VII. Nrs. 5351, Paris, 6 February 1801; 5354, Paris, 7
    February 1801; 5381, 5382, Paris, 15 February 1801; 5389, Paris,
    17 February 1801; 5441, Paris, 5 March 8101; 5486, Paris, 25
    March 1801.

5   Corr. VII. Nrs. 5373, Paris, 13 February 1801; 5419, 28 February
    1801; 5424, 1 March 1801; 5438, Paris, 4 March 1801; 5477, 5478,
    Paris, 20 March 1801; 5488, 5489, Paris, 25 March 1801; 5515,
    Paris, 8 April 1801. See also Lacour-Gayet, 298–9. In summer of
    1801 the *Nautilus* made several dives at Paris and Brest, descending
    on one occasion to a depth of eight meters and remaining sub-
    merged for nearly two hours. Technical difficulties caused
    Napoleon to lose interest, nor was he favorably impressed two years
    later when Fulton demonstrated his newest invention, the steam-
    boat, on the Seine. (See Bourrienne, II, 43; Méneval, 307.) Scoring
    no better with the English government, Fulton returned to the
    United States and in 1807 launched his first steamship on the
    Hudson river. The rest is history.

6   Corr. VII. Nrs. 5431, Paris, 3 March 1801; 5490, Paris, 28 March
    1801.

7   Corr. VII. Nrs. 5621, Paris, 27 June 1801; 5731, Paris, 5 September
    1801.

8   Corr. VII. Nr. 5349, Paris, 5 February 1801.

9   Chaptal, 287, 291, 355, 359.

10 Corr. VII. Nrs. 5368, Paris, 13 February 1801; 5399, Paris, 19
    February 1801; 5403, Paris, 20 February 1801; 5406, Paris, 21
    February 1801; 5413, Paris, 25 February 1801; 5482, Paris, 22
    March 1801; 5506, Paris, 3 April 1801; 5508, Paris, 5 April 1801;
    5509, Paris, 6 April 1801.

11 Corr. VII. Nrs. 5449, Paris, 7 March 1801; 5462, Paris, 16 March
    1801; 5470, Paris, 18 March 1801.

12 Corr. VII. Nrs. 5396, Paris, 18 February 1801; 5439, Paris, 4 March
    1801; 5440, Paris, 4 March 1801.

13 Corr. VII. Nr. 5417, Paris, 27 February 1801.

14 Corr. VII. Nrs. 5373, Paris, 13 February 1801; 5419, 5420, 5421,
    Paris, 28 February 1801; 5430, Paris, 2 March 1801; 5442, 5443,
    5445, 5446, Paris, 6 March 1801.

15   Savary, I, 342–61. See also Corr. VII. Nrs 5427, 5428, 5429, 2
     March 1801.
16   Corr. VII. Nr. 5516, Paris, 9 April 1801. See also Thiry (*Concordat*),
     25–9; Fouché, 174–5.
17   Rose (*Life*), I, 310.
18   Rose (*Life*), I, 315.
19   Tute, 111–12; Warner (*Baltic*), 99–101.
20   Corr. VII. Nrs. 5524, 5525, 5526, Paris, 12 April 1801; 5528, Paris,
     13 April 1801; 5545, Paris, 24 April 1801; 5550, Paris, 26 April
     1801.
21   Corr. VII. Nr. 5589, Paris, 28 May 1801.
22   Corr. VII. Nr. 5749, Paris, 17 September 1801.
23   Finley, 429–37.

CHAPTER THIRTY-EIGHT

THE CONQUERING HERO
JULY 1801–AUGUST 1802

*Never had a man been so popular as was the young Consul
in the spring of 1802.*

Louis Madelin[1]

NEITHER CZAR PAUL'S assassination nor Admiral Nelson's devastating strike at Copenhagen caused more than a momentary folding of Bonapartian wings. If the remaining months of 1801 were clouded by seemingly eternal diplomatic sparring, by the loss of Egypt to the British, by a bloody revolution in San Domingo and by a disputatious Spain and a recalcitrant Portugal, they were also marked by impressive progress in both domestic and foreign affairs.

If critical chatter in Parisian salons and in various republican and royalist strongholds over the Concordat negotiations and domestic legal reforms caused Napoleon to tighten censorship of journals and newspapers, much of that criticism (which rarely reached the general public) was muted by elaborate nationwide celebrations of Bastille Day (14 July), the overwhelming success of the ensuing arts and sciences fair in Paris, the signing of peace preliminaries with England in October and the conclusion of other favorable treaties including one with Russia.

"Faithful to your wishes and to its promises," Napoleon Bonaparte informed the nation on 9 November, anniversary of the founding of the Consulate, "the government has yielded neither to the ambition of more [military] conquests, nor to the temptation of bold and unusual enterprises." The task ahead was to consolidate the peace: "Let us join to the efforts of the government the efforts of its citizens to enrich and extend all parts of our vast territory."[2]

Ah, irony! While French citizens were reading this lengthy proclamation, bread and wine at hand, slavering over the good times ahead, General Leclerc was equipping an expedition of 20,000 troops which shortly would sail to put down Toussaint's rebellion in San Domingo. While Bonaparte dictated these optimistic words he was preparing to receive several hundred delegates from the Cisalpine republic, a meeting that took place at Lyons two months later to result in the establishment of the Italian republic with Bonaparte as president. (He would spend nearly a month in Lyons writing a constitution for the new republic, wooing the representatives, attending balls and fêtes with Joséphine and reviewing regiments only just returned from Egypt.)

If some citizens did not share their leader's stated confidence in a peaceful future their doubts vanished with the formal signing of the Treaty of Amiens the following March. For years the people had wanted peace, they had voted Napoleon dictatorial powers to achieve it – and now in the early spring of 1802 it was a reality.

Trade had been slowly reviving since the earlier signing of the peace preliminaries. Now it leapt ahead almost overnight as new markets opened within and without Europe. For the first time in the memory of young sailors, merchant ships set sail to ports in the Indies, east and west, in the Americas, north and south, without fear of being seized or sunk. Within a few months thousands of soldiers would be discharged, sons and husbands coming home at last. A peacetime army meant tremendous financial savings, money freed to support expensive domestic programs.

The effect on Napoleon was equally dramatic. Where ministers and councillors had been receiving a dozen directives and orders a day they now received twice as many or more. Where earlier the threat of renewed fighting had caused him to move with considerable circumspection now he was free to move in a score of different directions. Suddenly he had both money and a new labor force to carry out grandiose plans in rebuilding Paris and France. Increased money and manpower were hurled into programs already underway. Many of the projects such as canal and harbor repairs and enlargement would not be accomplished for years, but many others were completed in remarkably short order. Contemporaries close to Napoleon at this time have written that during the next two years no leader in history had ever worked harder on behalf of his country – and that is probably a fair judgment.

Not everyone appreciated Bonaparte's supercharged activity. Opposition remained generally mute however (except in elegant Parisian drawing rooms), the result in part of an active police force combined with government censorship of newspapers, journals, books, plays and even songs. When a strong opposition group led by Benjamin Constant in the tribunate protested that several clauses in the civil code were incompatible with republican principles, Bonaparte persuaded the senate to replace tribunate members (of whom one-fifth had to retire every year) with more sympathetic voices.[3]

Considerable remaining legislative opposition to increasingly dictatorial government was largely muted by the signing of the peace of Amiens. By raising Bonaparte's popularity to truly majestic levels the peace cleared the way for the enactment of perhaps his most controversial reform, the Concordat – the proposed religious contract with Rome.

Pope Pius VII (prompted by the papal curia) had fought tooth and nail to eliminate or at least ameliorate some of its clauses. Harassed however by Bonaparte's threats up to and including armed action against Rome he had given in little by little, a lengthy and complicated story told in interesting detail by among others Comte Boulay de la Meurthe, one of the more articulate and interesting participants.[4]

Napoleon got what he wanted in the end. Although the Concordat accepted Catholicism as the leading religion of France, it was not to be the national religion as under the *ancien régime*. Catholics, Jews, Protestants and Heretics were free to worship as they pleased, so long as they remained loyal to the state. The church would be subordinate to the state. Bonaparte and not the pope would appoint archbishops and bishops. The pope retained authority to canonize them, but they also would swear an oath of fidelity to the French constitution. As if these items were not sufficiently restrictive, Bonaparte subsequently attached a number of what he called "organic" articles to the documents, among them the invalidity in France of papal bulls or decrees issued by foreign synods. Catholic bishops could not assemble or even leave their dioceses without government permission, and similar restrictions governed Protestant ministers and Jewish rabbis. In partial compensation the state agreed to restore damaged churches and to pay the clergy of all faiths.[5]

The proposed pact with Rome had long since incurred the wrath of French revolutionary liberals including a powerful coterie of generals. So hostile was the air that a later historian, J. Holland Rose, concluded that "had not the infidel generals been for the most part seduced by mutual jealousies they might perhaps have overthrown Bonaparte."[6]

Other citizens scorned the pact as a patent move to increase centralized authority while paving the way for a return to royalist government. Joseph Bonaparte was said to have criticized it as "a retrograde and thoughtless step by the nation that submitted to it."[7] Pope Pius, while vigorously defending the pact to members of the curia as restoring the church's prestige in France, was well aware of the potential effects of what he regarded as humiliating clauses – and indeed these would haunt relations between the Roman church and the French state in the years to come.

The principals reached formal agreement in April 1802. Ratification was followed by an elaborate service in Notre Dame, marred only by the rude behavior of several diehard republican generals.[8] After hearing the *Te Deum* sung, Bonaparte somewhat nervously attended mass but refused to take the sacrament.[9]

This victory was followed by other sweeping measures. Plans were made to bring additional *émigrés* back to France under a general amnesty which the senate approved. Work continued on the civil code and was begun on supplementary codes. The assembly passed an education reform bill that bore the personal touch of the First Consul who "organized the new body of teachers and drew up the program of studies."[10] This was not the most satisfactory piece of work since it left primary schools under the aegis of often lackadaisical communes with only the *lycées* (state secondary schools) controlled by the government.[11]

At this point Bonaparte could do no wrong. Prompted by the wily Cambacérès, the newly chastened and now docile tribunate invited the senate "to give the consuls a proof of the nation's gratitude" for ending the war.[12] This resulted in a rather watery offer to the three consuls of a second ten-year term of office. Bonaparte had anticipated something more generous. The thorny question of succession had been on his mind certainly since the summer of 1800 when he discussed it with Roederer.[13] For at least two years his minions, astutely spurred by brothers Joseph and Lucien, had stirred people's fears as to what would happen to France should the First Consul be assassinated or killed in battle – or worse yet, voted from office at the end of his term. Was France to return to anarchy after Bonaparte had brought order and peace?

The minimum safeguard was surely to appoint him to office for life, and from time to time one even heard mention of the restoration of the monarchy. Great therefore was the hero's expectation, great therefore his disappointment. So incensed was he by the senate's pusillanimous offer that he would have refused it outright but for Cambacérès who cunningly advised him to accept only after a national plebiscite gave its approval. The people would vote yes or no to two questions framed by the council of state: should Napoleon Bonaparte become consul for life and, if yes, should he be allowed to name his successor? Suitably trapped, the senate perforce agreed and arrangements were made for a nation-wide vote to take place over the summer months.

Prior to this event the First Consul placed still another nail in the revolutionary coffin by a decision to form a Legion of Honor designed to reward past and present distinguished service to the nation, either civil or military. Thirty thousand such citizens were to be awarded specific ranks, each carrying special perquisites including cash payments. To an advisor who wished to limit membership to soldiers Napoleon replied in words as pertinent to this day as they were to his day:

> To do great things nowadays it is not enough to be a man
> of five feet ten inches. If strength and bravery made the
> general every soldier might claim the command. The
> general who does great things is he who also possesses civil
> qualities. The soldier knows no law but force, sees nothing
> but and measures everything by it. The civilian, on the
> other hand, only looks to the general welfare. The
> characteristic of the soldier is to wish to do everything
> despotically: that of the civilian is to submit everything to
> discussion, truth and reason. The superiority thus
> unquestionably belongs to the civilian.[14]

As with the Concordat, the Legion of Honor drew considerable criticism from those who considered it inappropriate to the principles of liberty and equality won by blood spilled in the revolution. To one important critic who regarded it as still another step toward monarchy because of its proclaimed elitism and penchant for colorful titles and elaborate crosses and ribbons, Bonaparte replied:

> Well, men are led by toys . . . I don't think that the French
> love liberty and equality: The French are not at all changed
> by ten years of revolution. They are what the Gauls were,
> fierce and fickle. They have one feeling, however. We must
> nourish that feeling: they must have distinctions.[15]

Bonaparte announced the formation of the Legion of Honor in July 1802. Shortly thereafter the nation learned the results of the plebiscite: some 3.5 million citizens had voted their assent for the First Consul to retain his office for life with the right to name his successor. Slightly over 8,000 citizens had voted down the proposals. On the first day of August 1802 a *senatus consultum* – a convenient device that avoided the necessity for assembly approval – confirmed the nation's vote. On 15 August, Napoleon's birthday, the nation celebrated the appointment.

The First Consul for life had turned 33.

Bonaparte was not surprised by the election results. He had expected nothing less and he was undoubtedly delighted to have turned the tables on the lukewarm senate. As a suggestion of things to come he no longer signed decrees and orders with his surname, Bonaparte, but rather in the royal tradition with his first name, Napoleon.

Any dullard who failed to get the message was soon awakened by a new "organic" law that replaced the old "list of notabilities" with departmental "electoral colleges." Members of these colleges were either selected by local assemblies or appointed directly by Napoleon from members of the Legion of Honor. Their main function was to supply qualified candidates eligible for appointment by the Consulate to various legislative, judicial and executive bodies. The tribunate, reduced to 50 members, was limited to secret debates in which, as Napoleon put it, "they might jabber as they liked," thus losing virtually all of its power as did the assembly.

The senate gained power, at least on paper. Increased to eighty members it absorbed many of the former functions of the tribunate and the assembly. It was authorized to dissolve the two legislative bodies and to quash "the verdicts of the tribunals on the score of illegality."[16] It was also empowered to interpret various points of the constitution and to debate the ratification of treaties. These important powers would be exercised only with care: Napoleon accorded himself the right to appoint forty of the eighty members and to submit the names of three candidates for each vacancy, one of which had to be selected.[17]

The council of state, also in theory, was strengthened by increasing its numbers to fifty. Real power however was transferred to a small coterie of favorites, a sort of privy council, which debated Napoleon's various ukases before they were carried to the senate for almost automatic approval.

Such was the temper of the general population that these and other measures were accepted almost without question. By autumn of 1802, Napoleon Bonaparte was the undisputed ruler of France.

Notes

1   Madelin (*Consulate*), 151.

2   Corr. VII. Nr. 5860, Paris, 9 November 1801.

3   Rose (*Life*), I, 321.

4   Boulay de la Meurthe (*Concordat*), Vols. II and III. See also Méneval, I, 81.

5   Rose (*Life*), I, 280–2.

6   Rose (*Life*), I, 281. See also Madelin (*Consulate*), 159–60.

7   Chaptal, 237–9.

8   Madelin (*Consulate*), 141–2.

9   Ludwig, 185. See also Madelin (*Consulate*), 148.

10 Madelin (*Consulate*), 154.

11 Rose (*Life*), I, 295–6.

12 Madelin (*Consulate*), 154.

13 Roederer (*Journal*), 10–14, 50–4.

14 Rose (*Life*), I, 285–6.

15 Rose (*Life*), I, 287.

16 Madelin (*Consulate*), 160–1. See also Roederer (*Journal*), 90–1.

17 Rose (*Life*), I, 342.

CHAPTER THIRTY-NINE

NAPOLEON THE MAN
1801–1802

*As a general rule he liked to talk in a familiar way. He was
fond of discussions, but did not impose his opinions, and made
no pretensions of superiority, either of intelligence or of rank.
When only ladies were present he liked to criticize their
dresses, or tell them tragical or satirical stories – ghost stories
for the most part.*

Private secretary Méneval describing the 33-year-old
First Consul at home[1]

THE NEW RULER had changed along with the nation. Each had
become stronger, in some ways ever more powerful. Napoleon
had long since divorced the concept of revolution to marry that of
republicanism. But the marriage had increasingly soured, to the
extent that in late 1802 he was preparing the country for a return
to monarchical rule. Some historians date the change in direction
from the coup of 18–19 Brumaire (9–10 November 1799), which
established Consulate rule, others from the Treaty of Amiens,
still others from his elevation to First Consul for life. The record
suggests however that he had probably decided on this goal at
least five years earlier as indicated by the pseudo-royal trappings
of Montebello castle, his splendid residence outside Milan.
Whatever traces of republicanism remained after the Italian campaigns were washed away by the continuing ineptitude of
Convention rule followed by the famous *coup d'état*.

Any question as to his ultimate goal vanished with his rule as
First Consul. Despite the council of state, ministers, tribunate,

assembly, senate, all suitably stroked when necessary, for almost two years Bonaparte had reigned as king without a crown. The Tuileries *was* a palace complete with a horde of lackeys, a team of chefs to prepare elaborate menus, a personal valet to shave and dress him, a body servant, secretaries, librarians, aides, footmen, coachmen, huntsmen – the works.

He had soon branched out domestically, first to Malmaison about eight miles west of Paris, an extremely comfortable country estate with beautiful gardens which were Joséphine's pride and a "small" amateur theater with "only" 200 seats. In autumn of 1801 Napoleon ordered the nearby dilapidated château of St. Cloud to be refurbished as a formal retreat for private state meetings and diplomatic receptions. The task was costly, over a million francs to repair the château, gardens, parks, ponds, stables, coach-houses and kitchens, as well as to supplement furnishings with paintings and statuary taken from Paris and Versailles museums along with rich tapestries from the Gobelin works in Paris and elsewhere.

Napoleon's new private secretary, 24-year-old Claude François de Méneval who replaced the disgraced Bourrienne in spring of 1802, was astounded by the complex human machinery of the Tuileries. Although Napoleon's office – his *cabinet* – was simple enough with a couple of desks, bookcases, cupboard, clock, some chairs, a settee, fireplace and a mantel holding a bronze equestrian statuette of Frederick the Great of Prussia, his staff was another matter. Adjacent to his *cabinet* was a map room manned by an army officer. There was a full-time librarian, a secretary-interpreter of oriental languages (Jaubert), a secretary-interpreter of northern languages, a governor of the palace (General Duroc), a military office headed by four generals (Lannes, Bessières, Davout and Soult), eight military aides, most of them colonels, four prefects or chamberlains, and to keep Joséphine company four quasi-ladies-in-waiting. "Already at that time," Méneval concluded, "the house of the First Consul resembled a court," an observation earlier made by Bourrienne in referring to life at Malmaison and St. Cloud.[2]

These and other perquisites were in keeping with his position as

Bessières, Jean Baptiste 1768–1813, Marshal of France

Soult, Nicolas Jean de Dieu 1769–1851 Marshal of France

head of state, and he was probably correct in assuming that the ordinary citizen wanted France to be represented by a certain amount of pompous grandeur. Although autocratic at times he was still reasonably accessible to councillors, generals, civil officials and politicians. Nevertheless, after peace had been made with England pomp and ceremony began to creep into official and social functions. Shortly before his precipitate departure from service, Bourrienne noted the introduction of "the habits and etiquette which brought to mind the ceremonies of sovereignty." One observer was struck by the royal grandeur of the ceremony to bless the Concordat, another by the elaborate launching of the Legion of Honor. Bourrienne described the "brilliant and numerous" functions at the Tuileries – "nothing was wanted but the reintroduction of [court] levées."[3]

The sea change became apparent after Napoleon was voted First Consul for life. No longer was he readily available to officials; appointments were necessary and were strictly regulated by the palace keeper, General Duroc. Uniformed chamberlains and prefects appeared as military dress vanished. Courtiers now wore expensively tailored breeches and jackets, silk stockings, black patent leather pumps with silver buckles. Guests at Malmaison and St. Cloud followed strict rules of etiquette including those of speech and rank. Fontainebleau castle, the hunting ground of kings since the twelfth century, was restored (despite the opinion of leading architects that it would have been cheaper to build a new one). Social scenes in these various country retreats increasingly resembled those of the *ancien régime* – or rather, in view of the backgrounds of most of the players, a thin imitation of such scenes.

Napoleon feigned aloofness to these changes, an attitude brusquely summed up by a remark to Bourrienne: "Men well deserve the contempt I feel for them. I have only to put some gold lace on the coats of my virtuous republicans, and they immediately become just what I wish them."[4] Aside from state affairs he continued to wear a simple military uniform and, as the English envoy Lord Malmesbury had noted earlier, on occasion to swear like a trooper.

He was now 33 years old. His health had declined in the second year of the Consulate, an abdominal problem with symptoms suggesting a stomach ulcer or an unhappy appendix. This had been remedied by Doctor Corvisart, henceforth his personal physician, who treated him with a series of blisters, the prohibition of too many hot baths (which were weakening him) and a regimen of exercise including the hunt.

His new secretary, Méneval, found him to be in excellent health, moderately stout, about five feet two inches tall, well built, a high forehead, short neck, broad shoulders and a prominent chest:

> His legs were well shaped, his feet were small and well
> formed. His hands, of which he was rather proud, were
> delicate and plump, with tapering fingers . . . eyes gray,
> penetrating and wonderfully mobile; his nose was straight
> and well shaped; his teeth were fairly good, the mouth
> perfectly modelled . . . his skin was smooth and his
> complexion pale . . . His very fine chestnut hair . . . was
> thin on the upper part of the head, and left bare on his
> forehead.[5]

A female observer described his cropped hair:

> his complexion, pale and sallow; his eyes gray, but very
> animated . . . his countenance is a pleasing melancholy,
> which, whenever he speaks, relaxes into the most agreeable
> and gracious smile you can conceive . . . He has more
> unaffected dignity than I could conceive in man . . . He
> speaks deliberately, but very fluently, with particular
> emphasis, and in a rather low tone of voice. While he
> speaks, his features are still more expressive than his
> words.[6]

His daily schedule in the Tuileries was almost unchanging. His secretary brought morning newspapers to his bedroom at 7 a.m.

While he read through them the secretary culled important letters from the morning mail which Napoleon either read or had read to him, often dictating immediate replies. After a hot bath he was either shaved by Roustam or shaved himself, the Mameluke holding the mirror to the light. Breakfast was at 9 o'clock, a matter of only a few minutes. He then returned to his papers until General Duroc announced the morning audience, mostly petitioners, which generally lasted until noon.

He lunched alone as a rule, content with simple dishes, a glass of Chambertin wine diluted with water, and a cup of coffee. During a luncheon break he relaxed with people whose company he enjoyed, usually savants or artists, but soon returned to his *cabinet* where, now and then taking a pinch of snuff, he worked until supper time – a slightly more formal meal shared by Joséphine and occasional visitors, the large staff dining separately. Eating was never a great pleasure for him and he often, particularly in critical times, left the table before the meal ended.

On Wednesdays, the usual day for the council of state to meet, he entertained various ministers and councillors at dinner. Important anniversaries and distinguished visitors were honored by elaborate receptions arranged and lorded over by gracious Joséphine while richly dressed generals and diplomats pranced about with jeweled members of Parisian society.

On occasion he and Joséphine attended the theater or opera, she far more often than he because his favorite repertoires were few, although the same cannot be said for the more seductive actresses. Normally he retired early, Joséphine joining him to read aloud from his favorite works. They usually slept in separate bedrooms, understandably since he often jumped out of bed in the middle of the night to summon a secretary for dictation.[7]

Once the peace of Amiens was ratified Napoleon lived mainly either at Malmaison or St. Cloud, only rarely visiting Paris. Although his daily routine did not greatly change – his large staff was always on hand, as were streams of couriers bringing the latest dispatches – life was considerably more relaxed in the country air where soft lawns invited leisurely walks in the beautiful parks. When not working, hunting or shooting he enjoyed long discussions with a variety of guests, scientists, artists, writers, dramatists, sculptors. Evening dinner was a family affair and unless work intervened was followed by coffee in the drawing-room where he played chess or conversed with his guests, the quiet behavior described by Méneval at the beginning of this chapter.

Joséphine obviously missed Parisian glamor, intimate meetings with friends and, not least, spending hours in expensive shops. She was a compulsive spender who ran up enormous bills and forced tradesmen to reduce them by half (to everyone's embarrassment but her own) before presenting them to Napoleon and responding to his tongue-lashings by tears and sulks – a ritual repeated throughout their marriage.

She was also adaptable and from all accounts was an extremely gracious and kind hostess either in Paris or in the country. Although she lacked accomplishments familiar to ladies of her day – according to Méneval she played only one tune on a harp in her bedroom – she had her "ladies" on hand to chat with while she sewed, and she also played a mean game of backgammon. Her particular interest and pride were gardens and hothouses filled with exotic flowers, plants and shrubs, many of them imported from English nurseries on the advice of London experts. Her receptions and dinner parties were well attended. Informal entertainment was largely homemade, card games, dice, amateur theatricals, dancing on Sundays (Napoleon joining in). She especially enjoyed the more witty and talented guests such as the great tragedian actor, François Joseph Talma, and the Italian sculptor, Antonio Canova, who prepared the first model of what became the famous fig-leaf figure of Napoleon while at Malmaison (it still graces the first Duke of Wellington's London mansion).[8]

Minister Chaptal later wrote of Napoleon's sudden displays of temper at Malmaison, of snapping blooms off Joséphine's precious plants with his riding crop or taking potshots with his carbine at her exotic swans. Roustam confirmed the latter practice but suggested that it was rare and more of a joke to annoy Joséphine than anything else.⁹

Méneval in contrast "had expected to find him [Napoleon] brusque, and of uncertain temper . . . [but instead] found him patient, indulgent, easy to please, by no means exacting, and sometimes of a charming *bonhomie*." His familiarity however was not to be reciprocated: "Napoleon played with men without mixing with them." That aside, Méneval felt entirely at ease in working for him and was particularly impressed by "his pleasant and affectionate ways with Joséphine, the assiduous devotion to his officers, the kindliness of his relations with consuls and ministers, and his familiarity with the soldiers . . . In his retreat at Malmaison Napoleon appeared like a father in the midst of his family."¹⁰

These bright colors were painted by a devoted and very loyal servant, but they are substantiated as one side of Napoleon's character by a host of diverse sources.

He was by nature a generous man in the material if not the emotional sense. His extravagant rewards to those who served him and France honestly and well were notorious. Official records are full of various gratuities of cash sums and pensions, sometimes both, to worthy persons, to old soldiers or their survivors, to citizens of other talents who had fallen on hard times. His generosity was almost unlimited to any soldier from general to private who had fought well. He unfailingly remembered former teachers, servants, companions in arms. He installed his old teacher, Abbé Dubois, as librarian at Malmaison. He furnished his friend Alexander des Mazis, who had exiled himself in the Portuguese army, with a letter of amnesty, and when the des Mazis brothers returned impoverished from exile in 1802 he loaned Alexander 10,000 francs and soon after appointed him to the lucrative position of director of the national lottery.¹¹

As private secretary Méneval also witnessed the other side of Napoleon's character, but good servant that he was we catch this only in passing, yet sufficiently when taken with numerous other accounts to realize that this extraordinary human being shared many of mankind's familiar faults.

Napoleon was quick to condemn anyone who failed to share his views or whom he believed had let him down by improper action, and he sometimes did this very rudely in a hot temper. But almost everyone who worked closely with him – Cambacérès, Berthier, Méneval, Talleyrand, Roederer, Chaptal, Fouché, assorted aides, Roustam, Constant, to name a few – described the lash of tongue or pen as temporary, usually resulting from professional frustrations.

Secretaries frequently held up hotly dictated communiqués to ministers and diplomats for two or three days, knowing that Napoleon would accept their toned-down editing. He was also prone to reconsider harsh reprimands, rarely if ever apologizing but almost always compensating by numerous generous gestures, cash gifts, promotion, praise, honors, whatever – a policy of personal reconciliation that eventually would become self-defeating.

How to explain this explosive and obstinate trait? It resulted from several factors – an enlarged ego hiding perhaps a basic inferiority complex, an exceedingly quick and brilliant mind, a refusal to suffer fools gladly, an almost limitless ambition, a Corsican heritage, a belief that whatever he wanted to happen *would* happen, combined with his faith in the validity of physical force to achieve his desires. He hated to have subordinates err because, having appointed them, in his mind he shared their failures. He did not hesitate to reprimand them, but now came the Corsican version of compassion – a person once punished, the crime was usually forgiven. Add to this a strong sense of loyalty mixed with deep gratitude and devotion for heroic and meritorious acts of the past.

Pertinent examples are evident at almost every turn of the long road leading to an emperor's crown and humiliating exile. In the case of the military he would overlook virtually any shortcoming in a commander who otherwise served him well. He ignored Masséna's corrupt practices up to a point because Masséna won battles. He brushed off instances of Bernadotte's treachery not only because Bernadotte was married to Joseph

Bonaparte's sister-in-law, Eugénie Désirée Clary – Napoleon's early love for whom he would always hold a tender regard – but because Bernadotte initially also won battles and therefore deserved to be showered with favors. He overlooked General Desaix's unfortunate signing of the armistice with the Turks in Egypt, not only because Desaix was one of his most able generals and closest friends but because General Menou had sent him on a diplomatic mission for which he was not trained. He reprimanded General Lannes, his ambassador at Portugal, only lightly for an unheard-of breach of diplomatic etiquette because Lannes was a hard-charging commander with a superb combat record.

Napoleon's lenient behavior with navy admirals is not as easy to explain. Perhaps he realized his own inadequacy when it came to matters naval, and that the long decline in the French navy would take many years to turn around; perhaps he understood that in view of the poor condition of the fleet, he was ordering missions made impossible by human and technical limitations. Whatever the reason, he was far too tolerant in the case of certain admirals who should have been relieved and even courtmartialed for professional dereliction of duty. He displayed a similar leniency toward General Menou upon the latter's return from Egypt despite his poor professional performance – possible a matter of conscience.

He treated important officials in the same manner, often relegating inadequate or even corrupt performers to lesser positions rather than demanding resignation and prosecution. Despite having known for some time of Bourrienne's corrupt practices, when the scandal broke he inwardly regarded the crime as his own. Upon dismissing the undeniably brilliant secretary he told him that he never wanted to see him again. Yet he shortly gave him employment and within a few years would receive him and send him on an important diplomatic mission (only to suffer for his kindness).[12] He expelled Fouché from the ministry but appointed him to the senate where he would continue his often damaging intrigues. He also appointed Roederer to the senate after hotly criticizing his performance as minister.[13]

This often misplaced generosity, no matter the motivation, did not rub off when it came to foreign affairs. Here Napoleon often vented pure Corsican hatred and a desire for revenge on those rulers whom he felt had crossed him.

Enter now a final and extremely important characteristic briefly touched on above: an impetuosity fueled by his respect for and reliance on physical force. In reprimanding subordinates Napoleon often threatened and rarely acted. In dealing with foreign powers he often threatened and often acted, which was almost invariably the case when it came to his arch-enemy, England.

Never was this more true than in the months after the Treaty of Amiens had been signed. Napoleon should have employed every diplomatic maneuver known to mankind to hold what he had gained from a favorable peace. His country was prospering, its citizens were happy, internecine feuds based on religion and politics were quieting. He had everything to gain from continued internal growth, further consolidation of his rule and repair and expansion of his navy, and everything to lose from a new war. Considering the conservatives' distaste for the treaty in England, perhaps it would have been impossible to avoid a new war, but it would have been to France's advantage to *try* to do so. Yet scarcely was the ink dry on the treaty before Napoleon had begun a series of bellicose actions that played directly into the hands of a small but vociferous war party in London intent on forming a new coalition against France.

Notes

1   Méneval, 121–1.
2   Méneval, 114–18.
3   Bourrienne, II, 99, 122.
4   Bourrienne, II, 99.
5   Méneval, 105.
6   Rose (*Life*) I, 328–9.
7   Méneval, 112–18.

8   Méneval, 122–3.
9   Chaptal, 333–4; Roustam, xxxiii, 188–9.
10 Méneval, 123–4.
11 Bartel, 253.
12 Méneval, 96, 103, 128–33.
13 Corr. VII. Nr. 6326, Paris, 15 September 1802.

CHAPTER FORTY

THE ROAD TO WAR
MARCH 1802–MAY 1803

It is impossible to understand why a great, powerful and
sensible nation [England] would want war with all its great
evils . . . over a miserable rock.

Napoleon to Lord Whitworth, English envoy to
France, concerning the dispute over the island of
Malta, Paris, 4 May 1803[1]

THE TREATY OF Amiens has been described as an armistice more
than a peace. This is fair enough considering the deep-seated
hatred between France and England that asserted itself up to the
signing of the document and would continue to do so.[2] It was
also tragic enough from the humanistic standpoint. Both the
French and English governments continued to stupidly ignore
those functions necessary to allow their citizens to live comfortably in peace after suffering almost a decade of war, although
England was a more flagrant offender than France.

Each country faced enormous internal problems, the ameliora-
tion or even the solution of which would have taxed all governing
talents for a good many years. France had still to consolidate the
social gains of the revolution, to ensure internal security, to build
a political and economic structure necessary to support a better life
for the bulk of its people.

England was staring at the burgeoning social disaster known as
the Industrial Revolution. Already hundreds of thousands of its
11 million people had been forced from the land to eke out miserable existences in towns and cities. Factories belching filthy

poisonous fumes were springing up everywhere. Even today's most chauvinistic British historians have written of seven-year-old naked girls dragging coal carts in Lancashire mines, of ten-year-olds working twelve hours a day under grueling conditions that included frequent beatings.[3]

Vast numbers of old, poor, hungry and illiterate citizens needed help which was not available. Schools and hospitals were few. Hungry, sometimes starving, children looked forward to a life as bleak as the walls of their ramshackle dwellings.

Yet in the midst of this human misery the nobility and upper classes, the large landowners, manufacturers and merchant kings were adding to already vast fortunes, many accruing from black slave laborers working themselves to early deaths in the fields and mines of ever-increasing overseas colonies. Social justice abroad was a joke. At home it was a rare, often non-existent, commodity, choked at every turn by those magic words trade and empire, by the monentary greed of the ruling classes dressed in the shimmering if time-worn costumes of national pride and honor.

The Treaty of Amiens was in some ways lopsided, the result of French military successes which isolated an exhausted England so as to cause Addington's weak government to give away far more than it gained. By the time the English government realized this it was too late to turn the otherwise joyful country around – except by obstructionism in carrying out a key term of the treaty which led to its final abnegation by England and to a new war.

Responsibility for the avoidable crime has to be shared. Napoleon's post-treaty actions formed a major factor in England's obstructionism. The English government was already upset by the hefty French military expedition sent to impose peace on San Domingo – the stepping-stone, many believed, to the building of a powerful presence in its newly acquired territory of Louisiana. Few people seemed to realize that France could not become a significant colonial power so long as it lacked a battle fleet commensurate with that of the Royal Navy, fewer still that new ships alone do not make a battle fleet worthy of the name. So addled was the English government's military thinking that with the arrival of peace it began to reduce naval strength while more than doubling army strength.[4] (Napoleon on the other hand placed his army on a peacetime footing while concentrating on trying to build up a battle fleet.) Nevertheless the Royal Navy maintained 40 warships on station with an additional reserve of over 60 that could quickly be mobilized.

Far more serious was Napoleon's truculent exclusion of English ships from French ports and colonies, a matter not taken up in the treaty but one that helped to turn general opinion in England against the First Consul when he refused to sign a commercial treaty. To England's protests Napoleon pointed to interference with French fishing boats and, far worse, to the English government's subsidizing of various Bourbon princes and troublesome French *émigrés*. Not only were those persons flooding England, France and Germany with virulent anti-republican pamphlets and sordid cartoons at Napoleon and Joséphine's expense, but English gold was supporting rebel movements in Brittany, the Vendée and the Midi, movements intent on ultimately assassinating the First Consul.

Feelings hardened as Napoleon accused the English of dragging their feet in implementing the terms of the treaty. One such called for England to evacuate the island of Malta, and the French the Taranto peninsula, within three months. Although Napoleon removed his troops on schedule England showed no sign of so doing. Upon learning that British troops still held the island after four months, Napoleon reasonably asked why.

For nearly two centuries many British historians have written around this vexing question while avoiding a direct and relatively simple answer. The answer is that England, having signed an unfavorable treaty, wished to renege on this particular item since it was determined to hold on to Malta as a necessary Mediterranean base.

In one sense its position is not difficult to understand. Despite the loss of the North American colonies it was building a vast overseas empire, its warships did rule the seas, and a large merchant fleet carried immensely valuable cargoes to and from colonial ports, a maritime-colonial success story that helps to explain its arrogance and haughtiness in that day's diplomacy.

England had agreed under the terms of the Treaty of Amiens to return Egypt to Turkey and the Cape of Good Hope to the Dutch. With its sea route to India, its most valued possession, placed in possible jeopardy, it now argued that Malta in other hands would endanger English trade with the Levant and close the land route to the east, and this was not acceptable to the world's foremost trading power.

But in another sense England's position was deplorable. If it had not been willing to yield Malta it should not have signed and ratified the treaty. Twist as it might – its leaders accusing Lord Cornwallis of having exceeded his negotiating authority, a ridiculous assertion in view of the ratification – the government had made a legal commitment familiar to all concerned powers to evacuate the island. It now set out to void this commitment without attracting outright the stigma of dishonorable behavior.

The first move in the stonewalling campaign was merely passive: the British garrison remained on the island after the agreed grace period, its defense being that a new Grand Master of the Knights of Malta had not been named. Although the treaty did not call for a time limit on this proviso, Napoleon persuaded Pope Pius VII to make the appointment which London refused to accept because the Russian czar had not approved it – more delay. Napoleon next arranged for the King of Naples to send a provisional garrison of 2,000 troops to the island. They duly arrived but were not permitted to man the forts, indeed they were shunted off to the countryside to be treated more as a potential enemy than an occupying force.

The word war heated up in late autumn when Napoleon agreed to mediate an incipient civil war in Switzerland, and when Addington's cabinet gained an important militant adherent, Lord Castlereagh. Although Britain was in no position to contest

Napoleon's mediation in Switzerland which ended in partial military occupation, its war party – the Pittites, Windhams, Grenvilles, Canning, Wellesley, Sheridan and others – unleashed a propaganda campaign second to none. Joined by former admirers of Napoleon such as the poets Coleridge, Southey and Wordsworth, the war party portrayed the First Consul as the embodiment of all evil who would have to be destroyed by Great Britain before Europe could again live in (quasi-feudalistic) peace. Thus pressured, Addington and his inept foreign minister, Lord Hawkesbury, sent a veteran and very bellicose diplomat, Lord Whitworth, to Paris as ambassador, his mission being to retain Malta at all costs – including renewed war.

Whitworth's first meeting with Napoleon, the six-footer towering over the First Consul, set the pattern of the next few months. Whitworth suggested that Britain should be compensated for French gains on the continent by retaining Malta. Napoleon countered that Britain already controlled large areas of the Americas, the West Indies and India, not to mention Gibraltar; and besides, Whitworth was talking outside treaty terms. Czar Alexander of Russia moreover had approved the pope's appointment of a new Grand Master for the island – so now nothing remained except British evacuation.

This was not to be. In a change of tack the English government next claimed that since the time limit for evacuation had expired the pertinent article was no longer valid. England now intended to hold the island for seven years.

This declaration at once brought renewed and increasingly angry protests from Napoleon, whose normal obduracy had been heightened by the failure of General Leclerc's mission in San Domingo. Leclerc had made a promising start in pacifying the country and the rebel Toussaint and his generals had surrendered the previous May, but by the time the rebellion had been quashed the dreaded yellow fever had reduced French strength to 12,000 soldiers. Napoleon's subsequent and ill-advised decision to reintroduce slave labor in the West Indies had brought on another serious revolt. The deadly fever continued to decimate the now ragged French force: Leclerc's death in November was followed by virtual annihilation of the expedition.

Even before this disaster Napoleon's geopolitical thinking had begun to shift from west back to east, back to his dream of building an Alexandrian-style eastern empire on the remains of what appeared to be a crumbling Ottoman empire. Toward this end he sent Colonel Sebastiani and Monsieur Jaubert, his eastern languages expert, on a "commercial mission" to Egypt (soon to be evacuated by British forces), St. Jean d'Acre (scene of his earlier disaster), Corfu and Smyrna. Theirs was an espionage mission to gather information necessary for a future French landing in Egypt.[5]

The two spies returned to Paris in early 1803 having accomplished very little despite widespread bribery of numerous local officials and native chieftains. Although the British government volubly disapproved of the expedition the matter would have ended there but for Sebastiani's vivid report to Napoleon: the Turkish situation in Egypt was desperate, he claimed; once the English force was evacuated "six thousand French would . . . be enough to conquer Egypt"; moreover the Ionian islands, Corfu and neighbors, "will declare themselves French as soon as an opportunity shall offer itself."[6]

Such overblown optimism so suited Napoleon's expansionist dreams that he now ordered a secret expedition to sail for India where France had been ceded Pondicherry by the Treaty of Amiens. Captain-General Decaen was to raise the French flag over the new territory and eventually win over native tribes to challenge British hegemony.[7] Although provocative, this move was legitimate enough and at least for the moment was secret. But now Napoleon made a very foolish move by having Sebastiani's report published in the *Moniteur* where against the wishes of his close advisers it appeared at the end of January.

Up to this point the Addington government, spurred on by the king and the war party, had continued to insist that Malta was only just compensation for Napoleon's gains on the continent, but this was mere diplomatic rhetoric. England's most persuasive spokesman, William Pitt, who along with his Tory colleagues regarded Napoleon as devil incarnate, remained silent at his country haunt where he was said to be enjoying an alcoholic sabbatical while his protégé Henry Addington ran the government. England's greatest orator, Charles James Fox, was openly sympathetic to the French demand for English withdrawal from Malta, as were many of his Whig cohorts.

Publication of Sebastiani's provocative report began to alter Addington's passivity. Whitworth was instructed to demand "a satisfactory explanation". In a stormy meeting Napoleon made it clear to the ambassador that the issue was not Egypt which was not worth a war since eventually it would fall to France. The issue on which peace or war rested was Malta. It was England's choice. If England evacuated the island and called off royalist propaganda and spies against France then the two countries – one master of the land, the other of the sea – could govern the world, an interesting suggestion that fell on deaf ears in London where the cabinet had no intention of allowing France to challenge control of its colonial empire.[8]

Napoleon followed this profitless meeting by reiterating his stand in a lengthy message to the senate and assembly. After reviewing the favorable state of the nation at home and abroad, its finances, industries, trade, public works, religious culture, education, armed forces, foreign relations and other ancillary subjects, he informed his audience that "the government guarantees the continental peace and is able to hope for the continuation of the maritime peace . . . in order to conserve it, the government will do everything compatible with national honor, essentially tied to the strict execution of treaties."

He went on to explain, somewhat inaccurately, that there was a struggle between the two English political parties, one being the party that had concluded the peace and wished to maintain it, the other that held "an implacable hatred" for France which explained "the fluctuating pacific and threatening attitudes." Until this struggle was decided, prudence dictated a French army

500,000 strong "ready to defend and avenge the country."
Although France need have no fear of the outcome of a war since
England had no continental allies, "let us hope that this will not
be the case, and let us believe rather that one will only hear in the
British cabinet sagacious counsels and the voice of humanity."9

If the arrogant confidence expressed in this message appealed
to French politicians, the reaction in England was explosive – a red
flag to an already angry John Bull. While Addington forced a
conciliatory step in having one of the most outrageous French
émigrés taken to court (and convicted) for publishing libelous
pamphlets against the French government, the war party jumped
on Napoleon's expansion of the army and his insult to British
arms. In early March, King George III addressed parliament to
point to Napoleon's expansionist intentions and the covert presence of French officers called "commercial agents" who were
surveying England's ports and harbors, and to request the call-up
of the militia and recruitment of 10,000 sailors, which was immediately passed.10

This in turn provoked an outburst from Napoleon to Lord
Whitworth a few days later at a ministerial reception when he
bluntly accused the English government of wanting war. To
Whitworth's denial he angrily replied: "You must respect treaties
then. Woe to those who do not respect treaties. They shall answer
for it to all Europe." With that, Whitworth reported, "he retired
to his apartment, repeating the last phrase."11

There was still room for maneuver had goodwill been a factor.
Each country had its strengths and weaknesses, the necessary
ingredients for continuing negotiations if not a peaceful settle-
ment. But such had been the intensity of almost a decade of war
that goodwill did not exist, a fatality followed by the demise of
common sense, the weapons of pride, honor, arrogance and ambition being not only fired by the leaders but by statesmen, generals
and ordinary citizens.

Napoleon clearly saw only struggle ahead. In January he had
ordered the cavalry to be remounted at a cost of 1.7 million francs,
the remounts to be young so that they would be strong enough "in

five or six years . . . to serve in several campaigns."[12] Also in
January, in dispatching Decaen's expedition to India he directed
him to evacuate Pondicherry in case of war and return to the
safety of Mauritania.[13]

Aware that he could not match England's naval superiority for
at least a decade, he already had written off San Domingo, his
gateway to the New World, and now in mid April he followed that
painful move by selling the rich territory of Louisiana to the
United States for a few pennies an acre.[14] Although Joseph and
Lucien Bonaparte among others vigorously opposed the sale
Napoleon remained firm, content in adding 60 million francs to
his hard-pressed treasury while at the same time denying the territory to England in case of war: "This accession of territory
affirms forever the power of the United States . . . [to give]
England a maritime rival which, sooner or later, will reduce its
arrogance."[15]

That arrogance was very much in evidence. In late April,
Whitworth delivered a new ultimatum: England to reduce its
occupation of Malta to ten years providing that France accepted
its earlier conditions. If not accepted, Whitworth was to leave
Paris for London within seven days.[16] Napoleon hotly rejected
this demand while his minions sought some kind of compromise
to prevent a bloody war being resumed for "a miserable rock."[17]

Whitworth was on the point of leaving when Talleyrand suggested that England turn the island over to Russian sovereignty.
Delaying his departure, Whitworth sent this proposal to London.
Meanwhile the English government had all but declared war by
placing its fleets on battle stations. It immediately dismissed the
new proposal as still another trick to stave off a decision until
French warships had safely returned to French harbors from San
Domingo waters, nor was it moved by news that Czar Alexander,
deemed to be under French influence, had agreed to mediate the
dispute.[18]

Lord Whitworth left Paris for Calais on 12 May. En route he
received a final proposal from a now apprehensive Napoleon:
Britain to retain Malta and France to occupy the Taranto peninsula

for ten years. Whitworth rejected this sensible compromise on the grounds that England could not yield what it did not own – an inadequate argument in view of England's influence over the King of Naples combined with the strong French presence in Italy.

Such was the situation when the English parliament met to debate the renewal of hostilities. Acrimonious words soon filled the small chamber. The Whigs intelligently argued against another war. The Tories whose bellicosity was enhanced by the fiery presence of William Pitt were not to be put down. The vote was called, the Tories were victorious – Britain would declare war on France.

Notes

1   Corr. VIII. Nr. 6725, Paris, 4 May 1803.
2   See, for example, Corr. VII. Nr. 5990, Paris, 12 March 1802, in which Napoleon complained to Talleyrand of the slowness of negotiations and the menacing attitude of the English government, "as if I needed to be forced to make the peace and as if, in reality the power and the strength of England were such that it was able to force me."
3   Bryant (*Victory*), 18–19.
4   Ziegler, 154–5.
5   Corr. VIII. Nrs. 6277, Paris, 29 August 1802; 6308, Paris, 5 September 1802; 6812, St. Cloud, 11 June 1803, which authorizes payment of 100,000 francs to Sebastiani for secret expenses.
6   Rose (*Life*), I, 413–4.
7   Rose (*Life*), I, 374–5.
8   Rose (*Life*), I, 416. See also Bryant (*Victory*), 41.
9   Corr. VIII. Nr. 6591, Paris, 20 February 1803.
10 Rose (*Life*), I, 418.
11 Rose (*Life*), I, 418. See also Corr. VIII. Nrs. 6630, Paris, 13 March 1803; 6636, Paris, 20 March 1803, for Napoleon's somewhat contradictory accounts of this confrontation.
12 Corr. VIII. Nr. 6536, Paris, 10 January 1803.
13 Rose (*Life*), I, 375. Decaen did not sail until early March 1803. The

naval force commanded by Admiral Linois counted four warships, two transports and some smaller vessels, the troops numbered some 1,800. The expedition reached Pondicherry in mid July, but meanwhile war had broken out between France and England and Linois was forced to return to Mauritania where the troops disembarked. His warships subsequently became the scourge of the ocean, sweeping "from the eastern seas British merchantmen valued at over a million [pounds] sterling." Rose (*Life*), I, 377–8.

14 Godlewski, 319–20. President Thomas Jefferson, upset by Napoleon's acquisition, already had sent James Monroe to Paris to try to purchase New Orleans and adjacent territory. Monroe was now pleasantly surprised when Talleyrand offered him the entire vast area, the first move toward what became the Louisiana Purchase. As finally worked out the United States paid 60 million francs ($12 million) in installments plus 20 million francs ($4 million) to pay off American creditors. The United States thus doubled its area at a cost of 30 centimes (six cents) per hectare (2½ acres) for some of the richest lands on the continent.

15 Godlewski, 320.

16 Bryant (*Victory*), 47.

17 Corr. VIII. Nr. 6725, Paris, 4 May 1803.

18 Bryant (*Victory*), 49.

CHAPTER FORTY-ONE

THE INVASION OF ENGLAND – I
JUNE 1803–FEBRUARY 1804

*However disastrous the war may be, it will never force the
French people, supported by justice and God, to bow before this
arrogant race which makes a mockery of all that is sacred on
earth, and which, above all for the last twenty years, has
taken an ascendancy and audacity in Europe that threatens the
industrial and commercial lifeblood of all nations.*

Napoleon to Talleyrand, 23 August 1803[1]

IT WASN'T MUCH of a war. All French ships in British harbors were
seized. An English fleet blockaded Brest, capturing two French
ships in the process, while Admiral Horatio Nelson sailed a fleet
to the Mediterranean to blockade Toulon. Napoleon could not
immediately retaliate at sea since over half of his battle fleet, small
and ineffective as it was, was in the West Indies. Admiral
Ganteaume at Toulon nevertheless was to place all available warships on high alert, "ready to sail any hour, day or night," if a
suitable opportunity for attack developed.[2]

Meanwhile General Mortier with a corps 25,000 strong
stormed into Hanover whose guardian army immediately surrendered. General Gouvion St. Cyr marched another force into the
Taranto peninsula (to be fed and clothed at the King of Naples'
expense). General Murat, commanding French forces in Italy,
declared the port of Leghorn "in state of siege" and General
Olivier marched a corps into Tuscany to enforce the decree, his
soldiers to be supported by the King of Etruria.

All British subjects in France and French-occupied countries

Destruction of French Gun-Boats, 1803

were arrested, all British ships and merchandise seized and all ports under French control closed to British vessels. Army commanders and civil ministers at Elba, Corsica, Genoa, Ancona, Italy and Holland were issued letters of marque, 24 to start with, which authorized civilian privateers to set out after British merchant ships.[3] Commanders of off-shore islands received orders to speed construction of defenses. Military and police officers in Brittany and the Vendée were to take special precautions to prevent infiltration of spies and troop landings.

These preliminary moves were ancillary to Napoleon's alleged intention to invade either England or Ireland – or both. The cross-channel invasion plan was relatively simple. Once a French fleet had lured away English ships guarding French ports, vast fleets of landing craft sailing from Boulogne, Étaples and Ambleteuse would land 100,000 French troops on Sussex and Kent beaches to push through allegedly feeble English defenses and run up the French flag on the Tower of London.

Napoleon's actual intentions are still the subject of considerable controversy among historians. Did he really intend to invade England or Ireland? Or was this a sham to disguise preparations for land attacks on the continent? A definitive answer will probably never emerge, but available facts indicate that at this point he was hell-bent on invading England. Else why would he – with multifarious domestic and foreign concerns whirling daily through the Tuileries – depart Paris at end of June for a six-week exhaustive tour of pertinent French and Belgian ports? Else why would he make enormous financial investments in the coming months to build landing craft and support vessels, money that otherwise could have been spent either on building more warships or on weapons and equipment for his armies, or on the host of public works and other civil projects so dear to his heart?

An accurate answer is not that important because it is doubtful if a more fatuous strategic and tactical plan ever existed. England's naval superiority, French ignorance of amphibious warfare, the incredible languor of senior French naval officers, the tremendous logistical and boat-building requirements, the mercurial state of European politics where partners changed beds with the frequency and intensity of a massive sexual orgy – all were ignored in vast preparations for the cross-channel invasion.

The operation was to be carried out by a flotilla of large- and medium-sized gunboats, pinnaces, caïques, fishing boats and flat-bottomed troop and horse carriers, these to the number of over 2,000 which Napoleon believed would be ready by late November.[4] This was crazy. France possessed neither the shipyards, standard or improvised, nor sufficient skilled workers nor the necessary materials to build such a fleet in a short time. Even if the craft were ready they would require thousands of trained seamen who were not available and, such was the ungainly design of troop and horse transports – large, flat-bottomed boats – that they either would have drifted away or have sunk in the first heavy wind.

Add to construction and manning requirements the armament and logistical needs: each gunboat armed with 1–4 cannon and several short-barrelled carronades; each carrying 15 days of food and 10 days of water for the crew, lesser quantities for soldiers, enormous amounts of pre-packaged weapons and ammunition, 1,200 rations of boxed biscuits, 1,200 rations of brandy, 8 copper boilers and 8 large water carriers. Each soldier would carry a heavy musket, pack, ammunition pouch holding 30 cartridges and three flints, 4 lbs of bread and a canteen full of wine. One or two field cannon were to be on board, with at least two harnessed artillery horses provided with a five day ration of oats, five of bran and sufficient water.[5]

Napoleon began a tour of the Channel coast in late June. As usual his organization was superb, aides and secretaries carefully chosen, communications with civil and military officials in Paris assured by a stream of couriers. As usual the pace was killing. In addition to conducting in-depth surveys of ports, harbors and coastal defenses from St. Valery on the Channel to Zeebrugge in Belgium, he received scores of local functionaries, attended innumerable illuminations, fêtes and formal banquets, inspected a variety of factories, regularly attended Catholic services and masses, and in long talks with bishops and priests implored them to end the quarrel between "constitutionals" and "non-constitutionals."

Often on horse for 5–8 hours, he frequently halted to drill sailors and soldiers before returning to headquarters to dictate replies to dispatches that had arrived during the day. At Calais he sent off some gunboats that, as he proudly reported to Paris, drove off two English frigates. The pattern continued as he moved up the coast into Belgium. Wherever he went it was a matter of intense observation, interrogation, issuance of corrective orders, of chivvying, scolding, encouraging and complimenting from the highest to the lowest ranks. Only in early August did he return to St. Cloud.

What was the result of this lengthy and exhausting tour?

On the positive side Napoleon was convinced that he held the people's support for whatever might come. Everywhere he appeared he was greeted by enormous cheering crowds that often held up his carriage. Surrounded by an immense number of enthusiastic citizens at Lille, he personally put the garrison through its paces on the drill-field.[6] His communiqués to Paris, mainly to Cambacérès and Berthier, form a solid paean of praise for the inhabitants. "I have reason to be very satisfied with the spirit of this city," he reported from Amiens early in the tour, "and of all the districts I have so far traveled through." The Somme country was very beautiful, he wrote, enjoying a high degree of prosperity. "After mass I received all the local authorities" (who thoughtfully presented him with the city's traditional gift of four swans).[7]

But if the spirit was willing the flesh was weak. Although he reported early in the trip "that construction is everywhere under way," he soon discovered that very little of anything had been completed. Important off-shore islands lacked proper defenses. Dunkirk was a disappointment: "I found the local administration badly organized and guided by unqualified advisers." Coast artillery defenses were not yet organized, no batteries existed from St. Valery to Étaples because of lack of gun carriages. The Boulogne pier had not been repaired to support the main battery owing to a turf war between army and navy engineers, nor was the furnace necessary to heat cannon-balls redhot in decent repair.

Strongpoints along the coast were not fortified. There was a crying need for ships' masts and hemp. One gunboat was armed with carronades of a small caliber which could not compete with better armed English boats – Napoleon had ordered 300 gunboats to be armed with heavier carronades three years ago: where were they, he asked Rear Admiral Denis Decrès, a survivor of Aboukir Bay and naval minister since 1801. English mortar galleys also possessed a greater range than those of the French – experiments were necessary to obtain parity. Boulogne had received no vessels for three months, "not a pinnacle, not a caïque, not a gunboat."[8]

Once again Napoleon was facing his old nemesis, the French navy which, as he complained to Decrès, was not energetically fulfilling its duties. He was disappointed with the commander of the Boulogne flotilla, Admiral Eustache Bruix, for not having countered a recent surprise bombardment of an important fort. To Bruix's claim that the enemy used better powder and thus its guns had greater range than his, Napoleon angrily replied that range was a matter of the degree of cannon elevation and not powder quality.

He followed this with another critical letter that lectured Bruix as to proper defense of the fort, and how to set a trap to attract and then destroy enemy raiders. The admiral should also shift his quarters from the town to the scene of the action: "In affairs of this sort, it is not unusual that the [commander in] chief is obliged to do everything." To Decrès: "I note from his [Bruix's] letters that he makes lengthy dissertations on the center, the right [and] the left of the [flotilla] divisions; this adds up to nothing. Every line has a center, a right and a left." And to Cambacérès: "Some functions of the naval ministry . . . are obviously neglected, and I am beginning to suspect that Decrès does not have the understanding of command and continuity, prime quality of an administrator.

However he has other qualities . . . [so despite] his carelessness over most important matters I decided to wait another three months to come to a decision because in the end there is little to gain from a change." Cambacérès was to tell the admiral that if he did not feel up to the job Napoleon would accept his resignation.[9]

Decrès felt perfectly up to the job he was not qualified to fill and he retained it as massive preparations for the crossing continued. That summer and autumn thousands of conscripts were called up and sent to rude coastal camps to be trained in embarkation and landing procedures.[10] Ovens were to be built to provide bread for 80,000 soldiers under the command of General Soult. Eighty thousand cloaks and 120,000 pairs of shoes were to be at embarkation ports by late September; 1.2 million packaged rations were to be delivered to St. Omer, along with 3 million rations of casked brandy by early October.

Elsewhere a variety of artillery trains were forming. They would require 10,000 horses of which only 4,000 were on hand.[11] Arsenals, factories, bakeries and distilleries in theory were working around the clock to found cannon, manufacture muskets, bayonets and ammunition, prepare food and drink.

All of this was very expensive. Even before his tour of the coast Napoleon had allotted 20 million francs for the purchase of masts and hemp. Subsequent manufactures would cost many millions more. Yet by late August only one 24-caliber cannon was being founded per day at Toulon instead of at least the normal ten because the company was owed 300,000 francs for the last two years. (Decrès was to contract for 250 cannon per month, pay the arrears and advance as much money as possible.) A couple of weeks later lack of funds threatened to halt all flotilla construction at Ostend and Dunkirk, a crisis surmounted only by shifting monies allotted elsewhere.[12]

Napoleon's supposition that European kingdoms and republics would either ally with him against tyrant-of-the-seas England or at least remain neutral began to unravel during his coastal tour. The first potential defector was the Spanish court which suddenly called up 100,000 militia to deploy between Valladolid and Burgos, uncomfortably close to the Spanish-French border. Talleyrand was to inform Prince Manuel Godoy that if Napoleon had the least reason to suppose a connivance between Madrid and London then this mobilization, taken with the partial disarmament of the Spanish fleet, would be regarded "as a commencement of hostilities."[13]

Napoleon employed equally strong language in a letter to Queen Marie Caroline of Naples, part of whose country his troops were occupying (at the kingdom's expense). Although his policy was conciliatory to his neighbors, he explained, so long as the kingdom of Naples, known as the Kingdom of the Two Sicilies, was governed more by a foreign prime minister (Sir John Acton) than by its own court, he would have to treat it "as a country governed by an English minister."[14]

He was much less aggressive when it came to Prussia, assuring King Frederick William that neither French armaments nor the occupation of Hanover were a cause for Prussian alarm. "I believe that England would not be able to sustain the war very long without the support of the continent, namely Prussia and Austria since Russia because of its distance could only play a secondary role." The Vienna court while behaving itself at the moment was an unknown quantity in view of the resentment caused from Austria's recent defeat by France.[15] Although he trusted Czar Alexander he did not trust his ministers. In a letter to the czar he thanked him for trying to keep the peace between France and England but he vigorously criticized the Russian ambassador in Paris, Markov, "for frequently involving himself in a disagreeable manner in the intrigues" of France.[16]

Portugal was misbehaving. French ambassador Lannes had been insulted several times, the country was arming, French citizens had been arrested and detained for several days without food. This was the doing of ministers in English pay who had sent 200,000 francs to the Chouans and other rebels in France. Talleyrand was to demand adequate compensation. Napoleon personally wrote a sharp warning to the Prince Regent: "It is impossible for me to consider Portugal as a neutral or friendly power if it is not governed by your Royal Highness instead of by ministers . . . who do not cease to greatly abuse French commerce."[17]

Spain having shown no signs of remorse by the time Napoleon returned to St. Cloud, he sent Talleyrand a lengthy list of complaints such as seizure of French ships and cargoes and maltreatment of French sailors forced to take refuge in Spanish harbors. Talleyrand was to determine whether Spain intended to declare war on England or, if remaining neutral, to pay the hefty subsidy to France called for by treaty; or if King Charles, blinded by the madness of Godoy and his ministers, wished to go to war against France.

The king had until early September to decide. Should he not respect Napoleon's demands, should he opt for alliance with England, then 80,000 French troops would pour into his country in early October. To avoid such unpleasantness Charles must disband the militia, pay 24 million francs in cash already owed to France, and pay an additional 72 million francs for the coming year. He must also expel the English ambassador, embargo all English ships, rearm Spain's warships and, in conjunction with French forces, attack Portugal and Gibraltar. King Charles defused this sharp ultimatum by declaring his intention to ally with France, either by declaring war against England or by paying subsidies to France if he remained neutral.[18]

Meanwhile news had reached St. Cloud of a new uprising in Ireland against English rule. Napoleon at once directed Admiral Decrès to offer Irish leaders in Paris 25,000 infantry, 40,000 muskets, all necessary artillery and munitions, and a promise that France would not make peace with England until Ireland gained independence – "providing, however, that 20,000 Irish, at least, join the French force during the first days of its debarkation on Irish shores."[19]

Despite some setbacks Napoleon saw no reason to slow down and rethink his position. The construction of an enormous flotilla would continue to breed massive problems, but with the nation behind him he was convinced of their solution. Although this would require a great deal of money he could expect massive funds from Spain and, once the American congress authorized the purchase of Louisiana, from the United States. Certain kingdoms including Spain, Portugal and Prussia would probably remain fractious, that was a fact of life, but as long as he commanded a large and powerful army there was nothing to worry about.

Napoleon however failed to realize that these various warts on the skin of France could become malignant, as indeed they had in the past. He should have known better – and he *would* have known better had his intense hatred of England not blinded him to anything but revenge. How could he otherwise have turned to Irish rebels who had already twice let France down?

His blindness became painfully obvious in late August when the Russian czar belatedly offered to mediate in the quarrel between France and England. Alexander came on stage a bit late. Napoleon had asked him to arbitrate the quarrel the previous year and he had refused. The offer now was to mediate only *after* the conditions had been set. The main condition was to give England the island of Lampedusa instead of Malta.

Napoleon refused to even consider the deal. In his opinion it was nonsensical for Russia to offer mediation at this stage, particularly under pre-set conditions. Lampedusa was nothing but another Malta, and a British fleet stationed there would spell death to French commerce with the Levant and the East. His reply stated old and new grievances but his conclusion remained the same. "England will never obtain from me a treaty other than that of Amiens," he informed Talleyrand. He would remove French troops from Taranto and Hanover once England evacuated Malta. If England refused to leave this island the war would continue.[20]

The war did continue, but at a slow pace during the winter of 1803–1804. Now and again prowling English cruisers pounced on a laggard French craft or fired a brace of Colonel Congreve's new rockets at a coastal port, puny efforts that caused little damage before being driven off by cannon fire that sometimes knocked off a mast or two.

To Napoleon the war meant only an invasion of England and Ireland. Ship construction continued at a frantic pace, not only in regular shipyards in France, Belgium and Holland, but in improvised hangars on convenient river banks where shipwrights and artisans worked day and night to provide and arm the requisite landing craft.

Troops from France and Italy continued to arrive in embarkation centers: 50,000 soldiers under Soult's command at Boulogne, 30,000 under Ney at Étaples, 30,000 at Bruges under Davout. Housed in rude barracks, the men spent their days in drilling or in embarking and debarking from the tiny craft, tiresome if dangerous sessions complemented by frequent inspections and target practice on land and spiced by swimming lessons in increasingly cold Channel waters.

Small craft of a dozen varieties continued to reach port, their skeleton crews filled out with volunteers and conscripts who had to learn all essential procedures including gunnery, but precious little seamanship owing to the English blockade. By November a broadside of more than a hundred craft guarded the Boulogne basin, with more arriving every week.[21]

Napoleon unexpectedly appeared in November to spend two weeks in Boulogne and neighboring ports, another exhausting period during which he daily faced rain and cold to inspect every facet of operations while frequently drilling troops when not entertaining local notables, dictating replies to urgent messages from Paris or attending mass at local churches. Heartened by the arrival of the first flat-bottomed transports he ordered Admiral Bruix to load one with 50 horses. Bruix was also to send small ships to reconnoitre the Kentish coast up to the river Thames – an optimistic order, as was that to form a company of guide-interpreters 117-strong, each of whom had lived in England, knew the land and could speak and translate the language.[22]

Probably no commander in chief has ever paid so much attention to the individual soldier's clothing and equipment, indeed to his well-being. If a unit drilled in mud, cold and rain it was frequently viewed by Napoleon. "The sea is horrible and the rain never ceases," he wrote Cambacérès. ". . . I have been constantly soaked . . . but have never felt better." The fatiguing inspections continued: "There is always something to see."[23] His letters remained very upbeat: "I have been here for ten days," General Augereau learned, "and I have reason to hope that within a reasonable time I shall achieve the goal awaited by Europe. We have six centuries of abuse to avenge."[24] Toward the end of his stay he informed Cambacérès that, "I have seen the coast of England from the heights of Ambleteuse . . . the houses and the traffic. This is a ditch that will be crossed when one has the nerve to attempt it."[25]

He returned to Paris in a buoyant mood. Minister of interior Chaptal was to have inspirational music written to familiar tunes to cheer on the troops. Light infantry regiments were to receive new and rather unusual companies of men under five feet in height armed with light fusils and trained "to follow the cavalry at a trot, holding on sometimes to the cavalier's boot, sometimes to the horse's tail, ready to leap behind the cavalier for faster movement."[26]

Despite these and other unlikely innovations Napoleon was once again a military Sisyphus, this time pushing up the huge boulder of invasion only to have it tumble down again.* Such were construction delays caused by material shortages, insufficient skilled workers, inefficient workshops and disorganized arsenals, such the lack of trained boat crews, shortage of cannon and financial crises caused by frequent embezzlements, that by late 1803 the weather closed in without the armada being anywhere near ready to sail.

Napoleon refused to be discouraged (and woe to him who car-

---

*The Greek errant whose punishment in the underworld was to roll uphill a huge stone which always fell back on him.

Davout, Louis Nicolas 1770–1823, Marshal of France

ried a long face). He counted each day a gain, problems be damned. In his mind the invasion was not *if* but *when,* and to a large degree he infused his major commanders and civilian officials with this positive attitude.

In Boulogne again during the first week of 1804 to inspect the rapidly growing flotilla, he boarded each ship while cannon boomed his presence to crews shouting "Vive la République!" and "Vive le Premier Consul!" Pleased with the overall spirit of the troops but distressed by the rain and muddy squalor of their camps, he ordered clogs to be sent along with theatrical troupes to entertain the men.

"Things seem to be going well at Boulogne," he informed navy minister Decrès – but the flotilla was still not ready to sail. "The season advances," he warned. "Those ships [from various dockyards] that do not arrive at Boulogne by mid February will no longer be of use to us."[27]

By February the armada was sufficiently formed to give him renewed hope for an early sailing. "Get well soon," he wrote the ailing General Davout, ". . . for the time approaches when the boats are going to sail."[28]

Notes

1   Corr. VIII. Nr. 7035, 23 August 1803.
2   Corr. VIII. Nr. 6762, Paris, 22 May 1803.
3   Corr. VIII. Nr. 6758, St. Cloud, 21 May 1803.
4   Corr. VIII. Nr. 7030, St. Cloud, 22 August 1803. See also Beaucour, 225–45; Chandler ("Fire"), 433–47.
5   Corr. VIII. Nr. 7026, St. Cloud, 22 August 1803.
6   Corr. VIII. Nr. 6890, Lille, 8 July 1803.
7   Corr. VIII. Nr. 6856, Amiens, 26 June 1803.
8   Corr. VIII. Nrs. 6869, Abbeville, 29 June 1803; 6876, 6877, 6878, Dunkirk, 3 July 1803; 6896, Lille, 9 July 1803; 6903, Bruges, 11 July 1803; 7023, St. Cloud, 21 August 1803.
9   Corr. VIII. Nrs. 7023, 7024, St. Cloud, 21 August 1803; 7028, St. Cloud, 22 August 1803; 7038, St. Cloud, 23 August 1803; 7049, St.

Cloud, 27 August 1803.

10   Corr. VIII. Nr. 6817, St. Cloud, 14 June 1803.

11   Corr. VIII. Nr. 6823, St. Cloud, 16 June 1803.

12   Corr. VIII. Nrs. 7052, St. Cloud, 27 August 1803; 7091, St. Cloud, 10 September 1803.

13   Corr. VIII. Nr. 6942, Brussels, 26 July 1803.

14   Corr. VIII. Nrs. 6950, 6951, Brussels, 28 July 1803.

15   Corr. VIII. Nr. 6956, Brussels, 29 July 1803.

16   Corr. VIII. Nr. 6957, Brussels, 29 July 1803. See also Seton-Watson, 85; Zawadzki, 28–9.

17   Corr. VIII. Nrs. 6878, 6879, Namur, 4 August 1803.

18   Corr. VIII. Nrs. 7007, St. Cloud, 14 August 1803; 7008, Paris, 16 August 1803.

19   Corr. VIII. Nr. 6994, Sedan, 8 August 1803.

20   Corr. VIII. Nr. 7032, St. Cloud, 23 August 1803.

21   Corr. IX. Nr. 7245, Boulogne, 5 November 1803.

22   Corr. IX. Nr. 7165, St. Cloud, 5 October 1803.

23   Corr. IX. Nrs. 7268, Boulogne, 11 November 1803; 7269, Boulogne, 12 November 1803. See also Thomazi, 115–29.

24   Corr. IX. Nr. 7273, Boulogne, 12 November 1803.

25   Corr. IX. Nr. 7279, Boulogne, 16 November 1803.

26   Corr. IX. Nr. 7415, Paris, 22 December 1803.

27   Corr. IX. Nr. 7468, Paris, 12 January 1804.

28   Corr. IX. Nr. 7516, Paris, 1 February 1804.

CHAPTER FORTY-TWO

The Late Duc d'Enghien
January–April 1804

It is worse than a crime, it is a blunder.

Statement attributed to either Fouché or
Talleyrand concerning Enghien's execution

I came to France to give her a king and I gave her an emperor.

Statement attributed to Georges Cadoudal, executed as
leader of the team assigned to assassinate
First Consul Napoleon Bonaparte

NAPOLEON'S PREPARATIONS FOR the invasion of England had for
some time put that government and a considerable part of the
population in a near state of panic. Only one of England's three
major weapons of war was immediately effective. This was the
Royal Navy whose ships were blockading Toulon (Admiral
Nelson), the Channel coast of France (Lord Cornwallis), the
Spanish ports of Cádiz and Ferrol (Admiral Pellew), with a
reserve squadron anchored off the Downs (Lord Keith).
Although the fleet numbered over 400 warships Prime Minister
Addington's peacetime economies had forced most of them into
temporary retirement, leaving about 55 on active duty (along
with several hundred support vessels). The French fleet in turn
counted slightly over 40 warships, but most of these were either
blockaded in French harbors or were in Caribbean waters. The
Royal Navy, blessed with an enormous merchant fleet from
which to draw experienced hands (augmented by the work of
brutal press gangs) would have little trouble in reinforcing its

fleet when necessary. Not so the tired and dispirited French navy.

Numbers aside, the Royal Navy was infinitely superior to any other navy of the day, its *esprit de corps* resulting from well over half a century of maritime supremacy hallmarked by aggressive strategy and tactics (that forever told against the French navy). Its younger admirals and captains, Nelson, Calder, Pellew and Cochrane, to name only a few, had been brought up by such masters as St. Vincent and Cornwallis whose solid teachings were daily passed on to young and eager subordinates.[1] The result was a cohesive and efficient fighting force that contrasted strongly with the slapdash fleets of France and Spain that with few exceptions were commanded by overly cautious admirals reluctant to face the enemy in battle.

England's army was a different matter, consisting of a great variety of privately owned regiments whose untrained officers bought promotions. When they fought, which was rare, it was generally according to private whim. The bulk of this "regular army" was stationed abroad at the outbreak of the new war with France. Home regiments were reinforced with provincial militias and even worse with volunteer units armed only with clubs and pikes. Napoleon was probably correct when he estimated that, once landed, it would take the French army five days to hang the tri-colored flag on the Tower of London.

England's second strength, not as immediately effective, was gold. The treasury had financed the first and second coalitions against France, providing money rather than men, and would soon finance a third effort, but that was of little use in the immediate crisis of supposed invasion.

England's third strength was related to gold applied in a different manner. This was a highly effective ongoing strategy of subversion carried out by numerous agents, royalists and mercenaries (often the same), covertly landed on the French Channel coast or infiltrated into France from European entities to carry out a wide variety of dirty tricks. The devilish activities of these agents were about to divert Napoleon from his cherished if stupid

plan of invasion – with results that would change not only the face
of war but the very history of the French nation.

Napoleon informed the senate in mid January 1804 "that all was
well in the interior of France."[2] This was not entirely accurate. His
efforts to bring about national reconciliation, though praiseworthy
enough, were only partially successful. Refractory priests, peasants
in the south and west, legislators, judges, publishers, authors,
dramatists, artists and critical coteries of Parisian intelligentsia –
all were susceptible targets for propaganda preached by infiltrated
royalist agents, their purses heavy with gold to further the major
·goal of restoring Bourbon rule. In addition Jacobin survivors
throughout France, including a number of senior generals, longed
to topple the Consulate to restore what they believed to be true
revolutionary principles of government.

The brief years of peace and soaring prosperity had dampened
but not extinguished these efforts, and they gained fresh impetus
with the outbreak of war in spring of 1803. By year's end subversive
movements had grown from a nuisance to a threat that increasingly
disturbed Napoleon as his correspondence of those months amply
demonstrates. "It would be difficult to imagine the anxieties, resulting in sleepless nights, which assailed the First Consul," his private
secretary, Méneval, wrote, ". . . during the month of January 1804
when plots, of which he knew nothing definite, were being woven
around him, and against which he fought in the dark; when he felt
the earth trembling beneath his feet, and each breath of air seemed
to bring with it the menace of some hidden danger."[3]

The most important threat was fired from London by a royalist group headed by the Comte d'Artois, the ambitious younger
brother of the pretender to the French throne, the Comte de
Provence (the future Louis XVIII). Artois and his minions had
been planning for some time to kill Napoleon and restore Bourbon
rule, a desire understandably shared by a good many patriotic
(and frightened) Englishmen. Aided financially and logistically by
the English government they now acted.

The new operation was spearheaded by General Jean Charles Pichegru, who had fled revolutionary ranks for exile in London, and the former Chouan leader, Georges Cadoudal, Napoleon's old nemesis in the Vendée. After secretly landing in a remote cove in Picardy they slipped into Paris, Pichegru to enlist retired General Moreau (sulking away on his nearby estate) and the most outspoken dissident Jacobin generals, including Bernadotte, Macdonald and Augereau, in the plot; Georges Cadoudal to recruit a band of killers to intercept Napoleon's lightly escorted carriage which traveled between Paris and St. Cloud or Malmaison. This effort was followed by the Royal Navy landing fifty or so senior French royalist officers in Normandy to work with resident agents and covert royalist bands in fomenting local rebellions.

These bold but somewhat optimistic plans were doomed almost from their inception, not only because French army patrols and General Savary's increasingly efficient *gendarmerie* had eliminated or at least identified most of the local insurgents, but also because of royalist propensity to talk to the wrong people. One such was an exiled veteran Jacobin named Mehée de la Touche, recruited by Fouché to travel to London in guise of a fiery royalist supporter. Having there learned essential details of the plot, Mehée traveled on to Munich where the British envoy, a notorious spymaster named Francis Drake, enlisted him as a spy and sent him back to Paris.

Informed of Mehée's findings an elated Napoleon ordered careful surveillance: "You must not be in a hurry about the arrests," he cautioned his police minister in early November.[4] He also devised an elaborate deception operation which through Mehée fed alleged top-secret information of French plans to Drake – a lurid tale told elsewhere.[5]

Continued surveillance paid off. Early in January 1804 the turncoat Pichegru was observed meeting with Moreau on three occasions in Paris. Meanwhile Savary's gendarmes had arrested a number of suspects in Normandy of whom several were summarily shot *pour encourager les autres* to talk.

One of them did so. By mid February police knew where Georges Cadoudal was living in Paris, and also of the intended landing of royalist officers in a cove not far from Dieppe. The party was said to include a "prince" thought to be the Comte d'Artois. Although the landing was aborted – Savary tells the exciting story in his memoirs[6] – police struck elsewhere, arresting General Moreau, then General Pichegru and finally Georges Cadoudal. A dejected Moreau – one more piece of flotsam from the shipwreck of the Bourbon monarchy – surrendered without a struggle, but Pichegru and Cadoudal were armed and put up strenuous resistance when seized.

Although this coup effectively ended the immediate Bourbon plot a few threads remained, one of which was soon spun into a controversial tapestry that still hangs on the wall of history. Among other suspects listed by the police investigation was the 32-year-old Duc d'Enghien, the sole heir to the ancient house of Bourbon-Condé. A former officer in the disbanded royalist Corps Condé, Enghien had settled at his country estate of Ettenheim (in the electorate of Baden) with his young and beautiful wife, ostensibly living the life of a country gentleman. French police agents claimed however, perhaps wrongly, that on at least one occasion the duke had slipped incognito into France in connection with the conspiracy. Mehée de la Touche, who among others had kept watch on the Ettenheim estate, reported that Enghien was away for days at a time. Still another source reported that the suspect was in close personal association with the infamous turncoat French general, Charles François Dumouriez (inaccurately since Dumouriez was then living in England).

Napoleon, in no mood to fine-tune supposed "facts," immediately jumped to the conclusion that Enghien was a key member of the assassination plot. He could not conveniently touch the Comte d'Artois in London, but he could neutralize Enghien by a quick raid into Baden.

Despite nearly two centuries of censure by royalist adherents, Napoleon's decision was understandable. He had been plagued by

English–Austrian-run spies for years, new cases were daily developing.[7] "The English are sending agents everywhere," he complained to General Soult at St. Omer, "they are making considerable sacrifices to achieve their ends . . . you are inundated with spies."[8] Soult and other flotilla commanders were to seal off their command areas and shoot any apprehended agent. As he received more reports on the assassination plot he became even more paranoiac. "The only thing that matches the profound stupidity of this entire plot is its wickedness," he complained to one general. "The human heart is an enigma that eludes all calculations. The most penetrating attempts are unable to understand it."[9]

Logic, if perhaps misplaced, also influenced him. Ettenheim was in neutral territory (the electorate of Baden), agents could easily come and go on the wooded estate, and it was close to the French border. It was also doubtful that either British intelligence or Comte d'Artois in London, or envoy Drake in Munich, would have overlooked the potential of either the person (an ardent royalist in English pay), his location or his convenient cover of gentlemanly retirement.

Not all of Napoleon's councillors agreed with his harsh decision to take out Enghien. He was strongly supported by assistant commissioner of police Réal, Talleyrand and Fouché, possibly for ulterior motives. Consul Lebrun of royalist sympathies correctly pointed to the adverse reaction the kidnapping would cause in European courts, a fear shared by consul Cambacérès who wisely did not wish to further antagonize Russia, Prussia and Austria at this delicate time in European affairs. Napoleon subsequently has been blamed for brushing off these and other objections without due consideration, but we should remember that as the repeated target of royalist assassination attempts he could be forgiven for seeking rash action against a supposed player. It is not unfair to regard his fury as the reverse side of the English coin that called for his own death.

The operation went quite smoothly. The Baden elector having been suitably muzzled, a small army-police task force slipped across the Rhine at Strasbourg and surrounded the estate. The duke surrendered and five days later was in a prison cell at the château Vincennes near Paris awaiting trial by courtmartial.

Subsequent events are disturbingly cloudy. Apparently Napoleon learned first that Enghien's alleged collaboration with General Dumouriez was false, next that the duke's personal papers which had been seized showed no connection with the conspiracy (which should surprise no one). Interrogation did reveal that he was in the pay of England and wished to participate "in the new war against France."

According to Madame Rémusat, one of Joséphine's "ladies," Joséphine and Joseph Bonaparte now intervened on Enghien's behalf, without effect – but Madame Rémusat is not the most trustworthy source. Whatever the facts, Enghien went before a military court convened at Vincennes. The court was allegedly under the strong influence of General Savary who, following Napoleon's orders, was present with a hand-picked squad of gendarmes. Enghien's two requests for personal interviews with Napoleon were reportedly denied on Savary's order. Condemned to death by the court, Enghien was led to the moat, shot by Savary's gendarmes and buried in a recently dug grave – all without, so it was said, the presence of a priest.[10]

There is some evidence that, owing to Joseph's urging, Réal, often employed by Napoleon for sensitive missions, was ordered to go to Vincennes to interrogate Enghien further in order to learn the names of French conspirators. Réal's servant allegedly received the order late at night in Paris and, not daring to awaken his exhausted master, presented it only the next morning. Arriving at Vincennes as Savary was leaving, Réal learned of the execution.

As Lebrun and Cambacérès had warned, Enghien's death provoked immediate uproar in English and European courts. Emperors, kings, aristocrats, nobles and the upper and middle classes, probably caressing their own necks, cursed it as the work

Manic Ravings or Little Boney in a strong Fit, May 1803

of a bloodthirsty tyrant while comfortably forgetting that it was a direct result of allied attempts to kill that same tyrant.

For the English government it was a definite plus to the propaganda effort at home and abroad. More important however, Czar Alexander of Russia (who was married to the Elector of Baden's daughter) denounced it as a crime, plunged the Russian court into mourning and a few months later broke off diplomatic relations with France. Although the Austrian emperor and the Prussian king were not so demonstrative their sympathies were clear to hovering diplomats, and London wasted little time in transforming resentment into the seeds of a new coalition that as usual would be amply fertilized with English gold.

In France it was a different story. Here too there was an outcry, however muted. According to valet Constant, a disheveled and distraught Joséphine pushed into Napoleon's bedroom early in the morning, crying, "The Duc d'Enghien is dead. Ah! my sweetheart, what have you done?"[11] (The difficulty here is that Savary would not bring the news until after noon.) Napoleon's mother, Letitia, was horrified to learn of the execution and, according to Madame Rémusat, severely upbraided Napoleon (doubtful indeed). General Caulaincourt who played a peripheral role in the abduction was said to have fainted upon hearing of the duke's death, and subsequently to have scolded Napoleon (even more doubtful). The venerable Chateaubriand, about to depart for Switzerland as French ambassador, resigned in protest. Madame de Staël of course burned the torch of disapproval at full heat and there was much wringing of hands in elegant Parisian salons. We willingly accept Constant's further testimony that Napoleon was upset and remained "sad and silent" for several days. It was also said that he shut himself in his office presumably in deep remorse, blaming everyone but himself.

Napoleon did shut himself in his *cabinet* but was neither sad nor silent as he dictated details of the dastardly assassination plot for publication at home and abroad, a counter-offensive that without doubt softened the egregious effect of enemy propaganda. Simultaneously he conducted business as usual – his numerous orders of state during this period are extant. Napoleon was not one to be upset by disapproval of family members, aides, ambassadors or Parisian society. He had his finger on the pulse of the nation and he firmly believed that not only was the duke's death justified (as he stated many years later in exile) but that the average Frenchman applauded rather than condemned Enghien's demise. As the French diplomat, Miot de Melito, later wrote, the people had retained "neither memory nor affection for the Bourbons" and they had been "too long accustomed to bloody scenes" to regard the execution as "more extraordinary and more distressing than any of the others." And as the editor of Caulaincourt's papers concluded over a century later: "In reality they judged the affair only by its immediate political consequences: the disappearance of endless plots that each day threatened to disturb the normal life of the country, and the strengthening of the recently established regime of order."[12]

Ironically it was these "immediate political consequences" that would prove so important to the future of France. The theory that a hereditary monarchy would tend to prevent further assassination attempts had earlier been bruited with no action taken. Napoleon's lieutenants, suitably prodded, now revived the subject with the added argument, for the sake of Jacobin support, that it would guarantee citizen rights won by the revolution. Electoral colleges quickly joined the bandwagon. Fouché introduced the subject in the senate where it was favorably received and put to committee for further discussion there and in the council of state.

Napoleon wisely played a waiting game, writing to General Soult in mid April that "up to now I have decided nothing; however I desire that you instruct me in great details as to the army's opinion."[13] The reply was evidently favorable for a month later Napoleon at his own insistence was decreed Emperor of the French by a *senatus consultum*, an act approved by the tribunate, the assembly and in general the nation.

During this sea change in French politics the leaders of the Bourbon plot were being variously interrogated and tried in court. Moreau was sentenced to two years in prison but Napoleon

A Tit Bit for a Russian Ambassador!

allowed his exile to America.[14] Pichegru was found mysteriously strangled in his cell – "a fine death for the conqueror of Holland," Napoleon sardonically remarked to Savary.[15] Georges Cadoudal and a number of his cohorts were executed.

By June the tempest had nearly passed. Napoleon had made his signal to would-be assassins, and indeed the attempts henceforth ceased. Tears would continue to flow over Enghien's death, but that did not worry Napoleon in the slightest. It was time now to get back to the invasion of England.

Notes

1   Mahan (*Sea Power*), 254 ff.

2   Corr. IX. Nr. 7482, Paris, 16 January 1804.

3   Méneval, 233.

4   Corr. IX. Nr. 7240, St. Cloud, 1 November 1803.

5   Méneval, 214–17. See also Rose (*Life*), I, 450.

6   Rovigo, II, 337–411.

7   Corr. IX. Nrs. 7579, Paris, 2 March 1804; 7584, Paris, 4 March 1804.

8   Corr. IX. Nr. 7594, Paris, 7 March 1804.

9   Corr. IX. Nr. 7598, Malmaison, 8 March 1804.

10   Rose (*Life*), I, 459–62. See also Masson (*Famille*), II, Chapter 13; Rovigo, II, 337–411; Méneval, 242–75; Savary, II, 12–64.

11   Constant, 34.

12   Caulaincourt, I, 57. See also Miot de Melito (*Mémoires*), II, 159; Méneval, 265; Masson (*Famille*), II, 332–3.

13   Corr. IX. Nr. 7683, St. Cloud, 14 April 1807.

14   Montgomery, 165–87. See also Thiébault, II, 106–8.

15   Rovigo, II, 81. See also Thiébault, II, 108: When it was suggested to Napoleon that he was responsible for Pichegru's death, he replied: "You do not dirty your hands with a coin that is out of circulation."

CHAPTER FORTY-THREE

THE INVASION OF ENGLAND – II
MARCH–OCTOBER 1804

*I have some 120,000 troops and three thousand barges and
gunboats which are awaiting only a favorable wind in order to
place the Imperial Eagle on the Tower of London.*

Napoleon to Marshal Brune, Pont de Briques,
27 July 1804[1]

FAILURE TO LAUNCH the invasion flotilla either prior to December,
when storms closed the Channel, or prior to March when nights
became too short to cloak the operation, necessarily postponed the
attempt until late autumn of 1804.

The Bourbon conspiracy and the Enghien affair had slowed
but not interrupted preparations. Heartened by the arrest of the
major conspirators, by "immense prizes" falling to French corsairs
in East Indian waters and by rumors of King George III of
England's approaching death, Napoleon continued to push army
and navy commanders to new efforts. Soult was to report if he had
sufficient sailors to man the transports, "for it would be very
unfortunate to have the boats and no sailors." Were field hospitals
organized? Napoleon asked. Did Soult have sufficient physicians,
surgeons and administrators? Admiral Decrès was to form a
flotilla of 288 barges, carefully organized according to Napoleon's
instructions. Grooms must be provided to care for 8,000 horses. "I
long to know if you have more than one hundred gunboats in
your ports," he wrote Soult. "I would very much like all battalions
to have at least eight hundred men." Improved coastal defenses
were a priority for all commanders: "This is the moment when the

war is going to take place between your harbor and the English. It is not necessary to spare the cannon-balls and the [mortar] bombs . . . from the moment that the enemy is within range, fire with the greatest activity." Shipyards at home and abroad were to continue working twenty-four hours a day in constructing not only ancillary flotilla craft but also warships including three-deckers of 80 guns.[3]

A variety of factors, some of which we have earlier discussed, frequently hindered preparations. For one reason or another boats built in other ports failed to sail for Boulogne. Other craft on arrival were armed with the wrong-caliber cannon. Desertion continued to be a problem that Napoleon blamed on agitation by English agents. A major setback emerged when logisticians discovered that it was extremely difficult, if not impossible, to load *one* horse, much less fifty, onto a flat-bottomed boat.[3]

Internal security remained a major threat as English-paid agents continued to stir up Chouan detritus and recalcitrant priests in the Morbihan and Normandy, and in towns and cities including Paris. While some alarms were ridiculous, such as the rumor of English ships landing bales of poisoned cotton on the beaches, others were sufficiently well-founded to keep mobile army units, Fouché's secret police and Savary's gendarmes, working at fever pitch.[4]

Despite his increasing political dominance in neighboring states Napoleon also faced people problems. The good citizens of Holland including soldiers and sailors were not happy with the constitution – the result, Napoleon believed, of agitation by civilian officials allied to England. For the moment he was content to await developments, but as he darkly informed Talleyrand, "I am not able to remain indifferent to all that passes there."[5] More dangerous was Czar Alexander's ostentatious disapproval of the Duc d'Enghien's execution. In instructing Talleyrand to recall the French ambassador from St. Petersburg, Napoleon wrote that "it is enough to have to put up with English insults on the seas without having to endure Russian impertinences." Should ambassador Hédouville see Prime Minister Vorontsov or the czar before departure, "he should be very firm and say that we can only be extremely pained to see Russia interfering in our internal affairs."[6]

However, his major concern remained the landing in England. He had finally come to recognize the futility of trying to protect the awkward invasion barges with small gunboats and the ridiculous "floating batteries," monstrous things to be propelled by a windmill![7] Whether he liked it or not, proper warships were necessary to hold off the English fleet until the troops were safely ashore on Kentish beaches.

In early June he gave the covering task to perhaps his most capable admiral, Louis de Latouche Tréville in Toulon, who was to sail for Egypt, slip past Nelson's watchdogs (no easy trick), then double back, pick up Spanish warships at Cádiz and French warships at Rochefort and sail for the Channel. Admiral Ganteaume meanwhile was to depart from Brest to give battle to Cornwallis' squadron cruising off Ushant island, thus clearing the way for Latouche Tréville's arrival. This was an immensely complicated and not very practicable plan but Napoleon obviously thought it would work. "Let us be masters of the [Dover] Straits for six hours," he wrote the admiral, "and we shall be masters of the world."[8]

While his admirals set about equipping their squadrons Napoleon moved to the coast in late July to oversee final preparations, his new headquarters being a rather dilapidated small house at Pont de Briques a few kilometers inland from Boulogne. "I am very satisfied with the spirit and appearance of the departments that I have traveled through," he informed Cambacérès, ". . . as well as with the condition and spirit of the army of land and sea."[9] More than ever he was anticipating the crossing. On a hill overlooking the beach from where Caesar was said to have sailed for the British Isles, he built a small house where he spent hours looking through a large telescope at the English fleet and coastline.[10]

To Joséphine who was about to leave on a triumphal tour to take the waters of Aix la Chapelle (her equipage of some fifty ladies and lackeys required 70 horses to pull the assorted carriages), he wrote: "During the four days that I have been away from you, I have been constantly on horse and in action with no ill effects on my health." He went on to describe an all-night rescue of a gunboat that had foundered on the rocks. Such was the fury of the sea that it seemed no one could survive – "the soul hovered between eternity, the sea and the night," but finally all were saved.[11]

He failed to report a later disaster that resulted from a mixture of his enlarged ego and severe frustration caused by ultra-conservative admirals, one of whom was commander in chief of the Boulogne flotilla, Eustache Bruix. Against Bruix's advice Napoleon continued to insist on holding gunboat drill despite heavy contrary winds, but Bruix was not to be intimidated. A decade older than his master and well aware of his own aristocratic lineage and contribution to the *coup d'état* that produced the First Consul, he was not overwhelmed by the imperial presence. Earlier he had been consulted by a group of court toadies as to a costume suitable for a proposed statue of Napoleon. "Sculpture him in the nude," was his reply, "so that it will be easier for you to kiss his ass."[12] Now, on a storm-swept beach with obvious evil weather closing in, he refused to give the necessary orders, an ugly scene ended in Napoleon relieving him (temporarily) of his command. The drill took place, a number of gunboats were broken up and their crews drowned – valet Constant who witnessed the débâcle put the number at 20 boats and 200 men. But Napoleon glossed over the tragedy in a letter to Talleyrand: "We have had some bad weather; a gust of wind has cost us the lives of fifteen men and three or four ships."[13]

Although Napoleon continued to insist that flotilla forces were in excellent condition he was well aware that more time was needed to complete preparations, and that even then all would depend on the arrival of Latouche Tréville's protective warships. Putting as favorable a face as possible on the situation he continued frantic peregrinations to various ports, on several occasions traveling by boat in defiance of the English blockade. "I hope that the [medicinal] waters do you as much good as all the activity and the sight of the fields and the sea do for me," he wrote Joséphine in early August. ". . . I very much want to see you. You are always necessary to my happiness." A week later he wrote from Ostend, complaining of her silence. "I have been here for eight days . . . I am very satisfied with the army and the flotillas. Eugène remains at Blois. Hortense might as well be in the Congo for all I hear from her."[14]

Returning to Boulogne he held a massive review of his forces, resumed relations with a mistress or two, distributed crosses of the Legion of Honor to numerous soldiers and silver eagles to their units. But now he suffered a great blow with the sudden death of Latouche Tréville from a heart attack. The admiral had revitalized the Toulon fleet and some ships had even gone to sea, if only to hurry back to port upon spotting Admiral Nelson's hovering cruisers. Who was to replace him? Of the few possibilities the competent and independently minded Admiral Missiessy would have been the best choice. Instead Napoleon bowed to his naval minister's recommendation and appointed the ultra-conservative Pierre de Villeneuve, another survivor of the disaster at Aboukir Bay.[15]

Napoleon now departed for a tour of the Rhineland. At his first stop, Aix la Chapelle, the shrine of Charlemagne, he joined Joséphine along with Talleyrand, assorted French diplomats and, not least, a favorite mistress – one of Joséphine's ladies-in-waiting, the beautiful Elisabeth de Vaudey – for a leisurely voyage down the Rhine.[16]

Although the purpose of the ensuing tour was political the Boulogne flotilla remained uppermost in his mind. If in general he was satisfied with it he was disappointed by the regular fleet, writing sarcastically to Admiral Decrès: "All naval expeditions undertaken since I have headed the government have failed because the misguided admirals have discovered, I know not where, that one can make war without taking any chances."[17]

Had Napoleon acted instead of grumbled he might still have put matters right. He had considered relieving Decrès, more a smooth-tongued courtier than a fighting admiral, months earlier but had failed to do so. He should have relieved Ganteaume and Villeneuve. He had some able junior admirals and captains, but whether they could have revived the moribund spirit of the fleet is a moot question. Not to have tried however was one of Napoleon's greatest failings, and he would continue to suffer dearly because of it. Meanwhile he went on hurling demanding directives at Decrès, often with no noticeable effect.

Part of the problem was the spirit of defeatism that had dogged the French navy long before the revolution, part was the exodus of a good many qualified royalist officers, but part also was Napoleon's refusal to listen to informed advice from his few competent admirals and senior captains. He had humiliated and sacked Truguet for his republican beliefs and refusal to endorse his imperial ambition,[18] he had held down the fiery and independent Missiessy and anyone else who disagreed with his theories of naval strategy and operations, and more recently he had petulantly overridden Bruix's sound professional advice, thereby bringing on an unnecessary disaster. His failure to admit to ignorance of naval warfare would continue to result in far too ambitious plans, with concomitant frustrations and temper tantrums when they failed.

Despite the unsatisfactory state of naval affairs Napoleon remained intent on invading England and possibly Ireland. A separate expedition of warships, frigates and brigs was to carry soldiers and arms to Martinique, Guadeloupe and St. Lucia in the West Indies, bombard English ports in Jamaica, return to Ferrol and bust the British blockade so as to release French warships in that harbor before sailing on to Rochefort. Another large expedition was to carry several thousand troops to French Guiana in South America in order to recover neighboring Surinam and other Dutch colonies from the English. A third large force sailing eastward was to drop off troops at Senegal and Goré in Africa, pick up some ships at Mauritius, attack and presumably seize the distant island of St. Helena and remain on station for several weeks, attacking any British ships in the area.[19]

All this seemed splendid on paper but in reality amounted to costly and time-consuming dreams that conflicted with the major task of invading England. The invasion force was still not ready to sail. Even if it had been, Villeneuve showed little inclination to carry out the involved operation that would culminate in a healthy fleet of warships appearing at the right time to protect the cumbersome barges from English interference.

At this crucial point Napoleon learned that over 3.5 million citizens had voted in favor of an hereditary crown, with only a few thousand against.[20] The navy and other serious problems would have to wait. The way was now clear for an imperial coronation which he was determined to make the greatest show on earth.

Notes

1   Corr. IX. Nr. 7874, Pont de Briques, 27 July 1804.

2   Corr. IX, Nrs. 7577, 7578, Paris, 1 March 1804; 7594, Paris, 7 March 1804; 7704, St. Cloud, 21 April 1804.

3   Corr. IX. Nrs. 7159, St. Cloud, 4 October 1803; 7558, Paris, 21 February 1804.

4   Corr. IX. Nr. 7635, Malmaison, 20 March 1804.

5   Corr. IX. Nr. 7718, St. Cloud, 27 April 1804.

6   Corr. IX. Nrs. 7745, 7746, St. Cloud, 13 May 1804; 7874, Pont de Briques, 27 July 1804. See also Seton-Watson, 69–75, 85–6 Zawadzki, 254–6, 262, 266.

7   The Naval War College Museum, Newport, Rhode Island, has a detailed German print of this incredible *Schwimmende Batterie*.

8   Thomazi, 132.

9   Corr. IX. Nr. 7862, Pont de Briques, 21 July 1804.

10 Méneval, 306.

11 Corr. IX. Nr. 7861, Pont de Briques, 21 July 1804.

12 Thomazi, 123–4.

13 Corr. IX. Nr. 7892, Pont de Briques, 1 August 1804.

14 Corr. IX. Nrs. 7907, Calais, 6 August 1804; 7931, Ostend, 14 August 1804.

15 Thomazi, 134–7.

16   Bruce, 359–60.
17   Corr. IX. Nr. 8018, Château de la Haye, 12 September 1804.
18   Thomazi, 132–3.
19   Corr. IX. Nr. 8060, Mainz, 29 September 1804.
20   Corr. IX. Nr. 7956, Pont de Briques, 24 August 1804. See also
     Roederer (*Mémoires*), 207.

CHAPTER FORTY-FOUR

THE EMPEROR TAKES A CROWN
MARCH–DECEMBER 1804

If only our father could see us now.

Napoleon to Joseph Bonaparte upon approaching the
coronation altar. 2 December 1804[1]

NAPOLEON'S SUDDEN ELEVATION to imperial status had brought mixed reactions at home and abroad. European rulers in general, including the English king, cautiously welcomed the move as indicating an end to the danger of revolution – Napoleon, so to speak, had joined the "family," albeit as an uncouth parvenu. A good many statesmen were not so optimistic, looking on the event as a consolidation of his power, a basis on which to build further mischief. Liberals everywhere were dismayed and saddened. Upon learning the news the composer Ludwig van Beethoven, who had just dedicated a new symphony to his hero, furiously tore up the dedication, retitled the work "Eroica" and dedicated it to "the memory of a great man."[2]

The approval or disapproval of rulers, statesmen and liberals did not worry Napoleon, but unpleasant family complications were another matter. The villain here was lack of a direct heir. Joséphine, the titular empress, was terrified that Napoleon would divorce her in order to remarry and father an heir. Joseph and Julie (née Clary) Bonaparte's two daughters were automatically excluded from succession. Lucien by his first marriage had only daughters; he subsequently sired a son by his mistress, Mademoiselle Jouberthion, whom he then married (thus theoretically putting a bastard in line for the throne). Joseph and Louis, considering themselves as heading the list of candidates, were infuriated when Napoleon refused to declare himself only to eventually name Louis and Hortense Bonaparte's son, Charles Napoleon, as his rightful heir – wicked tongues spoke noisily of Napoleon's alleged incestuous relationship with Hortense and asked if this were his child, a vicious canard that to Napoleon's fury gained wide currency in Europe and England.

Napoleon's relations with his mother, Letitia, had worsened owing to her loathing of Joséphine and disapproval of the Enghien affair, but she was soon to move to Rome, probably to her son's delight, "to escape the humidity and cold of Paris." Enghien's execution had further distanced Joseph and Louis, as had Napoleon's refusal to name them successors to the crown. Joseph in a huff now announced that he wished to join the invasion army. Napoleon arranged his departure from the senate and appointed him a colonel commanding a regiment. Louis, who had been hotly criticized by Napoleon for virtually abandoning Hortense shortly after their marriage and whose increasingly erratic behavior, presumably the result of a venereal disease, was causing tongues to wag, contented himself with frequent overt criticism of his brother while often quarreling furiously with Hortense. Lucien, always the fireball, refused the emperor's orders to divorce his former mistress, gave up his magnificent Paris mansion with its famous art gallery holding over 130 paintings of the masters, left his beautiful château of Plessis, resigned from the senate and moved his family to Rome where he would study "antiques and history."[3]

Napoleon's attempts to discipline his youngest brother, Jérôme, by naval service had badly misfired. While on shore leave in Baltimore 19-year-old Jérôme had married a rich merchant's daughter whom he wished to bring back to France. The news caused Napoleon almost to disown him. "I owe nothing to my brothers," he told Admiral Decrès, "who have reaped the abundant harvest of my success . . . They mean nothing to me if they

don't remain near me and if they take a road opposite to mine."
Jérôme had never respected his duties, he continued: "If he does
nothing for me, fate decrees that I should do nothing for him."
The French consul in Baltimore was to publicly state that
Napoleon "did not recognize a marriage contracted by a young
man of nineteen against the laws of his country."[4]

Sister Pauline, remarried to Prince Borghese and living in
Rome, was miserable and wanted only to return to Paris. This
drew little sympathy from Napoleon who advised her to "love
your husband and his family, be kind, accommodate yourself to
the Roman way of life and understand if at your age (twenty-four)
you allow yourself to act on poor advice you can no longer count
on me . . . if you fall out with [your husband] the fault will be
yours and then France will be closed to you."[5] Cardinal Fesch,
the French ambassador in Rome and Pauline's uncle, received the
awkward task of delivering the letter and explaining to her "that
she is no longer beautiful and will become less so in some years,"
thus she must make herself "kind and esteemed." In view of her
earlier life in Paris, her husband should however "allow her the
liberty which our women are accustomed to."[6] Napoleon's other
sisters, Caroline and Elisa, generally would remain in Paris to
criticize Joséphine on any given occasion and to complain of
Napoleon's parsimony at a time when they were living unwonted
lives of undeserved luxury.

Taken together the Bonapartes even at this early stage presented a tragic picture of familial dissension. Shortly before the
coronation Napoleon allegedly told councillor of state Roederer,
who had written a special report on the problem of succession,
that Joseph was less suited than Louis to inherit the crown: "You
forget that my brothers mean nothing to me, that my brothers are
grand only because I made them grand. There are several thousand Frenchmen who have rendered more services than they to
the state." In refusing to accept the responsibilities of rank and
office Joseph was "an enemy in disguise."[7] Judging from Joseph's
sadly prophetic words of this time, he may have recognized the
fragile structure of the house of Bonaparte: "Destiny seems to

*Bonaparte, Letitia 1750–1836 Napoleon's Mother, known as
Madame Mère*

blind us and intends, by means of our own faults, to restore France some day to her former rulers."[8]

Napoleon's imperial title had wrought changes familial more in form than substance. Joséphine became the uncrowned empress overnight, while after some delay and petulant entreaties his sisters and Joseph and Louis' wives were made imperial highnesses surrounded by ladies-in-waiting along with numerous lackeys. Mother Letitia was titled "Madame Mère" but enjoyed no lack of houses, servants and cash. Joseph and Louis received the rank of prince and the imposing titles of Grand Elector and Constable respectively. Cambacérès was named a prince and Archchancellor of the Empire, Lebrun a prince and Archtreasurer of the Empire. Other titles went to Talleyrand (Grand Chamberlain), Berthier (Grand Master of the Hounds), Duroc (Grand Master of the Palace), Caulaincourt (Master of the Horse), Cardinal Fesch (Grand Almoner), to name a few.

Fourteen active-duty generals of greatly varying talents received marshal's batons: Berthier, Masséna, Augereau, Murat, Lannes, Ney, Brune, Jourdan, Soult, Davout, Bernadotte, Moncey, Bessières and Mortier. Four older generals, Lefebvre, Perignan, Kellermann *père* (of Valmy fame) and Sérurier were appointed honorary marshals.

Palace protocol, already severe at the Tuileries, St. Cloud and Fontainebleau, now became incredibly stuffy with elegantly uniformed butlers pussyfooting in and out of gorgeously decorated salons, a footman behind each chair at dinners prepared by a corps of chefs, dozens of housekeepers and maids servicing luxurious suites, linens embroidered with the imperial seal that also appeared on silver, china and carriages. The imperial icons, the silver eagles of ancient Rome and the bees of an ancient French dynasty, covered furniture, drapes, carpets, cloaks, gowns, jacket-linings, carriages and saddles. Joséphine was soon sporting immensely beautiful baubles of diamonds, pearls and rubies taken from the public treasury and designated "jewels of the crown."[9]

Ney, Michel 1769–1815 Marshal of France

Soldiers would soon be dying to protect the silver eagles that topped each unit standard.

All this and more was to receive the hallmark of formal coronation scheduled for early December 1804. Originally planned to take place in the church of the Invalides, the venue was changed by Napoleon who objected that it was not large enough to house the many important guests and that money spent on embellishing the remotely located Invalides would be lost to Paris. Notre Dame, he insisted, had ample room for all and the money spent would be "permanent and durable" to the capital.

Napoleon personally drew up the elaborate plans. A cortège of thirty carriages would bring the imperial party from the Tuileries to the cathedral. The ceremony would last an hour, to be followed by various religious and civil functions. He noted in passing that some houses around Notre Dame would have to be knocked down, a justifiable expense in that it would clear the way for future state ceremonies.

Preparations continued for months and cost millions of francs. The artists Jean Baptiste Isabey and Jacques Louis David were given the immense task of designing the scores of gowns, uniforms and elaborate robes for all principals, and in addition of converting Notre Dame's interior into a semblance of a Graeco-Roman temple. At Napoleon's insistence and to the anger of numerous republican legislators and army commanders, the ailing Pope Pius VII was invited to Paris to give "the authority of the [Catholic] religion to the coronation of the first emperor of the French."[10] Despite strenuous objections by his anti-French cardinals the pope, hoping to reinstate church predominance in France, finally accepted without conditions – to Napoleon's great delight.[11]

A number of incidents, some unpleasant, occurred while vast preparations were under way. Brother Joseph's unwise demand that Joséphine must not be crowned empress brought down the emperor's wrath and the matter was dropped, at least for a time. (Joseph was not aware that Napoleon had yet to decide on this delicate matter. Ironically, persistent family objections caused him to rule in her favor only a few weeks before the coronation.) Napoleon's sisters next objected to having to bear Joséphine's train. After several acrimonious scenes a semantic compromise was reached: they along with Joseph and Louis' wives (Julie and Hortense) would merely "support" Joséphine's appendage.[12]

In late November the pope was met with considerable ostentation and escorted to regal lodgings in Paris where he was well received by the masses. Shortly before the ceremony he was approached by Joséphine who confessed that she and Napoleon had been married by only a civil ceremony. In that case, he told her, she could not be consecrated as empress. Napoleon resolved this embarrassing crisis by having Cardinal Fesch remarry them in a secret and highly irregular ceremony the night before the coronation.[13]

Coronation day also held a few surprises. A cold night gave way to late morning sunshine that nurtured the gaiety of thousands of waiting subjects lining the streets. The imperial procession left the Tuileries in mid morning, the earlier hours having been devoted to the cosmetic ministrations of artist Isabey endeavoring to erase the years from Joséphine's face.[14] His repairs were set off by a white satin gown "trimmed with silver and gold besprinkled with bees" and by a diamond necklace, a jeweled waist girdle and a diadem of diamonds and pearls.

Napoleon wore a formal red velvet coat richly hemmed with gold and partially covered by a short cloak decorated with embroidered bees and topped by the insignia of the Legion of Honor in diamonds, his head covered by a white plumed hat, hanging from his side a sword with a huge diamond mounted in the hilt. The imperial couple occupied a truly regal carriage with glass sides topped by four silver eagles "supporting a crown." Opposite were seated Napoleon's two sullen brothers, Joseph and Louis, each wearing beautifully tailored white velvet coats richly trimmed in gold.[15]

The ornate procession, led by squadrons of brilliantly arrayed chasseurs, cuirassiers and dragoons riding beautifully turned-out mounts and followed by a host of over-decorated carriages filled

Fêtes du Sacre et Couronnement de Leurs Majestés Impériales, 1804

with over-dressed officers and officials and their wives, wound through a maze of streets lined with soldiers to reach the archbishop's palace shortly before noon. Here Napoleon and Joséphine were helped into coronation robes of heavy red velvet adorned with embroidered bees and eagles and lined with ermine, Napoleon's elegant hat being exchanged for the traditional laurel wreath of Roman conquerors.[16]

Thus gowned the couple entered the packed cathedral and proceeded slowly to the altar presided over by Pope Pius VII resplendent in papal robes. It was an awesome moment and we can well believe that Napoleon, as later reported, whispered in Joseph's ear, "If only our father could see us now."[17]

At the altar Napoleon knelt to receive the triple unction, followed by Joséphine. He then proceeded up the altar steps and to general astonishment picked up the imperial crown and placed it on his head, after which he crowned Joséphine – the scene is portrayed in David's famous if inaccurate painting. Once seated on their thrones, the pair received the pope's blessing prior to sitting through a lengthy service followed by choral performances.

The newly crowned couple returned to the Tuileries via a lengthy route lighted by thousands of torches held by cheering citizens. Festivities continued for another two weeks after which Napoleon mounted a throne in the Bourbon palace to open, amidst wild enthusiasm, the new session of the legislative assembly.[18]

Notes

1   Rose (*Life*), I, 479–80.
2   Horward ("Beethoven"), 5; Rose (*Life*), I, 481.
3   Corr. IX. Nrs. 7618, Malmaison, 13 March 1804; 7708, St. Cloud, 22 April 1804. See also Masson (*Famille*), II, 173–5, 374–5.
4   Corr. IX. Nrs. 7699, St. Cloud, 20 April 1804; 7884, Pont de Briques, 30 July 1804.
5   Corr. IX. Nr. 7674, Paris, 6 April 1804.
6   Corr. IX. Nr. 7678, Malmaison, 10 April 1804.

7   Roederer, 209–15.
8   Rose (*Life*), I, 442–5. See also Miot de Melito (*Mémoires*), I, Chapter One; Masson (*Famille*), Vols. 1–7.
9   Corr. IX. Nr. 7858, St. Cloud, 17 July 1804.
10 Corr. IX. Nr. 8020, Cologne, 15 September 1804.
11 Ségur, II, 296–7; Rovigo, II, 110–18.
12 Rose (*Life*), I, 477. See also Bruce, 362–3.
13 Rose (*Life*), I, 475. See also Roederer, II, 215.
14 Rose (*Life*), I, 477. See also Ségur, II, 298–301.
15 Rose (*Life*), I, 479. See also Madelin (*Consulate*), 244.
16 Madelin (*Consulate*), 245.
17 Rose (*Life*), I, 479–80.
18 Madelin (*Consulate*), 245.

CHAPTER FORTY-FIVE

THE INVASION OF ENGLAND – III
THE END OF A DREAM
JANUARY–AUGUST 1805

I hope that you have arrived at Brest. Depart, do not lose a
moment, and with my [other] squadrons under your command,
enter the channel. England is ours. We are ready, everything
is embarked. Show yourself for twenty-four hours and
everything will be finished.

Napoleon to Admiral Villeneuve, Camp de Boulogne,
22 August 1805[1]

NAPOLEON OPENED THE new session of the legislative assembly in late December 1804, warning his audience that

> without a strong and paternal government France would have to fear the return of past evils. To be ruled by a weak supreme power is the most frightful calamity to befall humans. Soldier or First Consul, I have had only one thought; as Emperor I have no other: the prosperity of France . . . If death does not overtake me in the midst of my efforts, I hope to leave posterity a memory which will serve forever as an example of reproach to my successors.

After assuring his listeners of the healthy state of the empire's finances he made a curious pledge:

> I do not wish to increase the territory of France, but to maintain its [present] integrity. My ambition is not to

exercise a great influence in Europe but I do not wish to forfeit what I have acquired. No state will be incorporated into the empire, but I will not sacrifice my rights, nor the bonds that tie me to the state that I have created.[2]

A separate and very detailed report covered virtually every activity within the empire including the laws of succession, as well as reviewing relations with the European nations and with Russia, Turkey and England.

This report touched only indirectly on the postponed invasion: "London would be in agitation and despair if inexperience or weakness had not betrayed the most ably conceived project." Nonetheless:

Our soldiers and officers are learning to master the element which separates them from that island . . . Our fleets are constantly preparing for battle; and while those of our enemies are wearing themselves out [sailing] against the winds and the storms, ours are learning to struggle against them without destroying themselves . . . We are in better shape than ever to deliver some decisive blows to our enemies. Our navy is in the best shape it has been for ten years, our army larger, better trained and equipped than ever before . . . When England becomes convinced that France will never accept [peace] conditions other than those of [the Treaty of] Amiens, will never consent to grant England the right to break treaties at will in retaining Malta, then England will arrive at some peaceful thoughts.[3]

Snug in bulky imperial robes Napoleon was falling into a dangerous and quite unnecessary trap, the result of his failure to launch the cross-Channel invasion combined with lack of valid intelligence on which to base his political strategy. He had badly miscalculated the English strength of will which was reflected in a very stubborn prime minister (William Pitt, who replaced Addington in spring of 1804) and in England's able and determined navy. Napoleon could talk as much as he wished about English cruisers wearing out their crews on prolonged patrols in dreadful weather while French sailors remained comfortably in port. Life indeed was hard aboard English warships, what with miserable rations and overly harsh discipline. Most of the ships were old and creaky but they held together in wind and storm while quietly but effectively blockading key French ports.

They performed this onerous and often dangerous task very well. Horatio Nelson's squadron cruising off Toulon had earlier stymied Admiral Latouche Tréville. One of Nelson's tricks was to keep his main strength out of sight and then, when a French force emerged from port cocoon, to pounce and cause a hasty retreat. Latouche Tréville was too experienced not to realize that despite orders to the contrary he would never reach the Channel without giving battle. His successor, Admiral Villeneuve, had no intention of trying Nelson on for size and was quite content to remain in port, using contrary winds as an excuse.

The respite was fatal to Napoleon's plans. The British prime minister was determined to pursue the war against tyrant Napoleon. At first he did not have much to work with, but slowly he turned a defensive psychology that prevailed in the homeland into a desire to carry the war to Europe, and much of his effort early in office went toward building an army capable of fighting on the continent.

Pitt's other task was to reawaken a moribund alliance by forming a third coalition with Russia and Austria, hopefully to be joined by Prussia. The key here was Russia whose czar, still smarting from England's rejection of his offer to mediate the Malta impasse, probably would not have responded to Pitt's overtures but for anger brought on by the Enghien affair and Napoleon's insistence that Russian troops leave Corfu – issues eagerly embraced by his foreign affairs minister, Prince Adam Czartoryski, who had already decided that Napoleon must be eliminated.[4] Astute diplomacy aided by the magic clink of gold

coins and the promise of a British army to fight on the continent
would eventually bring the Russian court into a new coalition.

It was not easy going for Pitt. The Austrian and Prussian courts
and most of the smaller electorates and principalities, cowed by
French armies in Italy, Naples and the Rhineland and by
Napoleon's not-so-veiled threats to use them if necessary, at first
refused to join despite the allure of English gold. The Spanish
court, dominated by Prince Manuel Godoy who was under
Napoleon's thumb, also refused strident English overtures to the
degree that in early December England declared war on Spain.
Shortly afterward an English squadron intercepted a Spanish fleet
coming from the New World, and in the ensuing battle several
hundred Spaniards and an enormous treasure of Mexican silver
were lost when the flagship blew up and sank. Spain then joined
France in its war against England and promised to reinforce the
sorely pressed French fleet.

As rumors of England's new diplomatic offensive circulated in
European courts Napoleon seems to have realized that he was
approaching an uncertain crossroad. One road led to continuing
an expensive war with England, but with his flotilla blockaded in
Boulogne harbor and Villeneuve's battle fleet lying idle at Toulon,
matters appeared to be at impasse. Another road, not nearly so
clear in his mind, might well lead to a renewed war on the continent – which he did not want. Although he claimed Bavaria and
Württemberg as allies, Prussia was a doubtful quantity which
could swing in any direction, and he was particularly alarmed by
a reported build-up of Austrian arms.

Apparently unaware that the previous November Russia and
Austria had signed a defensive alliance designed ultimately to
destroy him, in early 1805 Napoleon had written to Emperor
Francis of Austria (whom in the regal style he addressed as
"Monsieur mon Frère" – my brother – undoubtedly to his annoyance), stating that the formation of Austrian armies in Carniola
and the Tyrol had obliged France to take counter-measures in

Italy and on the Rhine: "very costly operations . . . that can produce only new burdens for our peoples. They would be entirely
unnecessary if your Majesty shares my desire of maintaining
peace on the continent and putting himself on guard against the
instigations of the English who alone wish to upset it."[5]

He had also written a tentative to King George of England
(again, "Monsieur mon Frère," which must have brought on a
fresh attack of insanity), that expressed his "wish for peace." Your
Majesty's kingdom

> is at the greatest height of prosperity. What do you hope to
> gain by going to war? To form a coalition with some
> continental powers? The continent will remain tranquil; a
> coalition will only increase the preponderance and the
> continental grandeur of France. To renew interior troubles
> [in France]? The times are no longer the same. To destroy
> our finances? Finances founded on good agriculture will
> never be destroyed. To seize French colonies? Colonies for
> France are a secondary goal; and your Majesty, does he not
> have more of them than he can protect? If your Majesty
> thinks upon it, he will see that the war has no goal . . . The
> world is large enough that our two nations can live in it,
> and reason is sufficiently powerful for one to find a means
> of conciliation if both sides have the will to seek it.[6]

Whatever his hopes, the reply from the government (not the
palace) was so coldly negative that Talleyrand was instructed to
acknowledge it "by only three lines to Lord Harrowby."[7] The
Austrian court however replied that its build-up of troops in
Carniola and the Tyrol was merely to prevent importation of the
dreaded yellow fever, a patent lie but one nevertheless followed by
a slowdown of troop activities and a cordial letter from Emperor
Francis. Napoleon responded by cancelling some intended
marches in Italy: "the circumstances have changed . . . My relations with the Emperor . . . are already extremely intimate," he
informed his Italian war minister.[8]

Napoleon also tried to repair relations with Czar Alexander. When this failed he turned to the new Turkish ruler, Sultan Selim, warning of the grave danger to his empire by allowing Russia to maintain troops on Corfu, the fault of the sultan's councillors who had sold out to St. Petersburg. Selim was making a grave mistake by not joining Persia's war against Russia and by not respecting Turkey's traditional alliance with France, indeed he was putting Constantinople at risk of being seized by Russia. "Wake up, Selim. Call your friends to the ministry, chase out the traitors; trust in your true friends, France and Prussia, or you will lose your country, your religion and your family."[9]

Having probed north and east Napoleon turned south, pushing Godoy to meet treaty obligations by repairing the Spanish fleet and providing promised warships to the French navy. He was also sending a new ambassador to Portugal, General Andoche Junot, since it was vital to bring Lisbon into alliance with France and Spain.[10]

Meanwhile there remained the real enemy, England.

Heartened by the promise of Spanish warships Napoleon once again ordered his admirals at Toulon, Rochefort and Brest to sail the world's waters to join French corsairs in attacking England's merchant shipping and colonies.

Only one of these expeditions succeeded, that led by Admiral Missiessy whose fleet escaped from port to reach the West Indies and play such havoc with British merchant ships that London financiers came close to toppling Pitt's already unpopular government.[11]

Admiral Villeneuve, whose fleet carried a large troop contingent headed by General Lauriston, sailed from Toulon and evaded Nelson's squadron (which went on a wild goose-chase to Egypt). Nelson might as well have stayed put. Fear of the British admiral plus heavy seas which separated the French ships soon caused Villeneuve to return ingloriously to Toulon from where he tried to excuse his failure to Napoleon. Napoleon was not having it. "I

believe that your admiral has lacked resolution," he informed
Lauriston. The dispersals were nothing, he continued, a simple
order to rendezvous in the Canaries would have solved that problem; a leaking ship could have been repaired in Cádiz; a few
broken top masts in heavy seas were normal for a squadron putting to sea and could be put right with two days of good weather.
"The great fault of our navy," he added gratuitously, "is that the
captains are new to all the risks of command." As usual he did not
linger on failure. Lauriston was to debark his troops, maintain
them in the best possible order and stand by for new orders later
in the month.[12]

The new orders concerned the invasion of England. Napoleon
now came up with another convoluted plan to protect the Channel
crossing. In late March, Villeneuve in Toulon and Ganteaume in
Brest were to sail several thousand miles, eventually to rendezvous
at the island of Martinique in the Caribbean. After somehow
picking up Spanish and French warships blockaded in Cádiz and
Ferrol, and after delivering their troop cargoes to Martinique, they
were to wait, the one squadron for the other, for up to forty days.
Once united they would return to home waters. Meanwhile the
English guardians of the Channel having pursued them, they
would fight their way through whatever ships were left to guard
the Channel and reach Boulogne in late June to protect the short
sail of the invasion armada.

It was a poor plan at best. Ganteaume could not sail from Brest
without giving battle which Napoleon, perhaps foreseeing the outcome, forbade: "You have one goal only, to fulfill your mission.
Depart without battle."[13] Not being able to do so he remained in
port. Villeneuve, eventually pursued by Nelson, did reach
Martinique but seeing no sign of Ganteaume after a forty-day
wait sailed for home waters, inexplicably without even landing
Lauriston's troops.

While this complex naval drama unfolded, Napoleon made an
egregious error. He had decided earlier that the republic of Italy of

which he was president should become a kingdom under French hegemony, and had offered the crown to Prince Joseph Bonaparte providing that Joseph resigned his right to the imperial succession. When Joseph refused the offer, Napoleon – in a sharp reversal of his promise to the French legislature – promptly announced that he himself would wear the new crown.

Partly to shift attention from invasion preparations, the imperial procession ostentatiously departed in early April for Italy and a hastily arranged coronation ceremony. But first came a spectacular review of 30,000 troops on the battlefield of Marengo. So entranced was the emperor with the spectacle that he continued to drill the soldiers for several more days. He also ordered a large and expensive monument to be erected on the field.[14]

Having thus preserved his and the army's fame for posterity Napoleon continued on for the coronation in Milan cathedral, an elaborate ceremony attended by thousands of Lombardians who watched, probably with mixed feelings, as he placed on his head the iron crown that their kings had presented to Charlemagne nine centuries earlier. "The church was very beautiful," he informed Cambacérès. "The ceremony went as well as that in Paris with the difference that the weather was superb. In taking the crown of iron and putting it on my head, I added these words: 'God gives it to me, woe to him who touches it.'* I hope that this will be prophetic."[15] He already had decided to annex the republic of Genoa, which was soon accomplished at the formal request of the doge and senate.

The emperor remained in Italy until early July. He had appointed his 25-year-old stepson, Eugène Beauharnais, as viceroy of the new kingdom and had to settle him in the complicated job. He also had to deal with his youngest brother, the unruly 19-year-old Jérôme, who recently had arrived in Lisbon with his young American bride. Napoleon at once ordered him to come to Milan – alone. His unfortunate wife was to return to

---

*Napoleon was repeating the inscription on the crown.

America, her marriage "null in the eyes of religion as well as laws." If Mademoiselle Paterson, as Napoleon referred to her, agreed not to use the name Bonaparte upon her return to Baltimore, she would receive an annual life pension of 60,000 francs. Jérôme agreed to annul the marriage in return for the emperor's favor. "I am satisfied with his sentiments," Napoleon informed their sister Elisa, Grand Duchess of Tuscany, who was deputed to see that the young man remained good for his word.[16] Rehabilitation was swift. He was given command of a frigate and would soon command a squadron. "He has spirit, character and is decisive," Napoleon noted to Admiral Decrès, "and enough general knowledge of his profession to be able to profit from the ability of others."[17]

Napoleon meanwhile was paying close attention to flotilla affairs and the intended naval expeditions. Pleasing as was the news of Villeneuve's departure for Martinique it was modified by Admiral Ganteaume's enforced stay in Brest, his ships the prisoners of Admiral Cornwallis' prowling cruisers. In theory these cruisers should have chased Missiessy and Villeneuve to the Caribbean. Instead they had remained on station while Horatio Nelson took up the pursuit. In late June, Napoleon expressed to Admiral Decrès his fears that the English had learned of his plans from a secret agent. He nevertheless remained optimistic, anticipating Villeneuve's return to Ferrol (scheduled now for late July) and arrival at Boulogne in mid August. For the time being he could do nothing more than carry out myriad activities in Italy until his return to France in early July.[18]

Napoleon's return to Paris was anything but triumphant except perhaps in his own mind. A financial crisis was in the making, the fault of his inept treasury minister, Barbé-Marbois, who foolishly had drawn several million francs from the Bank of France to bail out a corrupt private business venture. This act, producing severe inflation at an awkward time, would plague the emperor for the next few months as bankruptcies multiplied and public confidence in the franc declined. Royalist agents in Paris were more active than ever, and police and soldiers were faced with serious insurrections in Normandy and Brittany. As July wore on, diplomatic reports continued to suggest unusual activity in European courts including renewed military preparations in Austria.

The reports were accurate. England and Russia had signed the Convention of St. Petersburg in April. This document called for a new coalition to declare war on France unless it returned to its "natural frontiers" by evacuating troops from Italy, Holland and Hanover. Despite persuasive diplomacy Austria and Prussia, though sympathetic, had refused to commit themselves to yet another war.

Napoleon's coronation in Italy however, followed by the annexation of the Genoese republic, played into anti-French hands in the courts of Vienna and Berlin. Although King Frederick William still held off, Emperor Francis was soon to join the new coalition.

The plan was threefold. A Russian-English corps from Corfu and Malta was to land in southern Italy while Archduke Charles, commanding an Austrian army 90,000 strong, stormed French fortresses on the Mincio river and seized former Habsburg territories in Italy. Archduke John with some 20,000 troops would hold the Tyrol. Simultaneously a smaller army of about 60,000 Austrians, under the titular command of Archduke Ferdinand but in reality of General Mack, would invade Bavaria and take up a defensive position on the Inn river around Braunau. Here he would be joined by Marshal Kutusov and some 35,000 Russians in mid October while two other Russian corps closed on Bohemia. Once Charles had defeated the French in Italy, Mack and Kutusov would advance to the upper Rhine to defeat whatever French forces stood in the way. Still another Russian corps was to land in Pomerania, join up with a Swedish corps and march on Hanover.[19]

Austria's refusal to evacuate troops from the Tyrol and Venice had given Napoleon a presentiment of this scenario. "I have good grounds to hope that the [new] war will not take place," he wrote Prince Eugène in late July, "however the preparations that the Austrians are making are such that I must make preparations."

Eugène was to keep a sharp eye "on the movements of Austrian troops beyond the Adige [river]."[20]

The looming threat made Napoleon more eager than ever to launch the stymied invasion of England. In the continuing belief that Missiessy and Villeneuve's expeditions had caused the major English guardians of French ports to abandon watch and sail after them,[21] and anticipating Villeneuve's arrival from Martinique, he had again ordered his other admirals to sail from Rochefort and Brest. Allemand's small squadron had departed without difficulty, but Ganteaume remained at Brest which earned him a veiled reprimand and urgent orders to move: "Be prudent, but also bold."[22]

August was to bring the moment of truth. Ever optimistic, Napoleon shifted headquarters to Pont de Briques early in the month. A few days later he learned that Villeneuve's sizeable fleet (upon return from Martinique) had engaged Admiral Calder's blockading squadron of 14 warships off Ferrol on the northwestern tip of Spain. Villeneuve early gained the weather gauge to send Calder running back to England with one ship sunk and three demasted. French ships suffered only light damage but two large Spanish ships had foundered and were seized by the English. Despite this loss Napoleon regarded the action as a victory, a splendid omen for the pending invasion. He now believed that he had 35 warships ready to sail from Ferrol to rendezvous with Ganteaume and Allemand and sail on to Boulogne.

He reckoned without two factors: one the Austrians, the other, Admiral Villeneuve. Despite Austrian denials of a military build-up, reports from the field continued to confirm that Austrian regiments were concentrating in the Tyrol and in Venice. Napoleon therefore concluded that the Vienna court had been writing sweet-nothings to him, playing for time until the Russians arrived. In early August he had informed Vienna that he wanted action, not words. "Who would say," he suggested to Talleyrand, "that [Austria] does not share the folly of Russia?"[23] In mid August as more of the war jinni oozed from General Mack's bottle, ambassador Cobenzl in Paris received an ultimatum: either the Austrian regiments in the Tyrol returned to home garrisons or France would declare war.[24]

Enter the naval factor. Napoleon still hoped for time to invade England, but the blurred shine of Villeneuve's victory had rapidly tarnished. He now learned that Villeneuve's ships were safely anchored in Ferrol harbor instead of having sailed to rendezvous with Ganteaume and Allemand, thus exposing the latter to great danger while further delaying the invasion. "Do you know where that fucking Villeneuve is?" he demanded of his civil councillor, Pierre Antoine Daru. "He is at Ferrol! . . . He has been beaten, he is hiding in Ferrol . . . What an admiral."[25] And to Decrès: "In my opinion Villeneuve does not have enough character to command a frigate . . . a man with neither firmness nor moral courage."[26]

At this point, late August, Napoleon was on the horns of a real strategic dilemma. While repeatedly ordering Villeneuve to sail for Boulogne, he continued to prepare for a land war. General Duroc was sent on a secret mission to Berlin to try to persuade the Prussian king to join the electors of Bavaria and Hesse-Darmstadt in a military alliance with France, his ultimate reward to be Hanover. Murat, Bertrand and Savary departed to make secret reconnaissances of the Rhineland. General Gouvion St. Cyr in Italy was alerted to invade Naples.

In the midst of this frenetic activity the emperor learned that Villeneuve had sailed from Ferrol in mid August, news that aroused his hopes and elicited the words quoted at the beginning of this chapter.[27]

All in vain. Villeneuve *had* sailed – but in another direction. He was now safely anchored in Cádiz harbor, his ships ringed by protective Spanish batteries. From here he could not be moved. Seeing now that the invasion could not take place, that probably it would never take place, Napoleon had no choice but to fight a land war which he did not want, yet one for which he was in part responsible. .

Notes

1   Corr. XI. Nr. 9115, Camp de Boulogne, 22 August 1805.

2   Corr. X. Nr. 8236, Paris, 27 December 1804.

3   Corr. X. Nr. 8237, Paris, 27 December 1804.

4   Corr. X. Nr. 8254, Paris, 2 January 1805. See also Fouché, 234–5.

5   Corr. X. Nr. 8250, Paris, 1 January 1805. See also Zawadzki, 269.

6   Corr. X. Nr. 8252, Paris, 2 January 1805.

7   Corr. X. Nr. 8258, Paris, 4 January 1805.

8   Corr. X. Nr. 8307, Paris, 1 February 1805.

9   Corr. X. Nr. 8298, Paris, 30 January 1805.

10   Corr. X. Nr. 8299, Paris, 30 January 1805.

11   Bryant (*Victory*), 110.

12   Corr. X. Nr. 8309, Paris, 1 February 1805.

13   Corr. X. Nr. 8480, Paris, 24 March 1805.

14   Corr. X. Nr. 8688, Alessandria, 6 May 1805. See also Ségur, II, 316–18.

15   Corr. X. Nr. 8796, Milan, 27 May 1805; Méneval, 146–8.

16   Corr. X. Nrs. 8690, 8691, 8692, Alessandria, 6 May 1805.

17   Corr. X. Nr. 8808, Milan, 29 May 1805.

18   Corr. X. Nr. 8959, Plaisance, 28 June 1805.

19   Rose (*Life*), II, 2–18; Wartenburg, I, 201–2, 207; Chandler (*Napoleon*), 382–3. See also Flayhart ("United Kingdom"), 113–15.

20   Corr. XI. Nrs. 9005, St. Cloud, 23 July 1805; 9015, St. Cloud, 25 July 1805.

21   Corr. XI. Nr. 9012, St. Cloud, 24 July 1805.

22   Corr. XI. Nr. 8998, St. Cloud, 20 July 1805.

23   Corr. XI. Nr. 9055, Boulogne, 7 August 1805.

24   Corr. XI. Nrs. 9068, 12 August 1805; 9070, Pont de Briques, 13 August 1805.

25   Ségur, II, 339. See also Méneval, 360–7.

26   Corr. XI. Nr. 9112, Camp de Boulogne, 22 August 1805.

27   Corr. XI. Nr. 9115, Camp de Boulogne, 22 August 1805.

CHAPTER FORTY-SIX

THE BATTLE OF ULM
SEPTEMBER–OCTOBER 1805

An army of 100,000 men has been destroyed as by magic.

Napoleon to Prince Cambacérès, reporting General
Mack's surrender at Ulm, Augsburg,
22 October 1805[1]

DURING THESE CONFUSED weeks of August 1805, Napoleon in various letters had touched briefly on his plans to fight a land war. In mid August he informed Talleyrand that if the Austrian court did not behave itself he would be at Vienna before the end of November in order to meet the approaching Russians (should they arrive).

Once he had buried hopes for a cross-Channel invasion he turned to the immense land task ahead. Almost overnight the army corps on the coast that comprised the Army of England became the nucleus of the new Grande Armée. After arranging for coastal defenses under Marshal Brune's command and the maintenance of the invasion fleet (the eventual hope was not quite extinguished), Napoleon returned to St. Cloud to work out the most minute details of the coming march – reconnaissances, unit orders, routes, supply and finances.

While Marshal Bernadotte's corps moved southward from Hanover another six corps, those of Marmont, Davout, Soult, Lannes, Ney and Augereau, would cross the Rhine to close on the enemy by three main routes, a total behemoth of 19 infantry divisions supported by artillery and 6 light cavalry divisions which, with allied contingents, would number over 200,000 men.

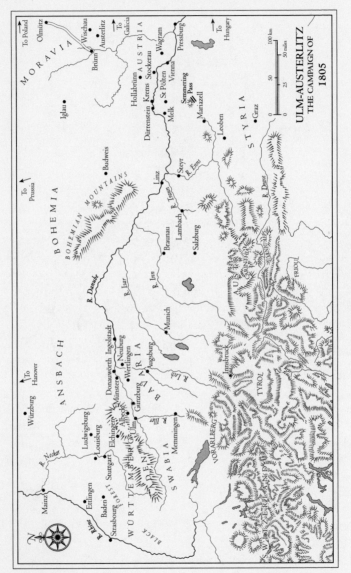

ULM-AUSTERLITZ
THE CAMPAIGN OF
1805

Ulm-Austerlitz The Campaign of 1805

Bosselman sc.

Gouvion St Cyr

Equally detailed plans were sent to Prince Eugène in Italy where General Masséna would shortly arrive to take command of the Army of Italy. Masséna, after sending General Gouvion St. Cyr with 25,000 troops to seize Naples and prevent a flank landing by Russian and English forces, was to fight a defensive war. Eugène was to provision all important forts in case of siege and transfer all cash in the provinces to Milan. (See map, Chapter 13.) If necessary he should retreat to Alessandria fortress, secretly taking Napoleon's crown of iron with him. All officers and government officials were to follow – if they did not, "upon my return I shall have them shot as traitors." Italy was secondary to the main effort but in case of extreme need Napoleon promised that he would come to Eugène's aid.[2]

Nor was the navy overlooked. The Napoleonic bile of years spilled over in early September when he informed naval minister Decrès that "[Admiral] Villeneuve is a villain to be ignominiously discharged. Without tactical ability, without courage, without general interest, he would sacrifice everything to save his own skin . . . Nothing is comparable to his ineptness."[3]

This harsh judgment was reinforced when Napoleon learned that Villeneuve in Cádiz had not yet passed the Gibraltar straits to pick up Spanish ships at Cartagena and carry out a new mission to reinforce General St. Cyr in Naples, his excuse being that he was blocked by a mere eleven English warships. Decrès was to send a special courier to him with orders to sail, "but as his excessive pusillanimity will prevent him from undertaking it," he was to be relieved by Admiral Rosily and sent back to France to answer for his conduct.[4] In addition to the expedition to Naples, Decrès was to arrange for expeditions to Mauritius and the islands of St. Helena and San Domingo, to Cayenne in South America and to African and Irish coasts, in all instances attacking English merchant shipping whenever possible.[5]

Napoleon next learned that General Mack's army had crossed the Lech river and was approaching Ulm. Kutusov's Russians had not yet reached Galicia but probably would arrive by end of September. The bulk of the French corps had reached Strasbourg and Marshal Murat had crossed the Rhine with a large cavalry corps. In late September, Napoleon joined the army at Strasbourg — but not until he had decreed that the revolutionary calendar so dear to Jacobin hearts would cease to function at year's end (a decree for which future historians would be ever grateful).

General Mack with an army of some 70,000 strong crossed the Inn river in early September to enter Bavaria. The Bavarian court and army hastily withdrew to Würzburg, and the Austrians occupied Munich.

The Austrian plan had been for Mack to wait for Kutusov's Russians before marching north but Mack saw no reason for this. The Russians were not expected until mid October and the French, he reasoned, could not reach the area until mid November. Far better to guard Swabia by basing the army on Ulm where he arrived in mid September.

Here his army turned to rebuilding fortress defenses on a dominance called Michelsberg while army outposts guarded the exits from the Black Forest to the west and the banks of the Iller river about 35 miles south to Memmingen where he posted Archduke Ferdinand with 25,000 troops, his supposition being that a French attack would come from this direction. Apparently it did not occur to him or to his staff that Napoleon possessed the will and capability to march *around* his position and attack from the right and rear.

The subsequent French victory over Mack at Ulm was a lopsided affair with little tactical interest other than the interworkings of various French corps and the outstanding performance of Napoleon and his marshals (apart from one or two errors), not to mention that of the troops. Mack was a political general, a fraud "who enjoyed a great reputation in Austria, probably because he was the only general who had suffered no great defeat."[6] Admiral Horatio Nelson had known him years earlier in Naples and had

his mark: "I know him to be a rascal, a scoundrel and a coward."[7]
Napoleon had met him briefly in 1800: ". . . one of the most
mediocre men I ever met . . . Full of conceit and vanity . . . and,
in addition, he is unlucky."[8]

Here is what happened: Marshal Bernadotte on the left of the
Grand Army marched southeast on Würzburg to be welcomed by
the fugitive Bavarian court and army. With Wrede and Deroy's
Bavarians on his left and Marmont's corps following, he continued
to march southeast, violating Prussian neutrality by crossing the
principality of Ansbach (to give Napoleon some future anxious
diplomatic moments with the Prussian court). Learning of this
development but discounting its significance, in early October
Mack sent General Kienmayer with some 18,000 troops to secure
his right in the area of Ingolstadt, Neuburg, Donauwörth and
Günzburg.

Marshal Murat, a flock of head plumes waving in the wind,
meanwhile had led his cavaliers across the Rhine, marching eastward but with a few detachments sent to make feint attacks on
Mack's guardians of the Black Forest to divert attention from the
main effort. Once Davout, Ney and Soult's columns had crossed
the river, Murat's main body of horse wheeled northward to form
Davout's right flank and slip undetected past Mack's front before
wheeling southward to begin Napoleon's extended envelopment.
Having junctioned in the areas of Münster and Augsburg the
corps now turned west to push in Austrian outposts before attacking Mack's army on the Michelsberg.

The initial deployment southeast of the target was carried out
with remarkable speed. As opposed to the slow march of Austrian
and Russian columns supported by ponderous wagon trains, the
French corps moved like the wind, miles ahead of their supply
columns, living off the land, eating mostly potatoes, slogging
through rain, mud and snow, gulping whatever brandy or wine
rations came their way, singing lusty marching songs and screaming their heads off upon sighting Napoleon – "Vive l'Empereur!
Vive l'Empereur!" – their oft-repeated vocal tribute to the most
recent cult of the leader.

As Napoleon had calculated, the real action began in the first week of October when Murat gained what the emperor termed *un petit succès* at Wertlingen to capture 3,000 generally demoralized enemy. Ney followed with a considerable victory at Günzburg to haul in another 1,500 enemy; after chasing the Austrians from Munich Bernadotte occupied the capital and went on to cleanse the land of enemy between the Isar and Lech rivers, thus protecting the French left while Soult closed on Archduke Ferdinand at Memmingen, forcing his corps of some 25,000 men to join Mack's army in Ulm.

Thinking that Mack would now withdraw to the Tyrol, Napoleon moved in Murat, Lannes and Ney's corps for the kill. Murat, temporarily commanding all three corps, pulled two of Ney's divisions across the Danube apparently without Napoleon's consent, leaving only General Dupont's infantry division around Albeck supported by Baraguey d'Hilliers' dragoons on the left or north bank of the river. Ney challenged the move but was overruled.

Mack with some 15,000 infantry and 10,000 cavalry now fell on Dupont's division perhaps 6,000 strong, a horrible battle of attack and counter-attack fought in heavy rain, at a cost to Dupont of 1,500 dead and wounded and a thousand men taken prisoner before he managed to withdraw to safety come evening. Ney furiously blamed Murat for the fiasco (as did Napoleon upon learning the details), the start of an enduring feud between the two marshals.[9]

Mack meanwhile enjoyed a brief opportunity to escape northward before the French closed the circle. Instead he insisted on remaining behind his Ulm defenses. Archduke Ferdinand however cut out to the northeast with some 6,000 cavalry. Murat's cavalry followed, a wild pursuit that ultimately captured not only most of the Austrian rearguard and baggage but thousands of garrison soldiers including 7 generals and 200 officers – Ferdinand with a small contingent only just escaping to the Bohemian mountains.[10]

Napoleon had already realized his error in assuming that Mack would try to withdraw to the Tyrol. Hastily reshuffling his corps, not without some confusion, he prepared for a final assault on the Austrians. Just over two weeks after crossing the Rhine, Ney and Lannes' corps opened the attack. Leading the advance guard Ney stormed the heavily defended bridge at Elchingen, a very brave feat later commemorated in his ducal title.

On the following day Ney's corps struggled through a field of mud to push in Austrian outposts before assaulting the Michelsberg. But now a beaten Mack, hoping to be saved by the Russians, asked for an eight-day armistice. Knowing that Kutuzov was still far away, Napoleon agreed, but a few days later the Austrian commander gave in and formally surrendered. At an elaborate ceremony with French troops drawn up on one side and Austrians on the other, the grief-stricken Mack handed Napoleon his sword, saying, "Here is the unfortunate Mack."[11]

The relatively easy victory nevertheless highlights the performance of Napoleon the commander vis-à-vis his executive instrument, the Grand Army. Other than one major miscalculation he was at his best. Not only did he pre-plan corps marches in minute and, as it turned out, accurate detail, but he closely followed these corps, daily issuing new orders, daily shifting divisions from one corps to another, daily prodding, inspecting, complimenting and scolding all ranks from marshal to private, all the while issuing frequent bulletins for publication in French, Italian and German newspapers.

His was an awesome performance in total contradiction to traditional command procedures. Often mounted on horse for hours he sometimes outran his staff. On one occasion he found himself in a tiny village, the rain beating down, his clothing sodden, with "no carriage, no desk, no nothing."[12]

What fired him? Mainly a desire for vengeance against both the Austrians "who had broken the peace to make us abandon our plan of maritime war" and perfidious Albion whose gold had propelled the march of the Austrians and Russians. But England was distant, Austria close at hand. Napoleon did not want a mere victory, he wanted every man of Mack's army captured – "if I had wished only to beat the enemy," he wrote Marshal Soult a few days before Mack's surrender, "I would not have needed so many marches."[13] At Ulm he had summoned Prince Liechtenstein, Mack's spokesman, to demand surrender of the entire garrison: if the troops did not lay down their arms they would be taken by assault and the prisoners put to the sword as he had done at Jaffa.[14]

His leadership in this campaign has few if any parallels. From 8 October, when heavy rains and occasional snow began falling, to the surrender of Ulm eight days later Napoleon had not removed his boots. Austrian generals taken prisoner were astonished to be interrogated by the bedraggled, soaked figure of the emperor wrapped in a mud-covered grey cloak, a sight all too familiar to French troops standing in mud and rain to hear his frequent encouraging harangues.

He handled his marshals and generals with the rare praise of Caesar mixed with the constant discipline of Sparta. "My cousin," he informed Prince Murat, "I am extremely satisfied with your account of my cavalry and especially of the dragoons yesterday . . . I am waiting for the eight standards and the prisoners that you have taken: 2,000, this is very few; I had hoped from your first report that the cavalry would have arrived in time to prevent the enemy from taking refuge in the woods."[15] With some he sympathized. To Marshal Lannes: "My cousin, I have seen with pleasure in your report the good conduct of the elite grenadiers. It is unfortunate that you did not have more than two hours of daylight; not a single man would have escaped . . . I pray God that he has you in His holy and worthy protection. My hearty embrace."[16]

Although he faced a frightened, disorganized and generally demoralized enemy and despite his desire to gain Ulm before the Russians arrived, as a rule he moved carefully, securing his flanks, frequently admonishing his marshals to maintain tactical unity – "march on the enemy wherever you find him," he ordered Murat, "but with precaution and cohesion."[17]

He was immensely proud of the army's performance and as usual he went to considerable lengths to let his non-commissioned officers and men know it. Grand Army bulletins almost always rang with the glorious deeds of individuals and units. "It is impossible to see soldiers more beautiful," he wrote of General Oudinot's grenadiers, "more animated with the desire to come to grips with the enemy, more full of honor and of that martial enthusiasm which presages the greatest success."[18] He openly praised the conscripts who "have shown as much bravery and readiness to fight as the old soldiers. Once under fire they lose the name of conscripts, thus all aspire to the honor of the title of soldier."[19] Since only one-sixth of the army saw battle action Napoleon decreed the entire thirty days of Vendémiaire should count as a campaign for service and pension purposes.[20]

As commanding general he was magnificent, as emperor he was majestical. From Strasbourg at the beginning of the campaign he reassured the Bavarian elector that he would soon return his fugitive court to Munich. The Swiss were forcefully advised to keep their frontiers closed to Austrian troops in order not to jeopardize their neutrality. He quietly pushed the Elector of Württemberg to hurry deployment of his promised 4,000 troops: "It will be obvious to your Highness that it is in the interest of all Swabian princes to move the war rapidly from Bavaria [and] to quell Austrian aggressions."[21]

The Emperor of France arrived at Strasbourg, the commander of the Grand Army departed from Strasbourg. "I am still here in good health," he wrote Joséphine from Ettlingen. "I am leaving for Stuttgart where I shall be this evening. The great maneuvers commence . . . I am in good position, and I love you."[22] Two days later he was the guest of the Württemberg elector in the "beautiful court" at Ludwigsburg where he enjoyed hearing the opera *Don Juan*, but, as he wrote minister Champagny, "the German melody appears to me however a trifle baroque. Has the [army] reserve marched? What is the state of conscription?"[23]

That was his last relaxation until the surrender of Ulm two weeks later, which was arranged from his headquarters in the abbey of Elchingen perched on a hill with a splendid view of the. beautiful countryside. From here he wrote Joséphine of his extreme fatigue after eight days of drenching rains and freezing feet, but a day of rest had made him feel better: "I have fulfilled my goal; I have destroyed the Austrian army by simple marches; I have taken 60,000 prisoners, 120 cannon, more than ninety standards and more than thirty generals . . . I am going after the Russians . . . Adieu, my Joséphine, a thousand lovely things everywhere. Prince Charles comes to cover Vienna."[24]

Napoleon arrived in Munich in late October to experience a city illuminated in his honor, a restored court and a citizenry paying constant homage to their deliverer, greeting his presence in the theater with wild applause and showering him and his entourage with adulation and every possible courtesy. In return he held a special concert for the ladies of the court and also attended mass in the palace chapel.

His stay was brief. Three days after his arrival he wrote Prince Joseph, "I am maneuvering against the Russian army which is in position behind the Inn [river], and is strong enough . . . I shall defeat them, but this probably will cost me some losses."[25]

Notes

1 Corr. XI. Nr. 9410, Augsburg, 22 October 1805.
2 Corr. XI. Nr. 9225, St. Cloud, 16 September 1805.
3 Corr. XI. Nr. 9179, Malmaison, 4 September 1805.
4 Corr. XI. Nr. 9220, St. Cloud, 15 September 1805.
5 Corr. XI. Nr. 9229, St. Cloud, 17 September 1805.
6 Rose (*Life*), II, 14. But see also Roider ("Habsburg"), 175–6.
7 Bryant (*Victory*), 152.
8 Wartenburg, I, 204. See also Rose (*Life*), II, 14, 21.
9 Rose (*Life*), II, 22–3; Chandler (*Napoleon*), 398–9.
10 Savary, II, 136–47. See also Rose (*Life*), II, 19–26; Wartenburg, I, 217–27; Chandler (*Napoleon*), 398–400.
11 Rose (*Life*), II, 25–6. See also Méneval, I, 391–2; Savary, II, 147–55; Wartenburg, 226–7; Chandler (*Napoleon*), 399–400. We are reminded of the fate of General Belisarius who, having lost favor with Emperor Justinian, was stripped of all honors and property

and then blinded. As a beggar he stood before the gates of the convent of Laurus and pleaded, "Give a penny to Belisarius the General." (See Asprey [*War in the Shadows*], I, 51.)

12   Corr. XI. Nr. 9359, Zusmarshausen, 10 October 1805.

13   Corr. XI. Nr. 9374, Augsburg, 12 October 1805.

14   Corr. XI. Nr. 9392, Elchingen, 18 October 1805.

15   Corr. XI. Nr. 9356, Donauwörth, 9 October 1805.

16   Corr. XI. Nr. 9357, Donauwörth, 9 October 1805.

17   Corr. XI. Nr. 9364, Augsburg, 11 October 1805.

18   Corr. XI. Nr. 9361, Zusmarshausen, 10 October 1805.

19   Corr. XI. Nr. 9370, Augsburg, 11 October 1805.

20   Corr. XI. Nr. 9406, Elchingen, 21 October 1805.

21   Corr. XI. Nr. 9283, Strasbourg, 29 September 1805.

22   Corr. XI. Nr. 9307, Ettlingen, 2 October 1805.

23. Corr. XI. Nr. 9331, Ludwigsburg, 4 October 1805.

24   Corr. XI. Nr. 9393, Elchingen, 19 October 1805.

25   Corr. XI. Nr. 9431, Munich, 27 October 1805.

CHAPTER FORTY-SEVEN

VICTORY IN AUSTRIA,
DEFEAT AT TRAFALGAR
OCTOBER–NOVEMBER 1805

*We are a few days from Vienna. We have only hurt
the Russians a little; as rapidly as we march, they
retreat more rapidly.*

Napoleon to Prince Cambacérès, Linz, Austria,
6 November 1805[1]

THE GRAND ARMY was not to be stopped. Mack might have been
eliminated but strong Russian armies were not far distant.
Archduke John still held the Tyrol and Archduke Charles commanded over 90,000 troops in North Italy, with what result
Napoleon did not know. One thing was certain, he could not
afford a link-up of the Russians and Charles' army, and this
could only be prevented by a drive east down the Danube while
other corps pushed south through central Austria, the strategy
being to knock out the Russians first before dealing with
Charles.

Napoleon was correct in respecting a potential threat from
Charles whose army was on its way home. Contrary to orders he
had sat on his predominant strength while Masséna, also defying
orders, moved across the Adige river, an unexpected development
that caused Charles to retreat on Caldiero. (See map, Chapter 13.)
Although he punished Masséna's attack here, Charles also learned
of Mack's catastrophe at Ulm and continued to withdraw, finally
to be joined by Archduke John's corps in Carinthia, a total of well
over 100,000 troops to threaten Napoleon's southern flank while

marching east in an attempt to reach Hungary and ultimately join the Russians at Olmütz.[2]

Foreseeing this possible scenario, Napoleon moved rapidly and well, setting up his defended supply line at Augsburg; guarding his rear and flanks; calling up Augereau's corps from France to screen Ulm and Augsburg; Ney and the Bavarians to occupy Innsbruck; Davout and Bernadotte along the Inn river to keep an eye on Kutusov and the Austrians; Marmont's corps to Steyr and Leoben to keep another eye on the Austrian left flank and the Austrians approaching from Italy. Finally, Murat, Lannes and Soult with Davout not far behind, defying rain, snow, cold and hunger to bridge the Inn and force Kutusov, once separated from his Austrian supporting corps, to a retreat down the right bank of the Danube that would end only a month later in Moravia.

Lannes' corps marching in a heavy snowstorm found Braunau hastily evacuated: "one of the keys of Austria," Napoleon wrote, "[with] . . . a beautiful walled fort and [supply] magazines of all types," – 40,000 rations of bread, 1,000 sacks of flour, tons of powder and munitions.[3] Some miles south on Lannes' right Bernadotte's corps occupied the lovely city of Salzburg, recently the headquarters of Emperor Francis. Everywhere the French advanced they found the enemy retreating, the Russians pillaging, raping and murdering, a sordid state of affairs that taken with Mack's disaster at Ulm had plunged Emperor Francis into deep melancholy. Napoleon nonetheless cautioned his marshals against exuberance: "It is necessary to march with caution. The Russians are still not hurt; they also know how to attack."[4]

Marshal Murat's corps supported by one of Davout's divisions first drew Russian blood in early November when some Russian battalions joined the Austrian defenders of Lambach. An infantry charge followed by cavalry sent the enemy running with a loss of 500 men taken prisoner including 100 Russians, not to mention a large amount of cash.

Napoleon at once moved imperial headquarters to the town where he replied to an ambiguous letter from Emperor Francis

proposing peace negotiations but with the apparent proviso that
Russia would participate. Whatever the case, Napoleon publicly
informed him, the peace would have to guarantee that Austria
would not join a fourth coalition. Austria, he emphasized, had
nothing to worry about from France. "My sole ambition is centered on the reestablishment of my commerce and navy [which]
England oppressively opposes."[5]

Francis should have come to terms. French corps were already
closing in on his capital, lusty columns marching down either side
of the Danube, bridging tributary rivers, stopping only for brief
bivouacs to huddle around fires while downing some sort of taste-
less gruel on rare occasion leavened by bread and wine. Linz fell
with its treasury of several hundred million florins, the Traun
river was crossed, then the Enns, the last line of defense of the
western approaches to Vienna. Aside from a few brief but sharp
actions there was little opposition, as Napoleon informed
Cambacérès in his letter of 6 November quoted at the beginning
of this chapter.

The action was heating up however. Deroy's Bavarians got
pommeled while outflanking an Austrian mountain position.
Although taking 600 prisoners, Deroy was wounded, and 12 of his
officers and 300 men were killed or wounded – a sacrifice given
eulogistic notice in an army bulletin.

Napoleon was still at Linz when General Count Gyulai arrived
with Emperor Francis' reply to his letter. This contained no suggestion of an armistice but again Napoleon answered politely,
pointing out that Austria and France were merely unwilling pawns
of an insane Anglo-Russian frolic; however much he wanted an
end to the war, he added, he feared "the delays and [Vienna court]
intrigues, the full bitterness of which I have experienced in past
negotiations."[6]

For a second time the Austrian ruler should have weighed his
enemy's words. Napoleon was talking from a position of ever
stronger tactical strength as his corps marched down the Danube
(Murat's cavalry scouting as far forward as Melk). From Linz he
ordered the preparation of a flotilla to carry the army across the

Danube should the need arise. He also formed a new corps of observation under Marshal Mortier whose three divisions once united would cross to the left bank of the Danube to keep an eye on any Russians in the vicinity.

Davout's corps meanwhile had caught a large Austrian force retreating on Mariazell, taking 4,000 prisoners and shattering the southwestern defenses of Vienna. Murat had now reached Melk and was marching on St. Pölten, hopefully to catch the remaining Russians before they escaped across the Danube.[7]

Napoleon arrived at Melk on 10 November, taking quarters in the famous abbey, which he described as "one of the most beautiful in Europe," – nothing like it in France or Italy. Parisian readers learned from an army bulletin that it was "one of the principal Roman outposts . . . called 'the House of Iron', built by the [Roman] emperor Commode. The caves and the cellars . . . [are full] of very good Hungarian wines, which have been of great help to the army."[8]

Up to this point almost everything had gone like clockwork. But now Murat, who had been ordered to stick on Kutusov's tail, had lost contact while moving on Vienna. Napoleon had all along extolled his brother-in-law's generalship (with the exception of the Dupont fiasco at Elchingen) both in personal letters and in frequent army bulletins, thus further enlarging an already gigantic ego. But now his unexpected move brought perhaps unduly harsh retribution:

> I can not approve your march [Napoleon informed him],
> you move like a harebrain and do not respect my orders.
> The Russians, instead of covering Vienna, have crossed the
> Danube to Krems . . . [but] you are going to rush my army
> on Vienna . . . I look in vain for reasons to explain your
> conduct. I have informed Marshal Soult not to march as
> you have ordered . . . I fear that you have strongly exposed
> [Marshal Mortier's corps], which would not have happened
> had you executed my orders . . . you have made me lose
> two days [of marches] in thinking only of the glory in

entering Vienna. There is only glory where there is danger,
and there is no danger in entering a defenseless capital.[9]

Napoleon's concern for Mortier was soon justified when General
Gazan's division about 4,000 strong was attacked by 38,000
Russians debouching from Dürrenstein. Napoleon had authorized
the marshal to retreat as far as Linz if necessary, but there was no
retreat. Gazan's troops not only held against the Russian ava-
lanche but, in conjunction with the opportune arrival of Dupont's
division, fell on the enemy columns which suffered "horrible carnage" more than 4,000 dead or wounded, 1,300 taken prisoner, the
remainder retreating northward leaving a large number of
wounded at Dürrenstein, many of whom fell victim to savage
French vengeance. French casualties, around 3,000 men, were
evacuated to the abbey of Melk "whose monks are rich enough to
nurse them in lieu of paying a contribution," Napoleon noted.
Surviving Russian casualties were taken to Vienna in order to
impress the citizenry with the enemy's great losses.[10]

The Russian defeat and the occupation of Vienna partially
redeemed Murat in the eyes of the emperor, now headquartered in
beautiful Schönbrunn palace. "I have seized the complete arsenal,
all artillery dumps; the cannon, muskets and munitions of all
types number thousands and thousands," Napoleon informed
Marmont, whose corps was guarding the Styrian passes against
Prince Charles' army approaching from Italy.[11] Murat gained further credit when he, Lannes and Bertrand by a clever ruse gained
control of the vital Vienna bridge across the Danube. Murat,
Lannes and General Suchet of Soult's corps were shortly in
Stockerau ready to march north, their orders to fall on the head
and flanks of the retreating army. Davout simultaneously was to
close on Pressburg to protect the army's new right flank and rear
in conjunction with Marmont screening the vital Semmering Pass.
Mortier once joined by Bernadotte's corps marching from
Salzburg would chase after the Russian rearguard.

But now more problems arose. True to form Bernadotte's
march did not reach the Danube on schedule, much less cross it.

"General Bernadotte has lost a day," Napoleon complained to Murat, "I have demonstrated my extreme displeasure to him."[12] The imperial wrath next shifted back to Murat who, having come on to Bagration's rearguard of 6,000 cavalry at Hollabrünn and wanting to gain time for Lannes' infantry to come up behind him, had thought to outwit the Russians by signing an armistice that, once accepted by Napoleon, called for Kutosov's withdrawal from Moravia. "It is impossible for me to find terms [sufficient] to express my displeasure," Napoleon informed the errant marshal. "You command only my advance guard and you do not have the right to make an armistice without my orders; you have made me lose the fruit of a campaign. Break the armistice immediately and march on the enemy."[13]

Napoleon's bad temper is easy to understand. The retreating Russians and the Austrian remnants would shortly join up with the main Russian army, General Buxhöwden's 55,000 or so troops based on Olmütz fortress in Moravia. Prince Charles was approaching Styria with a strong army and if neither Marmont nor Masséna stopped him he could march through Hungary to reach Olmütz. Even more threatening was King Frederick William of Prussia who, surrounded by anti-French advisers, had taken umbrage weeks earlier when Bernadotte's corps violated the Prussian principality of Ansbach. Napoleon had replied to initial protests by pointing out that in the last war the principality had not been considered as neutral and had been repeatedly violated by all involved powers. When this didn't wash, he wrote humbly and at length, reiterating the need to prevent Russia from encroaching on its neighbors and assuring the Prussian king of his lasting friendship – but Prussia nevertheless remained a dangerous threat.[14]

Shortly before Napoleon wrote this letter, Czar Alexander arrived in Berlin to try to persuade Frederick William to join the new coalition, a move greatly encouraged by Queen Louise with whose charms Alexander was smitten. Perhaps against his better judgment – the Prussian king did not trust Alexander any more than he did Napoleon – Frederick William signed the Treaty of

Potsdam by which he pledged "armed mediation." If Napoleon refused Prussia's chimerical demands to yield numerous territories under French control, Prussia would join the enemy coalition (in return for the czar's secret promise to give England's Hanover to Prussia). Count Haugwitz left Berlin in mid November to present Napoleon with this ultimatum.[15]

Napoleon knew none of these details but undoubtedly suspected the worst upon learning of Alexander's presence in Berlin. Prussia he knew could deploy 190,000 troops to strike his flank and rear, though probably not until mid December. More the urgency then to knock out the Russians which would end any armed threat from Prussia.

On the credit side, the immediate enemy was on the run along the line. Bernadotte's corps had finally crossed the Danube to fan out into Bohemia where Baraguey d'Hilliers' foot dragoons continued to push back a Russian corps. Mortier's corps, hastily repaired after Dürrenstein, dogged the Russians rear while Murat, Lannes and Soult, *l'épée dans les reins*, were fast closing on his flank.

Emperor Francis at Brünn wrote Napoleon still another inconclusive letter. Napoleon replied in detail, pointing to numerous Russian atrocities that were causing the Austrian ruler's subjects to lose faith in him – "The Russians are burning the most beautiful villages in their retreat. If your Majesty will assure me that they will evacuate all of his states, I will halt at Brünn and stop my pursuit of them."[16]

A day later Napoleon learned that Admiral Villeneuve's fleet of warships had been destroyed by Admiral Lord Horatio Nelson in the battle of Cape Trafalgar fought off the southern tip of Spain over 1,000 miles away. (See front endpaper map.)

While the Grand Army was marching through southern Germany into Austria the French navy remained blockaded in the ports of Brest, Ferrol, Toulon – and Cádiz. Vice-Admiral Pierre Villeneuve's combined French-Spanish fleet at Cádiz had been sufficiently strong, at least in theory, to break through Admiral Cuthbert Collingwood's meager covering force, had he acted promptly.

His delay allowed Collingwood to receive substantial reinforcements including a new commander, the legendary 47-year-old Horatio Nelson whose flag flew on HMS *Victory*. Nelson, who now commanded 23 warships, was looking at 33 enemy ships in Cádiz harbor, masts "as thick as a wood," wrote one observer.[17]

Nelson's task was not merely to fight a battle but to eliminate Villeneuve's battle fleet, just as Napoleon had wished to eliminate Mack's army at Ulm. "We have only one great object in view," Nelson wrote Collingwood, "that of annihilating our enemies."[18] Suspecting that Villeneuve intended to escape to the Mediterranean, Nelson left a squadron of frigates to observe him while keeping his main battle fleet out of sight as he had done earlier when screening Toulon.

Nelson was both right and wrong concerning Villeneuve's potential plans. Napoleon had instructed the reluctant admiral to carry 4,000 troops to General Gouvion St. Cyr at Naples. Aware that his career was already in serious jeopardy, he ordered preparations to sail despite the poor condition of most of his vessels which lacked adequate armament and trained crews. The decision was immensely unpopular with a number of his captains, particularly the Spanish captains and the Spanish Admiral Fédéric Gravina who pointed to the deplorable condition of the ships, a complete lack of training in combined operations and the signs of a dangerous approaching storm. Nelson's rumored arrival brought about a council of war to thrash out the matter, a noisy affair during which a Spanish commodore nearly drew his sword on one of Villeneuve's firebrand admirals who insisted on sailing.[19] Undoubtedly to Villeneuve's pleasure the council decided to disobey Napoleon's orders and remain in port. Nelson meanwhile had planned a suitable demise for the blockaded ships but could do nothing until they put to sea.

The standoff might have continued for months had Villeneuve not learned that French Admiral Rosily was at Madrid en route to relieve him of command. We feel sorry for Pierre Villeneuve, the victim of his own inadequacies so strikingly displayed by his precipitate departure from Aboukir Bay seven years earlier. Tested several times since beyond his moral strength, in general he had failed master and country. Was he now to find himself a craven object, perhaps to be courtmartialed, his name forever blemished? Could he not redeem himself by battle? Professionally he was an able sailor, he had more ships and thus firepower than the enemy, he had a fair notion of what Nelson would attempt. A victory would cancel calumny, would reap rich rewards. "About my brain," as Hamlet had it – after a suitably inspiring pep talk to his captains he ordered the fleet to sail.

The first ships left harbor on 19 October, the remainder on a fresh tide the following day. Nelson had sailed to screen the Gibraltar straits, but finding no enemy and learning from a frigate of activity in Cádiz harbor, he soon doubled back to sight the enemy fleet struggling to gain some semblance of order.

Early on 21 October this fleet had reached the waters off Cape Trafalgar, Villeneuve having characteristically decided to return to harbor. Two English divisions hoisted attack flags to move on a disorganized line of battle several miles long, Nelson commanding the first division and Collingwood the second.

"England expects that every man will do his duty," read the signal flag from HMS *Victory*. Every man did do his duty and many much more than their duty. The gloriously horrible battle began about noon as English ships closed on their targets. It was ship against ship, gun against gun – and finally man against man.

Nelson had led his division into action. An hour or two later while on the quarterdeck with Captain Thomas Hardy he was mortally wounded, but was still alive when Admiral Villeneuve surrendered his flagship. Captain Hardy reported to him later in the afternoon that 15 enemy ships had surrendered. "That is well," Nelson whispered, "but I had bargained for twenty."[20]

Nelson died before he learned the magnitude of his victory. The enemy fleet was all but eliminated. England had retained mastery of the seas.

Notes

1   Corr. XI. Nr. 9455, Linz, 6 November 1805.
2   Macdonald, 140–56; Chandler (*Napoleon*), 404–5.
3   Corr. XI. Nrs. 9437, 9441, Braunau, 30 October 1805.
4   Corr. XI. Nr. 9442, Braunau, 31 October 1805. See also Savary, II, 157–8.
5   Corr. XI. Nr. 9451, Lambach, 3 November 1805.
6   Corr. XI. Nr. 9464, 8 November 1805. See also Méneval, I, 387.
7   Wartenburg, I, 234–7. See also Ségur, II, 425–37.
8   Corr. XI. Nr. 9469, Melk, 10 November 1805.
9   Corr. XI. Nr. 9470, Melk, 11 November 1805.
10 Corr. XI. Nr. 9477, Schönbrunn, 14 November 1805. See also Méneval, I, 393–4; Wartenburg, I, 238–9.
11 Corr. XI. Nr. 9480, Schönbrunn, 14 November 1805. See also Chandler (*Napoleon*), 406.
12 Corr. XI. Nr. 9493, Schönbrunn, 15 November 1805.
13 Corr. XI. Nr. 9497, Schönbrunn, 16 November 1805.
14 Corr. XI. Nr. 9434, Munich, 27 October 1805. See also Metternich, II, 38–89.
15 Rose (*Life*), II, 30–2.
16 Corr. XI. Nr. 9503, Znaym, 17 November 1805.
17 Howarth (*Trafalgar*), 103. See also Collingwood, 109–10.
18 Tute, 117.
19 Howarth (*Trafalgar*), 94.
20 Bryant (*Victory*), 175.

CHAPTER FORTY-EIGHT

AUSTERLITZ:
THE DAY OF THE THREE EMPERORS
NOVEMBER–DECEMBER 1805

The positions that we are occupying are formidable, and while
[the enemy] marches to outflank our right they will present
their flank to me.

Napoleon's proclamation to the Grand Army on the eve
of Austerlitz, 1 December 1805[1]

NAPOLEON LEARNED OF the naval disaster at Trafalgar on 18
November at a time when his own war was approaching a climax.
According to his chief of staff, Berthier, he flew into a rage, shouting, "I can not be everywhere." Once calm he coldly replied to
Admiral Decrès' letter: "I await further details of what you have
told me before I form a final opinion on the nature of this affair."
But in true Napoleonic style he continued, "While waiting, I
hasten to inform you that this changes nothing concerning my
[planned naval] expeditionary projects; moreover I am annoyed
that they are not ready."[2]

Two days later he was comfortably ensconced in a château at
Brünn, the Austrian court and the Russian and Austrian troops
having retired on the fortress of Olmütz some 50 miles to the
northeast. In addition to a strong citadel capable of withstanding
prolonged siege Brünn had yielded six cannon, 300,000 lbs of
powder, large quantities of wheat and flour and a considerable
amount of clothing.

So long as Prince Charles did not reach Olmütz and so long as
Prussia remained neutral, Napoleon was in a relatively secure

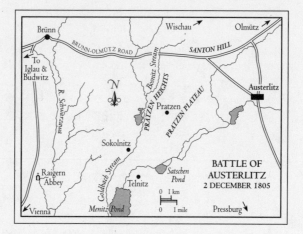

Battle of Austerlitz, 2 December 1805

position. Bernadotte was at Budwitz in Bohemia, about to move on Iglau as protector of the French left from Archduke Ferdinand's remnants licking their wounds in Bohemian hills. Murat had won a cavalry battle against the Russians northeast of Brünn where French outposts in and around Wischau now screened Napoleon's front, with patrols probing close to Olmütz fortress. The bulk of his army was about a march distant enjoying a well-earned rest in bivouac west of the small village of Austerlitz on the Pratzen plateau, a good position from which it could fall back on the bastion of Brünn if necessary. Davout was in Vienna with a portion of his corps at Pressburg, screening Napoleon's right. At the other end of the theater Marmont was standing guard around Graz in Styria, as was Ney at Innsbruck – "all of the Tyrol is occupied by our army," Napoleon noted on 24 November, with General Jellichich's Austrian corps caught between Ney and Augereau's corps at Ulm.[3] So all was well and good, but if he were to avoid a very dangerous situation he had to act soon.

What then should he do?

His options were limited. He could retreat along the line and abandon his German allies. That would not only end all hopes of establishing French hegemony in southern Germany but would also risk a severe military defeat followed by an invasion of France since undoubtedly it would bring Prussia into the enemy coalition. He could move on the enemy, but that would be insane in view of the defensive strength of fortress Olmütz and the surrounding terrain – even Frederick the Great had been forced to limit himself to besieging the place (an effort that resulted in disaster, as Napoleon would have known from his studies of Frederick's campaigns).[4] He could stay where he was, ready to fight if attacked, but hoping for a quick peace with Austria which would probably dissolve the new coalition and end the war.

He promoted the latter hope as best he could. When two Austrian envoys, Stadion and Gyulai, appeared at Brünn with authority to open peace negotiations, he received them politely and shunted them off to Talleyrand in Vienna, just as he would the Prussian ambassador, Haugwitz, in a secret audience a few days later. Talleyrand was instructed to treat them gently and make some concessions, but Napoleon accurately regarded their presence as an attempt to gain time for the arrival of Prince Charles' army. This left the singular possibility of an allied attack which seemed to be Napoleon's only real hope, one which he encouraged by sending General Savary to Czar Alexander with a suitably humble note of welcome presented by a face of deep concern.

The Russian czar had arrived at Olmütz about the time the French emperor reached Brünn. Owing to Kutusov's disastrous retreat Alexander was at first on the defensive, writing to the Prussian king: "Our position here is more than critical: we stand almost alone against the French, who are close on our backs. As for the Austrian army, it does not exist."[5]

Ever capricious, the mood of this 28-year-old ruler who desperately wanted to win laurels on the battlefield changed with the arrival of a strong reinforcement of troops that included 10,000 stalwarts of his splendidly turned out Imperial Guard, and it was not long before he was demanding an attack on the French.

This mood perfectly suited his senior commander, General Buxhöwden, his more aggressive younger aides such as Prince Dolgoruky, and the Austrian commander, General Weyrother, who was convinced that Napoleon was hurting, that he could not have more than 40,000 troops at best.[6] General Kutusov sharply disagreed, wisely counseling a further retreat eastward to let time and space do the work of spilled blood (while avoiding possible defeat), an opinion shared by the Russian foreign affairs minister, Prince Adam Czartoryski. Prince Schwarzenberg and to a lesser degree Emperor Francis also shied away from an offensive move but General Weyrother, as confident in his incompetence as he had been in Italy and more recently at Ulm, assured them that an enveloping attack over the Pratzen plateau would roll up the French right and the war would be over.

General Savary remained at Olmütz for three days, spreading careful word of French concerns over being attacked but also noting discord in the top allied commands. The war party was obviously dominant, Savary discovered, and he was probably not surprised when on 28 November a Cossack force fell on Wischau to capture some fifty French foot dragoons, prelude to the arrival of Alexander and the entire Russian army.[7]

Napoleon meanwhile had not been idle. Two days prior to the attack on Wischau he had issued a new brigade order of battle, the *ordre mince* which combined the fire of the line with the strength of the column *in defense*. General Caffarelli received orders that night to have his infantry division in position across the Brünn–Olmütz road early the next morning: "It is probable that a vigorous action will commence at eight a.m."[8] Bernadotte now at Iglau received orders to move out "without losing a moment" and to inform his troops "that there will be battle the other side of Brünn tomorrow or soon after."[9]

Shortly after dispatching these orders Napoleon reconnoitered enemy bivouac fires at Wischau in an attempt to determine enemy strength. Upon returning to headquarters he stopped by a small brook just off the main road about six miles from Brünn. After a suitable reconnaissance of the ground he turned to his staff and said, "Gentlemen, examine the ground carefully, it is going to be a battlefield."[10]

Savary now returned from Olmütz to report not only allied preparations for battle but also the prevalent discord in command ranks, and probably confirmation of the suspected allied plan of attack. This suited Napoleon who next abandoned the army's position on Pratzen plateau in favor of a night withdrawal to his recent discovery, the valley of the Goldbach stream, "as if [the army] had suffered a defeat."[11] He was now convinced that the enemy would attack his right flank thus exposing its own flank to his new positions – his right behind a series of frozen ponds, his center behind the Goldbach, his left anchored on the Brünn–Olmütz road. To encourage this move, the troops left and center were set to preparing ostentatious defensive works as if fearing a frontal attack.

The final deception took place when Napoleon received the czar's emissary who accompanied Savary, the bumptious and arrogant Prince Dolgoruky. Surrounded by what appeared to be disorganized and disheartened French soldiers, Dolgoruky rudely informed the French emperor that if he wished peace he must either evacuate Italy or lose all his provinces, that the crown of iron should henceforth be worn by the King of Sardinia. "He spoke to me," Napoleon wrote, "as if I were a Russian aristocrat about to be exiled to Siberia." Napoleon listened to the tirade in silence, his suppressed anger evident to his aides, and the prince returned to inform Alexander that the French army was in dire straits.[12]

Dolgoruky's arrogance convinced Napoleon that battle was imminent, as he informed Talleyrand. It was a matter now of properly deploying his corps along a 6–7 mile line. His decisions could scarcely be faulted: his left protected by a key terrain feature, a small conically shaped hill called the Santon where he placed one regiment of Suchet's division along with 18 cannon to cover the Brünn–Olmütz road; the remainder of Suchet's division was concealed behind the Santon with Caffarelli's division (also of Lannes' corps) on the right ready to march in line of brigades supported by Oudinot's grenadiers.

Next came all of Murat's cavalry deployed in columns so as to take as little space as possible, and on Murat's right Bernadotte's corps of two divisions forming the center; then Soult's powerful corps, Vandamme's division on the left, St. Hilaire's on the right, positioned in the ravine behind the junction of the Goldbach and Bosnitz streams, ready to move out in echelon, the right wing in advance, while one regiment of Legrand's division held the village of Sokolnitz. On Soult's right a gap showed behind the frozen ponds, honey for a hungry Russian bear, a sector to be defended by Friant's infantry division and a division of dragoons, both of Davout's corps, marching on the village of Telnitz to support Legrand.

Napoleon placed his command post, a hastily constructed thatched hut without roof, on a commanding height in center rear. Here he dictated final orders for delivery by an aide, General Junot, and here were held ten battalions of the Imperial Guard, foot, horse and artillery, and ten battalions of grenadiers commanded by Oudinot and Duroc – a reserve that in Napoleon's words counted as an army in its own right.

These deployments were being carried out none too soon. Although the last day of November passed without battle, Napoleon on the following morning watched "with unspeakable joy" as allied troops spilled onto the Pratzen plateau, their advance posts within cannon range, their formations strongly suggesting a march to strike the French right. He now issued a proclamation to the army, an excerpt from which is quoted at the beginning of this chapter.[13]

Word of battle on the following day, the anniversary of the emperor's coronation, further fired officers and men as did Napoleon's inspection of forward posts that night. Recognized upon his return, he was surrounded by thousands of soldiers burning improvised straw torches while shouting "Vive l'Empereur!" – an extraordinary demonstration that apparently went unreported by Russian outposts.

Meanwhile the allied army was marching to carry out General Weyrother's plan: Prince Bagration with some 14,000 cavalry to attack Napoleon's left; Grand Duke Constantine, the czar's towering brother, commanding about 10,000 men of the Imperial Guard to hold the French center; Buxhöwden and Kutusov's remaining corps along with some Austrian units, about two-thirds of the combined army, to march southwest in three columns across the plateau to strike the apparently weak French right between Telnitz and Sokolnitz, a grand encirclement maneuver intended to isolate and then destroy the Grand Army.

At least one modern historian has commented favorably on this idiotic plan. Weyrother and his fellows supposed that Napoleon was a fool, which he decidedly was not. They supposed that he . commanded 40–50,000 troops when the correct figure was over 70,000. They supposed that French cannon would remain mute and French infantry and cavalry immobile while over 50,000 enemy crossed their front. They also supposed that all Russian and Austrian generals understood and agreed to the plan which was not the case.

The arrogant Weyrother did not brief the generals until the night of 1–2 December, a good staff performance, big map, stick in hand, arrows, impressive diagrams, jump-offs, routes of attack, goals. The trouble was that quite a few Russian generals including Kutusov were drunk and uncaring, most did not understand the German language and the orders were as yet untranslated into Russian.

Here briefly is what happened.

On this beautiful sunny day of 2 December 1805, General Kienmayer's vanguard of about 5,000 horse reached the pot of honey (the French right) to ride down a spur of the plateau to the valley, there to push French defenders from Telnitz only to be stopped by cannon fire from Friant's regiments of Davout's corps coming up from Raigern Abbey.

As the following Russian tide of Buxhöwden's immense corps flowed over the defenders of Sokolnitz and Telnitz, Napoleon filtered in reinforcements from Soult's corps while praying that his right could hold until it was time to deliver the master stroke. Glass to eye he watched Buxhöwden's main body gradually clear the center while on the left Bagration's corps of infantry and horse, about 14,000 strong, was held by flanking fire from Santon Hill.

With Buxhöwden's force now committed on the enemy left, Napoleon ordered Soult to attack the center, an uncomfortable surprise for the enemy delivered by Vandamme's division supported by St. Hilaire and followed by Bernadotte's corps, a hot two-hour battle during which one of Vandamme's battalions was overrun and lost its eagle (a heinous crime) to expose the French flank. Grand Duke Constantine at once exploited this success by turning loose the Guard cavalry, a crisis finally resolved in French favor by Bessières' *cuirassiers* followed by more cavalry and one of Bernadotte's divisions fighting on ground already shaking from the rapid fire of some 400 cannon.

Bagration's infantry and cavalry attacks on the French left were meanwhile being ably fielded, first by Caffarelli and Suchet's infantry and artillery fire on Santon Hill, then by Lannes' infantry "marching in echelon . . . as if on an exercise."[14] Despite repeated charges supported by massive artillery fire, Bagration's corps instead of breaking through was broken through by a final fierce attack of Hautpol and Nansouty's *cuirassiers* which sent him back to Austerlitz and beyond.

The crisis in the center having been met, Soult's force wheeled right to follow Buxhöwden's torrent. That force of some 35,000 troops meanwhile had been checked by Legrand and Oudinot in and behind Sokolwitz and by Friant's indomitable division behind Telnitz, a total force about a third as strong as its enemy. With Soult's timely arrival on the heights, the enemy was suddenly caught between three fires. Whole columns were killed or taken prisoner, the fugitives throwing down their weapons in an attempt to escape over frozen ponds. But now Napoleon brought up another twenty cannon to join Soult's artillery in firing to break the ice and send an estimated 2,000 men to their death by drowning, a ghastly scene that reminded the emperor of the slaughter of Turkish soldiers some six years earlier in Aboukir Bay in Egypt.

The battle was over by early afternoon, the remnants of the allied army in full flight.[15] According to French figures 18,000 Russians had been killed, 7,000 wounded and 30,000 including 20 generals and hundreds of senior officers taken prisoner. Six hundred Austrians had been killed. General Buxhöwden was killed. Czar Alexander and his staff were lucky to escape capture as was the wounded General Kutusov. The enemy lost 45 battle standards and more than 150 cannon. Although these figures were (as usual) exaggerated, it seems probable that over a third of the Russian army had been destroyed, and that Alexander had lost all of his artillery and baggage.[16]

The French admitted to 900 dead and 3,000 wounded, figures which can safely be doubled and then some in view of the close-in fighting and murderous artillery fire. General St. Hilaire had been hit early in the action but continued to fight. General Valhubert would soon die from wounds. General Thiébault was shot through the shoulder and suffered seven fractures from the exiting bullet; Sebastiani, Kellermann, Rapp and others were also wounded while fighting brilliantly and would recover. Caffarelli had distinguished himself along with Nansouty, Hautpol and many more including General Friant who had four horses shot from beneath him.

Napoleon spent the rest of the afternoon and most of the night touring the battlefield with his staff, asking them to keep quiet so "that they could hear the cries of the wounded," frequently dismounting to examine wounded French soldiers, giving each a stiff drink of brandy and assurance that his wounds would soon be dressed and that he would be evacuated. He was generally good for his word but Russian wounded were not so fortunate – two days after the battle thousands were still waiting for treatment and evacuation.[17]

It was time now for laurels. Soon after the battle Napoleon ordered his chief *commissaire* to come up with 15 million francs (taken from Austrian holdings) so that the troops could have money to spend during a rest period. Many soldiers were already enjoying the fruits of victory, having ransacked abandoned enemy packs, thousands of wagons and some ornate carriages to find a great deal of gold and valuables.

This was only the beginning. Napoleon's largesse deserves to be reported not only from the humanitarian standpoint but because of its contrast to the day's normal practices. As part of pepping up morale prior to the battle he had decreed that any officer or man who had been wounded or *would be* wounded would receive a bonus of three months' pay, a promise subsequently respected as far as possible.[18] A few days after the battle he announced that the wives of those killed at Austerlitz would receive lifetime annual pensions ranging from 6,000 francs for a general's widow, 2,400 francs for those of colonels and majors and descending to 200 francs for the widows of soldiers. He was also adopting the children of the dead whom he would support and educate – each would be given the right to add the name of Napoleon to its own.[19]

Heroic personal deeds, heroic acts of battalions, squadrons, regiments, divisions and corps, of infantry, artillery, cavalry, all were enshrined in numerous bulletins published throughout France – every hero and every unit could not be listed "because it would be necessary to name everyone."[20] Allied generals and troops, Bavarians and the like, were singled out for praise both in bulletins and in private letters to their rulers. Numerous officers and men won promotions both in rank and in the Legion of Honor. Nor were commanders neglected – Berthier was ordered to divide 2 million francs between marshals, generals, adjutants-general and colonels.[21]

Napoleon sent the Archbishop of Paris 45 enemy standards to be displayed in the cathedral of Notre Dame, where an annual memorial service henceforth would be conducted in honor of "the brave dead." As a final tribute to the living he promised to hold *une grande fête* once the army returned to France: "the thought of seeing you all . . . gathered around my palace makes my heart smile."[22]

Notes

1 Corr. XI. Nr. 9533, In Bivouac, 1 December 1805.
2 Fouché, 237; Corr. XI. Nr. 9507, Znaym, 18 November 1805.
3 Corr. XI. Nr. 9522, 24 November 1805. See also Ségur, II, 445–7.
4 Asprey (*Frederick the Great*), 489–93.
5 Rose (*Life*), II, 33.
6 Rose (*Life*), II, 36, gives the figure of 50,000 men.
7 Savary, II, 190–8; Ségur, II, 444–55.
8 Corr. XI. Nr. 9530, Brünn, 28 November 1805.
9 Corr. XI. Nr. 9531, Brünn, 8 p.m., 28 November 1805.
10 Chandler (*Napoleon*), 412.
11 Corr. XI. Nr. 9541, Austerlitz, 3 December 1805.
12 Corr. XI. Nr. 9545, Austerlitz, 5 December 1805; Savary, II, 198.
13 Corr. XI. Nr. 9533, In Bivouac, 1 December 1805.
14 Corr. XI. Nr. 9541, Austerlitz, 3 December 1805.
15 Thiébault, II, 147–79; Savary, II, 194–209; Ségur, II, 462–75; Rose (*Life*), II, 36–42; Wartenburg, I, 256–63; Chandler (*Napoleon*), 412 ff.
16 Corr. XI. Nrs. 9544, 9546, Austerlitz, 5 December 1805; 9548, Austerlitz, 6 December 1805; 9550, Austerlitz, 7 December 1805. See also Ségur, II, 476–7.
17 Savary, II, 209; Corr. XI. Nr. 9546, Austerlitz, 5 December 1805.
18 Savary, II, 227.
19 Corr. XI. Nrs. 9529, Brünn, 28 November 1805; 9552, Austerlitz, 7 December 1805; 9610, Schönbrunn, 25 December 1805.
20 Corr. XI. Nr. 9546, Austerlitz, 5 December 1805.
21 Corr. XI. Nr. 9591, Schönbrunn, 19 December 1805.
22 Corr. XI. Nr. 9623, Schönbrunn, 27 December 1805.

SELECTIVE BIBLIOGRAPHY

Abrantès *see* Junot.

Abrantès, Laure Junot, Duchesse d'. *Mémoires.* 10 vols. Paris, n.d.

Adams, Henry. *History of the United States of America During the Administrations of Thomas Jefferson and James Madison.* N.Y.: Library Classics of the United States, 1986. 2 vols.

Adye, John. *Napoleon of the Snows.* London: Nash and Grayson, 1931.

Aldington, Richard. *Wellington.* London: Heinemann, 1946.

Alger, John I. "Jomini: A Man of Principle." *The Consortium on Revolutionary Europe,* 1980.

Ali *see* Saint-Denis.

Allgemeine Deutsche Biographie. Vols. I and II. Leipzig, 1875.

Altamira, Rafael. *A History of Spain.* N.Y.: Van Nostrand, 1949.

Antommarchi, François. *Mémoires . . . ou les derniers moments de Napoléon.* Paris: Barrois, 1825. 2 vols.

Arnold, Eric P. Jr. *Fouché, Napoleon and the General Police.* Washington (D.C.): University Press of America, 1979.

Asprey, Robert B. "The Peninsular War," *Army Quarterly,* April 1959.

———. *War in the Shadows: The Guerrilla in History.* Garden City, N.Y.: Doubleday, 1975. 2 vols.

———. *Frederick the Great: The Magnificent Enigma.* N.Y.: Ticknor & Fields, 1986.

Aubry, Paul V. *Monge – Le Savant Ami de Napoléon Bonaparte*. Paris: Gouthier-Villars, 1954.

Bainville, Jacques. *Napoleon*. Boston: Little, Brown, 1933. Tr. Hamish Miles.

Barahona, Renato. "The Napoleonic Occupation and its Political Consequences in the Basque Provinces (1808–1813)." *The Consortium on Revolutionary Europe*, 1985.

Bartel, Paul. *La jeunesse inédite de Napoléon*. Paris: Amoit-Dumont, 1954.

Bartual, Carlos Diaz. "Tropas Españolas al Servicia del Imperio." *Revista de Historia Militar*, Num. 38, 1975.

Bausset, L.F.J. de. *Mémoires* . . . Paris: Baudoin Frères, 1820–1827. 2 vols.

Beaucour, Fernand Émile. "Le Grand Projet Napoléon en l'Expédition en Angleterre: Mythe ou Realité?" *The Consortium on Revolutionary Europe*, 1982.

Belloc, Hilaire. *Napoleon*. Philadelphia: Lippincott, 1932.

Bellune, Duc de. *Extraits de Mémoires Inédits*. Paris: Dumaine et Laquionie, 1846.

Benoist-Méchin, J.G.P.M. *Bonaparte en Égypte*. Lausanne: Clairfontane, 1966.

Bernoyer, François. *Avec Bonaparte en Égypte et en Syrie 1798–1800*. Abbéville: Les Presses Françaises, 1976.

Berthier, le Général de Division. *Relation des Campagnes du Général Bonaparte en Égypte et en Syrie*. Paris: Didot, An VIII [1799].

Berthier, Louis-Alexandre. *Mémoires*. Paris: 1827. 2 vols.

Bertrand, Henri-Gratien. *Napoleon at St. Helena – the Journals of General Bertrand*. N.Y.: Doubleday, 1952.

Bertrand, L., and Petrie, C. *The History of Spain*. London: Eyre & Spottiswoode, 1934.

Beyle, Henri *see* Stendhal.

Biagi, G. *see* Masson, Frédéric.

Bierman, Stanley M. "The Peripatetic Posthumous Peregrination of Napoleon's Penis." *The Journal of Sex Research*, November 1992.

Bigelow, John. *Principles of Strategy*. Philadelphia: Lippincott, 1894.

Bingham, D.A. *The Letters and Despatches of the First Napoleon*. London: Chapman and Hall, 1884. Vol. 3.

Blond, Georges. *La Grande Armée 1804–1815*. Paris: Laffont, 1979.

Blythe, Legette. *Marshal Ney: A Dual Life*. N.Y.: Stackpole, 1937.

Bond, Gordon C. "Louis Bonaparte and the Collapse of the Kingdom of Holland." *The Consortium on Revolutionary Europe*, 1974.

Bosher, J.F. *The French Revolution*. London: Weidenfeld & Nicolson, 1989.

Boswell, James. *An Account of Corsica, The Journal of a Tour to that Island; and Memoirs of Pascal Paoli*. London: 1852.

Botzenhart, Manfred. "Metternich and Napoleon." *Francia*, 1: 584–594, 1973.

Boulay de la Meurthe, Comte. *Le Directoire et L'Expédition d'Égypte*. Paris: Hachette, 1885.

———— (ed.). "Correspondence de Talleyrand avec Le Premier Consul Pendant La Campagne De Marengo." *Extrait de la Revue d'Histoire Diplomatique*, April 1892.

Bourcet, Pierre. *Principes de la Guerre des Montagnes*. Paris: Imprimerie Nacionale, 1775.

Bourgogne *see* Cottin, Paul.

Bourrienne, Louis Antoine Fauvelet. *Memoirs of Napoleon Bonaparte*. N.Y.: Crowell, 1885. 4 vols.

Bouvier, Félix. *Bonaparte en Italie 1796*. Paris: Cerf, 1902.

Boyer, Ferdinand. "Quelques Considerations Sur les Conquêtes Artistiques De Napoléon," *R. Italiana di Studi Napoleonici*, 1968.

Brett-James, Antony. *Wellington at War, 1794–1815*. London: Macmillan, 1961.

Broadley *see* Wheeler.

Browning, Oscar. *The Boyhood and Youth of Napoleon*. London: John Lane, 1906.

Bruce, Evangeline. *Napoleon & Josephine – An Improbable Marriage*. London: Phoenix, 1996.

Bryant, Arthur. *The Years of Endurance 1793–1802*. London: Book Club Associates, 1975.

————. *Years of Victory 1802–1812*. London: Book Club Associates, 1975.

Burton, R.G. *Napoleon's Campaign in Italy 1796–1797 and 1800*. London: George Allen, 1912.

Byrd, Melenie, S. "Denon and the Institute of Egypt," *The Consortium on Revolutionary Europe*, 1989.

Caird, L.H. *The History of Corsica*. London: Unwin, 1899.

Callwell, E.C. *Small Wars – Their Principles and Practice*. London: HMSO, 1899.

Carnot, Lazare N.M. *Mémoires Historiques et Militaires*. Paris: Baudouin Frères, 1824.

Carr, Raymond. "Spain and Portugal – 1793 to c. 1840." *The New Cambridge Modern History*. London: Cambridge University Press, 1965. Vol. 9.

———. *Spain 1808–1975*. Oxford: Clarendon Press, 1982.

Carrington, Dorothy. "Les Parents de Napoléon d'Après des Documents Inédites." *Annales Historiques de la Revolution Française*, Vol. 52, 1980.

Castelot, André. *Bonaparte*. Paris: Librairie Academique, 1967.

——— *Napoleon*. N.Y.: Harper & Row, 1967. Tr. Guy Daniels.

Cate, Curtis. *The War of the Two Emperors: The Confrontation Between Napoleon and Tsar Alexander, Russia 1812*. N.Y.: Random House, 1985.

Caulaincourt, Général. *Mémoires du Général de Caulaincourt, Duc de Vicence*, Paris: Plon, 1933. 3 vols.

Caulaincourt, Duke of Vicenza, *Memoirs*. London: Cassell, 1950. 3 vols. Tr. H. Miles.

Chandler, David. *The Campaigns of Napoleon*. London: Weidenfeld & Nicolson, 1967.

———. "Fire Over England: Threats of Invasion That Never Came." *The Consortium on Revolutionary Europe*, 1986.

Chaptal, Comte de. *Mes Souvenirs Sur Napoléon*. Paris: Plon, 1893.

Charles-Roux, F. *Bonaparte: Governor of Egypt*. London: Methuen, 1937.

Chateaubriand, Vicomte de. *Mémoires d'outre tombe*. Paris: Flammarion, 1948. 4 vols.

Christiansen, Eric. *The Origins of Military Power in Spain 1800–1854*. London: Oxford University Press, 1967.

Chuquet, Arthur. *La jeunesse de Napoléon*. Paris: Armand Colin, 1897. 3 vols.

———. *Inédits Napoléoniens*. Paris: 1913. 2 vols.

Clausewitz, Carl P.G. von. *Clausewitz on War*. London: Penguin, 1968.

——— *The Campaign of 1812 in Russia*. London: John Murray, 1843.

Cobham, Alfred. *History of Modern France*. London: Penguin, 1957. 3 vols.

Colin, Jean. *L'education militaire de Napoléon*. Paris: R. Chapelot, 1900.

Constant (Wairy). *Mémoires de Constant*. Paris: Michel, 1909.

Cooper, Duff. *Talleyrand*. London: J. Cape, 1934.

Coston, Baron de. *Biographie des Premières Années de Napoléon Bonaparte*. Paris: Marc Aurel, 1890. 2 vols.

Cottin, Paul, and Heyault, Maurice. *Mémoires du Sergent Bourgogne*. Paris: Hachette, 1914.

Craig, Gordon A. *The Politics of the Prussian Army 1640–1945*. Oxford: Clarendon Press, 1955.

———. "Problems of Coalition Warfare: The Military Alliance Against Napoleon 1808–1814." *U.S. Air Force Academy*, 1965.

Crefeld, Martin Van. *Supplying War – Logistics from Wallenstein to Patton*. London: Cambridge University Press, 1977.

———. *Command in War*. Cambridge, Mass.: Harvard University Press, 1985.

Daline, V. "Napoléon Et Les Babouvistes." *Annales Historiques de la Révolution Français*, 1970.

Delderfield, R.F. *The Retreat from Moscow*. N.Y.: Atheneum, 1967.

Denon, Dominique Vivant, Baron. *Voyages dans la Basse et la Haute Égypte pendant les campagnes de Bonaparte en 1798 et 1799*. London: 1807. 2 vols.

Description de l'Égypte, ou recueil des observations et des recherches qui ont été faites en Égypte pendant l'expédition de l'armée française. Paris: 1809–1828. 24 vols.

Desgenettes, R. *Histoire Médicale de L'Armée D'Orient*. Paris: Chez Craullebois, 1802.

———. *Souvenirs d'Un Médicin de L'Expédition d'Égypte*. Paris: Calman-Lévy, 1893.

Doppet, Général. *Mémoires politiques et militaires*. Paris: 1820.

Driault, J.E. *Napoléon en Italie*. Paris: Félix Alcan, 1901.

Du Teil, Baron Joseph. *Napoléon Bonaparte et Les Généraux Du Teil*. Paris: Alphonse Picard, 1897.

Dufraisse, Roger. *Napoleon*. N.Y.: McGraw-Hill, 1992. Tr. Steven Englund.

Dumas, Mathieu. *Souvenirs de Lieutenant-Général Comte Mathieu Dumas, de 1770 à 1836*. Paris: Gosselin, 1839. 8 vols.

Dupont, Amiral Marcel. *L'Amiral Decrès et Napoléon*. Paris: 1991.

Dupuy, Trevor N. *A Genius for War – The German Army and Central Staff 1807–1945*. London: Macdonald and Janes, 1977.

Dupuy, Trevor N. et al. *The Harper Encyclopaedia of Military Biography*. New York: HarperCollins, 1992.

Elgood, P.G. *Bonaparte's Adventure in Egypt*. London: Oxford University Press, 1931.

Elting, John R. *see* Esposito.

————. "Jomini and Berthier." *The Consortium on Revolutionary Warfare*, 1989.

Epstein, Robert M. "Eugene de Beauharnais: A Military Commander or Macdonald's Puppet?". *The Consortium on Revolutionary Europe*, 1983.

————. "The Army of Italy at the Battle of Wagram: Turning Point of the Napoleonic Wars." *The Consortium on Revolutionary Europe*, 1989.

———— *Napoleon's Last Victory and the Emergence of Modern War*. Lawrence, Kansas: University Press of Kansas, 1994.

Esposito, Vincent J., and Elting, John R. *A Military History and Atlas of the Napoleonic Wars*. N.Y.: Praeger, 1964.

Fain, Baron du. *Manuscrit de Mil Huit Cent Douze*. Paris: 1827.

————. *Mémoires du Baron Fain*. Paris: Plon, 1908.

Falk, Minna R. "Stadion, Adversaire de Napoléon (1806–1809)," *Annales Historiques de la Révolution Française*, Vol. 34, 1962.

Finley, Milton C. Jr. "Reynier, Menou and the Final Siege of the Egyptian Campaign." *The Consortium on Revolutionary Europe*, 1983.

Fisher, H.A.L. *Napoleon*. London: Oxford University Press, 1945.

Flayhart, William H. "The United Kingdom in the Mediterranean: The War of the Third Coalition and the Anglo-Russian Invasion of Naples." *The Consortium on Revolutionary Europe*, 1980.

Flayhart, William Henry III. *Counterpoint to Trafalgar: The Anglo-Russian Invasion of Naples 1805–1806*. Columbia (S. Carolina): University of South Carolina Press, 1992.

Forester, C.S. *Nelson*. London: The Bodley Head, 1929.

————. *The Naval War of 1812*. London: 1957.

Forrest, Alan. *The Soldier of the French Revolution*. Durham (N. Carolina): Duke University Press, 1990.

Fortescue, B. *Napoleon's Heritage*. London: John Murray, 1934.

Fortescue, John. *Wellington*. London: Ernest Benn, 1925.

Fouché, Joseph. *Les Mémoires de Fouché*. Paris: Flammerion, 1945.

Fournier, August. *Napoleon I*. N.Y.: Henry Holt, 1911. Vol. I. Tr. A.E. Adams.

Fuente, Francisco de la. "Portuguese Resistance to Napoleon: Don Miguel Forjaz and the Mobilization of Portugal." *The Consortium on Revolutionary Europe*, 1983.

Fugier, André. *Napoléon et l'Espagne 1799–1808*. Paris: Felix Alcan, 1930. 2 vols.

———. *Napoléon et l'Italie*. Paris: Panin, 1947.

Fuller, J.F.C. *A Military History of the Western World*. N.Y.: Funk & Wagnalls, 1955. Vol. 2.

———. *The Conduct of War 1789–1861*. Rutgers (N. Jersey): Rutgers University Press, 1961.

Gates, David. *The Spanish Ulcer: A History of the Peninsular War*. N.Y.: Norton, 1980.

Gaxotte, Pierre. *The French Revolution*. N.Y.: 1932.

Geer, Walter. *Napoleon and His Family*. London: Allen and Unwin, 1923.

Geyl, Pieter. *Napoleon For and Against*. London: Jonathan Cape, 1949.

Gillespie, Charles. "The Scientific Importance of Napoleon's Egyptian Campaign." *Scientific American*, September 1994.

Godlewski, Guy. "Napoléon et Les-États-Amis," *La Nouvelle Revue Des Deux Mondes*, Juillet–Septembre, 1977.

Goldstein, Marc A. *The People in Counter-Revolutionary France*. London: Peter Long, 1988.

Görlitz, Walter. *The German General Staff – Its History and Structure 1657–1945*. London: Hollis & Carter, 1953.

Gotteri, Nicole. "La Lorgne d'Ideville et le service de renseignements . . . pendant la campagne de Russie (juin 1812–mars 1813)." *Revue d'Histoire Diplomatique*, 1984.

Gourgaud, Général Gaspard. *Campagne de Dix-Huit Cent Quinze . . .* Bruxelles: Aug. Wahlen, 1818.

———. *Mémoires pour servir à l'histoire de France sous Napoléon*. Paris: Didot, 1823. 2 vols.

———. *Sainte-Hélène: Journal inédit de 1815 à 1818*. Paris: Flammarion, 1899.

———. *The St. Helena Journal of General Baron Gourgaud 1815–1818*. London: John Lane, 1932.

Grab, Alexander I. "Popular Uprisings in Napoleonic Italy." *The Consortium on Revolutionary Europe*, 1989.

Grandmaison, Geoffrey De. *L'Espagne et Napoléon*. Paris: Plon, 1908 ff. 3 vols.

Guedalla, Philip. *Napoleon and Palestine*. London: Allen & Unwin, 1925.

Gum, Ert. "Eugene de Beauharnais and an Affair of Honor." *The Consortium on Revolutionary Europe*, 1974.

Guyon, Edouard-Felix. "Stendhal et la Campagne de Russie de 1812," *Revue Historique D'Histoire Diplomatique*, Vol. 98, 1984.

Hall, H.F. *see* Napoleon.

Harford, Lee S. Jr. "Bavaria and the Tyrol Under Napoleon." *The Consortium on Revolutionary Europe*, 1989.

Headley, J.T. *Napoleon and His Marshals*. N.Y.: Baker and Scribner, 1846. 2 vols.

Heles, Edward E.Y. *Napoleon and the Pope* . . . London: Eyre & Spottiswoode, 1962.

Henry, Peter A. "Clausewitz and the Campaign of 1812 in Russia." *The Consortium on Revolutionary Europe*, 1989.

Herold, J. Christopher. *Bonaparte in Egypt*. London: Hamish Hamilton, 1963.

Heyault, Maurice *see* Cottin, Paul.

Horne, Alistair. *How Far From Austerlitz? Napoleon 1805–1815*. London: Macmillan, 1996.

Horta, Nicolás Rodriguez. "Dos Estudios Sobre Las Guerrillas en La Guerra de la Independencia." *Revista de historia Militar*. Numero 8 (15), 1964.

———. "La Guerrilla del Cura Merino." *Revista De Historia Militar*. Numero 12 (25), 1968.

———. "Un Capuchino Vasco en la Guerra de la Independencia Española." *Revista De Historia Militar*. Numero 22 (44), 1978.

Hortense [Bonaparte]. *The Memoirs of Queen Hortense*. N.Y.: Cosmopolitan Book Corporation, 1927.

Howard, Donald D. "Napoleon and Berthier." *The Consortium on Revolutionary Europe*, 1980, Vol. II.

———. *Napoleon and Iberia: The Twin Sieges of Ciudad Rodrigo and Almeida*. Tallahassee [Florida]: Florida State University Press, 1984.

———. "Wellington and the Defense of Portugal (1808–1813)." *The Consortium on Revolutionary Europe*, 1987.

Howarth, David. *Waterloo: Day of Battle*. N.Y.: Atheneum, 1968.

———. *Trafalgar: The Nelson Touch*. London: Collins, 1969.

Iung, Th. *Bonaparte et Son Temps 1769–1799*. Paris: Charpentier, 1880–1881. 3 vols.

———. *Lucien Bonaparte et Ses Mémoires 1775–1840*. Paris: Charpentier, 1802.

Jackson, W.A.F. *Attack in the West. Napoleon's First Campaign*. London: Eyre & Spottiswoode, 1953.

Johns, Christopher M.S. "Portrait Mythology: Antonio Canova's Portraits of the Bonapartes." *Eighteenth-Century Studies*, Vol. 28, Nr. 1 (1994).

Jonquière, C. de la. *L'Expédition de l'Égypte*. Paris: 1900–1907. 5 vols.

Jomini, Antoine Henri, Baron de. *The Political and Military History of the Campaign of Waterloo*. N.Y.: Redfield, 1860.

———. *The Art of War*. Philadelphia: Lippincott, 1862.

Junot, Madame. *Memoirs of Madame Junot*. N.Y.: 1883, 3 vols.

Junot, Madame. *see* Abrantès.

Keegan, John. *The Mask of Command*. N.Y.: Viking, 1987.

Kircheisen, Friedrich M. *Memoirs of Napoleon Ier*. N.Y.: Duffield, 1929. Tr. Frederick Collins.

Kirchiesen, Gertrude. *Die Frauen um Napoleon*. Munich, 1912.

Klang, Daniel. "Bavaria and the War of Liberation, 1813–14." *French Historical Studies*, Vol. 4, 1965.

Knight, George D. "Lord Liverpool and the Peninsular Struggle, 1809–1812." *The Consortium on Revolutionary Europe*, 1989.

Koch, Général. *Mémoires de Masséna (1796–1797)*. Paris: Paulin et Lechevalier, 1848.

Korngold, Ralph. *The Last Years of Napoleon – His Captivity on St. Helena*. N.Y.: Harcourt Brace, 1959.

Lacour-Gayer, Robert. "Napoléon et Les États-Unis," *Revue d'Histoire Diplomatique*. Vol. 83, 1969.

Larchey, Lorédan. *Les Cahiers de Capitaine Coignet (1799–1815)*. Paris: Hachette, 1883.

Larrey, D.J. *Mémoires de Chirurgie Militaire Et Campagnes*. Paris: chez J. Smith, 1812. 4 vols.

Las Cases, Comte de. *Mémorial de Sainte-Hélène*. Bruxelles: P.J. de Mat, 1828. 4 vols.

Lavelette, Comte. *Mémoires et Souvenirs du Comte Lavelette*. Paris: Fournier, 1831. 2 vols.

Lefebvre, Georges. *Napoleon from Tilsit to Waterloo, 1807–1815*. N.Y.: Columbia University Press, 1970, Tr. J.E. Anderson.

Lloyd, E.M. *A Review of the History of Infantry*. London: Longmans, Green, 1908.

———. "The Third Coalition." *The Cambridge Modern History*. London: Cambridge University Press, 1904. Vol. 9.

Longford, Elizabeth. *Wellington – The Years of the Sword*. London: Weidenfeld & Nicolson, 1969.

Lucas-Dubreton. *Le Maréchal Ney 1769–1815*. Paris: Librairie Arthème Fayard, 1941.

Ludwig, Emil. *Napoleon*. Garden City (N.Y.): Garden City Publishing Company, 1926. Tr. Eden Cedar Paul.

Macartney, C.A. *The Habsburg Empire 1790–1912*. N.Y.: Macmillan,1969.

Macdonald, Marshal. *Recollections of Marshal Macdonald*. London: Richard Bentley, 1893. Tr. S.L. Simeon.

MacDonald, J.R.M. "The Terror." *The Cambridge Modern History*. London: Cambridge University Press, 1904. Vol. 8.

Mackesy, Piers. *Statesmen at War: The Strategy of Overthrow, 1798–1799*. London, 1974.

———. *War Without Victory: The Downfall of Pitt, 1799–1802*. Oxford, 1984.

———. *British Victory in Egypt, 1801*. London: Routledge, 1995.

Madelin, Louis. *Histoire du Consulat et de L'Empire*. Paris: Hachette, 1937–1954. 16 vols. Vol. 1: *La Jeunesse . . .*

———. *Histoire du Consulat et de L'Empire*. Vol. 3: *De Brumaire A Marengo*. Paris: Hachette, 1938.

———. *The Consulate and the Empire*. London: Heinemann, 1934. Tr. E.F. Buckley.

Mahan, Alfred. *The Influence of Sea Power upon the French Revolution and Empire 1783–1812*. London: Sampson, Low, Marston, 1892. 2 vols.

———. *The Influence of Sea Power upon History, 1660–1783*. London: Sampson, Low, Marston, 1900.

———. *Sea Power in Its Relations to the War of 1812*. London: Sampson, Low, Marston, c. 1905.

Maras, Raymond. "Napoleon and Levies on the Arts and Sciences." *The Consortium on Revolutionary Europe*, 1987.

Marbot, Général Baron de. *Mémoires du Général Baron de Marbot*. Paris: Plon, 1891. 3 vols.

Marcaggi, Jean Baptiste. *Le Souvenir de Napoléon à Ajaccio*. Ajaccio, Corse: Rombaldi, 1921.

Markham, Felix. *Napoleon*. London: Weidenfeld & Nicolson, 1963.

Marmont *see* Raguse.

Martin, Marc. "Les Journaux Militaires de Carnot." *Annales Historiques de la Révolution Française*. Vol. 49, 1977.

Martineau, Gilbert. *Napoleon's St. Helena*. N.Y.: Rand McNally, 1966.

Masséna, Marshal *see* Koch.

Masson, Frédéric. *Napoleon at Home*. Philadelphia: Lippincott, 1894. 2 vols. Tr. J.E. Matthew.

———. *Napoleon and the Fair Sex*. London: Heinemann, 1894.

———. *Napoléon et Sa Famille*. Paris: Ollendorff, 1898 ff. 14 vols.

———. *Napoléon dans Sa Jeunesse*. Paris: Ollendorf, 1907.

———. *Joséphine de Beauharnais 1763–1796*. Paris: Ollendorff, 1913.

——— et Biaggi, Guido. *Napoléon inconnu . . . Papiers Inédites*. Paris: Ollendorff, 1895.

Mathiez, Albert. *La Réaction Thermidorienne*. Paris: Armand Colin, 1929.

———. *Le Directoire*. Paris, 1934.

———. "Robespierre L'Histoire et la Legende." *Annales Historiques de la Révolution Française*. Vol. 49. 1977.

Maurois, André. *Napoleon – a pictorial biography*. London: Thames & Hudson, 1963. Tr. P.J.S. Thomson.

McLynn, Frank. *Napoleon*. London: Jonathan Cape, 1997.

Melchoir-Bonnet, Bernardine. *Le procès de Louis XVI*. Paris: Librairie Académique Perrin, 1992.

Méneval, Baron Claude François de. *Napoléon et Marie-Louise*. Paris: Amyot, 1844.

———. *Mémoires . . .* Paris: Dentu, 1893–1894.

———. *Memoirs to Serve for the History of Napoleon I from 1802 to 1815*. London: Hutchinson, 1894. Tr. R.W. Sherrard.

Metternich, Klemens, Prince de. *Mémoires-Documents et Écrits Divers Laissés par Le Prince de Metternich*. Paris: Plon, 1886. 2 vols (ed. Prince Richard de Metternich).

Meurthe *see* Boulay de la Meurthe.

Meyer, Jack Allen. *Wellington's Generalship – A Study of his Peninsular Campaign*. Columbia (S. Carolina): University of South Carolina Press, 1984.

Meyer, Frank. "Thirteen Critical Decisions at Waterloo." *Parameters*, Spring 1991.

Miot, Jacques-François. *Mémoires Pour Servir à L'Histoire Des Expéditions en Égypte et en Syrie*. Paris: Demonville, 1804.

Miot de Melito, Comte de. *Mémoires du Comte Miot de Melito*. Paris: Michel-Lévy Frères, 1858. 2 vols.

———. *Memoirs of Count Miot de Melito*. N.Y.: Charles Scribner's Sons, 1881. 2 vols. Tr. C. Hoey and J. Lillie.

Mollien, Nicolas-François, Comte de. *Mémoires d'un Ministre du Trésor Public*. Paris: Guillaumin, 1898. 2 vols.

Montholon, C.F.D., Comte de. *Récits de la captivité de l'Empereur Napoléon à Sainte-Hélène*. Paris: Paulin, 1847. 2 vols.

Montgomery, Frances. "General Moreau and the Conspiracy Against Napoleon in 1804: The Verdict of the Court and History." *The Consortium on Revolutionary Europe*, 1988.

Muller, Charles. *The Darkest Day: 1814*. Philadelphia: Lippincott, 1963.

Napier, W.F.P. *History of the War in the Peninsula and in the south of France from the Year 1807 to the Year 1814*. London and N.Y.: Routledge and Sons, 1878. 3 vols.

Napoléon. *Lettres de Napoléon à Joséphine pendant la première campagne d'Italie et Lettres de Joséphine à Napoléon et à Sa Fille*. Paris: Fermin Didot Frères, 1833. 2 vols.

Napoléon I. *Correspondance de Napoléon Ier*. Paris: Plon/Dumaine, 1858 ff. 32 vols.

Napoleon. *The Letters and Dispatches of the First Napoleon*. London: Chapman and Hall, 1884. 3 vols.

Napoléon Ier. *Lettres Inédites de Napoléon Ier*. Paris: Plon, 1897. 2 vols.

Napoleon. *Napoleon's Letters to Josephine 1796–1812*. London: J.M. Dent, 1901. Ed. and tr. F. Hall.

Napoléon. *Dernières Lettres Inédites de Napoléon Ier*. Paris: Honoré Champion, 1903. 2 vols.

Napoléon Bonaparte. *Lettres inédites de Napoleon Ier à Marie-Louise, écrites de 1810 à 1814*. Paris: 1933.

Napoleon Bonaparte. *The Letters of Napoleon to Marie-Louise*. London: Hutchinson, 1935. Commentary by Charles De La Roncière.

Napoléon. *Lettres D'Amour à Joséphine*. Paris: Fayard, 1981. Presentées par Jean Tulard.

Napoleon Bonaparte. *Supper at Beaucaire*. London: Cockerel Press, 1945. Tr. S. De Clair.

Nasica, T. *Mémoires sur l'enfance et la jeunesse de Napoleon*. Paris: Ledoyen, 1852.

Ney, Michel. *Mémoires du Maréchal Ney* . . . Paris: Fournier, 1833. 2 vols.

Nicolson, Harold. *The Congress of Vienna. A Study in Allied Unity: 1812–1822*. N.Y.: Harcourt Brace, 1946.

Oman, Carola. *Napoleon's Viceroy Eugene de Beauharnais*. N.Y. Funk and Wagnalls, 1966.

Oman, C.W.C. *A History of the Peninsular War*. London: Oxford University Press, 1902–1930. 7 vols.

———. *Studies in the Napoleonic Wars*. London: Methuen, 1929.

O'Meara, Barry E. *Napoléon en Exil*. Paris: Seignot, 1823. 4 vols.

———. *A Voice from St. Helena*. London: Simpkin and Marshall, 1922.

Palmstierna, C.F. *My dearest Louise. Marie-Louise and Napoleon 1813–1814*. London: Methuen, 1958. Tr. E.M. Wilkensen.

Paret, Peter. *Yorck and the Era of Prussian Reform 1807–1815*. Princeton (N. Jersey): Princeton University Press, 1966.

———. "Napoleon as Enemy." *The Consortium on Revolutionary Europe*, 1983.

Parker, Harold T. "Why did Napoleon Invade Russia? . . ." *The Consortium on Revolutionary Europe*, 1989.

Passant, E. *A Short History of Germany 1815–1945*. London: Cambridge University Press, 1962.

Petre, F. Loraine. *Napoleon's Campaign In Poland 1806–1807*. London: John Lane The Bodley Head, 1907.

Petrie, C. *see* Bertrand, L.

Pinaud, Pierre-Français. "Guerre et Finances de 1792 à 1815: La service de la Trésorie aux Armées." *Revue Historique*, Vol. 283, 1990.

Platonov, S.F. *History of Russia*. London: Macmillan, 1925. Tr. E. Arensberg.

Pokrovsky, M.N. *Brief History of Russia*. London: Martin Lawrence, 1983. 2 vols. Tr. D.S. Mirsky.

Pratt, Fletcher. *The Empire and the Glory – Napoleon Bonaparte 1800–1806*. N.Y.: William Sloane, 1949.

Priego, Juan Lopez. "Dos Acciones de Guerra del Cura Merino, Relatadas Por El Merino (16 y 28 De Abril De 1812)." *Revista de Historia Militar*, Número 12(25), 1968.

Priestley, E.C. *see* Cole, D.H.

Quimby, Robert S. *The Background of Napoleonic Warfare. The Theory of Military Tactics in Eighteenth Century France*. N.Y.: Columbia University Press, 1957.

Ragsdale, Hugh. "Russian Influence at Luneville." *French Historical Studies*, Nr. 3. 1968.

Raguse, Duc de. *Mémoires de Duc de Raguse*. Paris: Perrotin, 1857. 2 vols.

Rapp, Jean, Comte. *Mémoires du Général Rapp* . . . Paris: Gernier frères, 1895.

Ratcliffe, Bertram. *Prelude to Fame – An Account of the early life of Napoleon up to the battle of Montenotte*. London: Frederick Warne, 1981.

Reddaway, W.F. *A History of Europe from 1715 to 1814*. London: Methuen, 1959.

Reeves, Craig A. "Command and Control: Napoleon's Aides-de-Camp and Orderly Officers." *The Consortium on Revolutionary Europe*, 1990.

Reinhard, Marcel. *Avec Bonaparte en Italie – d'Après Les Lettres Inédites de Son Aide De Camp Joseph Sulkowski*. Paris: Hachette, 1946.

Rémusat, Paul D. (ed.). *Mémoires de Madame Rémusat 1802–1808*. Paris: Calmann Levy, 1880. 3 vols.

Ribiera, Aileen. *Factions in the French Revolution*. N.Y.: Holmes & Meier, 1989.

Roeder, Franz. *The Ordeal of Captain Roeder*. London: Methuen, 1960. Ed. and tr. Helen Roeder.

Roederer, Count P.L. *Journal du Comte P.-L. Roederer*. Paris. H. Daragen, 1909.

Roederer, Pierre-Louise. *Mémoires Sur La Révolution, Le Consulat et L'Empire*. Paris: Plon, 1942. Ed. Octave Aubry.

Rogers, H.C.B. *Napoleon's Army*. London: Ian Allen, 1974.

Roider, Karl A. *Baron Thugut and Austria's Response to the French Revolution*. Princeton (N. Jersey): Princeton University Press, 1987.

Rose, J. Holland. "The Despatches of Colonel Thomas Graham on the Italian Campaign of 1796–7." *The English Historical Review*, Nr. 53, Vol. XIV. January 1899.

————. *The Life of Napoleon*. London: George Bell & Sons, 1903. 2 vols.

————. "The Second Coalition." *The Cambridge Modern History*. London: Cambridge University Press, 1904. Vol. 8.

————. *Napoleonic Studies*. London: George Bell & Sons, 1904.

————. *The Personality of Napoleon*. London: George Bell & Sons, 1912.

————. *Pitt and Napoleon. Essays and Letters*. London: George Bell & Sons, 1912.

Ross, Steven T. "The Military Strategy of the Directory: The Campaign of 1799." *French Historical Studies*, Vol. 5, Nr. 1, 1967.

Rothenberg, Gunther E. *The Art of Warfare in the Age of Napoleon*. Bloomington (Indiana): Indiana University Press.

————. *Napoleon's Great Adversaries: The Archduke Charles and the Austrian Army*. Bloomington (Indiana): Indiana University Press, 1982.

————. "The Case of Archduke Charles." *The Consortium on Revolutionary Europe*, 1983.

Roustam, Raza. *Souvenirs de Roustam Mamelouck de Napoléon Ier*. Paris: Ollendorff, 1911.

Rovigo, Duc de. *Mémoires du Duc de Rovigo Pour Servir à L'Histoire de L'Empereur Napoléon*. Paris: A. Bossange, 1828. 8 vols.

————. *Memoirs of the Duke of Rovigo . . .* London: H. Colburn, 1828. 4 vols.

Saint-Denis, Louis-Etienne "Ali". *Souvenirs des mameluck Ali sur L'Empereur Napoléon*. Paris: Payot, 1926.

Saint-Hilaire, M. *Napoléon Au Conseil d'État*. Paris: Victor Magen, 1843.

Saunders, Edith. *Napoleon and Mademoiselle George*. London: Longman Green, 1958.

Savant, Jean. *Les Mamelouks de Napoléon*. Paris: Calmann-Lévy, 1949.

————. *Napoleon In His Time*. London: Putnam, 1958. Tr. K. John.

Savary, Général. *Memoirs of the Duke of Rovigo*. London: Henry Collins, 1828. 4 vols.

Savary, Jean-Marie-René *see* Rovigo, Duc de.

Savary, Jean-Julien. *Guerre des Vendéens et des Chouans contre la République Française . . .* Paris: Baudouin frères, 1824–7.

Schevill, Ferdinand. *The History of the Balkan Peninsula. From the Earliest Times to the Present Day*. N.Y.: Harcourt Brace, 1933.

Schom, Alan. *One Hundred Days: Napoleon's Road to Waterloo*. N.Y.: Atheneum, 1992.

———. *Napoleon Bonaparte*. N.Y.: HarperCollins, 1997.

Schroeder, Paul W. "The Collapse of the Second Coalition." *Journal of Modern History*. The University of Chicago Press, Vol. 59, June 1987.

Ségur, Le Général Comte de. *Histoire et Mémoires*. Paris: Firmin Didot, 1873. 3 vols.

Ségur, Count Phillippe Paul de. *Napoleon's Russian Campaign*. London: Michael Joseph, 1958. Tr. J.D. Townsend.

Serramon, Jean. "Operaciones en El Reino de Léon (May a Septiembre de 1811)." *Revista de Histoire Militar*, Número 9(19), 1965.

Seton-Watson, Hugh. *The Russian Empire 1801–1917*. Oxford: Clarendon Press, 1967.

Shanahan, W.O. *Prussian Military Reforms 1786–1813*. N.Y.: 1945.

Showalter, Dennis E. "Manifestation of Reform: The Rearmament of the Prussian Infantry, 1806–13." *Journal of Modern History*, University of Chicago Press, September, 1972.

Sloane, William. *Life of Napoleon Bonaparte*. N.Y.: 1909. 4 vols.

Soult, Jean de Dieu. *Mémoires du maréchal général Soult*. Paris: Anyot, 1854.

Standing, Percy Cross. *Guerrilla Leaders of the World*. London: Stanley Paul, 1912.

Stendhal (Henri Beyle). *Journal de Stendhal, 1801–1814*. Paris: Garnier, 1888.

———. *A Life of Napoleon*. London: The Rodale Press, 1956. Tr. Ronald Gant.

Stschepkin, E. "Russia Under Alexander I, and the Invasion of 1812." *The Cambridge Modern History*. London: Cambridge University Press, 1904. Vol. 9.

Suchet, Louis-Gabriel. *Mémoires du maréchal Suchet . . .* Paris: Bossange, 1928. 2 vols.

Sutherland, Christine. *Marie Walewska – Napoleon's Great Love*. London: Weidenfeld & Nicolson, 1979.

Talleyrand-Périgord, Charles Maurice de. *Mémoires du Prince de Talleyrand-Périgord . . .* Bruxelles: Société Belge de Libraire, 1838. 2 vols.

———. *Lettres Inédites de Talleyrand à Napoléon, 1800–1809*. Paris: Perrin, 1889. Ed. Pierre Bertrand.

———. *Mémoires du Prince de Talleyrand*. Paris: Calman Lévy, 1891–1892. Vols 1 and 2.

Tarlé, Eugène. *Napoleon's Invasion of Russia, 1812*. London: Allen & Unwin, 1942. Tr. G.M.

Teil *see* Du Teil.

Thackeray, William Makepeace. *Vanity Fair*. N.Y.: The Modern Library, n.d.

Thibaudeau, Antoine Claire. *Histoire de Napoléon*. Paris, 1827 ff. 5 vols.

———. *Mémoires sur le Consulat et l'Empire*. Paris, 1835 ff. 10 vols.

———. *Histoire de la campagne d'Égypte sous le règne de Napoléon-le-Grand*. Paris, 1839, 2 vols.

Thiébault, Paul, Baron. *The Memoirs of Baron Thiébault*. London: Smith, Elder, 1896. 2 vols. Tr. and condensed by A.J. Butler.

Thiers, Louis-Adolphe. *Histoire du consulat et de l'empire*. Bruxelles: 1845 ff. 20 vols.

———. *History of the Consulate and the Empire of France under Napoleon*. Philadelphia: Lippincott, 1861.

Thiry, J. *Aube du Consulat*. Paris: Berger-Levrault, 1948.

———. *Le Concordat et Le Consulat à Vie*. Paris: Berger-Levrault, 1956.

———. *Napoléon en Italie*. Paris: Berger-Levrault, 1973.

———. *Napoléon en Egypte*. Paris: Berger-Levrault, 1974.

———. *Années de Jeunesse de Napoleon Bonaparte*. Paris: Berger-Levrault, 1975.

Thomazi, Auguste Antoine. *Napoléon et ses marins*. Paris: Berger-Levrault, 1950.

Thompson, J.M. *Napoleon Bonaparte. His Rise and Fall*. Oxford: Basil Blackwell, 1952.

Tolstoy, Leo N., Count. *The Physiology of War: Napoleon and the Russian Campaign*. N.Y.: Crowell, 1888. Tr. H. Smith.

———. *War and Peace*. London: Heinemann, 1971. Tr. C. Garrett.

Tortel, Christian *see* Bernoyer.

Trenard, Louis. *La Révolution Française dans la Région Rhône-Alpes*. Paris: Perrin, 1992.

Trevelyan, George. *George the Third and Charles Fox*. London: Longman Green, 1914. 2 vols.

Turner, Martha L. "French Art Confiscation in the Roman Republic, 1798." *The Consortium on Revolutionary Europe*, Vol. II, 1980.

Tute, Warren. *The True Glory*. London: Macdonald, 1983.

United States Military Academy. *Atlas to Accompany Napoleon As A General* by Count Yorck von Wartenburg. West Point (New York), 1942.

———. *Great Captains Before Napoleon*. West Point (New York), 1948.

———. *Jomini, Clausewitz and Schlieffen*. West Point (New York), 1948.

Vallejo-Nágera, Antonio. *Yo El Rey*. Madrid: Planeta, 1985.

Van Crefeld *see* Crefeld.

Vandal, Albert. *Napoléon et Alexander I*. Paris: Plon, 1891 ff. 3 vols.

———. *L'Avènement de Bonaparte*. Paris, 1911.

Vann, James Allen. "Habsburg Policy and the War of 1809." *Central European History*, Vol. VII, 1974.

Vernadsky, George. *A History of Russia*. New Haven (Conn.): Yale University Press, 1945.

Vicenza *see* Caulaincourt.

Victor, Marshal *see* Bellune.

Volney, Constantin. *Voyage en Syrie et en Égypte*. Paris: 1787. 2 vols.

Volney, Count C.F. *Oeuvres Complêtes*. Paris: Bossange, 1821. Vol. 1.

Wairy *see* Constant.

Walach, Isser. *The French Veteran from the Revolution to the Restoration*. Chapel Hill (N. Carolina): University of North Carolina Press, 1979.

Walter, Jakob. *A German Conscript with Napoleon*. Lawrence (Kansas): University of Kansas, 1938.

Warner, Oliver. *The Battle of the Nile*. London: 1960.

Wartenburg, Count Yorck von. *Napoleon as a General*. London: K. Paul, Tench, Trubner, 1902. 2 vols. Ed. and tr. by W.H. James.

Watson, G.E. "The United States and the Peninsular War. 1808–1812." *The Historical Journal*, Vol 14, 4, 1976.

Wheeler, H.F.B., and Broadley, A.M. *Napoleon and the Invasion of England*. London: John Lane, 1908. 2 vols.

Wilkinson, Spenser. *The Rise of General Bonaparte*. Oxford: Clarendon Press, 1930.

Williams, David Hamilton. *Waterloo: New Perspectives: The Great Battle Reappraisal*. N.Y.: Wiley, 1994.

Williams, E.N. *The Ancien Régime in Europe 1648–1789*. London: The Bodley Head, 1970.

Wright, G.N. *Life and Campaigns of Arthur, Duke of Wellington*. London: Fisher, 1841. 4 vols.

Zawadzki, W.H. "Prince Adam Czartoryski and Napoleonic France.
    1801–1805. A Study in Political Attitudes." *The Historical Journal*,
    Vol. XVIII, 1975.
Ziegler, Philip. *Addington*. London: Collins, 1965.
Zweig, Stefan. *Napoleon*. London: Allen and Unwin, 1927.

INDEX

The abbreviation NB is used for Napoleon Bonaparte in the index
Page numbers in *italics* refer to illustrations and maps
A reference as 123n12 indicates page 123 note 12